D1413990

Handbook of Motivational Counseling

Handbook of Motivational Counseling
Concepts, Approaches, and Assessment

Edited by

W. Miles Cox
University of Wales, Bangor, UK
and
Eric Klinger
University of Minnesota, USA

JOHN WILEY & SONS, LTD

This publication is designed to provide accurate and authoritative information in regard to the
subject matter covered. It is sold on the understanding that the Publisher is not engaged in
rendering professional services. If professional advice or other expert assistance is required, the
services of a competent professional should be sought.

Other Wiley Editorial Offices

John Wiley & Sons Inc., 111 River Street, Hoboken, NJ 07030, USA

Jossey-Bass, 989 Market Street, San Francisco, CA 94103-1741, USA

Wiley-VCH Verlag GmbH, Boschstr. 12, D-69469 Weinheim, Germany

John Wiley & Sons Australia Ltd, 33 Park Road, Milton, Queensland 4064, Australia

John Wiley & Sons (Asia) Pte Ltd, 2 Clementi Loop #02-01, Jin Xing Distripark, Singapore 129809

John Wiley & Sons Canada Ltd, 22 Worcester Road, Etobicoke, Ontario, Canada M9W 1L1

Wiley also publishes its books in a variety of electronic formats. Some content that appears in print may not be
available in electronic books.

Library of Congress Cataloging-in-Publication Data

Handbook of motivational counseling : concepts, approaches, and assessment / edited by
W. Miles Cox and Eric Klinger.
      p.   cm.
Includes bibliographical references and index.
ISBN 0-470-84517-1 (alk. paper)
1. Counseling.   2. Psychotherapy.   3. Motivation (Psychology)   I. Cox, W. Miles.
II. Klinger, Eric, 1933–
BF637.C6H3172 2003
158′.3—dc21   2003005298

British Library Cataloguing in Publication Data

A catalogue record for this book is available from the British Library

ISBN 0-470-84517-1

Typeset in 10/12pt Times by TechBooks, New Delhi, India
Printed and bound in Great Britain by Antony Rowe Ltd, Chippenham, Wiltshire
This book is printed on acid-free paper responsibly manufactured from sustainable forestry
in which at least two trees are planted for each one used for paper production.

Contents

Part V: Conclusion

About the Editors

W. Miles Cox is Professor of Psychology of Addictive Behaviours, School of Psychology, University of Wales, Bangor. He is Founding Editor of *Psychology of addictive behaviors* (APA) and Past President of the APA Division on Addictions. His research and clinical activities focus on the interplay between drinkers' incentives in other life areas and their motivation to drink alcohol. A Fellow in the American Psychological Association and a Charter Fellow in the American Psychological Society, Miles Cox is the author of more than 100 publications, primarily in addictive behaviors. His prior books include:

Cox, W.M. (Ed.) (1983). *Identifying and measuring alcoholic personality characteristics.* San Francisco: Jossey-Bass.

Cox, W.M. (1986). *The addictive personality.* New York: Chelsea House.

Cox, W.M. (Ed.) (1987). *Treatment and prevention of alcohol problems: A resource manual.* Orlando, FL: Academic Press.

Cox, W.M. (Ed.) (1990). *Why people drink: Parameters of alcohol as a reinforcer.* New York: Amereon Press.

Eric Klinger is Professor of Psychology at the University of Minnesota, Morris and (adjunct) Minneapolis. His research activities focus on motivational processes, especially as these and emotional processes influence attention, recall, and thought content. He has contributed to the basic theory of motivation and its extension to substance use, treatment of alcoholism, and depression. A Fellow of the American Association for the Advancement of Science and of the American Psychological Association, and a Charter Fellow of the American Psychological Society, Eric Klinger is the author of more than 100 publications. His prior books include:

Klinger, E. (1971). *Structure and functions of fantasy.* New York: John Wiley & Sons.

Klinger, E. (1977). *Meaning and void: Inner experience and the incentives in people's lives.* Minneapolis: University of Minnesota Press.

Klinger, E. (Ed.) (1981). *Imagery: Concepts, results, and applications.* New York: Plenum.

Klinger, E. (1990). *Daydreaming.* Los Angeles, CA: Tarcher (Putnam).

Contributors

Monica L. Baskin   *Emory University, Department of Behavioral Sciences and Health Education, Rollins School of Public Health, 1518 Clifton Road, Atlanta, GA 30322, USA*

Nicola Baumann   *University of Osnabrück, F B Humanwissenschaften Lehreinheit Psychologie, Seminarstr. 20, 49069 Osnabrück, Germany*

Gijs Bleijenberg   *Department of Medical Psychology, UMC St. Radboud Nijmegen, PO Box 9101, 6500 HB Nijmegen, The Netherlands*

Arthur W. Blume   *Department of Psychology, Room 224, University of Texas at El Paso, El Paso, TX 79968-0553, USA*

Neil C. Chambers   *Department of Psychology, Carleton University, Ottawa, Ontario, K1S5B6, Canada*

Christopher J. Correia   *Department of Psychology, 226 Thach Hall, Auburn University, Auburn, AL 36849, USA*

W. Miles Cox   *School of Psychology, University of Wales, Bangor, Bangor LL57 2AS, UK*

Renate de Jong-Meyer   *Westfälische Wilhelms-Universität Münster, Psychologisches Institut I, Fliednerstr. 21, 48149 Münster, Germany*

Maria J. Emmen   *Amsterdam Institute for Addiction Research, Keizersgracht 818, 1017 EE Amsterdam, The Netherlands*

Arno Fuhrmann   *Alexianer-Krankenhaus GmbH, Alexianerweg 9, 48163 Münster, Germany*

Siegfried Gauggel   *University of Technology, Chemnitz, Department of Psychology, Wilhelm-Raabe-Str. 43, D-09120 Chemnitz, Germany*

Suzette V. Glasner   *VA San Diego Healthcare System, Psychology Service (116B), 3350 La Jolla Village Drive, San Diego, CA 92161, USA*

Thomas Heidenreich   *Wolfgang Goethe Institut Psychiatrie, Heinrich Hoffmannstr. 10, 60578 Frankfurt, Germany*

Allen W. Heinemann   *Rehabilitation Institute of Chicago, 345 East Superior Street, Chicago, IL 60611, USA*

Manfred Hillmann   *Lingener Strasse 61, 49716 Meppen, Germany*

Martina Hoop   *University of Technology, Chemnitz, Department of Psychology, Wilhelm-Raabe-Str. 43, D-09120 Chemnitz, Germany*

Jürgen Hoyer   *University of Technology, Dresden, Clinical Psychology and Psychotherapy, D-01062 Dresden, Germany*

Barry T. Jones   *Department of Psychology, University of Glasgow, Glasgow G12 8QQ, UK*

Hendrée E. Jones   *Department of Psychiatry and Behavioral Sciences, Johns Hopkins University, 4940 Eastern Ave., D-4-East, Baltimore, MD 21224, USA*

Reiner Kaschel   *Universität Osnabrück, FB Humanwissenschaften, Lehreinheit Psychologie, Postfach, 49069 Osnabrück, Germany*

Eric Klinger   *Division of Social Sciences, University of Minnesota, Morris, 600 East Fourth Street, Morris, MN 56267, USA*

Christoph Koban   *Faculty of Psychology, Department of Clinical Psychology and Psychotherapy, Ruhr-University Bochum, 44780 Bochum, Germany*

Julius Kuhl   *Universität Osnabrück, FB Humanwissenschaften, Lehreinheit Psychologie, Postfach, 49069 Osnabrück, Germany*

Brian R. Little   *Murray Research Center, Radcliffe Institute for Advanced Study, Harvard University, 10 Garden Street, Cambridge, MA 02138, USA*

G. Alan Marlatt   *Addictive Behaviors Research Center, University of Washington, Department of Psychology, Box 351525, Seattle, WA 98195-1525, USA*

Mary McMurran   *School of Psychology, University of Wales, Cardiff, CF10 3YG, UK*

Johannes Michalak   *AE Klinische Psychologie und Psychotherapie, Ruhr-Universität Bochum, D-44780 Bochum, Germany*

S. Vincent Miranti   *Schwab Rehabilitation Hospital and Care Network, 1401 S. California, Chicago, IL 60608, USA*

Santhi Periasamy   *Emory University, Department of Behavioral Sciences and Health Education, Rollins School of Public Health, 1518 Clifton Road, Atlanta, GA 30322, USA*

Simone S. Rahotep   *Emory University, Department of Behavioral Sciences and Health Education, Rollins School of Public Health, 1518 Clifton Road, Atlanta, GA 30322, USA*

Ken Resnicow   *School of Public Health, University of Michigan, 1420 Washington Heights, Am Arbor, MI 48109–2029, USA*

Loriann Roberson   *Arizona State University Main Campus, PO BOX 874006, Tempe, AZ 85287-4006, USA*

Stephen Rollnick   *Department of General Practice, University of Wales College of Medicine, Llanedeyrn Health Centre, Cardiff CF3 7PN, UK*

Gerard M. Schippers *Amsterdam Institute for Addiction Research, Keizersgracht 818, 1017 EE Amsterdam, The Netherlands*

Bernhard M. Schroer *Psychotherapeutische Praxis, Ludgeristr. 23, 48143 Münster, Germany*

David M. Sluss *Arizona State University Main Campus, PO Box 874006, Tempe, AZ 85287-4006, USA*

Maxine L. Stitzer *Department of Psychiatry and Behavioral Sciences, Johns Hopkins University School of Medicine, Behavioral Pharmacology Research Unit, 5510 Nathan Shock Drive, Baltimore, MD 21224, USA*

Ulrike Willutzki *Faculty of Psychology, Department of Clinical Psychology and Psychotherapy, Ruhr-University Bochum, 44780 Bochum, Germany*

Hub Wollersheim *Department of Quality Care, UMC St. Radboud Nijmegen, PO Box 9101, 6500 HB Nijmegen, The Netherlands*

Conrad J. Wong *Department of Psychiatry and Behavioral Sciences, Johns Hopkins University School of Medicine, Center for Learning and Health, 5200 Eastern Ave. Suite W142, Baltimore, MD 21224, USA*

Foreword

Peter E. Nathan
University of Iowa

Clinicians and researchers alike have long struggled to make sense of the fundamental paradox of substance abuse: why so many addicted individuals maintain their pattern of abuse despite the terrible consequences of doing so. For much of human history, this conundrum was understood to be an expression of abusers' disdain for society's expectations, a consequence of willful immorality, sociopathic personality disturbance, or both. As recently as *DSM-I* (1952) and *DSM-II* (1968), this understanding largely informed the work of psychiatric diagnosticians: alcohol and drug abuse, like antisocial behavior and sexual deviation, with which they were grouped, were seen as an expression of the abuser's decision to flaunt society's rules of proper conduct. Although not framed explicitly in motivational terms, this view of substance abuse nonetheless conceptualized the moral shortcomings of alcohol abusers as working hand-in-hand with their motivational deficits to maintain their abuse—although the mechanisms by which the two complemented each other could not be specified.

A markedly different explanation for the persistence of alcoholic behavior in the face of its adverse consequences underlies the basic tenets of Alcoholics Anonymous, founded in the mid-1930s; a similar view was proposed by E.M. Jellinek in his highly influential book *The disease concept of alcoholism* (1960). Both explained the abuser's self-destructive behavior as a manifestation of an otherwise unexplained biological predisposition or dysfunction that rendered alcohol particularly toxic to those whose use of it led to alcoholism. This view of substance abuse as primarily a neurobiological phenomenon has since gained strong support from a substantial number of genetic studies of twins (e.g., Kaij, 1960; Kendler & Prescott, 1998a, 1998b) and adoptees (e.g., Heath, 1995). Accordingly, a great deal of well-designed research now points to genetic predisposition to alcoholism and other substance-use disorders in individuals with a positive family history of substance abuse. These findings have led many to conclude today that, rather than representing a motivated act of defiance against society, substance use may simply be the phenotypic outcome of a genotype that makes it virtually impossible for the children of substance abusers to resist the siren call of abuse.

W. Miles Cox and Eric Klinger, editors of *Handbook of motivational counseling: Concepts, approaches, and assessment*, have worked collaboratively for more than 20 years both to identify the variables that account for the motivation to drink abusively and to develop techniques to change this motivation to abuse. This volume, the culmination of their highly productive partnership, offers us not only Cox and Klinger's latest thinking on their motivational model of alcohol abuse, but the thinking as well of a number of other researchers and clinicians, many influenced by Cox and Klinger's work, on motivation and abuse, its assessment, and its treatment.

I found Cox and Klinger's Chapter 7, "A motivational model of alcohol use: Determinants of use and change," to be especially helpful in confronting what I have referred to above as the fundamental paradox of substance abuse. In that chapter, the authors describe the 15-year process of development of their "motivational model of alcohol use" that, as well as any other model with which I am familiar, integrates the biological, psychological, and sociocultural factors affecting drinking, including abusive drinking, within a unifying, evidence-based framework. As such, then, the Cox and Klinger model accords with the most widely accepted current etiologic views of substance abuse and, for that matter, most other behavioral disorders. While a few disorders—for example, those that involve demonstrable changes in brain structure and function—must clearly emphasize the first of these explanations, most behavioral disorders reflect the impact of psychological and social factors as well. In fact, substance abuse may best epitomize this multifactorial model: while genetics and its neurobiological substrates clearly elevate risk for substance abuse in individuals with a family history of alcoholism or drug addiction, psychological factors, prominently including incentive motivation as well as related traits of personality, and social factors, especially peer and sociocultural group influences, also play documented roles in etiology, maintenance, and treatment.

With Cox and Klinger, as with the authors of the accompanying chapters in the first part of the book ("Basic concepts and theories"), I understand motivation and its accompaniments to represent an especially important determinant of behavioral change—or its absence—in persons whose problematic behavior may also have neurobiological and environmental determinants. Perhaps this role for motivation is expressed most familiarly in the Alcoholics Anonymous (AA) dictum that, before the alcoholic can benefit from involvement in AA, he or she must confront the denial that so commonly accompanies dependence. By implication, change in abusive patterns of consumption will not come about unless or until the abuser becomes motivated both to acknowledge the existence of the problem and do something about it. Formally recognized in one of the first of AA's Twelve Steps, and validated clinically to his satisfaction by Jellinek, who considered denial a hallmark of gamma and delta alcoholism, this basic motivational deficit in the substance abuser has long been seen by many as the key to any successful effort to confront a substance-abuse problem.

How, then, can we best understand Systematic Motivational Counseling (SMC), the central focus of this edited volume? A psychological intervention that derives from an extensive body of psychological theory and research on the role of incentives and goal striving in human behavior, much of which is described in this book, SMC would seem to fit comfortably within the historical context of broad-based efforts to understand and treat substance abuse. In that regard, the behavioral scientists for whom this book has been written will certainly appreciate the extensive empirical research on motivation, a good deal of it summarized in Chapter 1 ("Motivation and the theory of current concerns"), from which assumptions SMC makes about how motivational deficits lead to substance abuse and other behavioral disorders have been derived. The existence of this body of research contributes to the accessibility of this model to further empirical investigation. Clearly, SMC is an evidence-based intervention and, as such, firmly within that Zeitgeist. But beyond its strong base in psychological theory and research, SMC also reflects current views on the role of brain processes in complex behavioral phenomena. Notable, as well, is the respect SMC pays to the role of interpersonal phenomena in both the maintenance and cessation of substance abuse. The multifaceted theory and research that underlie SMC and constitute much of what is contained in this volume may represent one of the most fully realized biopsychosocial models of substance abuse currently available to us.

Like Motivational Interviewing (MI), an intervention with which it shares important similarities (both similarities and differences between MI and SMC are discussed in Chapter 24, "Motivational interviewing in health promotion and behavioral medicine"), SMC has now been extended beyond the individual to the group (Chapter 21) and beyond the addictive disorders to such diverse conditions as physical disabilities involving disturbed brain function (Chapter 15), criminal behavior (Chapter 16), and workplace problems (Chapter 14). Why does SMC appear to be effective across such a wide range of conditions? Perhaps because it is based on a comprehensive theory of motivation, a keystone to behavior change. Motivation, as the authors of many of the chapters in this volume affirm, is fundamental to understanding behavior. Perhaps Cox and Klinger have succeeded in harnessing techniques capable of modifying the diverse motivations that lead us to abuse substances or otherwise behave in ways not in our best interests. While substantially more empirical data must be gathered before we can be certain that these procedures will be consistently effective across a wide range of behavioral disorders, the data reviewed in this volume are certainly encouraging in this regard.

It is also noteworthy that SMC—again, like MI—involves continuous interaction between assessment and intervention: assessment *is* intervention in SMC and MI, just as intervention *is* assessment in the two. This melding of what are usually distinct clinical processes may contribute to the apparent robust effectiveness of these interventions. If the effort to change behavior begins when assessment begins, and continuous monitoring of behavior change extends beyond the assessment period, both assessment and intervention enjoy a notable value-added dimension.

If you, the reader, have come to agree that the biopsychosocial explanation of substance abuse and other behavioral disorders best explains them, I would then suggest that this volume best represents the evidence base for that model, one that integrates the neurobiological, the environmental, and, most particularly, the motivational and the psychological.

REFERENCES

American Psychiatric Association (1952). *Diagnostic and statistical manual of mental disorders.* Washington, DC: Author.

American Psychiatric Association (1968). *Diagnostic and statistical manual of mental disorders* (2nd edn.). Washington, DC: Author.

Heath, A.C. (1995). Genetic influences on alcoholism risk: A review of adoption and twin studies. *Alcohol Health and Research World, 19*, 166–171.

Jellinek, E.M. (1960). *The disease concept of alcoholism.* New Haven, CT: College and University Press.

Kaij, L. (1960). *Alcoholism in twins: Studies on the etiology and sequels of abuse of alcohol.* Stockholm: Almquist & Wiksell.

Kendler, K.S., & Prescott, C.A. (1998a). Cannabis use, abuse, and dependence in a population-based sample of female twins. *American Journal of Psychiatry, 155*, 1016–1022.

Kendler, K.S., & Prescott, C.A. (1998b). Cocaine use, abuse, and dependence in a population-based sample of female twins. *British Journal of Psychiatry, 173*, 345–350.

Preface

Motivation is an important topic for everyone who works in the helping professions, because people in need of help often lack the motivation to achieve the things that they want and need in life. Motivational deficits can prevent people from seizing opportunities that would enable them to lead fulfilling lives. The deficits can interfere with people's work productivity and their satisfaction with life. They can cause people to seek alternative but self-defeating ways to obtain satisfaction, such as through alcohol or other drug abuse. In still other cases, these deficits can result in psychological maladjustment and distress. This book shows how motivational problems develop, how they can be identified, and how they can be corrected.

Our work on motivational counseling started more than twenty years ago at the University of Minnesota, Morris. We both were interested in motivation from a theoretical perspective and in alcohol abuse, and were particularly interested in identifying the variables controlling people's motivation to drink excessively. Thus began our longstanding collaboration. As we embarked on the research, we were struck by the high incidence of relapse into abusive drinking by drinkers who had sought help for their problem drinking and whose problem had temporarily remitted. The return to problematic drinking shortly after treatment appeared to result from an eroding motivation not to drink rather than from any deterioration of the skills to cope with the drinking that had been learned during the treatment. Experiencing an abstinent or moderate-drinking lifestyle that was no more satisfying than the problem drinking one had been, recovering drinkers seemed to reach a point where they decided to resume drinking in an attempt to make their lives more bearable.

We next sought to find new techniques to improve problem drinkers' motivation to recover. We found important clues as to what our focus should be from several sources of evidence of differences between the majority of alcohol abusers who had relapsed after treatment and the minority who had not. Unlike the relapsing drinkers, the non-relapsing ones had found meaningful, satisfying lives to enjoy that did not include excessive drinking. Thus, we reasoned, rather than aiming for new strategies for dealing directly with the drinking, a more promising approach would be to target drinkers' goals and concerns apart from their drinking. Other researchers had similar ideas, as had Rudy Vuchinich in 1982 when he asked, "Have behavioral theories of alcohol abuse focused too much on alcohol consumption?"

The technique that we developed for addressing alcohol abusers' life concerns was Systematic Motivational Counseling (SMC). SMC is based on a theoretical point of view similar to other approaches that help problem drinkers gain access to healthy sources of reinforcement contingent on their not drinking (e.g., Sisson & Azrin, 1989). However, SMC is different from other techniques in that it aims to address directly the motivational basis for problem drinking. It is firmly grounded in motivational theory, and aims to correct drinkers' maladaptive patterns of goal-striving. Its strategy is to enhance the richness of the incentives in individuals' lives to the point of their competing successfully with the satisfactions gained by using alcohol, thus reducing the motivation to cope by drinking.

Although we originally used SMC as an individual counseling technique, it was subsequently adapted for use in various other formats and with a variety of psychological problems other than alcohol abuse. For some of these disorders, SMC is best used as a component to improve clients' receptiveness to a comprehensive treatment regimen. For other disorders, it may serve as a principal treatment, supplemented by other techniques as needed.

The purpose of the book is to present SMC, its theoretical basis and the work related to it, and other motivational counseling techniques that complement it. The book is organized into five parts. Part I lays the theoretical foundations for motivational counseling. Chapter 1 begins by presenting basic motivational terms, concepts, and findings in the context of the motivational theory of current concerns, and Chapter 7 shows how the theory is applied to alcohol abuse. Suzette Glasner, Christopher Correia, and Johannes Michalak and colleagues introduce and present important findings on additional motivational domains—incentive motivation, counseling economics, and goal conflicts, respectively—that amplify our understanding of how maladaptive motivations are formed and can be changed. Finally, Part I presents two additional motivational theories. Brian Little and Neil Chambers present the theory of personal projects and its similarities to and differences from the theory of current concerns. Reiner Kaschel and Julius Kuhl discuss the innovative new theory of personality systems interactions and its application to motivational assessment and counseling.

Part II deals with assessing motivation. Miles Cox and Eric Klinger present two closely related motivational assessment instruments, the Motivational Structure Questionnaire (MSQ) and Personal Concerns Inventory (PCI). Both Cox and Klinger and Nicola Baumann present research demonstrating that the MSQ (the older of the two instruments) is a valid, reliable, and clinically useful assessment device. Both instruments identify the content of respondents' concerns and their motivational patterns for reaching goals for resolving those concerns (i.e., their motivational structure).

The MSQ and PCI assess the motivational structure that impedes the ability of some respondents to reach their goals. Accordingly, Part III of the book shows how SMC, drawing on basic, empirically validated principles of motivation, can be used to reconfigure maladaptive motivational structures, leading participants to experience more satisfying and fulfilling lives. This part of the book describes how the SMC technique has been used in individual sessions with substance-abusing clients (by Cox and Klinger) and with those in rehabilitation for traumatic brain injuries (by Vincent Miranti and Allen Heinemann). It has also been adapted for use in group settings (by Bernhard Schroer, Arno Fuhrmann, and Renate de Jong-Meyer), in work settings (by Loriann Roberson and David Sluss), as a self-help manual (by Renate de Jong-Meyer), and for use with offenders (by Mary McMurran).

Part IV presents other motivational counseling techniques, all of which are theoretically consistent with SMC and some of which can be used in conjunction with it. Ulrike Willutzki and Christoph Koban, through their Elaboration of Positive Perspectives, and Manfred Hillmann, through logotherapy, discuss motivational issues with respect to clients in psychotherapy. The authors of four of the chapters present motivational techniques for helping problem drinkers reduce their alcohol consumption. Barry Jones shows how to reduce drinkers' positive expectancies about drinking and increase their negative expectancies. Maria Emmen, Gerard Schippers, and co-authors present the Motivational Drinker's Check-Up as a way to overcome drinkers' feelings of ambivalence about changing their

drinking. Arthur Blume and Alan Marlatt describe their intervention for excessively drinking college students, which includes education about alcohol, feedback about normative
drinking, and teaching coping skills. Conrad Wong, Hendree Jones, and Maxine Stitzer
describe contingency-management interventions for changing substance abusers' motivation to use. Finally, in Part IV, Siegfried Gauggel and Martina Hoop present their research
on goal-setting as a motivational strategy to help patients with brain injuries; and Ken
Resnicow and co-authors address the application of motivational interviewing in public
health, medical, and health-promotion settings.

In Part V, Cox and Klinger conclude the book by taking stock of the current issues and
developments in motivational counseling and suggest directions for the future.

The authors of the chapters are psychologists from a variety of perspectives and backgrounds. Geographically, they come from Europe (Germany, the Netherlands, and the United
Kingdom) and North America (Canada and the United States). Their varied expertise makes
for both an integrated understanding of the motivational bases for behavior and the motivational techniques for changing behaviors in desired directions. The book is expected to be
useful both to psychologists and to a variety of other specialists whose work involves helping to motivate people to change. These include psychiatrists, social workers, counselors,
nurses, and general practitioners. The book should also be useful to helping professionals
in training. Future practicing professionals need to acquire basic motivational techniques
that can be applied to a variety of psychological disorders whose treatment raises issues of
motivation for change.

We are grateful to the authors of the chapters for their excellent contributions. Over the
years, many individuals contributed to our work on motivational counseling other than those
who wrote chapters for the book. We cannot attempt to acknowledge everyone's contributions, but some notable examples do come to mind. The United States National Institute
of Mental Health Grant 1 RO1 MH24804, along with University of Minnesota support,
funded the early stages in the development and validation of current concerns theory and
assessment techniques. Steven G. Barta, Thomas W. Mahoney, and Madeline E. Maxeiner
were crucial members of the University of Minnesota, Morris, research team, in addition
to numerous other important members, that developed the early empirical methods and
data for this program. Sandra Rae Johnson helped to draft the earliest ancestors of the
Motivational Structure Questionnaire. Later stages of the research program were funded
by the United States National Institute on Alcohol Abuse and Alcoholism Grant R21
AA08265, United States National Institute on Disability and Rehabilitation Research Grant
H133A10014-93, British Economic and Social Research Council Grant R000239563, as
well as grants from the Norges Forskningsråd [Research Council of Norway]; Deutsche
Forschungsgemeinschaft [German Research Council]; University of Bergen, Norway; Uni-
versity of Minnesota, United States; University of Nijmegen, the Netherlands; the United
States Department of Veterans Affairs; the British Council; and the Deutscher Akademische
Austausch Dienst [German Academic Exchange Service]. During this stage of the research,
Daliah Bauer at the Chicago Medical School was a central player in data collection, analy-
sis, and reporting; Carolyn M. Parish and Suzette V. Glasner contributed important analyses
and write-ups at the University of Minnesota; and Javad S. Fadardi, Lee M. Hogan, and
Steven G. Hosier at the University of Wales, Bangor, were central to a variety of other
projects in the program. Our thanks also go to Joseph Blount, who assisted us on various
aspects of the research, as did other collaborators, including Renate de Jong-Meyer, Arno
Fuhrmann, František Man, Gerard M. Schippers, Bernhard M. Schroer, Arvid Skutle, and

Iva Stuchlíková. Throughout the planning and writing of the book, we were fortunate to be able to work with two excellent editors at Wiley Publications. First, Michael Coombs worked with us during the planning of the book. He encouraged us to submit the proposal and made valuable suggestions while we were preparing it. Second, we worked with Vivien Ward during the writing of the book. She promptly attended to our every request, and always seemed to have just the right answer to our every query. She was consistently optimistic and supportive. We are grateful for everyone's efforts on our behalf.

REFERENCES

Sisson, R.W., & Azrin, N.H. (1989). The Community Reinforcement Approach. In R.K. Hester & W.R. Miller (Eds.), *Handbook of alcoholism treatment approaches: Effective alternatives*. Elmsford, NY: Pergamon Press.

Vuchinich, R.E. (1982). Have behavioral psychologists focused too much on alcohol consumption? *Bulletin of the Society of Psychologists in Substance Abuse*, **1**(4), 151–154

PART I

Basic Concepts and Theories

CHAPTER 1

Motivation and the Theory of Current Concerns

Eric Klinger

University of Minnesota, Morris, USA

and

W. Miles Cox

University of Wales, Bangor, UK

Synopsis.—This chapter introduces basic concepts of motivation and goal pursuit within the framework of the theory of current concerns. Behavior and experience are organized around the pursuit and enjoyment of goals. Accordingly, this chapter first discusses basic motivational concepts, which address the processes involved in choosing and pursuing goals. It examines how people choose goals and traces the effects on a person of having a goal, up to the point at which the person attains or relinquishes the goal, and beyond that the consequences of the way the goal pursuit ends. Goal choice depends on the value assigned by the chooser to each alternative (*incentive*) and its perceived attainability. Commitment to a goal pursuit launches a latent, time-binding brain process (a *current concern*) that sensitizes the individual to notice, recall, think about, dream about, and act on cues associated with the goal pursuit. Goal pursuits vary according to whether the goal is an approach or an avoidance goal, the time frame for action, the anticipation of the details and difficulties of the goal pursuit, and the degree of conflict with other goals. Emotional responses determine incentive values, serve as evaluative feedback during goal pursuits, and accompany consummation of or disengagement from the goal. The process of disengagement normally entails a sequence of emotional changes: invigoration, anger, depression, and recovery. Each of these components of goal choice and pursuit can go awry, leading to a variety of difficulties that become reflected in anxiety, depression, alienation, interpersonal and occupational problems, substance use, suicide, and other forms of psychological disturbance. Counseling intervention needs to address the motivational problems that deter clients from committing to the goals that can potentially bring them happiness and fulfillment.

Vince Lombardi, renowned American football coach, is alleged to have said, "Winning isn't everything, it's the only thing" (Simpson, 1988, p. 388). In the same sense, successful pursuit of goals is not just the most important thing in the life of humans and other animals; it is ultimately the only thing that counts toward survival, life's bottom line.

All living organisms must meet life's challenges of obtaining nutrients, excreting toxic substances, locating hospitable places, and reproducing themselves. Plants and animals have evolved quite different strategies for addressing these challenges. Plants depend on their immediate environments to supply their needs. Their *sessile* (sitting in place) strategy requires massive procreation, and although a huge proportion of progeny die, enough survive

Handbook of Motivational Counseling. Edited by W. Miles Cox and Eric Klinger.

to carry on their species. Animals evolved a degree of freedom from the not-too-tender mercies of their most immediate environments. However, this freedom from total dependency also carries a price: the imperative to find, pursue, and consummate the substances and conditions that satisfy their needs. These substances and conditions constitute *goals*. Animals thus follow a *motile* (moving around) strategy that requires them to—in author and radio host Garrison Keillor's words (in innumerable radio broadcasts of Public Radio International's Prairie Home Companion)—"get up and do the things that need to be done," to pursue goals.

Human goals may be small or large—from a few moments of amusement or organizing a file to finding a mate, having and successfully rearing children, succeeding in a vocation, becoming rich, or achieving spiritual fulfillment. They may be positive (*appetitive*), like those just described, or negative (*aversive*), such as avoiding disease, a bully, or a bad reputation. Some are more obviously important than others, some more obviously bear on individual survival than others, and some may be perverted to jeopardize survival.

In psychology, the processes that make goal-striving possible are called *motivation*. This book and the approaches it contains are built around the notion that, to be effective, any psychological intervention must address the client's set of life goals, whether large or small, and the ways in which the client relates to those goals. Taken altogether, a client's goals and ways of relating to them are what this book refers to as the client's *motivational structure*. The approaches described in the chapters that follow focus on understanding, assessing, and intervening to modify clients' motivational structure. First, however, this chapter introduces some motivational definitions and concepts and maps out some of what scientific research has established about motivational systems—their nature, their influences on what people notice, recall, think about, feel, and do, and their implications for well-being, psychopathology, and treatment.

MOTIVATION FORMALLY DEFINED

Different psychologists define what they mean by motivation somewhat differently. Ferguson (1994) reflects a long tradition when he defined motivation as "the internal states of the organism that lead to the instigation, persistence, energy, and direction of behavior" (p. 429). That might seem to include everything that affects behavior, but the focus here is first of all on "internal states," which excludes the kind of direct physical impact that produces a broken leg or a patellar reflex, as when a physician taps a patient's patellar tendon and produces an involuntary knee jerk. Thus, Ferguson's definition includes the effects of drives such as hunger, emotional states such as anxiety and anger, and many other variations of inner states. Second, the definition lists the main qualities of behavior that motivation is defined to influence: its initiation, persistence, vigor, and direction.

Yet, this definition leaves out mention of a crucial component, which Chaplin (1968) included when he defined motivation as a concept "to account for factors within the organism which arouse, maintain, and channel behavior toward a goal" (p. 303). Chaplin's definition specifies an additional critical element of motivation that Ferguson's definition lacks—that motivation directs behavior toward specific *goals*. That is, motivated behavior is also goal-directed behavior. One could thus combine the two definitions of motivation: "the internal states of the organism that lead to the instigation, persistence, energy, and direction of behavior towards a goal." It is this combined definition that informs this chapter and most of the book.

THE CENTRALITY OF MOTIVATION IN BRAIN AND MIND

Motivation is not just one more set of psychological processes. If animals evolved with a motile strategy to go after the substances and conditions they need, the most basic requirement for their survival is successful goal-striving. In that case, all animal evolution, right up to humans, must have centered on natural selection of whatever facilitated attaining goals. This must mean that everything about humans evolved in the service of successful goal-striving—including human anatomy, physiology, cognition, and emotion. These other features of being human must therefore be understood in terms of their relationship to goal-striving and the motivational systems that make it possible.

In recent decades, neuroscientists have turned up dramatic evidence of the close connections between virtually all psychological processes and those associated with emotion and goal-striving. Ledoux (e.g., 1995) showed that, in the brain sensory systems, pathways bifurcate—some leading from sense organs to the cerebral cortex, and others from sense organs to the limbic system, which is heavily implicated in emotion. This suggests that sensory signals begin to trigger emotional reactions at least as quickly as they trigger cognitive processes that analyze the signals in order to make more detailed sense of them. There are also pathways from the limbic system to the cortex and from the cortex to the limbic system, which provides a system for mutual alerting, refinement, and correction between emotional and cognitive responses to the signal. Neurons in the anterior cingulate, a part of the limbic system, fire according to expectancy of reward (Shidara & Richmond, 2002). Thus, brain anatomy indicates that emotional response and closely related motivational processes are a central part of responding to something.

The centrality of emotional and motivational processes is also apparent in the work of Antonio and Hanna Damasio and their colleagues. They have, for example, shown that destruction of specific brain areas, such as the medial prefrontal cortex, leaves people unable to stay on course toward their goals, substantially crippling their ability to lead normal, satisfying lives (Damasio, 1994). The ventromedial prefrontal cortex appears to integrate emotion-related signals from the limbic system with signals from various cortical areas, including some that are necessary for planning and volition. Without this integration, people become impulsive, make unrealistic plans, and are easily distracted from their goals. Along similar lines, a controlled experiment showed that, unlike normal individuals, patients with ventromedial prefrontal damage were unable to learn to avoid risky or nonoptimal strategies in a laboratory game (Bechara, Tranel, & Damasio, 2000; Bechara et al., 1997). In the first of these two studies, the brain-damaged participants, in contrast to others, manifested no skin conductance responses when they chose risky strategies. Here skin conductance responses presumably reflect fear of taking a risk that would be inappropriate relative to the individual's goal in the task. Thus, the particular brain damage of these patients interfered with input from their emotional responses and correspondingly compromised their ability to make appropriate, goal-related decisions.

Mounting evidence such as this confirms the centrality of motivational and emotional processes in the organization of the brain. Correspondingly, it supports the parallel, older evidence of their centrality to psychological organization, and it underlines the importance for counselors and psychotherapists of understanding the interconnections with motivational processes and integrating applicable methods into treatment procedures.

IMPORTANT DISTINCTIONS REGARDING MOTIVATION

Motivational States versus Motivational Traits

There are also other important distinctions regarding motivation to keep in mind. The definitions introduced earlier suggest that motivation refers to short-lived internal states such as hunger or anger, but there is also in psychology a long history of conceptualizing and measuring motivational factors as relatively enduring dispositions or traits (e.g., Allport, 1937; Heckhausen, 1967, 1991; Jackson, Ahmed, & Heapy, 1976; McClelland et al., 1953; Murray, 1938). For example, an individual may not only be trying hard to build a strong business, which could reflect achievement motivation, but may also place high value on and invest much effort into doing many things better than others and into improving on a previous personal performance. This individual may then be described as generally achievement-motivated, which constitutes the enduring trait of high achievement motivation.

There are purposes for which conceiving motivation in terms of enduring dispositions is very useful. For example, as many search committees and search firms know, when one is selecting college professors or corporate executives, it would be helpful to ascertain the kinds of goals that typically interest them, because that knowledge may shed light on their likely performance and fitness for the position. However, characterizing someone in terms of motivational traits can also blind one to the fact that these traits are generalizations about an individual's goal pursuits, that each goal pursuit represents a decision that is influenced by a given set of factors, and that these factors, and the decisions they produce, are subject to change. Especially for counselors and therapists, the possibility of changing motivation, and the methods for producing change, are central to their enterprise. Thus, although motivational dispositions can be useful ways to describe individuals, they are not fixed quantities, but changeable.

Accordingly, this book is focused more on motivational states and conditions, which cumulatively may lead to traits, than on the motivational traits themselves. When one can change people's decisions about the kinds of goals to pursue, one has by that fact also changed motivational traits.

Motivation and Volition

Some writers on motivation, especially in the German psychological tradition (e.g., Heckhausen, 1991; Kuhl, 2001), restrict the term motivation to the processes and factors that determine which goals an individual will pursue; they then classify as *volition* (from the Latin root for the *will*) the factors that regulate *how* the individual carries out the pursuit—persistence, vigor, and efficiency. Thus, in this usage, the term *motivation* includes only the initial factors that determine an individual's choice of goals, leaving the rest to volition. In contrast, in the American tradition the term *motivation* includes volition; volitional processes are simply a subset of motivation. The difference is purely semantic, but the semantics entail advantages and disadvantages. The advantage of the German approach is that there is a separate term (motivation) for those factors that determine choice of goals, just as there is a term (volition) for how the goal is pursued. In the usual American usage there is no such generally accepted word for the factors that determine goal choice, because motivation covers the whole range of goal-related processes, from determining the choice of goals to the end of the pursuit. The advantage of the broader usage of the term *motivation* is that it provides a single term to refer to all goal-related processes. This chapter and most of the other chapters will abide by the broader definition of motivation.

What is important here is to keep in mind the importance of volitional processes. They are part of motivational structure, and they are part of what may need to change in counseling. For example, when an individual gives up too easily in the face of difficulty or uses self-defeating coping strategies such as procrastinating or ruminating, addressing these is part of effective intervention. Thus, a comprehensive approach to motivational counseling must include both a person's choices of goals and the volitional means of pursuing them.

Intrinsic versus Extrinsic Motivation

The field of motivational research has placed much importance on the distinction between intrinsic and extrinsic motivation (e.g., Ryan et al., 1996). Motivation is said to be intrinsic when an individual pursues a goal for its own sake. That is, reaching the goal is not just a step in attaining some further goal. For example, eating an ice cream cone for pleasure or marrying for love are intrinsically motivated acts. Motivation is said to be extrinsic when a goal is a stepping-stone to some further goal. For example, eating an ice cream cone solely to gain weight or marrying solely to improve one's social position are extrinsically motivated acts. Acts that are purely extrinsically motivated yield only one kind of satisfaction: the satisfaction of moving closer to attaining some other source of satisfaction.

The examples indicate that the same kind of act may be motivated intrinsically, extrinsically, or in both ways. However, some kinds of goal are generally more likely to be motivated intrinsically (e.g., visiting a national park) and others more likely to be motivated extrinsically (e.g., becoming rich). The balance of an individual's motivational structure in this regard—that is, whether the individual's motivation is more often intrinsic or extrinsic—is associated with overall feelings of well-being and satisfaction with life and work (Kasser & Ryan, 2001; Ryan et al., 1996; Schmuck, 2001).

Nevertheless, it is important to keep in mind that any extrinsically motivated act, which is a step toward some other goal, is part of a chain of acts and subgoals that ultimately lead to an intrinsically motivated goal. What may very well be more important than whether particular goals are intrinsically or extrinsically motivated is whether the intrinsically motivated goal at the end of the chain is appetitive (e.g., a happy home) or aversive (e.g., keeping from angering one's mate). People with more aversive goals are generally less satisfied with life and work than those with fewer aversive goals (Elliot & Sheldon, 1998; Roberson, 1989; Roberson & Sluss, Chapter 14, this volume). Satisfaction presumably also depends on whether the ultimate intrinsically motivated goal is worth all the bother of the extrinsically motivated activity leading up to it.

It is important not to confuse the intrinsic versus extrinsic distinction with whether a goal was self-chosen or chosen by someone else. Similarly, the distinction is not to be confused with whether another person plays a role in the rewards of attaining a goal. Goals imposed on one by others, or perhaps even just suggested by others, are likely to be extrinsically motivated, in that pursuing the goal is likely to have the further purpose of keeping the person who imposed it happy. Thus, the child will carry out the trash when asked to do so because of a desire to keep the parent's emotional support. Keeping that support, however, may be in part intrinsically motivated, in that the child enjoys for its own sake relating to a supportive parent. Conversely, self-chosen goals may be extrinsically motivated (for example, taking a difficult college course in order to upgrade one's credentials for future employment) as well as intrinsically motivated.

In summary, it is a mistake to equate—as some current writers appear to do—intrinsic motivation with desirable motivation and extrinsic with undesirable. Both are important and necessary. However, the balance between them in an individual's life and the concrete forms they take can affect overall happiness.

Other Motivational Constructs

This chapter is unable to review all of the motivational constructs. However, readers may wonder what happened to the traditional concepts that make up the main focus of conventional introductory textbooks, constructs such as drive (e.g., hunger, thirst, sexual arousal), need (e.g., for achievement or intimacy), and arousal.

The venerable concept of drive (e.g., Bindra, 1968; Hull, 1952) remains an important component of the motivational picture as an aroused internal state that both invigorates mental and motor activity and modulates the value of drive-related incentives. However, even Hull's (1952) theory supplemented it with incentive as a determinant of motivation, and subsequent evidence (e.g., Bindra, 1968; Black, 1965, 1968, 1969, 1976; Black & Cox, 1973; Klinger, 1971; Tomkins, 1962) supported the need for additional factors, or even just different factors, for motivational prediction of everyday human behavior. Following Bindra's analysis, drive may be considered to perform two functions: to activate and to modify, even if only temporarily, the values of various incentives. Thus, both rats and people, when hungry, become more restless and give heightened priority to getting something to eat.

The concept of need (e.g., Heckhausen, 1991; McClelland et al., 1953; Murray, 1938) is similarly alive and well. It has evolved into a construct that summarizes the value that an individual typically places on a certain class of incentives (i.e., potential goals). For example, an individual who places relatively high intrinsic value on achievement incentives, such as winning races or intellectual contests or doing well in one's work, is said to have a high need for achievement. Thus, like drive, need in this sense plays a role largely in relation to incentive value, which is a crucial component in decision-making regarding which goals to pursue (see also Correia, Chapter 3, and Glasner, Chapter 2, this volume).

GOAL PURSUITS, TIME-BINDING, AND THE CONCEPT OF CURRENT CONCERN

Pursuing a goal imposes some complex requirements on an individual. The first of these is that the pursuit be represented somehow in the brain between beginning the pursuit and ending it—otherwise, there would be no memory of the pursuit, in which case the individual would be distracted from it by every evocative stimulus that was encountered. Memory for the fact that one is pursuing a goal is an example of *prospective memory* (Brandimonte, Einstein, & McDaniel, 1996). When the memory is explicit and conscious, Kuhl (2000, 2001) calls it *intention memory*. However, goal pursuit requires more than a passive memory of the pursuit; it requires a continuing state of sensitization to stimuli relevant to the pursuit and readiness to act—to seize opportunities for attaining the goal. Furthermore, this state of sensitization needs to be an implicit, latent process; that is, the individual needs to be sensitized to goal-related cues and be ready to act even while not consciously thinking of the goal. Otherwise the goal pursuit would be very inefficient. As a later section of this chapter shows, there is now ample evidence confirming that goal pursuits are accompanied by a pervasive biasing of cognitive processing—attention, recall, and thought content—toward information associated with an individual's goal pursuits.

To give this hypothetical latent process a name, the construct of *current concern* refers to the state of an individual between two time points, the one of becoming committed to pursuing a particular goal and the other of either attaining the goal or giving up the pursuit. Because a current concern spans the duration of the pursuit and binds together psychological processes over that period, it constitutes a *time-binding* process.

It is worth reiterating two other properties of current concerns. First, there is a separate such process—a separate concern—corresponding to each goal. Second, it is a latent process, meaning that in and of itself it is not conscious. It certainly affects consciousness, and individuals are probably conscious of most, if not all, of the goals undergirded by their current concerns, but the concern construct refers to the underlying process, not just its conscious representation. The concept of current concern labels the process of having a goal.

Before and since the coining of the concept of current concern, other theorists have offered other, somewhat similar time-binding concepts. The concept of *Einstellung, Ustanovka,* or *set* (Ach, 1910; Uznadze, 1966), *intention* (e.g., Gollwitzer, 1990; Heckhausen & Kuhl, 1985; Irwin, 1971; Kaschel & Kuhl, Chapter 6, this volume; Kuhl, 2001), quasineed (Lewin, 1928), *force* (Lewin, 1938), and *personal project* (Little, 1983; Little & Chambers, Chapter 4, this volume) are all constructs with time-binding properties and have more or less overlap with the construct of current concern, but with variations in their theoretical properties. This is not the place for a detailed comparison of these constructs. The important point is that initiating a goal pursuit instates a persistent psychological process that influences cognition, action, and emotional response in ways that give the needs and course of the pursuit special priority.

Correspondingly, the concept of current concern provides a unifying framework for motivational processes in animal and human behavior and suggests important aspects of animal and human behavioral evolution. It also provides a useful framework for considering certain aspects of psychopathology and developing approaches to psychological intervention.

GOALS AND EMOTIONS

Goal pursuits are intimately and pervasively intertwined with emotions. Emotions play crucial roles in choosing goals, in assessing the pursuit of them, in steering cognitive processes within them, and in reacting to their outcomes. Subsequent sections of this chapter explore these propositions. The purpose of this section is to lay out the terrain and to examine some emotion-related concepts.

Emotions constitute states of organisms, directly or indirectly affecting virtually every process, psychological or biological. Emotional responses constitute changes in organismic states. They have long been recognized as components of instinctive behavior (e.g., Darwin, 1872/1985; McDougall, 1921) and as preparing an individual to act in particular ways. For example, participants were asked to look at letter strings on a screen and as quickly as possible either press a key (an approach response) or take their finger off a key (a withdrawal response) if the string was a word (Wentura, Rothermund, & Bak, 2000). Participants who were asked to press keys did so faster if the word was positively toned than if it was negatively toned, and those who were asked to withdraw their fingers did so faster if the word was negatively toned than if it was positively toned. The valences of the words presumably evoked incipient emotional responses, and these were evidently linked to a motor disposition to move accordingly—to approach positive things and withdraw from negative ones—that facilitated the corresponding acts of pressing or releasing a key on a keyboard.

Conversely, people were able to categorize or otherwise process emotionally positive words faster if they were flexing their arms or appeared to be approaching a computer screen, and they were able to process emotionally negative words faster if they were extending their arms or appeared to be receding from a computer screen (Neumann & Strack, 2000). Here the acts that physically represent approach (such as a flexed arm, often associated with bringing something closer) or an extended arm (as in pushing something away) appeared to facilitate dealing with the corresponding emotional information (positive and negative, respectively). Ideographs, which are presumably neutral stimuli to most American research participants, were evaluated more positively after association with arm flexion than after arm extension (Cacioppo, Priester, & Berntson, 1993). These three studies thus demonstrate the connections between emotional response and physical movement. Extensive evidence has also linked emotions to a wide range of neurohumoral states and immune function (e.g., Mayne, 2001). Emotions are thus much more than just the subjective feelings or the bodily sensations that people usually associate with them.

There are a number of other terms related to the term *emotion*, especially *feeling* and *affect*. Some writers use these synonymously with emotion, a few use affect to refer to physiological aspects of emotion, and some reserve feeling and affect for the conscious experience associated with emotion, in contrast to its physiological or nonconscious components. In this last usage, the term *emotion* includes affect and all of the many other components of emotion, for which there is no generally accepted separate term. This is the usage adopted here.

There is a growing consensus among emotion researchers (e.g., Cacioppo, Gardner, & Berntson, 1999; Kuhl, 2001; Watson et al., 1999) that the different emotions people feel can be organized within two dimensions or categories—that is, as either *positive* or *negative* affect. There is good reason to believe that these two dimensions correspond to separate reaction systems in the brain (Cacioppo, Gardner, & Berntson, 1999). When people experience positive affect, they feel pleasurably engaged with their environment; when they experience negative affect, they feel distressed and dissatisfied (Watson & Kendall, 1989).

An *affective change* is a change in affect from its present state. The change may be desirable (an increase in positive affect or a decrease in negative affect) or undesirable (a decrease in positive affect or an increase in negative affect). Affective change is a central motivational concept, because it is the ultimate essence of what people are motivated to achieve. As noted by innumerable writers from Aristotle (Stocker, 1996) onward, people strive for things that will make them feel better, by either giving them pleasure or relieving their discomfort.

Beyond this truism, important as it is, research has uncovered a remarkable range of other ways in which changing from a positive to a negative affective state or vice versa influences basic psychological functions. The changes involve peripheral physiology, neurophysiology, types of cognitive processing, and even the ability to consult one's own values and to learn from experience (e.g., Kaschel & Kuhl, Chapter 6, this volume; Kuhl, 2000, 2001).

The relation between emotion and goal-striving has become progressively better documented. Affect constitutes a person's basic system for recognizing the value of something, both of potential goals (or, negatively, of impediments and threats) and of progress toward goals (Damasio, 1994; Klinger, 1977; Pervin, 1983). When people are asked to rate the intensity of the emotions that words arouse in them and how closely the words are associated with their goal pursuits, the correlations tend to be about .60 (Bock & Klinger, 1986; et al.). Of course, the affective and broader emotional responses that lead to evaluative judgments are generally embedded in a more complex process that includes other components. Some emotional responses are innately hard-wired to certain schematic features of stimuli and hence require a perceptual process; others are responses to conditioned stimuli, which requires a learning history, and still others depend on even more complex inferences about the significance of a stimulus. Nevertheless, the weight of evidence strongly suggests that it is the emotional response or an anticipated emotional response that determines the value of an incentive and the evaluation of anything as good or bad for oneself.

Not everything to which an individual responds emotionally becomes a goal, but it does constitute a potential goal. To provide a term for this larger class of potential goals, the term *incentive* refers to an object or event that a person expects will bring about an affective change. Corresponding to the two broad kinds of affect, incentives can be either positive or negative. People would like to acquire *positive* incentives that would enhance their positive affect. They would like to get rid of *negative* incentives that would increase their negative affect.

A *goal*, then, is a particular incentive that a person strives to attain. The object of every goal-striving is an incentive, something that people expect will cause desirable changes in their affect. However, for various reasons, people do not strive to attain all of the incentives that could potentially bring them the changes that they would like. For example, they might (a) feel that they do not know how to go about attaining the goal that they want, (b) imagine that doing so would also bring them unhappiness, (c) believe that they are unlikely to succeed, or (d) find that time constraints force a choice among alternatives. Goals, therefore, constitute a limited selection from among a person's incentives.

HOW GOAL PURSUITS BEGIN

Commitment

Goal pursuits generally have an identifiable beginning when the individual selects an incentive and forms an inner *commitment* to pursuing it as a goal. This commitment instates a current concern about the goal and constitutes an irreversible change, in the sense that the goal cannot be relinquished without a psychological cost, such as disappointment or depression. Heckhausen and Gollwitzer (1987) have called this irreversibility the *Rubicon Effect*, an allusion to the irreversibility of Caesar's decision to cross the Rubicon River with his troops in an assault on rival forces before Rome. Having crossed, a painless retreat was no longer an option.

That commitments are discrete events is evident not only in the costs of relinquishment but also in the several changes that commitment to a goal produces. First, commitment to a goal changes the initial effects of sudden impediments; before commitment to a goal, impediments make pursuing the incentive as a goal less attractive, but after a commitment impediments initially lead to invigorated pursuit and deepened commitment (Klinger, 1975). Second, commitments also change *mind sets* (Gollwitzer, Heckhausen, & Steller, 1990). Before commitment, while the individual is still weighing alternatives and reserving the decision as to which incentive to pursue, the individual is in an *evaluative* mind set, characterized by relative objectivity about the alternatives and openness to a wide range of information. After commitment, the individual enters an *implemental* mind set characterized by partiality toward the chosen goal and a mental focus on the steps necessary to reach it. Third, as indicated in subsequent sections, the current concerns instated by commitments sensitize the individual to respond to cues associated with the goal pursuit.

Determinants of Commitment: Expectancy × Value Approaches

In any given circumstance, people are generally faced with choices of which incentives they will pursue. They face choices of playmates, careers or jobs, partners with whom to spend a coffee break or a lifetime, items on a restaurant menu, vacation destinations, whether to talk in class, and so on. Often one alternative is so much more attractive, or so much less unattractive, than the others that the individual may not feel as if there is a choice, but the choice is generally there.

If there is a choice, what determines which incentive the individual will choose as a goal? A long theoretical tradition in psychology and economics, which may loosely be termed *Value × Expectancy* formulations (e.g., Feather, 1982; Van Eerde & Thierry, 1996) holds that two important variables determine this choice: the value that the person attributes to each alternative incentive and the person's expectancy (subjective probability) of being able to attain it. In the simplest form of Value × Expectancy theory (which economists generally term *Subjective Expected Utility* theory), one multiplies the value by the expectancy of each alternative and predicts that the individual will choose the alternative yielding the highest product.

There are many elaborations, modifications, and qualifications of this approach, but its general outlines have survived. Although attempts to empirically test the nature of the relationship between value and expectancy remain inconclusive because of unresolved methodological problems (see Kuhl, 1986, pp. 409–410; Van Eerde & Thierry, 1996), the approach has proven useful in making concrete predictions of goal choice.

In terms of the motivational concepts described above, the value of each incentive—of each potential goal object—is the degree of affective change that the person expects to derive from it (Klinger, 1977; see also Loewenstein et al., 2001; Mellers, 2000). Insofar as an incentive has positive value, people expect that attaining it will increase their happiness more than their unhappiness, and they expect to experience sorrow if they fail to achieve it. In other words, people attribute value to their goal objects on the basis of the potential emotional payoffs for them.

Among the complications in applying this approach is the matter of how to assess or predict value. For example, the incentive may be something of relatively low absolute value (for example, going to see a particular film), but if the cost of pursuing this incentive is also modest and attaining it is likely to bring positive emotion, there is a good chance that the individual will pursue it. Value must therefore be balanced against costs. Furthermore, the value of an incentive may depend on a variety of extrinsic components, in that it affects the ability to reach other goals. For example, becoming a physician may be a positive incentive for someone because the individual expects high social status, respect, and financial returns and becoming more competitive in the search for a desirable mate, in addition to the intrinsic pleasure of feeling needed and making an important contribution to society. These positive components will be offset to some extent by the costs, such as many years of arduous study, exploitation as a hospital resident, limited time for one's family, increasing bureaucratization of the profession, and legal risks. Thus, the final value of an incentive may be a complex resultant of numerous components.

According to this view, both value and expectancy must be substantial for people to pursue a goal. Even if people greatly value particular incentives, they will not be motivated to pursue them if they do not expect to succeed. Likewise, even if the chances of reaching particular goals are judged to be high, individuals will not be motivated to pursue them if they do not expect a suitable benefit. As the theoretical multiplicative relationship between value and expectancy indicates, the two variables should moderate each other, such that if either value or expectancy is at zero there will be no motivation to attain the goal, regardless of how high the other might be.

The most important point here is that expected emotional return is probably the prime determinant of whether a person becomes committed to pursuing a particular goal. However, there are a number of important qualifications to this generalization.

First, the extent to which people take probability of success and incentive value into account varies, both from person to person (e.g., Shah & Higgins, 1997) and from time to time. For example, people are more likely to pay attention to the incentive value (i.e., emotional payoff) of far-off incentives than of those in which success or failure would be imminent, and more attention to probability of success for imminent incentives (Liberman & Trope, 1998).

Second, people often miscalculate their future emotional reactions to a particular event, which should theoretically distort their valuations. Thus, one's present state colors estimates of future emotion, especially when one is cognitively overloaded or if the future event is not specified with respect to the time of its occurrence (Gilbert, Gill, & Wilson, 2002).

Furthermore, people underestimate their future liking for things if they believe that once they receive them they will no longer be able to change their choice (Gilbert & Ebert, 2002). They tend to overestimate the intensity (Wilson, Meyers, & Gilbert, 2001) and duration (Gilbert et al., 1998; Wilson et al., 2000) of future emotional reactions to both positive and negative events. These distortions are reduced by having people consider in greater detail the context of their activities and lives at and after the time of the future event whose impact they are forecasting (Gilbert, Gill, & Wilson, 2002; Wilson et al., 2000), as well as reflecting on their inner emotional coping skills for reducing negative affect (Gilbert et al., 1998).

Finally, people are often willing to settle for good enough rather than insisting on getting the very best alternative. This is called *satisficing* (e.g., Gigerenzer & Goldstein, 1996; Schwartz et al., 2002; Simon, 1956). Nevertheless, despite all these qualifications, expected emotional gain remains the most reliable determinant of goal choice.

The Value × Expectancy framework has a number of implications for motivational counseling. For example, a depressed or substance-abusing client may be forgoing potentially satisfying nonsubstance incentives because of pessimism about being able to attain them. Depression lowers incentive values (see Klinger, 1993, for a review), which makes most incentives less attractive; and conflicts among goals (Michalak, Heidenreich, & Hoyer, Chapter 5, this volume) reduce their attractiveness, which further discourages people from pursuing them. Substance use competes with nonsubstance incentives and may be chosen if the nonsubstance incentives are sufficiently unattractive (Correia, Chapter 3, this volume; Cox & Klinger, Chapter 7, this volume; Glasner, Chapter 2, this volume). Sufficient lack of interest in earthly satisfactions may dispose people toward suicide (e.g., King et al., 2001; Klinger, 1977; Snyder, 1994; Williams, 1997). Here, motivational interventions to revalue incentives and instill reality-based optimism can change the balance of motivational structure and hence clients' behavior (Snyder, 1994—see also, in this volume: Cox & Klinger, Chapter 11; de Jong-Meyer, Chapter 13; Jones, Chapter 19; McMurran, Chapter 16; Miranti & Heinemann, Chapter 15; Roberson & Sluss, Chapter 14; Schoer, Fuhrmann, & de Jong-Meyer, Chapter 12; and Willutzki & Koban, Chapter 17).

HOW GOAL PURSUITS UNFOLD

The course of a goal pursuit can be thought of in terms of control theory (Carver & Scheier, 1998). There is a feed-forward component, in that the goal sets up criteria for the priority the individual will place on processing various future stimuli, as well as some specifications on how the individual will respond. Having decided to pursue a particular goal, a person becomes sensitized to respond to stimuli associated with that goal pursuit (Klinger, 1971, 1975, 1977, 1996b). The stimuli—*cues*—may be external (e.g., words or pictures related to the goal pursuit) or internal (e.g., thoughts or mental images related to the goal pursuit). Sensitization means that encountering one of these cues increases the likelihood of responding to them—with goal-directed actions if that seems appropriate or, more often, with mental activity such as the thoughts and mental images of mind-wandering. People are more likely to recall such cues and to think about them than they are to recall and think about other cues. Response is often extremely fast, making it clear that goal-related cues receive high priority in cognitive processing.

There is also a feedback component to goal pursuits (e.g., Carver & Scheier, 1998; Klinger, 1977). People continuously monitor the extent to which their thoughts and actions are advancing them toward their goals. If the feedback is favorable, they proceed according to plan; if the feedback is unfavorable, indicating that what they are doing is not helping as much as planned, they may adjust their actions to obtain better results. An important part of this feedback process—its evaluative component—is emotional. Positive emotions in reaction to events signal that the goal pursuit is on course; negative emotions—especially fear and depression—signal imminent or actual failures. This emotional component may occur before the person consciously recognizes what is going on (e.g., Winkielmann, Zajonc, & Schwarz, 1997; Zajonc, 1980).

Effects on Attention, Memory, Recall, Dreams, and Action

The evidence for the effects of current concerns on cognition is by now very strong. Initial investigations of this model asked participants to listen to series of two different but similar, simultaneous, 15-minute narratives on audiotape, one narrative to each ear. At particular time points, they heard passages in one ear that were associated with their own concerns, and, simultaneously, passages going to the other ear that were related to another's concerns. Participants spent significantly more time listening to passages associated with their own concerns than to the other's, recalled those passages much more often, and had thought content that (by ratings of blind judges) was much more often related to them (Klinger, 1978).

Automaticity of the Effects

Subsequent studies of both waking and sleeping participants indicated that these effects are apparently nonconscious and automatic rather than attributable to a conscious process, such as deliberately focusing on concern-related stimuli. In fact, concern-related stimuli seem to impose an extra cognitive-processing load even when they are peripheral and participants are consciously ignoring them (Young, 1987); when asked to judge as quickly as possible whether a string of letters on a screen constitutes a word, these apparently irrelevant distractor stimuli nevertheless slow the lexical decisions about the target words. Similar effects have been shown in yet another cognitive process, Stroop and quasi-Stroop procedures. In these procedures, people are presented with words on a screen and instructed to name the font color of the words as quickly as possible. Participants in these experiments name font colors more slowly when the words are related to one of their own concerns than when they are not (Bauer & Cox, 1998; Cox, Blount, & Rozak, 2000; Cox, Brown, & Rowlands, in press; Cox, Yeates, & Regan, 1999; Cox et al., 2002; Johnsen et al., 1994; Riemann, Amir, & Louro, 1995; Riemann & McNally, 1995; Sharma, Albery, & Cook, 2001; Stetter et al., 1995; Stormark et al., 1995, 2000; Williams, Mathews, & MacLeod, 1996). This slowing of response suggests that the brain gives processing priority to the concern-related features of the stimulus words, which defers the processing of other features and therefore slows judgments about these other features. Even when people are asleep, concern-related stimuli influence dream content much more reliably than do other stimuli (Hoelscher, Klinger, & Barta, 1981; Nikles et al., 1998). Taken together, these results confirm that the effects of concern-related cues on cognitive processing are substantially automatic and probably inexorable.

Goal-related cues, even nonconscious ones, also appear to exert automatic effects on goal-directed actions. A series of investigations (Bargh et al., 2001; Chartrand & Bargh, 1996, 2002) has shown that exposing participants to priming cues related to a particular goal influences how they perform on subsequent laboratory tasks. For example, when participants performed a first task that included unobtrusively embedded words related to achievement (versus receiving achievement-unrelated words), they performed better on a different second task, persisted longer, and were more likely to resume it if interrupted (Bargh et al., 2001). This was true even though no participant knew the true connection between the first and second tasks, meaning that the effect was probably nonconscious and in this sense automatic. Thus, nonconscious cues can affect performance in ways similar to the established effects (e.g., Locke, 1968, 2001) of setting conscious performance goals for oneself. Priming cues related to cooperation also had a comparable effect on participants' cooperative behavior (Chartrand & Bargh, 1996), showing that these effects are not restricted to just one kind of behavior.

Emotions and Attentional Processing

A number of indications from these and other data (e.g., Klinger, Barta, & Maxeiner, 1980) suggest that a critical property of current concerns is to dispose individuals to respond emotionally to cues associated with corresponding goal pursuits. The emotional response then induces a number of levels of cognitive processing, ending, at least under some conditions, with conscious thought. Because this hypothesis is hard to test with naturally occurring thought flow, the investigations to which it gave rise addressed effects on attention, recall, and physiological variables.

A reaction-time experiment (Schneider, 1987) produced effects of emotionally evocative cues (which participants were instructed to ignore) on choice reaction time similar to those obtained with current-concern-related words by Young (1987). Furthermore, participants who scored high on the Affective Intensity Measure (Larsen & Diener, 1987) were slowed by emotionally arousing distractors significantly more than other participants. Data also link current concerns to electrodermal responses of the kind often identified as orienting responses, and they link spontaneous electrodermal activity to current-concern-related ideation (Nikula, Klinger, & Larson-Gutman, 1993).

Emotions and Recall

Emotional arousingness of words also affects recall. Words rated by participants as either relatively emotionally arousing or concern-related were later recalled significantly more often than other words (Bock & Klinger, 1986; Klinger et al., in preparation). Concern-relatedness and emotional arousal value were strongly intercorrelated. Partialing emotionality and concern-relatedness of words out of each other suggested that much of the effect of current concerns on recall is mediated by the emotional responses that the concerns largely potentiated. This interpretation is consistent with other findings that people experience more emotion in relation to those autobiographical memories that are most closely associated with current goal pursuits and longer-term personal strivings (Singer & Salovey, 1993). Chemically impairing the ability to respond emotionally reduces recall of emotionally toned stimuli (Cahill et al., 1994).

These findings help to make sense of some other results in the literature, in which stimuli that arouse emotion facilitate cognitive processing of them when the stimuli are central to a task at hand and interfere with cognitive processing when the stimuli are distractors (see Klinger, 1996b, for a review). Close examination of procedures used in such studies suggests that people respond to cues as emotionally arousing insofar as the cues are related to current concerns. Thus, patients suffering from social phobias attend differentially more to socially threatening stimuli than to physically threatening ones, whereas people fearful of physical harm attend to the latter more than the former (Mogg, Mathews, & Eysenck, 1992; Williams, Mathews, & MacLeod, 1996).

Conclusion

In conclusion, then, having a goal sensitizes a person to respond to goal-related cues, one effect of which is to keep drawing the individual's perceptions, memories, thoughts, dreams, and actions back to the goal pursuit. Furthermore, the person's emotional reactions, whether of joy, fear, anger, or sadness, depend substantially on what is happening to the individual's goal pursuits. Taken together, these effects mold people's inner worlds around their individual sets of goals. If one placed two individuals into the identical objective world but with different sets of current concerns, they would experience quite different subjective worlds. What they would notice, recall, and think would be quite different, they would react with different emotions, and they would correspondingly act quite differently, which in turn would result in creating for them different objective circumstances.

These connections between goals on the one hand and perception, cognition, emotion, and action on the other are important points to remember in providing counseling. Apart from organic disorders, such as psychosis and brain damage, troublesome cognitions, emotions, and actions are tied to troubled goal pursuits. Whether the problem is rumination, boredom, depression, anxiety, or substance use, effective intervention requires examining and intervening in the related goal pursuits.

Other Influences on Goal Pursuits

A number of variables besides those already described also affect the level and quality of the motivation to pursue a goal. These and other aspects of motivated behavior are taken into account in the techniques for assessing motivation presented in Chapter 8.

Approach versus Avoidance Goals

One such variable is the valence of the desired goal object—whether it is positive or negative. There is growing evidence that positive and negative goals involve different neural systems for, respectively, approach and avoidance (e.g., Cacioppo, Gardner, & Berntson, 1999; Carver & Scheier, 1998; Watson et al., 1999). These different systems are associated with different effects on emotion, motivation, and health. Thus, people striving to achieve positive (*approach*) goals such as gaining a job promotion or better health are more likely to do so for the intrinsic value of the goal (Elliot & Harackiewicz, 1996) and less likely to experience negative feelings, poor health, or a negative outlook on themselves, than do people who are motivated more by a desire to avoid negative consequences (*avoidance goals*), as in striving not to be fired, not to become ill, or to rid oneself of negative incentives by which one feels burdened, such as a poor marriage or loud neighbors (Elliot & Church, 2002; Elliot & Sheldon, 1998).

However, these deleterious effects of avoidance goals may apply only to individuals with an independent outlook, which, on average, includes Americans and other Westerners; they appear not to apply to people with an interdependent outlook, such as, on average, residents of Asian countries (Elliot et al., 2001). This cultural difference aside, it may be beneficial for motivational counselors to help clients to reframe their avoidance goals into approach terms. For example, avoiding illness can be reframed as maintaining health; avoiding arguments with one's spouse can be reframed as improving one's marital relationship (see also Elliot & Church, 2002; Willutzki & Koban, Chapter 17, this volume).

There are important individual differences in the strength of these two hypothetical approach and avoidance systems. Some individuals respond more readily to approach goals, are more likely to experience positive emotions, and in these senses are said to be more *reward-dependent* (e.g., Cloninger, Svrakic, & Przybeck, 1993) or *reward-sensitive*, a characteristic that may be part of the essence of extraversion (Lucas et al., 2000). This difference among individuals is reflected in the different values that different people place on the same objective incentives and hence in their different choices of goals and other decisions.

Time Frame

The time course of the goal pursuit is another important consideration. Motivation is likely to be stronger when people pursue goals (or subgoals) that are achievable in the relatively near future, rather than having to wait far into the future to gain a sense of accomplishment (Miller, 1944). Breaking long-term goal pursuits into a tangible series of attainable nearer-term subgoal pursuits may improve motivation for staying on course.

Goal Conflicts

Yet another consideration is the impact that pursuing one goal will have on other goals for which one is striving (see Michalak, Heidenreich, & Hoyer, Chapter 5, this volume). For example, if one important goal interferes with the achievement of another one, the resulting conflict is bound to dampen the motivation to achieve either goal. People with more than average numbers of conflicts among their goals also experience more negative affect and poorer health (Emmons & King, 1988). Goal conflicts are necessarily an important target of counseling interventions.

Specificity of Intentions

People vary in regard to how concretely they imagine their goal pursuits. Sometimes they focus mainly on the end result—what it will be like and how it will feel to achieve the goal. Musing about the consummation of a romantic relationship or of a business deal can both be pleasant experiences. However, people are more likely to carry out their intended goal pursuits if they also imagine the steps necessary to reach their goals (e.g., Brandstaetter, Lengfelder, & Gollwitzer, 2001; Gollwitzer, 1999; Snyder, 1994) and take into account the difficulties before them (Oettingen, Pak, & Schnetter, 2001), especially if the goals also fit well with the individual's core values (Koestner et al., 2002). Counseling interventions can be targeted toward helping clients to form adequate conceptions of their goal pursuits so as to improve the quality of their tactics for attaining their goals (Cox & Klinger, Chapter 11, this volume).

HOW GOAL PURSUITS END

All goal pursuits must end, whether by reaching the goal, or by relinquishing it. Attaining a goal, especially an important goal that has many ramifications for one's future life, generally evokes some combination of joy, gratification, contentment, and pride. One marries, obtains a college degree, gets a desired job, buys a lovely house, or finds spiritual fulfillment. Attaining the goal ends the pursuit and deactivates the current concern. It is clearly the nice way for goal pursuits to end.

Unfortunately, life is rarely so kind as to spare people at least some failures. The relationship ends or the partner dies, the job goes to someone else, or the stock market collapses and takes one's savings with it. Obstacles to goal pursuits unleash a regular sequence of events, an *incentive-disengagement cycle* (Klinger, 1975, 1977). When the obstacle first arises, the effect is to invigorate goal-directed action. One tries harder, rethinks, tries alternatives, seeks help. If these tactics fail, invigoration turns to anger and possibly aggression. If this also fails to avert the obstacle, the individual experiences a souring of mood that can range from disappointment to depression. There is often a reduced interest in other pursuits (Klinger, 1993), lassitude, and fatigue. Eventually, the individual recovers from the failure or loss and returns to baseline levels of mood and activity. This may take from minutes to years, depending on the scale of the failure.

Although there are wide variations in the strength of these effects, they appear nearly universal, even when there is no apparent point to them. Thus, when someone learns that a loved one has unexpectedly died, the first reaction is often disbelief, checking on the accuracy of the report, and ascertaining that nothing can be done. This is often followed by anger and blame toward the departed, caretakers, medical personnel, relatives, or oneself. Then come the grieving and eventually the recovery.

When the cycle has run its course, the person is largely freed to go on to other things. The failed goal ceases to be a goal. However, its representation in the brain remains. Disengagement is almost certainly not a process of forgetting or deleting the goal but rather one of inhibiting responses to all but the most central cues associated with it. The failure or loss lives on, even though deeply suppressed. Thus, parents who have lost children never fully recover from the loss, at least for the several years that such losses have been followed up (Lehman, Wortman, & Williams, 1987).

Very likely, the reaction to failure or loss is a form of extinction, which has been studied extensively in this regard, especially in animals (Hutchinson, 1973; Lewinsohn, 1974). Extinction, which results from withholding reward that the animal had previously regularly experienced, also leads to a cycle of invigoration and depressed activity followed by recovery (e.g., Klinger, Kemble, & Barta, 1974; Lewis et al., 1992). Furthermore, the goal-striving is rapidly reinstated when the reward is again made available (e.g., Nakajima et al., 2000; Toyomitsu et al., 2002), suggesting that the previous extinction of response was by inhibition rather than deletion (see also Bouton & Swartzentruber, 1989).

These concepts of incentive-disengagement and extinction are important considerations in counseling depressed clients. Within limits, depression is a normal reaction to failure and loss. Individual differences in emotional responsiveness and in the ability to down-regulate negative affect (Kuhl, 2000, 2001; see also Kaschel & Kuhl, Chapter 6, this volume) may lead to psychopathological levels of depression. Nevertheless, it would appear to remain crucial for counselors and psychotherapists to work with the client's motivational structure, along with applying other well-established cognitive and interpersonal approaches (e.g., Beck, Rush, & Emery, 1979; Teasdale, Segal, & Williams, 1995; Teasdale et al., 2000) in treating depression. Chapters 11 to 24 of this volume describe the various motivational techniques in greater detail.

INCENTIVES, GOALS, WELL-BEING, AND THE SENSE THAT ONE'S LIFE IS MEANINGFUL

Perhaps the broadest measure of an individual's subjective success in life is the person's global sense of well-being (Kahneman, 1999). Another—closely correlated (Wong, 1998)—is the sense that one's life is meaningful. Both are closely related to having a range of satisfying personal goals and making reasonable progress toward attaining them (Brunstein, 1993; Klinger, 1977, 1998).

Any integration of past research on subjective well-being, or of the sense that one's life is meaningful, is bound to find that both depend substantially on people's perceptions that they have important goals and are progressing satisfactorily toward them. For example, most people place high value on finding and maintaining close relationships (Baumeister & Leary, 1995), and attaining these interpersonal goals is strongly related to their sense of well-being (Myers, 1999). Similarly, satisfaction with one's work, which subsumes another major set of personal goals, is related to the extent that the workplace fosters an employee's attainment of work-related and work-affected goals (Roberson, 1989; Roberson & Sluss, Chapter 14, this volume; Warr, 1999). Having a sense of interpersonal support in one's goal pursuits enhances well-being; a sense of others hindering one's goal pursuits detracts from well-being (Palys & Little, 1983; Ruehlman & Wolchik, 1988).

What is important in determining subjective well-being is a sense of progressing toward one's personal goals (Diener & Fujita, 1995), whatever they may be. By contrast, objective indices of personal resources and circumstances, such as income, education, and marital status, correlate rather poorly with subjective well-being. Similarly, a long-term longitudinal study (Halisch & Geppert, 1998) has found that life satisfaction and well-being depend on having goals that are attainable, and this is especially true for people highly committed to them. Mood was lower in the absence of affiliative and, for men, power-related activity.

However, not all personal goals carry equal weight in well-being. For example, progress on goals imposed by others or suggested by social pressures boost subjective well-being less than goals that correspond to one's individual core values (Brunstein, Schultheiss, & Graessman, 1998; Sheldon, 2001; Sheldon & Elliot, 1999). This suggests a point of departure for psychological intervention: assessing the self-concordance of a client's goals and modifying or eliminating those at variance with the client's core values.

There are also other important factors that moderate the relation of goal pursuits to subjective well-being. For example, some individuals (*state-oriented*) have more difficulty than other people in distinguishing self-chosen goals from goals suggested by others (Kuhl & Kazén, 1994; see also Kaschel & Kuhl, Chapter 6, this volume). Under pressure, they may be less able to discern their own values and interests in a situation and hence strive for suboptimally fulfilling goals. Individual differences in emotional response dispositions, partially described above, can determine the extent to which people pursue goals and the extent to which they derive satisfaction from them. These findings, too, suggest possible foci for psychological intervention.

Furthermore, a large proportion of the variance in subjective well-being can be accounted for by genetics (Lykken, 1999; Lykken & Tellegen, 1996). The genetic factors may, however, exert some of their effect through their influence on an individual's readiness to commit to positive goals and to reap the emotional gain from attaining them. Thus, to declare the disposition to subjective well-being to be heritable is not necessarily to gainsay its relation to goal pursuit. It would also be mistaken to conclude that its heritability prevents intervention from improving the individual's motivational structure and, with it, subjective well-being. Genes provide an input whose ultimate results depend on their interaction with the environment. Intervention can be part of that environment.

A substantial literature relates subjective well-being and the sense that one's life is meaningful to psychopathology and substance use (Baumeister, 1991; Cox & Klinger, 1988; Klinger, 1977, 1998—see also, in this volume: Correia, Chapter 3; Cox & Klinger, Chapter 7; and Glasner, Chapter 2). For example, a substantial student sample produced a correlation of $-.46$ between a rating of their lives' meaningfulness and depression scores (Klinger, 1977). In two samples of adolescents and young adults, Newcomb and Harlow (1986) found low-order but significant relationships between substance use and lacking direction, plans, or solutions. In a comparison of Czech students and demographically rather similar nonstudent alcoholic patients (Man, Stuchlíková, & Klinger, 1998), the clinical group listed 40% fewer goals, responded as if they needed richer incentives to form strong commitments to goal-striving, displayed marginally less average commitment to their goals, and, after other variables had been partialled out, expressed less ability to influence the course of goal attainment. These correlational findings cannot establish cause and effect, but, when combined with experimental studies of extinction, loss, and failure, it seems likely that goal pursuits affect moods and at least some forms of psychopathology.

Accordingly, efforts to modify clients' motivational structure form a promising avenue to clinical effectiveness with a variety of disorders and discontents. These methods form the focus of Parts III and IV of this volume.

REFERENCES

Ach, N. (1910). *Über den Willensakt und das Temperament*. Leipzig: Van Quelle & Meyer.

Allport, G.W. (1937). *Personality: A psychological interpretation*. New York: Holt, Rinehart & Winston.

Bargh, J.A., Gollwitzer, P.M., Lee-Chai, A., Barndollar, K., & Trötschel, R. (2001). The automated will: Nonconscious activation and pursuit of behavioral goals. *Journal of Personality and Social Psychology, 81*, 1014–1027.

Bauer, D., & Cox, W.M. (1998). Alcohol-related words are distracting to both alcohol abusers and non-abusers in the Stroop colour naming task. *Addiction, 93*, 1539–1542.

Baumeister, R.F. (1991). *The meanings of life*. New York: Guilford.

Baumeister, R.G., & Leary, M.R. (1995). The need to belong: Desire for interpersonal attachments as a fundamental human motivation. *Psychological Bulletin, 117*, 497–529.

Bechara, A., Damasio, H., Tranel, D., & Damasio, A.R. (1997). Deciding advantageously before knowing the advantageous strategy. *Science, 275*, 1293–1294.

Bechara, A., Tranel, D., & Damasio, A.R. (2000). Characterization of the decision-making deficit of patients with ventromedial prefrontal cortex lesions. *Brain, 123*, 2189–2202.

Beck, A.T., Rush, A.J., & Emery, G. (1979). *Cognitive therapy of depression*. New York: Guilford.

Bindra, D. (1968). Neuropsychological interpretation of the effects of drive and incentive-motivation on general activity and instrumental behavior. *Psychological Review, 75*, 1–22.

Black, R.W. (1965). On the combination of drive and incentive motivation. *Psychological Review, 72*, 310–317.

Black, R.W. (1968). Shifts in magnitude of reward and contrast effects in instrumental and selective learning: A reinterpretation. *Psychological Review, 75*, 114–126.

Black, R.W. (1969). Incentive motivation and the parameters of reward in instrumental conditioning. In W.J. Arnold & D. Levine (Eds.), *Nebraska symposium on motivation* (pp. 85–141). Lincoln: University of Nebraska Press.

Black, R.W. (1976). Reward variables in instrumental conditioning: A theory. In G.H. Bower (Ed.), *The psychology of learning and motivation* (pp. 199–244). New York: Academic Press.

Black, R.W., & Cox, W.M. (1973). Extinction of an instrumental running response in rats in the absence of frustration and nonreinforcement. *Psychological Record, 23*, 101–109.

Bock, M., & Klinger, E. (1986). Interaction of emotion and cognition in word recall. *Psychological Research, 48*, 99–106.

Bouton, M.E., & Swartzentruber, D. (1989). Slow reacquisition following extinction: Context, encoding, and retrieval mechanisms. *Journal of Experimental Psychology: Animal Behavior Processes, 15*, 43–53.

Brandimonte, M., Einstein, G.O., & McDaniel, M.A. (Eds.) (1996). *Prospective memory: Theory and applications* (pp. 53–91). Hillsdale, NJ: Erlbaum.

Brandstaetter, V., Lengfelder, A., & Gollwitzer, P.M. (2001). Implementation intentions and efficient action initiation. *Journal of Personality and Social Psychology, 81*, 946–960.

Brunstein, J.C. (1993). Personal goals and subjective well-being: A longitudinal study. *Journal of Personality and Social Psychology, 65*, 1061–1070.

Brunstein, J.C., Schultheiss, O.C., & Graessman, R. (1998). Personal goals and emotional well-being: The moderating role of motive dispositions. *Journal of Personality and Social Psychology, 75*, 494–508.

Cacioppo, J.T., Gardner, W.L., & Berntson, G.G. (1999). The affect system has parallel and integrative processing components: Form follows function. *Journal of Personality and Social Psychology, 76*, 839–855.

Cacioppo, J.T., Priester, J.R., & Berntson, G.G. (1993). Rudimentary determinants of attitudes. II: Arm flexion and extension have different effects on attitudes. *Journal of Personality and Social Psychology, 65*, 5–17.

Cahill, L., Prins, B., Weber, M., & McGaugh, J.L. (1994). Beta-adrenergic activation and memory for emotional events. *Nature, 371*, 702–704.

Carver, C.S., & Scheier, M.F. (1998). *On the self-regulation of behavior*. Cambridge, UK: Cambridge University Press.

Chaplin, J.P. (1968). *Dictionary of psychology*. New York: Dell.

Chartrand, T.L., & Bargh, J.A. (1996). Automatic activation of impression formation and memorization goals: Nonconscious goal priming reproduces effects of explicit task instructions. *Journal of Personality and Social Psychology, 71*, 464–478.

Chartrand, T.L., & Bargh, J.A. (2002). Nonconscious motivations: Their activation, operation, and consequences. In A. Tesser & D.A. Stapel (Eds.), *Self and motivation: Emerging psychological perspectives* (pp. 13–41). Washington, DC: American Psychological Association.

Cloninger, C.R., Svrakic, D.M., & Przybeck, T.R. (1993). A psychobiological model of temperament and character. *Archives of General Psychiatry, 50*, 975–990.

Cox, W.M., Blount, J.P., & Rozak, A.M. (2000). Alcohol abusers' and nonabusers' distraction by alcohol and concern-related stimuli. *American Journal of Drug and Alcohol Abuse, 26*, 489–495.

Cox, W.M., Brown, M.A., & Rowlands, L.J. (in press). The effects of alcohol cue exposure on non-dependent drinkers' attentional bias for alcohol-related stimuli. *Alcohol and Alcoholism*.

Cox, W.M., Hogan, L.M., Kristian, M.R., & Race, J.H. (2002). Alcohol attentional bias as a predictor of alcohol abusers' treatment outcome. *Drug and Alcohol Dependence, 68*, 237–243.

Cox, W.M., & Klinger, E. (1988). A motivational model of alcohol use. *Journal of Abnormal Psychology, 97*, 168–180.

Cox, W.M., Yeates, G.N., & Regan, C.M. (1999). Effects of alcohol cues on cognitive processing in heavy and light drinkers. *Drug and Alcohol Dependence, 55*, 85–89.

Damasio, A.R. (1994). *Descartes' error: Emotion, reason, and the human brain*. New York: Avon.

Darwin, C. (1872/1985). *The expression of the emotions in man and animals*. Chicago: University of Chicago Press.

Diener, E., & Fujita, F. (1995). Resources, personal strivings, and subjective well-being: A nomothetic and idiographic approach. *Journal of Personality and Social Psychology, 68*, 926–935.

Elliot, A.J., Chirkov, V.I., Kim, Y., & Sheldon, K.M. (2001). A cross-cultural analysis of avoidance (relative to approach) personal goals. *Psychological Science, 12*, 505–510.

Elliot, A.J., & Church, M.A. (2002). Client articulated avoidance goals in the therapy context. *Journal of Counseling Psychology, 49*, 243–254.

Elliot, A.J., & Harackiewicz, J. (1996). Approach and avoidance achievement goals and intrinsic motivation. *Journal of Personality and Social Psychology, 70*, 461–475.

Elliot, A.J., & Sheldon, K.M. (1998). Avoidance personal goals and the personality–illness relationship. *Journal of Personality and Social Psychology, 75*, 1282–1299.

Emmons, R.A., & King, L.A. (1988). Conflict among personal strivings: Immediate and long-term implications for psychological and physical well-being. *Journal of Personality and Social Psychology, 54*, 1040–1048.

Feather, N.T. (Ed.) (1982). *Expectations and actions: Expectancy-value models in psychology*. Hillsdale, NJ: Erlbaum.

Ferguson, E. (1994). Motivation. In R.J. Corsini (Ed.), *Encyclopedia of psychology* (Vol. 2; 2nd edn. p. 429). New York: John Wiley & Sons.

Gigerenzer, G., & Goldstein, D.G. (1996). Reasoning the fast and frugal way: Models of bounded rationality. *Psychological Review, 103*, 650–669.

Gilbert, D.T., & Ebert, J.E.J. (2002). Decisions and revisions: The affective forecasting of changeable outcomes. *Journal of Personality and Social Psychology, 82*, 503–514.

Gilbert, D.T., Gill, M.J., & Wilson, T.D. (2002). The future is now: Temporal correction in affective forecasting. *Organizational Behavior and Human Decision Processes, 88*, 430–444.

Gilbert, D.T., Pinel, E.C., Wilson, T.D., Blumberg, S.J., & Wheatley, T.P. (1998). Immune neglect: A source of durability bias in affective forecasting. *Journal of Personality and Social Psychology, 75*, 617–638.

Gollwitzer, P.M. (1990). Action phases and mind-sets. In E.T. Higgins & R.M. Sorrentino (Eds.), *Handbook of motivation and cognition: Foundations of social behavior* (Vol. 2; pp. 53–92). New York: Guilford.

Gollwitzer, P.M. (1999). Implementation intentions: Strong effects of simple plans. *American Psychologist, 54*, 493–503.

Gollwitzer, P.M., Heckhausen, H., & Steller, B. (1990). Deliberative and implemental mind-sets: Cognitive tuning toward congruous thoughts and information. *Journal of Personality and Social Psychology, 59*, 1119–1127.

Halisch, F., & Geppert, U. (1998). *Motives, personal goals, and life satisfaction in old age: First results from the Munich Twin Study (GOLD)*. Munich, Germany: Max Planck Institute for Psychological Research.

Heckhausen, H. (1967). *The anatomy of achievement motivation*. New York: Academic Press.

Heckhausen, H. (1991). *Motivation and action*. Berlin: Springer.

Heckhausen, H., & Gollwitzer, P.M. (1987). Thought contents and cognitive functioning in motivational and volitional states of mind. *Motivation and Emotion, 11*, 101–120.

Heckhausen, H., & Kuhl, J. (1985). From wishes to action: The dead ends and short cuts on the long way to action. In M. Frese & J. Sabini (Eds.), *Goal-directed behavior: Psychological theory and research on action* (pp. 134–160). Hillsdale, NJ: Erlbaum.

Hoelscher, T.J., Klinger, E., & Barta, S.G. (1981). Incorporation of concern- and nonconcern-related verbal stimuli into dream content. *Journal of Abnormal Psychology, 49*, 88–91.

Hull, C.L. (1952). *A behavior system*. New Haven: Yale University Press.

Hutchinson, R.R. (1973). The environmental causes of aggression. In J.K. Cole & D.D. Jensen (Eds.), *Nebraska Symposium on Motivation, 1972* (pp. 155–181). Lincoln, Nebraska: University of Nebraska Press.

Irwin, F.W. (1971). *Intentional behavior and motivation: A cognitive theory*. New York: Lippincott.

Jackson, D.N., Ahmed, S.A., & Heapy, N.A. (1976). Is achievement a unitary construct? *Journal of Research in Personality, 10*, 1–21.

Johnsen, B.H., Laberg, J.C., Cox, W.M., Vaksdal, A., & Hugdahl, K. (1994). Alcoholics' attentional bias in the processing of alcohol-related words. *Psychology of Addictive Behaviors, 8*, 111–115.

Kahneman, D. (1999). Objective happiness. In D. Kahneman, E. Diener, & N. Schwarz (Eds.), *Well-being: The foundations of hedonic psychology* (pp. 3–25). New York: Russell Sage Foundation.

Kasser, T., & Ryan, R.M. (2001). Be careful what you wish for: Optimal functioning and the relative attainment of intrinsic and extrinsic goals. In P. Schmuck & K.M. Sheldon (Eds.), *Life goals and well-being: Towards a positive psychology of human striving* (pp. 116–131). Seattle, Washington: Hogrefe & Huber.

King, R.A., Schwab-Stone, M., Flisher, A.J., Greenwald, S., Kramer, R.A., Goodman, S.H., Lahey, B.B., Shaffer, D., & Gould, M.S. (2001). Psychosocial and risk behavior correlates of youth suicide attempts and suicidal ideation. *Journal of the American Academy of Child and Adolescent Psychiatry, 40*, 837–846.

Klinger, E. (1971). *Structure and functions of fantasy.* New York: John Wiley & Sons.

Klinger, E. (1975). Consequences of commitment to and disengagement from incentives. *Psychological Review, 82*, 1–25.

Klinger, E. (1977). *Meaning and void: Inner experience and the incentives in people's lives.* Minneapolis: University of Minnesota Press.

Klinger, E. (1978). Modes of normal conscious flow. In K.S. Pope & J.L. Singer (Eds.), *The stream of consciousness: Scientific investigations into the flow of human experience* (pp. 225–258). New York: Plenum.

Klinger, E. (1993). Loss of interest. In C.G. Costello (Ed.), *Symptoms of depression* (pp. 43–62). New York: John Wiley & Sons.

Klinger, E. (1996a). The contents of thoughts: Interference as the downside of adaptive normal mechanisms in thought flow. In I.G. Sarason, B.R. Sarason, & G.R. Pierce (Eds.), *Cognitive interference: Theories, methods, and findings* (pp. 3–23). Hillsdale, NJ: Erlbaum.

Klinger, E. (1996b). Emotional influences on cognitive processing, with implications for theories of both. In P. Gollwitzer & J.A. Bargh (Eds.), *The psychology of action: Linking cognition and motivation to behavior* (pp. 168–189). New York: Guilford.

Klinger, E. (1998). The search for meaning in evolutionary perspective and its clinical implications. In P.T.P. Wong & P.S. Fry (Eds.), *The human quest for meaning: A handbook of psychological research and clinical applications* (pp. 27–50). Mahwah, NJ: Erlbaum.

Klinger, E., Barta, S.G., & Maxeiner, M.E. (1980). Motivational correlates of thought content frequency and commitment. *Journal of Personality and Social Psychology, 39*, 1222–1237.

Koestner, R., Lekes, N., Powers, T.A., & Chicoine, E. (2002). Attaining personal goals: Self-concordance plus implementation intentions equals success. *Journal of Personality and Social Psychology, 83*, 231–244.

Klinger, E., Kemble, E.D., & Barta, S.G. (1974). Cyclic activity changes during extinction in rats: A potential model of depression. *Animal Learning and Behavior, 2*, 313–316.

Kuhl, J. (1986). Motivation and information processing: A new look at decision making, dynamic change, and action control. In R.M. Sorrentino & E.T. Higgins (Eds.), *Handbook of motivation and cognition: Foundations of social behavior* (pp. 404–434). New York: Guilford.

Kuhl, J. (2000). A functional-design approach to motivation and self-regulation: The dynamics of personality systems and interactions. In M. Boekaerts, P.R. Pintrich, & M. Zeidner (Eds.), *Handbook of self-regulation* (pp. 111–169). San Diego: Academic Press.

Kuhl, J. (2001). *Motivation und Persönlichkeit: Interaktion psychischer Systeme* (Motivation and personality: Interaction of psychological systems). Göttingen: Hogrefe.

Kuhl, J., & Kazén, M. (1994). Self-discrimination and memory: State orientation and false self-ascription of assigned activities. *Journal of Personality and Social Psychology, 66*, 1103–1115.

Larsen, R., & Diener, E. (1987). Affect intensity as an individual difference characteristic. *Journal of Research in Personality, 21*, 1–39.

Ledoux, J.E. (1995). Emotion: Clues from the brain. *Annual Review of Psychology, 46*, 209–235.

Lehman, D.R., Wortman, C.B., & Williams, A.F. (1987). Long-term effects of losing a spouse or child in a motor vehicle crash. *Journal of Personality and Social Psychology, 52*, 218–231.

Lewin, K. (1928). Wille, Vorsatz und Bedürfnis (Will, intention, and need). *Psychologische Forschung, 7*, 330–385.

Lewin, K. (1938). *The conceptual representation and the measurement of psychological forces.* Durham, North Carolina: Duke University Press.

Lewinsohn, P.M. (1974). A behavioral approach to depression. In R.J. Friedman & M.M. Katz (Eds.), *The psychology of depression: Contemporary theory and research* (pp. 157–178). Washington, DC: Winston.

Lewis, M., Sullivan, M.W., Ramsay, D.S., & Alessandri, S.M. (1992). Individual differences in anger and sad expressions during extinction: Antecedents and consequences. *Infant Behavior and Development, 15,* 443–452.

Liberman, N., & Trope, Y. (1998). The role of feasibility and desirability considerations in near and distant future decisions: A test of temporal construal theory. *Journal of Personality and Social Psychology, 75,* 5–18.

Little, B.R. (1983). Personal projects: A rationale and method for investigation. *Environment and Behavior, 15,* 273–309.

Locke, E.A. (1968). Toward a theory of task motivation and incentives. *Organizational Behavior and Human Performance, 3,* 157–189.

Locke, E.A. (2001). Motivation by goal setting. In R.T. Golembiewski (Ed.), *Handbook of organizational behavior* (2nd edn; pp. 43–56). New York: Marcel Dekker.

Loewenstein, G.F., Weber, E.U., Hsee, C.K., & Welch, N. (2001). Risk as feelings. *Psychological Bulletin, 127,* 267–286.

Lucas, R.E., Diener, E., Grob, A., Suh, E.M., & Shao, L. (2000). Cross-cultural evidence for the fundamental features of extraversion. *Journal of Personality and Social Psychology, 79,* 452–468.

Lykken, D. (1999). *Happiness: What studies on twins show us about nature, nurture, and the happiness set-point.* New York: Golden Books.

Lykken, D., & Tellegen, A. (1996). Happiness is a stochastic phenomenon. *Psychological Science, 7,* 186–189.

Man, F., Stuchlíková, I., & Klinger, E. (1998). Motivational structure of alcoholic and nonalcoholic Czech men. *Psychological Reports, 82,* 1091–1106.

Mayne, T.J. (2001). Emotions and health. In T.J. Mayne & G.A. Bonanno (Eds.), *Emotions: Current issues and future directions* (pp. 361–397). New York: Guilford.

McClelland, D.C., Atkinson, J.W., Clark, R.A., & Lowell, E.L. (1953). *The achievement motive.* New York: Appleton-Century-Crofts.

McDougall, W. (1921). *An introduction to social psychology.* London: Methuen.

Mellers, B.A. (2000). Choice and the relative pleasure of consequences. *Psychological Bulletin, 126,* 910–924.

Miller, N.E. (1944). Experimental studies of conflict. In J.McV. Hunt (Ed.), *Personality and the behavioral disorders* (Vol. I; pp. 431–465). New York: Roland.

Mogg, K., Mathews, A., & Eysenck, M. (1992). Attentional bias to threat in clinical anxiety states. *Cognition and Emotion, 6,* 149–159.

Murray, H.A. (1938). *Explorations in personality.* New York: Oxford University Press.

Myers, D.G. (1999). Close relationships and quality of life. In D. Kahneman, E. Diener, & N. Schwarz (Eds.), *Well-being: The foundations of hedonic psychology* (pp. 374–391). New York: Russell Sage Foundation.

Nakajima, S., Tanaka, S., Urushihara, K., & Imada, H. (2000). Renewal of extinguished lever-press responses upon return to the training context. *Learning and Motivation, 31,* 416–431.

Neumann, R., & Strack, F. (2000). Approach and avoidance: The influence of proprioceptive and exteroceptive cues on encoding of affective information. *Journal of Personality and Social Psychology, 79,* 39–48.

Newcomb, M.D., & Harlow, L.L. (1986). Life events and substance use among adolescents: Mediating effects of perceived loss of control and meaninglessness in life. *Journal of Personality and Social Psychology, 51,* 564–577.

Nikles, C.D. II, Brecht, D.L., Klinger, E., & Bursell, A.L. (1998). The effects of current-concern- and nonconcern-related waking suggestions on nocturnal dream content. *Journal of Personality and Social Psychology, 75,* 242–255.

Nikula, R., Klinger, E., & Larson-Gutman, M.K. (1993). Current concerns and electrodermal reactivity: Responses to words and thoughts. *Journal of Personality, 61,* 63–84.

Oettingen, G., Pak, H., & Schnetter, K. (2001). Self-regulation of goal-setting: Turning free fantasies about the future into binding goals. *Journal of Personality and Social Psychology, 80*, 736–753.

Palys, T.S., & Little, B.R. (1983). Perceived life satisfaction and the organization of personal project systems. *Journal of Personality and Social Psychology, 44*, 1221–1230.

Pervin, L.A. (1983). The stasis and flow of behavior: Toward a theory of goals. In M.M. Page (Ed.), *Nebraska Symposium of Motivation, 1982* (pp. 1–53). Lincoln, Nebraska: University of Nebraska Press.

Riemann, B.C., Amir, N., & Louro, C.E. (1995). *Cognitive processing of personally relevant information in panic disorder.* Unpublished manuscript.

Riemann, B.C., & McNally, R.J. (1995). Cognitive processing of personally-relevant information. *Cognition and Emotion, 9*, 325–340.

Roberson, L. (1989). Assessing personal work goals in the organizational setting: Development and evaluation of the Work Concerns Inventory. *Organizational Behavior and Human Decision Processes, 44*, 345–367.

Ruehlman, L.S., & Wolchik, S.A. (1988). Personal goals and interpersonal support and hindrance as factors in psychological distress and well-being. *Journal of Personality and Social Psychology, 55*, 293–301.

Ryan, R.M., Sheldon, K.M., Kasser, T., & Deci, E.L. (1996). All goals are not created equal: An organismic perspective on the nature of goals and their regulation. In P. Gollwitzer & J.A. Bargh (Eds.), *The psychology of action: Linking cognition and motivation to behavior* (pp. 7–26). New York: Guilford.

Schmuck, P. (2001). Intrinsic and extrinsic life goals preferences as measured via inventories and via priming methodologies: Mean differences and relations with well-being. In P. Schmuck & K.M. Sheldon (Eds.), *Life goals and well-being: Towards a positive psychology of human striving* (pp. 132–147). Seattle, Washington: Hogrefe & Huber.

Schneider, W. (1987). *Ablenkung und Handlungskontrolle: Eine "kognitiv-motivationale Perspektive."* Unpublished Diploma thesis. University of Bielefeld.

Schwartz, B., Ward, A., Monterosso, J., Lyubomirsky, S., White, K., & Lehman, D.R. (2002). Maximizing versus satisficing: Happiness is a matter of choice. *Journal of Personality and Social Psychology, 83*, 1178–1197.

Shah, J., & Higgins, E.T. (1997). Expectancy * value effects: Regulatory focus as determinant of magnitude and direction. *Journal of Personality and Social Psychology, 73*, 447–458.

Sharma, D., Albery, I.P., & Cook, C. (2001). Selective attentional bias to alcohol related stimuli in problem drinkers and non-problem drinkers. *Addiction, 96*, 285–295.

Sheldon, K.M. (2001). The self-concordance model of healthy goal striving: When personal goals correctly represent the person. In P. Schmuck & K.M. Sheldon (Eds.), *Life goals and well-being: Towards a positive psychology of human striving* (pp. 18–36). Seattle, Washington: Hogrefe & Huber.

Sheldon, K.M., & Elliot, A.J. (1999). Goal striving, need satisfaction, and longitudinal well-being: The self-concordance model. *Journal of Personality and Social Psychology, 76*, 482–497.

Shidara, M., & Richmond, B.J. (2002). Anterior cingulate: Single neuronal signals related to degree of reward expectancy. *Science, 296*, 1709–1711.

Simon, H.A. (1956). Rational choice and the structure of the environment. *Psychological Review, 63*, 129–138.

Simpson, J.B. (1988). *Simpson's contemporary quotations.* Boston: Houghton Mifflin.

Singer, J.A., & Salovey, P. (1993). *The remembered self: Emotion and memory in personality.* New York: Free Press.

Snyder, C.R. (1994). *The psychology of hope.* New York: Free Press.

Stetter, F., Ackermann, K., Bizer, A., Straube, E.R., & Mann, K. (1995). Effects of disease-related cues in alcoholic inpatients: Results of a controlled "Alcohol Stroop" study. *Alcoholism: Clinical and Experimental Research, 19*, 593–599.

Stocker, M. (1996). *Valuing emotions.* Cambridge, UK: Cambridge University Press.

Stormark, K.L., Laberg, J.C., Bjerland, T., Nordby, H., & Hugdahl, K. (1995). Autonomic cued reactivity in alcoholics: The effect of olfactory stimuli. *Addictive Behaviours, 20*, 571–584.

Stormark, K.L., Laberg, J.C., Nordby, H., & Hugdahl, K. (2000). Alcoholics' selective attention to alcohol stimuli: Automated processing? *Journal of Studies on Alcohol, 61*, 18–23.

Teasdale, J.D., Segal, Z.V., & Williams, J.M.G. (1995). How does cognitive therapy prevent depressive relapse and why should attentional control (mindfulness) training help? *Behaviour Research and Therapy, 33*, 25–39.

Teasdale, J.D., Segal, Z.V., Williams, J.M.G., Ridgeway, V.A., Soulsby, J.M., & Lau, M.A. (2000). Prevention of relapse/recurrence in major depression by mindfulness-based cognitive therapy. *Journal of Consulting and Clinical Psychology, 68*, 615–623.

Tomkins, S.S. (1962). *Affect, imagery, consciousness. Vol. 1. The positive affects*. New York: Springer.

Toyomitsu, Y., Nishijo, H., Uwano, T., Kuratsu, J., & Ono, T. (2002). Neuronal responses of the rat amygdala during extinction and reassociation learning in elementary and configural associative tasks. *European Journal of Neuroscience, 15*, 753–768.

Uznadze, D.N. (1966). *The psychology of set*. New York: Consultants Bureau.

Van Eerde, W., & Thierry, H. (1996). Vroom's expectancy models and work-related criteria: A meta-analysis. *Journal of Applied Psychology, 81*, 575–586.

Warr, P. (1999). Well-being and the workplace. In D. Kahneman, E. Diener, & N. Schwarz (Eds.), *Well-being: The foundations of hedonic psychology* (pp. 392–412). New York: Russell Sage Foundation.

Watson, D., & Kendall, P.C. (1989). Understanding anxiety and depression: Their relation to negative and positive affective states. In P.C. Kendall & D. Watson (Eds.), *Anxiety and depression: Distinctive and overlapping features* (pp. 3–26). San Diego, CA: Academic Press.

Watson, D., Wiese, D., Vaidya, J., & Tellegen, A. (1999). The two general activation systems of affect: Structural findings, evolutionary considerations, and psychobiological evidence. *Journal of Personality and Social Psychology, 76*, 820–838.

Wentura, D., Rothermund, K., & Bak, P. (2000). Automatic vigilance: The attention-grabbing power of approach and avoidance-related social information. *Journal of Personality and Social Psychology, 78*, 1024–1037.

Williams, J.M.G., Mathews, A., & MacLeod, C. (1996). The emotional Stroop task and psychopathology. *Psychological Bulletin, 120*, 3–24.

Williams, M. (1997). *Cry of pain*. London: Penguin.

Wilson, T.D., Meyers, J., & Gilbert, D.T. (2001). Lessons from the past: Do people learn from experience that emotional reactions are short-lived? *Personality and Social Psychology Bulletin, 27*, 1648–1661.

Wilson, T.D., Wheatley, T., Meyers, J.M., Gilbert, D.T., & Axsom, D. (2000). Focalism: A source of durability bias in affective forecasting. *Journal of Personality and Social Psychology, 78*, 821–836.

Winkielmann, P., Zajonc, R.B., & Schwarz, N. (1997). Subliminal affective priming resists attributional interventions. *Cognition and Emotion, 11*, 433–466.

Wong, P.T.P. (1998). Implicit theories of meaningful life and the development of the Personal Meaning Profile. In P.T.P. Wong & P.S. Fry (Eds.), *The human quest for meaning: A handbook of psychological research and clinical applications* (pp. 111–140). Mahwah, NJ: Erlbaum.

Young, J. (1987). *The role of selective attention in the attitude–behavior relationship*. Doctoral dissertation, University of Minnesota.

Zajonc, R.B. (1980). Feeling and thinking: Preferences need no inferences. *American Psychologist, 35*, 151–175.

CHAPTER 2

Motivation and Addiction: The Role of Incentive Processes in Understanding and Treating Addictive Disorders

Suzette V. Glasner

University of Minnesota, USA

Synopsis.—This chapter provides a motivational analysis of learning-based theories of addiction. First, it demonstrates the relevance of principles of learning and conditioning to understanding addictive behavior patterns. The author argues that the motivational processes that control the pursuit of nondrug rewards share commonalities with those that control the pursuit of drugs of abuse. Next, the chapter introduces the utility of animal models as a means of investigating these processes and discusses methodological limitations in human addiction research. In efforts to bridge the gap between human and animal studies of motivation and addiction, it reviews parallel findings in animal and human addiction research and outlines the implications of these findings for the treatment of addictive disorders. Finally, it proposes a motivationally based theory of addiction phenomena, underscoring the fundamental role of incentive-motivation in understanding and treating addictive disorders.

In recent years, research in the addiction area has significantly advanced our understanding of risk factors in the development of substance abuse and dependence. These factors have been identified from a range of theoretical and methodological perspectives, and include genetic (e.g., Kendler et al., 1992; Noble, 1993; see Crabbe, Belknap, & Buck, 1994, for review), personality (e.g., Cloninger, 1987; Cloninger, Sigvardsson, & Bohman, 1988), and neurophysiological (e.g., McBride et al., 1993; Zhou et al., 1995) variables. In addition to research into vulnerability factors, these and various other approaches have been used in attempts to investigate another crucial issue in the study of substance-related problems: once initiated, what *maintains* addictive behavior in the face of its destructive life consequences?

In addition to those described above, a number of theoretical frameworks have been introduced in attempts to elucidate the mechanisms underlying the persistence of addictive behavior, including neurobiological (e.g., Robinson & Berridge, 1993; Wise & Bozarth, 1987), cognitive (e.g., Tiffany, 1999), and learning-based models (e.g., Solomon, 1977,

Handbook of Motivational Counseling. Edited by W. Miles Cox and Eric Klinger.
© 2004 John Wiley & Sons, Ltd.

1991; Stewart, de Wit, & Eikelboom, 1984). Notably, a basic assumption common to each of these theoretical formulations is that the addicted individual continually prefers to pursue and consume drug commodities in an environmental context in which nondrug alternative activities are available. Moreover, the broad objective of treatment for addictive disorders is to modify the addicted individual's persistent selection of substance-related activities, or factors that contribute to this selective behavior. Understanding the allocation of behavior (i.e., choice) among available drug- and nondrug-related activities is therefore a central empirical problem in the study and treatment of addictive disorders.

Although both nonaddicted and addicted humans often participate in laboratory studies of selective social and pathological substance use, respectively, the investigator's ability to induce and control the behaviors of interest with human participants is, in many aspects, limited. In the case of individuals with existing substance-use disorders, studies must, for example, rely on participants' self-reports in assessing historical variables that are of interest in addressing etiological questions, without the opportunity to directly observe these influences. Moreover, although scientists and clinicians have much to gain from understanding factors that influence the transition from social to pathological substance use, obvious ethical considerations preclude the use of experimental manipulations that might induce an addictive behavior in nonaddicted human participants. Nevertheless, these limitations can be overcome through the use of animal learning and conditioning paradigms.

The use of animal learning paradigms in the study of pathological drug-seeking and use, however, relies on the assumption that the observed behaviors in animal subjects are valid indicators of human addictive behavior patterns. There is, in fact, considerable evidence in support of this assumption, as described in a review by Griffiths, Bigelow, and Henningfield (1980), who demonstrated striking parallels between animal and human drug-seeking behaviors, and the factors that are presently known to impact these behaviors. Moreover, current evidence suggests not only that drug self-administration in animals and humans share commonalities, but these behaviors are consistent across various classes of drugs, ranging from alcohol to other drugs of abuse (Winger, Young, & Woods, 1983). Thus, in the absence of clear and compelling evidence to the contrary, this discussion assumes that the results of empirical investigations of drug self-administration and its underlying mechanisms in animal subjects may validly be generalized to human drug-seeking and drug-taking patterns in human populations.

Having accepted this assumption, animal learning and conditioning paradigms offer great utility in elucidating the learning-based processes that contribute to the initiation of addictive behavior, as well as the conditions that govern persistent selection of drug-seeking and drug-taking behaviors when alternative activities are available. If scientists can move closer to delineating these mechanisms, the results of our investigations will have very important and direct implications for the treatment of addiction. By understanding the genesis of addiction phenomena from this perspective, we can work to modify learning-based processes that support pathological drug-seeking behaviors.

The idea that addiction involves learning and conditioning processes is not new; in fact, as early as 1948, Abraham Wikler recognized that withdrawal phenomena could be conditioned by a process so sensitive that merely talking about drug use in psychotherapy could elicit "conditioned" withdrawal symptoms among abstinent opiate addicts. This discovery stimulated a growing interest in the role of learning and conditioning in substance abuse, and since that time several learning theories of drug and alcohol abuse have been developed (e.g., Siegel, 1983; Solomon, 1977; Stewart, de Wit, & Eikelboom, 1984; Wise, 1988). More recently, a few clinicians and researchers in the addiction area have developed treatment approaches based on principles of learning, motivation, and conditioning (e.g., Cox & Klinger, 1988; Drummond et al., 1995). The aim of this chapter, therefore, is to elaborate the learning and motivational mechanisms that support addictive behaviors, and, in so doing, demonstrate the relevance of studying these mechanisms to understanding and treating addictive disorders.

MOTIVATIONAL CONTROL OF GOAL-DIRECTED ACTION

The motivational processes that control the intake of alcohol and other drugs of abuse have recently received increasing attention in theory and research assessing the factors that determine drug-seeking behavior (e.g., Koob & Weiss, 1992; Newlin, 1992; Robinson & Berridge, 2001). An issue that has received relatively less focus, however, is the relationship between the motivational processes that control the pursuit of nondrug rewards and those that determine alcohol- and drug-seeking addictions. Nevertheless, understanding the commonalities between these processes has much to contribute to our current conception of addiction, particularly when considering that promotion of nondrug, alternative goal-directed activities is a central aspect of intervention for addictive disorders (e.g., Vuchinich & Tucker, 1998).

Instrumental actions aimed at nondrug rewards are controlled by two sources of information: (1) knowledge of the specific consequences of an action, and (2) evaluation of the incentive properties of those consequences (Balleine, 1992; Balleine, Ball, & Dickinson, 1994; Dickinson & Balleine, 1994, 1995). In addition, several studies have demonstrated that cues that predict those consequences can modulate instrumental actions in both single-action (Balleine, 1994) and choice (Colwill & Rescorla, 1985) situations. These findings are of interest in the study of addiction because incentive factors have received considerable recent attention in the development of treatment approaches to addiction as well as in the study of the motivational control of alcohol- and drug-seeking behavior.

Understanding the determinants of instrumental or goal-directed behavior for nondrug rewards is therefore a logical starting point for assessing the contribution of learning and motivational processes to addictive behavior. The following sections will address both historical and current concepts of motivation and incentive constructs, the relation of these constructs to theories of drug and alcohol addiction, and the implications of these relations for contemporary treatment approaches to substance-use disorders.

INTENTIONAL ACTION AND SURVIVAL

Following Skinner's early distinction between respondent and operant responses (Skinner, 1938), Dickinson and Balleine (1993) have described the "dual" nature of the behavioral repertoire of humans and animals, comprising "responses," or nonpurposive, reflexive behavior elicited by conditioned and unconditioned stimuli, and "actions," which refer to intentional, purposive behaviors undertaken in the pursuit of a goal-object. The adaptive nature of each of these modes of behavior is straightforward. One can imagine, for example, that the ability to predict biologically significant environmental events on the basis of knowledge about the relations between such events can allow an animal to respond adaptively to anticipate sources of food, water, and predation. Nevertheless, as a capacity to perform reflexive, automatic classes of responses, this ability carries a limited behavioral repertoire for the animal to draw upon in the face of changing environmental circumstances (see Balleine, 2000). Hence, somewhere between the beginning of life of the simplest living organisms and the evolution of humanity, animals were endowed with the ability to exercise flexibility in their behavioral responses to environmental stimuli and events. The resulting capacity for volitional control over behavior is manifest in the performance of actions that are *goal-directed*. The development of this class of behavior confers innumerable advantages to the organism; not only can the animal anticipate biologically significant events that promote its survival and present danger, but it now has the ability to seek out and select environmental resources to fulfill its basic needs and desires.

This capacity for intentional actions introduces a question that has long been the focus of investigation among learning theorists: how does a particular commodity, whether a food, fluid, sex partner, or drug, become established as a goal-object? We now turn to this question, drawing on historical and current views of learning and motivation to arrive at the argument that goal-directed behavior is grounded in incentive processes.

THE ROLE OF INCENTIVE PROCESSES IN GOAL-DIRECTED ACTION

Humans and many nonhuman animals can not only perform goal-directed actions, they can also learn to know the consequences of their actions. This principle was not obvious to early theorists and students of learning, who adopted a behaviorist approach to the analysis of instrumental action. According to S–R theorists such as Thorndike (1911), the consequence of an action served merely to strengthen an association between the action and contextual stimuli, thereby increasing the likelihood of subsequent performance of the action. According to this view, knowledge of the consequence of one's actions does not mediate or control instrumental performance. Considerable evidence has mounted against this position, lending support to the now widely accepted notion that animals and humans alike are able to encode or represent the outcome of their actions, which prompted a marked transition in the 1960s from behaviorist to cognitive theories of learning (see Balleine, 2000, for discussion).

Returning momentarily to the evolutionary account of goal-directed behavior, we might speculate that something more than knowledge of the contingency between one's actions and their consequences is required for goal-directed actions to promote survival. Namely, assuming that we can learn that performing action "A" results in "B," how do we know whether we need or desire "B"? Addressing this question requires an analysis of how our internal biological states interact with knowledge of action–outcome contingencies to produce behaviors that are instrumental or goal-directed.

Perhaps the clearest theoretical view of this relationship was presented by Tolman (1949a). According to his incentive theory, goal-directed behavior is established through the acquisition of a "cathexis," or a connection between a goal-object and a corresponding motivational state; that is, "the acquisition of a connection between a given goal-object or disturbance-object—i.e., a given type of food, a given type of drink, a given type of sex-object or a given type of fear object—and the corresponding drive of hunger, thirst, sex, or fright" (Tolman, 1949b, p. 144). Tolman further argued that direct experience with the goal-object was a necessary condition for acquiring a cathexis; that is, "by trying out the corresponding consummatory responses upon such objects and finding that they work" (p. 146). For Tolman, one consequence of acquiring a cathexis was the assignment of *incentive value* to the goal-object. In the case of attractive outcomes, Tolman referred to a "positive value" that corresponded to particular "types" of experienced goal-objects (Tolman, 1949a, pp. 360–361). Tolman's position serves to illustrate a central claim of incentive theories, that an organism's evaluation of the outcome of its actions mediates changes in performance. Based on this premise, it may be argued that an organism's evaluative beliefs with respect to a goal-object form its desires (cf. Balleine & Dickinson, 1998). Moreover, Tolman's incentive view suggests that factors modulating an individual's desire for a reward can modulate acts to obtain it.

Incentive theories suppose not only that animals and humans develop evaluative beliefs with respect to the goal-object; these form our expectations. If I believe that chocolate is delicious, and therefore has a "positive" incentive value, then I expect, while unwrapping a chocolate bar, that when I place a piece of it in my mouth, it will taste delicious. What is more, if I have not eaten for many hours and someone offers me a piece of chocolate, I may expect that the chocolate will be especially tasty. But how do I know that this is so? There is, in fact, a growing body of literature to suggest, consistent with Tolman's theory, that this expectation must be learned through direct consummatory experience with the chocolate when I am hungry.

Evidence that this experience is required before instrumental performance is affected comes from animal studies assessing the impact of shifts in motivational states on goal-directed behavior. In one study, Balleine (1992) trained free-feeding rats to perform a lever-press response for access to a novel food reward. During an extinction phase, half of the animals were food deprived and half were undeprived while they again had the opportunity to lever press but without food reward. If the shift from the food-undeprived to the deprived state had an immediate impact on the animals' evaluation of the incentive value of the reward, then shifting animals to the hungry state should increase their lever-press performance, relative to animals that were still undeprived. If, however, animals must *experience* the novel food pellets while hungry to learn that the reward had increased incentive value during hunger, then we should not predict any increase in lever pressing in the hungry group until after that experience. In fact, the latter prediction was confirmed; there was no difference between the performance of the deprived and undeprived animals. Nevertheless, when the animals were later given the opportunity to earn the reward, the hungry animals performed at a substantially higher rate than the undeprived animals. These data strongly suggest that consummatory contact with the pellets in the new, hungry motivational state was required to increase the frequency of the goal-directed behavior. In a subsequent experiment, Balleine, Ball, and Dickinson (1994) found that animals given the opportunity to consume a novel food reward following a shift from the undeprived to the hungry state, but prior to the extinction test, increased their lever pressing during extinction, relative to animals that were shifted but not allowed to experience the pellets while hungry. This provides evidence to support Tolman's original claim that the impact of shifts in motivational state on goal-directed behavior is mediated by experience with the goal-object. Moreover, in the case of the above-described experiments, it appears that this experience must take place while the organism is in a deprived state.

The process by which animals adjust their evaluation of an instrumental outcome conditional on a shift in motivational state has been termed *incentive learning*. It has importantly been suggested that animals and humans learn through this process that the new motivational state changes the instrumental outcome's affective impact (Dickinson & Balleine, 1994). Having defined incentive learning, we will now define the term *incentive*. In this discussion, an incentive is defined as an event that elicits biological and emotional effects (see Balleine, 2000, for discussion). Incentives can take either positive or negative values, depending on the particular biological and emotional responses that they elicit.

According to incentive learning theory, there is one key feature of the relationship between motivational states and the incentive value of a reward: once the agent has learned about the change in incentive value of an outcome in a particular motivational state (e.g., hunger), that motivational state acts to modulate the value of the reward. Returning to the chocolate example, if I have had both the experiences of eating chocolate when satiated (e.g., after dinner) and when hungry, I may learn that chocolate is more desirable (i.e., has a higher incentive value) when I am hungry than immediately after I have eaten a meal. Having had these two opportunities to learn about the differential values of chocolate when hungry and satiated, respectively, the incentive value of chocolate will subsequently be determined by my current motivational state. Likewise, the chocolate will take on the "higher" incentive value only when I am hungry; hence, this value comes under the conditional control of my current motivational state. In fact, a recent study of the relationship of chocolate craving to primary motivational states is consistent with this analysis; human subjects developed stronger subjective craving scores for chocolate after they had eaten it regularly several hours after a meal, rather than immediately after (Gibson & Desmond, 1999). Not only do these findings support incentive learning theory, but they suggest that the incentive properties of a reward can acquire the capacity to induce "craving" for a particular commodity.

Given that chocolate craving can be controlled by incentive processes, we may well expect that drug and alcohol craving, and possibly the pursuit of these commodities, are mediated by common incentive and motivational mechanisms. To assess this hypothesis, Glasner, Overmeir, and Balleine (2002) recently investigated the role of incentive learning in alcohol-seeking behavior in alcohol-dependent and nondependent animals. In that study, animals were trained to perform an instrumental action, lever pressing, in order to gain access to a small quantity of sweetened alcohol. Following instrumental training, half of the animals were made physically dependent on alcohol, with the remaining half nondependent. Then, in an extinction test on the lever, i.e., with no alcohol delivered, we assessed the impact of administering a priming dose of alcohol on alcohol-seeking behavior. This effect was assessed after both a single and a second cycle of alcohol dependency. If animals learn about the increased incentive value of alcohol through direct experience with alcohol while in the state of alcohol withdrawal, we should expect increased alcohol-seeking (i.e., lever pressing) among alcohol-primed subjects. This effect should not, however, be predicted among unprimed animals, for in the absence of direct experience with alcohol during the state of withdrawal, this group of subjects will not have had the opportunity to learn about the modified affective impact (i.e., the relieving properties) of alcohol during alcohol withdrawal. This prediction was confirmed with dependent, alcohol-primed subjects performing more lever-press responses during extinction, relative to dependent, unprimed subjects, Interestingly, however, this effect emerged only after two cycles of dependency and priming. In the nondependent group, the opposite pattern of results emerged, with primed subjects performing fewer lever-press responses relative to unprimed animals. These findings replicate an earlier report of the effects of alcohol priming in human subjects (Hodgson, Rankin, & Stockwell, 1979), in suggesting that a priming dose of alcohol has an "appetizing" effect on alcohol-dependent individuals, but a satiating effect in nondependent individuals. Moreover, these effects are manifest in instrumental performance only if animals are allowed to experience the impact of alcohol while in the dependent and nondependent motivational states, respectively. Hence, these data strongly suggest that incentive learning plays a role in the development of addictive behavior, thereby sharing a common mechanism with the processes that control instrumental performance for nondrug rewards.

These incentive-learning effects are not restricted to food or alcohol. There have been, in fact, numerous demonstrations of this phenomenon in the animal learning literature in actions earning access to fluids (Balleine & Dickinson, 1991), sex partners (Everitt & Stacey, 1987), and sources of heat (Hendersen & Graham, 1979), suggesting that motivational states do not affect goal-directed behavior directly but by interacting with the agent's evaluation of the incentive properties of the reward. Moreover, these incentive effects have been found in both single-action (Balleine, 1994) and choice (Balleine & Dickinson, 1998) paradigms, suggesting that these processes impact both the energization and selection of goal-directed activities.

In summary, there are two core determinants of motivated, goal-directed behavior: (1) knowledge of the consequences of one's actions, and (2) evaluation of the incentive properties of those consequences. Moreover, recent evidence suggests generality of the incentive processes that control goal-directed behavior for access to nondrug and drug rewards.

Although these assumptions appear to be fundamental to learning-based theories of drug and alcohol addiction as well as current treatment approaches to addiction, there has been little systematic investigation of incentive-learning processes in drug-dependent, as compared to nondependent, individuals. As a consequence, these governing principles have not been explicitly recognized in the addiction area, despite the importance of their implications for intervention. It is argued here, therefore, that the two core assumptions outlined above should be common to virtually all theories of drug and alcohol addiction, with a few exceptions (see Robinson & Berridge, 2001; Tiffany, 1999). The essential treatment implication of this view is that, through modification of incentive processes, the behaviors of addicted individuals can be redirected to alternative, nondrug incentives. This hypothesis will be elaborated below as we examine learning and motivationally based theories and intervention approaches to addiction.

INCENTIVE ASSUMPTIONS OF ADDICTION THEORIES

This section examines the incentive assumptions of three theoretical models of drug and alcohol use: expectancy theory, conditioned reinforcement, and the incentive-motivational model. We focus on these models for two reasons: (1) the fundamental assumptions of these models are applicable to various theoretical perspectives of addiction, allowing for generalizability of our learning-based analysis, and (2) because these views are explicitly based on principles of learning and motivation, recent evidence on the role of incentive learning in motivated behavior (see above section) may elaborate the mechanisms underlying the basic assumptions of these models.

Expectancy Theory

A core assumption of incentive theories of motivation is that expectations regarding the affective impact of a goal-object function to motivate or energize the appropriate instrumental behavior. This principle is explicitly essential to the expectancy theory of alcohol use (Goldman, Del Boca, & Darkes, 1999), which we examine below.

The expectancy interpretation of alcohol use among both alcoholics and social drinkers was stimulated by an early study by Marlatt, Demming, and Reid (1973) using a balanced placebo design. In this paradigm, one group of subjects received an alcoholic beverage, whereas a second group received a nonalcoholic tonic. Half of the subjects in each condition were instructed that they would be consuming alcohol, whereas the remaining half were instructed that they would be consuming tonic. Although the alcoholic subjects drank more than the social drinkers under both instruction conditions, both the alcoholic subjects and the social drinkers alike consumed more on the drinking test if they were instructed that they would be consuming alcohol, irrespective of the actual drink content. The suggestion by these data that an expectancy of receiving alcohol is a more powerful predictor of consumption than the actual drink content marked a turning point in laboratory research on alcohol use.

Concluding that expecting to receive alcohol can increase drinking fails to offer a mechanism to account for the behavior. These findings, however, raise several important questions: What is the nature of the expectancy? How does it arise? How does the expectancy impact alcohol-*seeking* behavior? Although anticipating alcohol may itself be a predictor of alcohol consumption, this form of expectation is not sufficient to establish a particular commodity as an incentive. Rather, understanding Marlatt et al.'s results from an incentive perspective requires consideration of the subjects' evaluative beliefs with respect to alcohol. In other words, to what extent is alcohol desirable to the subjects, and how does this desirability vary as a function of alcohol dependence?

These questions were addressed by Laberg (1987) in a replication and extension of Marlatt, Demming, and Reid's (1973) study using a within-participants balanced placebo design. This study demonstrated that instruction-induced expectations of receiving alcohol had a differential impact on subjective craving and autonomic responses as a function of the severity of subjects' dependency on alcohol. Before receiving the beverage, self-reported desire for alcohol in severely dependent participants was stronger than that of mildly dependent subjects—a finding that may be interpreted as evidence that severely dependent participants anticipated a greater affective impact of alcohol than was anticipated by other participants. Following consumption, however, severely dependent alcoholics who expected alcohol maintained the highest level of self-reported craving relative to all of the other participants, irrespective of drink content—again suggesting that in this subgroup the anticipation of receiving alcohol elicited a strong desire for alcohol.

Consistent with the above findings, a wealth of evidence has accumulated in recent years suggesting that expectancies are reliable predictors of drinking behavior (see Goldman, 1994, for review). According to expectancy theory, stimuli can acquire the ability to activate an expectancy template which, in turn, may activate an affective state. This affective state can then produce a behavior such as alcohol-seeking and/or consumption behavior (Goldman, Del Boca, & Darkes, 1999).

We endorse this conceptualization of expectancies, but place it in the framework of incentive-learning theory in order to account for the development of alcohol-related expectations and the impact of these expectations on alcohol-seeking and use. From this perspective, it is an *expectancy of the incentive value* of alcohol that impacts alcohol-seeking and consumption. The question, raised earlier, of how alcohol expectancies arise can be addressed by considering the incentive-learning process that occurs through experience with alcohol. Expectancy theorists have alluded to this learning process by advancing the argument that experience with alcohol is critical to the development of alcohol-related expectancies (see Goldman, 1994). Our explication of incentive processes, therefore, is intended to elaborate the mechanism through which such experience generates expectancies.

CONDITIONED REINFORCEMENT MODELS

We have considered the mechanisms through which alcohol expectancies arise, yet the question of the nature of these expectancies may be more thoroughly addressed by examining conditioned reinforcement models. These models similarly propose that drug and alcohol use are motivated by the individual's expectations of a particular affective consequence of consumption but focus largely on the role of associative learning in the formation of these expectancies.

Conditioned reinforcement models may be divided into positive reinforcement (e.g., Stewart, de Wit, & Eikelboom, 1984) and negative reinforcement (e.g., Solomon, 1977, 1991) views, each of which predicts that particular learned associations develop as a consequence of drug or alcohol use. According to positive reinforcement views, individuals who use drugs learn a relation between drug- or alcohol-associated stimuli and the pleasurable or positively rewarding effects of the drug. The resulting conditioned effect is manifest as a positive affective state in the presence of drug- or alcohol-associated cues. By this account, drug and alcohol use is motivated by a desire to re-experience the positive hedonic impact of consumption. On the other hand, negative reinforcement views, such as the conditioned withdrawal model (see Ludwig, Wikler, & Stark, 1974), propose that drug or alcohol use results in a learned association between drug-related cues and drug withdrawal symptoms. According to this view, environmental drug- or alcohol-associated stimuli can acquire the capacity to elicit a "conditioned withdrawal" state, comprising signs and symptoms of pharmacological withdrawal. From this perspective, drug use is motivated by a desire to attain relief from withdrawal symptoms.

When placed within an expectancy framework, positive reinforcement models suggest that drug or alcohol use is motivated by anticipating positive hedonic consequences of consumption, whereas negative reinforcement models suggest that two types of expectancies determine pathological drug- or alcohol-seeking and use: (1) the expectancy of withdrawal distress, resulting from a learned association between drug cues and withdrawal symptoms, and (2) the expectancy of relief from withdrawal distress, resulting from a learned association between drug or alcohol use and the experience of relief.

The assumption common to both expectancy and conditioned reinforcement models, that drinkers use alcohol to obtain expected emotional effects, is supported by a number of human laboratory and self-report studies. Consistent with the positive reinforcement view, drinkers report that they use alcohol on the basis of positive outcome expectancies, such as feeling more powerful (McClelland et al., 1972) and more optimistic (Klinger, 1977). Moreover, heavy drinkers in laboratory studies have been found to differ from social drinkers in their expectancies of the positive hedonic effects of alcohol, with severely dependent detoxified alcoholics reporting anticipation of higher "pleasant glow" during drinking, relative to moderately dependent and social drinkers (Laberg, 1987). Furthermore, when presented with alcohol-associated stimuli, heavy drinkers report expectations of more positively arousing effects of alcohol use and fewer sedative-like consequences, relative to social drinkers (Rather & Goldman, 1994).

Evidence in support of the negative reinforcement model may similarly be drawn from both human laboratory and self-report studies, yet many such studies have yielded equivocal findings. Although self-report studies have indicated that drinkers report using alcohol in efforts to reduce negative affect (e.g., Langenbucher & Nathan, 1983), a handful of studies have found that individuals in drug withdrawal or in negative mood states do not consistently report desires to reduce negative affect as the result of drug use. Rather, these individuals report desires for the pleasurable (i.e., positively rewarding) effects of the drug (e.g., Hufford, 2001; Topp, Lovibond, & Mattick, 1998). These findings underscore the important concept that positive and negative reinforcement mechanisms may not reflect independent or mutually distinct processes underlying the maintenance of addictive behavior (cf. Baker, Morse, & Sherman, 1987). Notably, one critical question that is raised by these findings is how negative affective states and associated alcohol expectancies differentially impact alcohol-seeking behavior among dependent, as compared to nondependent, individuals.

Recently, Randall and Cox (2001) addressed this question in a laboratory study of the impact of positive and negative mood induction procedures on alcohol use among individuals at high and low risk for alcohol problems. In their study, the negative mood induction procedure resulted in a more intense negative affective response among high-risk, relative to low-risk, individuals. In turn, high-risk individuals consumed more of a non-alcoholic beer beverage during a taste test following the negative mood induction, relative to individuals at low risk for alcohol problems. These findings strongly suggest that individuals at high risk for developing alcohol problems may be more reactive to negative mood-inducing stimuli, and are more likely to use alcohol in response to negative affect.

In summary, current evidence suggests that expectations of both positively and negatively reinforcing drug effects contribute to pathological drug- and alcohol-seeking behavior. These findings are consistent with conditioned reinforcement models, in suggesting that drug and alcohol use are motivated by expectations of affective consequences of consumption, whether these consequences are characterized in terms of relief or pleasure.

The body of previous findings thus suggests a model in which conditioned affective responses to alcohol-associated stimuli interact with incentive-learning processes to produce pathological alcohol- and drug-seeking behavior. By this account, conditioned positive affective states and conditioned withdrawal responses to alcohol-associated stimuli develop through associative learning. These conditioned affective states, however, do not immediately produce pathological alcohol- or drug-seeking behavior. Rather, the *experience* of alcohol consumption in the presence of these states gives alcohol its incentive value. Learning about the incentive value of alcohol in the presence of positive or negative affective states, in turn, forms our future expectations regarding the hedonic impact of alcohol consumption. As demonstrated throughout this chapter, these learned expectations motivate alcohol-seeking and use. On the basis of these assumptions, manipulating the incentive value of alcohol in relation to nondrug, alternative incentives within the individual's motivational nexus appears to be a promising approach to the treatment of addictive disorders. This approach is best captured by the incentive-motivational model of alcohol use, which we turn to next.

Incentive-Motivational Model

Cox and Klinger's motivational theory of alcohol use was, in part, influenced by the work of Jacqueline Wiseman (1970), whose careful observations of male Skid Row residents with devastatingly severe drinking problems serve as a powerful demonstration of the basic tenets of the incentive-motivational model. Wiseman observed and interviewed her subjects, following many of them through treatment, attempts to reintegrate into society, and their eventual return to Skid Row and alcohol abuse. In her analysis, Wiseman described quite compellingly the struggle and ultimate failure of these individuals in their pursuit of basic life incentives that might otherwise have replaced their pursuit of alcohol as a primary incentive:

> ... the majority of Skid Row residents are men alone, without families, whose heavy drinking orientation outweighs effort toward maintaining steady employment or improving living standards ... Skid Row is a world of sickness. The men ... there were sick with the all-pervading sickness of alcoholism ... Their goal each day was to drink enough wine to get them through the next. The next day was the same and the next day and the next day ... (Wiseman, 1970, p. 7).

Theoretically, Wiseman's observations prompt important questions. For example, how does the consumption of alcohol become the primary incentive in these individuals' lives? The incentive-motivational model assumes that a number of variables contribute to the selective pursuit of alcohol as a goal-object, including individual differences in biochemical reactivity to alcohol, personality, and sociocultural background. Moreover, the current sources of positive and negative affect in the individual's life, and the balance among these variables, is thought to impact the incentive to drink alcohol. Nevertheless, it is postulated that each of these contributing factors act to influence alcohol use through its effects on incentive motivation.

Based on the assumption in the above sections, that the pursuit of alcohol is largely determined by the expected emotional effects of consumption, the incentive-motivational model elaborates the interplay between these expectations, their impact on alcohol use, and the anticipated emotional effects from and pursuit of nondrug incentives. From this perspective, alcohol use is selected as a goal pursuit when the anticipated positive affective consequences of use exceed those expected from alternative, nondrug incentives. However, with sustained selection of drinking in the face of alternative, nondrug activities, a maladaptive cycle of affective change ensues: alcohol use modulates the agent's affective response to nondrug incentives, and the agent's modified affective response to nondrug incentives acts to modulate alcohol use. These affective changes result in a restructuring of the individual's expectations regarding the respective emotional impact of drug- and nondrug goal-objects, in effect altering the relative incentive values of these goal-objects. As a consequence of this incentive-learning process, the increased relative incentive value of alcohol guides the individual's persistent selection of instrumental, drug-seeking activities.

The fundamental assumption of the above hypotheses, that alcohol use can impact the agent's motivation to pursue nondrug incentives, is supported by animal studies of "incentive contrast effects." In this paradigm, the impact of changes in reward (e.g., increasing or de-creasing the size of a food reward, called *up- and down-shifts*) is assessed through the animal's running speed toward the reward. Early investigations of this phenomenon (e.g., Crespi, 1942) revealed that up- and down-shifts in the magnitude of a food reward following training produced corresponding shifts in instrumental performance, with up-shifts yielding increases in running speed (i.e., positive incentive contrast effects) and down-shifts pro-ducing decreases in running speed (i.e., negative incentive contrast effects). These findings marked a turning point for S–R learning theorists, in suggesting that response habits were not only energized by "drive," but that incentive properties of rewards could also exert a motivational influence on performance.

When animals are inebriated, however, changes in reward magnitude produce a different pattern of results from those observed by Crespi. Consistent with the earlier stated hypothesis that alcohol use can modulate the affective impact of nondrug incentives, Cox (1981) found that inebriated rats evidenced a pronounced positive contrast effect following an up-shift in food reward, suggesting that the positive affect elicited by the up-shift was enhanced when the rats were in the inebriated state. In a later study, Cox (1988) observed that inebriated rats evidenced an attenuated negative contrast effect in response to a down-shift in food reward, relative to sober rats. Moreover, although the inebriated animals in this study showed some reduction in their running speeds, they were notably slower to recover following the down-shift, relative to sober rats. These findings demonstrate not only that alcohol use can modulate an organism's immediate response to losing a nondrug incentive, but that the course of recovery from the incentive loss may be impeded by alcohol use.

Taking into consideration the richness and complexity of the motivational nexus of the human relative to the animal, we consider an example of the above-demonstrated principle in a hypothetical addicted human. Consistent with Cox's findings, alcohol use may, for example, dampen the affective impact of aversive events, including problems that result from pathological alcohol use itself. If significant intimate relationships (i.e., nondrug incentives) become strained as a result of an individual's alcohol use, the person may find alcohol use more emotionally rewarding than engaging in and/or pursuing these relationships. The sustained selection of alcohol-related activities, in turn, may result in (1) a reduced ability to derive positive affect from the intimate relationship, thereby increasing the relative incentive value of alcohol, and (2) a dampened negative affective response to the conflict in the intimate relationship which, when weighed against the intensity of the negative affect produced by the relationship in the absence of alcohol, may similarly act to promote continued alcohol use.

Recent investigations of the relationship between affect and alcohol use are, in fact, generally consistent with these hypotheses. For example, Hussong et al. (2001) found that young adults with fewer and less supportive intimate relationships evidenced more negative affect than their peers, and were more likely to consume alcohol in response to such negative affect (e.g., feelings of sadness and hostility) than individuals with a richer social support system. Moreover, consistent with the incentive-motivational model, there was a cyclical relationship between negative affect and alcohol use, with drinking episodes induced by negative affect predicting, in turn, successive elevations in negative affect the following week. These findings highlight three key concepts of a motivational approach to understanding addiction: (1) the affective changes experienced as a consequence of nondrug incentives can influence alcohol use; (2) alcohol use can predict negative affective changes; and (3) *availability* of nondrug incentives (e.g., supportive relationships) may influence an individual's degree of negative affect, which may, in turn, impact alcohol use.

The third item above has, in fact, been the subject of a growing body of literature in the areas of behavioral choice theory and behavioral economics (see Carroll, 1999; Correia, Chapter 3, this volume; Vuchinich & Tucker, 1998). This line of research was stimulated by the seminal work of Premack (1965) and Herrnstein (1970), who demonstrated the dependence of engagement in a particular goal-directed activity on the availability, relative reinforcement value, and accessibility of alternative available activities. In elaborating the contextual conditions that control choice within addicted populations, a number of studies have found a direct relationship between substance use and constraints on access to nondrug incentives (Carroll, 1996; Higgins, 1997; Vuchinich & Tucker, 1988) and an inverse relation between substance use or abuse and accessibility of the substance (Bickel, DeGrandpre, & Higgins, 1993; DeGrandpre & Bickel, 1996; Vuchinich & Tucker, 1988). Consistent with the incentive-motivational model, these findings underscore the importance of considering the life context in which the addicted individual continually allocates goal-directed behavior between substance- and nonsubstance-related activities, an essential treatment implication that will be elaborated below.

In summary, Cox and Klinger's motivational model represents a synthesized account of the role of learning and motivationally based processes reviewed in this chapter in pathological alcohol-seeking and use. The core assumption of this view, that alcohol-seeking and use are motivated by the individual's expectations regarding the affective impact of alcohol, is supported by empirical investigations of incentive-learning processes and their role in instrumental behavior for both nondrug and drug rewards, the role of alcohol outcome expectancies in alcohol use, and the relation between affect and alcohol use. Moreover, the model is consistent with, and serves to complement, many of the currently dominant theoretical views of alcohol use and abuse, including conditioned reinforcement models, expectancy theory, and behavioral choice theory. The synthesis of principles of learning, motivation, and behavior allocation in Cox and Klinger's conceptualization of substance use importantly draws attention to a key issue of empirical and clinical relevance; namely, the function of learning and motivationally based mechanisms in the pursuit of both drug and nondrug goals, and the interaction between these mechanisms. By drawing the focus of scientific and clinical approaches to addiction to this issue, the scope of investigation and treatment of addiction phenomena is broadened from its traditional emphasis on reducing drug-seeking and consumption to considering (1) the nature and extent of alternative valued activities available within the environmental context in which addictive behaviors occur, and (2) the mechanisms underlying the addict's emergent preference for substance use, relative to these activities. These considerations are essential in extending the aim of current intervention approaches from the problem of "how to reduce/eliminate substance use" to "what, if not the drug, will the addict strive to attain in life?" and, as addressed by the Systematic Motivational Counseling (SMC) technique, "how might we help the addict to identify and successfully pursue an appropriate set of nondrug incentives?" In the section below, we elaborate this approach and the relevance of its principles to other existing treatment modalities for addiction.

TREATMENT IMPLICATIONS

Since Wikler's early observations of conditioned withdrawal during group therapy, a number of learning and conditioning approaches to addiction treatment have been developed. The aim of these interventions varies from extinguishing or eliminating drug-craving and use in response to drug-associated cues, as emphasized by the cue-exposure technique (Drummond et al., 1995), to providing positively reinforcing and punishing consequences for abstinence and drug use, respectively, as is central to the contingency management approach (Higgins & Petry, 1999; Wong, Jones, & Stitzer, Chapter 22, this volume).

The SMC technique, although somewhat different in scope from other approaches, is highly consistent with the therapeutic objectives of the above-described model, and various others (e.g., relapse prevention, motivational-enhancement therapy, community reinforcement approach, Matrix model; see Fuller & Hiller-Sturmhöfel, 1999, for review). The broad aim of this model is to promote reallocation of the addicted individual's behavior to nondrug, alternative activities. As demonstrated in this chapter, current evidence suggests that (1) the selective pursuit of substances of abuse is largely determined by the addicted individual's expectations of relatively more positive affective changes resulting from substance use, as compared to nonsubstance-related activities, and (2) these "relative expectations" are learned through experience with the substance and the nondrug incentives. The SMC method, therefore, aims to restructure these expectations by facilitating a new and emotionally satisfying experience with respect to the client's pursuit and attainment of nondrug incentives.

The SMC approach is described in detail elsewhere (Cox & Klinger, Chapter 11, this volume) and is described here only briefly. Using this technique, the clinician works with the addicted client to identify the positive and negative incentives in his or her life, the conflicts among them, and the affective changes that the individual derives or could potentially derive from these incentives. The identification of these "current concerns" of the client is achieved through the administration of the Motivational Structure Questionnaire (MSQ; see Cox & Klinger and Klinger & Cox, Chapters 8 and 9, this volume) to the client. The clinician's interpretation of the client's response patterns, in turn, facilitates the formulation of client-specific strategies for the successful pursuit and attainment of positive incentives, and the elimination of negative incentives or other sources of negative affect (see also Cox, Klinger, & Blount, 1996). Although this strategy does not focus directly on promoting drug abstinence, it targets modulation of learning- and incentive-based mechanisms that appear to play a critical role in maintaining the addictive behavior.

As noted earlier, the consistency in the aims of the SMC approach and other models is quite clear. Among the key themes of the relapse prevention approach (Marlatt & Gordon, 1985), for example, are (1) promoting the development and/or enrichment of the client's social network, (2) teaching the client to cope effectively with negative affect, and (3) helping the client to establish a balanced lifestyle, in part, through the development of "substitute indulgences" (see Daley & Marlatt, 1997, p. 459). Similarly, clinicians employing the contingency management (CM) and community reinforcement (CR) models provide rewards such as voucher incentives and clinic privileges as reinforcing consequences both for abstinence and for completion of nondrug activities such as seeking employment and attending to medical heath concerns (see Higgins & Petry, 1999; Wong, Jones, & Stitzer, Chapter 22, this volume). Moreover, outcome research has shown that clients who meet pre-established nondrug treatment goals using this incentive approach are more likely to remain abstinent, relative to those who do not meet their nondrug goals (Bickel et al., 1997). By offering a systematic approach to establishing and helping the client to work toward such nondrug goals, the SMC technique may serve as a useful adjunct to these models, apart from its established efficacy as a primary intervention strategy among brain-injured populations (Cox et al., in press-a; Miranti & Heinemann, Chapter 15, this volume) and other populations (de Jong-Meyer, Chapter 13, this volume).

CONCLUSIONS

At present, we appear to be entering an era in addiction research in which the importance of learning and motivationally based mechanisms in understanding and treating addictive disorders is becoming increasingly recognized and emphasized. In light of the mounting evidence supporting an integral role of incentive processes in the development of addictive behaviors, it seems reasonable to suggest that addiction phenomena reflect, at least in part, a disorder of motivation.

An earlier section of this chapter examined the adaptive significance of the capacity to perform goal-directed actions. This capacity, it was argued, developed as a means of promoting survival, in expanding the behavioral repertoire of animals and, subsequently, humans, to include the ability to seek out and pursue environmental resources to fulfill our basic needs and desires. Our desires, in turn, are formed on the basis of our evaluative beliefs concerning the affective consequences of the goal-object. Seeking out commodities that bring positive emotional consequences may be viewed as adaptive because such activities promote psychological well-being which, in evolutionary terms, may be considered an essential aspect of "fitness." Although the addict's pursuit of substances of abuse results in a gross imbalance between adaptively significant positive and negative outcomes (e.g., loss of employment, family, physical health), this imbalance is not sufficient to eliminate the behavior, and hence we recognize the individual as having an addictive "disorder."

Although defining the concept of "mental disorder" is a subject of contentious debate in the field of psychopathology, Wakefield (1992, p. 373) offers a compelling analysis of this concept as comprising both scientific and societal value components:

> ...a disorder exists when the failure of a person's internal mechanisms to perform their functions as designed by nature impinges harmfully on the person's well-being as defined by social values and meanings.

By Wakefield's definition, an addictive behavior comprises a "mental disorder" insofar as the harm to the addict's well-being results from a failure of some internal mechanism to function as intended by evolution and natural selection. It is argued here, therefore, that the capacity to perform goal-directed actions, an ability that developed as a means of promoting survival, is the core function that is disturbed among individuals with addictive disorders. More specifically, the selective performance of substance-related activities in the face of its maladaptive consequences reflects a failure of a *motivational mechanism* to perform its intended function, i.e., to select behaviors that promote the addicted individual's well-being.

Although speculative, the suggestion that addiction reflects a disorder of motivation is supported by recent evidence that individuals with a dysfunctional motivational structure, as measured by the MSQ, are at higher risk for heavy alcohol use, as compared to individuals with an adaptive motivational structure (Cox et al., in press-b). The addiction literature is in its infancy, however, in terms of exploring the relative predictive power of motivational variables, as compared to other factors (e.g., personality, genetic, neurobiological) that are associated with substance-related problems. Likewise, within the animal literature, we are only beginning to delineate the basic learning and motivational mechanisms that impact substance use in drug-dependent, relative to nondependent, individuals. Thus, the truth behind the suggestion that addiction phenomena reflect a disorder of motivation can be unveiled only with future investigation and integration of human and animal research into motivational mechanisms. With knowledge of the incentive and motivational constructs, and the corresponding etiological and intervention models presented in this chapter, scientists and clinicians are in an excellent place to begin.

REFERENCES

Baker, T.B., Morse, E., & Sherman, J.E. (1987). The motivation to use drugs: A psychobiological analysis of urges. In C. Rivers (Ed.), *The Nebraska Symposium on Motivation: Alcohol use and abuse* (pp. 257–323). Lincoln: University of Nebraska Press.

Balleine, B. (1992). Instrumental performance following a shift in primary motivation depends on incentive learning. *Journal of Experimental Psychology, Animal Behavior Processes, 18,* 236–250.

Balleine, B. (1994). Asymmetrical interactions between thirst and hunger in Pavlovian-instrumental transfer. *Quarterly Journal of Experimental Psychology, 47B,* 211–231.

Balleine, B. (2000). Incentive processes in instrumental conditioning. In R. Mowrer & S. Klein (Eds.), *Handbook of contemporary learning theory* (pp. 307–366). Hillsdale, NJ: Erlbaum.

Balleine, B.W., Ball, J., & Dickinson, A. (1994). Benzodiazepine-induced outcome revaluation and the motivational control of instrumental action in rats. *Behavioral Neuroscience, 108,* 573–589.

Balleine, B.W., & Dickinson, A. (1991). Instrumental performance following reinforcer devaluation depends upon incentive learning. *Quarterly Journal of Experimental Psychology, 43B,* 279–296.

Balleine, B.W., & Dickinson, A. (1998). The role of incentive learning in instrumental outcome revaluation by sensory-specific satiety. *Animal Learning and Behavior, 26* (1), 46–59.

Bickel, W.K., Amass, L., Higgins, S.T., Badger, G.J., & Esch, R.A. (1997). Effects of adding behavioral treatment to opioid detoxification with buprenorphine. *Journal of Consulting and Clinical Psychology, 65,* 803–810.

Bickel, W.K., DeGrandpre, R.J., & Higgins, S.T. (1993). Behavioral economics: A novel experimental approach to the study of drug dependence. *Drug and Alcohol Dependence, 33,* 173–192.

Carroll, M.E. (1996). Reducing drug abuse by enriching the environment with alternative nondrug reinforcers. In L. Green & J. Kagel (Eds.), *Advances in behavioral economics: Vol. 3. Substance use and abuse* (pp. 37–68). Norwood, NJ: Ablex.

Carroll, M.E. (1999). Prevention and treatment of drug abuse: Use of animal models to find solutions. In M.D. Glantz, C.R. Hartel (Eds.), *Drug abuse: Origins and interventions* (pp. 149–159). Washington, DC: American Psychological Association.

Cloninger, C.R. (1987). Neurogenetic adaptive mechanisms in alcoholism. *Science, 236,* 410–416.

Cloninger, C.R., Sigvardsson, S., & Bohman, M. (1988). Childhood personality predicts alcohol abuse in young adults. *Alcoholism: Clinical and Experimental Research, 12,* 494–505.

Colwill, R., & Rescorla, R.A. (1985). Postconditioning devaluation of a reinforcer affects instrumental responding. *Journal of Experimental Psychology: Animal Behavior Processes, 11,* 120–132.

Cox, W.M. (1981). Simultaneous incentive constrast effects with alcoholic and nonalcoholic beverages as the discriminanda for reward magnitude. *Physiological Psychology, 9,* 276–280.

Cox, W.M. (1988). Effects of alcohol on successive incentive contrast. *Bulletin of the Psychonomic Society, 26,* 67–70.

Cox, W.M., Heinemann, A.W., Miranti, S.V., Schmidt, M., Klinger, E., & Blount, J. (in press-a). Outcomes of systematic motivational counseling for substance use following traumatic brain injury. *Journal of Addictive Diseases.*

Cox, W.M., & Klinger, E. (1988). A motivational model of alcohol use. *Journal of Abnormal Psychology, 97,* 168–180.

Cox, W.M., Klinger, E., & Blount, J.P. (1996). *Systematic Motivational Counseling: A treatment manual.* Copyrighted manual available from W.M. Cox.

Cox, W.M., Schippers, G.M., Klinger, E., Skutle, A., Stuchlíková, I., Man, F., King, A.L., & Inderhaug, R. (in press-b). Motivational structure and alcohol use of university students with consistency across four nations. *Journal of Studies on Alcohol.*

Crabbe, J.C., Belknap, J.K., & Buck, K.J. (1994). Genetic animal models of alcohol and drug abuse. *Science, 264*, 1715–1723.

Crespi, L.P. (1942). Quantitative variation of incentive and performance in the white rat. *American Journal of Psychology, 55*, 467–517.

Daley, D.C., & Marlatt, G.A. (1997). Relapse prevention. In J.H. Lowinson, P. Ruiz, R.B. Millman, & J.G. Langrod (Eds.), *Substance abuse: A comprehensive textbook* (3rd edn.; pp. 458–467). Baltimore, MD: Williams & Wilkins.

DeGrandpre, R.J., & Bickel, W.K. (1996). Drug dependence as consumer demand. In L. Green & J.H. Kagel (Eds.), *Advances in behavioral economics: Vol. 3. Substance use and abuse* (pp. 1–36). Norwood, NJ: Ablex.

Dickinson, A., & Balleine, B. (1993). Actions and responses: The dual psychology of behavior. In N. Eilan, R.A. McCarthy et al. (Eds.), *Spatial representation: Problems in philosophy and psychology* (pp. 277–293). Malden, MA: Blackwell Publishers Inc.

Dickinson, A., & Balleine, B.W. (1994). Motivational control of goal-directed action. *Animal Learning and Behavior, 22*, 1–18.

Dickinson, A., & Balleine, B.W. (1995). Motivational control of instrumental action. *Current Directions in Psychological Science, 4*, 162–167.

Drummond, D.C., Tiffany, S.T., Glautier, S., & Remington, B. (1995). *Addictive behaviour: Cue exposure theory and practice.* New York: John Wiley & Sons.

Everitt, B.J., & Stacey, P. (1987). Studies of instrumental behavior with sexual reinforcement in male rats (*Rattus norvegicus*): II. Effects of preoptic area lesions, castration, and testosterone. *Journal of Comparative Psychology, 101*, 407–419.

Fuller, R.K., & Sturmhöfel, S. (1999). Alcoholism treatment in the United States: An overview. *Alcohol Research & Health*, 23, 69–77.

Glasner, S.V. (2002). *Motivational control of alcohol-seeking behavior.* Unpublished doctoral dissertation, University of Minnesota, Minneapolis.

Glasner, S.V., Overmier, J.B., & Balleine, B.W. (2002). Unpublished data. University of Minnesota, MN.

Gibson, E.L., & Desmond, E. (1999). Chocolate craving and hunger state: Implications for the acquisition and expression of appetite and food choice. *Appetite, 32*, 219–240.

Goldman, M.S. (1994). The alcohol expectancy concept: Applications to assessment, prevention, and treatment of alcohol abuse. *Applied and Preventive Psychology, 3*, 131–144.

Goldman, M.S., Del Boca, F.K., & Darkes, J. (1999). Alcohol expectancy theory: The application of cognitive neuroscience. In H. Blane & K. Leonard (Eds.), *Psychological theories of drinking and alcoholism* (pp. 233–262). New York: Guilford.

Griffiths, R.R., Bigelow, G.E., & Henningfield, J.E. (1980). Similarities in animal and human drug-taking behavior. In N.K. Mello (Ed.), *Advances in substance abuse: Behavioral and biological research* (Vol. 1; pp. 1–90). Greenwich, CT: JAI press.

Hendersen, R.W., & Graham, J. (1979). Avoidance of heat by rats: Effects of thermal context on the rapidity of extinction. *Learning and Motivation, 10*, 351–363.

Herrnstein, R.J. (1970). On the law of effect. *Journal of the Experimental Analysis of Behavior, 13*, 243–266.

Higgins, S.T. (1997). The influence of alternative reinforcers on cocaine use and abuse: A brief review. *Pharmacology, Biochemistry and Behavior, 57*, 419–427.

Higgins, S.T., & Petry, N.M. (1999). Contingency management. Incentives for sobriety. *Alcohol Research and Health, 23*, 122–127.

Hodgson, R., Rankin, H., & Stockwell, T. (1979). Alcohol dependence and the priming effect. *Behavior Research and Therapy, 17*, 379–387.

Hufford, M.R. (2001). An examination of mood effects on positive alcohol expectancies among undergraduate drinkers. *Cognition and Emotion, 15* (5), 593–613.

Hussong, A.M., Hicks, R.E., Levy, S.A., & Curran, P.J. (2001). Specifying the relations between affect and heavy alcohol use among young adults. *Journal of Abnormal Psychology, 110* (3), 449–461.

Kendler, K.S., Heath, A.C., Neale, M.C., Kessler, R.C., & Eaves, L.J. (1992). A population-based twin study of alcoholism in women. *JAMA, 268*, 1877–1882.

Klinger, E. (1977). *Meaning and void: Inner experience and the incentives in people's lives.* Minneapolis, MN: University of Minnesota Press.

Koob, G.F., & Weiss, F. (1992). Neuropharmacology of cocaine and ethanol dependence. *Recent Developments in Alcoholism, 10*, 201–233.

Laberg, J.C. (1987). Psychophysiological indicators of craving in alcoholics: Effects of cue exposure. *British Journal of Addiction, 82* (12), 1341–1348.

Langenbucher, J.W., & Nathan, P.E. (1983). The "wet" alcoholic: One drink...then what? In W.M. Cox (Ed.), *Identifying and measuring alcoholic personality characteristics.* San Francisco: Jossey-Bass.

Ludwig, A.M., Wikler, A., & Stark, L.H. (1974). The first drink: Psychobiological aspects of craving. *Archives of General Psychiatry, 30* (4), 539–547.

Marlatt, G.A., Demming, B., & Reid, J.B. (1973). Loss of control drinking in alcoholics: An experimental analogue. *Journal of Abnormal Psychology, 81* (3), 233–241.

Marlatt, G.A., & Gordon, J.R. (Eds.) (1985). *Relapse prevention.* New York: Guilford.

McBride, W.J., Chernet, J.E., Dyr, W., Lumeng, L., & Li, T.K. (1993). Densities of dopamine D2 receptors are reduced in CNS regions of alcohol preferring P rats. *Alcohol, 10*, 387–390.

McClelland, D.C., Davis, W.N., Kalin, R., & Wagner, F. (1972). *The drinking man: Alcohol and human motivation.* New York: Free Press.

Newlin, D.B. (1992). A comparison of drug conditioning and craving for alcohol and cocaine. *Recent Developments in Alcoholism, 10*, 147–164.

Noble, E.P. (1993). The D2 dopamine receptor gene: A review of association studies in alcoholism. *Behavior Genetics, 23* (2), 119–229.

Premack, D. (1965). Reinforcement theory. In D. Levine (Ed.), *Nebraska Symposium on Motivation* (pp. 123–180). Lincoln: University of Nebraska Press.

Randall, D.M., & Cox, W.M. (2001). Experimental mood inductions in persons at high and low risk for alcohol problems. *American Journal of Drug and Alcohol Abuse, 27* (1), 183–187.

Rather, B.C., & Goldman, M.S. (1994). Drinking-related differences in the memory organization of alcohol expectancies. *Experimental and Clinical Psychopharmacology, 2*, 167–183.

Robinson, T.E., & Berridge, K.C. (1993). The neural basis of drug craving: An incentive sensitization theory of addiction. *Brain Research: Brain Research Reviews, 18* (3), 247–291.

Robinson, T.E., & Berridge, K.C. (2001). Incentive-sensitization and addiction. *Addiction, 96* (1), 103–114.

Siegel, S. (1983). Classical conditioning, drug tolerance, and drug dependence. In Y. Israel, B.F. Glaser, H. Kalant, R.E. Popham, W. Schmidt, & R.G. Smart (Eds.), *Research advances in alcohol and drug problems* (Vol. 7; pp. 207–246). New York: Plenum.

Skinner, B.F. (1938). *The behavior of organisms: An experimental analysis.* Englewood Cliffs, NJ: Prentice-Hall.

Solomon, R.L. (1977). Acquired motivation and affective opponent processes. In J.D. Maser & M.E.P. Seligman (Eds.), *Psychopathology: Experimental models* (pp. 66–103). San Francisco: Freeman.

Solomon, R. (1991). Acquired motivation and affective opponent processes. In J. Madden (Ed.), *Neurobiology of learning, emotion, and affect* (pp. 307–348). New York: Raven Press.

Stewart, J., de Wit, H., & Eikelboom, R. (1984). Role of unconditioned and conditioned drug effects in self-administration of opiates and stimulants. *Psychological Review, 9*, 251–268.

Thorndike, E.L. (1911). *Animal intelligence: Experimental studies.* New York: Macmillan.

Tiffany, S.T. (1999). Cognitive concepts of craving. *Alcohol Research and Health, 23* (3), 215–224.

Tolman, E.C. (1949a). The nature and functioning of wants. *Psychological Review, 56*, 357–369.

Tolman, E.C. (1949b). There is more than one kind of learning. *Psychological Review, 56*, 144–155.

Topp, L., Lovibond, P.F., & Mattick, R.P. (1998). Cue reactivity in dependent amphetamine users: Can monistic conditioning theories advance our understanding of reactivity? *Drug and Alcohol Review, 17* (3), 277–288.

Vuchinich, R.E., & Tucker, J.A. (1988). Contributions from behavioral theories of choice to an analysis of alcohol abuse. *Journal of Abnormal Psychology, 97* (2), 181–195.

Vuchinich, R.E., & Tucker, J.A. (1998). Choice, behavioral economics, and addictive behavior patterns. In W.R. Miller & N. Heather (Eds.), *Treating addictive behaviors* (pp. 93–104). New York: Plenum.

Wakefield, J.C. (1992). The concept of mental disorder: On the boundary between biological facts and social values. *American Psychologist, 47*, 373–388.

Winger, G., Young, A.M., & Woods, J.H. (1983). Ethanol as a reinforcer: Comparison with other drugs. In B. Kissen & H. Begleiter (Eds.), *The biology of alcoholism: The pathogenesis of alcoholism* (Vol. 7; pp. 107–132). New York: Plenum.

Wise, R.A. (1988). The neurobiology of craving: Implications for understanding and treatment of addiction. *Journal of Abnormal Psychology, 97* (2), 118–132.

Wise, R.A., & Bozarth, M.A. (1987). A psychomotor stimulant theory of addiction. *Psychological Review, 94*, 469–492.

Wiseman, J.P. (1970). *Stations of the lost: The treatment of skid row alcoholics.* New York: Prentice-Hall.

Zhou, F.C., Zhang, J.K., Lumeng, L., & Li, T.K. (1995). Mesolimbic dopamine system in alcohol-preferring rats. *Alcohol, 12*, 403–412.

CHAPTER 3

Behavioral Economics: Basic Concepts and Clinical Applications

Christopher J. Correia
Auburn University, Auburn, USA

Synopsis.—This chapter provides an introduction to behavioral economics, a relatively new development in behavioral psychology that is well suited to understanding choice behavior. Throughout the chapter, an effort is made to focus on the concepts and clinical applications of behavioral economics. The chapter begins with a review of the historical factors that led to the development of behavioral economics, and with a discussion of the advantages of integrating behavioral psychology and economic theory. An overview of consumer demand theory is provided, which includes examples of four economic variables—income, price, alternative reinforcers, and reinforcer delay—that influence choice behavior. The behavioral choice perspective on substance abuse is offered as an example of how behavioral economics is able to synthesize results from the laboratory and the natural environment, and how it has been applied to "real world" clinical problems. Finally, the chapter discusses two clinical implications of the behavioral economic literature: increasing alternative reinforcers, and developing a tolerance for delayed rewards. These specific treatment elements were chosen because they highlight some of the overlap between behavioral economics and cognitive-motivational treatment approaches.

INTRODUCTION

Life is full of choices. During the course of normal daily living and social interaction, most individuals contact a variety of potentially reinforcing or rewarding stimuli. Some choose to allocate the majority of their time and energy toward healthy, productive, and fulfilling behaviors. Others devote much of their time to unhealthy, unproductive, and potentially dangerous behaviors. This chapter is designed to demonstrate how behavioral economics— a relatively new development in the field of behavioral psychology—attempts to describe and predict the choices people make.

Introductions to behavioral economics often include somewhat complex mathematical formulations and equations. Although the mathematical approach is an important aspect of behavioral economics, many find it daunting and impractical. This chapter is designed to make the theory and application of behavioral economics accessible and relevant to

Handbook of Motivational Counseling. Edited by W. Miles Cox and Eric Klinger.

as wide an audience as possible. Thus, the chapter makes only limited reference to the mathematical foundations of behavioral economics. Instead, the chapter focuses on how behavioral economic research has been used to increase our understanding of real world clinical problems. One goal is to enable readers to gain a better understanding of how the behavioral economic perspective could inform their own research and clinical work. A second goal is to discuss the relationship between behavioral economics and cognitive-motivational treatment approaches, including motivational counseling.

THEORETICAL FOUNDATIONS

Behavioral economics draws from a rich foundation of empirically supported principles. This section begins by describing some of the seminal theoretical and empirical statements on the selection of preferences, and discusses how this research contributed to the development of behavioral economics.

Traditional theories of reinforcement have tended to focus on the relationship between an individual reinforcer and behavior (e.g., Skinner, 1938). However, as reinforcement theory has developed over time, there has been a tendency to focus on the context within which reinforcement occurs. Thus, in addition to asking how behavior is influenced by one particular reinforcer, behavioral theorists are now also asking how an individual establishes preferences and allocates his or her behavior among an array of simultaneously available reinforcers.

Premack (1965) operationally defined a preference as the ordering a participant gives to a set of stimuli, and suggested that preferences for a particular stimulus are determined in the context of all other competing stimuli. Herrnstein (1970) formalized the relationship between reinforcers with the matching law, a mathematical account of choice behavior particularly well suited to understanding preference selection in a broader environmental context. The theory and accompanying equations specify that an individual's behavior is distributed across concurrently available options in proportion to the amount of differential reinforcement received for engaging in each behavior. Simply put, the frequency of a given behavior is a function of its reinforcement, relative to the reinforcement obtained from all other possible activities. Thus, the amount of reinforcement received from a behavior *relative to other options* is viewed as more predictive of choice behavior than the *absolute amount* of reinforcement received. Reviews of the literature suggest that the matching law can adequately describe human choice behavior in both controlled and natural environments (cf. McDowell, 1988).

The work of Premack and Herrnstein revealed that behavior allocation is affected by environmental conditions and, more specifically, the reinforcement associated with all of the activities available within the environment. This work also opened the door for a productive synthesis between the fields of economics and behavioral psychology. Vuchinich and Tucker (1998, p. 95) summarized how the above developments gave rise to this merger:

> It was soon recognized that the task of describing the behavioral allocation of animals in the laboratory shared essential features with the task of describing the resource allocation of human consumers in the economy (e.g., Rachlin et al., 1976). This connection led some behavioral psychologists to use concepts from consumer demand theory in economics and led some economists to use behavioral methods, which resulted in a mutually beneficial merger now known as behavioral economics (Kagel, Battalio, & Green, 1995).

Behavioral economics is the application of economic principles to the study of behavior. Behavioral economics combines the rigor and precision of the psychologist's laboratory-based experimental analysis of behavior with the economist's rich set of concepts and principles (Green & Kagel, 1996). The application of behavioral methods to consumer behavior has allowed economists to conduct exacting experimental tests of their theories and postulates. Economic theories, on the other hand, have proven useful as a means of organizing seemingly disparate data from behavioral experiments. Moreover, the extension of operant psychology to the "real world" problems of economics provides a powerful demonstration of how basic behavioral principles can be used to better understand and address a variety of complex clinical phenomena (Winkler & Burkhard, 1990).

To summarize, behavioral economics is a useful way of understanding the factors that control choice behavior in both laboratory and natural environments. The next section introduces some of the basic economic variables that influence consumer behavior. Many of the economic principles relevant to the study of behavioral economics are derived from consumer demand theory.

OVERVIEW OF CONSUMER DEMAND THEORY

Consumer demand theory is the study of how an individual's behavior is influenced by a variety of economic and environmental factors (Pearce, 1992). When talking about consumer demand, economists are interested in two primary variables: consumption and spending. Consumption refers to the use of goods and services, and can include a broad range of activities such as eating a meal, buying gasoline for an automobile, or utilizing health care. Spending refers to the amount of money, time, or effort an individual allocates to obtaining and consuming a particular good, product, or service.

Although terms like consumption, spending, and price are traditionally thought of as economic variables, they can be easily translated into more general behavioral terms. Behavioral economics is the study of how behavior is allocated among all available reinforcing activities. Within this context, "goods and services" are conceptualized as reinforcers; "price" refers to the money, time, or effort required to obtain access to a given reinforcer; and "spending" refers to how an individual allocates resources among the available reinforcers (Madden, 2000). Put another way, "reinforcers and commodities are both classes of things that a subject will do something to get" (Lea, 1978, p. 443). The remainder of this section describes how four important variables—income, price, the availability of alternative activities, and reinforcement delay—have been shown to influence consumer demand, or the way individuals allocate their behavior among available reinforcers.

Income

Economists define income as the amount of money, goods, or services available to an individual at a given time (Pearce, 1992). In behavioral terms, income can be defined as the amount of total reinforcement available during an experimental session (DeGrandpre & Bickel, 1996); the density of positive reinforcement available in the natural environment (Correia, Carey, & Borsari, 2002); or the amount of money, time, energy, or other resources that can be allocated to various reinforcers. In all cases, it is easy to see how income is a main factor, and perhaps the primary factor, constraining our choices (Chaloupka & Pacula, 2000). In other words, the more reinforcers that are available, and the more resources you have to allocate to those reinforcers, the more choices you have.

Increased income can make us more likely to choose some reinforcers, and less likely to choose other reinforcers. Consider for following example:

> If any of us had significantly more income, there are probably several products and services that we either would stop purchasing or would purchase at a reduced rate (e.g., used vehicles, whatever beer is on sale, and cleaning products), and several on which we would begin spending our newfound wealth (e.g., new cars, craft-brewed beers, and a maid). (Madden, 2000, p. 20)

This quotation highlights the fact that increases in income are not associated with increased consumption of every available good or reinforcer. Rather, we allocate more of our resources to some goods, and less of our income to other goods.

Price

Generally speaking, as the price of a good increases, consumption of it decreases. This principle has been formalized as the Law of Demand. However, just as increases in income do not lead to increased consumption of all reinforcers, there is not always a perfect correlation between increased prices and decreased consumption. A reinforcer's elasticity is one way of describing how its consumption is influenced by price changes. Demand for a reinforcer is said to be elastic when increases in price lead to proportional decreases in consumption. Examples of goods that are typically thought of as elastic include luxury and leisure items such as first-class airline tickets, meals in restaurants, and clothing purchased at expensive boutiques. Alternatively, demand for a reinforcer is said to be inelastic when consumption remains fairly stable despite increases in price. In other words, the behavior is resistant to change despite the increase in the cost.

In considering the effects of price on behavior, it is important to recognize that the behavioral economic definition of price goes beyond the simple monetary cost. Chaloupka and Pacula (2000) provided a comprehensive review of a variety of factors that can influence decisions about smoking, including the monetary costs of smoking, restrictions on where and when people can smoke, the fines and other legal consequences of smoking at unauthorized locations, and awareness of the short- and long-term health risks associated with smoking. More generally, the full price of any good, service, or reinforcer consists of four basic components: (1) monetary cost, (2) time and effort costs, (3) potential legal cost, and (4) potential health cost. The full price concept is useful in trying to calculate the cost–benefit ratio of a particular behavior.

Alternative Sources of Reinforcement

As previously mentioned, the work of Premack and Herrnstein altered the course of behavioral research and led to the development of behavioral economics. Rather than simply focusing on the reinforcing value of one particular stimulus, behavioral economics explicitly recognizes that preference for a particular reinforcer also depends on the availability of other competing reinforcers. There are a variety of ways to conceptualize the availability of rewarding or potentially reinforcing behaviors. One rather broad conceptualization is Cautela's (1984) General Level of Reinforcement (GLR), which is defined as the number, quality, and duration of reinforcers operating during a given unit of time. A number of factors can lead to a low GLR, including a punishing environment in which few reinforcers are available, individual differences in sensitivity to reward and punishment, and individual differences in the skills needed to take advantage of potentially rewarding situations. Regardless of the reasons for low GLR, when a person is in a state of deprivation, all existing reinforcers become more powerful.

In addition to the number or density of reinforcers, behavioral economics investigates the competition that takes place among those reinforcers that are available. Economists use the concept of substitutability to describe the degree to which one commodity or reinforcer can take the place of another. Reinforcers that share important properties with one another are referred to as substitutes. For example, potato chips and tortilla chips share a number of properties; they are both crunchy, salty, and make for a convenient snack. Because of these similarities, one of them could likely be substituted for the other. If the price of potato chips suddenly increased, its consumption would likely decrease, while consumption of tortilla chips would increase. Similarly, some studies have demonstrated that various drugs, such as heroin and valium, can serve as substitutes for one another (Petry & Bickel, 1998). Indeed, the use of methadone for the treatment of opioid dependence is based on the notion that methadone is a reasonable substitute for heroin.

When considering the degree to which two reinforcers can be substituted for each other, it is important to recognize that substitutability is driven by the function of the reinforcers. Thus, two reinforcers can be qualitatively very different and yet serve as substitutes for one another. A good example is cigarette smoking and social support. Recent studies have reported that positive role models, community involvement, and spending time with organized groups serve as protective factors against cigarette smoking (Atkins et al., 2002; Elder et al., 2000). Earlier studies had reported that increased rates of smoking are associated with divorce, separation, single marital status, widowhood, and lack of a confidant (Fisher, 1996). Although these results can be interpreted in a variety of ways, they are consistent with Fisher's (1996) view that social support can serve as a commodity, and that it can function as a substitute for smoking under certain contexts. The following quotation summarizes his proposition:

> The review of [social supports] effects and those of nicotine suggest that social support and nicotine may be substitutable for each other. Both (a) appear to enhance task performance, (b) have positive benefits on mood, and (c) appear to have enhanced utility in the face of distress. These similar values of social support and nicotine might be the basis for their serving as substitutes for each other in times of stress, low mood, and desire for energized performance. (Fisher, 1996, p. 215)

The commodity view of social support has been applied to other forms of substance use (Rachlin, 2000), binge-eating (Krug-Porzelius et al., 1994), and diabetes (Fisher et al., 1997), and might prove useful in understanding a variety of other behaviors.

Understanding how alternative reinforcers influence decision-making and choice behavior may be one of the most important contributions that behavioral economics has to make. It also provides the most obvious link between behavioral economics and the motivational counseling techniques described in this book. An expanded view of alternative reinforcers is presented in the section on behavioral theories on choice, and again in the final section on the clinical and motivational implication of behavioral economics.

Reinforcer Delay and Impulsivity

Impulsivity is mentioned in the DSM-IV criteria for a number of disorders and has been implicated as a symptom or correlate of a wide range of problematic behaviors, including antisocial and borderline personality disorders; bipolar disorder, depression, and suicide; ADHD and conduct disorder; substance abuse; gambling and excessive spending; binge-eating and failure to exercise; and aggressive, delinquent, and criminal behaviors (Bickel & Marsch, 2000; Evenden, 1999; Moeller et al., 2001).

Impulsivity has traditionally been defined as a trait or personality feature. Alternatively, Logue (2000) provided a more operational definition of impulsivity: the choice of immediate, but ultimately less valuable, rewards. Self-control, on the other hand, can be defined as the choice of delayed, but ultimately more valued, rewards. The behavioral economic literature on impulsivity utilizes an operant model that measures preferences for rewards of various sizes and delivers after delays of various lengths. This research is generally referred to as delay or temporal discounting, and results have demonstrated that individuals tend to discount future consequences as a function of their delay. Delay discounting research has also uncovered some interesting individual differences. For example, a recent study (Bickel, Odum, & Madden, 1999) compared current cigarette smokers ($n = 23$) to never-smokers ($n = 22$) and ex-smokers ($n = 21$) on the degree to which they would discount hypothetical monetary rewards. All participants made choices between various combinations of monetary amounts (ranging from $1 to $1000) delivered immediately or after a delay (ranging from one week to 25 years). The results indicated that current smokers discounted the value of the delayed money more than either comparison group, and that the never-smokers and ex-smokers did not differ from each other. Thus, in this study, impulsive decisions could be partially attributed to characteristics of the individuals (smoking status), and partially attributed to the environmental context (the delay of the reward). The fact that never-smokers and ex-smokers did not differ from each other suggests that the degree to which an individual discounts future rewards can change over time and across situations.

Laboratory-based measures of delay discounting have been related to a variety of other naturally occurring behaviors, such as alcohol use (Vuchinich & Simpson, 1998), opiate abuse (Madden et al., 1997), and risky sexual behaviors (Farr, Vuchinich, & Simpson, 1998). As with alternative reinforcers, there are some interesting ways to link delay discounting and cognitive-motivational treatments, and these will be discussed later in the chapter.

PULLING IT ALL TOGETHER: THE BEHAVIORAL CHOICE PERSPECTIVE ON SUBSTANCE USE

Thus far, this chapter has detailed the development of behavioral economics, and, in fairly general terms, discussed the effects of income, price, alternative reinforcers, and reinforcer delay on behavioral allocation. In this next section, the behavioral choice perspective is presented as an example of how the behavioral economic literature has been applied successfully to substance use (the terms *behavioral choice perspective* and *behavioral economics* are often used interchangeably). Vuchinich and Tucker (1983) proposed the behavioral theories of choice as a framework for understanding the environmental context surrounding substance use and abuse. These authors described the behavioral choice perspective as a molar account of how organisms allocate their behavior among a set of available activities, with the full set of available activities constituting the surrounding context. Thus, the behavioral choice perspective recognizes that preferences for substances arise within a broader context involving the availability or utilization of other competing reinforcers and their associated environmental constraints. Analyses emerging from this perspective aim to identify the variables that control the reinforcing value of substance use relative to the reinforcing value of other available activities (Vuchinich & Tucker, 1988).

After reviewing the work of Premack (1965), Herrnstein (1970), and other behavioral choice researchers, Vuchinich and Tucker (1983) proposed the following generalization: If constraints on a particular reinforcer are increased, there is a tendency for its consumption to be reduced and for behavior to be reallocated among the other available reinforcers. When applied to the use of psychoactive substances, the generalization suggests that the context surrounding alcohol use can be investigated as a function of two classes of variables: (a) the direct constraints imposed on access to substance use, and (b) reinforcers other than substance use that are available and the constraints imposed on access to them.

Direct Constraints on Access to Substances

Vuchinich and Tucker's conceptualization of constraints is very similar to the behavioral economic notion of total price. Constraints usually refer to changes in the price of a substance, but can include any factor that limits the availability or devalues substance use, including the introduction of negative consequences contingent on substance use. Constraints can be the result of an experimental manipulation, such as the response required to obtained a reinforcer, or conditions existing in the natural environment.

In one early study (Liebson et al., 1971), alcoholics receiving inpatient treatment earned credits by doing laundry work, tutoring other patients, and performing other types of service. The credits could then be exchanged for a variety of goods and services, including health care, entertainment, and alcohol. Increasing the amount of work required to obtain alcohol resulted in decreased alcohol consumption. These results were later replicated in a study of alcohol self-administration in moderate drinkers (Van Etten, Higgins, & Bickel, 1995). Three male volunteers could earn a designated amount of beer (2 oz. or 4 oz.) by pulling a lever a designated number of times (100, 200, 400, 800, or 1600). Thus, the experimenters manipulated both the available dose and the response requirement. As in the earlier study with alcoholics, moderate drinkers showed decreased alcohol consumption as schedule requirements increased.

Griffiths, Bigelow, and Henningfield (1980) reviewed the literature on the relationship between substance self-administration and response requirement, including studies utilizing both human and nonhuman participants. These authors concluded that the "results have shown a relationship which is remarkably generalizable across species, across drugs, and across settings; as response requirement increases, the amount of drug self-administered typically decreases" (p. 30). Research on response requirement is important in demonstrating that behavior can sometimes be controlled with relatively simple environmental and economic manipulations

Alternative Reinforcers: Availability and Constraints

Direct constraints on access to substances can have a powerful effect on substance use. However, constraints on nondrug alternative reinforcers may be more salient determinants of actual consumption, because direct constraints on alcohol are relatively rare in most natural environments (Vuchinich & Tucker, 1988). In other words, decisions to *not* drink are usually the result of competition from substance-free alternatives, rather than from the effects of prohibitive constraints. Studies from both the laboratory and naturalistic settings have been used to demonstrate the inverse relationship between substance use and alternative reinforcers.

Laboratory Studies

Numerous laboratory studies have demonstrated that substance use decreases as alternative reinforcers are made available, and that substance use increases when previously available alternative reinforcers are removed. Preference for alcohol consumption among nonalcoholic males was studied as a function of the value and delay of an alternative reinforcer (Vuchinich & Tucker, 1983). Participants could earn points by responding with button presses, and the points could be redeemed for either money or alcohol. All alcohol earned in the study had to be consumed during the experimental session. The investigators manipulated the monetary value of the points (2¢ or 10¢) and the delay before money was received (no delay, two-week delay, or eight-week delay); the price of alcohol remained the same across conditions. As predicted, participants showed greater preference for alcohol under the low money condition, and participants in both delay conditions preferred alcohol more than participants in the no-delay condition.

Vuchinich and Tucker (1988, 1996a) reviewed numerous operant-based laboratory studies, and concluded that substance use may emerge as a highly preferred activity when constraints on psychoactive substances are minimal and alternative reinforcers are either sparse, delayed, or difficult to acquire. Carroll (1996a) reached similar conclusions when she analyzed the optimal environmental conditions for preventing drug abuse or dependence. In doing so, she reviewed laboratory-based drug self-administration studies in which the availability of nondrug reinforcers was manipulated. The review concluded that the availability of nondrug alternative reinforcers reliably and effectively reduces drug self-administration, can slow or prevent acquisition of drug self-administration, and may suppress withdrawal under some conditions. Findings tend to generalize across species, drugs of abuse, types of alternative reinforcers, and routes of administration.

Natural Environment Studies

Building on earlier laboratory findings, Vuchinich and Tucker (1996b) tested an application of the behavioral-choice perspective to the problem of alcohol relapse. The decision to consume alcohol after treatment was likened to choosing an immediate but small reward over delayed but larger rewards that are often contingent on maintaining abstinence, such as improved health, work performance, and family relations. Participants were 26 male veterans in an aftercare program following inpatient treatment for alcohol dependence. They provided daily records of alcohol consumption, and an explanation of why they drank. Participants also recorded significant positive and negative life events and a rating of their impact on mood. As predicted, drinking episodes preceded by negative events were more severe. The authors proposed that certain life events (e.g., separation from a spouse) led to a reduction in the future availability of nondrinking reinforcement, thus increasing the relative reinforcing value of alcohol consumption.

Correia and colleagues conducted a series of studies on the relationship between substance use and substance-free reinforcement. An initial study with college undergraduates (Correia et al., 1998) demonstrated that predictions of substance use improved when both substance-free and substance-related reinforcement were taken into account. Specifically, a negative relationship was observed between substance-free reinforcement and the frequency of substance use, indicating that as reinforcement from substance-free activities decreased, the frequency of substance use increased. The addition of a reinforcement ratio, based on Herrnstein's (1970) matching law equations and designed to measure reinforcement received from substance-related activities relative to total reinforcement, accounted for additional unique variance. A related study (Correia & Carey, 1999) reported similar relationships between the frequency of substance use and substance-free reinforcement in a sample of substance-using psychiatric outpatients. A third study (Correia, Carey, & Borsari, 2002) extended the research by demonstrating a relationship between substance-related reinforcement and measures of substance use quantity and related negative consequences.

Van Etten and colleagues (1998) compared the density of naturally occurring positive reinforcement experienced by cocaine abusers to the density experienced by a matched control group. Cocaine abusers reported a lower frequency of engagement in nonsocial, introverted, passive outdoor, and mood-related activities relative to the control group. Similar findings were reported in a study of college student binge-drinkers (Correia et al., 2003). Relative to the comparison group of lighter-drinking undergraduates, students who engaged in frequent binge-drinking derived less reinforcement from a variety of substance-free activities.

All of the studies reviewed in this section are consistent with previous experimental research and further highlight the connection between substance-related behaviors and alternative reinforcers. They also support the notion that the behavioral choice perspective is able to account for substance-related behavior in the natural environment. Thus, in both the laboratory and the natural environment, the frequency, quantity, and negative consequences of substance use is tied to the broader economic context. The behavioral choice perspective serves as an excellent example of how the behavioral economic perspective is able to integrate basic human and animal research with studies conducted in the natural environment. It also demonstrates how the behavioral economic literature has been applied to real-world clinical problems.

APPLICATION OF BEHAVIORAL ECONOMICS: CLINICAL AND MOTIVATIONAL IMPLICATIONS

This chapter began with the integration of laboratory-based behavioral psychology and consumer-demand theory. The chapter now ends with a discussion of another potentially fruitful integration. The behavioral economic perspective and cognitive-motivational treatment approaches, including motivational counseling, converge in some important ways. Many of the techniques described in this book can be linked to more basic behavioral research. Thus, both human and animal studies lend theoretical and empirical support to a number of related treatment techniques. In turn, research supporting the effectiveness of certain cognitive-motivational treatment techniques provides external validity for more basic behavioral-economic research. Thus, there exists the potential to use both frameworks—behavioral economic and cognitive motivational—to experimentally develop and test a wide range of empirically supported treatment approaches. Basic research can be used to provide an experimental analysis of the behavioral processes and mechanisms that underlie the development of unhealthy behaviors. Applied research on treatment process and outcome can build on these more basic findings, and provide the impetus for future laboratory studies. What follows are two examples of general treatment strategies that enjoy supportive research from both the behavioral-economic and cognitive-motivational paradigms: increasing alternative reinforcers and developing a tolerance for delayed rewards.

Increasing Alternative Reinforcers

One of the clearest implications of the behavioral-economic literature is the importance of alternative reinforcers. The behavioral-economic perspective suggests that the reinforcing value of any particular behavior depends on the availability of alternative reinforcers. When overall levels of reinforcement are low, existing reinforcers become more powerful. Research in both the laboratory and the natural environment suggests that increasing alternative reinforcers is one way of reliably decreasing behaviors that are unhealthy or detract from other goals and incentives.

A number of behavioral treatment approaches attempt to alter the consequences of an individual's behavior, such that rewards for alternative behaviors begin to outweigh the rewards for unwanted target behaviors. For example, contingency management programs have been used to decrease the reinforcing value of substance use by increasing the value of abstinence and substance-free reinforcers. Contingency management programs have been used to decrease the use of a number of substances, including cocaine (Higgins et al., 1991), opioids (Silverman et al., 1996), alcohol (Petry et al., 2000), and cigarettes (Corby et al., 2000). Wong, Jones, and Stitzer (Chapter 22, this volume) provide a full discussion on the use of contingency management and other behavioral treatments for substance abuse.

Epstein and colleagues have applied the behavioral-economic framework to the problem of obesity. Their laboratory research has shown that the presence of an alternative reinforcer, such as the chance to earn money, can be used to decrease preference for food (Lappalainen & Epstein, 1990). In discussing the relationship between obesity and activity preferences, Epstein (1992) observed that many obese individuals not only find exercise unrewarding, but also find more sedentary behaviors highly reinforcing. Subsequent studies demonstrated that preferences for active and sedentary lifestyles could be shifted by increasing the environmental constraints on sedentary behaviors and decreasing the environmental constraints on active behaviors (Epstein, Saelens, & O'Brien, 1995; Epstein et al., 1997; Raynor, Coleman, & Epstein, 1998). These results suggest that obesity can be treated in a variety of ways that go beyond simply decreasing food consumption. Increasing the rewards for engaging in alternative behaviors, or altering the contingencies associated with active and sedentary lifestyles, are additional ways of fostering behavioral change.

Marlatt and Kilmer (1998) suggested that treatment strategies derived from the behavioral-choice perspective could emerge as effective components in broader cognitive-motivational treatments for substance use. These authors specifically mentioned motivational interviewing (Miller & Rollnick, 2002; Resnicow et al., Chapter 24, this volume), which uses feedback regarding substance-related behaviors and consequences to promote contemplation or initiation of behavior change. For example, one study with college students (Kilmer et al., 1998) used time-allocation data to assess the relationship between drinking and environmental constraints limiting engagement in preferred activities. The results revealed a positive relationship between perceived constraints and time engaged in drinking, such that perceived constraints on preferred activities were associated with increased drinking. The authors suggested that information regarding constraints on access to valued substance-free activities could be used as sources of motivational feedback. Thus, patients could be encouraged to consider how constraints on preferred activities could be reduced, and how alcohol use imposed additional contraints on other potentially rewarding activities. As a second example, Marlatt and Kilmer (1998) reminded us that many relapse-prevention programs are designed to teach patients alternative coping behaviors that will replace drug use (see Carroll, 1996b; Marlatt & Gordon, 1985) and that a functional analysis of drug-taking behavior often yields useful information about alternative activities that may be substituted for drug use.

Motivational counseling also explicitly recognizes the importance of alternative reinforcers. Cox and Klinger's (1988; and Chapter 7, this volume) model of alcohol use, for example, suggests that drinking occurs when the expected utility of alcohol use outweighs the expected utility of not drinking. For alcoholics, repeated decisions to drink alcohol are often linked to an inadequate number of nonchemical incentives and goals. It follows that a major component of motivational counseling for alcohol abuse is helping patients to increase the degree to which nonchemical sources of reinforcement can foster emotional satisfaction and replace the reinforcement gained from drinking. Indeed, one of the tenets of motivational counseling for alcoholism is that "any treatment technique will be doomed to failure if it enables alcoholics to stop drinking but does not provide them with alternative sources of emotional satisfaction" (Cox & Klinger, 1988, p. 176).

Cox and Klinger (Chapter 11, this volume; Cox, Klinger, & Blount, 1991, 1999) suggest a number of strategies for increasing alternative sources of reinforcement, such as shifting from negative goals that require a decrease in behavior ("eat less so I can lose weight") to goals that promote engagement in more attractive alternative behaviors ("become more physically fit and attractive through increased exercise and good nutrition"), and identifying new goals and incentives that might take the place of alcohol abuse and other unwanted behaviors. The revised Pleasant Events Schedule (PES; MacPhillamy & Lewinsohn, 1982; see also Correia, Carey, & Borsari, 2002) is one tool that could be used to identify new goals or incentives. It is a self-report measure of the frequency and subjective pleasure of potentially reinforcing events and activities, which could be used, for example, to help clients to identify activities that are highly pleasurable but engaged in infrequently, and these activities could then be targeted as possible substitutes for unwanted behaviors. Alternatively, people with very few or no highly pleasurable activities (e.g., psychiatric patients) could benefit from treatment programs that expose them to novel sources of reinforcement, such as activity-oriented groups (i.e., ceramics, hiking). The PES could also be used to demonstrate, empirically, the relationship between unhealthy behaviors like substance use and other sources of reinforcement, such as family relations or occupational success. To achieve this goal, clients could complete one reinforcement survey to document their actual activities, and one to document the sources of reinforcement that would be available to them if they reduced or eliminated their substance use (see MacPhillamy & Lewinsohn, 1974, for a similar strategy used in depression research). This type of information, if presented early in treatment, may help to motivate clients who are reluctant to give up the reinforcement derived from substance use by making them more aware of underutilized substance-free sources of reinforcement.

Develop a Tolerance for Delayed Rewards

Delayed consequences of behavior, both positive and negative, are discounted relative to more immediate consequences. It is important to keep in mind that many of the long-term goals involve fairly abstract and uncertain outcomes. For example, one benefit of quitting smoking, exercising, and improving nutrition is the prospect of living a longer, healthier life. In making these changes, clients are sacrificing the short-term rewards of smoking, engaging in sedentary behaviors, and eating fatty foods in favor of something much less tangible. In a similar vein, the benefits of abstinence for an alcoholic might include improved health and greater levels of interpersonal and occupational satisfaction. However, these benefits will not be realized immediately, whereas taking a drink will produce instant gratification. Thus, clients often need to shift their perspective beyond the short-term impact of their behavior to better appreciate the benefits of working toward the delayed rewards often associated with their more important incentives and goals.

Bickel and Marsch (2000) suggested a number of ways in which increased attention to impulsivity and laboratory measures of delay discounting could increase our understanding of decision-making. For example, delay discounting research might foster an experimental analysis of the variables affecting discounting, and provide a description of the behavioral processes that lead to impulsivity and loss of control. Such a research program might also result in interventions for impulsive behavior, and outcome measures to determine the impact of interventions designed to increase self-control.

Logue (2000, p. 176) provided the following example of how impulsivity and delay discounting could be addressed in treatment:

> One particular technique may help people to increase self-control by increasing their awareness of the existence of larger, more delayed outcomes. This technique involves teaching people how to think about self-control situations in terms of cost–benefit rules. People are taught to analyze a choice situation in terms of all of the possible costs and benefits associated with each possible choice, including what opportunities may be lost through making a particular choice (a type of cost). They are also taught to weigh carefully the relative net value of each outcome before making a decision.

An important aspect of teaching self-control is the cost–benefit analysis. The decisional balance exercise, often used in cognitive-behavioral and motivational interventions, is one way of helping clients consider the full range of negative and positive consequences of their behaviors. The exercise follows from the notion that a behavior will change when the perceived costs of the behavior begin to outweigh the perceived benefits, and is very similar to behavioral-economic principles of price and total cost. Thus, both perspectives suggest that decision-making can be a rational process of carefully considering how a behavior fits into the larger context of a person's life.

The decisional balance and other techniques used in motivational counseling also help clients to develop the self-control needed for goal achievement. For example, clients are taught to construct goal ladders (Cox & Klinger, Chapter 11, this volume; Cox, Klinger, & Blount, 1991, 1999) in order to break long-range goals into smaller, more attainable subgoals. In doing so, clients begin to see how everyday decisions and behaviors are connected to the achievement of longer-term incentives and goals. The technique also enables the therapist to identify skill deficits that are preventing clients from reaching their goals, and then provide them with training in those areas. Finally, as clients make their way up their goal ladders, they experience the immediate rewards of subgoal attainments. When these components are used with the Motivational Structure Questionnaire (Cox & Klinger, Chapter 8, this volume; Klinger & Cox, Chapter 9, this volume; Klinger, Cox, & Blount, in press), clients can see how their behaviors that bring short-term rewards aid or impede their progress toward longer-term incentives and goals.

SUMMARY AND CONCLUSIONS

This chapter gives a conceptual overview of behavioral economics, and demonstrates some of its clinical implications and applications. Behavioral economics provides a set of empirically validated concepts and research procedures that have proven very useful in understanding choice behavior. By focusing on economic variables like price, alternative reinforcers, and reinforcer delays, the behavioral-economic perspective views behavior in its broader environmental context. Behavioral economics and motivational counseling share a number of conceptual features, and arrive at some similar treatment recommendations. Continued integration of the two fields could be mutually beneficial, especially by providing useful bridges between basic behavioral research and clinical theory and practice.

REFERENCES

Atkins, L.A., Oman, R.F., Vesely, S.K., Aspy, C.B., & McLeroy, K. (2002). Adolescent tobacco use: The protective effects of developmental assets. *American Journal of Health Promotion, 16*, 198–205.

Bickel, W.K., & Marsch, L.A. (2000). The tyranny of small decisions: Origins, outcomes, and proposed solutions. In W.K. Bickel & R.E. Vuchinich (Eds.), *Reframing health behavior change with behavioral economics* (pp. 341–392). Mahwah, NJ: Erlbaum.

Bickel, W.K., Odum, A.L., & Madden, G.J. (1999). Impulsivity and cigarette smoking: Delay discounting in current, never, and ex-smokers. *Psychopharmacology, 146*, 447–454.

Carroll, M.E. (1996a). Relapse prevention as a psychosocial treatment: A review of controlled clinical trials. *Experimental and Clinical Psychopharmacology, 4*, 46–54.

Carroll, M. E. (1996b). Reducing drug abuse by enriching the environment with alternative non-drug reinforcers. In L. Green & J. Kagel (Eds.), *Advances in behavioral economics* (Vol. 3; pp. 37–68). Norwood, NJ: Ablex.

Cautela, J.R. (1984). General levels of reinforcement. *Journal of Behavioral Therapy and Experimental Psychiatry, 15*, 109–114.

Chaloupka, F.J., & Pacula, R.L. (2000). Economics and antihealth behavior: The economic analysis of substance use and abuse. In W.K. Bickel & R.E. Vuchinich (Eds.), *Reframing health behavior change with behavioral economics* (pp. 89–114). Mahwah, NJ: Erlbaum.

Corby, E.A., Roll, J.M., Ledgerwood, D.M., & Schuster, C.R. (2000). Contingency management interventions for treating the substance abuse of adolescents: A feasibility study. *Experimental and Clinical Psychopharmacology, 8,* 371–376.

Correia, C.J., & Carey, K.B. (1999). Applying behavioral theories of choice to drug use in a sample of psychiatric outpatients. *Psychology of Addictive Behaviors, 13,* 207–212.

Correia, C.J., Carey, K.B., & Borsari, B.E. (2002). Measuring substance-free and substance-related reinforcement in the natural environment. *Psychology of Addictive Behaviors, 16,* 28–34.

Correia, C.J., Carey, K.B., Simons, J., & Borsari, B. (2003). Relationships between binge drinking and substance-free reinforcement in a sample of college students: A preliminary investigation. *Addictive Behaviors,* **28,** 361–368.

Correia, C.J., Simons, J., Carey, K.B., & Borsari, B.E. (1998). Predicting drug use: Application of behavioral theories of choice. *Addictive Behaviors, 23,* 705–709.

Cox, W.M., & Klinger, E. (1988) A motivational model of alcohol use. *Journal of Abnormal Psychology, 97,* 168–180.

Cox, W.M., Klinger, E., & Blount, J.P. (1991). Alcohol use and goal hierarchies: Systematic motivational counseling for alcoholics. In W.R. Miller & S. Rollnick (Eds.), *Motivational interviewing* (pp. 260–271). New York: Guilford.

Cox, W.M., Klinger, E., & Blount, J.P. (1999). *Systematic motivational counseling: A treatment manual.* Unpublished manuscript. University of Wales, Bangor.

DeGrandpre, R.J., & Bickel, W.K. (1996). Drug dependence as consumer demand. In L. Green & J. Kagel (Eds.), *Advances in behavioral economics* (Vol. 3; pp. 1–36). Norwood, NJ: Ablex.

Elder, J.P., Campbell, N.R., Litrownik, A.J., Ayala, G.X., Slymen, D.J., Parra-Medina, D., & Lovato, C.Y. (2000). Predictors of cigarette and alcohol susceptibility and use among Hispanic migrant adolescents. *Preventative Medicine, 31,* 115–123.

Epstein, L.H. (1992). Role of behavior theory in behavioral medicine. *Journal of Consulting and Clinical Psychology, 60,* 493–498.

Epstein, L.H., Saelens, B.E., Myers, M.D., & Vito, D. (1997). The effects of decreasing sedentary behaviors on activity choice in obese children. *Health Psychology, 16,* 107–113.

Epstein, L.H., Saelens, B.E., & O'Brien, J.G. (1995). Effects of reinforcing increases in active behavior versus decreases in sedentary behavior for obese children. *International Journal of Behavioral Medicine, 2,* 41–50.

Evenden, J.L. (1999). Varieties of impulsivity. *Psychopharmacology, 146,* 348–361.

Farr, C.A., Vuchinich, R.E., & Simpson, C.A. (1998, May). *Delayed reward discounting in sexual risk-takers and non-risk-takers.* Poster session presented at the meeting of the Association for Behavior Analysis, Orlando, FL.

Fisher, E.B. Jr. (1996). A behavioral-economic perspective on the influence of social support on cigarette smoking. In L. Green & J.H. Kagel (Eds.), *Advances in behavioral economics* (Vol. 3; pp. 207–236). Norwood, NJ: Ablex.

Fisher, E.B. Jr., La Greca, A.M., Greco, P., Affken, C., & Schneiderman, N. (1997). Directive and nondirective support in diabetes management. *International Journal of Behavioral Medicine, 4,* 131–144.

Green, L., & Kagel, J.H. (Eds.) (1996). *Advances in behavioral economics* (Vol. 3.). Norwood, NJ: Ablex.

Griffiths, R.R., Bigelow, G.E., & Henningfield, J.E. (1980). Similarities in animal and human drug-taking behavior. In N.K. Mello (Ed.), *Advances in substance abuse*: *Behavioral and biological research* (Vol. 1; pp. 1–90). Greenwich, CT: JAI Press.

Herrnstein, R.J. (1970). On the law of effect. *Journal of the Experimental Analysis of Behavior, 13,* 243–266.

Higgins, S.T., Delaney, D.D., Budney, A.J., Bickel, W.K., Hughes, J.R., Foerg, F., & Fenwick, J.W. (1991). A behavioral approach to achieving initial cocaine abstinence. *American Journal of Psychiatry, 148,* 1218–1224.

Kagel, J.H., Battalio, R.C., & Green, L. (1995). *Economic choice theory: An experimental analysis of animal behavior.* New York: Cambridge University Press.

Kilmer, J.R., Larimer, M.E., Alexander, E.N., & Marlatt, G.A. (1998, November). *Bait for the hook in motivation enhancement programs: Contributions from molar behavioral theory of choice.* In J.R. Kilmer (Chair), Interventions with college student drinkers: Reducing alcohol-related harm.

Symposium conducted at the meeting of the 32nd annual convention of the Association for the Advancement of Behavior Therapy, Washington, DC.

Klinger, E., Cox, W.M., & Blount, J.P. (in press). Motivational Structure Questionnaire (MSQ) and Personal Concerns Inventory (PCI). In J.P. Allen & M. Columbus (Eds.), *Assessing alcohol problems: A guide for clinicians and researchers* (2nd edn.). Washington, DC: US Department of Health and Human Services.

Krug-Porzelius, L., Houston, C.A., Smith, M., Arfken, C.L., & Fisher, E.B. Jr. (1994). Comparison of a behavioral weight loss treatment and a binge eating weight loss treatment. *Behavior Therapy, 26*, 119–134.

Lappalainen, R., & Epstein, L.H. (1990). A behavioral economics analysis of food choice in humans. *Appetite, 14*, 81–93.

Lea, S.E.G. (1978). The psychology of economics and demand. *Psychological Bulletin, 85*, 441–466.

Liebson, I.A., Cohen, M., Faillace, L.A., & Ward, R.F. (1971). The token economy as a research method in alcoholics. *Psychiatric Quarterly, 45*, 574–581.

Logue, A.W. (2000). Self-control and health behavior. In W.K. Bickel & R.E. Vuchinich (Eds.), *Reframing health behavior change with behavioral economics* (pp. 167–192). Mahwah, NJ: Erlbaum.

MacPhillamy, D.J., & Lewinsohn, P.M. (1974). Depression as a function of desired and obtained pleasure. *Journal of Abnormal Psychology, 83*, 651–657.

MacPhillamy, D.J., & Lewinsohn, P.M. (1982). The pleasant events schedule: Studies on reliability, validity, and scale intercorrelation. *Journal of Consulting and Clinical Psychology, 50*, 363–380.

Madden, G.J., Petry, N.M., Badger, G.J., & Bickel, W.K. (1997). Impulsive and self-controlled choices in opioid-dependent patients and non-drug-using control participants: Drug and monetary rewards. *Experimental and Clinical Psychopharmacology, 5*, 256–263.

Madden, G.J. (2000). A behavioral economics primer. In W.K. Bickel & R.E. Vuchinich (Eds.), *Reframing health behavior change with behavioral economics* (pp. 3–26). Mahwah, NJ: Erlbaum.

Marlatt, G.A., & Gordon, J.R. (Eds.) (1985). *Relapse prevention: Maintenance strategies in the treatment of addictive behaviors*. New York: Guilford.

Marlatt, G.A., & Kilmer, J.R. (1998). Consumer choice: Implications of behavioral economics for drug use and treatment. *Behavior Therapy, 29*, 567–576.

McDowell, J.J. (1988). Matching theory in natural human environments. *The Behavior Analyst, 11*, 95–109.

Miller, W.R., & Rollnick, S. (2002). *Motivational interviewing* (2nd edn.). New York: Guilford.

Moeller, F.G., Barratt, E.S., Dougherty, D.M., Schmitz, J.M., & Swann, A.C. (2001). Psychiatric aspects of impulsivity. *American Journal of Psychiatry, 158*, 1783–1793.

Pearce, D.W. (Ed.) (1992). *The MIT dictionary of modern economics* (3rd edn.). Cambridge, MA: MIT Press.

Petry, N.M., & Bickel, W.K. (1998). Polydrug abuse in heroin addicts: A behavioral economic analysis. *Addiction, 93*, 321–335.

Petry, N.M., Martin, B., Cooney, J.L., & Kranzler, H.R. (2000). Give them prizes, and they will come: Contingency management for the treatment of alcohol dependence. *Journal of Consulting and Clinical Psychology, 68*, 250–257.

Premack, D. (1965). Reinforcement theory. In D. Levine (Ed.), *Nebraska Symposium on Motivation* (pp. 123–180). Lincoln, NE: University of Nebraska Press.

Rachlin, H. (2000). The lonely addict. In W.K. Bickel & R.E. Vuchinich (Eds.), *Reframing health behavior change with behavioral economics* (pp. 145–166). Mahwah, NJ: Erlbaum.

Rachlin, H., Green, L., Kagel, J., & Barralio, R. (1976). Economic demand theory and psychological studies of choice. In G. Bower (Ed.), *The psychology of learning and motivation* (pp. 129–154). New York: Academic Press.

Raynor, D.A., Coleman, K.J., & Epstein, L.H. (1998). Effects of proximity on the choice to be physically active or sedentary. *Research Quarterly for Exercise and Sport, 99*, 103.

Skinner, B.F. (1938). *The behavior of organisms: An experimental analysis*. Englewood Cliffs, NJ: Prentice-Hall.

Silverman, K., Wong, C.J., Higgins, S.T., Brooner, R.K., Montoya, I.D., Contoreggi, C., Umbritch-Schneiter, A., Schuster, C.R., & Preston, K.L. (1996). Increasing opiate abstinence through voucher-based reinforcement therapy. *Drug and Alcohol Dependence, 41*, 157–165.

Van Etten, M.L., Higgins, S.T., & Bickel, W.K. (1995). Effects of response cost and unit dose on alcohol self-administration in moderate drinkers. *Behavioural Pharmacology, 6*, 754–758.

Van Etten, M.L., Higgins, S.T., Budney, A.J., & Badger, G.J. (1998). Comparison of the frequency and enjoyability of pleasant events in cocaine abusers vs. non-abusers using a standardized behavioral inventory. *Addiction, 93*, 1669–1680.

Vuchinich, R.E., & Simpson, C.A. (1998). Hyperbolic temporal discounting in heavy and light social drinkers. *Experimental and Clinical Psychopharmacology, 6*, 292–305.

Vuchinich, R.E., & Tucker, J.A. (1983). Behavioral theories of choice as a framework for studying drinking behavior. *Journal of Abnormal Psychology, 92*, 408–416.

Vuchinich, R.E., & Tucker, J.A. (1988). Contributions from behavioral theories of choice to an analysis of alcohol abuse. *Journal of Abnormal Psychology, 97*, 181–195.

Vuchinich, R.E., & Tucker, J.A. (1996a). The molar context of alcohol abuse. In L. Green & J. Kagel (Eds.), *Advances in behavioral economics* (Vol. 3; pp. 133–162). Norwood, NJ: Ablex.

Vuchinich, R.E., & Tucker, J.A. (1996b). Alcohol relapse, life events, and behavioral theories of choice: A prospective analysis. *Experimental and Clinical Psychopharmacology, 4*, 19–28.

Vuchinich, R.E., & Tucker, J.A. (1998). Choice, behavioral economics, and addictive behavior patterns. In W.R. Miller & N. Heather (Eds.), *Treating addictive behaviors: Processes of change* (2nd edn.; pp. 93–104). New York: Plenum.

Winkler, R.C., & Burkhard, B. (1990). A systems approach to behavior modification through behavioral economics. In L. Green & J.H. Kagel (Eds.), *Advances in behavioral economics* (Vol. 2; pp. 288–315). Norwood, NJ: Ablex.

CHAPTER 4

Personal Project Pursuit: On Human Doings and Well-Beings

Brian R. Little

Harvard University, Cambridge, USA

and

Neil C. Chambers

Carleton University, Ottawa, Canada

Synopsis.—Personal projects are extended sets of personally salient action that range from the daily doings of typical Thursdays (e.g., "put out the cat, quickly") to the self-defining passions of a life-time (e.g., "transform Western thought, slowly"). We propose that analysis of the content, structure, appraisal, and impact of personal project systems offers an effective way of augmenting motivational counseling.

Personal Projects Analysis (PPA) is the assessment device through which projects and related personal action construct (PAC) units are investigated. We describe several core modules and their potential for providing clinically useful information. The Project Elicitation Module asks clients to generate a list of current projects. We propose that aspects of the content of personal projects, such as their relative infrequency, linguistic features, or their lack of balance across different life domains, provide insights into potentially problematic aspects of a person's life. The Project Appraisal Module, similarly, explores how projects are evaluated on dimensions having both theoretical and clinical significance. Well-being is shown to be related to the extent to which individual projects are appraised as high on meaning, structure, community, and efficacy and as relatively unstressful. Cross-impact matrices allow us to examine project conflict and congruency both within and between individuals.

Our central theoretical proposition is that both the quality of life and the course of therapy depend critically on whether a person is engaged in the sustainable pursuit of core projects. Difficulties in negotiating life transitions and resistance to therapeutic interventions are likely to be encountered if one's core projects are threatened. Sustainability, moreover, has both an internal and an external face: it is related to a person's capacity for self-regulation and to the facilitating or frustrating contextual forces within which projects are played out. The shape of human lives, we conclude, is determined both by the latent dynamics of current concerns and the manifest destinies of the personal projects we pursue.

Handbook of Motivational Counseling. Edited by W. Miles Cox and Eric Klinger.
© 2004 John Wiley & Sons, Ltd.

CURRENT CONCERNS AND PERSONAL PROJECTS:
LATENT DYNAMICS AND MANIFEST DESTINIES
OF GOAL PURSUIT

Current concerns and personal projects are units of analysis for psychological research that have lived parallel lives for many years. The two constructs emerged out of different intellectual traditions at virtually the same time, using methodological probes that were strikingly similar. The research stimulated by both units examined the complexities and perplexities of human cognition, motivation, and action. Each construct provided a perspective for confronting problems in living and enhancing human flourishing.

The similarities between current concerns and personal projects are clear. Both are based on the evolutionary premise that humans, like all animal species, are creatures of action, pursuing goals that will sustain them and impact on their eco systems (Klinger, 1975, 1987a, 1998; Little, 1972, 1976, 1999a). Both assume that goal pursuit begins with an acknowledgment of a state of affairs that needs to be maintained or attained and ends with the completion of the envisioned goal, or with disengagement from it (Klinger, 1975; Little, 1983). Both perspectives emphasize that individuals pursue multiple goals simultaneously, and that these may be in harmony or conflict. Both trace the dynamics of motivation and potential risks for psychopathology, to interruptions of vital goal pursuit. Each has generated a program of research with applied and therapeutic implications (Christiansen, Little, & Backman, 1998; Cox, Klinger, & Blount, 1999; Klinger, Barta, & Maxeiner, 1981; Little, 1987c, 1998, 2000a; Little & Chambers, 2000).

The major difference in the two constructs is one of emphasis: current concerns theory has been relatively more focused on elucidating the internal dynamics of goal pursuit (Klinger, 1977). A current concern is a latent state occasioned by a person's commitment to a goal and continues until its consummation or abandonment.[1] The present volume is a testament to the extensive research that has explored how current concerns influence information processing, thought flow, and regulatory processes (Cox & Klinger, 1988; Klinger, 1990, 1996; Klinger & Cox, Chapter 1, this volume; Klinger et al., 1996). Although we are mindful of the conative[2] factors undergirding project pursuit, personal projects analysis places relatively more emphasis on the external, social-ecological aspects of goal pursuit, particular the social physical, and temporal contexts within which projects are embedded. Thus, beyond the internal viability of personal projects, we explore their external facilitation or frustration. In short, we are concerned with the overall *sustainability* of a person's pursuits through the vicissitudes of daily life.

We have suggested (Little, 1989, 2000a, 2000b) that both current concerns and personal projects are exemplars of a new generation of units of analysis in psychology. They are personal action construct (PAC) units that are, relative to other analytic units, dynamic, contextually sensitive, middle level, and integrative (see Little, 2000b). Related PAC units include personal strivings (Emmons, 1986), life tasks (Cantor et al., 1986), possible selves (Markus & Nurius, 1986), and personal goals (e.g., Karoly, 1993; Nurmi, 1993). These units

---

[1] It is important here to distinguish Klinger's use of commitment from the more general usage which implies, typically, the emergence of specific action. Klinger defines commitment more generally as "a structural change in (a person's) response tendencies, a change that cannot ordinarily be abandoned without psychological cost..." (Klinger, 1987a, p. 339). Thus action is not an inevitable sequella of a concern.

[2] From the Latin, conor, "to try," the term conative emphasizes the volitional, purposeful nature of action.

can be aligned along an inner–outer continuum. Personal strivings and current concerns are deflected toward the internal, personal end. Life tasks anchor the external, contextual end. Personal projects occupy a middle position, linking internal motivational propensities and external, ecological hindrances and affordances (Little, 1996, 2000a).

Given their similarities, our goal is not to contrast current concerns and personal projects approaches, but, by reviewing developments in projects theory and methodology, to provide links to the common venture of a systematic motivational counseling.

PERSONAL PROJECTS AS ANALYTIC UNITS: ASSUMPTIONS AND ASSESSMENT

The methodological details of Personal Projects Analysis (PPA) have been given elsewhere (Little, 1983; 2000b); we focus here on their counseling implications. PPA is a flexible methodology, a generalized assessment system explicitly designed to be applicable to a broad range of theoretical and applied questions. Unlike a traditional fixed test, PPA is more like an assessment system board, accommodating a variety of assessment modules.

We conceive of personal projects neither as exclusively "person" units nor as "environmental" units of analysis. Rather, personal projects are interactional *carrier units* (Little, 1987b) allowing us to design intervention strategies involving reconstruals of action by the client as well as the modification or creation of new living contexts. PPA focuses on the tractable aspects of human conduct, those aspects of action impelled by inner intention, embedded in contextual realities, but subject to reconstrual and revision.

Our scientific goal is to elucidate intentional action in context and to explore the dynamics and impacts of action. This has involved several different programs of research. One program generated a formal set of social ecological propositions for studying persons in context across the life span (Little, 1999b, 2000a; Little & Ryan, 1979) and another developed measurement criteria for the integration of individual and normative levels of assessment of personal projects (Little, 2000b). More empirically focused research examines the factors influencing the content, appraisal, and impact of personal projects and provides comparative tests of alternative models of project pursuit and well-being (e.g., Little, 2000b; McGregor & Little, 1998; Palys & Little, 1983).

Our applied goal is to use our basic research to inform and enhance the quality of decisions about individuals and their environments. This applied work spans the spectrum from individually focused therapy (Little, 1987c; Little & Chambers, 2000) to organizational and community psychology (Little, 1999b). Our applied work on personal projects brings us squarely into the domain of ethical concerns about the shape of human lives and how we might promote well-being. Although we do not believe that psychology has a distinctive *adjudicative* role here, our empirical results can inform philosophers and policy analysts who grapple with the problems of promoting human flourishing in a just and sustainable way.

As our concern here is counseling, we focus on how the formulation, appraisal, and impact of an individual's projects may contribute to problems in living and may frustrate (or facilitate) the implementation of therapeutic programs. Therapists adopting PPA provide methods for the reformulation of project systems, encourage clients to invest in new projects that are estimable undertakings and to address the ecological strictures that impede project sustainability.

PPA is based upon a set of twelve measurement criteria that can be organized under four major methodological goals (Little, 1989, 2000b). These overarching goals promote methods that are constructivist (e.g., rely on personally salient information generated by the participant), contextualist (e.g., bring features of the daily ecology of the individual into focus), conative (e.g., recognize the volitional nature of human pursuits), and consilient (e.g., integrate affective, cognitive, and behavioral aspects of human conduct). In these respects, PPA contrasts with traditional assessment methodologies (see Krahé, 1992; Little, 2000b).

Although PPA is based on formal measurement criteria, the actual development, modification, and accretion of new project dimensions and modules has been rather more *ad hoc*, influenced by the exigencies of particular settings and the necessary inventions demanded by distinctive research questions such as the acculturation of Indochinese refugees (Little, 1997), the passions and problems of doctoral students (Pychyl & Little, 1998), and project phrasing in the elderly (Chambers, 2000). Over the years, however, a set of standard dimensions and core modules have been retained as useful to most inquiries into personality and well-being. We will briefly summarize this core methodology and then discuss its counseling implications.

PERSONAL PROJECTS ASSESSMENT: MODULES FOR ELICITATION, APPRAISAL, AND CONTEXTUAL ANALYSIS

A basic PPA comprises modules for the elicitation, appraisal, and contextual analysis of the individual's personal projects. For details regarding PPA, including printable and interactive PPA matrices, see www.PersonalProjectsAnalysis.com.

Personal Project Elicitation

Respondents are given a brief written description of what is meant by a personal project. Typically, ten examples drawn from a relevant eco-setting or group are given (e.g., students, rehabilitation patients, executives, etc.). These are designed to show the diversity of content subsumed under the concept of personal projects. Personal projects can range from the tedious tasks of a soggy Thursday, to the passionate commitments of a lifetime, and we wish to encourage the full range of such pursuits in the elicitation phase of PPA. In particular, we do not want respondents only to list projects that are restrictively formal.[3] After reading the instructions, individuals are asked to list their own personal projects, typically within about 10 to 15 minutes and without any restriction as to how many they list. Typically 15 projects are generated. They are then asked to select a subset of their projects, typically 10, which are then explored in greater detail with the other modules.

The prompt for selecting the ten projects has changed over the years. Originally we were interested in those projects likely to be engaged in over the next few months. Subsequently we have encouraged respondents to select projects that will provide an informative picture of

---

[3] This has proven important with older individuals who frequently view daily activities as insufficiently structured to warrant the label "project." In a study with individuals in their seventies and eighties expanding the label to read "personal projects/daily activities" led to more inclusive construal of personal action (Chambers, 2000).

themselves and their current life situation.[4] More fine-grained focusing is also possible. For example, we have examined "work" projects (Phillips, Little, & Goodine, 1997), projects being actively worked on (Chambers, 2000), or those "on hold" or "shelved" (Hotson, 2001). Projects of specific clinical interest may be solicited, such as those relating to weight control or those that are highly emotionally charged (Little, 1997). This flexibility permits the clinician to elicit projects relevant to the presenting problem (e.g., choose those projects that may help us to understand your relationship difficulties, or your drinking problems, etc.).[5]

Project Appraisal: Dimensional Analysis

Clients then appraise each of their selected personal projects on a set of dimensions that have been chosen in terms of both their theoretical and applied importance. They rate each project on each appraisal dimension using an 11-point scale (from 0 to 10). Brief descriptions of the scales, including verbal anchors of high and low scores, are provided. The original unpublished versions of PPA contained only a few appraisal dimensions, and the original published article describing the methodology used 17 dimensions, including some "open columns" in which individuals are asked to specify "with whom" and "where" each project is undertaken (Little, 1983).

Because of the modular nature of PPA, and the desirability of creating *ad hoc* dimensions attuned to the eco-setting being explored, there has been an increase in the dimensions that have been operationalized for use in PPA (for a comprehensive review of these *ad hoc* dimensions, see Chambers, 1997a). Although the modal number of dimensions within any personal projects investigation has remained at about 20, there has been "dimensional creep" over the years (for example, McGregor & Little, 1998, used 35 dimensions). Fortunately, dimensions usually can be collapsed into robust and coherent factors or clusters, obviating some of the problems relating to statistical power.

Project Context Modules

In addition to the elicitation and appraisal modules, the original publication (Little, 1983) contained modules designed to examine several other features of projects, particularly their contextual and systemic nature and their impact on the social ecology in which they are embedded. The project cross-impact matrix has individuals appraise the impact of each project on others within the system (positive, negative, ambivalent, etc.) and has been adopted or adapted for research with other PAC units (e.g., Cox, Klinger, & Blount, 1999; Emmons & King, 1988).

A joint cross-impact matrix examines the same phenomenon for two or more people (e.g., marital or work partners). Recent refinements have looked at the impact of an organization's

---

[4] Although the number of personal projects used in our laboratory has been ten, other researchers have used as few as one project (randomly chosen from a set of projects undertaken in different time frames). The active group of Finnish researchers using PPA has tended to use three projects (Nurmi & Salmela-Aro, in press; Salmela-Aro, 1992); Sheldon and Kasser (1998) used five, and Brunstein (1993) used six projects. For extensive analysis of the psychometric foundations of PPA, see Gee (1998).

[5] Indeed, projects that are regarded as criterial for a particular clinical group may be added to the project list if they do not spontaneously appear in the original elicitation list.

climate and its impact on employee projects (Phillips, Little, & Goodine, 1997). Another of the early PPA modules, adapted from Kellian methodology (Hinkle, 1965), explored the superordinate reasons for undertaking each project and the subordinate acts through which they are enacted, thus revealing the level in a hierarchy of action occupied by each project (Little, 1983). Several other modules have been developed for both clinical and research exploration (e.g., Little, 1987c; Little & Chambers, 2000; McDiarmid, 1990), some of which will be described in a later section.

ANALYSES OF PPA MODULES: A COUNSELING ASSESSMENT PRIMER

We turn now to an overview of how we analyze PPA, again with specific attention being drawn to issues of quality of life and well-being and of potential therapeutic use.

Personal Project Elicitation: The Scope and Substance of Projects

Even before we know "how it's going" with a client, it is informative to know "what are you up to?" The number and nature of personal projects generated during the elicitation phase, or project dump, may provide clinically useful information. Six kinds of analysis can be distinguished.

Project Load

The number of projects generated during the elicitation phase (colloquially referred to as the "project dump") may have diagnostic significance. For typical PPA administrations fewer than three and more than 50 projects are statistically rare. Given that projects are sources of meaning, structure, and community in lives, too many or too few projects may be problematic. Too few projects, particularly among youth, may indicate pervasive boredom, an impoverished sense of opportunity, and risk of depression. Activities to help stimulate possible pursuits, or identify barriers that prevent their being acted upon, will be therapeutically helpful (Little & Chambers, 2000). Project overload is a frequent complaint, likely to be linked to clinical symptoms ranging from stress and anxiety to hypomania. Though an optimal number of personal projects is theoretically compelling, the nature and level of complexity of the projects make this a complex matter in practice, because projects differ in their scope and their complexity. Thus, the shortest project list we have seen had one project "to serve God." But a little probing indicated that this pursuit subserved a diversity of spiritual strivings and daily devotions optimal for flourishing in this particular eco-setting, a convent. Similarly, a large number of lower level projects may be viable as long as the person can "chunk" these into larger coherent projects (McDiarmid, 1990).

Category Frequency

The normative infrequency of categories of project content may be instructive. For example, in college student populations, the two highest frequency categories of personal project are academic and interpersonal projects while, in work settings, occupational and interpersonal

Table 4.1 Samples of personal projects by category

Category	Definition	Sample project
Academic	School/university-related projects	Get my teaching certificate Study harder for exams
Occupational	Job-related projects such as job tasks or job-related courses	Find a more rewarding career Finish inventory by Tuesday
Health/Body	Activities relating to appearance, health, or fitness in which the goal is clearly fitness related and not recreational	Lose ten pounds Drink more water, less pop
Interpersonal	Projects dealing with others on a personal level. Includes family, friends, and intimate others	Try to figure out Susie Visit my parents more
Intrapersonal	Projects dealing with outlook and attitudes relating to the self, including self-improvement, spiritual and philosophical projects, and coping or adjustment projects	Stop being so antisocial Work on my self-esteem
Leisure	Recreational activities done alone or with others	Go bungee jumping with Mike Read more for pleasure
Maintenance	Projects relating to organization and administration, including household and financial maintenance activities, pet maintenance, paperwork, etc.	Clean out the basement Get the car tuned up

projects predominate. Table 4.1 provides definitions and samples of projects in each of seven major categories.

Project lists from students containing no instances of these highly normative pursuits are statistically abnormal, but may also point to clinical concerns. The absence of projects that are restorative in some sense (e.g., leisure pursuits) may signify the lack of significant incentives in the person's daily pursuits (see Cox, Klinger, & Blount, 1999). Clients listing no projects relevant to their presenting symptoms (e.g., no interpersonal projects for those seeking marital therapy or no projects relating to self-regulation for those with addiction problems) may represent a conscious avoidance of dealing with a concern as an explicit project for public disclosure.

Sequencing of Categories

Cantor and her colleagues have shown that the *sequencing and timing* of different project categories affects student adaptation to university life (Cantor et. al., 1986). Those who, over the course of a term, first give priority to interpersonal projects and then clamp down on academic projects are the most likely to flourish.

Linguistic Analysis of Project Content and Syntax

How individuals phrase their projects may have subtle but powerful influences on adaptation (see also Pennebaker, Mayne, & Francis, 1997). Phrasing projects as things to avoid (e.g., "don't be so angry") is associated with lower well-being (Chambers & Little, 2002a; Elliot, Sheldon, & Church, 1997). This may reflect the never-ending anxiety associated with such endeavors, which undermines any positive feelings of accomplishment that accompany completing an onerous project. Similarly, projects phrased as "tryings" (e.g., "try to be outgoing") are associated with lower efficacy and well-being than those phrased as direct doings (e.g., "be outgoing") (Chambers & Little, 2002a). More subtly, individuals phrasing projects as ongoing activities ("eat healthily") report higher well-being than those constantly working toward project completion (Chambers, 2000). This may stem from the beneficial low-level positive affect of happy engagement as opposed to the short-lived but stronger rush of successful completion (Diener, Sandvik, & Pavot, 1991).

"Problematic" Categories

Certain project categories may be diagnostic of problems in the pursuit of one's projects. For example, the relatively high frequency of intrapersonal (e.g., self-focused) projects is associated with depressive affect (Little, 1993; Salmela-Aro, 1992).[6] Such projects are essentially related to changing, modulating, or acquiring new aspects of the self—such as changing a personality trait. These may give rise to ruminative worrying, which may be depressogenic, particularly in women (Nolen-Hoeksema, Parker, & Larsen, 1994), although research in our laboratory has shown that intrapersonal project frequency does not invariably lead to depressive affect (Blake, 1994). Indeed, there is evidence that aspects of intraproject appraisal may characterize openness to experience and creativity (Little, 1997).

Although rarely found in projects listed by nonclinical populations, it is possible that bizarre or disturbing projects may be listed. Even in nonclinical samples of students we occasionally find projects that imply or state a concern with harming oneself or with suicide. Obviously, their presence calls for appropriate professional attention to be mobilized directly.

Balance in Project Categories

Irrespective of the load of a project system, balance in the types of categories of projects may be beneficial (Little, 1983). Christiansen (2000) has made a strong case for personal project balance, citing this as a foundational premise in the beginnings of occupational therapy (Meyer, 1922; see also Miranti & Heinemann, Chapter 15, this volume). A system dominated by one type of project (even if it is normatively important) is likely to be less adaptive than one showing a diversity of areas of project pursuit, if only because it may indicate a rigidly, overspecialized way of confronting one's social ecology (Baltes, 1997; Freund, Li, & Baltes, 1999; Little, 1972, 1976).

Thus, even before we begin to look at the appraisal of projects, their irregularity, their eccentricity, their focus, and their lopsidedness may all figure importantly as possible influences in a person's well-being and capacity for successful therapy.

---

[6] However, see Nurmi regarding the life stage specificity of this finding (Nurmi & Salmela-Aro, in press).

Project Appraisals: Dimensions and Factors for Normative and Individual Levels of Analysis

PPA was explicitly developed as a technique that could be used for both normative/comparative *and* idiographic inquiry (Little, 1983). Psychometrically, this involves two kinds of PPA measurement. The first, normative measurement, obtains appraisals on dimensions for each project (described below). Mean scores on each of these dimensions are then calculated for each individual and used, much like conventional test items, to examine linkages between project dimensions, with traits and contextual variables, and with diverse measures of well-being. The second, idiographic alternative in PPA measurement is to examine the relationships between dimensions within the single case, by correlating ratings on dimensions across projects.

For present purposes we will focus upon the counseling relevance of normative measurement. However, for each analysis proposed, an equivalent analysis can be carried out at the idiographic level.

Standard Normative Dimensions: Five Factors of Project Appraisal

Normative analysis of personal project appraisals takes the mean score for each project dimension (summed across typically ten projects). These scores can then be compared with appropriate norm groups much as in traditional multidimensional trait inventories and in current concerns analysis (e.g., Cox & Klinger, 2000). Personal Project Profile sheets have been used in both z score and T score forms. Due to printing constraints the profile sheet is not reproduced here, but Table 4.2 provides sample norms for both standard and affective dimensions. The standard project dimensions fall under one of five major theoretical factors: project meaning, structure, community, efficacy, and stress. Well-being is typically associated with pursuing personal projects that are meaningful, well-organized, supported by others, and, in particular, seen as efficacious and not too stressful (Christiansen et al., 1999; Little, 1989).

It should be emphasized that the five-factor personal project model of "standard" PPA dimensions is primarily a heuristic template guiding the creation of project dimensions. Although the five factors frequently appear in factor analyses, their emergence is contingent on whether there is a roughly equivalent number of dimensions sampled from each of the five domains. For example, studies that include primarily efficacy or competency dimensions, but few dimensions tapping other theoretical factors, will obviously yield a single factor rather than five (e.g., Salmela-Aro, 1992).

Ad Hoc *Dimensions: Appraisals Sensitive to Particular Eco-Settings*

Besides the "standard" project dimensions, we have encouraged the use of *ad hoc* dimensions specially suited to the particular investigation. Clearly the strength of such dimensions is their distinctive ecological representativeness for the setting under consideration, and these new dimensions are frequently those most strongly associated with well-being for a particular sample. For example, a sample of pregnant mothers was asked to state the

Table 4.2 Means and standard deviations for standard and affective project appraisal dimensions[a]

Standard dimension (n = 1176)	M	SD	Affective dimension (n = 179–506)	M	SD
Meaning			*Positive affect[b]*		
Importance	7.29	1.31	Happy	5.84	2.09
Enjoyment	6.01	1.61	Hopeful	6.95	2.07
Value congruency	7.47	1.31	Excited	5.20	2.16
Self-identity	6.74	1.57	Proud	5.75	2.23
Absorption	6.46	1.46			
Structure			*Negative Affect[b]*		
Control	7.29	1.37	Sad	1.86	1.77
Initiation	7.11	1.56	Fearful	2.45	1.91
Time adequacy	5.36	1.65	Guilty	1.86	1.99
Positive impact	6.58	1.63	Fearful/scared	2.45	1.91
Negative impact	3.18	1.62	Angry	1.68	1.71
Community					
Visibility	5.68	1.69			
Others' view of					
importance	6.48	1.59			
Efficacy					
Progress	5.20	1.64			
Likelihood of success					
(outcome)	7.18	1.28			
Stress					
Stress	4.78	1.74			
Difficulty	5.43	1.61			
Challenge	6.15	1.62			

[a]Data from SEAbank.
[b]In factor solutions including the affective dimensions, the standard dimensions enjoyment and stress (Little, 1983) regularly load on the two affective factors.

extent to which each project was seen as helpful to the new baby; a sample of migraine sufferers was asked about the impact of their migraines on each project; and the impedance of language requirements on project progress was explored in a sample of Indo-Chinese refugees (see Chambers, 1997a; Little, 1997).

Affect Dimensions: Feelings about Doings

One set of dimensions, originally used in an *ad hoc* manner, have assumed sufficient prominence in research on personal projects that they have led to a revision of the five-factor-project analytic model and have added significantly to the prediction of human well-being. In early versions of PPA the dimensions of enjoyment and stress were the only clearly affective dimensions in the appraisal matrix and were thus used as general indicators of positive and negative affective tone. Stress was found to be the best predictor of well-being or, inversely, depression (Gee, 1993; Wilson, 1990). Goodine (1999) demonstrated that people readily apply discrete emotion terms to their projects. Moreover, these specific emotion terms are predictable from knowledge of how their project is appraised on the standard dimensions (Chambers, Goodine, & Little, 1999). We have recently modified the standard PPA package to include a separate rating matrix in which individuals appraise each project along several core emotion terms (Little & Chambers, 2000). This provides the clinician with additional insight into how projects are progressing. Aberrant associations, such as high frustration ratings on a project rated as progressing well, may serve as clues to underlying project system conflicts that need addressing. Some clients may also be more comfortable in an emotional "register" (e.g., "I know I feel angry over this project, but I am not sure why") than a predominantly cognitive focus (e.g., "This project is going well [high progress] but is not that meaningful [low self-identity] and I'd rather not be doing it").

Although the normative base for assessing affective dimensions of personal projects is still very small compared with the Social Ecology Assessment Data Bank (SEAbank), the database housing 25 years of personal project assessment data, Table 4.2 displays the means and standard deviations associated with various emotions explored in recent studies with the affective module of PPA.[7]

Finally, reflecting the modular and open-ended nature of PPA, we have retained the open column introduced by Goodine (1999) which asks individuals to list other emotions that they feel are associated with each project. This ensures that respondents are not pigeon-holed into using emotion terms that may not be relevant to them and can also highlight problems of emotional fluency.

Cross-Impact and Joint Cross-Impact Matrices

Projects are embedded in an intrapersonal and an interpersonal ecology that entails tradeoffs, potentiations, and conflicts that may help to explain the subtle dynamics of a person's life. We examine intraindividual project dynamics by the use of a *cross-impact matrix* that examines how each project facilitates or frustrates other projects in the system (Little, 1983). The clinician is able to determine both the overall conflict or consiliency within a single person's project system by determining, for each project, the total positive, total negative, and differential positive impact of that project on others. Summing across all projects will give an estimate for the system as a whole (see Michalak, Heidenreich, & Hoyer, Chapter 5, this volume). It is often instructive to examine those projects that contribute the most conflict or provide the greatest facilitation to other projects in the system as well as to examine those that are in essence dominated by other project pursuits or radically dependent on them. Although there is an intuitive appeal to the use of cross-impact matrices, and respondents often report that it is the most informative module within PPA, the empirical yield of cross-impact scores has been less impressive than that found with dimension scores such as stress or efficacy in predicting outcome measures of effectiveness and well-being (see Christiansen, Little, & Backman, 1998; Little, 1998). One reason for this is probably that the various cross-impact scores are likely to be moderated by the extent to which the projects are *core projects*. Only to the extent that a given project has a strong impact upon a core project is it

---

[7] Norms for both traditional and affective dimensions should be developed at the local level given the importance of stable contextual (as well as personal contextual) influences on project pursuit; however, these are provided as a guide for interpretation pending the development of more geographic, age, and culturally specific norms.

likely to substantially affect well-being. On the other hand, a core project that has positive impacts on all the other undertakings of an individual is likely to be particularly salutary.

The *joint cross-impact matrix* takes the social ecological contexts of people's lives into account in a systematic fashion. Following essentially the same logic as the cross-impact matrix for the single person, the joint cross-impact matrix has individuals rate the impact of the projects of a significant other person (e.g., spouse, coworker) on their projects. Although several variations are possible (e.g., estimating the impact that a client's projects have on each of his or her spouse's projects and looking at the discrepancy score), there has not been sufficient empirical work with joint cross-impact matrices to justify a conclusion about their practical or therapeutic benefits (see, however, Yard, 1980, in Little, 1997, for some promising initial findings). Again, however, core projects will have the greatest overall impact on the lives of clients and on those with whom they share their lives.

Laddering and Latticing: The Hierarchical Analysis of Personal Projects

In the original methodological publication on PPA it was suggested that some projects may be higher on a molar–molecular spectrum, where molar projects subsume other projects and molecular ones are primarily the means through which other projects are accomplished (Little, 1983, p. 296). Indeed, some projects may essentially be accomplishable acts with a very short time frame. Other projects, such as "grow as a person," may have an inordinately complex set of ill-specified subprojects which need to be completed before it is finally, if ever, accomplished. We assumed that there is a kind of meaning–manageability tradeoff, with higher levels of molarity associated with more complex tactical steps of implementing a project. The lower the level of molarity, the less meaningful a project is likely to be (see also Vallacher & Wegner, 1987). Procedures adopted from Hinkle's (1965) "laddering" technique allowed us to operationalize molarity level for projects. For each project individuals are asked, iteratively, "why are you engaged in this project" and "how will you carry out this project" with the "Why" laddering leading to a "terminal value" and the "Act" laddering leading to a schedulable act (see Little, 1983; Little & Chambers, 2000). This procedure has been expanded to allow for more complex relations among projects based on initial findings that a linear association oversimplified the more lattice-like nature of project systems (Chambers, 1997b).

Getting to the Core: Alternative and Emerging Paths for Assessment

A central tenet of PPA is that the sustainable pursuit of core projects is essential to human well-being. Theoretically, the concept of "core" means that it ramifies throughout the system and is important partly because of its centrality to the operation of all other projects. Were it to be removed from the system as a whole, it would cause the greatest degree of change in the system. That is, although a single project may be of considerable importance, we would not regard it as a core project if, when it is cordoned off from other projects, it serves as neither a major frustration nor a facilitator of those projects. We have explored this with variations on techniques used in personal construct methodology (see McDiarmid, 1990). For each project we can ask what implications it would have on the rest of the projects if it were abandoned (or removed from the system). The greater the number of other projects impacted, the more "core" that project will be. We also ask how resistant the person would be to giving up each project. As Hinkle (1965) has shown with repertory grids, these two variables—degree of implicative linkages and resistance to change—are highly correlated. Thus a personal project that holds the rest of the system together by reason of its centrality and binding qualities would be regarded as a core project.

Though of increasing importance to project analytic theory, the *assessment* of core projects is still being developed. There is some evidence that different measures of core project status correlate sufficiently well with standard dimensions, such as importance or self-identity, that the latter can be used as proxy measures of this construct. However, for clinical purposes we strongly recommend measuring the degree to which a project is a core project contributing to the system as a whole.

HUMAN FLOURISHING AS THE SUSTAINABLE PURSUIT OF CORE PROJECTS: INTERNAL REGULATION AND EXTERNAL REALITY

Human flourishing, under a project analytic view, comprises the sustainable pursuit of core projects. We believe that the varieties of human misery result both from the inability to identify core projects and the presence of internal and external factors that make their pursuit unsustainable. Thus there are two major sources of sustainability in project pursuit: those that involve inner, regulatory functions and those that arise from external, ecological factors.

Internal Sustainability: Self-Regulatory and Volitional Competencies

A project may be sustained by internal motivational appraisals of the intrinsic worth or of the instrumentality of a project to more superordinate concerns. Thus, each of the major factors discussed above can serve to maintain or attain the desired state of affairs undergirding a project. Projects that are construed as meaningless, as unmanageable, or as overwhelmingly negative in affective tone are unlikely to be successfully pursued to completion. Consistent with earlier speculations (Little, 1983), Taylor and Gollwitzer (1995) showed that, at the initial stages of project planning (the deliberative stage), individuals typically show "balanced" appraisals of the likely sustainability of a project. Once committed to the project and launched upon it, however (the implemental stage), individuals adopt the illusory-glow view that gives preferential access to cues and information supportive of continued action on the project. Similarly, Baldwin, Carrell, and Lopez (1990) showed that graduate students who were primed (through subliminal stimulation) with the face of a threatening professorial authority figure were more likely to generate projects of a poorer quality.

External Sustainability: Ecological Affordances and Competencies

The last example shows the difficulties of sharply differentiating between internal and external sources of project sustainability or threats to sustainability. The image of a threatening figure may be as much a personal construction by a highly anxious person as a realistic appraisal of a genuine environmental impediment to a project. Indeed, an essential aspect of clinical skill is distinguishing between distorted and more realistic projections of a potential project's trajectory.

Our perspective proposes that construal of a course of action is sustainable to the extent that it is based on an accurate appraisal of ecosystem resources and constraints (Little, 1999a). This is no easy task. It requires not only an awareness of current and potential forces militating against the pursuit of a particular project; it also requires a reasonably accurate forecasting of the individual's affective state at various project stages (Gilbert & Ebert, 2002).

For example, some individuals may be unaware of how difficult it may be to actually bring a core project to termination (Klinger, 1977). Indeed, part of the successful management of a project system may lie precisely in knowing how to live comfortably with interminable projects, some of which may reach to the deepest core of ourselves and thus be better conceived of as enduring commitments or core concerns. Other people may need assistance in reformulating and revising projects that have become "stuck" or have lost their motivating force. We suspect it is precisely the ability to revisit our ongoing projects, including those that have been put on hold or temporarily shelved, that constitutes a central component of wisdom in managing our lives (Baltes & Baltes, 1990).

External factors can lead to premature foreclosure on a project or prevent us from even considering it as a possible pursuit; these may range from simple social norms operating in a social microsystem to pervasive proscriptions arising out of major cultural traditions (Sarbin, 1996). Some of these constraints on action may be blatantly unjust; others may be reasonable constraints that will allow an equitable apportioning of project space within which other individuals may pursue their own projects with impunity. Lomasky (1984) has provided a rich philosophical account of precisely these issues in his theory of how project pursuit can provide a theoretical framework on human rights as a component of a theory of justice.

CONCLUDING REMARKS

This chapter has attempted to show the parallel interests and potential mutual benefits of research deriving from the current concerns and personal projects perspectives. Our key theoretical assertion has been that human well-being is intimately linked to the sustainable pursuit of personal projects. This has several consequences for motivational counseling.

One consequence of this is that therapeutic effectiveness is likely to be enhanced to the extent that the therapeutic regimen (e.g., in alcoholism relapse prevention programs) does not impede core personal projects. We have argued that core projects provide both the motivational stabilizing forces in human behavior and that therapeutic regimens that impede them are likely to be overtly or covertly resisted. To be aware of those core projects is likely to provide more sophisticated grounds for discussions with clients about the values that undergird their lives and of the likely success of the therapy that is going to be attempted.

Research on current concerns and motivational counseling might benefit from more explicit consideration of some of the social ecological concepts and assessment modules used in personal projects research. For example, the joint cross-impact matrices for looking at project conflict and support between spouses and the organizational-climate hindrance and facilitation scales may be incorporated into the standard personal-concerns assessment tools and allow a greater integration with some of the contextual features that both generate and perpetuate the personal concerns of our clients.

Finally, there is a need for greater normative, cross-national research on both current concerns and personal projects. Though the focus of convenience of research, discussed in this and other chapters of this volume, has been on motivational counseling, particularly within the context of substance abuse, the study of current concerns and personal projects, singly and as integrated components of a multimodal assessment system, will cast light upon the subtle dynamics of human actions and how an understanding of them can contribute to the enhancement of well-being.

REFERENCES

Baldwin, M.W., Carrell, S.E., & Lopez, D.F. (1990). Priming relationship schemas: My advisor and the pope are watching me from the back of my mind. *Journal of Experimental Social Psychology, 26*, 435–454.

Baltes, P.B. (1997). On the incomplete architecture of human ontogeny: Selection, optimization, and compensation as a foundation of developmental theory. *American Psychologist, 52*, 366–380.

Baltes, P.B., & Baltes, M.M. (Eds.) (1990). *Successful aging: Perspectives from the behavioral sciences.* Cambridge: Cambridge University Press.

Blake, C. (1994). *Personal projects, depressive affect and coping styles.* Unpublished master's thesis, Carleton University, Ottawa.

Brunstein, J.C. (1993). Personal goals and subjective well-being: A longitudinal study. *Journal of Personality and Social Psychology, 65*, 1061–1070.

Cantor, N., Norem, J.K., Niedenthal, P.M., Langston, C.A., & Brower, A.M. (1986). Life tasks, self-concept ideals, and cognitive strategies in a life transition. *Journal of Personality and Social Psychology, 53*, 1178–1191.

Chambers, N. (1997a). *Personal project analysis: The maturation of a multidimensional methodology.* Unpublished paper. Carleton University, Ottawa, Canada.

Chambers, N. (1997b). *Onwards and upwards: From ladders and lattices to nests and trees in project pursuit.* Unpublished paper. Carleton University, Ottawa, Canada.

Chambers, N. (2000). *Time and personal action: Tenses and aspects of project pursuit.* Unpublished doctoral dissertation. Carleton University, Ottawa, Canada.

Chambers, N., Goodine, L.A., & Little, B.R. (1999). *Discrete emotions in goal vs. event-based appraisal.* Poster presentation at the 107th American Psychological Association Conference in Boston, Massachusetts.

Chambers, N., & Little, B.R. (2002a). *Just do it!: The implications of "trying" to do and other systematic differences in personal project phrasing.* Manuscript submitted for publication.

Chambers, N., & Little, B.R. (2002b). *How do you feel about what you are doing? Exploring discrete emotional responses to one's personal projects.* Manuscript submitted for publication.

Christiansen, C. (2000). Identity, personal projects and happiness: Self construction in everyday action. *Journal of Occupational Science (Australia), 7*, 98–107.

Christiansen, C.H., Backman, C., Little, B., & Nguyen, A. (1999). Occupation and subjective well being: A study of personal projects. *American Journal of Occupational Therapy, 54*, 25–34.

Christiansen, C.H., Little, B., & Backman, C. (1998). Personal projects: A useful approach to the study of occupation. *American Journal of Occupational Therapy, 52*, 439–446.

Cox, W.M., & Klinger, E. (1988). A motivational model of alcohol use. *Journal of Abnormal Psychology, 97*, 168–180.

Cox, W.M., & Klinger, E. (2000). *Personal Concerns Inventory.* Unpublished manuscript, University of Wales, Bangor.

Cox, W.M., Klinger, E., & Blount, J.P. (1999). *Systematic motivational counseling: A treatment manual.* Unpublished manuscript. University of Wales, Bangor.

Diener, E., Sandvik, E., & Pavot, W. (1991). Happiness is the frequency, not the intensity, of positive vs. negative affect. In F. Strack & M. Argyle (Eds.), *Subjective well-being: An interdisciplinary perspective*. Elmsford, NY: Pergamon Press.

Elliot, A.J., Sheldon, K.M., & Church, M.A. (1997). Avoidance personal goals and subjective well-being. *Personality and Social Psychology Bulletin, 23*, 915–927.

Emmons, R.A. (1986). Personal strivings: An approach to personality and subjective well-being. *Journal of Personality and Social Psychology, 51*, 1058–1068.

Emmons, R.A., & King, L.A. (1988) Conflict among personal strivings: Immediate and long-term implications for psychological and physical well-being. *Journal of Personality and Social Psychology, 54*, 1040–1048.

Freund, A.M., Li, Z.H., & Baltes, P.B. (1999). Successful development and aging: The role of selection, optimization and compensation. In J. Brandtstädter & R.M. Lerner (Eds.), *Action and self-development: Theory and research through the life span* (pp. 401–434). Thousand Oaks, CA: Sage.

Gee, T. (1993). *Emotion, cognition and personal projects: A nonmetric meta-analysis focusing on depression*. Unpublished manuscript. Carleton University, Ottawa, Canada.

Gee, T.L. (1998). *Individual and joint-level properties of personal project matrices: An exploration of the nature of project spaces*. Unpublished Ph.D. dissertation. Carleton University, Ottawa, Canada.

Gilbert, D.T., & Ebert, J.E.J. (2002). Decisions and revisions: The affective forecasting of changeable outcomes. *Journal of Personality and Social Psychology, 82*, 503–514.

Goodine, L.A. (1999). *A personal projects analysis of commitment*. Unpublished doctoral dissertation. Carleton University, Ottawa, Canada.

Hinkle, N. (1965). *The change of personal constructs from the viewpoint of a theory of construct implications*. Unpublished doctoral dissertation. Ohio State University, Ohio.

Hotson, H. (2001). Lives interrupted: The impact of inactive personal projects on well-being. Unpublished master's thesis. Carleton University, Ottawa, Canada.

Karoly, P. (1993). Mechanisms of self-regulation: A systems view. *Annual Review of Psychology, 44*, 23–52.

Kelly, G.A. (1955). *The psychology of personal constructs*. New York: Norton.

Klinger, E. (1975). Consequences of commitment to and disengagement from incentives. *Psychological Review, 82*, 1–25.

Klinger, E. (1977). *Meaning and void: Inner experience and the incentives in people's lives*. Minneapolis: University of Minnesota Press.

Klinger, E. (1987a). Current concerns and disengagements from incentives. In F. Halisch & J. Kuhl (Eds.), *Motivation, intention and volition*. Berlin: Springer.

Klinger, E. (1990). *Daydreaming*. Los Angeles, CA: Tarcher.

Klinger, E. (1996). Emotional influences on cognitive processing, with implications for theories of both. In P.M. Gollwitzer (Ed.), *The psychology of action: Linking cognition and motivation to behavior* (pp. 168–189). New York: Guilford.

Klinger, E. (1998). The search for meaning in evolutionary perspective and its clinical implications. In P.T. Wong & P.S. Fry (Eds.), *The human quest for meaning* (pp. 27–50). Mahwah, NJ: Erlbaum.

Klinger, E., Barta, S.G., & Maxeiner, M.E. (1981). Current concerns: Assessing therapeutically relevant motivation. In P.C. Kendall & S.D. Hollon (Eds.), *Assessment strategies for cognitive-behavioral interventions*. New York: Academic Press.

Klinger, E., Goetzman, E.S., Hughes, T., & Seppelt, T.L. (1996). *Microinfluences of protoemotional reactions and motivation on cognitive processing*. Paper presented at the annual Midwestern Psychological Association Conference, Chicago (May).

Krahé, B. (1992). *Personal and social psychology: Toward a synthesis*. London: Sage.

Little, B.R. (1972). Psychological man as scientist, humanist and specialist. *Journal of Experimental Research in Personality, 6*, 95–118.

Little, B.R. (1976). Specialization and the varieties of environmental experience: Empirical studies within the personality paradigm. In S. Wapner, S.B. Cohen, & B. Kaplan (Eds.), *Experiencing the environment* (pp. 81–116). New York: Plenum.

Little, B.R. (1983). Personal projects: A rationale and method for investigation. *Environment and Behavior, 15* (3), 273–309.

Little, B.R. (1987b). Personality and the environment. In D. Stokols & I. Altman (Eds.), *Handbook of environmental psychology* (Vol. 1; pp. 206–244). New York: John Wiley & Sons.

Little, B.R. (1987c). Personal Projects Analysis: A new methodology for counselling psychology. *Natcom, 13*, 591–614.

Little, B.R. (1988). *Personal Projects Analysis: Method, theory and research*. Ottawa: Final Report to the Social Sciences and Humanities Research Council.

Little, B.R. (1989). Personal projects analysis: Trivial pursuits, magnificent obsessions, and the search for coherence. In D. Buss & N. Cantor (Eds.), *Personality psychology: Recent trends and emerging directions* (pp. 15–31). New York: Springer-Verlag.

Little, B.R. (1993). Personal projects and the distributed self: Aspects of a conative psychology. In J. Suls (Ed.), *Psychological perspectives on the self* (Vol. 4; pp. 157–181). Hillsdale, NJ: Erlbaum.

Little, B.R. (1996). Free traits, personal projects and idio-tapes: Three tiers for personality research. *Psychological Inquiry, 8*, 340–344.

Little, B.R. (1997). *Annotated bibliography of personal project research*. Unpublished manuscript. Carleton University, Ottawa, Canada.

Little, B.R. (1998). Personal project pursuit: Dimensions and dynamics of personal meaning. In P.T.P. Wong & P.S. Fry (Eds.), *The human quest for meaning: A handbook of research and clinical applications*. Mahwah, NJ: Erlbaum.

Little, B.R. (1999a). Personality and motivation: Personal action and the conative evolution. In L.A. Pervin & O.P. John (Eds.), *Handbook of personality theory and research* (2nd edn.; pp. 501–524). New York: Guilford.

Little, B.R. (1999b). Personal projects and social ecology: Themes and variations across the life span. In J. Brandtstädter & R.M. Lerner (Eds.), *Action and self-development: Theory and research through the life span* (pp. 197–221). Thousand Oaks, CA: Sage.

Little, B.R. (2000a). Free traits and personal contexts: Expanding a social ecological model of well-being. In. W.B. Walsh, K.H. Craik, & R. Price (Eds.), *Person–environment psychology* (2nd edn.; pp. 87–116). New York: Guilford.

Little, B.R. (2000b). Persons, contexts, and personal projects: Assumptive themes of a methodological transactionalism. In S. Wapner, J. Demick, T. Yamamoto, & H. Minami (Eds.), *Theoretical perspectives in environment-behavior research* (pp. 79–88). New York: Plenum.

Little, B.R., & Chambers, N. (2000). Analyse des projets personnels: Un cadre intégratif pour la psychologie clinique et le counselling. [Personal Project Analysis: An integrative framework for clinical and counselling psychology]. *Revue québecoise de psychologie, 21*, 153–190.

Little, B.R., & Ryan, T. (1979). A social ecological model of development. In K. Ishwaran (Ed.), *Childhood and adolescence in Canada* (pp. 273–301). Toronto: McGraw-Hill Ryerson.

Lomasky, L.E. (1984). Personal projects as the foundation of human rights. *Social Philosophy and Policy, 1*, 35–55.

Markus, H., & Nurius, P. (1986). Possible selves. *American Psychologist, 41*, 954–969.

McDiarmid, E. (1990). *Level of molarity, project cross-impact and resistance to change in personal project systems*. Unpublished master's thesis. Carleton University, Ottawa, Canada.

McGregor, I., & Little, B.R. (1998). Personal projects, happiness and meaning: On doing well and being yourself. *Journal of Personality and Social Psychology, 74*, 494–512.

Meyer, A. (1922). The philosophy of occupational therapy. New York: Ravena Press.

Nolen-Hoeksema, S., Parker, L., & Larsen, J. (1994). Ruminative coping with depressed mood following loss. *Journal of Personality and Social Psychology, 67*, 92–104.

Nurmi, J.-E. (1993). Adolescent development in an age-graded context: The role of personal beliefs, goals, and strategies in the tackling of developmental tasks and standards. *International Journal of Behavioral Development, 16*, 169–189.

Nurmi, J.-E., & Salmela-Aro, K. (in press). Goal construction reconstruction and well-being in a life-span context: A transition from school to work. *Journal of Personality*.

Palys, T.S., & Little, B.R. (1983). Perceived life satisfaction and the organization of personal project systems. *Journal of Personality and Social Psychology, 44* (6), 1221–1230.

Pennebaker, J.W., Mayne, T.J., & Francis, M.E. (1997). Linguistic predictors of adaptive bereavement. *Journal of Personality and Social Psychology, 72*, 863–871.

Pervin, L.A. (1996). *The science of personality*. New York: John Wiley & Sons.

Phillips, S.D., Little, B.R., & Goodine, L.A. (1997). Reconsidering gender and public administration: Five steps beyond conventional research. *Canadian Journal of Public Administration, 40*, 563–581.

Pychyl, T.A., & Little, B.R. (1998). Dimensional specificity in the prediction of subjective well-being: Personal projects in pursuit of the Ph.D. *Social Indicators Research, 45*, 423–473.

Salmela-Aro, K. (1992). Struggling with self: The personal projects of students seeking psychological counseling. *Scandinavian Journal of Psychology, 33*, 330–338.

Sarbin, T.R. (1996). *The poetics of identity*. Henry Murray Award Address, presented at the annual meeting of the American Psychological Association, New York.

Sheldon, K.M., & Kasser, T. (1998). Pursuing personal goals: Skills enable progress, but not all progress is beneficial. *Personality and Social Psychology Bulletin, 24*, 1319–1331.

Taylor, S.E., & Gollwitzer, P.M. (1995). The effects of mind-sets on positive illusions. *Journal of Personality and Social Psychology, 69*, 213–226.

Vallacher, R.R., & Wegner, D.M. (1987). What do people think they are doing? Action identification and human behavior. *Psychological Review, 94*, 3–5.

Wilson, D.A. (1990). *Personal project dimensions and perceived life satisfaction: A quantitative synthesis*. Unpublished master's thesis, Carleton University, Ottawa.

CHAPTER 5

Goal Conflicts: Concepts, Findings, and Consequences for Psychotherapy

Johannes Michalak*

University of Bochum, Germany

Thomas Heidenreich

University of Frankfurt, Germany

and

Jürgen Hoyer

Technical-University of Dresden, Germany

Synopsis.—Conflicts between goals and strivings, as well as their lack of integration in psychotherapy clients, contribute to the psychotherapeutic process in several ways. First, as pathogenic factors these conflicts influence the onset and maintenance of psychological disorders. Second, as motivational factors, they contribute to the extent in which a client engages in therapy. This chapter elaborates on the role that goal conflicts can play in the therapeutic process and presents two methodological approaches for assessing goal conflicts (i.e., Computerized Intrapersonal Conflict Assessment and Conflict Matrixes). Research findings from basic and clinical research are presented that describes the possible influences goal conflicts can impose on the therapeutic process: (1) as a pathogenic factor they are associated with decreased well-being and heightened levels of psychopathological symptoms; (2) as a motivational factor they are associated with a lack of active involvement of clients in therapy and decreased therapy motivation. In the last section of this chapter, therapeutic interventions that can be used to resolve conflicts and promote the integration of clients' goals are discussed. If clients show only vague representations of their conflicts, a first step toward interventions should be to gain further clarification and elaboration of essential aspects of their conflicts. When all important aspects of a conflict are sufficiently represented, or if the client starts therapy with a well-elaborated understanding of his or her conflicts, specific interventions for reducing or solving the conflict, or for increasing integration of goals, can be used (e.g., elaborating alternative ways of goal-striving, reformulating or abandoning goals, or promoting the acceptance of the conflict).

---

* Please send correspondence to Johannes Michalak.

Handbook of Motivational Counseling. Edited by W. Miles Cox and Eric Klinger.
© 2004 John Wiley & Sons, Ltd.

GOAL CONFLICTS IN THE THERAPEUTIC PROCESS

Psychotherapy clients have their personal or even idiosyncratic hopes, expectations, and goals concerning their treatment. Although this idea may seem trivial, the systematic integration of clients' goals in conceptualizations of the psychotherapeutic process is not obvious. It is neither established in a practical perspective, nor has psychotherapy research investigated the topic adequately. Recently, stimulated by concepts from social and motivational psychology (Austin & Vancouver, 1996; Brunstein & Maier, 1996; Emmons, 1996; Klinger, 1977; Pervin, 1989), the topic "clients' goals" has attracted more attention in clinical research (Cox & Klinger, 1988, 1990; Michalak, 2000; Pöhlmann, 1999; Schulte-Bahrenberg, 1990).

In the therapeutic process clients usually strive for a variety of goals concerning the outcome of their treatment. Such explicit therapeutic goals could be the relief from agoraphobic anxieties, the improvement in their domestic partnership, or a life without using alcohol. However, beyond these explicit therapy goals, the clients' behavior is regularly influenced by a variety of other personal goals (Austin & Vancouver, 1996) and plans (Caspar, 1997). These goals can be related to topics such as partnership, occupation, friendship, or independence and are organized in a complex overall goal structure.

In addition to the properties of each single goal, such as the importance of the goal or the likelihood of goal attainment (Austin & Vancouver, 1996), the relation between the goals and the features of the overall goal structure could have a crucial influence on the therapeutic process. For instance, different goals can support each other, considering that the attainment of one goal might have a positive influence on the attainment of others, in which case the overall goal structure is well integrated. If, for example, the attainment of the explicit therapeutic goal "relief from agoraphobic anxieties" supports the goals "having success at work" or "spending more time with friends," these goals are well integrated. Conversely, the attainment of important personal goals might support the explicit therapeutic goal (e.g., the goal "having more time for relaxing" supports the explicit goal "overcoming agoraphobic anxieties").

However, it is also possible that goals impede each other, creating a conflictive relation. The term *goal conflict* refers to situations in which "a goal that a person wishes to accomplish interferes with the attainment of at least one other goal that the individual simultaneously wishes to accomplish" (Emmons, King, & Sheldon, 1993, p. 531). If, for example, the attainment of the explicit therapeutic goal "overcoming agoraphobic anxieties" destabilizes the patient's partnership — i.e., if the client only gets attention and mutual affection from the partner in states of anxiety — the symptoms might have a functional meaning. In such a case the explicit therapeutic goal has a conflictive relation to other relevant personal goals (i.e., goals related to the client's partnership). Furthermore, important personal goals can impede the explicit therapeutic goal. If, for example, the attainment of the important personal goal "having success at work" increases the client's stress level, it could interfere with the goal "reducing panic attacks."

What are the consequences of goal conflicts on the therapeutic process? Psychoanalytical (e.g., Freud, 1927; Horney, 1945; Horowitz, 1988; Jung, 1953), behavioral (e.g., Miller, 1944; Wolpe, 1958), motivational (e.g., Hovland & Sears, 1938; Lewin, 1931), and cognitive (e.g., Epstein, 1982; Lecky, 1945) approaches discuss this issue. Reviewing the theoretical perspectives reveals two main assumptions concerning the concept of conflict. The first of these is that conflicts play a major role as a *pathogenic factor* in the onset and the maintenance of psychological disorders. From Freud's (1927) theory of neurosis to recent consistency theoretical conflict theories (Grawe, 2003), this assumption has had a formative influence on various psychopathological theories. Apart from this pathogenic role, conflicts were also regarded as a *motivational factor* that influences experience and behavior; they can cause behavior inhibition, motivational deficits, and difficulties in action control (e.g., Emmons & King, 1988; Emmons, King, & Sheldon, 1993; Miller, 1944, 1959).[1]

According to these considerations, conflicts (also conflicts between the client's goals) may influence the therapeutic process twofold. First, they can be the cause for the onset and maintenance of psychological disorders and symptoms. Second, they can be a motivational factor that influences the client's therapy motivation. Clients whose personal goals (e.g., goals related to topics such as partnership, occupation, friendship, independence) are in conflict with each other should be less motivated to strive actively for such goals. If, in particular, the explicit therapeutic goal (e.g., reducing panic attacks, stop drinking alcohol) interferes with other relevant goals that the clients wish to accomplish simultaneously (e.g., stabilizing partnership, be more relaxed in social situations), the clients should hesitate to take an active role in the therapeutic change process, because striving for the explicit therapy goal interferes with the attainment of other relevant personal goals.

These two ideas (i.e., goal conflicts as a pathogenic factor and as a motivational factor) are not necessarily exclusive. While conflicts can directly cause psychopathological symptoms, as postulated by the theories cited above, they can also indirectly influence the maintenance of symptoms by diminishing the motivation to challenge these symptoms actively. For example, in their motivational model of alcohol use, Cox and Klinger (1988) postulated that goal conflicts diminish the probability of emotionally satisfying goal attainment. Because of that, goal conflicts have an unfavorable effect on the balance between the satisfaction that alcoholics expect to find by drinking alcohol and the emotional satisfaction they expect to obtain nonchemically, thus undermining their motivation to use active change strategies without using alcohol.

In the long run, goal conflicts as a pathogenic factor as well as a motivational factor should have a significant influence on the progress and success of treatment. Accordingly, therapists should carefully monitor their clients' goal structure for conflictful constellations and should intervene adequately to resolve or reduce those conflicts between goals.

The following sections present newly developed methods for the assessment of goal conflicts. Empirical studies and research findings that demonstrate the relevance of goal conflicts as a pathogenic or motivational factor will be introduced. Finally, we discuss therapeutic interventions that could reduce goal conflicts and increase the integration of the client's goals.

METHODS TO ASSESS GOAL CONFLICTS

Although various psychotherapeutic approaches emphasize the concept of conflict on a theoretical level, empirical studies are rare. However, recently developed and ecologically valid methods to assess goal conflicts now make an empirical analysis possible. The following

---

[1] Aside from the dysfunctional consequences of goal conflicts for psychopathology and motivation, Emmons, King, and Sheldon (1993) point out that conflicts can be a beneficial force in human life. For example, they can be important in a developmental perspective as a necessary step that promotes developmental changes from a less sophisticated level of organization to a more sophisticated one (see Turiel, 1974).

section introduces two methods that have been successfully implemented in empirical research.

Computerized Intrapersonal Conflict Assessment

The Computerized Intrapersonal Conflict Assessment (CICA) developed by Lauterbach (1996a; Lauterbach & Newman, 1999) allows the investigation and quantification of intrapsychic conflicts. CICA assesses conflicts between goals or other areas of personal concern, such as values or personal attitudes. The method is based on the well-elaborated sociopsychological theories of (im)balance and (in)consistency (see Heider, 1946, and Insko, 1984, for reviews).

In this section, the central concepts of CICA will be presented in a brief and simplified form (for more detailed information, see Lauterbach, 1996a; Lauterbach & Newman, 1999). Based on Heider's principle of (im)balance, a "conflict" is defined as an inconsistency between two concepts (e.g., "success at work" and "leisure time"). To determine whether there is a conflict between these concepts, the attitude toward each concept and the beliefs about their interactions are assessed. *Attitudes* (relationship between the concept "myself" and another element) are identified by asking participants to judge the positive or negative value the concepts have for them (e.g., "is it a good thing or a bad thing to work?"; "is it a good or bad thing to have (much) leisure time?"). By modifying this question, it is also possible to assess attitudes toward personal goals (e.g., "is the goal 'success at work' a goal you strive for or you avoid?"). Additionally, participants are asked to estimate the *relationship* between the concepts, describing the positive or negative effects they may have on each other in the participants' belief system. For example, one concept may (positively) promote or (negatively) impede the other (e.g., "being more successful at work" may impede "leisure time"). The extent of cognitive inconsistency is assessed at the level of substructures of triads, i.e., structures of three cognitive concepts or elements (e.g., goals) and their subjective relationships, as described above (the three elements in the example given are "myself," "having a regular occupation," and "leisure time"; see Figure 5.1). According to Heider's (1946) balance theory, a triad is balanced if zero or two relationships are negative. A triad is imbalanced if one or three relations are negative (Figure 5.1).

CICA is usually done with more than just three concepts. Typically, conflicts in a field of eight to ten elements (e.g., goals) are assessed simultaneously. All possible relationships—i.e., attitudes toward the elements, and beliefs about the relationships between the elements—are presented to the participant as items ranging from -10 to $+10$. All possible triads, each comprising three items, are constructed post hoc by the computer and their balance is calculated. The number of triads far exceeds the number of concepts: e.g., in a cognitive field with ten concepts the number of possible triad constellations is 960 (including circular triads; Lauterbach, 1996a). Thus, the test does not contain any direct questions concerning "conflict," but assesses conflict indirectly according to the theory of Heider (1946).

Several conflict indices can be computed. For example, a *global conflict index* C_g, describing the magnitude of conflict in the entire field, is defined as the overall percentage of imbalanced triads (triads with one or three negative elements) of all triads (balanced and imbalanced) in the field. Conflict indices for single concepts or goals can also be computed. The *concept-conflict-size* gives information about the amount of conflict a single concept or goal introduces into the entire field. The more specific *value-conflicts* arise when a positively

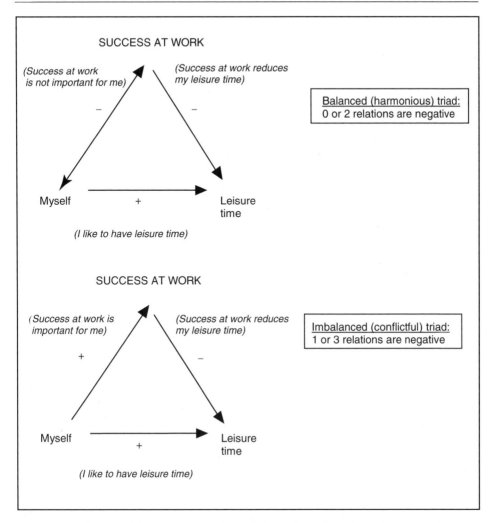

Figure 5.1   A balanced (harmonious) and an imbalanced (conflictual) triad. Relations between concepts ("myself," "success at work," "leisure time") are formulated as items in the Online Conflict test (e.g., "Is success at work important for you?" relating the concepts "myself" and "success at work"). Answers are analyzed with respect to their contradictoriness on the basis of triads

evaluated concept or goal has an undesirable effect, regardless of what a person's reality is (e.g., if the goal "quit drinking alcohol" has undesirable effects on the goal "being more relaxed in social situations"; for a detailed discussion of different indices, see Lauterbach & Newman, 1999). Results validating this approach are presented below.

Conflict Matrices

Several approaches use conflict matrices to examine the interrelationship and possible conflicts among goals. Emmons and King (1988) developed the Striving Instrumentality

	Trying to be more successful	Trying to do more sport	Trying to quit smoking	•••	Trying to reduce panic attacks
Trying to be more successful	—	–1	–2	•••	–1
Trying to do more sport	+2	—	+1	•••	+2
Trying to quit smoking	–1	+2	—	•••	+2
•••	•••	•••	•••	•••	•••
Trying to reduce panic attacks	+2	+1	0	•••	—

Figure 5.2   An example of a Striving Instrumentality Matrix

Matrix (SIM), Palys and Little (1983) the Personal Project Matrix, and Cox, Klinger, and Blount (1999) the Motivational Structure Questionnaire (MSQ) Goal Matrix. The procedure to establish a conflict matrix is comparable in these approaches: conflicts between idiographically generated personal goals are assessed directly and consciously by the participants.

For example, in order to create an SIM, Emmons and King (1988) first ask their participants to generate a list of idiographic personal strivings. Participants are told that a personal striving is "an objective that you are typically trying to accomplish" (Emmons, 1986, p. 1060). They are also given examples of personal strivings (e.g., "trying to seek new and exciting experiences," "trying to do more sport"). Michalak (2000; Michalak & Schulte, in 2002) supplemented this instruction for psychotherapy clients: If the clients themselves do not mention the explicit therapy goal "relief from symptoms" (or some equivalent goal), it was added to the participants' list. In this way the interrelationship between the clients' explicit therapy goal and other relevant personal goals can be examined.

The list of strivings is then used to construct the SIM. The rows and columns of the matrix are labeled with the participants' strivings. In order to measure the amount of conflict that exists between the strivings, participants compare each striving with every other striving and ask themselves, "Does being successful in this striving have a helpful, a harmful, or no effect on the other striving?" This rating is a scale ranging from -2 (*very harmful*) to $+2$ (*very helpful*). An example of an SIM is shown in Figure 5.2.

Two kinds of conflict scores can be computed. A total conflict score is obtained by averaging the ratings of the whole matrix. A conflict score for each goal (e.g., for the explicit therapy goal "relief from symptoms") can be computed by averaging the ratings for the column and the row that contains this goal. Emmons and King (1988) report a split-half reliability coefficient for the SIM of $r_s = .91$, and a one-year test–retest reliability coefficient of $r_{tt} = .58$.

Cox, Klinger, and Blount (1999) defined conflict in the Goal Matrix they embedded in the MSQ in a very similar way: participants estimate the effect that each goal identified in the MSQ has on the attainment of the other goals. As above, conflict is defined as "goals that are expected to interfere with the attainment of other goals" (Cox, Klinger, & Blount, 1999, p. 45).

It should be noted that Michalak (2000) reported only very low associations between conflict matrix and CICA conflict scores. The correlation between the total conflict scores of the SIM and the CICA was $r = .07$, between the conflict scores for the goal "relief from symptoms" $r = .05$. Besides qualifications that arise from the small sample size ($N = 24$) on which these correlations are based, this remarkable lack of association might be attributable to a variety of methodological differences between the two approaches: SIM uses self-generated goals, the conflict assessment is totally conscious, and the goals are often formulated very concretely; in the CICA approach concepts or goals are introduced into the test by the researcher (or therapist), the conflict assessment is more indirect, and goals are often defined in a more abstract way. Further research is needed to elucidate which of these methodological differences is most relevant—in particular, whether it is necessary to further differentiate the conflict concept into different facets with accompanying different methodological approaches.

RESEARCH FINDINGS

Conflicts as a Pathogenic Factor

Although there is an abundance of clinical literature concerning the assumption that conflicts as a pathogenic factor play a major role in the onset and maintenance of psychological disorders, empirical studies are relatively scarce. However, in the past two decades several studies within the scope of the personal goal paradigm were conducted that demonstrated the role of conflicts as a pathogenic factor in nonclinical as well as in clinical samples.

To our knowledge, the first study that demonstrated detrimental effects of conflicts between personal goals was conducted by Palys and Little (1983). In a sample of undergraduates and in a community sample, they found associations between conflicts among personal projects (Little, 1983), measured with the Personal Project Matrix, and life satisfaction.

Emmons and King (1988) conducted two studies with undergraduate samples to investigate the association between conflicts among personal strivings and well-being. They measured conflicts with the SIM and well-being with diary and experience sampling methods, measures for physical and psychological symptoms (Hopkins Symptom Checklist by Derogatis et al., 1974), and by accessing students' health center records. Conflict was associated with high levels of negative affect, depression, neuroticism, and psychosomatic complaints. Conflicts were also associated with health center visits and illness over the past year. A one-year follow-up demonstrated that conflict predicted psychosomatic complaints over time.

However, two recent studies failed to replicate the findings of Emmons and King (1988). Püschel (2000) found no associations between the SIM conflict score and psychological symptoms measured with the SCL-90-R (Derogatis, 1986) in an undergraduate sample ($N = 53$). In addition, Michalak (2002) could not replicate the association between SIM conflict scores and psychological symptoms, measured with the SCL-90-R and the Beck Depression Inventory in a sample of outpatients ($N = 65$) with anxiety and affective disorders.

Perring, Oatley, and Smith (1988) studied the associations between conflicts among personal plans and psychiatric symptoms in four different nonclinical samples (three student sets, roughly in order of age, and a sample of nonstudent adults). First, they identified broad categories of how the participants spent time ("activities"). Explicit conflicts among activities were assessed by asking participants, "How severe would you say the conflict is that you experience between this activity and others in your life?" (Perring, Oatley, & Smith, 1988, p. 169). Thus, participants directly estimated the amount of conflict that is associated with one activity without using a matrix approach. Psychiatric symptoms were measured with Goldberg's (1972) General Health Questionnaire. Results showed significant correlations between conflicts surrounding participants' principal activity and psychiatric symptoms in the three student samples but not in the nonstudent adults.

Research using the CICA found positive relations between intrapsychic conflicts and negative mood (Lauterbach, 1975, who used a paper-and-pencil version of the conflict test). Other CICA studies showed a negative relation between conflicts and positive mood (Rinner, 1991). Studies using clinical samples—alcoholics and patients with psychosomatic disorders (Hoyer, 1992); patients with anxiety disorders (Bogovic, 2001); psychotherapy patients with heterogeneous diagnoses (Renner & Leibetseder, 2000)—also showed largely consistent positive relations between intrapsychic conflicts and the degree of psychopathological symptoms. Furthermore, studies comparing psychotherapy in- and outpatients and controls—e.g., heroin addicts and controls (Völp, 1984); alcoholics and abstinent alcoholics (Hoyer, 1995); patients with psychosomatic disorders and controls (Hoyer, 1992)—showed consistently higher conflict scores in patient groups and supported the validity of the approach. There are also positive correlations between conflicts and dysfunctional self-awareness, which is regarded as an inflexible and exaggerated way of dealing with personal problems (Hoyer, 2000). Other studies showed a reduction of intrapsychic conflicts during inpatient treatment of alcoholics (Heidenreich, 2000; Hoyer et al., 2001; Roweck, 1990) and outpatients with anxiety disorders (Michalak, 2000). Interestingly, in these studies the cognitive-behavior therapies reduced conflicts without having an explicit rationale for doing so.

In summary, most studies reveal a relation between intrapsychic conflicts and people's psychopathological status. However, because of the correlational nature of the majority of the presented results, a causal hypothesis that intrapersonal conflicts lead to psychopathological symptoms cannot yet be verified.

Conflicts as a Motivational Factor

Goal conflicts are associated with the onset and maintenance of psychological disorders, but they can also influence motivational processes. Emmons and King (1988, Study 3) examined the influence of goal conflicts on undergraduates' thoughts and activities. Goal integration was assessed with the SIM. The authors recorded naturally occurring activities and thoughts using an experience-sampling method over a three-week period following the conflict assessment. Results show that participants were less likely to act on conflictful strivings (i.e., success in these strivings has a harmful effect on other strivings; however, for a detailed discussion of the construct validity of the SIM, see below) but spent more time thinking about these strivings. However, it should be noted that associations between the goal conflict scores and acting and thinking were rather low, with correlation coefficients of $r = -.27$ and $r = .14$, respectively.

If goal conflicts are linked to the motivation to strive for personal goals actively, are they also associated with the motivation to participate actively in the psychotherapeutic process? Michalak (2000) and Michalak and Schulte (2002) investigated the relation between patients' goal conflicts and basic behavior in a sample of 55 outpatients with anxiety disorders. The term "basic behavior" (Schulte & Michalak, in preparation) refers to client characteristics such as motivation for cooperation, self-disclosure, testing out new patterns of behavior, and the tendency to show resistance and drop-out of treatment.

Michalak (2000) measured goal conflicts using the CICA at four times during treatment (pretreatment, after the 7th and 15th sessions, and after the treatment). In a subgroup of 24 outpatients, goal conflicts were additionally assessed with the (SIM) either after the 7th or the 15th treatment session. Basic Behavior was measured with the Basic Behavior Questionnaire (BBQ; Michalak, 2000; Schulte & Michalak, in preparation). This questionnaire consists of 15 items and was regularly completed by the study therapists after each treatment session. Schulte and Michalak (in preparation) identified five types of behavior as separate factors: seeking treatment (vs. dropping out), cooperation (high vs. low), self-disclosure (vs. refusal), willingness to test new patterns of behavior, (no) resistance.

The CICA conflict scores correlated only moderately with basic behavior. However, marked correlations emerged between basic behavior and the SIM conflict scores. Both the total conflict score and the conflict score for the explicit therapeutic goal "relief from symptoms" of the SIM correlated highly with all subscales of the BBQ (the subscales were aggregated for the five sessions following conflict assessment). Correlations between conflicts and the BBQ subscales ranged from $r = .44$ to $r = .62$. Furthermore, basic behavior correlated with treatment outcome. Marked associations emerged between basic behavior and retrospective measures of success (e.g., global assessment of success and goal attainment scaling by patients and therapists at the end of therapy; see Michalak et al., 2003.). This means that treatment is more successful for clients who show more cooperation, self-disclosure, and willingness to test new patterns of behavior and less resistance. However, only moderate correlations emerged between basic behavior and change scores computed as pre–post effect sizes.

It should be noted that clients seldom rated their goals as conflictful in the SIM. The mean total conflict score was $M = .92$ ($SD = .51$); the mean conflict score for the goal "relief from symptoms" was even lower: $M = 1.25$ ($SD = .51$) (note that positive values indicate integration of goals). Similarly, in their original study with undergraduates, Emmons and King (1988) reported comparable means for their scores in the nonconflictful range. In recent studies very similar conflict scores were also reported for other clinical and undergraduate samples (Fasbender, 2001; Püschel, 2000). Taken as a whole, these descriptive findings suggest that the SIM seems to be a method of assessing a greater or lesser degree of integration between a person's goals rather than a measure of intrapsychic conflict.

Integration means that individuals perceive their goals as being helpful or instrumental to each other. The region of the scale indicating conflictful goals is used only rarely.

Accordingly, the pronounced associations between conflict scores and basic behavior indicate that patients who perceive their goals—including their explicit therapy goal "relief from symptoms"—as helpful and instrumental are more committed to therapy. They are more motivated to participate actively in the course of treatment and to show the required basic behavior. Thus coherence (Sheldon & Kasser, 1995) of clients' goal systems seems to facilitate motivational support of goal enactment in psychotherapy.

In two other studies, Heidenreich (2000) investigated associations between conflicts and therapy motivation. A first study with 32 inpatients treated for drug addiction showed marked negative associations between the amount of conflict concerning "personal change" (measured with the CICA) and attitudes toward change-relevant topics. These attitudes, which are regarded as essential for change, were operationalized according to the transtheoretical approach developed by Prochaska, DiClemente, and Norcross (1992): Willingness to contemplate changing problematic substance abuse ("Contemplation") and to actively cope with the abuse ("Action"). A second longitudinal study in an alcohol inpatient treatment setting yielded analogous findings (Fecht et al., 1998). Results of both studies suggest that patients who perceive their explicit therapeutic goal, "changing in treatment," as conflictful are less motivated to change problematic and dysfunctional behaviors. Taken as a whole, findings of Michalak (2000; Michalak & Schulte, 2002) and Heidenreich (2000) support the notion that goal conflicts and therapy motivation are tightly associated. However, the design of the studies precludes firm conclusion about causal relations between goal conflicts and therapy motivation.

THERAPEUTIC IMPLICATIONS

If goal conflicts and the integration of goals is relevant for the onset and maintenance of symptoms as well as for clients' therapy motivation, therapeutic interventions to resolve conflicts and to promote the integration of clients' goals should be crucial. Especially in situations when clients' problems and symptoms are resistant to standard clinical treatment and when motivational problems have a detrimental effect on treatment success, a closer look at conflictful relations between clients' goals should be useful. Diagnostic procedures like CICA or conflict matrixes can be used to identify conflicts between goals or poorly integrated goal hierarchies. If there is evidence that clients' goals are conflictful or poorly integrated, what can be done to resolve conflicts or to further the integration of clients' goals?

The first aspect to deal with is the degree of awareness and elaboration of clients' conflict representation. Clients may formulate their conflicts vaguely and only parts of the conflicts may be fully recognized and experienced. In particular, the emotional aspects of conflicts, with their strong impact on behavior, may seldom be completely conscious (see Emmons, King, & Sheldon, 1993; Greenberg, 1984; Greenberg & Safran, 1987). If clients show only vague representations of their conflicts, interventions to further the clarification and elaboration of essential aspects of their conflicts should be utilized. For example, techniques from goal-oriented, client-centered psychotherapy (Sachse, 1992, 1998; Sachse & Maus, 1991) focus on the explication of emotions and motives that are just partially aware and understood by the client. In addition, focusing (Gendlin, 1981) could be a useful technique to promote a more elaborate experiencing and recognition of emotions associated with various aspects of the conflict. For this purpose, focusing uses the so-called "felt sense," a holistic bodily feeling associated with the conflict. Beyond this, gestalt therapy developed several techniques to lead clients to a better understanding of their conflicts and to promote the resolution of conflicts (Fagan & Shepherd, 1970). For instance, the two-chair technique is used to differentiate the two opposing sides of the conflict and make them explicit.

If all aspects of a conflict are sufficiently represented or if the client starts therapy with a well-elaborated understanding of his or her conflicts, there are different interventions for reducing or solving the conflict or for increasing the integration of goals. An important issue for further steps in the therapeutic process is to determine the central feature of the conflict. Wilensky's (1983) differentiation of various types of conflicts could be useful in this context: goals can show conflictful structures, because the *end states*, which are represented in the goals, are mutually exclusive (e.g., choice between two attractive full-time jobs). In this situation, goals can be reformulated, the goal hierarchy can be modified (e.g., change of priorities), or irreconcilable goals may have to be abandoned. Furthermore, when clients are unable to resolve or reduce the conflict in this way, therapists can help them to acknowledge and accept the conflict as part of their life and assist them to find ways to live with the conflict (Hayes & Batten, 2000; Hayes, Strosahl, & Wilson, 1999).

On the other hand, goals can be conflictful even if the end states are compatible. If the *resources* (e.g., material or psychological) to attain the goals are limited or if the *strategies* the person has chosen to strive for the goals are mutually exclusive, goal conflicts emerge. Dysfunctional strategies to stabilize partnerships by (e.g., agoraphobic) symptoms are an example of this last type of conflict. In this case a conflict between the explicit therapeutic goal "relief from symptoms" and a goal concerning the stability of the partnership is apparent. This type of conflict can be resolved by elaborating alternative ways to attain goals or to change circumstances. Cox, Klinger, and Blount (1999) include techniques to resolve conflicts as a special component in their Systematic Motivational Counseling for alcohol problems. Giving several clinical examples, they (p. 56) note that "Resolving conflicts generally involves identifying alternative means for clients to satisfy one or the other (or both) of the goals involved in their conflicts." This process of restructuring the goal hierarchy and identifying alternative means of goal attainment can be supported by techniques for problem-solving and decision-making (D'Zurilla & Goldfried, 1971; Janis & Mann, 1977; Wheeler & Janis, 1980). Figure 5.3 illustrates diagnostic decisions and therapeutic targets in the process of goal-conflict resolution.

Beyond these interventions that try to resolve conflicts in the narrower sense, approaches that facilitate the integration of goals—or, more comprehensively, the integration of personality—may complete the strategies described above. In humanistic therapies this aspect was traditionally of great importance. One example of an approach that tries to facilitate personal integration is Frankl's logotherapy (Frankl, 1963; Hillmann, Chapter 18, this volume; Wong & Fry, 1998). The central issue of logotherapy is to encourage clients to perceive their experiences and concerns as part of their search for meaning. This means that people should learn to adjust their lives to something that goes beyond themselves and transcends their existence. It can be assumed that people who sense that their life has meaning should experience more personality integration and more coherence of their goals. Thus, encouraging clients to perceive their current concerns and life situation (including symptoms)

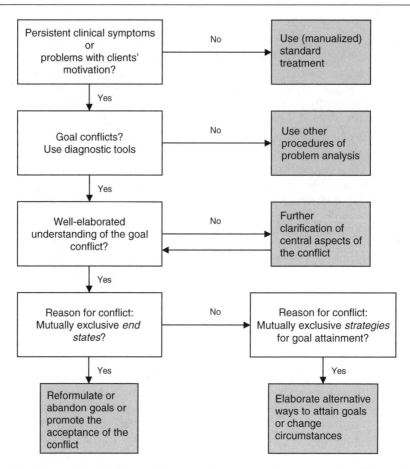

Figure 5.3   Diagnostic decisions and therapeutic targets in the process of conflict resolution

under this broadened perspective could facilitate goal integration and could help them to live their lives in a more committed and resourceful way.

Taken as a whole, different interventions to resolve conflicts and to promote the integration of goals have been developed. However, aside from a few case studies (Greenberg, 1984; Lauterbach, 1996b; Lauterbach & Newman, 1999) and correlational clinical studies (Heidenreich, 2000; Hoyer et al., 2001; Renner & Platz, 1999), controlled studies systematically investigating the effectiveness of these interventions are lacking. Considering that empirical conflict research is just beginning to evolve, it comes as no surprise that interventions to resolve conflicts and to promote goal integration are just beginning to be systematically investigated. However, a more detailed analysis of how conflicts affect the therapeutic process should promote the development of appropriate therapeutic interventions and should, as a "side-effect," increase the integration of different therapeutic approaches.

REFERENCES

Austin, J.T., & Vancouver, J.B. (1996). Goal constructs in psychology: Structure, process, and content. *Psychological Bulletin, 120*, 338–375.

Bogovic, J. (2001). *Der Zusammenhang zwischen Zielkonflikten, Symptombelastung und Krankheits-folgen bei Angstpatienten* [*The association between goal conflicts, symptom strain, and consequences of being ill*]. Unpublished diploma thesis. Ruhr-University, Bochum, Germany.

Brunstein, J.C., & Maier, G.W. (1996). Persönliche Ziele: Ein Überblick zum Stand der Forschung [Personal goals: A review]. *Psychologische Rundschau, 47*, 146–160.

Caspar, F. (1997). Plan analysis. In T.D. Eells (Ed.), *Handbook of psychotherapy case formulation* (pp. 260–288). New York: Guilford.

Cox, W.M., & Klinger, E. (1988). A motivational model of alcohol use. *Journal of Abnormal Psychology, 97*, 168–180.

Cox, W.M., & Klinger, E. (1990). Incentive motivation, affective change, and alcohol use: A model. In W.M. Cox (Ed.), *Why people drink: Parameters of alcohol as a reinforcer*. New York: Gardner Press.

Cox, W.M., Klinger, E., & Blount, J.P. (1999). *Systematic motivational counseling: Treatment manual*. Unpublished manuscript. University of Wales, Bangor, UK.

Derogatis, L.R. (1986). Symptom-Check-Liste (SCL-90-R) [Symptom-check-list (SCL-90-R)]. In Collegium Internationale Psychiatrieae Scalarum (Ed.), *Internationale Skalen für Psychiatrie* (3. Aufl.). Weinheim, Germany: Beltz.

Derogatis, L.R., Lipman, R.S., Rickels, J., Uhlenhuth, E.H., & Covi, L. (1974). The Hopkins Symptom Checklist: A measure of primary symptom dimensions. In P. Pichot (Ed.), *Psychological measurements in psychopharmacology: Modern problems in pharmopsychiatry* (pp. 77–110). Basel, Switzerland: Karger.

D'Zurilla, T.J., & Goldfried, M.R. (1971). Problem solving and behavior modification. *Journal of Abnormal Psychology, 78*, 107–126.

Emmons, R.A. (1986). Personal strivings: An approach to personality and subjective well-being. *Journal of Personality and Social Psychology, 51*, 1058–1068.

Emmons, R.A. (1996). Striving and feeling, personal goals and subjective well-being. In P.M. Gollwitzer & J.A. Bargh (Eds.), *The psychology of action: Linking cognition and motivation to behavior* (pp. 313–337). New York: Guilford.

Emmons, R.A., & King, L.A. (1988). Conflict among personal strivings: Immediate and long-term implications for psychological and physical well-being. *Journal of Personality and Social Psychology, 54*, 1040–1048.

Emmons, R.A., King, L.A., & Sheldon, K. (1993). Goal conflict and the self-regulation of action. In D.M. Wegner & J.W. Pennebaker (Eds.), *Handbook of mental control. Century psychology series* (pp. 528–551). Englewood Cliffs, NJ: Prentice-Hall.

Epstein, S. (1982). Conflict and stress. In L. Goldberg & S. Breznitz (Eds.), *Handbook of stress* (pp. 49–68). New York: Free Press.

Fagan, J., & Shepherd, I.L. (1970). *Gestalt therapy now: Therapy, techniques, applications*. Palo Alto, CA: Science and Behavior Books.

Fasbender, J. (2001). *Der Einfluss von Zielkonflikten und Motiv-Ziel-Diskrepanzen auf das Basisver-halten* [*The impact of goal conflicts and discrepancies between motives and goals on basic behavior*]. Unpublished diploma thesis. Ruhr-University, Bochum, Germany.

Fecht, J., Heidenreich, T., Hoyer, J., Lauterbach, W., & Schneider, R. (1998). Veränderungsstadien bei stationärer Alkoholentwöhnungsbehandlung: Probleme der Diagnostik [Stage of change with in-patient treatment for alcoholism: Problems of diagnosis]. *Verhaltenstherapie und psychosoziale Praxis, 30*, 403–419.

Frankl, V.E. (1963). *Man's search for meaning* (I. Lasch, Trans.). Boston: Beacon Press. (Original work published 1959.)

Freud, S. (1927). *The ego and the id* (J. Riviere, Trans.). London, England: Leonard and Virginia Woolf at the Hogarth Press, and the Institute of Psycho-Analysis.

Gendlin, E.T. (1981). *Focusing*. New York: Bantam.

Goldberg, D.P. (1972). *The detection of psychiatric illness by questionnaires: A technique for the identification and assessment of non-psychotic illness.* London: Oxford University Press.

Grawe, K. (2003). *Psychological therapy.* Seattle, WA: Hogrefe.

Greenberg, L.S. (1984). A task analysis of intrapersonal conflict resolution. In L.N. Rice & L.S. Greenberg (Eds.), *Patterns of change: Intensive analysis of psychotherapy process.* New York: Guilford.

Greenberg, L.S., & Safran, J.D. (1987). *Emotion in psychotherapy.* New York: Guilford.

Hayes, S.C., & Batten, S.V. (2000). Acceptance and commitment therapy. *European Psychotherapy, 1*, 2–9.

Hayes, S.C., Strosahl, K., & Wilson, K.G. (1999). *Acceptance and commitment therapy: An experiential approach to behavior change.* New York: Guilford.

Heidenreich, T. (2000). *Intrapsychische Konflikte und Therapiemotivation in der Behandlung der Substanzabhängigkeit [Intra-psychic conflict and therapy motivation in the treatment of substance addiction].* Regensburg, Germany: Roderer.

Heider, F. (1946). Attitude and cognitive organization. *Journal of Psychology, 2*, 107–112.

Horney, K. (1945). *Our inner conflicts.* New York: W.W. Norton.

Horowitz, M.J. (1988). *Introduction to psychodynamics.* New York: Basic Books.

Hovland, C.I., & Sears, R.R. (1938). Experiments on motor conflict: I. Types of conflicts and their modes of resolution. *Journal of Experimental Psychology, 23*, 477–493.

Hoyer, J. (1992). *Intrapsychischer Konflikt und psychopathologische Symptombelastung [Intra-psychic conflict and psychopathological symptom-strain].* Regensburg, Germany: Roderer.

Hoyer, J. (1995). Kognitive Konflikte bei Alkoholpatienten und Abstinenten Alkoholikern. *Sucht, 41*, 252–264.

Hoyer, J. (2000). *Dysfunktionale Selbstaufmerksamkeit [Dysfunctional self-awareness].* Heidelberg, Germany: Asanger.

Hoyer, J., Fecht, J., Lauterbach, W., & Schneider, R. (2001). Changes in conflict, symptoms, and well-being during psychodynamic and cognitive-behavioral alcohol inpatient treatment. *Psychotherapy and Psychosomatics, 70*, 209–215.

Insko, C.A. (1984). Balance theory, the Jordon paradigma, and the Wiest tetrahedron. *Advances in Experimental Social Psychology, 18*, 89–140.

Janis, I.L., & Mann, L. (1977). *Decision making. A psychological analysis of conflict, choice and commitment.* New York: Free Press.

Jung, C.G. (1953). Psychology and alchemy. In H. Read, M. Fordham, & G. Adler (Eds.), *Collected works* (Vol. 13). Princeton, NJ: Princeton University Press.

Klinger, E. (1977). *Meaning and void: Inner experience and the incentive in people's lives.* Minneapolis, MN: University of Minnesota Press.

Lauterbach, W. (1975). Assessing psychological conflict. *British Journal of Social and Clinical Psychology, 14*, 43–47.

Lauterbach, W. (1996a). The measurement of personal conflict. *Psychotherapy Research, 6*, 213–225.

Lauterbach, W. (1996b). The changing structure of Tanya's conflicts: A case of on-line conflict assessment in psychotherapy. *Psychotherapy Research, 6*, 277–290.

Lauterbach, W., & Newman, C.F. (1999). Computerized intrapersonal conflict assessment in cognitive therapy. *Clinical Psychology and Psychotherapy, 6*, 1–18.

Lecky, P. (1945). *Self-consistency: A theory of personality.* New York: Island Press.

Lewin, K. (1931). *Die psychologische Situation bei Lohn und Strafe.* Leipzig, Germany: Hirzel.

Little, B.R. (1983). Personal projects: A rational and method for investigation. *Environment and Behavior, 15*, 273–309.

Michalak, J. (2000). *Zielkonflikte im therapeutischen Prozess [Goal conflicts in the therapeutic process].* Wiesbaden, Germany: Deutscher Universitätsverlag.

Michalak, J. (2002). [*Conflicts and psychological symptoms*]. Unpublished research data.

Michalak, J., Kosfelder, J., Meyer, F., & Schulte, D. (2003). Messung des Therapieerfolgs—Veränderungsmessung oder retrospektive Erfolgsbeurteilung [Assessment of treatment success—change-scores or retrospective outcome ratings]. *Zeitschrift für Klinische Psychologie und Psychotherapie, 32*, 91–103.

Michalak, J., & Schulte, D. (2002). Zielkonflikte und Therapiemotivation [Goal conflicts and therapy motivation]. *Zeitschrift für Klinische Psychologie und Psychotherapie, 31*, 213–219.

Miller, N.E. (1944). Experimental studies of conflict. In J.McV. Hunt (Ed.), *Personality and the behavioral disorders* (Vol. I; pp. 431–465). New York: Roland Press.

Miller, N.E. (1959). Liberalization of basic S–R concepts: Extensions to conflict behavior, motivation, and social learning. In S. Koch (Ed.), *Psychology: A study of science*. New York: McGraw-Hill.

Palys, T.S., & Little, B.R. (1983). Perceived life satisfaction and the organization of personal project systems. *Journal of Personality and Social Psychology, 44*, 1221–1230.

Perring, C., Oatley, K., & Smith, J. (1988). Psychiatric symptoms and conflict among personal plans. *British Journal of Medical Psychology, 61*, 167–177.

Pervin, L.A. (1989). *Goal concepts in personality and social psychology*. Hillsdale, NJ: Erlbaum.

Pöhlmann, K. (1999). Persönliche Ziele: Ein neuer Ansatz zur Erfassung von Patientenzielen [Personal goals: A new approach for the assessment of patient goals]. *Praxis Klinische Verhaltensmedizin und Rehabilitation, 12*, 14–20.

Prochaska, J.O., DiClemente, C.C., & Norcross, J.C. (1992). In search of how people change. Applications to addictive behaviors. *American Psychologist, 47*, 1002–1114.

Püschel, O. (2000). *Auswirkungen von Motiv-Ziel-Diskrepanzen auf Volition und Symptombelastung [Impact of discrepancies between motives and goals on volition and symptoms]*. Unpublished diploma thesis. Ruhr-University, Bochum, Germany.

Renner, W., & Leibetseder, M. (2000). The relationship of personal conflict and clinical symptoms in a high-conflict and a low-conflict subgroup: A correlational study. *Psychotherapy Research, 10*, 321–336.

Renner, W., & Platz, T. (1999). Kognitive und symptombezogene Effekte standardisierter Verhaltenstherapie: Evaluation eines ambulanten Gruppenprogramms [Cognitive and symptom-related effects of standardized behavioral therapy: Evaluation of an ambulant group treatment]. *Zeitschrift für Klinische Psychologie, Psychiatrie und Psychotherapie, 47*, 271–292.

Rinner, K. (1991). *Intra-individuelle Konfliktmessung an stationär behandelten Alkoholikern [Intra-individual conflict assessment with in-patient alcoholics]*. Unpublished dissertation. University of Innsbruck, Austria.

Rosen, H. (1989). Piagetian theory and cognitive therapy. In A. Freeman, K.M. Simon, L.E. Beutler, & H. Arkowitz (Eds.), *Comprehensive handbook of cognitive therapy*. New York: Plenum.

Roweck, M. (1990). *Intraindividuelle Konfliktveränderung bei Alkoholkranken im Therapieverlauf [Intra-individual conflict assessment with alcoholics in the course of therapy]*. Unpublished diploma thesis. Johann Wolfgang Goethe-University, Frankfurt a.M., Germany.

Sachse, R. (1992). *Zielorientierte Gesprächspsychotherapie. Eine grundlegende Neukonzeption [Goal-oriented client-centered psychotherapy. A fundamental new concept]*. Göttingen, Germany: Hogrefe.

Sachse, R. (1998). Goal-oriented client-centered psychotherapy of psychosomatic disorders. In L.S. Greenberg (Ed.), *Handbook of experiential psychotherapy* (pp. 295–327). New York: Guilford.

Sachse, R., & Maus, C. (1991). *Zielorientiertes Handeln in der Gesprächspsychotherapie [Goal-oriented acting in client-centered psychotherapy]*. Stuttgart, Germany: Kohlhammer.

Schulte, D. (1996). *Therapieplanung [Planing therapy]*. Göttingen, Germany: Hogrefe.

Schulte, D. (1997). Die Bedeutung der Therapiemotivation in Klinischer Psychologie und Psychotherapie [The significance of therapy motivation in clinical psychology and psychotherapy]. In W. Rockstroh, H. Watzl, & Th. Elbert (Ed.), *Impulse für die Klinische Psychologie. Festschrift zum 65. Geburtstag von R. Cohen* (pp. 129–141). Göttingen, Germany: Hogrefe.

Schulte, D., & Michalak, J. (in preparation). *Der BAV-96—ein Fragebogen zur Erfassung des Basisverhaltens [The BAV-96—a questionnaire for assessing basic behavior]*. Manuscript in preparation.

Schulte-Bahrenberg, T. (1990). *Therapieziele, Therapieprozeß und Therapieerfolg [Therapy goals, therapeutic process and therapy success]*. Pfaffenweiler, Germany: Centaurus-Verlagsgesellschaft.

Sheldon, K.M., & Kasser, T. (1995). Coherence and congruence: Two aspects of personality integration. *Journal of Personality and Social Psychology, 68*, 531–543.

Turiel, E. (1974). Conflict and transition in adolescent moral development. *Child Development, 45*, 14–29.

Völp, A. (1984). *Entwicklung und Anwendung eines Konfliktfragebogens zum Vergleich von Drogenabhängigen und religiös Gebundenen [Development and application of a conflict questionnaire for the comparison of drug dependent and religious people]*. Unpublished diploma thesis. Johann Wolfgang Goethe-University, Frankfurt a.M., Germany.

Wheeler, D.D., & Janis, I.L. (1980). *A practical guide for making decisions*. New York: Free Press.

Wilensky, R. (1983). *Planning and understanding—A computational approach to human reasoning.* Reading, MA: Addison-Wesley.

Wolpe, J. (1958). *Psychotherapy by reciprocal inhibition*. Stanford, CA: Stanford University.

Wong, P.T.P., & Fry, P.S. (Eds.) (1998). *The human quest for meaning: A handbook of psychological research and clinical applications*. Mahwah, NJ: Erlbaum.

CHAPTER 6

Motivational Counseling in an Extended Functional Context: Personality Systems Interaction Theory and Assessment

Reiner Kaschel

and

Julius Kuhl

University of Osnabrück, Germany

Synopsis.—A new theory of personality (PSI theory) is summarized and applied to motivational counseling. This theory focuses on interactions among seven levels of personality such as temperament and affect, holistic and analytical cognitive systems on low ("irrational") and on high ("rational") levels of integration, needs and motives, coping styles and self-regulatory functions. In contrast to dualistic approaches, a four-systems architecture is proposed on the two cognitive levels. The four-systems view avoids confounding rationality with analytical intelligence by adding to the rational (high-level) form of analytical processing (i.e., thinking, intention memory, and conscious ego) a low-level ("irrational") form of analytical processing that generates figure-ground separation, decontextualized objects, and dichotomous categories ("object recognition"). In a similar vein, the traditional (irrational) form of intuition is complemented by a high-level (rational) form of intuition (implicit extension memory and personal self). In two *modulation assumptions*, positive and negative affect modulate the interaction and communication between two pairs of mental systems. Restoring positive affect facilitates the interaction between two behavioral systems (intention memory and intuitive behavior control). Down-regulating negative affect facilitates the interaction between two experiential systems (integration of new isolated experiences into extension memory and the self, which integrates all experiences). An in-depth discussion of a clinical case illustrates the application of a new assessment system derived from PSI theory. This system scans seven levels of personality functioning and aims at the detection of one or a few key functions that bear a high potential for personal development (Evolvement-Oriented Scanning [EOS]). In counseling based on EOS, those key functions are used for formulating a simple and clear-cut message with regard to promising areas of self-development. Additional case studies are briefly summarized.

Handbook of Motivational Counseling. Edited by W. Miles Cox and Eric Klinger.
© 2004 John Wiley & Sons, Ltd.

PERSONALITY SYSTEMS INTERACTION THEORY

The theory of personality systems interactions (PSI) postulates seven levels of personality functioning: (1) simple cognitive operations (object recognition and intuitive behavior control); (2) temperament (motor activation and sensory arousal); (3) positive and negative affect; (4) emotional coping (regressive vs. progressive modes); (5) motives (based on autobiographical knowledge as to how needs for achievement, affiliation, power, etc., are satisfied in various contexts); (6) high-level cognition (analytical thinking and intentional planning vs. holistic and extended autobiographical experience); and (7) self-regulation (e.g., goal-centered self-control vs. creative self-regulation).

Although the new theory of personality and the new assessment techniques described in this chapter may at first glance appear very complex, the reader will discover with growing practice and familiarity that the new system actually simplifies the complexity of personality dynamics—of behavior, emotion, and cognition—that therapists typically encounter on the surface level (unless they decide to ignore it). We intend to show how two simple PSI principles (the two modulation assumptions) are sufficient to explain the variety of phenomena observed on the surface. Participants of our workshops learn after some practice to navigate quickly through the many indices provided by EOS assessment and derive new goals for therapy at each of its phases. The success of these attempts can be evaluated by applying EOS assessment repeatedly as demonstrated in the clinical case study.

On each of the two cognitive levels (i.e., levels 1 and 6), PSI distinguishes between analytical and parallel holistic forms of processing, which yields four cognitive macrosystems: intention and extension memory (IM and EM) as two high-level ("intelligent") systems, and intuitive behavior control (IBC) and discrepancy-sensitive object recognition (OR) as two low-level systems.

Extension memory (EM) is defined as a (right hemispheric) extended semantic network that provides simultaneously and implicitly available representations of many possible meanings of a word, an emotion, or an act, and an extended network of possible options for action as well as different (sometimes even contradictory) emotional and motivational responses linked to various parts of the network. Thinking or planning is subserved by a left frontal system called *intention memory* (IM). It forms specific intentions, maintains goals on a conscious and analytical level, and controls (with the help of positive affect) a behavioral output system, IBC, which provides intuitive routines (presumably supported by right hemispheric posterior and other brain systems such as basal ganglia and cerebellum). Feedback of outcome is registered via an elementary perceptual system that (especially under the influence of negative affect) is disproportionately sensitive to discrepancies, contradictions, and distinct isolated events (presumably supported by left posterior and other brain systems). Perceptions and feedback that differ from expectations, and other new experiences encoded by the OR system, should at best be integrated into the second frontal system, the self-system. The self-system, which is part of EM, subserves self-maintainance by maintaining extended representations of personal preferences (supported by the right prefrontal cortex and other systems). When guided by IM, people are striving for a concrete goal (narrowly defined) which may or may not be congruent with the self-system, whereas behavioral guidance by EM is characterized by self-congruence, emotional support ("self-motivation"), and creative and flexible problem-solving (because the extended network typically provides alternative routes for action should one route fail).

The functional characteristics of IM and EM are adapted to their respective purposes: Intention memory is optimized for preparing the performance of intended action steps which requires linear, step-by-step processing and a *reduction of information* to whatever is relevant to the concrete action at hand (on the basis of explicit declarative knowledge). In contrast, the holistic feeling system (EM) is optimized for fast and simultaneous (parallel rather than sequential) activation of *integrated knowledge*, derived from vast experience. This is needed to make complex self-congruent decisions quickly (e.g., during social interaction) or to provide an integrated representation of one's own needs and values (and other aspects of the self) in relation to their social context. This holistic system relies upon the implicit and simultaneous activation of cross-modality representations of the self and respective long-term motives (extension memory). According to their sequential vs. simultaneous processing characteristics, both intelligent frontal systems (i.e., IM and EM) can be used for different kinds of control and regulation processes. Whereas IM deals with conscious goal-oriented self-control ("self-discipline"), especially in difficult and/or new situations, simultaneous processing of EM allows for satisfying multiple constraints and is therefore prone to produce compromises between external and internal needs, explicit and implicit motives, etc. Motives (which are defined in terms of the need-related portion of the self and EM) are defined in terms of *intelligent needs*, that is, needs (for food, achievement, affiliation, power, etc.) embedded within an extended network of options for actions, expected outcomes, and consequences. This motive-related knowledge, like other EM networks, is based on abstractions from vast personal experience across a variety of contexts.

On the level of self-regulation, PSI theory distinguishes between *self-control* which yields clear-cut intentions or decisions resembling a dictatorial regime, and *self-maintenance* (or *self-regulation* in a narrower sense of the word) which acts as its counterpart in a more "democratic" way (dedicated to self-maintenance but also to the integration of contradictory long-term aims and goals). The dictatorial flavor of self-control is based on its reliance on left hemispheric (IM-based) reduction to only one path for action (suppressing other options provided by the extended self-system), whereas the democratic flavor of *self-maintenance* derives from the parallel holistic format of implicit self-representations which facilitate satisfaction of multiple constraints from many sources in the system (integrating many, even opposing feelings, attitudes, needs, etc.).

Two modulation assumptions of PSI theory specify how positive and negative affect, respectively, modulate the activation of and communication between the four macrosystems. The *first modulation assumption* describes the effects of positive affect and its inhibition. First of all, as planning requires the formation of difficult or long-term intentions, loading an intention into IM inhibits positive affect (which is the typical result of a confrontation with some sort of difficulty). Later on, externally provided encouragement or internally generated positive affect ("self-motivation") abolishes this inhibition at the appropriate moment and thus effectuates the respective intentions through IBC.

Whereas IM and behavioral routines are thus linked via positive affect (i.e., the reward system), the discrepancy-sensitive perceptual system interacts with EM (including the self and motives) via negative affect (i.e., the punishment system). According to the *second modulation assumption*, integration of new perceptions (from OR) into the extended self (i.e., learning from new experience provided by the OR system) requires a reduction of negative affect (which otherwise inhibits the self-system).

Both volitional functions—enactment of intentions and self-integration of new experiences—are diffentially vulnerable. Self-controlled goal-enactment requires the transition from IM to enactment (IBC), which in turn requires positive affect. This transition can be impaired when positive affect is not externally provided and the subject is unable to generate it internally. The construct of *prospective state* (*vs. action*) *orientation* describes an impaired ability to remove inhibition from positive affect (recall that this "volitional" inhibition is elicited when difficult or frustrating situations are encountered). In this situation, explicit intentions and even unrealistic ideals can be activated, but their execution is impeded because positive affect is missing, and it is needed to connect IM with IBC.

The second type of volition is self-regulatory integration (into EM) of new discrepant sensations or findings (from OR). This form of volition is impaired when individuals are unable to reduce negative affect by their own means. The construct of *state orientation after failure* (SOF) describes an impaired ability to reduce negative affect without external support. Perseverating negative affect inhibits activation of EM (including its self-related parts) with the effect that new experiences (from OR) stay isolated and cannot be integrated into a growing and coherent self-system. In extreme cases, this lack of integration leads to inconsistent behavior, dissociative experience, and other symptoms of a disintegrated personality.

THE STAR MODEL OF PERSONALITY STYLES AND DISORDERS

On the basis of PSI theory, personality styles and disorders can be explained in terms of distinct configurations of affective and cognitive systems. According to the first two modulation assumptions, preferences for certain cognitive systems can be caused by preferences for (or "fixations" on) affective dispositions. For example, according to the first modulation assumption, a disposition toward the inhibition of positive affect ("frustration tolerance") can produce a preference for analytical thinking and for loading IM with difficult tasks. According to the second modulation assumption, a strong disposition toward down-regulation of negative affect ("high threshold for negative affect") can produce a preference for the activation of EM which provides an overview (cognitive map) of autobiographical knowledge relevant for a given situation. The STAR[1] model assigns each personality style or disorder a specific combination of high, medium, or inhibited dispositions toward positive and negative affects (Figure 6.1). For example, paranoid personality styles and disorders are presumably associated with the combination of low (inhibited) positive affect and low (inhibited) negative affect (Figure 6.1). Paranoid symptoms characteristic of this style can then be derived on the basis of the modulation assumptions: when positive affect is often inhibited, intentions can be activated (in IM), but they cannot be enacted unless positive affect can be generated (first modulation assumption). Failures to enact one's own intentions can be attributed internally ("I do not have the energy and motivation to enact my intentions") or externally ("Others have bad intentions: they are to be blamed for the fact that things never work out my way"). From a functional point

---

[1] The letters of the acronym STAR summarize the basic parameters of the model, that is "**S**patial" vs. "**T**emporal" modes of information processing and "**A**cceptance" vs. "**R**ejection," which relate to the affective conditions for activating those modes of information processing: Acceptance (which is the summary term for positive affect and down-regulation of negative affect) activates the two intuitive ("spatial") modes (i.e., IBC or EM, respectively) and Rejection, (which is the summary term for negative affect and inhibited positive affect) activates the two analytical modes (i.e., OR or IM, respectively).

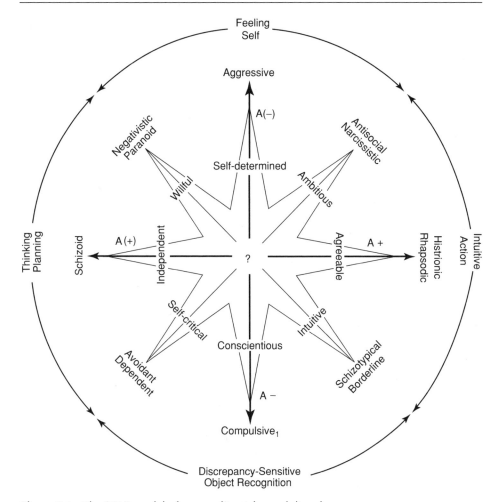

Figure 6.1   The STAR model of personality styles and disorders

of view, internal attribution of failure (i.e., self-criticism) requires the ability to inhibit one's self-representations for a while, which in turn requires a low threshold for negative affect (emotional sensitivity). To the extent that paranoid personalities have a high threshold for negative affect[2] (Figure 6.1), they should not be capable of much self-criticism. As a result, they are likely to externalize their failure to enact their own intentions. In other words, they attribute the fact that things don't work out their way to others' bad intentions. In this way, the basic characteristic of distrust can be derived from the combination of two hypotheses: first, that paranoid individuals are characterized by low positive and low negative affect (Figure 6.1) and, second, that the two modulation assumptions hold.

---

[2] It should be noted that "negative" affect has a narrower than usual meaning in PSI theory: Negative affect relates to states that have an inhibitory impact on behavior. Accordingly, associations between seemingly "negative" states such as hostility and paranoid personality would not be inconsistent with the hypothesis that this personality style is associated with a high threshold for "negative affect" in the narrower sense of this term.

A recent empirical study (Scheffer, 2000) confirmed this functional account of the paranoid system configuration. Mothers scoring high on the paranoid scale (reporting much distrust even toward friends and partners) enforced their own current intentions on their babies during a face-to-face interaction, especially when raters stated that the baby was in a negative mood. According to the STAR model, the high threshold (or low tolerance) for negative affect associated with paranoid styles or disorders activates the self when signs of negative affect are discovered (e.g., the baby's negative mood). A strong activation of the self should result in stubborn pursuit of one's own goals and external attributions of failures to enact them.

NEW ASSESSMENT TOOLS BASED ON PSI

Evolvement-Oriented Scanning (EOS) is based on a new assessment system. This system (called "Scan") provides a comprehensive, resource-oriented, battery of questionnaires for the assessment of these four macrosystems and their phasic and tonic interactions. Because of the powerful influence attributed to affect in the modulation of systems interactions, the actual level of distress is also measured. For each case referred from an industrial, educational, or clinical setting, we list individual results of various components on each of the seven levels of personality functioning. In addition, we search for the key function that explains the interaction of macro- or microsystems, current mood states, and stress levels that might account for specific problems reported by this client. Furthermore, resources to cope with the respective deficits are identified. Tables 6.1 and 6.2 depict the scales that belong to the short version of this Scan battery.

PSI theory is needed to make sense of the otherwise hard-to-handle complexity of findings characteristic of a given person. First of all we assess which of the four macrosystems is preferably used by the respective client. For example, if EM outweighs other systems, this person may prove self-confident or behave assertively in social situations. If the preponderance of EM becomes extremely exaggerated, features of an antisocial personality may develop. In this case the individual may hardly be able to integrate new, painful, or unexpected experiences into his or her self-system, including knowledge about the needs and expectations of others when they differ from his or her own. Note that, according to the second modulation assumption, some tolerance for negative affect is needed in order to focus on discrepant information (from OR) such as the needs or expectations of others when they differ from one's own. As a result, a chronically high threshold for, or intolerance of, negative affect, as assumed for antisocial personality (Figure 6.1), leaves the self at an immature stage of development.[3] In sum, a relative dominance of one or several macrosystems, driven by the dominance of the relevant affective disposition, is conceptualized as a personality style, whereas an extreme bias toward a certain cognitive and affective style can merge into a personality disorder.

This pattern of personality styles and disorders corresponds to common personality assessment inventories and clinical taxonomies (e.g., DSM-IV). Although conventional

---

[3] The assumption that high threshold for negative affect is associated with antisocial personality ("psychopathy" as defined by chronic antisocial behavior) is confirmed by findings that show low aversive conditionability in psychopaths (Lewis, 1991) and an extremely low level of cortisol responsivity even under stress in consistently aggressive or antisocial children (Flinn & England, 1995). The STAR hypothesis of antisocial personality does not exclude, however, the possibility that subforms of antisocial behavior exist that are not associated with low negative emotionality.

assessment of personality styles or disorders typically claims to provide a comprehensive description of the person under consideration, we propose that personality assessment of this sort omits highly significant aspects of personality functions, such as interactions among the four macrosystems and modulation of these systems through factors such as mood, stress levels, motives, and self-regulatory styles. According to recent findings, even extreme scores on scales assessing personality styles or disorders (e.g., paranoid, borderline, or schizoid styles or disorders) can be associated with a healthy, fully functioning personality, provided self-regulatory abilities are intact (Kuhl, 2000a, 2001; Kuhl & Kaschel, in press). Personality styles based on affective dispositions (e.g., high or low arousability of reward or punishment) or the cognitive styles that can be derived from those dispositions according to the modulation assumptions (e.g., a preponderance of analytical, self-controlled processing resulting from low arousability of positive affect) describe the first rather than the second emotional or cognitive response to new situations, respectively. High emotional sensitivity (i.e., low threshold for experiencing negative affect) need not be maladaptive; it may even turn into a resource when the first affective (even "oversensitive") response can be down-regulated later, that is, when the secondary response differs from the primary. This active down-regulation of negative affect can be interpreted as successful coping, which heavily draws upon self-regulatory abilities. Affect regulation should be more relevant for psychological and somatic health than the primary affective response, because affect regulation determines the *duration* of emotional responses.

On the basis of these theoretical and empirical arguments, a first addition to our personality inventory is the Volitional Components Inventory (VCI[4]), which provides information about the interaction of macrosystems. Even when IM scores are high (according to respective scales from the Personality Styles and Disorders Inventory: PSDI[5]), indicating a person who prefers to make plans for difficult situations, the realization of *difficult* intentions may be blocked if the individual is unable to remove the inhibition of positive affect (which normally occurs when forming difficult intentions). This inability is described by the construct of prospective state orientation, and its consequences are captured by the concept of volitional (as opposed to behavioral) inhibition. A person who is characterized by a strong arousability of positive affect as a primary response (e.g., an extraverted or histrionic person) has sufficient command over behavioral facilitation, but he or she may at the same time lack volitional facilitation. The latter condition means being unable to recover easily from a loss of positive affect, as, for instance, when confronted with a difficult task. Similarly, the PSDI may yield high scores on dispositional activation of EM (self) due to high threshold for negative affect as a first response, but EM may not be able to develop its integrative power when the ability to down-regulate negative affect, once it is aroused, is impaired (i.e., when SOF or other negative events is high). This weak ability to reduce negative affect once aroused can also occur in a robust person who has a high threshold for negative affect in the first place (e.g., in an antisocial person). Failure-related state orientation prevents the self-system from integrating new experiences (i.e., from learning and self-development).

Since affects are not considered the only determinants of cognitive styles and vice versa, the former should be assessed independently of the latter. Prevailing mood states, especially

---

[4] The German label for the VCI is "SSI."
[5] The German label for the PSDI is "PSSI."

the presence or absence of negative or positive affect or sensorimotor temperament, are assessed by an adjective checklist (i.e., Mood Checklist: MCL[6]) which combines various factors from several published mood checklists. This checklist assesses the arousability of positive and negative affects (i.e., the primary emotional response) by asking participants to rate the frequency of affective states in everyday life. (Recall that state orientation, which is to capture the secondary emotional response, relates to the duration rather than the frequency of respective moods.) Another questionnaire taps more longlasting consequences of positive or negative affect which might be reflected, for example, by somatic symptoms (Psychological Symptoms Questionnaire: PSQ[7]). These two questionnaires add qualitatively distinct information to the individual pattern.

Last but not least, the strengths of motives are assessed on an explicit level with the Motive Enactment Test (MET[8]). A modified Operant Motive Test (OMT), following the idea of the Thematic Apperception Test, uses self-generated implicit associations to drawings. Questionnaire scores describing explicit aims and goals show a close relationship to goal attainment (through IM) in explicitly structured situations (e.g., the degree of achievement motivation in an exam) whereas self-generated fantasies or associations may indicate whether this individual feels more or less driven by needs for achievement, affiliation, and/or power in less clearly structured situations that leave more room for spontaneous action (McClelland, Koestner, & Weinberger, 1989). Recent findings confirm the hypothesis that the discrepancy between explicit (MET) and implicit (OMT) motives is a powerful predictor of psychosomatic symptoms (Küster & Wittenberg, 2002). For example, a client might explicitly report having a strong achievement motive (in the MET). In contrast, his strong affiliation but rather low achievement motive according to implicit measures (OMT) might shed a completely different light on this person. This discrepancy between a strong explicit and a weak implicit motive predicts avoidance of difficulty unless confrontation with difficult tasks is unavoidable (e.g., when explicitly instructed to finish a difficult task).

The remaining sections of this chapter provide a detailed description of a case study that illustrates the use of the Scan instruments in planning therapy. In addition, they discuss dissociations among seemingly similar (sometimes highly correlated) Scan measures that reflect typical problems of clients in educational, industrial, or clinical settings.

PSYCHOTHERAPEUTIC CASE STUDY

A 34-year-old social worker asked for psychotherapy because he suffered from a moderately severe depressive episode after his girlfriend had left him six times during the past eight years. She had always returned to him on these preceding occasions. The client's father had committed suicide when the client was 13 years old and his mother was seriously depressed for many years. He explicitly stated that therapy should not only help him to overcome the current episode but also help him to become more independent in managing his life.

He reported that he was addicted to this woman and that he also adopted her way of living in order to prevent conflicts. His depression started when she left him again for

---

[6] The German label for the MCL is "BEF."
[7] The German label for the PSQ is "BES."
[8] The German label for the MET is "MUT."

good (i.e., the sixth time) without giving an explanation. Interestingly, he was not able to express any aggression. Inhibition of aggression was a key feature of the emotional climate in his family (with several members involved in medical professions). Conflicts were not expressed overtly among family members.

Standardized T-scores from all Scan tests of this client are listed in Tables 6.1 and 6.2. Progress is documented pre- and post-therapy and after a nine-month follow-up interval. From February 2000 to September 2001 a total of 40 sessions were provided at a decreasing rate (1/week; 1/fortnight; 1/month). Therapy was accompanied by the cessation of the social-worker job and professional reorientation toward becoming a physiotherapist. Follow-up data were collected in June 2002. In September 2001 he enrolled in a school for physical therapists, moved to the place of his new school, and was able to form a new intimate relationship.

The discussion starts with motive-related scores from the first measurement when he had just entered therapy (see first of the three scores in each row of the client's column in Table 6.2). In sharp contrast to his modest attitude expressed explicitly, the OMT indicates a strong unconscious tendency toward having an impact (power) on others. The affiliation motive was well developed when the client entered therapy ($T = 57$). In contrast, the implicit achievement motive ($T = 37$) scored below the normative range ($40 < T < 60$). These T-scores are based on the number of responses given on OMT levels 1–4, which are approach categories (as opposed to level 5 which reflects the complete lack of active coping attempts).

The explicit representation of these motives as assessed through the self-report motive scale (MET) corresponds to the overt behavioral and verbal data of this client (see Table 6.1). On the explicit-declarative level, the client underestimated his power motive (see MET Scale 7 in Table 6.2). Conversely, the affiliation motive (Table 6.2: MET Scale 1) showed the highest score among the three explicit motives ($T = 52$). Dissociations among explicit and implicit motives are also evident for the achievement motive, which scored higher in the explicit compared to the implicit measure (see Table 6.2: MET Scale 13 and OMT Scale L).

Table 6.1 provides some additional information. First of all, measures of mood do reflect his seriously depressed condition. All mood scales (MCL) are consistent with this pattern and suggest both a lack of positive affect and an overwhelming negative affect (e.g., listlessness, negative mood). This pattern was confirmed by a high score of 36 in the Beck Depression Inventory (not shown in Table 6.1), which indicates a condition of serious depression (pre-therapy score).

Apart from mood, Table 6.1 depicts cognitive styles of this client. At the beginning of therapy the client had elevated scores on paranoid and negativistic scales. According to the STAR model of personality styles and disorders, these two styles or disorders should be associated with a strong activation of EM and the integrated self, especially when negative affect is aroused, because that would trigger the dispositional inhibition of negative affect presumably associated with those disorders (see Figure 6.1). Apart from the risks associated with paranoid and negativistic cognitive styles (Beck & Freeman, 1990), the STAR model suggests a positive side of those styles. The high-level version of parallel-distributed ("holistic") intelligence (i.e., EM), presumably associated with paranoid and negativistic styles, indicates a potential resource for psychotherapy. On the other hand, a more fine-grained analysis showed that this function is not used adequately for the realization of specific motives. This client does not enact his power motive via EM (Table 6.2: MET Scale 8), nor does he take advantage of his EM resource when enacting the

Table 6.1 Personality inventory (VCI, ACS, MCL, BES-K, and PSDI Scales)
*Internal consistencies of some micro-components of Evolvement-Oriented Scanning (EOS)
and standardized T-scores (M = 50/SD = 10) of client BS before psychotherapy (pre), after
the end of regular sessions provided over a period of six months (post) and nine months after
the cessation of therapy (follow-up).*[a]

Macro functions	Micro functions	Client BS (T-scores) pre/post/ follow-up	Cron-bach's α
Self-regulatory abilities (Volitional Components Inventory: VCI)			
A. *Self-regulation* (self-maintenance and goal formation)	1. *Self-motivation*	43/38/57	.82
	2. Activation control	27/31/40	.81
	3. Self-determination	42/42/64	.81
B. *Goal enactment* (Volitional facilitation)	4. Initiative (under load)	36/32/52	.85
	5. *Activity (under load)*	37/41/56	.83
	6. Concentration (under load)	42/28/57	.90
C. *Self-control* (Action control)	7. Cognitive self-control	50/46/54	.79
	8. Affective self-control	43/46/54	.72
D. *Self-access under stress* ("ego resilience")	9. Non-conformity (under threat)	37/42/50	.85
	10. Coping with failure (under threat)	27/31/49	.84
E. *Life stress*	11. *Load (e.g., difficult or unfinished intentions)*	70/78/43	.82
	12. *Threat (e.g., adaptation to change, fears, pressure, etc.)*	83/74/62	.85
Action-/State orientation (ACS)			.81
F. **Action control**	1. AOD: Action orientation (post-decisional)	34/30/51	.78
	2. AOF: Action orientation (after failure)	34/41/55	.70
Mood checklist (MCL)			
A. *Affective dispositions*	1. Positive mood	18/38/76	.91
	2. Negative mood	81/81/34	.80
	3. Activation (energy)	11/28/71	.74
	4. Tension (arousal)	72/79/40	.86
	5. Listlessness	88/60/37	.73
	6. Relaxation	16/33/56	.87
	7. Anger	39/47/39	.82
Well-being (BES-K)			
B. *Affective states*	1. Severity of symptoms	53/56/25	.89
	2. Dissatisfaction	64/58/14	.89
	3. Activation (energy)	27/54/71	.91
	4. Relationships (satisfaction)	29/46/83	.85
	5. Somatic complaints	58/50/13	.80
Personality styles (and disorders) inventory (PSDI): Affective-cognitive styles (SEKS)			
C. *Cognitive-emotional primary responses*	1. Self-assertive (antisocial)	37/47/41	.86
	2. Determined (paranoid)	73/64/44	.79

Table 6.1 *(continued)*

Macro functions	Micro functions	Client BS (*T*-scores) pre/post/ follow-up	Cron-bach's α
	3. Reserved (schizoid)	55/55/42	.81
	4. Apprehensive (avoidant)	63/51/40	.79
	5. Conscientious (compulsive)	49/52/42	.84
	6. Intuitive (schizotypical)	50/74/55	.85
	7. Ambitious (narcissistic)	48/55/41	.76
	8. Critical (negativistic)	59/71/47	.78
	9. Loyal (dependent)	69/66/47	.83
	10. Spontaneous (borderline)	65/72/42	.85
	11. Emotional (histrionic)	46/49/57	.79

[a] Short test versions are available for applications in which lower reliabilities are acceptable (i.e., $\alpha \approx .70$).

affiliation motive (Table 6.2: MET Scale 2). Note that the MET assesses the degrees to which each of the four cognitive systems (i.e., IM, EM, IBC, OR) are utilized for enacting intentions related to each of the three motives (i.e., affiliation, achievement, and power motives). Motive enactment through EM (and the integrated self that is part of it, according to PSI theory) is a prerequisite for intrinsic motivation. The self integrates unconscious needs (i.e., the basis of intrinsic motivation: cf. Ryan, 1995) with personal feelings (the basis for emotional identification) and extended personal knowledge about possible options for actions across a variety of situations (Kuhl, 2000a). Indeed, the client reported some occasions where he did not take into account his intrinsic preferences. For example, he could not give reasons for becoming a social worker after a similarly chaotic choice of other disciplines when starting college (from sports to ethnology). Taken together, EOS assessment suggests that, at the time when he started psychotherapy, the cognitive macrosystem of EM was well developed but not adequately exploited in the realization of the (subconsciously) dominant power motive.

The picture may be completed by looking at other affective dispositions and cognitive macrosystems: For example, the client showed high arousability of negative affect (see Table 6.1: "negative mood" and "tension") which should, according to the second modulation assumption of PSI theory, lead to an elevated sensitivity for discrepancies or errors in object recognition. According to the first modulation assumption of PSI theory (see above), the client's high inhibition of positive affect (see Table 6.1: "listlessness") should result in an increased tendency to use high-level analytical rather than holistic processing resources (i.e., planning, reasoning, and IM). The negative consequences of high arousability of inhibitory mood states (e.g., negative affect and listlessness) is aggravated by a low score on the self-regulation scale assessing the ability to terminate states of inhibited positive affect such as listlessness and hesitation (Table 6.1: action-state orientation section F: AOD). According to the first modulation assumption of PSI theory, the high tendency to enter listless states (Table 6.1: high "listlessness") combined with the low ability to terminate such states (Table 6.1: low AOD) should, ceteris paribus, impair the ability to enact personal goals. Of all VCI scores at this pretreatment stage, this low prospective action orientation as well as low scores for coping with failure (under threat: AOF) show the most

Table 6.2 Personality inventory (MET and OMT Scales)
Motivation Scan: Internal consistencies of some micro-components of Evolvement-Oriented Scanning (EOS) and standardized T-scores (M = 50/SD = 10) of client BS (pre/post/follow-up).[a]

Macro functions	Micro functions	Client BS (T-scores) pre/post/ follow-up	Cron-Bach's α
Motivational abilities: A. Conscious motives (Motive Enactment Test: MET)			
Enactment of affiliation *Making and maintaining social relationships*	1. *Explicit affiliation*	**52/57/57**	**.86**
	2. Integrative affiliation (enactment through EM)	33/38/44	.79
	3. Intuitive affiliation (enactment through IBC)	58/58/62	.86
	4. Controlled affiliation (enactment through IM)	47/52/38	.80
	5. Anxious affiliation (passive expression through OR)	**67/63/35**	**.84**[c]
	6. Extroversion (subtype of 3)	32/47/51	.70
Enactment of power *Autonomous, assertive impact on others*	7. *Explicit power*	**37/28/35**	**.72**
	8. Integrative power (enactment through EM)	41/45/49	.80
	9. Intuitive power (enactment through IBC)	46/51/32	.82
	10. Controlled power (enactment through IM)	36/36/40	.80
	11. Anxious power (passive expression through OR)	**44/48/44**	**.88**[c]
	12. Altruistic power (subtype of 9)	41/41/48	.75
Enactment of achievement *Acquisition of competences and learning*	13. *Explicit achievement*	**45/42/42**	**.79**
	14. Integrative achievement (enactment through EM)	25/39/45	.83
	15. Intuitive achievement (enactment through IBC)	68/65/57	.74
	16. Controlled achievement (enactment through IM)	34/34/34	.86
	17. Anxious achievement (passive expression through OR)	**60/60/53**	**.92**[c]
	18. Competitive achievement (subtype of 16)	39/36/39	.86
Motivational abilities: B. Unconscious motives (Operant Motive Test: OMT)			r_{ttb}
Enactment of affiliation *Making and maintaining social relationships*	A. *Implicit affiliation: Approach* (sum of A1–A4)	**57/49/32**	**.63**
	A1. Intimacy (personal encounter)		.68
	A2. Sociability (fun and excitement)		.68
	A3. Personal coping (through love or networking)		.56
	A4. Security (through closeness and attachment)		.54
	A5. Anxious affiliation (loneliness, rejection)		.22[c]

Table 6.2 *(continued)*

Macro functions	Micro functions	Client BS (T-scores) pre/post/ follow-up	Cron-Bach's α
Enactment of power (M)	M. *Implicit power: Approach* (sum of M1–M4)	**57/57/57**	.68
Autonomous, assertive impact on others	M1. Integrative power (prosocial)		.76
	M2. Object power (status)		.47
	M3. Personal coping ("ice-breaker")		.50
	M4. Dominant power (incl. inhibited power)		.39
	M5. Anxious power (humiliation)		.27[c]
Enactment of achievement	L. *Implicit achievement: Approach* (sum of 1–4)	**37/43/50**	.66
Acquisition of competencies and learning	L1. Intuitive achievement (intrinsic; flow)		.42
	L2. Standard of excellence (teamwork)		.50
	L3. Mastery orientation (learning from failures)		.34
	L4. Competitive achievement (pressure)		.52
	L5. Achievement anxiety (helplessness)		.58[c]

[a] Short test versions are available for applications in which lower reliabilities are acceptable (i.e., α ≈ .70).

[b] The assumptions that underlie the estimation of reliability on the basis of internal consistency (Cronbach's α) are not valid for OMTs (Atkinson, 1981). Therefore, reliability was estimated through retest reliability (r_{tt}); repeated measurements were two-weeks apart (Scheffer Kuhl, & Eichstaedt, 2003 in preparation). Retest values above .50 can be interpreted in terms of sufficient test reliability because retest reliability is lowered by factors that are not related to reliability (e.g., variable conditions for motive arousal, motivational consummation effects, or—when several weeks or months elapse between repeated measurements—changes in motive strength).

[c] The anxiety component of motives can on theoretical and empirical grounds be more reliably (and more validly) assessed through self-report scales (Atkinson, 1958). This old insight is confirmed here when one compares the anxiety components of the self-report motive (MET Scales 5, 11, and 17) with the anxiety component of operant motive assessment (OMT). Nonetheless, the comparison between operant and self-report measures of anxiety components can be heuristically interesting.

extreme scores. These indications for a strong degree of state orientation were confirmed by a low realization rate of direct goals indicated by a self-monitoring exercise concerning goal enactment conducted over a period of 14 weeks. According to the first modulation assumption, when positive affect is lacking—as it was for this client when he entered therapy—initiation of action is hampered, which is not uncommon in depression. For example, the client reports long-term idealistic goals, as, for example, the goal to find an adequate profession that would satisfy all his needs and values, but he was hardly able to reach short-term goals—even overlearned daily routines were blocked (e.g., he often could not leave bed until lunchtime). Furthermore, according to Table 6.1, a low degree of self-determination (VCI Scale 3) was assessed, which can be regarded as an indication that goals and intentions often fail to be integrated in and supported by the self-system. Additional results describe his way of dealing with initiative and intuition. He did not use intuitive initiative to satisfy his power motive (Table 6.2: MET Scale 9; $T = 46$), whereas it was utilized for the enactment of affiliation (Table 6.2: MET Scale 3; $T = 58$) and achievement motives (Table 6.2: MET Scale 15; $T = 68$).

In general, his low self-determination seems to be associated with a dependent personality structure (Table 6.1: PSDI Scale 9), which might be attributable to the early loss of his

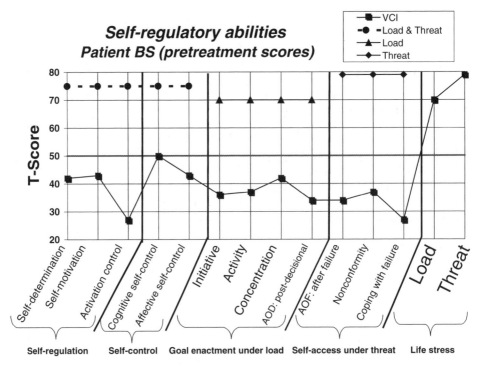

Figure 6.2   Assessment of self-regulation functions

father, who acted more like a friend than an authority before divorcing from his family. Other dependent features comprise the focus on this girlfriend and on his mother, who both claim to know better the right way to continue his professional career.

The Scan inventory contains two scales that assess two components of life stress: load and threat (Table 6.1: VCI Scales 11 and 12). There were strong discrepancies between levels of life stress reported and the related self-regulatory skills necessary to cope with them. In each of the self-regulatory domains depicted in Figure 6.2, levels of life stress exceeded the self-regulatory skills needed to cope with those stress components. Taking the first entries in the client column of Table 6.1 (VCI Scales), Figure 6.2 depicts the pre-therapeutic status. Discrepancies were pronounced in the prospective (related to initiative and volitional facilitation) and in the retrospective volitional modes (related to coping with failure and self-facilitation under stress). First, the capability to initiate actions (see "Goal enactment" in Figure 6.2) was not sufficient to cope with the excessive load deriving from uncompleted tasks that render initiation of new activities difficult, according to the first modulation assumption. Secondly, his self-regulatory skills for coping with failures and other negative episodes (see "Self-access under threat" in Figure 6.2) were insufficient to master the high level of threat in life stress that renders access to self-representations difficult (see Table 6.1: VCI Scales 11 and 12).

Psychotherapeutic interventions comprised the following steps:

- Contract for not committing suicide and for asking for help in case of suicidal ideas
- Not calling the girlfriend by phone despite strong tendencies to do so
- Reduction of negative stress and enhancement of positive mood
- Improvement of self-determination.

These aims were implemented as steps in a hierarchical procedure. Before specific targets could be selected for therapy from the personality functioning profile (Tables 6.1 and 6.2), the risk of suicidal attempts and the depressive symptoms had to be alleviated. Reduction of depression followed the application of standard behavior therapy techniques. As soon as suicidal and depressive symptoms were reduced, the dependent personality structure was chosen as the main target of intervention (cf. Table 6.1: PSDI Scale 9). In contrast to classical intervention approaches, Scan-informed therapy does not focus on the critical target behavior only (e.g., dependent behaviors). When personality scanning reveals some hidden source of the critical behavior, this personality function becomes a target in addition to any direct interventions focusing on the overt psychopathological symptoms. Specifically, even after alleviating depressive symptoms, Scan assessment revealed perseveration of the initially assessed inability to generate personal goals and identify with them (see low score for self-determination, that is, VCI Scale 3, in Table 6.1 at the first measurements of pre- and post-treatment: $T_1 = 42$ and $T_2 = 42$) and the inability to generate energy for action (see low scores for activation control, initiative, activity, and action orientation in Table 6.1 [i.e., VCI Scales 2, 4, and 5 and ACS Scales 1 and 2] for these first two points of measurement). It was hypothesized that the dependent personality style was caused by the energy generation deficit. This client needed others in order to compensate for his energy deficit (in other cases dependent styles can have quite different causes). Interestingly, the initial ability to generate and perceive positive incentives (see initial self-motivation score of client BS in Table 6.1) was not as severely impaired as the four components of action control just mentioned.

This dissociation between (intermediate-level) self-motivation and (very-low-level) action control can be interpreted in terms of the discrepant primary and secondary responses concerning EM access. Finding positive sides of a difficult or unpleasant activity (i.e., self-motivation) is facilitated by the extended networks of relevant autobiographical experiences provided by EM. Insofar as EM access is facilitated by his strong paranoid and negativistic styles as a *first* response to new situations, this could explain why his self-motivational competence is still at an intermediate level. However, his ability to generate global energy for action (see *activation control*, VCI Scale 2 in Table 6.1) in *difficult* situations was strongly impaired, as demonstrated by his very low ability to generate energy for initiating and maintaining action once this energy had been lost (see Table 6.1: initiative and activity, respectively) and to remove inhibition of positive affect in difficult situations (see Table 6.1: AOD). Note that energy deficit in difficult situations depends on a different level of personality functioning (i.e., self-regulation of affect as described in Level 7 of PSI theory) than the first cognitive and affective response to new unproblematic situations. The latter response relates to the second and third levels of personality functioning (emotional sensitivity described by the rate of affective arousal or "initiation gradient" rather than affect regulation or "cessation gradient").

On the basis of this pattern of Scan findings, it was decided to focus on EM access as a first therapeutic step. The assumed underlying source of the loss of EM access *in difficult and stressful situations* (i.e., lack of affect regulation, low initiative, low action orientation) was not chosen as an immediate target for therapy for the following reason: self-regulation training always involves a risk because it contains a self-confrontation component. For example, self-regulation of the positive affect needed for initiative, activity, and action control in difficult situations (cf. Table 6.1) requires maintenance or restoration of self-access even when confronted with difficult tasks. When one accesses the self, the likelihood increases that one encounters personal experiences, including negative or even traumatic ones. People who have a differentiated self or facilitated self-access are indeed more likely to develop symptoms unless the self has developed mature coping skills and stress exceeds a critical threshold (cf. the aggravating main effect of self-complexity on symptom formation: Linville, 1987). In light of the strong depressive and suicidal disposition of this client, it was decided to intensify and extend his facilitated EM access during the initial phase of therapy without touching too much upon the more complex self-referential aspects of EM (e.g., one's sense of personal identity; the personal meaning of traumatic experiences). For example, divergent thinking techniques such as brainstorming exercises were used to stimulate EM. Self-related components of EM were given special attention during the initial phase of therapy when they referred to positive experiences.

Toward the ultimate aim of developing more personal autonomy, therapeutic techniques were designed to take advantage of the high level of this client's EM functioning in relaxed contexts (outside the self-related part of EM). According to the STAR model of personality styles and disorders, paranoid and negativistic styles (Table 6.1: PSDI Scales 2 and 8) are typically associated with privileged access to EM and the self (see Kuhl, 2000b). To the extent that personality styles describe *primary* (arousal-dependent) rather than secondary (self-regulatory) responses of affective and cognitive systems, the high scores for paranoid and negativistic styles combined with the low score for action orientation (ACS scores in Table 6.1 for the first two measurement points) suggest that EM access is likely to be facilitated only as an initial response that is quickly counteracted by strong state orientation as a secondary response when difficulties are encountered (see low scores on action orientation scales in Table 6.1: VCI Scales, part F). Nonetheless, the high *initial* readiness to activate EM could be utilized in the relaxed therapeutic setting in which (secondary) action-oriented regulation of adverse affect was not needed, as here the client's low action orientation was not expected to impair his EM access. (The paranoid mothers in Scheffer's study became self-centered only when their babies were in a bad mood.) To utilize and improve EM access, divergent thinking techniques such as brainstorming were applied to reveal hidden preferences and resources associated with autobiographical knowledge. When the client discovered some of his implicit preferences, the easy-going atmosphere of brainstorming sessions, including music, yielded a variety of personal resources associated with those preferences. For example, the client remembered a couple of journeys to different countries, former sports experiences, a guitar at the house of his mother, and some friends he had not contacted for years.

In addition to these attempts to intensify EM access (amplifying available resources) to remove one source of his dependent personality (which the client wanted to change), strategies for coping with traumatic experiences were developed when needed. For example, when depression recurred after he saw (by chance) his former girlfriend with another man in a music club one night, he was taught to use the following strategy. Whenever feelings, images, the odor or words of the former girlfriend came to his mind, he was not to try to avoid these memories but to confront himself by practicing the following Yoga exercise which was combined with the subsequent expression of aggression, reframing, and self-reinforcement. If any memories of his girlfriend came into his mind more than three times a day, at fixed points of his schedule (Premack principle) he looked for a quiet place and took a deep breath while standing with his back to a wall, but without touching it. Then he closed his eyes, imagined the traumatic moment when the girl entered the music club, and imagined that this picture pressed him against the wall as if it were a live person. His job was to extend his arms with opened palms and press this imagined picture away from his breast and body. He did this in synchrony with his breathing—i.e., while exhaling he pushed away the image of the girl. The image then fell down from the gallery where both became visible for him at this evening. The gallery changed to the top of the hill in the Bavarian mountains which he loved and which was the place were he had gone during his childhood whenever he encountered trouble. The image then fell down from the hill and he enjoyed the view from this mountain.

From a practical point of view, the client acquired some sort of "self-regulation" during this phase of therapy. However, the process of self-regulation as defined in PSI theory was not the target of intervention in this exercise, because the client was still dependent upon an external model demonstrating the sequence of steps. Strictly speaking, modeling the therapist's behavior is still under "external" control unless this process is integrated into the self-system and becomes automatic (see Deci & Ryan, 2000, for a similar view). Recall that PSI theory distinguishes between two types of volition: IM-based self-control, which may be still largely under external control, and EM-based self-regulation (or self-maintenance), which is based on an implicit, automatic, top-down modulation of emotion and cognition Kuhl & Koole, 2003. As mentioned, the therapist decided to confine intervention to externally supported self-control in order to protect the client from the vulnerability (self-confrontation) component of the self-system. In accordance with such attempts to improve access to EM without modifying self-regulatory skills in the strict sense of this concept, changes during therapy (pre- vs. post-therapy) were most pronounced in the cognitive styles (primary cognitive reaction) and mood (primary affective response), whereas no improvements were found with regard to self-regulatory functions such as self-determination, initiative, activity, or action orientation (see VCI Scales in Table 6.1 for the first two measurements).

After improvements in primary affective and cognitive responses were secured, therapy started to focus on consolidating those advances by teaching self-regulatory skills. It was hypothesized that, after some improvement of primary cognitive and affective styles, self-regulation training could be conducted with a reduced risk of relapse due to the self-confrontation component of self-regulation training. In accordance with this shift in focus, scores related to self-regulation (secondary responses to difficulties and stress) changed remarkably during the follow-up period (that is, from the second to the third measurement). For example, whereas high state-orientation scores did not change in the first six months (i.e., from the first to the second measurement) they considerably changed during follow-up (see Table 6.1: ACS Scales 1 and 2). This trend confirmed the predictions and the therapeutic rationale applied. Whereas the pushing-away component in his Yoga-like exercise relied on explicit strategies that were largely under explicit and external control (i.e., following the therapist's steps toward relaxation on the basis of an explicit "introject"), this and other relaxation procedures were gradually brought under the control of the *implicit* self-system in the final period of therapeutic sessions.

Self-regulation of affect is faster and more future- and resource-oriented than the self-control that follows an explicit sequence of steps Kuhl & Koole, 2003. During this self-focused period of therapy, experiences were more and more elaborated as to their emotional implications for personal needs, values, and other self-aspects. In addition, self-expressions were encouraged in an understanding interpersonal context and frequently followed by prompt attempts by the therapist to counterregulate expressed negative (or low positive) affect. The therapist responded to expressed personal pain with attempts to reframe the experience (e.g., introducing positive or meaningful sides of a negative experience) and responded to expressed discouragement with encouraging, resource- and action-oriented comments. According to the systems-conditioning model of PSI theory (Kuhl, 2000a), the temporal contiguity of activating the self-system (elicited by self-expression) and externally controlled counterregulation of affect strengthens the connectivity between the self-system (right prefrontal cortex) and affect-regulating (limbic) systems of the brain. Being largely an implicit and right hemispheric process, self-regulation has, compared to explicit self-control, the advantage of faster and more efficient self-regulation; that is, the right, implicit, hemisphere is more densely connected with the autonomic nervous system involved in affect generation (see, for example, Dawson & Schell, 1982, or Wittling, 1990). The transition from explicit, largely externally supported, to implicit, self-regulated affect management was reflected in an automatization of the relaxation response. Whenever the client faced any stressors, he quickly repeated the breathing and hand-moving exercise described above, but turned to the "top-of-the hill image" more rapidly than before and utilized aspects of the brainstorming in which he was previously trained to integrate even negative aspects into his images. From the "top of the hill" he not only visualized new aims and how it felt to reach them, but in the follow-up measurement session he reported that it was not necessary to deliberately "push away" the image of his girlfriend, as in the externally controlled therapeutic period, as he spontaneously "moved to the hill" whenever he felt distressed.

We provided this detailed description of one case study to illustrate how Scan-informed therapy, which takes advantage of dynamic changes of all important personality functions during the therapy process, can help to utilize elements from diverging schools in an informed rather than an eclectic way. Whereas a more technical interaction similar to procedures derived from behavior therapy was chosen for the first and second phases of therapy (e.g., the deliberate step-by-step imaging and relaxation procedure), more "client-centered" and interactional procedures reminiscent of humanistic approaches to therapy (e.g., Perls, 1973; Rogers, 1961) were emphasized during the final phase of therapy (e.g., exploring the implicational network associated with personal experiences, encouraging self-expressions, and the prompt and responsive regulation of affect provided by the therapist contingent on self-expressions of discouragement or distress). Scan assessment can be used not only to decide which type of therapy is best for which client (e.g., a humanistic approach for clients who have a strong need for meaning and self-congruence), but also to decide within clients which type of therapy is indicated during the course of an individual's therapy (e.g., encouraging self-expression, mutual understanding on a personal level, and exploration of personal implications of difficult experiences at a later stage in therapy after primary affective and cognitive responses have improved).

ADDITIONAL CASE STUDIES: PSI-SUPPORTED MOTIVATIONAL COUNSELING

The remaining part of this chapter reports evidence for the benefits of counseling and coaching. For most of the clients who received counseling, the detailed feedback of their results in the battery of tests described above had a major motivational impact. The typical response was that they expressed their surprise and curiosity because they had never seen such an extended array of figures about facets of their own personality. Furthermore, during the process of explaining these patterns to the client, he or she was actively involved in finding everyday evidence for corresponding strengths and weaknesses. For example, a 52-year-old manager reported two months after such a feedback session (which did not even include any specific counseling or coaching) that he felt more sense in what he was doing. Additionally, he claimed to have improved the expression of his emotions. Whereas feedback of test results proves sufficient for a variety of cases, others do need additional coaching. In order to illustrate typical features we summarize a few of these interventions.

A 43-year-old manager of a software company complained about a low degree of support from his colleagues and felt the same way when he made innovative suggestions to his boss. Scan assessment yielded a high implicit power motive (high scores on OMT categories M1 to M4) and an extreme preference for logical–analytical cognitive strategies, which were used in the realization of the power and affiliation motive (high scores on MET Scales 4 and 16). He reported that he often had emotional outbursts and a lack of patience in dealing with his colleagues. The coaching taught him less analytical and more high-level intuitive skills when dealing with others at his work. The strong implicit power motive was explained to him as a potential resource for taking responsibility and exercising leadership. He soon discovered during the counseling process that he could utilize those resources when he learned more intuitive, self-congruent ways of interacting with others. For example, he learned to present his ideas about innovations to his colleagues spontaneously without premeditating specific goals to be reached and without specific expectations as to how they should react. In this way his social behavior appeared less manipulative than it used to appear when he approached social interactions in a planful way centered around his own goals, leaving little room for the ideas and suggestions of others. When his personal EOS profile was discussed with him he realized that his emotional outbursts had been caused by the narrow perception of others as potential intruders into his sphere, interfering with his plans and goals. When his social interactions became less planful and more open to others' suggestions, the outbursts rapidly became less frequent, and to the degree that he learned social skills for situations at work (e.g., empathy for less creative colleagues), he was more tolerant and even satisfied with the reactions of others to his ideas.

PSI-oriented testing may also be applied to the selection of appropriate personnel. For example, a company from the new economy branch urged us to screen four candidates for two jobs that were known to place high demands on them (e.g., a high level of stress). Whereas one candidate suffered from volitional inhibition when several difficult goals had to be accomplished (low score on prospective action orientation: see VCI Scale F1, AOD, in Table 6.1), another was unable to resist wishes of others (low score on VCI Scale 9; see Table 6.1). Since these two features seemed incompatible with the job description, the two remaining candidates were recommended to be invited for personal interviewing.

Apart from clinical and organizational domains, PSI-supported testing is also applied to educational settings. For example, a 13-year-old pupil with high intellectual abilities (according to IQ scores and his former grades) reported that since his parents had divorced he had conflicts with his mother and his siblings. His grades in school dramatically worsened and he claimed that if he was no longer able to show optimal performance he would no longer be interested in learning. Testing showed that intuitive skills (cf. IBC in PSI theory) were not used in social situations (Table 6.2: low score on MET Scale 3, "Intuitive affiliation") where they are much more needed than in achievement contexts. This lack of IBC corresponded to his complete lack of "small talk" or other social skills and his strong tendency toward analytical style (not only in achievement-related discussions, but also in social interaction). A second problem area identified on the basis of EOS assessment was related to his low self-motivation skills when confronted with unpleasant tasks (Table 6.1: low score on VCI Scale 1, "Self-motivation"). Specifically, he had problems to motivate himself for routine tasks that he had to finish for homework—a problem not uncommon in gifted and underachieving children. When confronted with this issue during coaching, this bright young man spontaneously concluded from looking at his low self-motivation scores (in a diagram similar to Figure 6.2) that he would need someone as an external "prosthesis" to motivate him. Even before he was able to recruit a former teacher for this kind of coaching, the use of a diary in which he protocoled difficult steps to perform beforehand bypassed this self-motivation deficit.

CONCLUSION

Therapy and counseling supported by EOS assessment has helped to speed up the process of finding a specific focus of intervention in each individual case. Taking into account the full range of the many functional components in each of the seven levels of personality functioning would be an almost unrealistic aim without the help of a comprehensive approach to personality functioning provided by PSI theory. In the context of this theory, we and the participants of our workshops learn to identify the one (or few) pivotal element(s) in the network of interacting personality functions of the client that seem to hold the many personal characteristics together. After identifying this key element, the complex picture of interacting personality functions can often be reduced to a simple message that becomes the target of individual counseling or therapy, respectively. In the context of this new dynamic systems approach to personality assessment, simplicity is not something forced onto personal assessment from the beginning (as is often the case with fashionable summary concepts such as "positive thinking," "self-efficacy," etc.). From the perspective of PSI theory, there is no such thing as one simple psychological function that would suffice to explain most psychological symptoms. The success of simplified summary constructs is based on their predictive rather than their explanatory power. Unfortunately, prediction and explanation are often confounded: summary constructs predict psychological functioning comparable to the prediction one can make when one pushes the power button of a stereo amplifier. Only in the rare cases when the prediction fails (i.e., when the music does not start after pushing the button because of a breakdown in some electronic circuit), we realize that behind this apparent simplicity of a button-push, a tremendously complex system is working. The rationale underlying PSI-supported intervention based on the EOS assessment system can be summed up by saying that "life becomes simple only *after* we accept (and understand) its complexity."

REFERENCES

Atkinson, J.W. (1958). *Motives in fantasy, action, and society.* Princeton, NJ: Van Nostrand.
Atkinson, J.W. (1981). Studying personality in the context of an advanced motivational psychology. *American Psychologist, 36,* 117–128.
Beck, A.T., & Freeman, A. (1990). *Cognitive therapy of personality disorders.* New York: Guilford.

Dawson, M.E., & Schell, A.M. (1982). Electrodermal responses to attended and nonattended significant stimuli during dichotic listening. *Journal of Experimental Psychology: Human Perception and Performance, 8*, 315–324.

Deci, E.L., & Ryan, R.M. (2000). The "What" and "Why" of goal pursuits: Human needs and the self-determination of behavior. *Psychological Inquiry, 11*, 227–268.

Flinn, M.V., & England, B.G. (1995). Childhood stress and family environments. *Current Anthropology, 36*, 854–866.

Kuhl, J. (2000a). A functional-design approach to motivation and volition: The dynamics of personality systems interactions. In M. Boekaerts, P.R. Pintrich, & M. Zeidner (Eds.), *Self-regulation: Directions and challenges for future research* (pp. 111–169). New York: Academic Press.

Kuhl, J. (2000b). A theory of self-development: Affective fixation and the STAR model of personality disorders and related styles. In J. Heckhausen (Ed.), *Motivational psychology of human development: Developing motivation and motivating development*. Amsterdam: Elsevier.

Kuhl, J. (2001). *Motivation und Persönlichkeit: Interaktionen psychischer Systeme [Motivation and personality: Interactions of mental systems]*. Göttingen, Germany: Hogrefe.

Kuhl, J., & Kaschel, R. (in press). Entfremdung als Krankheitsursache: Selbstregulation von Affekten und integrative Kompetenz [Alienation as a determinant of mental disorders: Self-regulation of affects and integrative competence]. *Psychologische Rundschau*.

Kuhl, J. & Koole, S.L. (2003). Workings of the will: A functional approach. In J. Greenberg, S.L. Koole & T. Pyszcynski (Eds.), *Handbook of experimental existential psychology*. New York: Guilford.

Küster, F., & Wittenberg, H. (2002). *Burnout im Spiegel der PSI-Theorie [Burn-out in the context of PSI theory]*. Unpublished diploma thesis. University of Osnabrück.

Lewis, C.E. (1991). Neurochemical mechanisms of chronic antisocial behavior (psychopathy): A literature review. *Journal of Nervous and Mental Disease, 179*, 720–727.

Linville, P.W. (1987). Self-complexity as a cognitive buffer against stress-related illness and depression. *Journal of Personality and Social Psychology, 52*, 663–676.

McClelland, D.C., Koestner, R., & Weinberger, J. (1989). How do self-attributed and implicit motives differ? *Psychological Review, 96*, 690–702.

Perls, F. (1973). *The Gestalt approach and eye witness to therapy*. Palo Alto Science and Behavior Books, CA.

Rogers, C.R. (1961). *On becoming a person: A therapist's view of psychotherapy*. Boston: Houghton Mifflin.

Ryan, R.M. (1995). Psychological needs and the facilitation of integrative processes. *Journal of Personality, 63*, 397–427.

Scheffer, D. (2000). *Implizite Motive: Entwicklungskontexte und modulierende Mechanismen [Implicit motives: Developmental contexts and modulating mechanisms]*. Unpublished dissertation. University of Osnabrück.

Scheffer, D., & Kuhl, J., & Eichstaedt, J. (2002). Der Operante-Motiv-Test (OMT): Inhaltsklassen, Auswertung, psychometrische Kernwerte und Validierung [The operant motive test (OMT): Content categories, scoring, psychometric properties, and validation]. In J. Stiensmeier-Pelster & F. Rheinberg (Eds.), *Tests und trends: Diagnostik von Motivation und Selbstkonzept* (Tests and trends: Diagnosis of motivation and self-concept; Vol. 2, pp. 151–167. Göttingen: Hogrefe.

Wittling, W. (1990). Psychophysiological correlates of human brain asymmetry: Blood pressure changes during lateralized presentation of an emotionally laden film. *Neuropsychologia, 28*, 457–470.

CHAPTER 7

A Motivational Model of Alcohol Use: Determinants of Use and Change

W. Miles Cox
University of Wales, Bangor, UK
and
Eric Klinger
University of Minnesota, Morris, USA

Synopsis.—This chapter presents a motivational formulation of alcohol use. The model accounts for the biological, psychological, and sociocultural determinants of drinking behavior, showing how each kind of variable is channeled through a motivational pathway leading to decisions to drink or not to drink. Although drinking involves decisional processes, there is mounting evidence that drinkers are unaware of, and cannot directly control, many of the variables contributing to their drinking decisions. The determinants of drinking carry different weights both for different people and for given individuals at different points in their drinking career, rendering some people susceptible to problematic drinking. For such a person, drinking alcohol has high incentive value, and the person is strongly motivated to drink in an effort to regulate affect (either to reduce negative affect, increase positive affect, or for both reasons). The incentive value of drinking alcohol competes with other incentives in the person's life. If people do not have compelling incentives to strive for these incentives, or the motivational structure needed to acquire them, they will be more likely to resort to alcohol as a means of coping, particularly if drinking alcohol is valued as a result of the other converging motivational influences. Some people who begin to drink excessively are strongly motivated to reduce their drinking, but other excessive drinkers lack this motivation. To be motivated to change, the drinker must perceive both the negative consequences of drinking and the benefits of changing, which requires believing both that adequately attractive benefits exist and that they will accrue if the drinking changes.

INTRODUCTION

The desire to drink alcohol, or not to do so, can be a powerful motivator of behavior. For some people, alcohol is a highly attractive incentive and the goal of drinking it is pursued relentlessly, even at the expense of potentially more fulfilling, less destructive goal pursuits. Other people know that drinking alcohol can interfere with their health and happiness, and

Handbook of Motivational Counseling. Edited by W. Miles Cox and Eric Klinger.
© 2004 John Wiley & Sons, Ltd.

seek to avoid drinking it at all costs. Still others feel highly ambivalent about drinking; they want to drink, but also see the downside of doing so. Such people might waver in their resolve not to drink, but eventually give in to their temptations. Even among alcohol-dependent people who undergo apparently successful treatment and resolve never to drink again, the strong motivation to drink often quickly returns, leading to a vicious cycle (Dimeff & Marlatt, 1998; Hunt, Barnett, & Branch, 1971).

How can we account for such perplexing behavior? Originally, univariate explanations for alcohol-seeking behavior prevailed. For instance, alcohol problems were regarded as resulting from moral weakness or a disease (Parks, Marlatt, & Anderson, 2001), an addictive personality (Barnes et al., 2000; Cox, 1987; Cox et al., 2001), or a need to reduce tension (Greeley & Oei, 1999). By contrast, research conducted during the past several decades has made it clear that alcohol problems have multiple determinants. Today there is a general consensus that *biopsychosocial* models—showing how the various biological, psychological, and sociocultural variables interact with one another—are necessary to understand how excessive drinking develops and how drink-related problems can best be addressed (see Heather, 2001, p. 252; Nathan, 1990).

Cox and Klinger's (1988, 1990) motivational model of alcohol use brings together the biological, psychological, and sociocultural determinants of drinking in a unifying motivational framework. The model shows how each variable that contributes to drinking is channeled through a motivational pathway, either distally or proximally affecting individuals' expectations of affective change from drinking versus not doing so. The purpose of this chapter is to summarize the motivational model, showing how various kinds of motives for drinking are formed and how harmful patterns of drinking can be changed through motivational interventions. The model takes the perspective that drinking motivations are intertwined with the wishes, aspirations, and goals that people have (or do not have) in other areas of their life. Examining the motivational context in which drinking motivations are formed provides a valuable means for understanding why some people drink too much and how we can better help them to change.

ALCOHOL USE FROM A MOTIVATIONAL PERSPECTIVE

For a motivational account of alcohol use, the motivational model uses the motivational constructs presented in Chapter 1, including incentive value, expected affective change, goal, and current concern. In this view, an incentive acquires value to the extent that the person (or animal) expects to derive either positive or negative changes in affect from it. Drinking alcohol is a positive incentive when people expect that drinking will bring about desirable changes in their affect; a negative incentive when they expect undesirable changes; and more often than not it has both positive and negative incentive value simultaneously. Drinking alcohol can become a goal that a person actively pursues, just like any other goal. A person committed to such a goal pursuit would have a current concern for drinking alcohol—an internal motivational process that would direct that person's attention, thoughts, emotions, and behavior toward the act of drinking. This chapter presents an explanatory framework for how drinking alcohol can become a person's overriding current concern, so that it overshadows other goal pursuits in the person's life and conflicts with their attainment.

Although expectation and affect are central constructs in this view, they need not be conscious processes at the time they influence decision processes. There is ample evidence of nonconscious, implicit effects on decision processes, both through the automatization of cognitive and goal-directed processes (e.g., Bargh et al., 2001) and through preconscious, protoemotional processes (e.g., Klinger, 1996; Klinger & Cox, Chapter 1, this volume) that can influence cognition and action without awareness of the influence. In addition, cortical dysfunctions in substance abusers, presumably caused by the substances, can lead to decision-making deficits (Bechara et al., 2001).

Expectations of how one will react affectively in the future are also subject to error from several possible sources. These include biasing by current emotional state (Gilbert, Gill, & Wilson, 2002), the extent to which a choice seems irreversible (Gilbert & Ebert, 2002), focusing too much on a particular outcome rather than on the likely future context (Wilson et al., 2000), and the general tendency to overestimate the intensity (Wilson, Meyers, & Gilbert, 2001) and duration (Gilbert et al., 1998; Wilson et al., 2000) of a future emotional reaction. Such errors in estimating future affective reactions, and hence in assigning values to prospective goals, provide one focal point for motivational counseling. Nevertheless, it appears that anticipated affective reactions to future goal attainment, however flawed and whether implicit or explicit, provide a basis for assessing the values of one's potential goals.

The motivational model is also a decision model. That is, whether consciously or not, it treats each integrated unit of behavior as the motivated result of a decision to do one thing rather than another. If taking an individual drink is an integrated behavioral unit, it is the result of a decision. If drinking to intoxication is an integrated behavioral unit—integrated in the sense of having been repeated enough times to have become automatized—then the whole drinking episode is the result of a motivated decision. The decision may be made by default if the individual is unaware of more attractive alternative incentives that are incompatible with the drinking episode. The decision may be encumbered by changes inflicted by a long history of alcohol use on attitudes, neurochemistry, and other processes that change the relative appeal of factors in the decision process. The motivational influences on it may be relatively direct—a clear, conscious preference for one alternative over another— or complex and indirect, through effects of motivational factors on cognitive responses to external and internal cues. In any event, this motivational model assumes that behavior is the outcome of a decision process, whether explicit or tacit and however flawed, that can be modified by altering the array of alternatives from among which the individual chooses.

Although treating alcoholic behavior as outcomes of a motivated decision process may seem at odds with traditional perspectives, it is actually a framework for analyzing the components of the behavior. It parallels a growing literature within the field of behavioral economics that has led to formal models of decision-making in addictions (Bernheim & Rangel, 2002; see also Correia, Chapter 3, this volume). Its validity will ultimately be established by its ability to generate useful predictions and treatments.

Viewing alcohol use from a motivational perspective offers a number of advantages. It allows us to identify etiology, in that it permits analyzing the factors that, at the various stages of an individual's use patterns, went into the individual's decisions to drink. It has heuristic value, in that it enables one to focus on the weighting of the various factors that drove the decision-making and may thus reveal something about the features of these factors that make them more or less compelling. It thus also generates hypotheses that lead to testable predictions. It can encompass biological, psychological, and sociocultural factors, and ultimately their neurological underpinnings, as all of these factors traverse the common final pathway of the decision to drink. Finally, it has distinct implications for treatment and other kinds of interventions for overcoming excessive drinking or avoiding it altogether.

THE MOTIVATIONAL MODEL

An abridged version of the motivational model (Cox & Klinger, 1988, 1990) is shown in Figure 7.1. The pathway that the model depicts ends with a person's decision to drink, or not to do so, on any particular occasion. As others have suggested (Drobes, Saladin, & Tiffany, 2001; Marlatt, 1985; Tiffany, 1990, 1995; Tiffany & Conklin, 2000), decisions about drinking can be highly automatic, with drinkers often being unaware of the factors that influence their decisions (e.g., Wiers et al., 2002). Nevertheless, drinking alcohol itself is a voluntary act. Although drinkers may perceive that they are unable to control their drinking, the motivational model holds that taking a drink of alcohol is a volitional act that is preceded by decisional processes with both rational and emotional components. As Figure 7.1 shows, the most proximal determinant of the decision to drink is the positive versus negative changes in affect that the person expects from drinking versus not drinking. If the net expected effect is positive, the decision will be to drink; otherwise, it will be not to drink.

The contribution of each of the variables in the model to decisions about drinking varies from one person to another. For example, one individual, who is predisposed to experience positive biochemical reactions to alcohol and few negative reactions, will have greater weight contributed by expectations of positive affective changes from the chemical effects of alcohol than another person who does not have this predisposition. Or consider the example of a person who has become unemployed, and the person has difficulty finding new employment. This person might turn to alcohol as a way of coping with the unpleasant situation. In this case the motivation for drinking would come largely from the lack of positive incentives in another area of the person's life. The weight contributed by the different variables also varies within particular individuals from one point in their drinking career to another. For example, a college student who regularly goes out to drink with his friends might well be motivated to drink heavily because of the approval that he gets from his peers for doing so, rather than the pleasure that he gets from the pharmacological effects of the alcohol. However, if he continues his pattern of heavy drinking, he might develop physical dependence on alcohol, so that physiological variables come to play a greater role in his drinking.

Alcohol Expectancies versus Motives for Drinking

Considerable research has been conducted to investigate drinkers' expectancies about the positive and negative effects of alcohol, and how these expectancies are related to actual drinking behavior and excessive drinkers' ability to change (Goldman, Del Boca, & Darkes, 1999; Jones, Chapter 19, this volume; Jones & McMahon, 1998; Vik, Carrello, & Nathan, 1999). Alcohol expectancies, however, differ from motives or reasons for drinking. "Expectancies [are the] ... cognitive representations of an individual's past direct and indirect learning experiences with alcohol. In contrast, reasons for drinking are an individual's specific motivations for using alcohol, that is, the outcomes they hope to attain by drinking"(Collins & Bradizza, 2001, p. 327). In other words, expectancies are people's beliefs about what will happen if they (or other people) drink alcohol, whereas motives are the value placed on the particular effects they want to achieve, which motivate them to drink, or

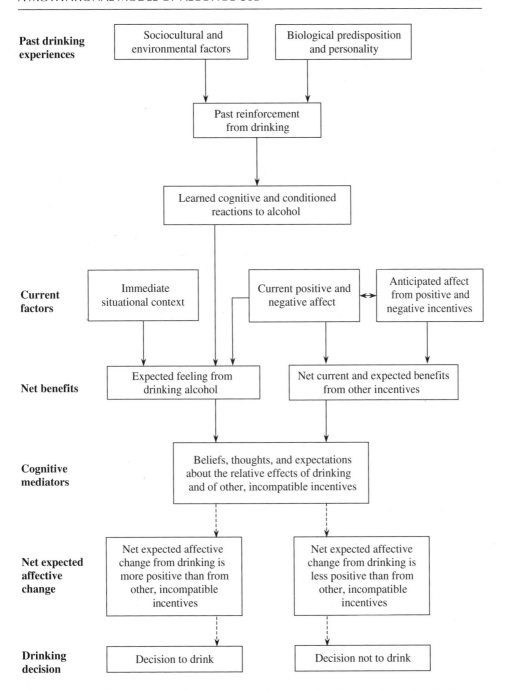

Figure 7.1 An abbreviated version of a motivational model of alcohol use (Cox & Klinger, 1988, 1990)

the effects that they want to avoid, motivating them not to drink. In the motivational model, expectations about affective change from drinking reflect the expected consequences from drinking that the person wants to have or to avoid and are the most proximal determinant of the actual behavior. Therefore, expectations about affective change from drinking correspond more closely to motives for drinking than to alcohol expectancies. Prior research has shown that drinking motives are stronger predictors of actual drinking behavior than are alcohol expectancies (e.g., Cooper et al., 1995; Cronin, 1997).

The motivational model proposes four categories of motives for drinking. Each category is determined by (a) the valence of the expected affective change from drinking (enhancement of positive affect or reduction of negative affect), and (b) whether the change occurs directly from the pharmacological effects of the alcohol or instrumentally through the effects of drinking alcohol on other incentives. That is, the four motive categories are (a) increased positive valence from direct pharmacological effects, (b) increased positive valence from instrumental effects of drinking, (c) reduced negative valence from direct pharmacological effects, and (d) reduced negative valence from instrumental effects of drinking.

Regardless of how the affective change comes about, if the net expected affective change from drinking alcohol is more positive than from other, incompatible incentives, the decision will be to drink. If the net expected affective change from drinking alcohol is less positive than from other, incompatible incentives, the decision will be not to drink.

Testing the conceptual validity of Cox and Klinger's (1988) motivational model, Cooper (1994) identified four categories of drinking motives among adolescent drinkers that she called social, coping, enhancement, and conformity, each of which was related to a distinct pattern of antecedents and consequences of drinking. These four categories of drinking motives correspond roughly but not exactly to those of Cox and Klinger. They differ somewhat in that, for instance, drinking to enhance positive affect through instrumental means is not restricted to social motives for drinking, and drinking to counteract negative affect instrumentally has a broader meaning than Cooper's conformity motives. In any event, Cooper concluded that the results supported both the conceptual validity of the motivational model and the utility of measuring the four kinds of motives for clinical and research purposes across a diverse range of adolescent populations. Additional support for the categorical drinking motives has been found both with young adults and adolescents (e.g., Carey & Correia, 1997; Cooper et al., 1992, 1995).

Distal Determinants: Past Drinking Experiences

An important source of people's current expectations of affective change from drinking is their own past drinking experiences. In turn, these experiences are molded by each person's diathesis and the environmental influences that place the person at risk for drinking excessively or protect the person from doing so. These factors, represented by the first row of boxes in Figure 7.1, include (a) each person's neurochemical and metabolic reactions to alcohol and the extent to which alcohol is experienced as positive or negative, (b) that person's personality characteristics that promote or protect against excessive drinking, and (c) the drinking practices in the person's society that help to mold that person's own drinking.

Regarding diathesis, there is now considerable evidence that genetic factors play a significant role in determining people's risk for developing alcohol-related problems or their protection from doing so (Cook & Gurling, 2001; McGue, 1999). The evidence comes largely from twin and adoption studies, which have shown that as the biological related-ness between two people increases, so does the concordance rate for alcohol-related prob-lems. Moreover, genetic-marker studies have identified some of the mechanisms through which inherited, biological factors exert their influence on people's alcohol consumption and alcohol-related problems. Perhaps the best established evidence for such a genetic effect is the alcohol-flushing syndrome, due to a chromosomal mutation, which causes a subjective, aversive reaction to alcohol (Cook & Gurling, 2001). The syndrome occurs fre-quently among people of Asian ancestry, but infrequently among Caucasians, thus rendering the former individuals biologically protected against drinking excessively and developing alcohol-related problems.

Additional evidence helps to clarify the role that neurotransmitters and other neurochem-ical substances in the brain play in determining the acute positive and negative effects of alcohol that mediate the motivation to drink. Reviewing this literature, Fromme and D'Amico (1999) concluded that alcohol's effects on dopamine and the opioid peptides are largely responsible for the positive mood-enhancing effects that promote alcohol-seeking behavior, whereas the enhancing effects of alcohol on gamma-aminobutyric acid serve to mediate the anxiolytic effects of drinking. The alcohol-mediated release of dopamine in the brain may thus bring about pleasurable feelings directly, but they may also do so indi-rectly by directing the organism's attention to cues in the environment that signal reward. Fromme and D'Amico proposed a separate neurochemical account of alcohol's effects on higher-order cognitive processes that augment motivations to drink. These processes include associative and cognitive reactions to alcohol-related stimuli, in the absence of alcohol itself, which might help to explain the intractable nature of positive alcohol expectancies in spite of negative drinking-related consequences. Similarly, according to Robinson and Berridge's (1993, 2000, 2001) incentive-sensitization theory, repeated administration of alcohol causes the brain to become sensitized to alcohol and its associated stimuli. In turn, these stimuli can trigger a conditional motivational state in the sensitized brain, leading the organism to search for alcohol and ingest it, but without experiencing the pleasure previously associated with doing so ("drug wanting" in the absence of "drug liking"). Of course, knowing how alcohol affects the brain's neurotransmitters and other brain processes does not in itself clarify the wide variance among people in their motivation to drink.

Personality characteristics constitute a second category of individual-difference variables that place people at risk for excessive drinking or protect them from it (Cox et al., 2001; Sher et al., 1999). The large body of research on personality and alcohol abuse has established both that (a) personality characteristics often predate alcohol-related problems, and (b) alcohol-dependent people often have personality characteristics that distinguish them from nondependent people. That is, the personality characteristics of young people who in the future will develop alcohol problems can be distinguished from those who will not. The most commonly observed characteristics that distinguish future problem drinkers from others are their antisocial, aggressive, and impulsive behaviors.

The most commonly observed characteristics of people currently dependent on alcohol are behavioral disinhibition (impulsivity, an inability to profit from mistakes, and difficul-ties forming close interpersonal relationships) or negative emotionality (Cox et al., 2001; Finn et al., 2000). This behavioral pattern has been observed with lesions of the medial prefrontal cortex and related structures. Although there is no neuroanatomical evidence of such systematic injury in alcoholic individuals, there is now neurochemical evidence from a small sample of post-mortem analyses pointing to differences in the brains of alcoholic and nonalcoholic individuals: a lower serotonin transporter density in a region of the anterior cingulate (Mantere et al., 2002). Damasio (1994) describes the anterior cingulate as a region "where the systems concerned with emotion/feeling, attention, and working memory interact so intimately that they constitute the source for the energy of both external action (movement) and internal action (thought animation, reasoning)" (p. 71). For perhaps some people who manifest alcoholism, therefore, a neurochemical deficiency in this integrative region may be part of the diathesis. Whether it is part of the etiology of alcoholism or a result of prolonged heavy alcohol consumption is still unclear, but the evidence that some of the associated personality characteristics predate alcoholism suggest a role in the etiology.

Thus, it would appear that some personality characteristics precede the drinking problems and contribute to them, whereas others result from the excessive drinking. In any case, alcohol-dependent people are heterogeneous with respect to personality, leading some researchers to conclude that personality factors do not reliably differentiate alcohol abusers from nonabusers (Nathan, 1988). Other researchers (Babor et al., 1992; Cloninger, 1983; Morey & Skinner, 1986; Zucker, 1986) have identified two primary *types* of dependent people. People of one type are antisocial, impulsive, and disinhibited, and their problem drinking begins at an early age. People of the other type experience strong negative affect and develop drinking problems at a later age, sometimes in reaction to negative life events. People representing the two types would appear to have different motives for drinking. Those high on impulsivity and behavioral disinhibition drink to fulfill enhancement motives; those high on negative emotionality drink to fulfill coping motives (see Cooper, 1994; Cooper et al., 1995).

It should be noted that the biological influence on the development of alcohol problems can be partly accounted for by variations in personality (Gerra et al., 1999; McGue, 1999; Tarter, Moss, & Vanyukov, 1995). It is also noteworthy that people who are at high risk for developing alcohol-related problems because of their personality characteristics (viz., behavioral disinhibition) obtain greater stress-dampening effects from alcohol than those not at risk (Sher, 1987; Sher & Levenson, 1982) and that neurochemical differences have been found between the former and latter individuals (Sher et al., 1994). These findings again underscore the value of *biopsychosocial* models that identify interactions among the different categories of variables that contribute to the motivation to drink. Like other models (e.g., Petraitis, Flay, & Miller, 1995; Sher & Trull, 1994), the motivational model views personality as moderating the effects of other kinds of diathesis. For instance, people who are at risk for alcohol problems because they experience strong positive and weak negative biochemical reactions to alcohol, will be at still greater risk if they also have personality characteristics that promote excessive drinking.

The final category of variables that determine people's past reinforcement from drinking is the society and culture in which they live (i.e., sociocultural variables). Societies differ widely in both per capita alcohol consumption and patterns of consumption (e.g., typical frequency of drinking and typical amount drunk per occasion; e.g., Partanen & Simpura, 2001). Societies also have widely varying *attitudes* about drinking, especially with regard to the acceptability of excessive drinking and the behaviors that accompany it. In fact, it has long been argued (MacAndrew & Edgerton, 1969) that the manner in which people conduct themselves while under the influence of alcohol is learned through the transmission of cultural values, rather than being due to the chemical effects of alcohol itself. Both the patterns of drinking in a society and the behaviors that accompany it are learned because people model their behavior after that of other people, and they receive implicit or explicit social reinforcement for doing so (Heath, 2000). In each society, there are additional, broadly based, macroenvironmental influences on drinking, such as governmental regulation of the price and availability of alcohol (Pacula & Chaloupka, 2001). From the perspective of the motivational model, people learn to expect that they will achieve desirable changes in affect if they drink in the manner that their society expects them to, and undesirable changes in affect if they do not do so.

To the extent that people's biochemical reactivity to alcohol has been positive, their personality characteristics have promoted drinking, and they live in a society that reinforces frequent or heavy drinking, or both, they will have been reinforced for drinking, and will have acquired expectations of being able to regulate their affect in a positive manner when they drink alcohol. Through their direct drinking experiences, people will have developed conditioned and learned cognitive reactions to alcohol-related stimuli (e.g., Shapiro & Nathan, 1986). Traditionally, classically conditioned responses to alcohol stimuli have been classified as either appetitively based or withdrawal based (Feldtkeller et al., 2001); however, on balance the evidence suggests that conditioned reactions to alcohol resemble the direct, stimulatory effects of alcohol (Drobes, Saladin, & Tiffany, 2001). There has been much interest in the link between alcohol cue reactivity and urges to drink and its implications for treatment (Drummond et al., 1995). However, the evidence is mixed regarding the prediction that alcohol cue exposure will produce urges to drink (see, for example, Drobes, Saladin, & Tiffany, 2001; Monti, Rohsenow, & Hutchison, 2000), suggesting that exposure to alcohol cues alone is insufficient to motivate drinking. One determining factor is the drinker's mood at the time of the exposure. Among alcohol-dependent people, urges in the presence of cues are more likely to occur during negative moods (Cooney et al., 1997; Rubonis et al., 1994). Regarding cognitive reactions, habitual drinkers selectively attend to alcohol-related cues (see Klinger & Cox, Chapter 1, this volume). The attentional bias for these stimuli contributes to drinkers' preoccupation with alcohol and their perceptions that they are unable to control their urges to drink (see McCusker, 2001; Roberts & Koob, 1997). The response to these potent cues, involving the evaluative processes of the limbic system and ventromedial prefrontal cortex, presumably contributes to the flawed decisions to drink too much or to break abstinence (Bernheim & Rangel, 2002; Damasio, 1994). The distal influences are thus brought to a focus at the moment of decision.

In summary, the distal influences on decisions about drinking discussed in this section will funnel through the motivational pathway and be modified by influences that are more proximal to the actual decision to drink, or not to drink, at a particular time and in a particular place. For example, to the extent that a person has experienced reductions in negative affect (e.g., anxiolytic effects) from drinking alcohol in the past, that person will currently entertain expectations of obtaining such effects. When such a person encounters situations that are anxiety provoking, the likelihood that the person will drink alcohol in order to cope will be increased. To the extent that a person has experienced mood-enhancing effects from drinking in the past, this person will currently entertain expectations of being able to do so.

Proximal Determinants: Current Factors

The expectations of affective changes that individuals have formed on the basis of their past drinking experiences can be modified by the situation that they are in when a decision about drinking is about to be made. Relevant factors include the physical setting, whether or not alcohol is present, and the degree to which the situation encourages drinking. For example, many people would expect greater positive affective change from drinking while in a convivial atmosphere where drinking is expected than while alone in a sterile environment. Furthermore, the attentional biases and judgmental lapses manifested by alcoholic individuals can be to some extent overridden in the presence of sufficiently salient cues for more prudent behavior, as in decisions about using condoms (MacDonald et al., 2000). On the other hand, responses to threatening features of stimuli, relatively unimpaired during intoxication if they are the only ones and hence salient, are reduced more under alcohol than when sober if attention is divided by the need to process additional stimulus features (Curtain et al., 2001). Thus, alcohol reduces fearful responses and presumably leads to less prudent behavior particularly under higher cognitive loads. These kinds of influences are called microenvironmental (McCarty, 1985) and are distinguished from the pervasive sociocultural influences discussed above. In addition, when in the presence of alcohol, habitual drinkers are likely to show classically conditioned and learned cognitive responses to alcohol-related stimuli, and these responses serve to increase the person's expectations of desirable changes in affect from imbibing.

It has long been established that the value that animals and humans attribute to incentives is not absolute. Rather, they evaluate incentives relative to the other incentives available (Black, 1968; Carroll, 1996; Correia, Chapter 3, this volume; Cox, 1975; Flaherty, 1996; Glasner, Chapter 2, this volume). Accordingly, expected affective changes from drinking occur in the context of the affective changes that a person expects from other incentives in his or her life. Drinking alcohol becomes relatively more valued when people are unable to derive emotional benefits that they are seeking through other incentives. For instance, they drink to feel more optimistic (e.g., Klinger, 1977) or less anxious and depressed (Abrams et al., 2002; Hussong et al., 2001; Kalodner, Delucia, & Ursprung, 1989; Langenbucher & Nathan, 1990). Those whose personality impedes their access to satisfying, healthy, and enduring incentives are likely to engage in various problem behaviors, including alcohol and drug abuse (Donovan, Costa, & Jessor, 1994). Experimental studies have demonstrated that as people's access to other incentives decreases, their motivation to drink alcohol increases (Vuchinich & Tucker, 1996, 1998). Inverse relationships have also been shown between problem drinkers' ability to change their drinking and the degree to which they have other satisfying incentives to enjoy (Perri, 1985; Tucker, Vuchinich, & Rippens, 2002a, 2002b). University students' ability to moderate their drinking in the face of drinking-related problems appears related to how well they can facilitate attainment of their other important goals (Cox et al., 2002). Alcohol-dependent people are more likely to relapse after treatment if they return to a stressful life situation without adequate resources to cope (Moos, Finney, & Cronkite, 1990). Relapse is also more likely if recovering drinkers encounter negative life events, such as those related to employment, finances, and interpersonal relationships (Tucker, Vuchinich, & Pukish, 1995). Finally, contingency management procedures that reinforce healthy, competing behaviors can dramatically improve the functioning of alcohol-dependent people, by simultaneously reducing their use of alcohol and improving the quality of other areas of their lives (see Wong, Jones, & Stitzer, Chapter 22, this volume).

Net Expected Benefits from Drinking

As the earlier discussion illustrates, there are two ways in which people can expect that drinking alcohol can change their affect. The first kind of expectation comes from the direct pharmacological effects of alcohol on affect. Alcohol can rapidly and reliably change affect in *positive* ways through its effects on neurotransmitters in the brain (Fromme & D'Amico, 1999). It can do so either by alleviating negative affect such as depression or anxiety or enhancing positive affect, such as optimism or enthusiasm. However, there are also both acute and delayed *negative* effects, which different people perceive to different degrees and to which they attribute different degrees of importance.

The second kind of expectation comes from the indirect, instrumental effects that drinking alcohol can have on a variety of other incentives. There are four ways in which this can occur. First, drinking alcohol can have *positive* effects on other *positive* incentives, leading people to expect that drinking alcohol can help them to gain access to positive incentives that they want (enhancing their motivation to drink). For example, some people might be motivated to drink because they perceive that doing so enables them to socialize with other people or gain other people's approval. Second, people might expect that drinking will *interfere* with their access to other positive incentives (enhancing their motivation not to drink). Drinking might (a) sour relationships with their family or friends who disapprove of the person's drinking, or (b) jeopardize employment or financial security. Third, drinking alcohol can have desirable effects on negative incentives of which the person would like to be rid. For example, people might believe that drinking alcohol helps them to cope with the pain caused by a physical disease. Finally, drinking can also have undesirable effects on other negative incentives, perhaps leading people to expect alcohol to exacerbate their physical or psychological suffering. Each person will assign different degrees of importance to the different kinds of effect. Thus, in the final analysis, whether the person is motivated to drink or not will depend on whether the net expected effects of drinking are positive or negative. If the net expected change in affect is positive, the decision will be to drink. If it is negative, the decision will be not to drink.

Net Expected Benefits from Other Incentives

If people and animals evaluate incentives relative to one another (Black, 1968; Carroll, 1996; Correia, Chapter 3, this volume; Cox, 1975; Flaherty, 1996; Glasner, Chapter 2, this volume), the attractiveness of drinking must compete as a goal with the attractiveness of doing something else. In that case, the decision to drink depends on the other incentives in the individual's life. Efforts to change drinking patterns must then theoretically attend not only to clients' relation to alcohol use but also to the array of their other incentives.

There is a growing literature, reviewed in Chapter 1 of this volume, on the kinds of goals and relationships to goals—i.e., motivational structure—that are associated with well-being. These include satisfying interpersonal goals, satisfaction with one's work, having a sense of interpersonal support in one's goal pursuits, a sense of progressing toward one's personal goals, and goals that correspond to one's individual core values. (See Chapter 1 for a fuller account and references.)

There is ample reason to believe that the availability of attractive alternatives to alcohol reduces use. For example, having supportive relationships can serve as a buffer against urges to drink. In one study, "[y]oung adults with less intimate and supportive friendships, as compared with their peers, showed risk for greater drinking following relative elevations in sadness and hostility. Such drinking episodes, in turn, predicted subsequent elevations in these same negative moods the following week" (Hussong et al., 2001, p. 449), thus initiating a potentially vicious cycle. Newcomb and Harlow (1986) found substance use associated with lacking direction, plans, or solutions. Compared with a group of Czech students, a group of demographically similar alcoholic patients listed 40% fewer goals, responded as if they needed richer incentives to form strong commitments to goal-striving, displayed marginally less average commitment to their goals, and, after other variables had been partialled out, expressed less ability to influence the course of goal attainment (Man, Stuchlíková, & Klinger, 1998).

Clearly, alternatives matter. Closely controlled experimental work with monkeys (Carroll, Bickel, & Higgins, 2001; Carroll, Carmona, & May, 1991) has demonstrated that the presence of ready saccharine alternatives reduced self-administration of the drug phencyclidine. Parallel work with human participants has produced similar results when, for example, pitting monetary incentives against alcohol (Tucker, Vuchinich, & Rippens, 2002b; Vuchinich & Tucker, 1988). Some treatment programs for human drug users have already tried building nondrug incentives into clients' lives as a way of weaning them away from drugs (e.g., Iguchi et al., 1997). A review of these (Carroll, Bickel, & Higgins, 2001) indicates their effective contribution to treatment outcome.

Cognitive Mediators

The distal and proximal determinants and net expected benefits discussed above give rise to cognitive processes, either implicit or explicit, that mediate between the influences earlier in the motivational pathway and the final drinking decision. These cognitions include memories, perceptions, and thoughts about the relative effects of drinking and of other, incompatible incentives on the drinker's positive and negative affect. They will be related to positive and negative effects of drinking versus those of other incentives, and to both immediate and delayed effects of both kinds of incentives. Weight will be added to the decision to drink to the extent that the drinker entertains (a) strong positive and weak negative thoughts about the negative effects of drinking, and (b) thoughts of not being able to derive satisfaction from positive incentives and of being troubled by negative incentives. Empirical research has shown that explicit and implicit cognitions such as these are strong predictors of actual drinking (e.g., Stacy, 1997; Wiers et al., 2002), although the cognitions do not, of course, necessarily correspond to reality (Epps et al., 1998; Rohsenow & Marlatt, 1981). Furthermore, cognitions about drinking can be altered through experimental alcohol challenges (Corbin, McNair, & Carter, 2001; Dunn, Lau, & Cruz, 2000; Goldman, 1999; Jones, Chapter 19, this volume).

THE MOTIVATION TO CHANGE

As a result of the impact of the variables that contribute to the motivation to drink, some people begin to drink excessive amounts of alcohol. After having reached that point, people vary greatly in their ability to moderate or discontinue their drinking. What follows considers the factors that affect people's motivation to alter their excessive drinking.

Many excessive drinkers express a strong commitment to change. Many also try very hard to change but do not succeed. There are several key motivational factors that determine excessive drinkers' motivation to change and their success in doing so. If the value of any of the variables is low, the motivation to change is likely also to be low. One of the variables is the drinker's perceived benefits and negative consequences of drinking (Cunningham et al., 1997), which will have been formed through the mechanisms discussed in the previous sections. By definition, drinking alcohol has high incentive value for excessive drinkers. They have drunk alcohol in an effort to bring about affective changes that they wanted to achieve; therefore, they must have strong expectations about the benefits of drinking. When they are trying to reduce their intake or stop, many heavy drinkers will continue to view alcohol as a valuable positive incentive. The resulting feelings of ambivalence about wanting to change their drinking habits and at the same time not wanting to do so is one of the very reasons why many drinkers find it so difficult to change. Consequently, if they are to change, drinkers must understand the negative consequences of their drinking (Jones, Chapter 19, this volume). If they do not realize the harmful effects of their drinking on other valuable incentives in their life, such as their health, relationships, work, or finances, they will not be motivated to change. The issues surrounding drinkers' expectations about positive versus negative consequences of drinking have been extensively addressed previously (Jones & McMahon, 1998).

Another key variable affecting the motivation to change is the benefits that drinkers expect will accrue for them if they change. Sometimes the benefits of drinking less are simply the opposite of the negative consequences of drinking too much. For example, drinkers might view drinking as damaging their health and anticipate that changing their drinking will restore their health. In other cases, the benefits of changing do not amount to removal of the negative consequences of drinking, although the expected benefits will not occur unless the drinker changes. For instance, if the person stops drinking (or drinks less), the time and money previously spent on drinking can be devoted to accomplishing other goals in various areas of the person's life. The latter kind of benefit of changing sometimes amounts to finding an activity to enjoy that will serve as a substitute for drinking alcohol (Correia, Chapter 3, this volume; Perri, 1985; Wong, Jones, & Stitzer, Chapter 22, this volume). As discussed earlier, there is considerable empirical evidence to support the view that the motivation to change one's drinking habits is closely tied to the availability of other positive incentives and the person's ability to gain access to them.

Nevertheless, the degree to which drinkers will be motivated to change their drinking will not depend simply on the intensity of the negative affect that they feel from drinking and the intensity of the positive affect that they imagine not drinking would bring them. The effort that they exert to change their drinking habits will also be vitally dependent on their expected chances of actually succeeding in achieving the changes in affect that they desire. To what extent does the person expect that the harmful effects that drinking has caused in his or her life will be reversed if he or she changes? How firmly does the drinker believe that desirable consequences will actually materialize if he or she changes? Expected affective change and expected chances of success are two key aspects of the person's motivational structure (see Cox & Klinger, Chapter 8, this volume; Klinger & Cox, Chapter 1, this volume) that will determine his or her motivation for change. Some drinkers' motivational structure will enable them to focus their resources on the pursuit of healthy incentives that can bring them happiness and fulfillment, without the need to resort to excessive drinking. By contrast, other drinkers will be less able to do so, because the emotional satisfaction that they receive from other goal-strivings will be low and they will continue to seek short-term relief by drinking alcohol. Systematic Motivational Counseling (see Cox & Klinger, Chapter 11, this volume) is a way to change the latter kind of motivational patterns.

REFERENCES

Abrams, K., Kushner, M.G., Medina, K.L., & Voight, A. (2002). Self-administration of alcohol before and after a public speaking challenge by individuals with social phobia. *Psychology of Addictive Behaviors, 16* (2), 121–128.

Babor, T.F., Hofmann, M., Del Boca, F.K., Hesselbrock, V.M., Meyer, R.E., Dolinsky, Z.S., & Rounsaville, B. (1992). Types of alcoholics: I. Evidence for an empirically derived typology based on indicators of vulnerability and severity. *Archives of General Psychiatry, 49*, 599–608.

Bargh, J.A., Gollwitzer, P.M., Lee-Chai, A., Barndollar, K., & Trötschel, R. (2001). The automated will: Nonconscious activation and pursuit of behavioral goals. *Journal of Personality and Social Psychology, 81*, 1014–1027.

Barnes, G.E., Murray, R.P., Patton, D., Bentler, P.M., & Anderson, R.A. (2000). *The addiction prone personality.* New York: Plenum.

Bechara, A., Dolan, S., Denburg, N., Hindes, A., Anderson, S.W., & Nathan, P.E. (2001). Decision-making deficits, linked to a dysfunctional ventromedial prefrontal cortex, revealed in alcohol and stimulant abusers. *Neuropsychologia, 39* (4), 376–389.

Bernheim, B.D., & Rangel, A. (2002). *Addiction and cue-conditioned cognitive processes.* Working Paper 9329. Cambridge, MA: National Bureau Of Economic Research. 〈http://www.nber.org/papers/w9329〉

Black, R.W. (1968). Shifts in magnitude of reward and contrast effects in instrumental and selective learning: A reinterpretation. *Psychological Review, 75*, 114–126.

Carey, K.B., & Correia, C.J. (1997). Drinking motives predict alcohol-related problems in college students. *Journal of Studies on Alcohol, 58* (1), 100–105.

Carroll, M.E. (1996). Reducing drug abuse by enriching the environment with alternative nondrug reinforcers. In L. Green & J. Kagel (Eds.), *Advances in behavioral economics: Vol. 3. Substance use and abuse* (pp. 37–68). Norwood, NJ: Ablex.

Carroll, M.E., Bickel, W.K., & Higgins, S.T. (2001). Nondrug incentives to treat drug abuse: Laboratory and clinical developments. In M.E. Carroll & J. Bruce Overmier (Eds.), *Animal research and human health* (pp. 139–154). Washington, DC: American Psychological Association.

Carroll, M.E., Carmona, G., & May, S.A. (1991). Modifying drug-reinforced behavior by altering the economic conditions of the drug and nondrug reinforcer. *Journal of the Experimental Analysis of Behavior, 56*, 361–376.

Cloninger, C.R. (1983). Genetic and environmental factors in the development of alcoholism. *Journal of Psychiatric Treatment and Evaluation, 5*, 487–496.

Collins, R.L., & Bradizza, C.M. (2001). Social and cognitive learning processes. In N. Heather, T.J. Peters, & T. Stockwell (Eds.), *International handbook of alcohol dependence and problems* (pp. 317–337). Chichester, UK: John Wiley & Sons.

Cook, C.C.H., & Gurling, H.H.D. (2001). Genetic predisposition to alcohol dependence and problems. In N. Heather, T.J. Peters, & T. Stockwell (Eds.), *International handbook of alcohol dependence and problems* (pp. 257–279). New York: John Wiley & Sons.

Cooney, N.L., Litt, M.D., Morse, P.A., Bauer, L.O., & Gaupp, L. (1997). Alcohol cue reactivity, negative-mood reactivity, and relapse in treated alcoholic men. *Journal of Abnormal Psychology, 106* (2), 243–250.

Cooper, M.L. (1994). Motivations for alcohol use among adolescents: Development and validation of a four-factor model. *Psychological Assessment, 6*, 117–128.

Cooper, M.L., Frone, M.R., Russell, M., & Mudar, P. (1995). Drinking to regulate positive and negative emotions: A motivational model of alcohol use. *Journal of Personality and Social Psychology, 69* (5), 990–1005.

Cooper, M.L., Russell, M., Skinner, J.B., Frone, M.R., & Mudar, P. (1992). Stress and alcohol use: Moderating effects of gender, coping, and alcohol expectancies. *Journal of Abnormal Psychology, 101* (1), 139–152.

Corbin, W.R., McNair, L.D., & Carter, J.A. (2001). Evaluation of a treatment-appropriate cognitive intervention for challenging alcohol outcome expectancies. *Addictive Behaviors, 26* (4), 475–488.

Cox, W.M. (1975). A review of recent incentive contrast studies involving discrete trial procedures. *Psychological Record, 25*, 373–393.

Cox, W.M. (1987). Personality theory and research. In H.T. Blane & K.E. Leonard (Eds.), *Psychological theories of drinking and alcoholism* (pp. 55–89). New York: Guilford.

Cox, W.M., & Klinger, E. (1988). A motivational model of alcohol use. *Journal of Abnormal Psychology, 97* (2), 168–180.

Cox, W.M., & Klinger, E. (1990). Incentive motivation, affective change, and alcohol use: A model. In W.M. Cox (Ed.), *Why people drink: Parameters of alcohol as a reinforcer* (pp. 291–314). New York: Amereon Press.

Cox, W.M., Schippers, G.M., Klinger, E., Skutle, A., Stuchlíková, I., Man, F., King, A.L., & Inderhaug, I. (2002). Motivational structure and alcohol use of university students with consistency across four nations. *Journal of Studies on Alcohol, 63* (3), 280–285.

Cox, W.M., Yeates, G.N., Gilligan, P.A.T., & Hosier, S.G. (2001). Individual differences. In N. Heather, T.J. Peters, & T.R. Stockwell (Eds.), *Handbook of alcohol dependence and International problems* (357–374). New York: John Wiley & Sons.

Cronin, C. (1997). Reasons for drinking versus outcome expectancies in the prediction of college student drinking. *Substance Use and Misuse, 32* (10), 1287–1311.

Cunningham, J.A., Sobell, L.C., Gavin, D.R., Sobell, M.B., & Breslin, F.C. (1997). Assessing motivation for change: Preliminary development and evaluation of a scale measuring the costs and benefits of changing alcohol or drug use. *Psychology of Addictive Behaviors, 11* (2), 107–114.

Curtain, J.J., Patrick, C.J., Lang, A.R., Cacioppo, J.T., & Birbaumer, N. (2001). Alcohol affects emotion through cognition. *Psychological Science, 12*, 527–531.

Damasio, A.R. (1994). *Descartes' error: Emotion, reason, and the human brain*. New York: Avon.

Dimeff, L.A., & Marlatt, G.A. (1998). Preventing relapse and maintaining change in addictive behaviors. *Clinical Psychology: Science and Practice, 5* (4), 513–525.

Donovan, J.E., Costa, F.M., & Jessor, R. (1994). *Beyond adolescence: Problem behavior and young adult development*. Cambridge: Cambridge University Press.

Drobes, D.J., Saladin, M.E., & Tiffany, S.T. (2001). Classical conditioning mechanisms in alcohol dependence. In N. Heather, T.J. Peters, & T. Stockwell (Eds.), *International handbook of alcohol dependence and problems* (pp. 281–297). New York: John Wiley & Sons.

Drummond, D.C., Tiffany, S.T., Glautier, S., & Remington, B. (1995). *Addictive behaviour: Cue exposure theory and practice*. Chichester, UK: John Wiley & Sons.

Dunn, M.E., Lau, H.C., & Cruz, I.Y. (2000). Changes in activation of alcohol expectancies in memory in relation to changes in alcohol use after participation in an expectancy challenge program. *Experimental and Clinical Psychopharmacology, 8* (4), 566–575.

Epps, J., Monk, C., Savage, S., & Marlatt, G.A. (1998). Improving credibility of instructions in the balanced placebo design: A misattribution manipulation. *Addictive Behaviors, 23* (4), 427–435.

Feldtkeller, B., Weinstein, A., Cox, W.M., & Nutt, D. (2001). Effects of contextual priming on reactions to craving and withdrawal stimuli in alcohol-dependent participants. *Experimental and Clinical Psychopharmacology, 9*, 343–351.

Finn, P.R., Sharkansky, E.J., Brandt, K.M., & Turcotte, N. (2000). The effects of familial risk, personality, and expectancies on alcohol use and abuse. *Journal of Abnormal Psychology, 109* (1), 122–133.

Flaherty, Charles F. (1996). *Incentive relativity*. Cambridge: Cambridge University Press.

Fromme, K., & D'Amico, E.J. (1999). Neurobiological bases of alcohol's psychological effects. In K.E. Leonard & H.T. Blane (Eds.), *Psychological theories of drinking and alcoholism* (2nd edn.; pp. 422–455). New York: Guilford.

Gerra, G., Avanzini, P., Zaimovic, A., Sartori, R., Bocchi, C., Timpano, M., Zambelli, U., Delsignore, R., Gardini, F., Talarico, E., & Brambilla, F. (1999). Neurotransmitters: Neuroendocrine correlates of sensation-seeking temperament in normal humans. *Neuropsychobiology, 39* (4), 207–213.

Gilbert, D.T., & Ebert, J.E.J. (2002). Decisions and revisions: The affective forecasting of changeable outcomes. *Journal of Personality and Social Psychology, 82*, 503–514.

Gilbert, D.T., Gill, M.J., & Wilson, T.D. (2002). The future is now: Temporal correction in affective forecasting. *Organizational Behavior and Human Decision Processes, 88*, 430–444.

Gilbert, D.T., Pinel, E.C., Wilson, T.D., Blumberg, S.J., & Wheatley, T.P. (1998). Immune neglect: A source of durability bias in affective forecasting. *Journal of Personality and Social Psychology, 75*, 617–638.

Goldman, M.S. (1999). Risk for substance abuse: Memory as a common etiological pathway. *Psychological Science, 10* (3), 196–198.

Goldman, M.S., Del Boca, F.K., & Darkes, J. (1999). Alcohol expectancy theory: The application of cognitive neuroscience. In K.E. Leonard & H.T. Blane (Eds.), *Psychological theories of drinking and alcoholism* (2nd edn.; pp. 203–246). New York; Guilford.

Greeley, J., & Oei, T. (1999). *Alcohol and tension reduction.* In K.E. Leonard & H.T. Blane (Eds.), *Psychological theories of drinking and alcoholism* (2nd edn.; pp. 14–53). New York: Guilford.

Heath, D.B. (2000). *Drinking occasions: Comparative perspectives on alcohol and culture.* Philadelphia: Brunner/Mazel.

Heather, N. (2001). Editor's introduction. In N. Heather, T.J. Peters, & T. Stockwell (Eds.), *International handbook of alcohol dependence and problems* (pp. 252–255). New York: John Wiley & Sons.

Hunt, W., Barnett, L., & Branch, L. (1971). Relapse rates in addiction programs. *Journal of Clinical Psychology, 27,* 455–456.

Hussong, A.M., Hicks, R.E., Levy, S.A., & Curran, P.J. (2001). Specifying the relations between affect and heavy alcohol use among young adults. *Journal of Abnormal Psychology, 110,* 449–461.

Iguchi, M.Y., Belding, M.A., Morral, A.R., Lamb, R.J., & Husband, S.D. (1997). Reinforcing operants other than abstinence in drug abuse treatment: An effective alternative for reducing drug use. *Journal of Consulting and Clinical Psychology, 65* (3), 421–428.

Jones, B.T., & McMahon, J. (1998). Alcohol motivations as outcome expectancies. In W.R. Miller & N. Heather (Eds.), *Treating addictive behaviors* (2nd edn.; pp. 75–92). New York: Plenum.

Kalodner, C.R., Delucia, J.L., & Ursprung, A.W. (1989). An examination of the tension reduction hypothesis: The relationship between anxiety and alcohol in college students. *Addictive Behaviors, 14* (6), 649–654.

Klinger, E. (1977). *Meaning and void: Inner experience and the incentives in people's lives.* Minneapolis: University of Minnesota Press.

Klinger, E. (1996). Emotional influences on cognitive processing, with implications for theories of both. In P. Gollwitzer & J.A. Bargh (Eds.), *The psychology of action: Linking cognition and motivation to behavior* (pp. 168–189). New York: Guilford.

Langenbucher, J., & Nathan, P.E. (1990). The tension reduction hypothesis: A reanalysis of some crucial early data. In W.M. Cox (Ed.), *Why people drink: Parameters of alcohol as a reinforcer* (pp. 131–168). New York: Gardner Press.

MacAndrew, C., & Edgerton, R.B. (1969). *Drunken comportment: A social explanation.* Chicago: Aldine.

MacDonald, T.K., Fong, G.T., Zanna, M.P., & Martineau, A.M. (2000). Alcohol myopia and condom use: Can alcohol intoxication be associated with more prudent behavior? *Journal of Personality and Social Psychology, 78,* 605–619.

Man, F., Stuchlíková, I., & Klinger, E. (1998). Motivational structure of alcoholic and nonalcoholic Czech men. *Psychological Reports, 82,* 1091–1106.

Mantere, T., Tupala, E., Hall, H., Särkioja, T., Räsänen, P., Bergström, K., Callaway, J., & Tiihonen, J. (2002). Serotonin transporter distribution and density in the cerebral cortex of alcoholic and nonalcoholic comparison subjects: A whole-hemisphere autoradiography study. *American Journal of Psychiatry, 159,* 599–606.

Marlatt, G.A. (1985). Cognitive assessment and intervention procedures for relapse prevention. In G.A. Marlatt & J.R. Gordon (Eds.), *Relapse prevention: Maintenance strategies in the treatment of addictive behaviors* (pp. 128–200). New York: Guilford.

McCarty, D. (1985). Environmental factors in substance abuse: The microsetting. In M. Galizio & S.A. Maisto (Eds.), *Determinants of substance abuse: Biological, psychological, and environmental factors* (pp. 247–281). New York: Plenum.

McCusker, C.G. (2001). Cognitive biases and addiction: An evolution in theory and method. *Addiction, 96* (1), 47–56.

McGue, M. (1999). Behavioral genetic models of alcoholism and drinking. In K.E. Leonard & H.T. Blane (Eds.), *Psychological theories of drinking and alcoholism* (2nd edn.; pp. 372–421). New York: Guilford.

Monti, P.M., Rohsenow, D.J., & Hutchison, K.E. (2000). Toward bridging the gap between biological, psychological and psychosocial models of alcohol craving. *Addiction, 95* (8), 229–237.

Moos, R.H., Finney, J.W., & Cronkite, R.C. (1990). *Alcoholism treatment: Context, process, and outcome.* New York: Oxford University Press.

Morey, L.C., & Skinner, H.A. (1986). Empirically derived classifications of alcohol-related problems. In M. Galanter (Ed.), *Recent developments in alcoholism* (pp. 145–168). New York: Plenum.

Nathan, P.E. (1988). The addictive personality is the behavior of the addict. *Journal of Consulting and Clinical Psychology, 56* (2), 183–188.

Nathan, P.E. (1990). Integration of biological and psychosocial research on alcoholism. *Alcoholism: Clinical and Experimental Research, 4* (3), 368–374.

Newcomb, M.D., & Harlow, L.L. (1986). Life events and substance use among adolescents: Mediating effects of perceived loss of control and meaninglessness in life. *Journal of Personality and Social Psychology, 51*, 564–577.

Pacula, R.L., & Chaloupka, F.J. (2001). The effects of macro-level interventions on addictive behavior. *Substance Use and Misuse, 36* (13), 1901–1922.

Parks, G.A., Marlatt, G.A., & Anderson, B.K. (2001). Cognitive-behavioural alcohol treatment. In N. Heather, T.J. Peters, & T. Stockwell (Eds.), *International handbook of alcohol dependence and problems* (pp. 557–573). New York: John Wiley & Sons.

Partanen, J., & Simpura, J. (2001). International trends in alcohol production and consumption. In N. Heather, T.J. Peters, & T. Stockwell (Eds.), *International handbook of alcohol dependence and problems* (pp. 379–394). Chichester, UK: John Wiley & Sons.

Perri, M.G. (1985). Self-change strategies for the control of smoking, obesity, and problem drinking. In S. Shiffman & T.A. Wills (Eds.), *Coping and substance use* (pp. 295–317). Orlando, FL: Academic Press.

Petraitis, J., Flay, B.R., & Miller, T.Q. (1995). Reviewing theories of adolescent substance use: Organizing pieces in the puzzle. *Psychological Bulletin, 117* (1), 67–86.

Roberts, A.J., & Koob, G.F. (1997). The neurobiology of addiction: An overview. *Alcohol Health and Research World, 21* (2), 101–106.

Robinson, T.E., & Berridge, K.C. (1993). The neural basis of drug craving: An incentive-sensitization theory of addiction. *Brain Research Reviews, 18* (3), 247–291.

Robinson, T.E., & Berridge, K.C. (2000). The psychology and neurobiology of addiction: An incentive-sensitization view. *Addiction, 95* (Supplement 2), S91–S117.

Robinson, T.E., & Berridge, K.C. (2001). Incentive-sensitization and addiction. *Addiction, 96* (1), 103–114.

Rohsenow, D.J., & Marlatt, G.A. (1981). The balanced placebo design: Methodological considerations. *Addictive Behaviors, 6* (2), 107–122.

Rubonis, A.V., Colby, S.M., Monti, P.M., Rohsenow, D.J., Gulliver, S.B., & Sirota, A.D. (1994). Alcohol cue reactivity and mood induction in male and female alcoholics. *Journal of Studies on Alcohol, 55* (4), 487–494.

Shapiro, A.P., & Nathan, P.E. (1986). Human tolerance to alcohol: The role of Pavlovian conditioning processes. *Psychopharmacology, 88* (1), 90–95.

Sher, K.J. (1987). Stress response dampening. In H.T. Blane & K.E. Leonard (Eds.), *Psychological theories of drinking and alcoholism* (pp. 227–271). New York: Guilford.

Sher, K.J., Bylund, D.B., Walitzer, K.S., Hartmann, J., & Ray-Prenger, C. (1994). Platelet monoamine oxidase (MAO) activity: Personality, substance use, and the stress-response-dampening effect of alcohol. *Experimental and Clinical Psychopharmacology, 21* (1), 53–81.

Sher, K.J., & Levenson, R.W. (1982). Risk for alcoholism and individual differences in the stress-response-dampening effect of alcohol. *Journal of Abnormal Psychology, 91* (5), 350–367.

Sher, K.J., & Trull, T.J. (1994). Personality and disinhibitory psychopathology: Alcoholism and antisocial personality disorder. *Journal of Abnormal Psychology, 103* (1), 92–102.

Sher, K.J., Trull, T.J., Bartholow, B.D., & Vieth, A. (1999). Personality and alcoholism: Issues, methods, and etiological processes. In K.E. Leonard & H.T. Blane (Eds.), *Psychological theories of drinking and alcoholism* (2nd edn.; pp. 54–105). New York: Guilford.

Stacy, A.W. (1997). Memory activation and expectancy as prospective predictors of alcohol and marijuana use. *Journal of Abnormal Psychology, 106* (1), 61–73.

Tarter, R.E., Moss, H.B., & Vanyukov, M. (1995). Behavior genetics and the etiology of alcoholism. In H. Begleiter & B. Kissin (Eds.), *Alcohol and alcoholism (Vol. 1): Genetic factors and alcoholism* (pp. 294–326). New York: Oxford University Press.

Tiffany, S.T. (1990). A cognitive model of drug urges and drug-use behavior: Role of automatic and nonautomatic processes. *Psychological Review, 97,* 147–168.

Tiffany, S.T. (1995). The role of cognitive factors in reactivity to drug cues. In D.C. Drummond (Ed.), *Addictive behavior: Cue exposure theory and practice* (pp. 137–165). Chichester, UK: John Wiley & Sons.

Tiffany, S.T., & Conklin, C.A. (2000). A cognitive processing model of alcohol craving and compulsive alcohol use. *Addiction, 95* (Supplement 2), S145–S153.

Tucker, J.A., Vuchinich, R.E., & Pukish, M.M. (1995). Molar environmental contexts surrounding recovery from alcohol problems by treated and untreated problem drinkers. *Experimental and Clinical Psychopharmacology, 3* (2), 195–204.

Tucker, J.A., Vuchinich, R.E., & Rippens, P.D. (2002a). Environmental contexts surrounding resolution of drinking problems among problem drinkers with different help-seeking experiences. *Journal of Studies on Alcohol, 63* (3), 334–341.

Tucker, J.A., Vuchinich, R.E., & Rippens, P.D. (2002b). Predicting natural resolution of alcohol-related problems: A prospective behavioral economic analysis. *Experimental and Clinical Psychopharmacology, 10* (3), 248–257.

Vik, P.W., Carrello, P.D., & Nathan, P.E. (1999). Hypothesized simple factor structure for the Alcohol Expectancy Questionnaire: Confirmatory factor analysis. *Experimental and Clinical Psychopharmacology, 7* (3), 294–303.

Vuchinich, R.E., & Tucker, J.A. (1988). Contributions from behavioral theories of choice to an analysis of alcohol abuse. *Journal of Abnormal Psychology, 97* (2), 181–195.

Vuchinich, R.E., & Tucker, J.A. (1996). Alcoholic relapse, life events, and behavioral theories of choice: A prospective analysis. *Experimental and Clinical Psychopharmacology, 4* (1), 19–28.

Vuchinich, R.E., & Tucker, J.A. (1998). Choice, behavioral economics, and addictive behavior patterns. In W.R. Miller & N. Heather (Eds.), *Treating addictive behaviors* (2nd edn.; pp. 93–104). New York: Plenum.

Wiers, R.W., Van Woerden, N., Smulders, F.T.Y., & de Jong, P.J. (2002). Implicit and explicit alcohol-related cognitions in heavy and light drinkers. *Journal of Abnormal Psychology, 111,* 648–658.

Wilson, T.D., Meyers, J., & Gilbert, D.T. (2001). Lessons from the past: Do people learn from experience that emotional reactions are short-lived? *Personality and Social Psychology Bulletin, 27,* 1648–1661.

Wilson, T.D., Wheatley, T., Meyers, J.M., Gilbert, D.T., & Axsom, D. (2000). Focalism: A source of durability bias in affective forecasting. *Journal of Personality and Social Psychology, 78,* 821–836.

Zucker, R.A. (1986). The four alcoholisms: A developmental account of the etiologic process. In P.C. Rivers (Ed.), *Alcohol and addictive behavior: Nebraska Symposium on Motivation* (pp. 27–83). Lincoln: University of Nebraska Press.

PART II

Assessment and Relationships to Behavior

Measuring Motivation: The Motivational Structure Questionnaire and Personal Concerns Inventory

W. Miles Cox

University of Wales, Bangor, UK

and

Eric Klinger

University of Minnesota, Morris, USA

Synopsis.—This chapter introduces and describes two idiothetic instruments for assessing individuals' motivational structure: the Motivational Structure Questionnaire (MSQ) and Personal Concerns Inventory (PCI). They are idiothetic in the sense that respondents begin by providing idiographic lists of their current goals, which they then rate using nomothetic rating scales. These ratings can be processed to provide indices and profiles that characterize the individual's motivational structure.

There is, to be sure, a history of motivational assessment using other means, especially thematic apperceptive methods and psychometric questionnaires. In their present state of development, however, these lack the combination of having both specificity and comprehensiveness in describing an individual's motivational structure. The MSQ and PCI provide these properties.

This chapter is purely descriptive. Subsequent chapters provide evidence regarding the reliability, factor structure, and validity of the information provided by the MSQ and PCI, as well as their application in motivational counseling.

Deciding how to measure something assumes a certain definition of the construct being measured. In the field of psychology, motivation has been viewed in different ways by different writers. In this book, the basic concepts and definitions related to motivation are detailed in Chapter 1. To summarize, the definition of motivation used here, a fusion of those offered by Ferguson (1994) and Chaplin (1968), is "the internal states of the organism that lead to the instigation, persistence, energy, and direction of behavior towards a goal." An individual's array of goals and ways of relating to them is denoted here as *motivational structure.*

Handbook of Motivational Counseling. Edited by W. Miles Cox and Eric Klinger.
© 2004 John Wiley & Sons, Ltd.

MOTIVATIONAL MEASUREMENT IN HISTORICAL PERSPECTIVE

There have been numerous approaches to measuring motivation, but the two main approaches have entailed the Thematic Apperception Test (TAT; Morgan & Murray, 1935) or variations on it (e.g., Atkinson, 1958; Heckhausen, 1967), and measures devised in the tradition of the psychometric questionnaire. The TAT measures were designed to assess certain of the needs (also called motives) described by Murray (1938), especially the needs for achievement, affiliation, and power. Although many psychometric questionnaires have contained motivationally related scales (e.g., Achievement via Independence and Sociability scales of the California Psychological Inventory [Gough, 1956]), the true–false Personality Research Form (PRF; Jackson, 1964) and the forced-choice Edwards Personal Preference Schedule (Edwards, 1954) were specifically designed to measure a wide range of Murray's (1938) needs. The Action Control Scale (Kuhl, 1994) and the Volitional Components Inventory (Fuhrmann & Kuhl, 1998) measure volitional attributes of individuals—how they behave in the face of obstacles or difficulty in pursuing their goals. However, the latter two instruments do not assess what these goals might be. There have also been efforts to meld the TAT and psychometric approaches by using picture stimuli and asking respondents to choose from among a set of predetermined responses (e.g., Schmalt, 1977).

There may be gifted TAT practitioners who can divine valid information from intuitive analyses of TAT stories, but this appears not to be the general case. When TAT predictions are made through intuitive (so-called *clinical*) inference, the evidence indicates questionable validity (e.g., Keiser & Prather, 1990), whereas scores based on rigorous TAT scoring systems attain reasonable levels of validity (e.g., Avila-Espada, 2000; Garb et al., 2002; Holt, 1999; McAdams & Zeldow, 1993). Many such scoring systems have been developed, but those available for motivational assessment are aimed at relatively broad classes of psychological needs.

Although both formally scored TAT stories and psychometric measures of needs have compiled defensible records for validity (e.g., Schmalt & Sokolowski, 2000; Spangler, 1992; Tuerlinckx, De Boeck, & Lens, 2002), cognate scales from the two approaches (e.g., TAT need for achievement and PRF achievement) have been found to be virtually uncorrelated. Subsequent evidence (McClelland, Koestner, & Weinberger, 1989) suggested that the two kinds of assessment actually tap two different kinds of motives. TAT-like methods assess *implicit* motives and predict *operant* behaviors (which are emitted [initiated] without obvious elicitation by situations), whereas psychometric methods assess *self-attributed* motives and predict so-called *respondent* behaviors, which people perform upon situational elicitation.

Despite the validity of the scores obtained by these methods, they pose a number of difficulties in applied settings. First, the needs or motives that they assess represent broad dispositions that make it difficult to predict specific behaviors. For example, the achievement motive could be manifested in a large variety of specific goals—athletic, academic, entrepreneurial, etc.—that may vary sharply among different individuals who have the same scores. TAT stories are laborious to score and scoring them reliably requires training. Although it is theoretically possible to derive more specific information about individual motivational structure from TAT stories and psychometric methods, and there are many special-purpose scales available, we are unaware of a general assessment tool that provides both specific and reasonably comprehensive information about individual motivational structure and also permits ready quantitative analysis and comparison.

At present, therefore, both TAT-based and psychometric measures of motivation provide limited information regarding the ways in which respondents relate to their goals. Such scores also typically represent relatively enduring dispositions and hence are poorly designed to predict day-to-day or even month-to-month changes in behavior. They are therefore of limited utility in making concrete predictions about individual decision-making and in working with individuals in counseling or clinical contexts.

One response to these difficulties has been the development of *idiothetic* methods (to use the term coined by Lamiell, 1981) for assessing motivational structure. These methods ask respondents first to list specific attributes, such as their current goals, thus yielding highly individualized (*idio*graphic) data. Then they ask respondents to apply standard rating scales to the things they have just listed, thus providing quantitiative, descriptive (nomo*thetic*) data. These ratings permit comparisons among an individual's goals, and they can be averaged within individual respondents and the averages (or proportions) compared across individuals. This is the strategy followed by the Motivational Structure Questionnaire (MSQ) and Personal Concerns Inventory (PCI), which are described further in subsequent sections of this chapter. It is also the strategy developed for assessing personal projects (Little & Chambers, Chapter 4, this volume) and personal strivings (an individual's typical goals; Emmons, 1986). Because of the specificity that these methods provide regarding an individual's current goals or strivings, at the same time that they permit the development of summary indices for individuals' motivational structures, they lend themselves well to application in counseling and therapeutic contexts.

THE MSQ

Current Format

The MSQ (Klinger, Cox, & Blount, in press) is shown in Appendix 8.1, to which reference is made in the following discussion. It has three parts: the Test Booklet, a list of Action Words, and Answer Sheets. The Test Booklet introduces respondents to the MSQ by telling them its purpose and structure. Subsequently, instructions for completing each of 12 steps are given one at a time, prior to the completion of each step.

The purpose of the MSQ is to identify respondents' most important current concerns and the manner in which they strive to reach goals to resolve their concerns. As discussed in Chapter 1, a *current concern* is a person's motivational state between the point in time of commitment to a goal pursuit and the point when either the goal is reached or its pursuit relinquished. It is a technical motivational construct that is presumed to correspond to underlying brain processes. Therefore, in developing a questionnaire for assessing current concerns, one task was to convey to respondents in a nontechnical way what the concept means, and in a way that enables them to access their most important concerns. The General Instructions in the Test Booklet do this by explaining that the purpose of the questionnaire is to find out about the things that concern the respondent—his or her goals, interests, activities, and problems—and then it gives some additional elaboration of the concept. Because people often understand *concerns* to mean problems, the instructions emphasize that the questionnaire is asking about *both* the things that respondents consider to be problems *and* the things that bring them joy and happiness, i.e., goals in general for which they are striving.

The Idiographic Part

The idiographic part of the assessment begins by asking respondents to read the list of areas of life on the Example Answer Sheet (see the MSQ in Appendix 8.1) about which they might have concerns. The list was compiled on the basis of areas in which prior respondents most frequently named concerns. The use of the list structures the exercise for respondents and helps them to remember important concerns that they may otherwise forget to name.

Next are the instructions for Step 1, which asks respondents to describe briefly in their own words each of their important concerns in each of the areas, although it is stressed that an individual respondent may have no concerns in certain areas. Next, in Step 2, respondents are asked to read the *action words* (verbs) in the list of Action Words (see the MSQ in Appendix 8.1) and then, one concern at a time, choose the word that best describes the action they would like to take to resolve each concern. Just after each word is chosen, it is used to write a short sentence describing what the person wants to do to resolve that concern (i.e., the goal that he or she wants to reach). Having respondents formulate their goals by using the action-word categories allows one to classify the valence of each goal (e.g., whether it is positive or negative). This is important, because the descriptions of concerns alone do not allow the valence of each goal-striving to be unambiguously classified. For example, in the area of Health and Medical Matters, someone may express a concern about being overweight. The additional information that the person wants to *get rid of my weight problem* indicates that the goal-striving is *aversive* (the person wants to be rid of a negative incentive). If, on the other hand, the person had written, *I want to get a more healthy body*, the goal-striving would be *appetitive* (aimed at a positive incentive). The motivation for resolving the same concern would be qualitatively different in the two cases.

After finishing Steps 1 and 2, respondents will have described all of their important concerns and named their goal for resolving each of them. These two steps comprise the idiographic portion of the assessment.

The Nomothetic Part

Steps 3 to 12 form the basis for the nomothetic assessment. These steps comprise ten different rating scales, on each of which respondents rate each of the goals they named in Step 2. The numerical ratings allow a variety of motivational indices to be calculated, which make it possible to compare the motivational patterns of different individuals with each other and with normative samples.

Role and Commitment

The first two scales are Role and Commitment. On the Role scale (Step 3), respondents choose one of six options to indicate how actively they are participating (if at all) in the goal-striving, ranging from "take part, and know what action to take" to "neither take part nor watch, but this is a concern of mine because another person who is important to me is involved." The Commitment scale (Step 4) asks respondents how committed they feel to attaining each goal (or the amount of effort they are willing to expend). There are six choices, ranging from "I do not intend to make the thing happen" to "I fully intend to if I possibly can." Dimensions of the goal-strivings that subsequent steps assess (e.g., the value and expectancy scales) are determinants of the level of commitment. Placing the commitment scale early in the questionnaire allows global estimates to be provided, without respondents' having first seen the components that are likely to affect commitment.

Value and Expectancy

The value of incentives has been measured in different ways by different motivational theorists. Behavioral psychologists, for instance, have physically measured the quality (e.g., degree of sweetness; level of praise) or quantity (e.g., number of food pellets; amount of money) of the incentive. Another option is to ask people to globally assess the value they place on the incentive. In our view of motivation, the measure of value most closely linked to a person's level of motivation is the *affect* that the person anticipates experiencing if the incentive were acquired (or if the person failed to acquire it). In turn, anticipated affect has three components, each of which is assessed by separate MSQ value scales.

In Step 5, respondents are asked to imagine the *joy* (i.e., positive affect) that they would feel if they succeeded in reaching each of the goals that they named in Step 2. For each one, they then choose from the rating scale a number that best matches their anticipated joy. The nine-point scale ranges from "no joy at all" to "the most joy I can imagine feeling about anything."

Even though reaching desired goals enhances positive feelings, it might also simultaneously cause people to feel unhappy (i.e., increase their negative affect). For example, the usual great joy at graduating from college is often tinged with sadness at leaving behind good friends and, for many, an enjoyable lifestyle. Thus, in Step 6, individuals taking the MSQ are asked to rate the *unhappiness* (i.e., negative affect) that they imagine feeling if they *succeeded* in reaching each goal. Like the Joy scale, the Unhappiness one has nine points ranging from "no unhappiness at all" to "the most unhappiness I can imagine feeling about anything." The Joy and Unhappiness scales are used together to assess the ambivalence that respondents feel about particular goal-strivings. Feelings of ambivalence are important to know about, because they affect both individuals' subjective well-being and the likelihood that they will take action to resolve the things about which they are concerned. For people completing the MSQ, it is often helpful to clarify the reason for having both the Joy and Unhappiness scales by providing an example of a concern about whose resolution the person feels conflicted, expecting both strong joy and strong unhappiness if the goal were reached. Such an example is given in the instructions for Step 6 in the Test Booklet.

The third scale assessing value is the Sorrow scale (Step 7). Whereas some people are motivated by excitement about anticipated goal achievements (i.e., joy), other people are motivated by avoiding disappointment from not reaching their goals (or a fear of failure). The Sorrow scale evaluates this aspect of motivation by asking respondents to rate the degree of sorrow that they expect to feel if they were *unsuccessful* in resolving their concerns in the way that they want to. Like the first two value scales, the Sorrow scale has nine scale points.

There are two expectancy scales. Using the first scale, Chances of Success (Step 8), respondents judge their expected overall likelihood of succeeding with each goal. The judgments are made on a ten-point scale on which the probability of success is expressed in increments of 10% each—from "almost no chance—a 0–9% chance" to "almost certain— at least 90% sure." Sometimes people might expect that things will turn out the way they want, even if they do nothing to make them happen (Heckhausen, 1977). Thus, the second expectancy scale asks about respondents' expectations of succeeding if they take no action. The answers are scaled in the same manner as on the Chances of Success scale.

Temporal Dimensions

There are two dimensions related to the time course of goal-strivings that affect motivational patterns. One is the time pressure before the person must do something about reaching the goal. On the MSQ, this dimension is assessed in Step 10, Time Available. Respondents are asked to indicate how soon they must start taking action if they are to succeed with each of the goals they named in Step 2. The second dimension is distance in time before the goal achievement will occur. It is assessed with the Goal Distance scale in Step 11. In both Steps 10 and 11, the person specifies a timeframe that he or she has in mind, expressing it in terms of the number of days, months, or years.

Alcohol and Drug-Use Instrumentality

Much of our work with the MSQ has been related to alcohol and other drug abuse. Accordingly, the final scale of the MSQ asks respondents to judge the effects that drinking or other drug use would have on their succeeding with each of the actions they named in Step 2. This scale is completed in Step 12, Effect of Drinking and Other Drug Use on Successful Action. The points on the scale range from "+5: *Virtually assure* my chances of success" to "0: *Have no effect on* my chances of success" to "−5: *Entirely prevent* my chances of success." People who abuse alcohol or other drugs may, of course, correctly perceive that their use helps them to achieve some goal, although it is likely to be a short-term and maladaptive solution. For example, the use might help to facilitate the person's interactions with drinking companions, or it might help him or her cope with feelings of despondency. Such information is helpful to know when the aim is to get the person to adopt healthier, more adaptive motivational patterns for reaching goals. More often, abusers of alcohol or drugs readily acknowledge the harmful effects that their use has on the important concerns in their lives that they are trying to resolve, but they have not managed to find more adaptive ways to cope. Again, the details about the interplay between the effects of using and acquiring the other incentives that the person would like to have are important for helping the person to change. In work with individuals other than those with substance-use disorders, MSQ Step 12 could be simply omitted or replaced by another scale specific to the other kind of problem.

Options for Administration

When used clinically, the most common way for respondents to complete the MSQ is alone in their spare time. The purpose of the MSQ is explained to them, and they are then given the Test Booklet, Action Words, and Answer Sheet to complete. Most respondents readily understand what is intended, and they seem to enjoy performing the exercise. However, in some situations the client's counselor prefers to complete the MSQ along with the client,

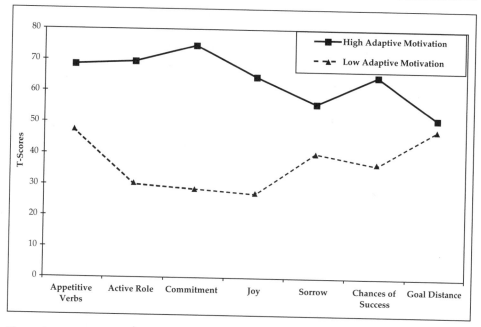

Figure 8.1   Two contrasting MSQ profiles

much like a structured interview. The advantage of doing this is that the counselor is immediately aware of the client's concerns and the thought processes that go into rating them, eliminating the necessity for the client to reconstruct this information later. On the other hand, it opens the door to the counselor's preconceptions influencing the respondent's responses. In some situations, a group of participants or patients complete the MSQ together, with a test administrator present to guide respondents through the steps. This procedure is used, for instance, in treatment units that have a large number of newly admitted patients each week who can efficiently complete the assessment in a group setting.

MSQ Indices and Profiles

After respondents complete the MSQ assessment, a motivational profile is plotted for each of them on the basis of computer-generated motivational indices that correspond to each of the nomothetic rating scales. The indices are either the ratings averaged for each scale across all of the life areas, or the ratings averaged for each life area separately, depending on the required depth of analysis. In the latter case, there would be a profile for each of the areas in which the person named any concern(s). Examples of the two contrasting MSQ profiles are shown in Figure 8.1. The profile of one person reflects an adaptive motivational structure. This person is actively pursuing goals, feels strongly committed to them, expects to feel strong happiness if the goals are attained and strong sorrow if they are not, and believes that the goals are attainable. The other profile reflects a pattern of indifference, a maladaptive motivational structure. This person does not feel strongly committed to goals, is not actively involved in pursuing them, and does not expect strong emotional benefits if the goals are achieved. Although both people report having experienced drinking problems in the past, the person with the adaptive motivational structure managed to stop drinking, whereas the person with the maladaptive motivational structure continues to drink. Thus, it would appear that a person with an adaptive motivational structure can better control an alcohol-related problem than a person with a maladaptive pattern.

More elaborate indices can also be calculated. For example, a respondent's "Ambivalence" index takes into account both the Happiness and Unhappiness ratings for each concern. The index is calculated in such a way that as the difference between these two ratings decreases, the Ambivalence index increases.

The Inappropriate Commitment index is calculated as the difference between a respondent's stated commitment to goal pursuits and the level of commitment that would be predicted from the product of his or her expected chances of succeeding times anticipated happiness if successful. High scores on this index reflect stronger commitments than would be expected from this product and, hence, the person's readiness to commit to pursuing goals. A high score represents a low threshold for commitment.

The Composite Emotional Intensity index is the average sum of the respondent's Joy, Unhappiness and Sorrow ratings for each concern averaged across all of the concerns.

THE PCI

The PCI (Cox & Klinger, 2000; see Appendix 8.1) is a modified and abridged version of the MSQ, written to be as simple and as user-friendly as possible. Like the MSQ, the PCI has three parts: Test Booklet, Rating Scales, and Answer Sheets. Respondents are introduced to the PCI in the same way as to the MSQ, but with less elaboration. Then they are given the instructions for completing each of the three steps to: (a) describe their concerns in different areas of life, (b) describe what they would like to do in order to resolve each concern, and (c) rate each goal along ten different dimensions. Like the instructions, the list of areas of life (shown in the Test Booklet) has been condensed from the list used with the MSQ.

The PCI ratings scales differ in several ways from those on the MSQ. First, each was changed to a 0-to-10 scale, to provide consistency across the scales and because 0-to-10 scales are intuitively meaningful. Second, only the original scales judged to be most useful in working with people clinically were retained: *Commitment, Happiness, Unhappiness, Chances of Success*, and *Goal Distance*. Others were omitted: *Sorrow if Unsuccessful, Chances of Success if No Action*, and *Time Available to Take Action*. One new scale was added: *Importance* of resolving the concern. Finally, two scales were transformed. The original *Role* scale was dropped as such and replaced with *Control* and *Know What to Do* scales. The bipolar *Alcohol and Other Drug Effects* scale was replaced by separate *Alcohol and Drugs Help* and *Alcohol and Drugs Hinder* scales. PCI indices are calculated, and motivational profiles based on them are produced in the same way as for the MSQ. Two contrasting PCI profiles are shown in Figure 8.2.

Computer-Administered PCI

Using the computer-administered version of the PCI, respondents interact with a computer as they describe their concerns and goals, typing them into the computer and rating each goal using the ten PCI rating scales. The computer produces a summary of all of the

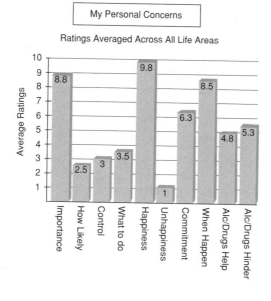

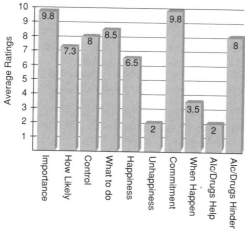

Figure 8.2 Two contrasting profiles from the computerized PCI

person's concerns and goals, corresponding motivational profiles, which can be viewed on the screen, printed, or both. When the PCI is used in clinical settings, there are additional options to use, such as forms for a PCI-based treatment plan and progress reports related to it.

As with the MSQ, an index is plotted for each of the rating scales in an individual's basic profile. The indices are either the ratings averaged for each scale across all of the life areas, or they are averaged for each life area separately, depending on the depth of analysis that is needed. In the latter case, there would be a profile for each of the areas in which the person named any concerns.

CONCLUSION

The MSQ and PCI provide clinically useful information about a client's motivational structure. They detail the clients' nontrivial goals and permit the easy calculation of scores and score profiles. This chapter has described these instruments and their advantages over existing TAT and psychometric measures of motivation. Chapter 9 presents evidence for their reliability, factor structure, and validity, and Baumann extends the evidence for construct validity in Chapter 10. Chapters 11 to 16 then describe treatment methods, especially Systematic Motivational Counseling, that have been built on the foundation provided by the MSQ and PCI.

REFERENCES

Atkinson, J.W. (1958). *Motives in fantasy, action and society : A method of assessment and study.* Oxford, UK: Van Nostrand.

Avila-Espada, A. (2000). Objective scoring for the TAT. In R.H. Dana (Ed.), *Handbook of cross-cultural and multicultural personality assessment* (pp. 465–480). Mahwah, NJ: Erlbaum.

Chaplin, J.P. (1968). *Dictionary of psychology.* New York: Dell.

Cox, W.M., & Klinger, E. (2000). *Personal Concerns Inventory.* Unpublished manuscript. University of Wales, Bagnor.

Edwards, A.L. (1954). *Edwards personal preference schedule.* New York: Psychological Corporation.

Emmons, R.A. (1986). Personal strivings: An approach to personality and subjective well-being. *Journal of Personality and Social Psychology, 51,* 1058–1068.

Ferguson, E. (1994). Motivation. In R.J. Corsini (Ed.), *Encyclopedia of psychology* (Vol. 2; 2nd edn.; p. 429). New York: John Wiley & Sons.

Fuhrmann, A., & Kuhl, J. (1998). Decomposing self-regulation and self-control: The Volitional Components Inventory. In J. Heckhausen & C. Dweck (Eds.), *Lifespan perspectives on motivation and control.* Hillsdale, NJ: Erlbaum.

Garb, H.N., Wood, J.M., Lilienfeld, S.O., & Nezworski, M.T. (2002). Effective use of projective techniques in clinical practice: Let the data help with selection and interpretation. *Professional Psychology: Research and Practice, 33,* 454–463.

Gough, H.G. (1956). *California Psychological Inventory.* Palo Alto, CA: Consulting Psychologists Press.

Heckhausen, H. (1967). *The anatomy of achievement motivation.* New York: Academic Press.

Heckhausen, H. (1977). Achievement motivation and its constructs: A cognitive model. *Motivation and Emotion, 1,* 283–329.

Holt, R.R. (1999). Empiricism and the Thematic Apperception Test: Validity is the payoff. In L. Gieser & M.I. Stein (Eds.), *Evocative images: The Thematic Apperception Test and the art of projection* (pp. 99–105). Washington, DC: American Psychological Association.

Jackson, D.N. (1964). *The Personality Research Form.* London, Ontario: Research Psychologists Press.

Keiser, R.E., & Prather, E.N. (1990). What is the TAT? A review of ten years of research. *Journal of Personality Assessment, 55,* 800–803.

Klinger, E., Cox, W.M., & Blount, J.P. (in press). Motivational Structure Questionnaire (MSQ) and Personal Concerns Inventory (PCI). In J.P. Allen & M. Columbus (Eds.), *Assessing alcohol problems: A guide for clinicians and researchers* (2nd edn.). Washington, DC: US Department of Health and Human Services.

Kuhl, J. (1994). Action versus state orientation: Psychometric properties of the Action Control Scale (ACS-90). In J. Kuhl & J. Beckmann (Eds.), *Volition and personality: Action versus state orientation* (pp. 47–59). Seattle, WA: Hogrefe & Huber.

Lamiell, J.T. (1981). Toward an idiothetic psychology of personality. *American Psychologist, 36,* 276–289.

McAdams, D.P., & Zeldow, P.B. (1993). Construct validity and content analysis. *Journal of Personality Assessment, 61*, 243–245.

McClelland, D.C., Koestner, R., & Weinberger, J. (1989). How do self-attributed and implicit motives differ? *Psychological Review, 96*, 690–702.

Morgan, C.D., & Murray, H.A. (1935). A method for investigating fantasies: The thematic apperception test. *Archives of Neurology and Psychiatry, 34*, 289–306.

Murray, H.A. (1938). *Explorations in personality*. Oxford, UK: Oxford University Press.

Schmalt, H.-D. (1977). Convergent and discriminant validity of various components of achievement motivation. *Psychologie und Praxis, 21*, 112–117.

Schmalt, H.-D., & Sokolowski, K. (2000). Zum gegenwaertigen Stand der Motivdiagnostik (The current status of motive measurement). *Diagnostica, 46*, 115–123.

Spangler, W.D. (1992). Validity of questionnaire and TAT measures of need for achievement: Two meta-analyses. *Psychological Bulletin, 112*, 140–154.

Tuerlinckx, F., De Boeck, P., & Lens, W. (2002). Measuring needs with the Thematic Apperception Test: A psychometric study. *Journal of Personality and Social Psychology, 82*, 448–461.

Motivational Structure Questionnaire *and* Personal Concerns Inventory

Motivational Structure Questionnaire

TEST BOOKLET

GENERAL INSTRUCTIONS

The purpose of this questionnaire is for us to get a picture of what your life is like *now* and the way you feel *now*. We would like you to tell us about your interests, the activities you are involved in, your problems, the things that concern you, your goals, joys, disappointments, hopes, and fears.

We are interested *both* in the things that you consider to be problems *and* in the things that bring you joy and happiness. In other words, we want to know about all of the things that you feel are important in helping us to know you better—the things that make you feel good, as well as the things that make you feel bad.

The questionnaire is divided into different steps. Each step of the questionnaire has its own instructions, which you will read just before you complete that step. Read each set of instructions carefully, and feel free to ask us about anything that is not clear to you.

When you are asked to do so, please turn the page and read the instructions for STEP 1.

Instructions for Step 1

BRIEF DESCRIPTIONS OF THE THINGS IN YOUR LIFE

In STEP 1, we simply want you to *list briefly* the things that affect your life: your interests, the activities you are involved in, your problems, the things that concern you, your goals, joys, disappointments, hopes, and fears. Later in STEPS 2 to 12, you will have an opportunity to tell us what you would like *to do* about the things, and to describe them in greater detail.

For STEP 1, do these three things:

1. Before you write anything, turn through the pages of the Answer Sheet* and read the Life Area categories in the left column, so that you are familiar with the different life areas.
2. Next, start with the first category on page 1 of the Answer Sheet and think of all the things in your life that fall into that category. Briefly describe each thing that falls into Life Area #1 in the left column of the Answer Sheet, beginning each one on a separate line.
3. Continue in this manner with all of the life-area categories. In some areas you may have several things to list; in other areas only one or none. List as many things as you can in order to let us know what your life is like.

NOW DO STEP 1

WHEN YOU HAVE COMPLETED STEP 1, TURN TO THE NEXT STEP

* An Example Answer Sheet is presented on page 170.

Instructions for Step 2

ACTION WORD

Now that you have listed the things that affect your life, what would you like to do about each one? For example, let's suppose that you described being bored with your present job. What would you like to do about this? One possibility is that you may want to *find out more about* other interesting jobs to change to.

For STEP 2, do these things:

1. Read the separate ACTION WORDS sheet,* which lists 13 groups of Action Words with examples. Notice that the words in each group have similar meanings.
2. Go to the list of things that you wrote in the left column of your Answer Sheet under STEP 1.
3. Decide what you would like to do (or are now doing) about each thing that you listed by choosing an Action Word from the ACTION WORDS list.
4. In the right column of the Answer Sheet labeled STEP 2,[†] write a brief sentence to describe what you want to do (or are now doing). The sentence should begin, "I want to . . ." Complete the sentence by writing

   (a) the *number* of the group in which you found the Action Word
   (b) the *particular Action Word* that best fits the thing, and
   (c) any *other words* that you need in order to make the sentence a complete thought.

5. Continue until you have written a sentence for each thing that you listed in STEP 1.

Here is an example. Suppose that in STEP 1 you wrote "Kitten needs rabies shot." You want to get the kitten its shot and you find the word "get" in Group #1, "get, make, obtain, accomplish, gain, attain." So under STEP 2 you would write, "I want to *#1 get* the kitten its rabies shot." Another person may have thought about the shot differently and may have written "I want to *#7 prevent* rabies."

NOW DO STEP 2

WHEN YOU HAVE COMPLETED STEP 2, TURN TO THE NEXT STEP

---

* See list of Action Words on page 169.
[†] See Example Answer Sheet on page 170.

STEPS 3 to 12

For the rest of the questionnaire (STEPS 3 to 12), we would like you to *rate* the things you wrote in STEP 2. First, fold out each page of your answer sheet booklet,* in order to see the columns where you will write your answers for STEPS 3 to 12. We will continue to give you the instructions for each step just before you are to complete it. However, this part of the questionnaire will not take as much time or writing as the first two steps.

* Owing to limitations on space, we cannot reproduce the entire booklet; however, an Example Answer Sheet is shown on page 170.

Instructions for Step 3

ROLE

For each sentence that you completed in STEP 2, tell us what *role* you are now playing (or expect to play) with regard to the action that you named. Below are six ways to describe your role.

Note that the scale ranges from the MOST ACTIVE Role to the LEAST ACTIVE Role.

1. Take part, and know what action to take.
2. Take part, but don't know what action to take.
3. Watch only, but would like to take part.
4. Watch only.
5. Watch only, but this is a concern of mine because another person who is important to me is involved.
6. Neither take part nor watch, but this is a concern of mine because another person who is important to me is involved.

Decide which of the six choices best describes how you are involved in the action that you named and write that number in the STEP 3 column of the Answer Sheet.* If none of the choices fully describes your role, pick the one that fits best. Do this for all of the actions that you wrote in STEP 2. Remember that you may choose *a different number* for each action.

NOW DO STEP 3

WHEN YOU HAVE COMPLETED STEP 3, TURN TO THE NEXT STEP

* See the Example Answer Sheet on page 170.

Instructions for Step 4

COMMITMENT

Find the column on your Answer Sheet labeled STEP 4—Commitment. Please mark your answers in this column. Tell us how committed you are to taking the action that you named in STEP 2, using the scale below.

Be careful to choose a number that represents your *commitment*, not something else. For example, suppose Bob insults you and you want to *ignore* his insults. Then, you would express your commitment to *ignoring Bob's insults*; you would *not* express your commitment to the insults, which you dislike.

Note that the scale ranges from the LEAST Commitment to the MOST Commitment.

1. I do not intend to make the thing happen.
2. I am not sure whether I want to put out the effort.
3. I am prepared to try but not go out of my way.
4. I am prepared to make a medium effort.
5. I am definitely prepared to try very hard.
6. I fully intend to if I possibly can.

NOW DO STEP 4

WHEN YOU HAVE COMPLETED STEP 4, TURN TO THE NEXT STEP

Instructions for Step 5

JOY

For each sentence that you completed in STEP 2, imagine that you have succeeded with the thing the way you wanted to. Try to imagine how much joy you would feel when you know you have succeeded. For example, suppose that in STEP 2 you wrote, "I want to get a new friend." Imagine how happy you'd feel when you finally did make a new friend.

Find the column on your Answer Sheet labeled STEP 5—Joy. Please mark your answers for STEP 5 in this column, using the scale below.

Note that the scale ranges from the LEAST Joy to the MOST Joy.

1. no joy at all
2. very little joy
3. some joy
4. an amount of joy between "some" and "medium"
5. a medium amount of joy
6. an amount of joy between "medium" and "pretty strong"
7. pretty strong joy
8. great joy
9. the most joy I can imagine feeling about anything

NOW DO STEP 5

WHEN YOU HAVE COMPLETED STEP 5, TURN TO THE NEXT STEP

Instructions for Step 6

UNHAPPINESS

For each sentence that you completed in STEP 2, again imagine that you have *succeeded* with the action the way you wanted to. This time try to imagine how much *unhappiness* you would feel when you know you have *succeeded*.

It may seem a little odd to say that you are *unhappy* because you *succeeded* with something that you wanted. Sometimes, though, even successes bring some unhappiness with them. For example, a student might be very happy to finally graduate from high school, but doing so may also bring some *unhappiness* because it means leaving friends and places the student has grown attached to.

In the column labeled STEP 6—Unhappiness, indicate how much unhappiness you would feel if you succeeded at each action that you named in STEP 2, using the following scale:

Note that the scale ranges from the LEAST Unhappiness to the MOST Unhappiness.

1. no unhappiness at all
2. very little unhappiness
3. some unhappiness
4. an amount of unhappiness between "some" and "medium"
5. a medium amount of unhappiness
6. an amount of unhappiness between "medium" and "pretty strong"
7. pretty strong unhappiness
8. great unhappiness
9. the most unhappiness I can imagine feeling about anything

NOW DO STEP 6

WHEN YOU HAVE COMPLETED STEP 6, TURN TO THE NEXT STEP

Instructions for Step 7

SORROW

For each sentence that you completed in STEP 2, now imagine that you were *unable to succeed* with the action the way you wanted to. This time try to imagine how much *sorrow* you would feel when you know you have *not* succeeded.

For each of the actions that you named in STEP 2, choose a number from the scale below to indicate the amount of sorrow that you would feel if you did *not* succeed. Place each number in the column marked STEP 7.

Note that the scale ranges from the LEAST Sorrow to the MOST Sorrow.

1. no sorrow at all
2. very little sorrow
3. some sorrow
4. an amount of sorrow between "some" and "medium"
5. a medium amount of sorrow
6. an amount of sorrow between "medium" and "pretty strong"
7. pretty strong sorrow
8. great sorrow
9. the most sorrow I can imagine feeling about anything

NOW DO STEP 7

WHEN YOU HAVE COMPLETED STEP 7, TURN TO THE NEXT STEP

Instructions for Step 8

CHANCES OF SUCCESS

Overall, how likely are you to succeed with each action that you named in STEP 2? That is, what are your *chances of success*? For each sentence that you wrote in STEP 2, please write in the STEP 8 column of the Answer Sheet the number that best matches your chances of succeeding with the action that you want to take. Use the scale below.

Note that the scale ranges from the LOWEST Chances to the HIGHEST Chances.

0. almost no chance—a 0–9% chance
1. a 10–19% chance
2. a 20–29% chance
3. a 30–39% chance
4. a 40–49% chance
5. a 50–59% chance
6. a 60–69% chance
7. a 70–79% chance
8. an 80–89% chance
9. almost certain—at least 90% sure

NOW DO STEP 8

WHEN YOU HAVE COMPLETED STEP 8, TURN TO THE NEXT STEP

Instructions for Step 9

CHANCES OF SUCCESS IF NO ACTION

In some cases you might succeed with something that you want to happen without doing anything yourself, that is, without taking any action at all. For example, you might very much want the weather to turn warmer (or cooler) and would be very happy if this were to happen, even though you did nothing to make it happen.

To do STEP 9, choose from the scale below the number that best matches the chances that you will succeed with each of the things that you named in STEP 1, *even if you don't try.*

Note that the scale ranges from the LOWEST Chances to the HIGHEST Chances.

0. almost no chance—a 0–9% chance
1. a 10–19% chance
2. a 20–29% chance
3. a 30–39% chance
4. a 40–49% chance
5. a 50–59% chance
6. a 60–69% chance
7. a 70–79% chance
8. an 80–89% chance
9. almost certain—at least 90% sure

NOW DO STEP 9

WHEN YOU HAVE COMPLETED STEP 9, TURN TO THE NEXT STEP

Instructions for Step 10

TIME AVAILABLE

How soon must you *start taking action* if you are *to succeed* with each of the sentences that you wrote in STEP 2? Must you start today? Can you wait a week, a month, a year, or even longer and still succeed?

Please answer this question by writing the approximate number of days, months, or years before you must start taking action in the column marked STEP 10. First, write the *number* that you have in mind, and then write "Da," "Mo," or "Yr" to indicate whether the number refers to *days*, *months*, or *years*.

If you have already started, or you have to start today, you would write a "0." Try your best to specify the time available for each sentence. However, if you cannot do so, write an "X" in the STEP 10 column. Remember that you may choose *a different time available* for each sentence that you wrote in STEP 2.

NOW DO STEP 10

WHEN YOU HAVE COMPLETED STEP 10, TURN TO THE NEXT STEP

Instructions for Step 11

GOAL DISTANCE

Do you have a certain time in mind when you expect to succeed at each of the actions you wrote in STEP 2? If so, how soon is it? For example, if you wrote "I want to get my diploma," and if you expect to complete it in 1 month, you would write "1 Mo" for STEP 11.

Just as you did in STEP 10, please answer this by writing the approximate number of days, months, or years in the column marked STEP 10. First, write the *number* that you have in mind, and then write "Da," "Mo," or "Yr" to indicate whether the number refers to *days*, *months*, or *years*.

Please make every effort to give an answer. However, if you cannot do so, then write an "X" in the column for STEP 11. For example, for certain of the Action Words, it may not make sense to try to state a time when you expect to reach your goal. These are Action Words like "Continue," "Maintain," "Keep," "Prevent," "Avoid," and "Ignore." Remember that you may choose *a different goal distance* for each action that you wrote about in STEP 2.

NOW DO STEP 11

WHEN YOU HAVE COMPLETED STEP 11, TURN TO THE NEXT STEP

Instructions for Step 12

EFFECT OF DRINKING AND OTHER DRUG USE
ON SUCCESSFUL ACTION

What effect would your drinking alcohol or using other drugs have on your succeeding at each of the actions that you wrote in STEP 2? Select from the scale
below the number that best expresses this effect, and place the number on the
Answer Sheet under STEP 12. Be sure to include the "+" or the "−" with the
number as shown on the scale.

*Note that the scale ranges from the MOST POSITIVE effect to the MOST NEGA-
TIVE effect.*

Drinking alcohol or using other drugs would:

+ 5. *Virtually assure* my chances of success.
+ 4. *Very strongly improve* my chances of success.
+ 3. *Strongly improve* my chances of success.
+ 2. *Moderately improve* my chances of success.
+ 1. *Somewhat improve* my chances of success.
  0. *Have no effect on* my chances of success.
− 1. *Somewhat impair* my chances of success.
− 2. *Moderately impair* my chances of success.
− 3. *Strongly impair* my chances of success.
− 4. *Very strongly impair* my chances of success.
− 5. *Entirely prevent* my chances of success.

This is the end of the questionnaire. Thank you for taking the time to complete it,
and for sharing with us the things in your life. We would appreciate any comments
you have about the questionnaire. For example, did you enjoy or dislike filling it
out? Your opinions can help us to make any needed changes in it. Please write
any comments that you have about this questionnaire on the *back of your Answer
Sheet*. Thank you.

ACTION WORDS

1. *get*, *make*, *obtain*, *accomplish*, *gain*, *attain*: for example, *get* a project done, *obtain* a raise, *gain* control over emotions.

2. *keep*, *maintain*, *continue*: for example, *keep* a job, *maintain* a good driving record.

3. *fix*, *repair*, *get back*: for example, *restore* a friend's trust in you, *repair* a car.

4. *do*: for example, *do* skiing, *do* swimming, *do* going for a stroll.

5. *get rid of*, *abandon*, or *change* the thing by removing it: for example, *get rid of* an unreliable car, *change* friends.

6. *avoid* or *ignore* the thing by removing yourself before the negative thing can take effect: for example, *avoid* a family argument, *ignore* a friend's rudeness.

7. *prevent* the thing by taking action to block it: for example, *prevent* getting into a car accident by driving carefully.

8. *escape* the thing after bad effects have already begun: for example, *escape* job stress by calling in sick, *escape* an abusive relationship by breaking it off.

9. *attack*: for example, *attack* a friend by breaking his/her things, *attack* spouse by hitting him/her, *attack* a coworker by cussing him/her out.

10. *find out more about* or *resolve questions about* a positive thing: for example, *find out more about* chances for a new job, *find out more about* a positive thing in your life.

11. *find out more about* or *resolve questions about* a negative thing: for example, *find out about* your child's school problems.

12. *find out more about* a thing which you don't consider to be positive or negative, that is, it is neutral.

13. *Other.* You may use this category for concerns for which none of the other action words fit. If you choose this category, make certain that you write down the name of the particular other action word that you have in mind.

MSQ EXAMPLE ANSWER SHEET

My Current Concerns and Goals in Major Life Areas Step 1	Action Word Step 2	Role Step 3	Commitment Step 4	Joy Step 5	Unhappiness Step 6	Sorrow Step 7	Probability of Success Step 8	Probability of Success if no Action Step 9	Time Available Step 10	Nearness Step 11	Alcohol Instrumentalist Step 12
1. Family and Home											
A. Immediate family and other relatives (for example, problems and achievements of your children; your sister's upcoming marriage; a gift for your mother-in-law)											
•											
•											
•											
•											
B. Roommates and nonrelatives (for example, a roommate who is never home; noisy people who live upstairs; needing to find a roommate)											
•											
•											
•											
•											
•											
C. Home and House keeping (for example, raking the yard; planting the garden; painting the woodwork; buying a home; grocery shopping)											
•											
•											
•											
•											
D. Pets (for example, a dog who chews furniture; getting a kitten; cleaning an aquarium; buying new fish)											
•											
•											
•											
•											

Personal Concerns Inventory

INTRODUCTION

Undoubtedly, you have concerns about different areas of your life. You may also have in mind things that you would like to change in order to resolve these concerns. If these changes were to happen, it might make it easier for you to change your use of alcohol or other drugs.

By "concerns" we do NOT mean only problems. You might have concerns about unpleasant things that you want to "get rid of," "prevent," or "avoid." Or you might have concerns about pleasant things that you want to "get," "obtain," or "accomplish."

INSTRUCTIONS, PART 1

Read through the Areas of Life listed below, and think carefully about each of them. Then tick the areas in which you have important concerns or things that you would like to change. For now, ONLY TICK the areas that apply.

—— Home and Household Matters (Area #1)

—— Employment and Finances (Area #2)

—— Partner, Family, and Relatives (Area #3)

—— Friends and Acquaintances (Area #4)

—— Love, Intimacy, and Sexual Matters (Area #5)

—— Self Changes (Area #6)

—— Education and Training (Area #7)

—— Health and Medical Matters (Area #8)

—— Substance Use (Area #9)

—— Spiritual Matters (Area #10)

—— Hobbies, Pastimes, and Recreation (Area #11)

—— Other Areas (not included above) (Area #12)

INSTRUCTIONS, PART 2

You have been given a sheet that corresponds to each of the Areas of Life that you ticked.* These are the Areas of Life in which you have important concerns about which you might like to do something. On the following sheets, please do three things.

- First, think carefully about each Area of Life, and jot down in the spaces provided *at the left* of the Answer Sheet the important concerns that come to your mind. Notice that each Area of Life has spaces for you to list up to six concerns. In some of these Areas of Life, you might have only one concern (or no concern at all). In other Areas of Life, you might have two, three, or more concerns. Use as many of the spaces as you need to describe your different concerns.
- Second, in the spaces *at the centre* of the Answer Sheet describe what you would like to happen. That is, how would you like things to turn out?
- Third, refer to the Rating Scale Sheet on page 174. Then choose the numbers that best describe how you feel about each of the goals and concerns that you have described. Fill in these numbers at the boxes *at the right side* of the Answer Sheet.

* See Sample Answer Sheet on page 175.

PCI RATING SCALE SHEET

Importance: How important is it to me for things to turn out the way I want? Choose a number from 0 to 10, where

0 is not important at all, and 10 is very important

How likely: How likely is it that things will turn out the way I want? Choose a number from 0 to 10, where

0 is not likely at all, and 10 is very likely

Control: How much control do I have in causing things to turn out the way I want? Choose a number from 0 to 10, where

0 is no control at all, and 10 is much control

What to do: Do I know what steps to take to make things turn out the way I want? Choose a number from 0 to 10, where

0 is not knowing at all, and 10 is knowing exactly

Happiness: How much happiness would I get if things turn out the way I want? Choose a number from 0 to 10, where

0 is no happiness at all, and 10 is great happiness

Unhappiness: Sometimes we feel unhappy, even if things turn out the way we want. How unhappy would I feel if things turn out the way I want? Choose a number from 0 to 10, where

0 is no unhappiness at all, and 10 is great unhappiness

Commitment: How committed do I feel to make things turn out the way I want? Choose a number from 0 to 10, where

0 is no commitment at all, and 10 is strong commitment

When will it happen? How long will it take for things to turn out the way I want? Choose a number from 0 to 10, where

0 is very short (e.g., days), and 10 is very long (e.g., years or never)

Will alcohol/drugs help? Will using alcohol or drugs help things to turn out the way I want? Choose a number from 0 to 10, where

0 is not helpful at all, and 10 is very helpful

Will alcohol/drugs interfere? Will using alcohol or drugs interfere with things turning out the way I want? Choose a number from 0 to 10, where

0 is not interfere at all, and 10 is interfere very much

PCI SAMPLE ANSWER SHEET

Area #1: Home and Household Matters. When you think of this area, what concerns come to mind?

Step 1. Jot down your concerns	Step 2. Describe what you want to have happen	Step 3. Choose numbers from Rating Scale Sheet and fill in boxes

Concern #1

What I would like to have happen is . . .

→ Importance: _____
→ How likely: _____
→ Control: _____
→ What to do: _____
→ Happiness: _____
→ Unhappiness: _____
→ Commitment: _____
→ When it will happen: _____
→ Alcohol/drugs help: _____
→ Alcohol/drugs interfere: _____

Note. The Answer Sheet continues in this format, allowing the respondent to list up to 6 concerns in each of the 12 Life Areas named in *Instructions, Part 1* (page 172).

CHAPTER 9

The Motivational Structure Questionnaire and Personal Concerns Inventory: Psychometric Properties

Eric Klinger
University of Minnesota, Morris, USA
and
W. Miles Cox
University of Wales, Bangor, UK

Synopsis.—This chapter presents the psychometric properties of the Motivational Structure Questionnaire (MSQ; Cox & Klinger, Chapter 8, this volume; Klinger, Cox, & Blount, 1995) and Personal Concerns Inventory (PCI; Cox & Klinger, 2000b), with a focus on their reliability, factor structure, and validity. These closely related instruments are designed unconventionally in an idiothetic format, in that respondents first list idiographically recorded goals and then rate these goals along quantitative dimensions that permit deriving nomothetic scores. Their test–retest and internal-consistency reliability have been established with a variety of participant groups, including both individuals in clinical treatment and others drawn from universities and communities. Although the stability of these measures is variable because the goals with which they start are changeable, the internal consistency of their scales is within conventionally acceptable limits. The validity of these measures has been established by relating participants' responses on the questionnaire to a wide variety of other, independent measures of their motivational patterns. These have included measures from the following domains: (a) physiological and cognitive processes (e.g., from skin-conductance responses to attentional biases for concern-related stimuli), (b) mental processes (e.g., the content of thoughts and dreams), (c) life style (e.g., participants' daily activities), (d) workers' characteristics (e.g., employee satisfaction and work patterns in industrial settings), (e) various personality measures, and (f) treatment outcome (e.g., symptom remission and psychological functioning one-year post-treatment). This chapter reviews this research, which has demonstrated that the MSQ is a reliable, valid, and useful psychological assessment device.

Handbook of Motivational Counseling. Edited by W. Miles Cox and Eric Klinger.
© 2004 John Wiley & Sons, Ltd.

CHALLENGES AND SOLUTIONS IN ASSESSING RELIABILITY OF THE MSQ

The Need for Reliability and Validity in Motivational Assessment

No system of psychological intervention in people's affairs can reach its full potential without a scientific basis, and no science can succeed without effective ways to quantify its variables. That requires adequate measurement.

The two kinds of standards conventionally used to evaluate measures are reliability and validity. Reliability refers ultimately to the ability of a measure, when applied to the same object repeatedly under identical conditions, to produce the same reading. Given that, in reality, there are never identical conditions, how can one best assess degree of reliability in an idiothetic measure of changeable objects—goals—such as the MSQ?

Validity is essentially a matter of truth in labeling. A measure's validity is always validity with respect to some construct, so that no measure is universally valid. A measure of anxiety, however valid for assessing anxiety, typically has little validity for assessing intelligence or conscientiousness, and vice versa. But what criteria are there for the motivational constructs tapped by the MSQ? The difficulties are clear, but developing evidence shows that they are not insurmountable.

Limitations of Standard Reliability Measures for State or Process Constructs

Assessing either the reliability or the validity of motivational measures presents special challenges. This is especially true when the instrument is aimed at states such as moods or at Personal Action Construct units (PAC units; Little & Chambers, Chapter 4, this volume) such as current concerns (Klinger & Cox, Chapter 1, this volume) or personal projects (Little & Chambers, Chapter 4, this volume), rather than at long-lasting traits, and especially if the measuring technique departs from conventional multi-item, response-limited, respondent questionnaires.

Standard procedures for determining reliability (apart from face validity) take one of three forms: interobserver agreement, test–retest measures of stability, and internal consistency. Motivational states and current concerns are, of course, not readily observable by others, thus limiting the possibilities for interobserver agreement.

Any stability measure of reliability confounds unreliability with changes in the thing being measured, with the result that stability measures of states provide a lower bound on reliability, with potentially considerable underestimation of its true size. Thus, for instance, most moods, other emotional states, and goal pursuits may change from hour to hour, day to day, week to week, and certainly year to year. Scores on such states achieved at a momentary Time 1 are therefore likely to be at best only moderately correlated with those achieved at a momentary Time 2. This lack of stability is, however, attributable to changes in these states themselves in addition to deficient reliability of the instrument, and the extent to which state change is responsible is indeterminate without some other way to estimate true reliability.

Attempting to assess the reliability of measuring PAC units such as current concerns or personal projects through internal consistency encounters the problem that existing methods of measuring individual PAC units lack a multi-item format, and also that PAC units are idiographic, with little direct, quantitative comparability across respondents. Typically, in such procedures respondents list their current goal pursuits, with each such PAC unit listed only once. The reliability of such a listing is beyond the reach of internal consistency measures. Consequently, assessing reliability must fall back on stability measures.

However, the MSQ and the Personal Projects Assessment methods (as well as measures of personal strivings, which are somewhere between current concerns or personal projects and traits in their durability; Emmons, 1986) are *idiothetic* methods (Lamiell, 1981). That is, they begin with *idio*graphic listings and perhaps descriptions of PAC units but then ask respondents to rate each unit listed on a series of standard scales, a nomo*thetic* component. Because respondents typically list numerous PAC units, these methods afford the opportunity to regard each PAC unit listed as a kind of item and then to examine the internal consistency with which respondents apply any given scale to each of the PAC units. At least the scores assigned to respondents on the basis of their aggregated scale ratings of PAC units are therefore amenable to internal-consistency measures of reliability.

Meaning and Findings Regarding Internal Consistency of MSQ Scores

The scales of the MSQ (see Cox & Klinger, Chapter 8, this volume) that are applied to each listed goal include the kind of consummation intended for that goal (Action Word; e.g., to attain, keep, restore, avoid, or prevent the goal event), the extent to which the respondent is an actor in relation to the goal (Active Role), Commitment, anticipated joy at goal attainment (Joy), anticipated displeasure (i.e., ambivalence) at goal attainment (Unhappiness), the degree of sorrow anticipated if the goal can finally not be attained (Sorrow), subjective Probability of Success, subjective Probability of Success If No Action is taken to attain the goal, amount of Time Available before having to begin action to attain the goal, amount of time anticipated before attaining the goal (Goal Distance), and, in alcohol-related applications, the extent to which drinking alcohol advances or impedes goal pursuit (Alcohol Instrumentality). Because most respondents apply these scales to dozens of their own listed goals, it is possible to characterize a respondent through their mean ratings. Thus, one can compute a respondent's mean level of Commitment to his or her goals, mean Joy anticipated at goal attainment, mean Probability of Success, etc.

Taken across all of a respondent's goals, these means then enable one to describe an individual as highly or weakly committed, as anticipating much or little joy from goal attainments, as optimistic or pessimistic about goal attainments, etc. By the same token, one can treat the ratings on a particular scale as equivalent to responses to the items on a conventional questionnaire and hence subject them to standard internal-consistency measures.

The internal consistency of the 11 main MSQ scales, using Cronbach's alpha coefficients, was calculated on MSQ data from an American sample of 182 college student volunteers. These results are provided in Table 9.1 for the first 20 goals listed by those respondents who listed at least 20 goals. Cronbach's alpha coefficients for internal consistency of these scales ranged from .56 to .97 (Table 9.1). For the seven conventionally scaled variables the range is .81 to .97 and hence satisfactory.

The reason that only respondents with at least 20 goals are included and coefficients were calculated for only the first 20 goals is that the Cronbach's alpha computational program requires each respondent to have responded to all items. For all 240 participants in this

Table 9.1   Internal consistency (Cronbach's alpha) of 11 scales of the MSQ

MSQ scale	Alpha coefficient	Scale range	Mean	Standard deviation	N
Role	.80	1 to 6	4.53[a]	.72[a]	171
Commitment	.81	1 to 6	3.58	6.81	170
Joy	.84	1 to 9	6.32	1.18	172
Unhappiness	.92	1 to 9	6.46	1.29	173
Sorrow	.87	1 to 9	2.62	1.80	171
Probability of Success	.83	0 to 9	1.86	.578	170
Probability of Success If No Action	.90	0 to 9	5.57	1.42	171
Drinking Utility	.97	−5 to +5	1.98	1.13	170
Verb (Appetitive vs. Avoidant)	.56	1 to 13	4.39[a]	2.69[a]	174
Time Available (Years) before active Pursuit	.68	Unlimited	0.64	0.87	72[b]
Goal Distance (years to goal)	.83	Unlimited	1.80	3.85	22[b]

Note: Because of occasional missing ratings, *N* values for particular scales range from 170 to 173. Alpha coefficients, means, and standard deviations were computed for the first 20 goals listed by respondents. Only respondents with at least 20 goals are included. The sample had a median age of 19, was 68% female, and was in most cases unmarried and Caucasian.
[a] These figures are not particularly meaningful because the variable uses a nominal scale, with scale levels ordered only roughly.
[b] These *N* values are much reduced because respondents had the option of indicating that specific time intervals were inapplicable to a goal (e.g., maintaining a relationship, avoiding an illness). The *N* values reflect the number of respondents who made no use of this option for their first 20 goals.

sample, the mean and median number of goals listed was 27 with a standard deviation of 11 and mode of 32. Number of goals ranged from 4 to 75. With such variable numbers of items per respondent, it was necessary to exclude some respondents and yet desirable to decide on a number of items (i.e., concerns) that would be provided by a reasonable number of respondents. The 20-goal criterion for inclusion retained 76% of the 240 participants in the original sample. The decision for 20 goals thus provided both a large respondent sample and a substantial number of goals.

Comparisons of Internal Consistency and Other MSQ Properties with those of the Personal Projects Analysis and the Personal Strivings Assessment

Another, smaller sample (*N* = 79, 18 men and 61 women, mostly American, Caucasian, single, college undergraduates) provided an opportunity to compare alpha coefficients for the MSQ, Personal Projects Analysis (PPA; Little, 1983 and Chapter 4, this volume), and Personal Strivings Assessment (PSA; Emmons, 1986, 1999). The latter two usually restrict numbers of PAC units analyzed to respectively 10 and 15. As a result, the analysis confounds numbers of PAC units with differences in scaling instructions. The latter differences are, however, sufficiently small that differences in alpha coefficients can be considered largely attributable to different numbers of PAC units.

Method

This investigation included three rating scales that were either virtually identical or essentially cognate scales among the three methods: Commitment, Joy/Happiness, and Chances of Success. The investigation also included scales for Importance (part of both the PSA and PPA) and Level (part of the PSA). For purposes of this investigation, all responses were recorded on identical 11-point scales ranging from 0 to 10.

The instructions to respondents as to what to write down on the answer sheet followed the different standard instructions for the various instruments. For the MSQ (see the appendix to Chapter 8, this volume), these included the following language:

> We would like you to tell us about your interests, the activities you are involved in, your problems, the things that concern you, your goals, joys, disappointments, hopes, and fears. We are interested *both* in the things that you consider to be problems *and* in the things that bring you joy and happiness.

For the PPA, the comparable instructions were:

> We would like you to take 10 minutes and write down on the next page as many personal projects as you can think of that you are engaged in or considering, including the everyday kinds of activities or concerns that characterize your life at present. We call these kinds of activities and concerns that people have over the course of their lives *personal projects*.

For the PSA, the wording was:

> We are interested in the things that you typically or characteristically are trying to do. We might call these objectives "strivings."

Reliability Comparisons

The Cronbach's alpha coefficients, as well as means and standard deviations for the five scales, are presented in Table 9.2. Although alphas obtained from larger numbers of PAC units tended to be on average higher than those obtained from smaller numbers of PAC units, this trend was by no means uniform. Furthermore, although PPA scores, based on only 10 PAC units, yielded uniformly lower alphas than MSQ scores based on 20 or 30 PAC units, their alphas were uniformly higher than scores based on 10 PAC units obtained under PSA instructions. Because of the small sample sizes and unexpected result, this latter regularity would need to be replicated before forming the basis of a conclusion about the relative reliability of the two procedures.

Comparisons of Rating Means

The only appreciable differences in mean scores among the three instructional conditions were that MSQ instructions produced lower Importance scores over all PAC units rated than PSA and PPA instructions did (Table 9.3). The only other difference was that the 61 women scored on average significantly higher on Commitment and Joy/Happiness than the 18 men did (Table 9.4). There were no appreciable interactions between instructional conditions and sex.

Table 9.2 Internal consistency (Cronbach's alpha), rating means, and standard deviations of respondents' mean ratings for five scales under MSQ, PSA, and PPA instructions with varying numbers of PAC units

Scale	Instrument	Number of PAC units	Alpha coefficient	Mean	Standard deviation	N
Commitment	MSQ	30	.77	7.30	.98	19
	MSQ	20	.65	7.32	.96	23
	MSQ	15	.66	7.25	1.12	23
	MSQ	10	.64	7.23	1.35	25
	PSA	15	.73	7.61	.89	25
	PSA	10	.50	7.57	.83	25
	PPA	10	.64	7.37	1.02	21
Joy/Happiness	MSQ	30	.83	7.39	1.18	19
	MSQ	20	.83	7.55	1.33	23
	MSQ	15	.80	7.41	1.46	23
	MSQ	10	.75	7.24	1.69	25
	PSA	15	.67	7.89	.85	25
	PSA	10	.55	7.94	.82	25
	PPA	10	.74	8.30	1.09	21
Chances of success	MSQ	30	.77	6.98	1.04	19
	MSQ	20	.72	6.91	1.11	23
	MSQ	15	.76	6.80	1.38	23
	MSQ	10	.76	6.88	1.68	25
	PSA	15	.67	7.51	.82	25
	PSA	10	.58	7.39	.91	25
	PPA	10	.59	7.69	.90	21
Importance	MSQ	30	.71	7.03	.95	19
	MSQ	20	.68	7.18	1.04	23
	MSQ	15	.66	7.15	1.17	23
	MSQ	10	.70	7.32	1.49	25
	PSA	15	.73	7.79	.96	25
	PSA	10	.59	7.74	.95	25
	PPA	10	.68	8.02	1.06	21
Level	MSQ	30	.77	5.94	1.13	19
	MSQ	20	.75	6.09	1.20	23
	MSQ	15	.71	5.96	1.29	23
	MSQ	10	.65	5.70	1.51	25
	PSA	15	.74	6.13	1.34	25
	PSA	10	.58	6.32	1.27	26
	PPA	10	.68	6.22	1.29	21

Note: MSQ = Motivational Structure Questionnaire; PSA = Personal Strivings Assessment; PPA = Personal Projects Analysis. Within a given instrument, the data reported for varying numbers of PAC units are from the same participants.

In general, then, the three instructional conditions produced similar mean ratings on the five scales used here except for the Importance scale. The lower Importance mean under MSQ instructions may be attributable to the different instructions for selecting and ordering goals. The MSQ procedure provides a list of life areas within which respondents can organize the listing of their goals. Although respondents are instructed to read through all life-area categories before beginning to list their goals, most respondents follow the order

Table 9.3 Differences in effects of MSQ instructions from effects of instructions in PPA and PSA on mean importance ratings

Importance statistic	MSQ	PPA	PSA
Mean	7.07	7.84	7.73
Standard deviation	1.18	1.00	1.09
t (1, 73)[a]	—	2.37	2.28
p-Value of t[a]	—	.020	.026
Tukey HSD p-value[a]	—	.034	.079
LSD p-value[a]	—	.013	.031
Pillai's F (10, 140)[b]		2.43	
p-Value of Pillai's F[b]		.011	
Partial Eta^2[b]		.15	
Univariate F (2, 73)[b]		3.61	
p-Value of F[b]		.032	
Partial Eta^2[b]		.09	

[a] Statistics are for comparisons with the MSQ.
[b] Statistics are for tests of differences among the three means.

Table 9.4 Sex differences in Commitment and Joy/Happiness

Statistic	Commitment		Joy/Happiness	
	Male	Female	Male	Female
Mean	6.89	7.56	7.11	8.11
Standard deviation	.97	.98	1.32	.88
Univariate F (1, 73)[a]	5.82		15.09	
p-Value of F[a]	.018		.000	
Partial Eta^2[a]	.074		.17	
Pillai's F (5, 69)[b]		4.56		
p-Value of Pillai's F[b]		.001		
Partial Eta^2[b]		.25		

Note: There were 18 men and 61 women in the sample.
[a] Statistics are for comparisons between sex within scale type.
[b] Statistics are for tests of sex differences in all five scales administered.

of the categories in their listings. Because categories such as job, education, religion, and health come later than several interpersonal categories, the MSQ may distribute important goals across the list. Selecting just the first 20 such goals therefore does not systematically select the respondents' most important goals. In contrast, when respondents are asked to pick 10 or 15 goals, they presumably list their most important PAC units, with the result that restricting numbers of PAC units, as in the PPA and PSA, selects for, on average, more important PAC units.

However, the differences, although clearly significant, are not very large. This suggests that PAC units listed later, although on average slightly less important, probably contain some reasonably important items. In some cases, respondents may also list important concerns later if they feel less comfortable in communicating them. Thus, restricting numbers of PAC units may exclude items that are clinically important.

Meaning and Findings Regarding Stability of the MSQ

Even though test–retest correlations of MSQ scores confound reliability with the stability of the underlying construct—for example, reliability with the extent to which a person's depth of commitment remains the same—it is of interest to know about the relative stability over time of the information the MSQ yields. This stability can be examined at two different levels of generality: the level of the individual goal and the level of the scores (such as an individual's average level of commitment) that are based on multiple goals.

Stability of Listing Particular Goals

The stability of the individual goals listed by respondents has been assessed only once (Church, Klinger, & Langenberg, 1984; Klinger, 1987). In this study, 12 well-motivated respondents, mostly University of Minnesota students, took the Interview Questionnaire (IntQ) twice, one month apart. The IntQ is the immediate and very similar predecessor of the MSQ, differing primarily in that its phrasing was somewhat less accessible, its wording encouraged listing more goals and interests, and its instructions were longer than those of the MSQ. After the second administration, respondents were asked to identify for each goal listed in each administration the corresponding goal, if any, in the other administration. For goals that appeared in only one administration, respondents indicated the reason, ranging from having forgotten to list the goal to having already attained the goal before the second administration or having not yet adopted the goal at the time of the first administration.

This procedure made it possible to assess the rate at which goals recurred on individuals' goal lists and the fate of those that did not. The mean number of goals listed was 53 (median = 47, SD = 25) on the first administration and 36 (median = 25, SD = 26) on the second. Of the first-administration goals, 64% recurred on the second administration. Disregarding goals that had been attained by the time of the second administration, 74% recurred. Only 19% failed to recur because of forgetting. Considering all of the goals listed on the second administration, 50% had been listed on the first, and of those listed on the second administration that had already been adopted as goals by the time of the first administration, 78% occurred both times.

These figures indicate that, although not perfect, there is a reasonable degree of stability in the goals listed. The listings are not simply capricious. There is no way of knowing how many of respondents' goals failed to show up on either administration, but, of those we know about, the great majority found their way into each IntQ.

Stability of MSQ Scores

Two investigations (Cox et al., in press; Klinger & Cox, 1986) have assessed stability of MSQ scores. Because for the majority of these patients the two administrations bracketed treatment programs dedicated to change, these figures may represent lower-bound estimates of stability.

Table 9.5 Test–retest correlations for three samples of patients

	Patient groups and test–retest intervals			
		Traumatically brain-injured patients		
	SA inpatients	SMC		No SMC
IntQ or MSQ scale	1 month	10 months	19 months	13 months
Number of Goals	.66***	.17	−.03	.39**
Appetitive Action	.42**	−.22	−.17	.06
Active Role	.41**	.19	.15	.14
Commitment	.07	.63***	.47***	.50***
Joy	.31*	.39*	.22	.43**
Unhappiness	.22	.17	.01	.22
Sorrow/No Success	.19	.33*	.28	.25
Chances of Success	.47***	.29	.28	.68***
Chances/No Action	.20	.12	.09	.18
Time Available	.77***	.18	.06	.21
Goal Distance	.22	.01	.03	−.05
Substance Effects Beliefs	.64***	.72***	.48***	.24

Note: SA = Substance Abuse; SMC = Systematic Motivational Counseling; TBI = traumatically brain-injured. N values for the columns are as follows: SA, 42; TBI-SMC, 40; TBI-No-SMC, 54.
$* p < .05$ $** p < .01$ $*** p < .001$

The first sample consisted of 42 inpatients in a unit of a Minnesota regional treatment center for substance-abusing patients who were tested within one week of intake and again a month later at the end of a conventional 30-day substance-use treatment program. The second sample consisted of 94 traumatically brain-injured (TBI) outpatients of two Chicago rehabilitation centers, many of whom were also substance abusers. Of these 94, 40 received Systematic Motivational Counseling (SMC; Chapters 11 to 15, this volume) between the first and second of three administrations of the MSQ. The three administrations took place at the start and end of SMC (an average of 10 months that encompassed 12 SMC sessions) and again at a follow-up averaging another 9 months later. The remaining 54 patients, who served as a control group, received only standard rehabilitation treatment and two administrations of the MSQ 13 months apart.

Stability varied markedly among scales, treatment regimens, and time intervals (Table 9.5). Thus, Commitment was reasonably stable for both TBI groups and all TBI time intervals (10, 13, and 19 months), the test–retest coefficients ranging from .47 to .63; but, unaccountably, the correlation was only .07 for the Minnesota substance-abusing group, even though its interval was only one month. Test–retest coefficients for Anticipated Joy at goal attainment ranged from .22 to .43, Anticipated Sorrow in response to failure from .19 to .33, Chances of Success from .28 to .68, and Substance Effects Beliefs (in the Minnesota group, concerns about avoiding alcohol; in the TBI groups, the extent to which substance use facilitates or impedes attainment of other goals) from .24 to .72. Other scales evinced low or extremely erratic coefficients.

Thus, some MSQ scales are somewhat stable even over the course of extended treatment aimed at changing motivational structure. The variability in coefficients can probably be explained by differences in treatment experiences. Thus, Chances of Success was most stable for the groups that received no SMC, which focuses, among other things, on reassessing expectancies. Similarly, it is likely that all treatment programs would tend to stabilize substance-effects beliefs, as in the Minnesota and SMC groups, which may account for the greater stability of Substance Effects Beliefs there than in the TBI group that received no SMC. With regard to Appetitive Action (the proportion of goals cast in appetitive rather than avoidant terms), respondents tended on average to list about 70 to 80% of their goals as appetitive. This means that for MSQ responses with an average of 21 goals listed, as in the TBI groups, only about four or five of these goals would on average be avoidant. Small shifts in this number could therefore substantially alter a respondent's ranking and hence lower test–retest coefficients. This seems especially likely during the longer intervals used with the TBI groups.

Summary of Reliability Results for the MSQ

Overall, MSQ scales satisfy conventional criteria for internal consistency. Because stability has been assessed primarily in groups of patients before and after treatments aimed at changing motivation, stability in normal populations is hard to estimate. Nevertheless, some MSQ scales show a degree of stability comparable to many personality variables. Others show little stability in the groups studied to date, which may reflect changes in the motivational structure that the MSQ is designed to assess. Scales showing the most promising stability are Commitment, Joy (anticipated at goal attainment), and Chances of Success.

FACTOR STRUCTURE OF MSQ AND PCI SCALES

Evidence regarding the factor structure of the MSQ and PCI comes from principal components analyses performed as parts of several different investigations, five of which are highlighted here. In the first, the MSQ data were drawn from 370 students in four countries: the Czech Republic, the Netherlands, Norway, and the United States (Table 9.6; Cox et al., 2002b). The MSQ used was a shortened form that omitted some scales of the full MSQ. Because the factor structures were substantially similar in each of these country samples, the analysis of the combined data is presented here. The second study (Cox et al., 2000a; Table 9.6) drew its MSQ data from a group of inpatients in a US Veterans Affairs Medical Center. The results of these two studies were remarkably similar: in both cases, the results pointed to a two-factor solution, and in both cases the solution was not materially improved by rotation. The third, fourth, and fifth studies examined PCI data from British participants—the third study (Cox, Pothos, & Hosier, in preparation) from a mixed sample of 94 community residents and university students, the fourth study (Hosier, 2002; Hosier & Cox, 2002; abridged PCI that limited participants to one most important concern in each of five life areas) from a sample of 111 university students, all of whom were self-described excessive drinkers, and the fifth study (Fadardi, in preparation; Fadardi & Cox, 2002; abridged PCI that limited participants to one most important concern in each of eight life areas) from a sample of 87 university students (Table 9.7). As Tables 9.6 and 9.7 indicate, the factor structures for these rather different samples are remarkably similar in the case of Component 1, despite somewhat different sets of scales. Component 2 yielded similar loadings

Table 9.6 Factor structure of MSQ scales from two sets of samples

MSQ scale	Component[a]		Component[b]	
	1	2	1	2
Appetitive Action	—	.59	—	.56
Active Role	.49	.69	—	.74
Commitment	.78	—	.73	—
Joy Anticipated at Success	.79	−.37	.76	—
Sorrow Anticipated at Failure	.59	−.53	.69	—
Chances of Success	.69	—	.57	.44
Goal Distance	—	—	−.43	—

Note: The solutions were obtained by unrotated principal components analysis.
[a] From Cox et al. (2002b). $N = 370$ university students from four nations. Mean number of concerns was 29.39 with a standard deviation of 22.20. Only loadings > .35 are shown.
[b] From Cox et al. (2000a). $N = 77$ American veterans in treatment for substance abuse. Only loadings > .40 are shown.

Table 9.7 Factor structure of PCI scales

PCI scale	Component[a]		Component[b]		Component[c]	
	1	2	1	2	1	2
Commitment	.69	−.48	.89	—	.77	—
Happiness Anticipated at Success	.45	−.76	.82	—	.64	—
Chances of Success	.74	—	.72	−.38	.80	—
Importance	.39	−.69	.86	—	—	—
Control	.59	.55	.35	−.73	.65	—
Knowledge	.71	.40	.36	−.61	.72	—
Unhappiness Anticipated at Success	—	.49	—	.56	—	—
Distance (Time) from Goal Attainment	−.55	—	—	.48	—	—
Alcohol Interference with Goal Attainment	—	.43	—	.54	NU	NU
Alcohol Help for Goal Attainment	—	—	—	—	NU	NU
Hope	NU	NU	NU	NU	.71	.39
Sadness Anticipated at Failure	NU	NU	NU	NU	.49	—
Index of Appetitive Motivation	NU	NU	NU	NU	.56	−.74
Index of Aversive Motivation	NU	NU	NU	NU	—	.87

Note: Only loadings > .35 are shown. PCI = Personal Concerns Inventory. NU = scale not used.
[a] From Cox, Pothos, and Hosier (in preparation). $N = 94$. The solution was obtained by unrotated principal components analysis. Mean number of concerns was 4.45 with a standard deviation of 1.68.
[b] From Hosier (2002) and Hosier and Cox (2002). $N = 111$. The solution was obtained by principal components analysis with Oblimin rotation. This PCI version limited participants to their most important goal in each of five life areas.
[c] From Fadardi (in preparation) and Fadardi and Cox (2002). $N = 87$. The solution was obtained by principal components analysis without rotation. This PCI version limited participants to their most important goal in each of eight life areas.

for the two MSQ analyses but rather different loadings from the PCI analyses. In all cases, however, Components 1 and 2 lend themselves to interpretation as respectively adaptive and maladaptive factors of motivation.

In all data sets, Component 1 has high loadings from Commitment, Joy (or Happiness) Anticipated at Success, and Chances (or Likelihood) of Success. Participants who scored high on this component were on average more strongly committed to their goals, expected greater enjoyment from attaining them, and were more optimistic that they would attain them. Of the remaining scales, the only one that is shared by both instruments and did not yield a consistent loading > .35 is Distance (in time from goal attainment), which had a moderate negative loading in one MSQ analysis and one PCI analysis but not in the other MSQ analyses or in the two abridged-PCI analyses. Insofar as this result is interpretable, it means that participants who scored higher on Component 1 expected on average a somewhat sooner attainment of their goals. The loadings from scales that occur on only some of the instruments indicate consistently that people scoring higher on Component 1 considered their reported goals more important, had a greater sense of control over the outcomes and of knowing how to attain them, and would feel greater sorrow if they finally failed to attain them. In short, in comparison with participants who scored lower on this component, they cared more deeply about their goals and viewed success as likelier.

Component 2 is more variable. In two data sets, one MSQ and the other PCI, Component 2 has a negative loading on Joy (Happiness) at Goal Attainment. Of the other scales with loadings greater than absolute .35, two scales shared by the two instruments yielded inconsistent results: Commitment had trivial loadings in the MSQ analyses and in two PCI analyses but a moderate negative loading in the other PCI analysis, where participants scoring higher on Component 2 reported on average less commitment to their goals. Goal distance (in time) had trivial Component 2 loadings in both MSQ analyses and one PCI analysis but a positive loading in a second PCI analysis and a near miss (.31) in the third. The trend here is that people scoring higher on Component 2 expected that reaching their goals will take longer. To summarize, insofar as there are interpretable trends among these analyses, people who scored higher on Component 2 reported less anticipated joy at goal attainment, less commitment, and a longer wait to goal attainment.

As viewed from the scales not shared by all of these instruments, high scorers on Component 2 were on average more likely to be actively involved with appetitive (approach) goals in both MSQ analyses but *less* actively involved with appetitive goals in the one PCI study that used this variable. High scorers on Component 2 also anticipated less sorrow (one MSQ analysis) if they should fail but greater unhappiness (two PCI analyses) should they succeed (i.e., greater ambivalence). They vested their goals with less importance (one PCI analysis), and viewed alcohol use as a greater impediment to goal attainment (both PCI analyses that included this scale). Sense of control and knowing how to proceed produced opposite Component 2 loadings in two PCI analyses and a trivial loading in the third.

In a principal components analysis of a German MSQ version, Schroer (2001) arrived at a three-component Varimax-rotated solution. His Component 1 resembles in most respects the corresponding Component 1 in the MSQ and PCI analyses described above and in Tables 9.6 and 9.7. His Components 2 and 3 vary considerably from the Component 2 reported in the MSQ and PCI analyses. This may be in part the result of the different scales entered into these analyses, especially scales omitted from the short form of the MSQ and from the PCI, and the decision to rotate.

At least the first component of these solutions may therefore be considered reasonably robust. The second factor may be more variable with different combinations of MSQ-like scales. In any event, as seen below, the factor scores based especially on Component 1 have theoretically important relationships to people's responses to problems stemming from alcohol use.

EVIDENCE ON THE VALIDITY OF MSQ-LIKE INSTRUMENTS

The evidence on the validity of the MSQ and the rather similar PCI takes several forms:

- The ability of investigators using the raw content of individual goals listed by respondents to create stimulus materials that have the effects predicted for them.
- The ability of judges perusing lists of goals to distinguish whose goal lists are associated with whose reported real-life activities.
- Intraindividual relationships of descriptions and ratings of goals with people's subsequent diary-based reports of goal-related activities.
- Correlations of scale scores with patterns of alcohol consumption, abuse, and diagnosis, as well as with response to treatment.
- Evidence that scale scores are largely unrelated to personality dimensions that have no perceptible theoretical connection with them but are related to personality dimensions and mood traits to which they should theoretically be related.

Validity of Raw MSQ Content Measures

Attention, Orienting, Recall, and Thought Content

Raw MSQ content here means participants' idiographic accounts of their current goals, as these are elicited in the first steps of the MSQ, the PCI, and their predecessor instruments. In the earliest stages of our research program on current concerns, before the creation of these questionnaires, investigators interviewed participants about their concerns and gave them additional goal-identification questionnaires to ascertain current goal pursuits. On the basis of this information, these investigators then inserted individually tailored cues (words and phrases) seamlessly into audiotaped narratives as stimuli. When played for the participants, participants paid much more attention to these modified passages, recalled many more of them, and had thoughts related to them much more often than to control passages (Klinger, 1978). These highly significant effects on a range of cognitive processes validated the interview procedure, which evolved into the IntQ and then into the MSQ.

Another investigation showed that words related versus unrelated to a participant's goals (as assessed by a Concern Dimensions Questionnaire [Klinger, Barta, & Maxeiner, 1980]) produced significantly more skin-conductance responses than words related only to other participants' goals (Nikula, Klinger, & Larson-Gutman, 1993). This extends validation of the goal-assessment procedure to effects on a completely nonverbal domain of response.

Effects on Dreams

Subsequent research applied the questionnaire methods for assessing goals to effects on dream content. This formed the basis for identifying goal-related and goal-unrelated words and phrases, which were then read to sleeping participants. Concern-related stimuli influenced dream content that participants reported during periodic awakenings from sleep significantly more than other stimuli did (Hoelscher, Klinger, & Barta, 1981). Later, based on MSQ responses to identify participants' goals, presleep suggestions to dream about goal-related topics led to significantly more dreaming about suggested topics than if the topics were unrelated to participants' goals (Nikles et al., 1998). Apart from suggested topics, dreams were in general more closely related to these participants' own goal pursuits than to the goal pursuits of others. These results, then, provide a kind of validation for the assessment instruments whose results formed the basis of stimulus construction.

Cognitive Interference

If, as theory suggests (Klinger, 1996a, 1996b), people are bound to process goal-related stimuli, even when these distract from a momentary task, presenting goal-related stimuli should slow down processing related to that task. Two such investigations (Riemann, Amir, & Louro, 1995; Riemann & McNally, 1995) used a modified MSQ to identify goals and the emotional Stroop procedure to assess interference. They asked participants to name the font colors of words that varied according to whether they were emotionally neutral or were highly or only slightly related to participants' positive or negative current concerns. Responses were quickest for neutral words and slowest for words highly related to concerns.

The emotional Stroop test has also been used to compare drinkers' response times to alcohol-related, concern-related, and neutral stimuli. Cox, Blount, and Rozak (2000b) found that alcohol abusers (whose goals were assessed with the MSQ), unlike nonabusers, showed greater attentional distraction for alcohol-related than other goal-related words. This outcome was expected, because procuring and imbibing alcohol is a compelling goal of alcohol abusers that often exceeds the importance of their other goal pursuits.

Cox and colleagues (2002a) assessed alcohol abusers' and nonabusers' goals with an interview analog of a reduced MSQ. Using the same three categories of stimuli as Cox, Blount, and Rozak (2000b), they assessed participants' reaction times on the Stroop task at two time points: upon the alcohol abusers' admission to inpatient treatment and immediately before discharge four weeks later, and at similar time points in the case of the nonabusers. Several findings of this study are noteworthy. First, compared to control participants and alcohol abusers who completed the four weeks of treatment, those who did not complete treatment were highly distracted by concern-related stimuli at treatment admission. These alcohol abusers seemed to have low motivation for treatment and great distraction for the concern-related stimuli because of serious financial, housing, relationship, and health problems that burdened their lives. Second, during the four weeks of inpatient treatment there was a significant increase in attentional distraction for alcohol stimuli but only among the alcohol abusers who at a later three-month follow-up had either relapsed or lost contact with the treatment service. Thus, attentional bias for disorder-related stimuli measured during treatment predicted later outcome.

Using a short form of the PCI to assess cognitive and motivational variables related to college students' alcohol use, Fadardi (in preparation) and Fadardi and Cox (2002) identified adaptive and maladaptive motivational factors similar to those described above. Although both maladaptive motivation and alcohol attentional distraction on the emotional Stroop task were positively and significantly related to the amount of alcohol that participants consumed, only attentional bias remained a significant predictor after maladaptive motivation and other variables had been controlled.

The various results on cognitive interference from participants' idiographic concern-related stimuli taken from their MSQ responses add to evidence for the construct validity of the MSQ.

Association of Assessed Goals with Subsequent Actions

Action is an imperfect guide to motivation, because equally important goals may entail different time frames and during a given time period may entail different amounts of activity. Nevertheless, one might expect at least a loose relationship between levels of motivation for particular goals and amounts of activity directed toward attaining them. These relationships have been investigated in at least three studies.

In the first (Church, Klinger, & Langenberg, 1984; Klinger, 1987), 12 university students and staff took the IntQ twice at one-month intervals and, beginning a week after the first IntQ, maintained a diary of their daily activities. At the end of their participation, they indicated toward which of the goals listed on their IntQ responses each activity was primarily directed. The percentage of diary activities related to any one of the goals listed on their previous IntQ ranged from 81% on the first diary day (a week after their first IntQ) to 56% ten days later. It was still 60% 28 days after taking the first IntQ. Thus, at least in participants' own view, the IntQ goals predicted a large proportion of their subsequent activities.

To investigate the question of whether participants' ratings of their goals predict the amount of activity they engage in toward attaining those goals, Church, Klinger, and Langenberg (1984) reduced all the scores on each scale to standard z scores within each participant's data and, separately for each participant, correlated these scores with (a) the number of activities reported in diaries over the three-week reporting period and (b) the number of days on which at least one activity was directed toward each goal. These correlations were then pooled across the 12 participants. Both activity measures were significantly predicted by IntQ ratings of goals on five scales: Commitment, anticipated Joy at goal attainment, anticipated Sorrow at final failure to attain the goal, Probability of Success, and Internality (Probability of Success If No Action is taken to attain the goal). The best predictor was the product of Sorrow and Internality, which correlated .36 with number of days on which goal-related activity occurred and .34 with the number of goal-related activities (for both correlations $p < .01$ by one-sample t-tests of the 12 z-transformed individual-participant correlations).

A second investigation administered a variant of the MSQ adapted to employment settings, the Work Concerns Inventory (WCI; Roberson, 1989; Roberson & Sluss, Chapter 14, this volume), to 37 employees of a nonprofit community service agency and then sampled their activities with programmed signals to record current activity over the following five work days. Of the 665 activities recorded, 76% were related to one or more of the goals listed on the WCI. As in the study by Church, Klinger, and Langenberg (1984) the WCI scale ratings of each goal were correlated separately within each employee's data with the number of reported activities that were directed toward the respective goals. The mean multiple correlation of the scale ratings as predictors of number of activities was .43 ($t\,[26] = 18.70, p < .001$), providing impressive evidence for the validity of the WCI. The scales that contributed significantly to prediction were Commitment, Valence (roughly parallel to Joy/Happiness), and Time Available (for beginning action toward a goal). Unhappiness was also significantly and negatively correlated with number of activities but did not have a significant regression coefficient when entered with the set of other WCI predictors.

In a third investigation (Baumann, 1998 and Chapter 10, this volume; Baumann & Kuhl, in press; Kazén, Baumann, & Kuhl, 2002), after taking a German translation of the MSQ (Cox et al., 1995) 41 participants returned a week later and rated their MSQ goals on their having taken actions to attain them. A number of MSQ scale scores significantly predicted taking action: Commitment, .40 ($p < .01$), Inappropriate Commitment (which can be viewed as low threshold for committing to a goal), .32 ($p < .05$), Probability of Success, .37 ($p < .05$), and Internality/Efficacy (.34, $p < .01$). These correlations, which are in strong agreement with those found in the other investigations, indicate the robustness of the relationship between MSQ-style measures of individuals' goals and activity undertaken to attain them.

Discriminability of Individual Behavior Patterns from MSQ Content

It might be argued that with the similarity in human activity patterns, especially in a relatively homogeneous university-related group, anyone's activities would have a good chance of matching anyone else's IntQ or MSQ list of goals. To check on this possibility, Church, Klinger, and Langenberg (1984) enlisted the help of five judges who were uninformed about which IntQ respondent generated which activities during the subsequent one-month interval. Each judge received the separate IntQ goal lists of two participants of the same sex and a list of their activities from their first diary day, with the activities from the two participants randomly intermixed in a single activity list. Different judges worked with different pairs of respondents. The judges' task was to guess which activity came from which participant, based only on knowledge of their respective IntQ goal lists. Their judgments were correct far more often than chance: 77% of the time (χ^2 [1, $N = 96$ activities] $= 28.2$, $p < .001$). This yielded a *phi* coefficient of .54 versus a maximum possible value of .78. Thus, the IntQ goals permitted clear-cut discrimination between pairs of participants.

The judges were also asked to rate the likelihood that each activity was directed toward each goal listed on the previous IntQ. Taking those activities rated as at least "highly likely" to have been directed at particular goals, 50% of the activities were judged to be related to the goals of the participant who reported the activities, and only 24% of the activities were judged to be related to goals listed by the other participant in the pair (t [9] $=$ 2.46, $p < .001$). Thus, the relation of activities to IntQ goals cannot be attributed purely to similarities among participants. The goal lists permitted real distinctions among individuals and hence characterized them as individuals.

Validity of MSQ-Like Scale Scores

In addition to the relationships described in previous sections, which involve the raw contents of respondents' goal lists, scale scores from the MSQ, the WCI, the PCI, and related instruments have been found correlated with numerous other variables in theoretically meaningful ways. These correlations support the construct validity of these measures.

Some of this evidence is discussed in other chapters of this volume and hence need not be elaborated here. In those instances, this section samples these findings and refers readers to other chapters that discuss the evidence at greater length.

Relationships with Goal and Personality Attributes

Baumann (1998 and Chapter 10, this volume; Baumann & Kuhl, in press) described important relationships between German MSQ scales and other properties of goals, as well as volitional personality traits. Thus, for instance, individuals' mean Commitment scores were correlated with the mean self-congruence of their goals. Commitment was correlated positively with trait persistence at goal-striving and inversely with the trait of ruminating about failures. Individuals' mean Inappropriate Commitment (also interpretable as low threshold for forming commitments) was strongly negatively correlated with rumination about failure, perhaps suggesting that commitments are easier to form if the emotional costs of failure, as represented by rumination, are more modest.

The MSQ index Sorrow in Excess of Joy (i.e., anticipating more sorrow at failure to reach goals than joy at attaining them) was correlated inversely with the self-congruence of the individual's goals. This Sorrow index was also higher for goals that constituted duties rather than self-generated wishes, and was correlated, as was Hopelessness, with the subjective effortfulness of striving for goals.

Goal Distance (tending to commit to longer-range goals) and Inefficacy were correlated with both depression and anxiety. So were Ambivalence and Hopelessness, although their correlations with depression fell just short of significance.

Unpublished data collected by the first author of this chapter from a sample of 122 American students indicates little correlation of MSQ scales with scales of the Multidimensional Personality Questionnaire (MPQ; Tellegen, 1982; Tellegen et al., 1988). This suggests that the motivational variables tapped by the MSQ are substantially independent of traditional personality dimensions and therefore add new perspectives on their respondents. Those correlations that exist, however, make conceptual sense. Thus, the second-order MPQ Positive Affectivity scale correlated significantly ($N = 121$, $p < .05$) with MSQ (individual mean) Joy anticipated at goal attainment (.19), subjective Probability of Success (.23), and Sorrow anticipated at failure to attain goals (.22). Second-order MPQ Constraint correlated significantly with Joy (.20) and Probability of Success (.21). One component of MPQ Positive Affectivity, Well-Being, correlated with Probability of Success at r [119] $= .36$, $p = .000$.

Within a group of Czech alcoholic inpatients, a state-oriented group (given to ruminating after failure and hesitating unduly before making decisions) were marked by greater MSQ "feelings of ineffectiveness, hopelessness and emotional ambivalence, with higher passivity and with tendency to choose disproportionately [more] aversive goals" (Stuchlíková & Man, 1999, p. 63). As in Baumann's findings with a German sample (Chapter 10, this volume), rumination was inversely related to Inappropriate Commitment (low threshold for committing to goals), suggesting that this is a robust finding.

Associations with Alcohol and Other Substance Consumption and Abuse

The first of the two factors based on MSQ scales, described above as adaptive and maladaptive motivation (Cox et al., 2000a, 2002a), has a very modest first-order correlation with amount of alcohol consumed by college students but a significant interaction with scores on the short Michigan Alcohol Screening Test (SMAST) in its effects on alcohol consumption (Cox et al., 2002b). The SMAST in essence assesses the number of life problems encountered by respondents as a result of their drinking. For those who experienced no such problems, the correlation between MSQ Factor 1 and amount of alcohol consumed annually was essentially zero. For those who experienced any problems, r [154] $= -.22$, $p < .01$. Within this problem group, the more problems respondents had experienced, the higher the correlation between MSQ Factor 1 and alcohol consumption, reaching r [27] $= -.45$, $p < .01$, for those who reported three or more problems caused by drinking alcohol. These relationships were remarkably similar across the four different country samples in the study.

These results both demonstrate the predictive validity of MSQ Factor 1 (adaptive motivation) and make an important theoretical point: Motivational structure is irrelevant to drinking patterns unless drinking poses a problem to solve. Then, the greater the problem, the more important adaptive motivation is to solving it. People with no reason to reduce alcohol use are unlikely to do so, regardless of their motivational soundness. For those who have reason to reduce their drinking, adaptive motivation—satisfying goals to pursue other than drinking—is associated with reduced drinking.

In other studies, Fadardi (in preparation) and Fadardi and Cox (2002) found that maladaptive motivation, as assessed with a short form of the PCI, was positively related to the amount of alcohol that participants consumed. Hosier (2002) and Hosier and Cox (2002) found that maladaptive motivation as measured by the short PCI predicted the number of alcohol-related problems that college students experienced, in this case after alcohol consumption and other alcohol-use variables had been controlled.

Two other investigations compared groups of Czech alcoholic patients with socioeconomically similar students (Man, Stuchlíková, & Klinger, 1998) or community adult groups (Stuchlíková, Man, & Popov, 1999). In the first, smaller sample, the alcoholic patients listed 40% fewer goals, scored lower on Inappropriate Commitment (presumably because of greater reluctance to commit to goals), reported marginally less average commitment to their goals, and, after other variables were partialed out, reported greater Inefficacy (i.e., less feeling of control over goal attainment). In the second investigation, the groups differed in the proportion of goals that were avoidant and in which anticipated sorrow after failure exceeded anticipated joy at goal attainment, and, again, in less feeling of control over goal attainment.

An investigation using a German version of the MSQ (Zielaktivierung und Zielklärung [ZAK]; Schroer, 2001; Schroer, Fuhrmann, & de Jong-Meyer, Chapter 12, this volume) compared a group of alcoholic patients with nonalcoholic controls. Like the findings of Man, Stuchlíková, and Klinger (1998), the alcoholic patients reported fewer goals than the controls did; a depressed group reported even fewer. However, in this instance the alcoholic group reported higher Probability of Success, Commitment, and anticipated Sorrow upon failure than the comparison group did.

Prediction of Responses to Alcohol Treatment Programs

There have been a number of investigations of the ability of IntQ, MSQ, and PCI scales to predict response to treatment for alcohol abuse. The first of these (Klinger & Cox, 1986) examined IntQ scales in relation to a dichotomized assessment of treatment outcome:

satisfactory or not. A stepwise discriminant analysis and correlational analyses indicated that successful outcomes were significantly related to having positive treatment goals, lacking concerns about avoiding alcohol, and expecting early attainment of goals.

In an investigation of a group version of Systematic Motivational Counseling (Schroer, 2001; Schroer, Fuhrmann, & de Jong-Meyer, Chapter 12, this volume), ZAK (German MSQ version) Component 1 (the adaptive motivation factor) was inversely related to health-related quality of life at the start of treatment but positively related to subjective well-being at the end of treatment.

Another investigation (Glasner et al., 2001; see also Glasner, Chapter 2, this volume) cluster-analyzed MSQs of 202 alcoholic veterans entering a 30-day treatment program, identifying two clusters, which were significantly related to post-treatment drinking patterns assessed at 12-month follow-up. One cluster, which was characterized by more active pursuit of more readily attainable goals other than substance use, reported more feelings of guilt upon relapse and were more likely to relapse in social drinking settings. The other cluster, marked by more passive pursuit of nonchemical goals that were on average more often inappropriate or unrealistic, was more likely to drink heavily when they relapsed, tended more toward binge-drinking, experienced stronger mood changes in response to drinking, and manifested more externalizing behaviors while drinking, such as illegal acts, arguing, and fighting. Here, again, a healthier motivational structure as assessed by the MSQ was associated with a different, socially less undesirable drinking outcome.

Cox and colleagues (2000a) sought to identify the motivational context in which substance abusers pass through the precontemplation, contemplation, action, and maintenance stages of change (Prochaska & DiClemente, 1986, 1992). Using the MSQ and the University of Rhode Island Change Assessment (URICA; McConnaughy, Prochaska, & Velicer, 1983), regression analysis revealed that the adaptive motivational-structure component of the MSQ was a negative predictor of problem denial. The adaptive component was also a positive predictor of determination to change; that is, the adaptively motivated participants both recognized the problem and were motivated to change it.

Prediction of Work Satisfaction

Roberson's investigation of an employee group (1989 and Chapter 14, this volume) described above had as its principal objective the prediction of work satisfaction. The best psychological predictors of work satisfaction were a number of WCI scales. The more satisfied workers scored higher on Commitment, perceived higher Chances of Success, and reported fewer negative goals.

SUMMARY

Despite their unconventional design, assessments of motivational structure using idiothetic techniques such as the MSQ and PCI attain acceptable levels of reliability and construct validity. The scales they generate have produced reasonably replicable and useful factor structures. They have produced theoretically interesting results and, as indicated in Chapters 11 to 15 of this volume, clinical and organizational psychologists have found them useful tools around which to build interventions.

REFERENCES

Baumann, N. (1998). *Selbst- versus Fremdbestimmung: Zum Einfluß von Stimmung, Bewußtheit und Persönlichkeit* [*Self- versus other-determination: The influence of mood, consciousness, and personality*]. Unpublished dissertation. Osnabrück, Germany: University of Osnabrück.

Baumann, N., & Kuhl, J. (in press). Self-infiltration: Confusing assigned tasks as self-selected in memory. *Personality and Social Psychology Bulletin.*

Church, A.T., Klinger, E., & Langenberg, C. (1984). *Combined idiographic and nomothetic assessment of the current concerns motivational construct.* Unpublished manuscript.

Cox, W.M., Blount, J.P., Bair, J., & Hosier, S.G. (2000a). Motivational predictors of readiness to change chronic substance abuse. *Addiction Research, 8,* 121–128.

Cox, W.M., Blount, J.P., & Rozak, A.M. (2000b). Alcohol abusers' and nonabusers' distraction by alcohol and concern-related stimuli. *American Journal of Drug and Alcohol Abuse, 26,* 489–495.

Cox, W.M., Heinemann, A.W., Miranti, S.V., Schmidt, M., Klinger, E., & Blount, J. (2003). Outcomes of Systematic Motivational Counseling for substance use following traumatic brain injury. *Journal of Addictive Diseases.*

Cox, W.M., Hogan, L.M., Kristian, M.R., & Race, J.H. (2002a). Alcohol attentional bias as a predictor of alcohol abusers' treatment outcome. *Drug and Alcohol Dependence, 68,* 237–243.

Cox, W.M., & Klinger, E. (2000b). *Personal Concerns Inventory.* Copyrighted test available from W. Miles Cox.

Cox, W.M., Klinger, E., Fuhrmann, A., & de Jong-Meyer, R. (1995). *Fragebogen zu gegenwärtigen Anliegen* (FGA). (German adaptation of the MSQ.) Unpublished manuscript. Münster, Germany: University of Münster.

Cox, W.M., Pothos, E.M., & Hosier, S.G. (in preparation). *Determinants of alcohol abusers' success in changing.* Unpublished investigation.

Cox, W.M., Schippers, G.M., Klinger, E., Skutle, A., Stuchlíková, I., Man, F., King, A.L., & Inderhaug, R. (2002b). Motivational structure and alcohol use of university students with consistency across four nations. *Journal of Studies on Alcohol, 63,* 280–285.

Emmons, R.A. (1986). Personal strivings: An approach to personality and subjective well-being. *Journal of Personality and Social Psychology, 51,* 1058–1068.

Emmons, R.A. (1999). *The psychology of ultimate concerns: Motivation and spirituality in personality.* New York: Guilford.

Fadardi, J.S. (in preparation). *Motivational structure and executive control as determinants of attentional bias for alcohol-related stimuli: Therapeutic implications.* Ph.D. dissertation. University of Wales, Bangor, UK.

Fadardi, J.S., & Cox, W.M. (2002, September). *Two predictors make a more robust prediction: Motivational structure and attentional bias as predictors of alcohol use among university students.* Poster presented at the Addiction 2002 Conference, Eindhoven, The Netherlands.

Glasner, S.V., Cox W.M., Klinger, E., & Parish, C. (2001). *The relation of motivational structure to post-treatment drinking behavior in a male alcoholic sample.* Paper presented at the annual meeting of the American Society of Addiction Medicine, Los Angeles, April, 2001.

Hoelscher, T.J., Klinger, E., & Barta, S.G. (1981). Incorporation of concern- and nonconcern-related verbal stimuli into dream content. *Journal of Abnormal Psychology, 49,* 88–91.

Hosier, S.G. (2002). *An evaluation of two brief interventions aimed at reducing college students' alcohol use.* Unpublished doctoral dissertation. University of Wales, Bangor, UK

Hosier, S.G., & Cox, W.M. (2002, September). *Factors predicting heavy alcohol use and alcohol-related problems among university students.* Poster presented at the Addiction 2002 Conference, Eindhoven, The Netherlands.

Kazén, M., Baumann, N., & Kuhl, J. (2002). *Self-infiltration vs. self-compatibility checking in dealing with unattractive tasks and unpleasant items: The moderating influence of state vs. action-orientation.* Unpublished manuscript. Osnabrück, Germany: University of Osnabrück.

Klinger, E. (1978). Modes of normal conscious flow. In K.S. Pope & J.L. Singer (Eds.), *The stream of consciousness: Scientific investigations into the flow of human experience* (pp. 225–258). New York: Plenum.

Klinger, E. (1987). The Interview Questionnaire technique: Reliability and validity of a mixed idiographic–nomothetic measure of motivation. In J.N. Butcher & C.D. Spielberger (Eds.), *Advances in personality assessment* (Vol. 6; pp. 31–48). Hillsdale, NJ: Erlbaum.

Klinger, E. (1996a). The contents of thoughts: Interference as the downside of adaptive normal mechanisms in thought flow. In I.G. Sarason, B.R. Sarason, & G.R. Pierce (Eds.), *Cognitive interference: Theories, methods, and findings* (pp. 3–23). Hillsdale, NJ: Erlbaum.

Klinger, E. (1996b). Emotional influences on cognitive processing, with implications for theories of both. In P. Gollwitzer & J.A. Bargh (Eds.), *The psychology of action: Linking cognition and motivation to behavior* (pp. 168–189). New York: Guilford.

Klinger, E., Barta, S.G., & Maxeiner, M.E. (1980). Motivational correlates of thought content frequency and commitment. *Journal of Personality and Social Psychology, 39*, 1222–1237.

Klinger, E., & Cox, W.M. (1986). Motivational predictors of alcoholics' responses to inpatient treatment. *Advances in Alcohol and Substance Abuse, 6*, 35–44.

Klinger, E., Cox, W.M., & Blount, J.P. (1995). Motivational Structure Questionnaire (MSQ). In J.P. Allen & M. Columbus (Eds.), *Assessing alcohol problems: A guide for clinicians and researchers* (pp. 399–411). Washington, DC: US Department of Health and Human Services.

Lamiell, J.R. (1981). Toward an idiothetic psychology of personality. *American Psychologist, 36*, 276–289.

Little, B.R. (1983). Personal projects: A rationale and method for investigation. *Environment and Behavior, 15*, 273–309.

Man, F., Stuchlíková, I., & Klinger, E. (1998). Motivational structure of alcoholic and nonalcoholic Czech men. *Psychological Reports, 82*, 1091–1106.

McConnaughy, E.A., Prochaska, J.O., & Velicer, W.F. (1983). Stages of change in psychotherapy: Measurement and sample profiles. *Psychotherapy: Theory, Research and Practice, 20*, 368–375.

Nikles, C.D. II, Brecht, D.L., Klinger, E., & Bursell, A.L. (1998). The Effects of current-concern- and nonconcern-related waking suggestions on nocturnal dream content. *Journal of Personality and Social Psychology, 75*, 242–255.

Nikula, R.M.K., Klinger, E., & Larson-Gutman (1993). Current concerns and electrodermal reactivity: Responses to words and throughts. *Journal of Personality, 61*, 63–84.

Prochaska, J.O., & DiClemente, C.C. (1986). Toward a comprehensive model of change. In W.R. Miller & N. Heather (Eds.), *Treating addictive behaviors: Processes of change*. New York: Plenum.

Prochaska, J.O., & DiClemente, C.C. (1992). In search of how people change: Applications to addictive behaviors. *American Psychologist, 47*, 1102–1114.

Riemann, B.C., Amir, N., & Louro, C.E. (1995). *Cognitive processing of personally relevant information in panic disorder*. Unpublished manuscript.

Riemann, B.C. & McNally, R.J. (1995). Cognitive processing of personally-relevant information. *Cognition and Emotion, 9*, 325–340.

Roberson, L. (1989). Assessing personal work goals in the organizational setting: Development and evaluation of the Work Concerns Inventory. *Organizational Behavior and Human Decision Processes, 44*, 345–367.

Schroer, B.M. (2001). *Zielaktivierung und Zielklärung (ZAK): Evaluation einer gruppentherapeutischen Kurzintervention in der Entzugsbehandlung alkoholabhängiger Menschen [Goal activation and goal clarification (ZAK): Evaluation of a group therapeutic brief intervention in the addiction treatment of alcohol-dependent people]*. Unpublished doctoral dissertation. Westfällische Wilhelms-Universität Münster, Germany.

Stuchlíková, I., & Man, F. (1999). Motivational structure of state and action oriented alcoholics. *Studia Psychologica, 41*, 63–72.

Stuchlíková, I., Man, F., & Popov, P. (1999). Motivacni struktura alkoholove zavislych v porovnani se vzorkem populace (Motivational structure of alcoholic and nonalcoholic Czech persons). *Ceskoslovenska Psychologie, 43*, 193–204.

Tellegen, A. (1982) *Brief manual for the Differential Personality Questionnaire*. Unpublished manuscript. University of Minnesota, Minneapolis.

Tellegen, A., Lykken, D.T., Bouchard, T.J., Wilcox, K.J., et al. (1988). Personality similarity in twins reared apart and together. *Journal of Personality and Social Psychology, 54*, 1031–1039.

CHAPTER 10

Volitional and Emotional Correlates of the Motivational Structure Questionnaire: Further Evidence for Construct Validity

Nicola Baumann
University of Osnabrück, Germany

Synopsis.—This chapter presents relationships between the Motivational Structure Questionnaire (MSQ) and personality and clinical questionnaires as well as behavioral measures that contribute to the construct validity of the MSQ. The MSQ showed theoretically consistent relationships with a personality disposition toward state versus action orientation and clinical measures of depression and anxiety. In addition to interindividual differences in motivational structure, MSQ indices reflected intraindividual differences in motivational characteristics between wishes, duties, and intentions. Furthermore, MSQ indices predicted difficulties with subsequent actual goal enactment, as retrospectively rated by participants. Consistent relationships were found not only for self-report measures but also for implicit, nonreactive measures of self-infiltration (i.e., false self-attribution of externally controlled goals or activities) and alienation (i.e., difficulties in perceiving and enacting emotional preferences). The experimental data suggest that specific motivational structures may be interpreted as instances of volitional inhibition or self-inhibition. In sum, findings contribute to the validity of the MSQ.

The study on which the present chapter* is based was originally designed to examine determinants of self-infiltration (Baumann & Kuhl, 2003; Kazén, Baumann, & Kuhl, in press), and to explore self-infiltration effects in the context of personal goals and goal pursuit (Baumann, 1998). Self-infiltration is defined in terms of a confounding between self-congruent and self-alien (e.g., assigned) goals and activities. Operationally, misperceiving an assigned activity as self-selected in retrospective memory is taken as a measure of self-infiltration. Self-infiltration can be regarded as an indicator of poor self-awareness

---

* The author gratefully acknowledges the contribution of Julius Kuhl to this chapter.

Handbook of Motivational Counseling. Edited by W. Miles Cox and Eric Klinger.
© 2004 John Wiley & Sons, Ltd.

and self-accessibility. When people lose access to self-related knowledge, their ability to discriminate between self-congruent and externally controlled goals and actions is impaired. Consequently, they may strive for more goals with which they do not identify (e.g., striving because they believe in the importance of a goal) but introjected (e.g., striving because they feel that they ought to and because they would feel ashamed or guilty if they didn't). The type of internalization (or degree of self-integration of goals) and appropriate commitment are important aspects of motivation that have consequences for effort investment, goal attainment, and subjective well-being (Baumann, 1998; Brunstein, Schultheiss, & Graessman, 1998; Deci & Ryan, 2000; Sheldon & Elliot, 1998; Sheldon & Kasser, 1995).

Individual differences in the maintenance of self-access when exposed to aversive experiences (e.g., failure) are captured by the personality disposition toward *state versus action orientation* (Kuhl, 1994a). It consists of three components:

1. Failure-related action orientation (AOF) describes the ability to return to action quickly after a negative experience in contrast to ruminating about it (disengagement versus preoccupation). It is associated with the ability to self-regulate or top-down reduce negative affect and to maintain self-access in the presence of aversive events.
2. Decision-related action orientation (AOD) describes the ability to act upon decisions quickly instead of hesitating to initiate an intended activity (initiative versus hesitation). It is associated with the ability to self-generate positive affect that is needed for action, especially when difficult intentions are active and uncompleted.
3. Performance-related action orientation (AOP) describes the ability to become immersed in a pleasant activity in contrast to premature shifting between activities (persistence versus volatility). These individual differences in volitional action control are thought to influence a person's current concerns and motivational structure.

As clinical parameters, depression and anxiety were assessed in the study described in this chapter. Depression has been related to negative thinking (Beck, 1967; Dykman, 1996; Rude et al., 2001; Wenzlaff & Bates, 1998), unrealistic belief systems (Chang, 1997; Ellis, 1977), and—as a common pathway to various aspects of depression—the maintenance of degenerated intentions (Kuhl & Helle, 1986). These aspects of depression should be reflected in typical patterns of MSQ indices. In turn, individuals with a dysfunctional motivational structure should experience higher depressive and anxious symptoms over time.

Other data reported in this chapter show that MSQ indices meaningfully differentiate between different categories of goal pursuits (i.e., wishes, duties, and intentions) and demonstrate theoretically consistent relationships with additional goal characteristics (e.g. "self-congruence," "perceived effort") and actual goal performance after one week. In addition, there were interesting relationships between MSQ indices and measures of self-infiltration and alienation from one's preferences. Findings further contribute to the validity of the MSQ and are discussed in the context of the theory of Personality Systems Interactions (PSI; Kuhl, 2000) on which the study is based.

THEORETICAL BACKGROUND OF THE STUDY

A central assumption of PSI theory is that the activation of cognitive systems (intention memory, behavioral output control, extension memory, and an object recognition system) is modulated through positive and negative affect. Different modes of volitional action control can be described in terms of typical interactions of the four cognitive and two affective systems (see Kuhl, 2000; Kuhl & Fuhrmann, 1998). The activation dynamics of these basic systems may also contribute to differences in motivational structure. For example, finding appropriate and self-compatible goals is supported by a broad associative network system (*extension memory*) providing implicit self-representations of one's own feelings, preferences, and needs, and making many action alternatives simultaneously available on the basis of autobiographical experiences (Kuhl, 2000). The self-related aspects of extension memory are called the *self-system*. An example of a content of extension memory that is not part of the self-system is a polysemantic representation of a word including simultaneous implicit awareness of its alternative meanings (e.g., "bank" of a river and as a money transaction place) and its relationships with other concepts. It is assumed that the representation of *persons* (including oneself and other people) requires this representational format of extended parallel and implicit semantic networks because of the complexity of persons. Without access to this holistic system, a person cannot be perceived in his or her full complexity (i.e., as a whole), but only in terms of specific aspects that are singled out from the full, holistic representation—for instance, because these aspects are instrumental for the perceiver's current intentions and purposes.

The *negative affect modulation hypothesis* of PSI theory states that unless negative affect can be down-regulated, it reduces access to the self-system and facilitates elementary sensations and attentional orienting toward novel or self-incongruent stimuli. The inability to down-regulate negative affect once aroused is expected to reduce the ability to view people (oneself and others) as a whole and increase the tendency to perceive them as "objects." According to PSI theory, object perception is supported by a system that isolates a bunch of details forming an "object" from the context. This decontextualization is useful when attention is to be focused on unexpected or dangerous details and when these details are to be recognized on a later occasion (e.g., as a warning cue). However, self-integration and realization of personal goals often require top-down inhibition of the unexpected or unwanted thoughts and feelings that are ushered in by negative affect. State-oriented preoccupation is conceived of as a low ability to self-regulate negative affect. When negative affect (e.g., life-stress) is high, state-oriented individuals lose self-access and have difficulties in integrating social expectations, personal needs, and preferences and in developing self-determined goals and life perspectives.

The *positive affect modulation hypothesis* of PSI theory states that positive affect facilitates the implementation of difficult intentions through re-establishing the connection between the intention memory and its output system (Kuhl, 2000). One crucial adaptive function of forming an intention is to inhibit its immediate enactment because a problem needs to be solved or an appropriate opportunity needs to be awaited (Kuhl & Kazén, 1999). This inhibition is released through positive affect. When situational demands are high and intentions are difficult, people may lack the positive affect to put their intentions into action. State-oriented hesitation is conceived of as a low ability to self-generate positive affect. It can lead to a motivational structure characterized by conscious awareness of intentions, high motivation, and feelings of low efficiency in the implementation of intentions.

To summarize, PSI theory predicts a modulating influence of positive and negative affect on cognitive systems. Individual differences in self-regulated coping with affect (i.e., action versus state orientation) lead to specific system configurations that are expected to correlate with motivational structure.

DESCRIPTION OF THE STUDY

Forty-seven participants (30 women and 17 men) were recruited through flyers around the University of Osnabrück. Their mean age was 28 years (range 19 to 51). Participants, who were remunerated for their participation, were tested individually. At the beginning of the experimental session they filled out a mood adjective checklist with four negative items ("sad," "depressed," "anxious," "sorrowful") and four positive items ("happy," "joyful," "sociable," "interested"), the Action Control Scale (ACS-90; Kuhl, 1994b), the Beck Depression Inventory (BDI; Beck, 1967), and the Beck Anxiety Inventory (BAI; Beck et al., 1988). As part of a nonreactive method to measure self-infiltration, they were introduced to a computer-aided simulation of a secretary's working day (Kuhl & Kazén, 1994). First, participants rated the attractiveness of 48 simple office activities (e.g., "sharpening pencils," "sorting letters"). Office activities were median split into items of high versus low attractiveness. Taking the role of a secretary, participants selected some of the activities for later enactment. The experimenter, taking the role of the boss, additionally assigned some activities to them while other activities remained not chosen. The computer program allowed for complete balancing of item attractiveness, self-selection, and external assignment. Thus, equal numbers of highly attractive and unattractive activities were originally (a) selected by both participant and experimenter, (b) self-selected by the participant, (c) assigned by the experimenter, and (d) unselected and unassigned, respectively.

A German adaptation of the MSQ was administered (Cox et al., 1995). Participants listed their current concerns and rated them along several dimensions that allowed calculation of the following MSQ indices:

> (1) *Number of Concerns*, that is, the total number of concerns that participants named throughout a list of major life areas. (2) *Commitment*, that is, the degree to which participants feel committed to achieving the goals that they have named. (3) *Inappropriate Commitment*, that is, (a) the degree to which participants are committed to achieving goals for which they expect little chance of success and/or (b) from which they expect to derive little emotional satisfaction. (4) *Anticipated Sorrow in Excess of Joy*, that is, the number of concerns that participants have in which the amount of sorrow that they expect to experience if they do *not* reach their goal exceeds the amount of joy that they expect to experience if they *do* reach their goal. (5) *Ambivalence*, that is, the number of goals for which participants expect to experience joy and unhappiness that are close in intensity. (6) *Emotional Intensity*, that is, the sum of participants' anticipated affect upon reaching or failing to reach their goals. (7) *Hopelessness*, that is, the degree to which participants feel that they have little chance of success in reaching their goals. (8) *Inefficacy*, that is, the degree to which participants feel that their chances of succeeding at their goals are the same, regardless of whether or not they take action. (9) *Goal Distance*, that is, the degree to which participants perceive that their actual attainment of the goals that they are striving for will occur far in the future. (10) *Preparation Time*, that is, the degree to which participants perceive that there is a long interval between (a) the time that they must start taking action if they are to succeed at their goals, and (b) the time of their actual goal attainment. (Cox, Klinger, & Blount, 1999).

Subsequently, an unexpected memory test was carried out for the initial source of office activities. Participants were asked to classify each activity as previously self-selected or not self-selected. Self-infiltration was assessed by a significantly higher rate of false self-ascriptions of assigned unattractive activities compared to unassigned and unselected unattractive activities (i.e., falsely classifying an assigned activity as self-chosen in the retrospective memory test). Finally, participants made a final choice about the office activities. They were asked to successively mark any 24 activities according to their preferred order of enactment. *Alienation* was assessed by a deficit in making final choices according to one's preferences—that is, a low tendency to select highly attractive activities earlier and more often than unattractive activities. The experimental session lasted about 90 minutes. A follow-up questionnaire was administered after one week.

STATE AND ACTION ORIENTATION

State-orientated preoccupation is conceived of as a low ability to self-regulate or reduce negative affect. As a result, state orientation (i.e., low AOF) should be associated with a decreased access to holistic representations and an increased focus on single, decontextualized objects such as thoughts, emotions, and persons perceived as "objects" rather than in their complexity. As long as access to self-representations can be maintained, a person has an extended feeling of what belongs to his or her current concerns, goals, and preferences and what does not. Access to this implicit knowledge is necessary to identify and inhibit whatever is not wanted at the moment—for example, distracting thoughts and emotions. Thus, for state-oriented individuals, whose distracting thoughts ushered in by negative affect and other unwanted experiences are not inhibited as long as negative affect that impairs self-access cannot be down-regulated, goals may not be checked for self-compatibility, and an extended network of action alternatives is not available.

As shown in Table 10.1, AOF or disengagement (from rumination and unrealistic goals) was associated with more current concerns, lower commitment as well as lower inappropriate commitment, lower emotional intensity, and shorter goal distance. Interestingly, the number of current concerns was not indicative of preoccupation and low volitional control. In a similar vein, Klinger and Murphy (1994) found action-oriented individuals to engage in daydreams to the same extent as state-oriented individuals but to feel more accepting of their daydreams. Rumination or daydreaming per se can be controllable or uncontrollable (Klinger, 1981; Martin & Tesser, 1989). In the present study, current concerns were indeed related to uncontrollable (state-oriented) preoccupation when they referred to goals that promised little chance of success and/or little emotional satisfaction (i.e., inappropriate commitment). Action-oriented individuals were less committed to achieving such inappropriate goals. In contrast, they identified more short-term goals. Concentrating on smaller subgoals and concrete action steps might increase chances of success and facilitate disengagement in case of failure because they are alternative means to an end. The finding that failure-related state orientation (i.e., low AOF) is associated with increased commitment combined with increased inappropriate commitment is consistent with the theoretical assumption that state orientation is characterized by an impaired access to self-representations when exposed to failure or other aversive events. When personal needs and priorities and personal experiences concerning the attainability of a goal are not readily accessible, it is difficult to identify inappropriate commitments—that is, commitments that are not compatible with one's needs and priorities or that cannot be expected to be accomplished on the basis of one's personal experiences with comparable goals and activities. This view is also compatible with the assumption that inappropriate commitment may represent a low threshold for commitment (Man, Stuchlíková, & Klinger, 1998; see also Klinger & Cox, Chapter 1, this volume). Action-oriented individuals need to feel self-compatibility before committing to goals, but state-oriented individuals may commit themselves to goals even without feeling self-compatibility and merely because of social expectations. The positive

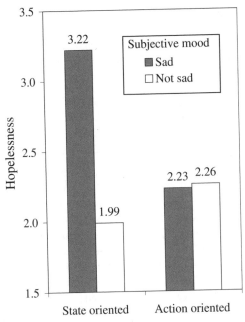

Figure 10.1 Mean hopelessness as a function of failure-related state and action orientation and subjective sadness

correlation between inappropriate commitment and self-infiltration (discussed below) further supports this assumption.

Another way to test state-oriented participants' reduced self-access when negative affect is high was to look for interaction effects between state and action orientation and subjective mood. Therefore, MSQ indices were analyzed using a 2 (state versus action orientation) by 2 (low versus high subjective sadness) analysis of variance. Results yielded a marginally significant AOF × Subjective Sadness interaction for "Hopelessness," $F (1, 43) = 3.80$, $p < .06$. As depicted in Figure 10.1, state-oriented participants reporting high sadness were more pessimistic about their chances of success than state-oriented participants reporting low sadness. The independent-samples t test was significant, $t (22) = 3.47, p < .002$. Action-oriented participants were less influenced by their momentary mood. They did not feel very hopeless in either mood state.

In addition, there was a significant AOF × Subjective Sadness interaction for "Inefficiency," $F (1, 43) = 4.19, p < .05$. As depicted in Figure 10.2, state-oriented participants who were sad felt more inefficient in goal attainment than state-oriented participants who were not sad. The independent t test was significant, $t (22) = 4.15, p < .001$. In contrast, action-oriented participants did not feel inefficient, irrespective of their momentary mood.

According to PSI theory, these findings can be explained on the basis of the functional characteristics of extension memory, which integrates numerous personal experiences (constituting the self). Subjective expectancies are based on implicit access to extended networks (in extension memory) of personal experiences that specify successful action alternatives (Kuhl, 2001, p. 261). According to this view, a person has a high expectancy of success when he or she *feels* (on the basis of past experiences) that there are several action alternatives

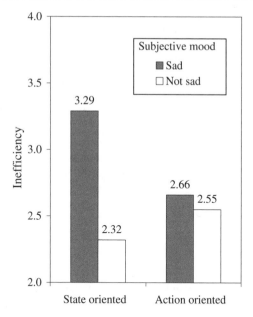

Figure 10.2 Mean inefficacy as a function of failure-related state and action orientation and subjective sadness

available even if these alternatives cannot be consciously enumerated. When the number of successful personal experiences retrieved from implicit autobiographical memory (extension memory) is low, either because one has not experienced a sufficient number of successes or because access to this knowledge base is inhibited (e.g., due to a momentary sad mood), subjective probability of success and analogous efficacy judgments should be reduced. The present findings are consistent with this assumption.

Prospective AOD was not significantly correlated with AOF ($r = 0.15$) and showed a different pattern of correlations with MSQ indices (see Table 10.1). Initiative (i.e., high AOD) was associated with stronger commitment, higher emotional intensity, less hopelessness, and less inefficacy. State-oriented hesitation (i.e., low AOD) can be conceived of as a low ability to self-generate positive affect when positive affect is dampened after nonattainment of a goal or after formation of a difficult intention (i.e., an intention that cannot be carried out immediately). Thus, intentions remain disconnected from intuitive behavioral routines necessary for their implementation as long as that dampened positive affect cannot be restored. The motivational structure of action-oriented individuals characterized by high commitment, high efficacy, and low hopelessness confirms this system configuration. An individual's commitment toward achieving a goal can be interpreted in terms of an activation of an intention. According to this interpretation, the feeling, associated with prospective state orientation (i.e., low AOD), that one has little chance of success in reaching a goal (i.e., feelings of inefficacy) reflects the actual difficulty in releasing the inhibition between intention memory and its output system; and the fact that state-oriented participants (i.e., those scoring low on AOD) cannot easily restore positive and facilitating affect after forming a difficult intention can explain their feeling of inefficacy. In sum, these findings confirm the assumption that feelings of hopelessness and inefficacy can be interpreted as consequences

Table 10.1 Correlations between MSQ indices and Failure-related Action Orientation (AOF), Decision-related Action Orientation (AOD), Performance-related Action Orientation (AOP), Beck Depression Inventory (BDI), and Beck Anxiety Inventory (BAI) ($N = 47$)

	AOF	AOD	AOP	BDI	BAI
Number of Concerns	.28[†]	−.15	−.19	.14	.13
Commitment	−.33*	.29*	.45**	−.20	−.20
Inappropriate Commitment	−.49**	.08	.30*	.00	.04
Sorrow in Excess of Joy	.20	−.04	−.01	.09	.03
Ambivalence	−.13	.11	.16	.25[†]	.30*
Emotional Intensity	−.27[†]	.27[†]	.42**	.10	.13
Hopelessness	−.04	−.39**	−.32*	.26[†]	.31*
Inefficacy	−.06	−.33*	−.25	.31*	.32*
Goal Distance	−.25[†]	−.03	.14	.47**	.39**
Preparation Time	−.22	−.07	.23	.37**	.25[†]

[†] $p < .10$ (2-tailed)   * $p < .05$ (2-tailed)   ** $p < .01$ (2-tailed)

of volitional inhibition, that is, the inhibition of the pathway between the memory for difficult intentions and the system that controls behavior (Kuhl & Kazén, 1999). In contrast to preoccupied participants (i.e., those scoring low on AOF) who have reduced access to the extended memory system on which subjective expectancies are based, hesitant participants (i.e., those scoring low on AOD) probably have experienced a smaller number of successes due to actual difficulties in enacting goals, or may have invested more effort to reach their goals despite these difficulties.

Whereas AOD and AOF describe the ability to escape a state-oriented mode of action control when necessary, AOP describes the ability to stay in an action-oriented mode while performing a pleasurable activity. It was not significantly correlated with AOD ($r = .16$) and negatively correlated with AOF ($r = −.37$, $p < .01$). As shown in Table 10.1, motivational persistence (AOP) was associated with stronger commitment, higher inappropriate commitment, higher emotional intensity, less hopelessness, and less inefficacy. It seems plausible that commitment, intense emotions, and volitional efficacy help to stay involved in activities and, vice versa, a dispositional tendency to become immersed in pleasant activities increases experiences of commitment, intense emotions, and volitional efficacy. However, the correlation with inappropriate commitment is less plausible. On the one hand, persisting in pleasant activities should reduce the probability for becoming involved in goals that offer few chances of success and/or few emotional satisfactions. On the other hand, a dispositional tendency to become immersed might be associated with a lower threshold for commitment to any kind of goals—even those with few chances of success and/or little emotional satisfaction. An alternative approach was to check whether the relationship was due to the significant correlation between AOP and AOF dimensions in the present sample. Whereas partial correlations between AOP and commitment, emotional intensity, hopelessness, and inefficacy remained significant, there was no significant relationship between AOP and inappropriate commitment ($r = .13$) when controlling for AOF. In contrast, AOF was still significantly correlated with inappropriate commitment ($r = −.43$, $p < .05$) when controlling for AOP. Findings suggest that motivational persistence is more related to "appropriate commitment" and autonomous reasons for acting (Sheldon & Elliot, 1998) than to inappropriate commitment.

DEPRESSION AND ANXIETY

The many possible antecedents of depression (e.g., separation, loss) are thought to lead to a depressive disorder only when they result in the overmaintenance of degenerated intentions (Kuhl & Helle, 1986). According to this model, a fully-developed intention is characterized by four components: (1) a context component specifying conditions (e.g., time and place) for action; (2) a subject component specifying the self as the agent of an intended action; (3) an object component specifying actions or action alternatives to reach a desired goal state; and (4) a relation component specifying the degree of commitment through which the other components are connected ("related"). If one or more components are missing or ill-defined, the intention is degenerated. Some MSQ indices are examples of ill-defined components: A large goal distance and a long preparation time indicate that conditions for action are not well specified or concrete action steps are missing. Hopelessness and inefficacy indicate that actions are not elaborated or that action alternatives are not available. Ambivalence points to an ill-defined relation component because individuals have a problem with their commitment when the expected unhappiness about reaching a goal is close in intensity to the expected experience of joy. These examples of maintenance of degenerated intentions were thought to correlate with depressive symptoms as measured by the Beck Depression Inventory (BDI).

Interestingly, the BDI had a similar pattern of correlations with MSQ indices as the Beck Anxiety Inventory (BAI). This may be due to the highly significant correlation between BDI and BAI ($r = .85$, $p < .001$). Both showed positive correlations with ambivalence, hopelessness, inefficacy, goal distance, and preparation time. Findings were consistent with the theoretical link between degenerated intentions and depression. Furthermore, individuals with dysfunctional motivational structures were found to develop more depressive and anxious symptoms.

ADDITIONAL GOAL CHARACTERISTICS

In addition to MSQ ratings, participants were asked to categorize each goal as something they desire even if it is unrealistic (*wish*), something they must do even if they do not like to (*duty*), or as something they are personally committed to do (*intention*). According to Kuhl and Goschke (1994), these goal categories differ along two dimensions: realizability and self-compatibility. Intentions are high in realizability and high in self-compatibility, whereas duties are high in realizability and low in self-compatibility. In contrast, wishes are low in realizability and high in self-compatibility. As shown in Table 10.2, these goal characteristics were reflected in MSQ indices that were calculated separately for different goal categories. Consistent with Kuhl and Goschke (1994), participants listed more intentions and wishes than duties. Anticipated sorrow was higher and emotional intensity lower for duties than for wishes, indicating their lower self-compatibility or self-congruence. Hopelessness and inefficacy were significantly higher for wishes than for duties and intentions, indicating their low realizability. MSQ indices not only distinguish individuals according to their motivational structure but also meaningfully differentiate between different goal categories.

The correlations between MSQ indices and some additional goal ratings were in accord with theoretical expectations and might further contribute to evidence for the validity of

Table 10.2 Mean MSQ indices (SD) for different goal categories ($N = 37$)

	Wishes	Duties	Intentions	Effect size (η^2)
Number of Concerns	6.73[a] (3.94)	2.95[b] (2.12)	7.50[a] (5.42)	.279
Sorrow in Excess of Joy	.10[a] (.13)	.25[b] (.34)	.17 (.23)	.095
Emotional Intensity	15.09[a] (2.63)	13.40[b] (4.11)	14.58 (2.93)	.128
Hopelessness	3.15[a] (1.74)	1.57[b] (1.57)	2.02[b] (1.11)	.335
Inefficacy	3.19[a] (1.06)	2.13[b] (.95)	2.45[b] (.87)	.329

Note: Different superscripts indicate significant differences between goal types in post-hoc comparisons.

Table 10.3 Correlations between MSQ indices and additional goal ratings during an experimental session ($N = 46$) and after one week ($N = 41$)

	Self-congruence	Perceived effort	After one week Action opportunities	Goal enactment
Commitment	.36*	−.21	.39*	.40**
Inappropriate commitment	.21	−.02	.32*	.32*
Sorrow in excess of joy	−.49**	.34*	.24	.02
Emotional intensity	.41**	−.18	−.08	.13
Hopelessness	−.24	.30*	−.41**	−.37*
Inefficacy	−.09	.28[†]	−.45**	−.34*

[†]$p < .10$ *$p < .05$ **$p < .01$ (2-tailed)

MSQ indices. As shown in the left column of Table 10.3, there was a negative correlation between self-congruence of goals and anticipated sorrow in excess of joy: Participants with higher anticipated sorrow reported less self-congruent goals. Alternatively, one might argue that the possibility of not attaining important, self-congruent goals should be associated with high sorrow. However, anticipated joy upon goal attainment should be equally high or even higher if a goal is really important and self-congruent. Consequently, anticipated sorrow upon failure exceeding anticipated joy upon success indicates extrinsic rather than intrinsic motivation and, more specifically, a guilt-driven, internally controlled (i.e., introjected) type of regulation (Deci & Ryan, 2000). Consistent with this interpretation, anticipated sorrow was characteristic of duties (see Table 10.2). There were positive correlations between self-congruence and commitment and emotional intensity. Participants with stronger commitment and higher emotional intensity reported more self-congruent goals. In addition, there were positive correlations between perceived effort of enactment and anticipated sorrow and hopelessness (see Table 10.3): The higher participants scored in anticipated sorrow and hopelessness the higher was their perceived effort of enactment, which has been associated with a more controlled type of regulation (Kuhl, 2001; Sokolowski, 1993).

GOAL PURSUIT

In a follow-up questionnaire one week after the experimental session, participants had to rate their goals along several dimensions. How often participants thought about their goals during the past week was highly correlated with emotional intensity ($r = .50$, $p < .001$):

Participants with emotionally intense goal structures reported more thoughts about their goals. Although intensity has emerged as an important predictor of uncontrollability of thoughts (England & Dickerson, 1988), participants did not seem to experience their goal-related thoughts as particularly uncontrollable in the present study. There was no significant correlation between emotional intensity of goal structure and controllability of thoughts about goals ($r = -.20$, $p < .22$). However, emotional intensity had different effects for state- and action-oriented participants (i.e., scoring low and high on AOF, respectively). Whereas there was no significant relationship between intensity and controllability for action-oriented participants ($r = .05$), state-oriented participants with higher emotional intensity were less able to control their thoughts ($r = -.43$, $p < .05$). One possible explanation for this finding is that there is no relationship between emotional intensity and control for the lower part of the distribution of emotional intensity and a moderate to strong relationship for the higher part of the distribution. Accordingly, state-oriented participants would have difficulties in controlling thoughts about emotional intense goals because they have a tendency to experience higher levels of emotional intensity ("overmotivation" or "overcommitment") as shown in Table 10.1. However, state orientation is defined as a difficulty in self-regulating affect. Thus, the tendency for state-oriented participants to experience higher levels of emotional intensity is more likely to be one of the results of their low volitional control than its cause. In any case, the negative relationship between emotional intensity and control underlines the state-oriented participants' need for help when self-regulation of emotional reactions is required.

MSQ indices had meaningful relationships with goal pursuit. As shown in the right-hand column of Table 10.3, the percentage of actually enacted goals was positively correlated with commitment and inappropriate commitment, and negatively correlated with hopelessness and inefficacy. The higher participants' commitment and the lower their feelings of hopelessness and inefficacy, the more goals they enacted during one week. Moreover, and somewhat counter-intuitively, the higher participants' inappropriate commitment, the more goals they enacted during one week. The same pattern of correlations was found for perceived opportunities to enact the goals during the past week (see Table 10.3). Perceiving an action opportunity was positively correlated with commitment and inappropriate commitment, and negatively correlated with hopelessness and inefficacy. The higher participants' commitment and inappropriate commitment, the more action opportunities they had (or recognized) during one week. The higher participants' hopelessness and inefficacy, the fewer action opportunities they had (or recognized) during one week.

According to PSI theory, the positive correlation between inappropriate commitment and goal enactment may be explained in terms of behavioral facilitation through preprogramming of intuitive behavioral routines, a mechanism that is similar to Gollwitzer's (1999) delegation hypothesis—i.e., when time and place of execution and the action steps are specified, no volitional intervention is needed because the behavior will automatically be performed as soon as relevant cues are encountered. This type of automatic behavior control can work not only without volitional support, but also without motivational support (as exemplified by the two aspects of inappropriate commitment: little chance of success and little emotional satisfaction). Automatic behavior control is mediated by a system that is largely independent of self-compatibility and incentive checking. On the neurobiological level, this system can be related to the nigrostriatal dopaminergic system, which can facilitate behavior through a route that does not include the limbic or prefrontal systems. In everyday life we experience this type of behavioral facilitation when we rely on habits and routines (e.g., I brush my teeth in the morning automatically, no matter whether or not I enjoy it or have access to my self-congruent feeling about dental care). Therefore, the paradoxical relationship between enactment and inappropriate commitment can be explained in terms of the functional characteristics of automatic behavior control (Kuhl, 2001, pp. 420ff).

Correlations between goal enactment and MSQ indices were not significant when controlling for action opportunities. However, the correlation between action opportunities and inefficacy was still significant when controlling for goal enactment ($r = -.32$, $p < .05$). This suggests that inefficacy (i.e., the degree to which chances for success are not rated higher due to one's own action compared to taking no actions) is more strongly associated with a deficit in perceiving action opportunities than in actually taking action when given the opportunity to do so. These findings are consistent with the negative affect modulation assumption of PSI theory: When access to extension memory is inhibited, participants cannot perceive action opportunities and become inefficient.

SELF-INFILTRATION

The experimentally derived measure of self-infiltration (baseline corrected number of false self-ascriptions of externally controlled activities) was correlated with MSQ indices. There was a positive partial correlation between inappropriate commitment and false self-ascriptions ($r = .26$, $p < .09$): With higher inappropriate commitment participants had higher rates of false self-ascription of unattractive activities originally assigned by the experimenter, controlling for rates of false self-ascription of unattractive activities that were neither chosen by the participant nor by the experimenter in the self-infiltration experiment described earlier. Participants who were committed to unrealistic goals and to goals providing little satisfaction in their life showed a tendency to be "invaded" by the intentions of others in an experimental setting.

Although the correlation between inappropriate commitment and self-infiltration reached only marginal significance, it is striking because it relates a self-report measure of introjection generated in the broad context of personal goals to an implicit measure of introjection experimentally derived within the restricted context of office activities. The process of self-infiltration may cause participants to become committed to goals that provide little satisfaction in the first place. Reliance on automatic behavior control is an example of a process that is characterized as an uncoupling of behavior control from motivational and volitional systems, thus increasing the risk of alienation, that is, performance of activities that are neither self-congruent nor need-satisfying and pleasant. Pursuing goals that are unrealistic and provide only little satisfaction may in turn increase frustration and negative affect. According to the negative-affect modulation assumption of PSI theory (Kuhl, 2000), unattenuated negative affect reduces access to an extended associative network system (extension memory) and the implicit self. Thus, high levels of inappropriate commitment may further reduce access to the very system that is needed for finding alternative ways to actually reach goals and for generating more self-congruent, satisfying goals. In extreme cases, the person can be trapped in a vicious cycle of increasing alienation from his or her needs, emotional preferences, and self-congruent values.

ALIENATION

As expected on the basis of the foregoing discussion, MSQ indices showed meaningful relationships with experimentally derived measures of alienation. Theoretically, two forms of alienation can be distinguished. Whereas *manifest alienation* refers to a failure to plan, initiate, or maintain emotionally preferred behavior, *latent alienation* refers to an impaired perception of emotional preferences or needs (Kuhl & Beckmann, 1994). The measures used in the present study may be interpreted in terms of manifest alienation, that is, a volitional inefficiency to behave according to one's preferences.

The proportion of highly attractive activities selected during the final choice was significantly correlated with anticipated sorrow ($r = -.35$, $p < .02$): With increasing scores in anticipated sorrow fewer attractive compared to unattractive activities were selected in a free-choice period. Anticipated sorrow can be interpreted in terms of avoidance motivation (or prevention focus): Behavioral facilitation is more strongly guided by the concern to prevent an aversive state from occurring than by positive concerns. Mean selection positions were calculated for unattractive activities. Lower scores (i.e., early selection positions) indicated an earlier choice and greater willingness to enact an activity. Thus, for both indices (selection proportion of attractive activities and position of unattractive ones) lower scores meant orientation toward activities of lower attractiveness (i.e., higher alienation). Selection positions of unattractive activities were significantly correlated with commitment ($r = .39$, $p < .01$), hopelessness ($r = -.34$, $p < .02$), and inefficacy ($r = -.38$, $p < .01$): The weaker participants' commitment and the stronger their feelings of hopelessness and inefficacy in dealing with current concerns, the earlier they selected unattractive office activities and the later they selected highly attractive activities in a free-choice period.

Alternatively, one might argue that these participants were not alienated from their preferences but somehow "liked" unattractive office activities. This alternative interpretation was discounted by the fact that there were no significant correlations between MSQ indices and attractiveness ratings, neither for the median-split subsamples of 24 unattractive and 24 highly attractive activities nor for the total sample of 48 activities.

Anticipated "sorrow in excess of joy" means that participants feel that they have a lot to lose if they are unable to reach their goals, but not much to gain if they do reach their goals (stronger focus on prevention of aversive events than promotion of positive events). Anticipated sorrow is correlated with duties ("must"), low self-congruence, and effortful goal pursuit. This type of motivation is typical of a controlling mode of regulation characterized by rigid protection of introjected goals and suppression of conflicting needs and the self. In the loss-of-autonomy cycle, Kuhl and Beckmann (1994) describe how excessive control and self-suppression lead to accumulation of conflict, uncontrollable intrusive thoughts, and impairments of self-regulatory efficiency. In an effort to compensate for these impairments, participants may increase attempts to gain control and further suppress counter-intentional information and conflicting needs and preferences. It is not surprising that individuals with this self-controlled mode of regulation do not gain satisfaction from their goals and do not behave hedonistically in a free-choice situation. Findings further support the suggested link between anticipated sorrow and lack of commitment and a controlled mode of regulation and self-inhibition.

REFERENCES

Baumann, N. (1998). *Selbst- versus Fremdbestimmung: Zum Einfluß von Stimmung, Bewußtheit und Persönlichkeit* [*Self- versus other-determination: The influence of mood, consciousness, and personality*]. Unpublished dissertation. University of Osnabrück, Germany.

Baumann, N., & Kuhl, J. (2003). Self-infiltration: Confusing assigned tasks as self-selected in memory. *Personality and Social Psychology Bulletin, 29*, 487–497.

Beck, A.T. (1967). *Depression: Causes and treatment.* Philadelphia, PA: University of Philadelphia Press.

Beck, A.T., Epstein, N., Brown, G., & Steer, R.A. (1988). An inventory for measuring clinical anxiety: Psychometric properties. *Journal of Consulting and Clinical Psychology, 6*, 893–897.

Brunstein, J.C., Schultheiss, O.C., & Graessman, R. (1998). Personal goals and emotional well-being: The moderating role of motive dispositions. *Journal of Personality and Social Psychology, 75*, 494–508.

Chang, E.C. (1997). Irrational beliefs and negative life stress: Testing a diathesis-stress model of depressive symptoms. *Personality and Individual Differences, 22*, 115–117.

Cox, W.M., Klinger, E., & Blount, J.P. (1999). *Systematic motivational counseling: A treatment manual.* Unpublished manuscript. University of Wales, Bangor, UK.

Cox, M.W., Klinger, E., Fuhrmann, A., & de Jong-Meyer, R. (1995). *Fragebogen zu gegenwärtigen Anliegen (FGA).* German adaptation of the MSQ. Manuscript. University of Münster, Germany.

Deci, E.L., & Ryan, R.M. (2000). The "what" and "why" of goal pursuits: Human needs and the self-determination of behavior. *Psychological Inquiry, 11*, 227–268.

Dykman, B.M. (1996). Negative self-evaluations among dysphoric college students: A difference in degree or kind? *Cognitive Therapy and Research, 20*, 445–464.

Ellis, A. (1977). The basic clinical theory of rational-emotive therapy. In A. Ellis & R. Grieger (Eds.), *Handbook of rational-emotive therapy.* New York: Springer.

England, S.L., & Dickerson, M. (1988). Intrusive thoughts; unpleasantness not the major cause of uncontrollability. *Behaviour Research and Therapy, 26*, 279–282.

Gollwitzer, P.M. (1999). Implementation intentions: Strong effects of simple plans. *American Psychologist, 54*, 493–503.

Kazén, M., Baumann, N., & Kuhl, J. (in press). *Self-infiltration vs. self-compatibility checking: The moderating influence of state vs. action-orientation.* in press/Motivation and Emotion

Klinger, E. (1981). The central place of imagery in human functioning. In E. Klinger (Ed.), *Imagery: Concepts, results and applications* (Vol. 2; pp. 3–16). New York: Plenum.

Klinger, E., & Murphy, D.M. (1994). Action orientation and personality: Some evidence on the construct validity of the action control scale. In J. Kuhl & J. Beckmann (Eds.), *Volition and personality: Action versus state orientation* (pp. 79–92). Göttingen, Germany: Hogrefe.

Kuhl, J. (1994a). A theory of action and state orientation. In J. Kuhl & J. Beckmann (Eds.), *Volition and personality: Action versus state orientation* (pp. 9–46). Göttingen, Germany: Hogrefe.

Kuhl, J. (1994b). Action versus state orientation: Psychometric properties of the Action Control Scale (ACS-90). In J. Kuhl & J. Beckmann (Eds.), *Volition and personality: Action versus state orientation* (pp. 47–59). Göttingen, Germany: Hogrefe.

Kuhl, J. (2000). A functional-design approach to motivation and self-regulation: The dynamics of personality systems interactions. In M. Boekaerts, P.R. Pintrich, & M. Zeidner (Eds.), *Self-regulation: Directions and challenges for future research* (pp. 111–169). New York: Academic Press.

Kuhl, J. (2001). *Motivation und Persönlichkeit [Motivation and personality].* Göttingen, Germany: Hogrefe.

Kuhl, J., & Beckmann, J. (1994). Alienation: Ignoring one's preferences. In J. Kuhl & J. Beckmann (Eds.), *Volition and personality: Action versus state orientation* (pp. 375–390). Göttingen, Germany: Hogrefe.

Kuhl, J., & Fuhrmann, A. (1998). Decomposing self-regulation and self-control: The volitional components checklist. In J. Heckhausen & C. Dweck (Eds.), *Motivation and self-regulation across the life span* (pp. 15–49). New York: Cambridge University Press.

Kuhl, J., & Goschke, T. (1994). State orientation and the activation and retrieval of intentions in memory. In J. Kuhl & J. Beckmann (Eds.), *Volition and personality: Action versus state orientation* (pp. 127–153). Göttingen, Germany: Hogrefe.

Kuhl, J., & Helle, P. (1986). Motivational and volitional determinants of depression: The degenerated-intention hypothesis. *Journal of Abnormal Psychology, 95*, 247–251.

Kuhl, J., & Kazén, M. (1994). Self-discrimination and memory: State orientation and false self-ascription of assigned activities. *Journal of Personality and Social Psychology, 66*, 1103–1115.

Kuhl, J., & Kazén, M. (1999). Volitional facilitation of difficult intentions: Joint activation of intention memory and positive affect removes Stroop interference. *Journal of Experimental Psychology: General, 128*, 382–399.

Man, F., Stuchlíková, I., & Klinger, E. (1998). Motivational structure of alcoholic and nonalcoholic Czech men. *Psychological Reports, 82*, 1091–1106.

Martin, L.L., & Tesser, A. (1989). Toward a motivational and structural theory of ruminative thought. In J.S. Uleman & J.A. Bargh (Eds.), *Unintended thought* (pp. 306–326). New York: Guilford.

Rude, S.S., Covich, J., Jarrold, W., Hedlund, S., & Zentner, M. (2001). Detecting depressive schemata in vulnerable individuals: Questionnaires versus laboratory tasks. *Cognitive Therapy and Research, 25*, 103–116.

Sheldon, K.M., & Elliot, A.J. (1998). Not all personal goals are personal: Comparing autonomous and controlled reasons for goals as predictors of effort and attainment. *Personality and Social Psychology Bulletin, 24*, 546–557.

Sheldon, K.M., & Kasser, T. (1995). Coherence and congruence: Two aspects of personality integration. *Journal of Personality and Social Psychology, 68*, 531–543.

Sokolowski, K. (1993). *Emotion und Volition [Emotion and volition]*. Göttingen, Germany: Hogrefe.

Wenzlaff, R.M., & Bates, D.E. (1998). Unmasking a cognitive vulnerability to depression: How lapses in mental control reveal depressive thinking. *Journal of Personality and Social Psychology, 75*, 1559–1571.

PART III

Systematic Motivational Counseling and its Applications

Systematic Motivational Counseling: The Motivational Structure Questionnaire in Action

W. Miles Cox

University of Wales, Bangor, UK

and

Eric Klinger

University of Minnesota, Morris, USA

Synopsis.—Sufferers of many forms of psychological disturbance show maladaptive patterns of motivation, which significantly cause or contribute to the disorder. Systematic Motivational Counseling (SMC) is a technique for assessing and changing these maladaptive patterns, aiming to guide people to happier and more fulfilling lives. The Motivational Structure Questionnaire (MSQ) or Personal Concerns Inventory (PCI) is an integral part of SMC and is used to assess clients' concerns, goals, and motivational structure. Once a client's maladaptive motivational patterns are identified as the targets for change, SMC motivational restructuring components are used to help the person to find better ways to resolve important concerns. These components include setting treatment goals, constructing goal ladders, setting between-session goals, improving the ability to meet goals, resolving conflicts among goals, disengaging from inappropriate goals, identifying new incentives to enjoy, shifting from an aversive to an appetitive lifestyle, and re-examining sources of self-esteem. SMC has been used with clients with alcohol- and other substance-abuse disorders, affective disorders, personality disorders, psychosis, and traumatic brain injuries. It has also been used in work settings to improve employee job satisfaction and work performance. The SMC technique has been used in individual and group counseling and developed as a self-help format. Evaluations have been consistently favorable.

Systematic Motivational Counseling (SMC) was developed on the premise that many forms of psychological disturbance are disorders of motivation, i.e., maladaptive ways in which people commit themselves to the pursuit of their goals. As argued in Chapter 1, people's behavior and experiences are organized around the pursuit and enjoyment of goals, so that committing oneself to appropriate goals is essential for healthy psychological functioning. In the normal course of events, people are able to find realistic goals to pursue that make their lives meaningful and satisfying, and they are able to give up goals that

Handbook of Motivational Counseling. Edited by W. Miles Cox and Eric Klinger.
© 2004 John Wiley & Sons, Ltd.

become psychologically disadvantageous to pursue. Some people, however, repeatedly commit themselves to goals that are socially undesirable or self-destructive, as in the case of alcohol or other substance abuse. Other people have difficulties finding desirable and fulfilling goals, as in the case of depressed people or those who lack the motivation to achieve. Still other people give undue time and energy to goal pursuits that would better be relinquished, as in the case of those with debilitating anxieties and phobias, or in the case of state-oriented individuals (e.g., Kuhl, 1994), who have great difficulty in disengaging from unattainable goals (Maier & Brunstein, 1999). Therefore, motivational counseling of people with difficulties such as these involves helping those individuals to establish, terminate, maintain, modify, or initiate new goal pursuits. This chapter presents the strategies that SMC uses for helping people to achieve these ends.

Using the Motivational Structure Questionnaire (MSQ) or the Personal Concerns Inventory (PCI) (Cox & Klinger, Chapter 8, this volume; Klinger & Cox, Chapter 9, this volume; Klinger, Cox, & Blount, in press) as the starting point, SMC first systematically assesses clients' goals and their manner of relating to their goals, i.e., their *motivational structure*. This process allows maladaptive motivational patterns to be identified that will become the focus of systematic change through individually selected counseling components. Cox and Klinger's work using SMC started in the area of substance abuse, which serves as the basis for many of the clinical examples in this chapter. However, it should be emphasized that the SMC technique has a much broader application than to people abusing substances.

ALCOHOL ABUSE AND DEPENDENCE

The use of SMC with alcohol abusers began with the observation that relapses among alcohol-dependent people run rampant (Donovan & Chaney, 1985; Hunt, Barnett, & Branch, 1971; Marlatt & Gordon, 1985). At that time, a substantial proportion of drinkers returned to abusive drinking within a few months after treatment—a pattern that continues today (Dimeff & Marlatt, 1998; Whitworth et al., 1996). Although existing treatment techniques were effective in helping alcohol-dependent persons to stop drinking temporarily, they did not bring permanent remissions (Riley et al., 1987).

In the effort to identify components necessary for a treatment for alcohol dependence whose effects would endure, it became clear that the motivation to reduce one's drinking occurs in the context of other incentives in the drinker's life, and when those other incentives gain sufficient value to compete successfully with alcohol use, drinking subsides (Cox & Klinger, 1988, 1990, and Chapter 7, this volume). Therefore, it appeared that a treatment technique that specifically helped alcohol-dependent people to develop enduring sources of emotional satisfaction as an alternative to drinking alcohol would be highly promising.

Cox and Klinger next tried to identify mechanisms for finding emotional satisfaction that a motivational intervention could target. Obviously, whether or not recovering alcohol-dependent people are able to find emotional satisfaction through nonchemical means is not due simply to the *good* and *bad* events that happen to them. Rather, it seemed to depend largely on a person's own motivational patterns. These patterns include commitment to pursuing healthy, positive incentives as alternatives to drinking alcohol; the ability to cope with the negative incentives that cause them discomfort and that they want to remove; implementation of goals that they have formed (or have failed to form) for obtaining or removing these incentives; and the manner in which they strive for their goals. SMC, therefore, specifically targets problem drinkers' motivation for change by helping them to develop adaptive motivational patterns for increasing their nonchemical sources of emotional satisfaction that are incompatible with drinking, thereby shifting the motivational balance—the decision matrix—in favor of decisions *not* to drink.

SMC is not necessarily conceived as a stand-alone treatment. In substance-abuse disorders, its role would be to supplement standard treatment modules to render clients more receptive to them and better able to maintain gains after the period of intensive treatment. It is also compatible with other conceptual frameworks. For example, it can help to move clients through the contemplation, preparation, action, and maintenance stages of Prochaska and DiClemente's model of change (DiClemente & Prochaska, 1998; Prochaska, Johnson, & Lee, 1998). It has points in common with Scott's (1999) "problem-solving pilgrim" and it readily serves as a framework within which to use cognitive and cognitive-behavioral techniques (Dobson, 2001). Its focus on helping clients to achieve their goals—together with its diagnostic components that may indicate the need for social, vocational, and educational support—provides a useful potential interface with social-services, vocational counseling, and rehabilitation personnel. It can therefore be a versatile component of a variety of treatment programs.

USING SMC WITH ALCOHOL-DEPENDENT CLIENTS: INITIAL STEPS AND OVERVIEW

Getting Started

As with any therapeutic endeavor, the counselor who intends to use SMC spends some time initially in getting to know the client, establishing rapport, and beginning a therapeutic bond. At the same time, the counselor also sets the tone for SMC. Doing so involves (a) introducing SMC to the client and explaining its rationale, and (b) determining the client's reactions and interest in proceeding. If the client wants to go forward, the counselor then begins trying to understand how the client's presenting problem is linked to his or her incentives in other areas of life. For instance, in the case of alcohol abuse, it is important to determine (a) why the person values drinking alcohol so highly, and (b) what the person is unable to get from nonchemical incentives, turning instead to alcohol.

Some Initial Issues to Address with Alcohol Clients

The degree to which the counselor focuses on particular issues will, of course, vary from one client to another. However, some of the questions addressed are as follows:

• *What are the circumstances surrounding the client's beginning counseling?* It can be helpful to determine why the client entered counseling at the particular time. Was there some *final straw*? Did the person come of his or her own volition, or did someone else (e.g., a spouse, the courts) press the person to do so? This information can indicate how actively or passively clients are involved in the goals they want to achieve.

Clients often enter counseling in the midst of a crisis *vis-à-vis* other incentives. For example, the person may be under threat of dismissal from a job or separation or divorce from a partner or spouse, or legally required to enter treatment. If there is no single precipitating event, the person probably decided that life in general was going so badly that help was required. Identifying the incentives whose actual or potential loss motivates clients to change can be important grist for the mill in beginning to work with clients. But what exactly has gone wrong and why? How have clients' maladaptive motivational patterns gotten them into their present situation, and what can be done to correct these patterns? What things are in jeopardy in clients' lives as they perceive them? Are these incentives real sources of emotional satisfaction, or are they replaceable?

- *What is the history of the client's use of alcohol?* One way to answer this question is chronologically, beginning with the first time the person drank alcohol. Was the experience strongly reinforcing, or did the person react negatively? How did the client's alcohol use progress from then until the present? What problems has drinking alcohol caused the client, and when did they begin? Has the client sought help before? What of value does the person get from drinking? Have the reasons changed during the course of the drinking career?

- *How does the client view the problem?* Clients differ widely in what they perceive the *problem* to be, what caused it, and how it can be overcome. Some minimize the problem or deny it. Others feel undecided, still weighing the evidence. When clients feel ambivalent, motivational interviewing (Miller & Rollnick, 2002; Resnicow et al., Chapter 24, this volume) can be useful to help the person, for example, to recognize problems that were not previously acknowledged. Still other clients see themselves as *alcoholic*. If they do, it can be useful to explore what the term means. They might also believe that they have inherited a disease—a belief that can have major implications for controlling the drinking. Finally, it is important to know how clients perceive counseling. If, for instance, they view themselves as a passive recipient of treatment, that faulty view needs to be addressed.

- *What are the client's goals for counseling?* Goal formulation is an integral part of SMC. Clients can be asked informally during the initial sessions about their goals—those both for drinking and for changes in other areas of their lives. Does the person want to stop drinking, or drink moderately? If the goal is moderation, it is important to explore with the person how realistic and appropriate this goal is. When clients are clearly committed to abstinence, they can be helped to acquire the skills needed to maintain it while building a satisfying lifestyle that does not involve alcohol. In either case, there are two useful questions for counselors to ask: *What about your life would you like to change? What about your life must change in order for you to change your drinking?*

- *Why does the client drink?* When the initial interviews have been completed, it can be useful for the counselor to summarize the factors contributing to the client's motivation to drink and to change. Reviewing the factors discussed in the motivational model (Cox & Klinger, 1988, 1990, and Chapter 7, this volume) might help to answer the question. For example, regarding situational factors, has the client drunk to enjoy the camaraderie of other people? Has the client drunk more heavily while in situations that promoted heavy drinking? Regarding other incentives, what incentives are lacking from other areas of the client's life for which he or she is trying to compensate by drinking?

A Motivation-Enhancing Exercise

A useful exercise can be completed early in the counseling for increasing motivation for change during the subsequent counseling. The client makes an inventory of the gains and losses to be derived from continuing to drink versus those from drinking less or discontinuing. In clients' minds, there are both positive and negative aspects of drinking and not drinking, with both kinds of feelings together contributing to ambivalence about changing. It is important, however, to specify exactly what the advantages and disadvantages are for each person. To do so, the client can complete a *balance sheet* (see Janis & Mann, 1977), similar to Marlatt's (1985) decision matrix. It is a simple table with two columns (labeled *Gains* and *Losses*) and two rows (labeled *Drinking* and *Not Drinking*). The counselor can help the client to think of the various consequences to be placed in each of the four categories.

Completing the balance sheet serves two functions. First, it helps clarify the advantages and disadvantages of drinking for a particular client. This is important because people with alcohol problems often overvalue the immediate positive consequences of drinking and the negative consequences of not drinking, while discounting the delayed, negative consequences of drinking and the positive consequences of not drinking. Second, the balance sheet can be a useful tool during the later part of counseling, when clients begin to waver in the commitment not to drink. At that point, the counselor can use the previously completed balance sheet as a tangible reminder of the gains that will accrue from not drinking and the losses that will be taken if the client resumes the old pattern.

Changing Problem Drinkers' Motivational Structure

SMC seeks to directly modify the motivational basis for problem drinking. It does so by first assessing drinkers' motivational structure with the MSQ (or PCI) and attempting to change their motivational structure through the SMC components discussed below. The aim is to maximize the emotional satisfaction that drinkers derive from nonchemical incentives, thereby reducing their motivation to seek emotional satisfaction by drinking alcohol. The technique is individualized, in that it does not use a session-by-session agenda that is identical for all clients. Although certain components are used with all clients, other components may or may not be used with individual clients, depending on the particular characteristics of their motivational structure. The sequence in which the individual components are used might also vary among individual clients.

SMC COUNSELING COMPONENTS

This section presents in general terms the components of SMC. The specific actions taken by the counselor in treating a particular client will, of course, vary according to what makes sense with that individual. However, the detailed implementation of the various SMC components presented below will presumably draw on general principles of motivation. These are laid out in Part I, Chapters 1 through 7 of this volume, and hence not repeated or systematized here.

Preliminary Counseling Components

Component 1: Reviewing Clients' Goals and Concerns

Completing the MSQ is an integral part of the initial counseling. Thus, after an initial discussion of SMC with clients, and soon after they indicate that they want to continue, they complete the MSQ. High-functioning outpatients might complete the questionnaire at home. Some inpatients can complete it in the clinic during their spare time. In situations where a number of inpatients need to complete the questionnaire at the same time, they might do so in a group under the guidance of a test administrator. The MSQ then needs to be scored and the client's motivational profile drawn, which can be done immediately by using the computer-administered version.

Review of MSQ Results with Client

As soon as the history-taking, the rapport-building, the MSQ, and other exercises have been completed, the counselor reviews the results with the client. The time required to do so will vary from client to client, but it can take several sessions. Reviewing the results allows counselors to determine which characteristics of clients' motivational structure would be the best focus of change and which counseling components could best be used to try to bring about the changes. With the client, the counselor goes over the goals that were written in MSQ Step 2, asking the client to clarify each one. This process allows the counselor the opportunity to better understand the client's goals and concerns and begin to get a feeling for the client's motivational structure. The counselor will also have a chance to explore ideas formed about the client's motivational structure from having viewed his or her motivational profile.

Next, the counselor asks the client about the ratings of the goals that were provided in MSQ Steps 3 through 12 (see Cox & Klinger, Chapter 8, this volume). Doing so provides additional insights into the client's motivational structure. When exploring clients' ratings of their goals, there are generally three things that counselors try to clarify: whether the ratings accurately depict clients' goals and concerns and the extent to which the chosen goals are appropriate and realistic. Clients, for instance, may have provided inaccurate ratings of their goals and concerns because they underestimated or overestimated the value actually attributed to them (see Klinger & Cox, Chapter 1, this volume, for a brief review of evidence on such valuing errors). Or clients may have provided unrealistic ratings, either underestimating or overestimating their chances of succeeding. Finally, clients' ratings may be inappropriate, because they attributed too much or too little value to their goals for the degree of emotional satisfaction they will ultimately derive. The discussion between the client and counselor helps to identify these discrepancies and enables the client to begin to re-evaluate inaccurately described, inappropriate, and unrealistic goals. The discrepancies will also serve as *flags* for the subsequent counseling sessions.

It is not necessary for the counselor to ask about every goal and every rating. To do so would be too tedious and time-consuming. Instead, it is sufficient to *spot check* individual goals and ratings. Counselors continue in this manner until they feel confident that they have uncovered clients' most significant goals and the major inaccurate, inappropriate, and unrealistic ratings. In short, by exploring the goals and ratings counselors try to accurately characterize each client's motivational structure, thereby gathering valuable information for the future sessions. Some of the specific aspects of the MSQ ratings about which clients are queried are described in Table 11.1.

Clinical Example

Reviewing one client's MSQ revealed that he placed great value in acquiring material possessions, wanting especially to have a new car and nice clothes. Although these incentives might have been emotionally satisfying in their own right, this client exaggerated the extrinsic implications of having them, believing that people would rebuff him if he did not drive a new car and wear expensive clothes. Because, currently, he could not afford these material possessions, he avoided social contacts. This pattern, in turn, interfered with a number of the client's interpersonal goals (e.g., "obtain true, honest friends," "keep friendly toward people," "obtain a healthy, caring relationship") and promoted his tendency to drink alcohol to cope with his present loneliness. As the client said, "I might as well be drinking if I have to live like this." Hence, one goal of the counseling was to help the client to place less value on material possessions and help him to reach his interpersonal goals without first acquiring a new car and expensive clothes.

Component 2: Analysis of Goal Interrelationships

In addition to identifying clients' individual goals and the ratings of them, it is important to understand interrelationships among the goals. In fact, people's life satisfaction is related to whether or not their personal goals facilitate or interfere with one another (see Michalak, Heidenreich, & Hoyer, Chapter 5, this volume). Conflict among goals is associated with negative affect, depression, neuroticism, and psychosomatic complaints (Emmons & King, 1988).

To examine goal interrelationships, the client completes a *goal matrix* (see Figure 11.1), either alone or through dialog with the counselor. The matrix is similar to Emmons and King's (1988) striving instrumentality matrix and Little's project cross-impact matrix (Little & Chambers, Chapter 4, this volume). The MSQ goal matrix requires the client to judge the effect that each MSQ goal will have on the attainment of each of the other MSQ goals. When the matrix is completed, a score is obtained for each goal. A positive score indicates that a goal is expected to facilitate other goals; negative scores, that it will interfere. Clients are generally encouraged to pursue facilitating goals that are also judged to be appropriate and realistic. Such goals may potentiate each other. On the other hand, clients are helped to minimize goal interference through the resolution of goal conflicts (see Component 7 below).

Clinical Example

A portion of one client's completed goal matrix is shown in Figure 11.2. It reveals that Goal #8, "get back to having a meaningful relationship with a woman," critically facilitated the client's attainment of a number of other goals (e.g., "accomplish more time with young sister," "keep commitments," "maintain watching my weight," "prevent my emotions running amok," "accomplish having some money in bank," "accomplish being more dependable," "accomplish exercising more," "get back going out more," "get father to have better

Table 11.1 How to probe clients' MSQ ratings

Role	When clients indicate that they are actively involved in goal-strivings (e.g., *take part, and know what action to take*), the counselor might ask in what way they are actively involved, especially when inaccurate ratings are suspected. When clients indicate that they are *not* actively involved in goal-strivings (e.g., *watch only, but an important other person is actively involved*), the counselor tries to establish why they are not involved and explore ways in which they could become more involved.
Commitment	When clients indicate that they are fully committed to particular goals (e.g., *I fully intend to if I possibly can*), it is important to ask whether the commitment is *appropriate* (i.e., whether the degree of commitment is proportional to the expected chances of success and anticipated positive affect). On the other hand, when clients express lack of commitment to their goals (e.g., *I do not intend to . . . the thing*), it is important to determine why they do not feel committed and explore ways to help them to become more committed.
Joy, Unhappiness, and Sorrow	It is important to establish whether clients' anticipated positive and negative affect accurately reflects their likely actual affect if they succeed in reaching their goals, or if they do not. That these anticipations are often in error, and the conditions that affect such errors, are increasingly well established (see Klinger & Cox, Chapter 1, this volume). The *Joy* and *Unhappiness* ratings are best considered together, because the more nearly equal the two ratings are, the greater the ambivalence that the client is likely to experience. High *Sorrow* ratings are also noteworthy, especially when they are high relative to *Joy* ratings. In the latter case, it would be important to consider why clients feel they have a lot to lose but not a lot to gain. Finally, it is important whether clients' expected affect upon reaching their goals is proportional to their stated commitment.
Chances of Success and Chances of Success/No Action	The counselor asks whether clients' judged *Chances of Success* in reaching their goals match their actual chances (i.e., whether the expectations of success are realistic). They also explore the reasons behind *hopeless* (i.e., low expected chances of succeeding) and *ineffective* feelings (i.e., success that does not depend on one's actions).
Time Available	Perceiving that one has a lot of time before taking action might indicate a tendency to procrastinate, and ultimately that little progress will be made in achieving goals. Perceiving that there is *little* time, on the other hand, could reflect exaggerated feelings of pressure.
Goal Distance	Clients with distant goals probably need help to reformulate them as subgoals. Doing so helps to concretize the steps needed to reach the ultimate goal, and it helps to give clients a sense of self-efficacy as they reach successive subgoals. By contrast, if goals are primarily short term, they are likely to be trivial and not to contribute much to the person's long-range emotional satisfaction.
Alcohol Effects	When clients perceive that drinking alcohol will facilitate their attainment of other goals, the accuracy of the judgment needs to be checked out (i.e., *Does drinking really help?*). If confirmed, the client should be helped to find ways to facilitate goal attainments other than by drinking alcohol. Clients should also be made aware of the ways that drinking alcohol can interfere with their goal attainments.

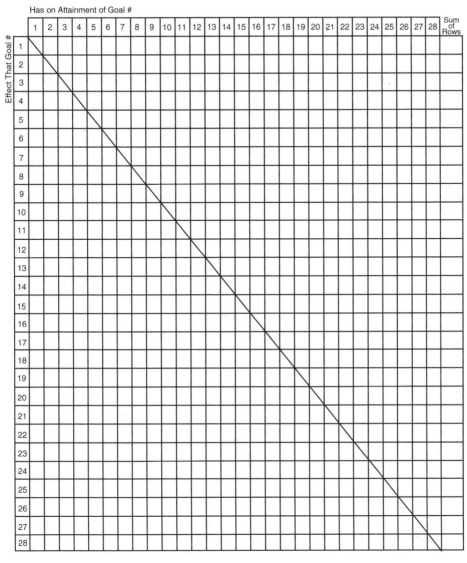

Has on Attainment of Goal #

Effect That Goal #

+2   = Strongly Facilitate
+1   = Facilitate
Leave Blank = No Effect
-1   = Interfere
-2   = Strongly Interfere

Figure 11.1 MSQ goal matrix

understanding of alcoholism"). Thus, in the subsequent counseling sessions, the counselor focused on helping this client to achieve Goal #8. With this support, he did, in fact, attain his goal. He established a meaningful relationship with a woman, whom he later married, and with whom he continued to have a satisfying relationship. The attainment of this goal, moreover, had the expected positive impact on the client's other goals.

Has on Attainment of Goal #

Effect That Goal #	1	2	3	4	5	6	7	8	9	10	11	12	13	14	15	16	17	18	19	20	21	22	23	24	25	26	27	28	Sum of Rows
4	-1										+1			+1			+2							+1	+1				5
5		-1		+1							+1			+1			+1							+1	+1		+1		6
6				-1			+1				-1						-2					-1	-1		+2	+1	-1		-3
7				+1							-1						-2					-1	-1		+1	+1	+1		-1
8	+2	+2					-2	-1		-1	-1	+2			+2	+2	+1		+2				-1		+2	+2	-1	+1	11
9																													
10				-2	-1	-2	+1	+1	-1				+1	+1	+1		+2								+2	+1	-1		3
11		-1				-2																					-1		-4
12																													

Figure 11.2   Portion of a completed goal matrix

Goal-Setting Components

Before beginning the goal-setting components, counselors provide clients with feedback from their MSQ profile and goal matrix. The distinctive features of the person's motivational structure are discussed, along with patterns of facilitation and interference among the goals. However, instead of presenting the results as *facts* about clients, the counselor introduces the results as *working hypotheses*, asking clients themselves to help decide whether the results accurately reflect the kind of person they are. When presented in this manner, clients usually help to build a case for the accuracy of the results. At this time, it is also helpful to deal with the client's goal for drinking. Because there will be both gains and losses from either drinking or not doing so, it is important to explore the motivational conflicts associated with reaching the drinking goal.

This process prepares the transition to the goal-setting components, of which there are three kinds: (a) setting treatment goals, (b) constructing goal ladders, and (c) setting between-session goals. Extensive evidence indicates the value of explicitly setting goals (e.g., Gauggel & Hoop, Chapter 23, this volume; Locke & Latham, 1990). The prominence of the goal-setting exercises should, however, not be taken to mean that SMC only helps clients to set and reach goals. Counselors use whatever techniques are at their disposal for changing clients' self-defeating motivational patterns and maximizing their long-range, healthy sources of emotional satisfaction. Nevertheless, the extent to which goal-setting exercises are used varies from client to client. In general, clients who are cognitively more concrete seem to profit most from structured goal-setting activities.

Component 3: Setting Treatment Goals

Setting treatment goals involves a process of active negotiation between client and counselor. Neither decides unilaterally what the list of goals will be. As these goals are formulated, it is helpful to make a written list of them, stating them as concretely as possible. Counselors sometimes draw up a contract with the client to specify reinforcement contingencies that will be enforced, depending on goal achievements. It is also helpful to specify what would constitute achievement or nonachievement of each goal. Goals-Attainment Scaling (Gauggel & Hoop, Chapter 23, this volume; Kiresuk, Smith, & Cardillo, 1994) is one way to

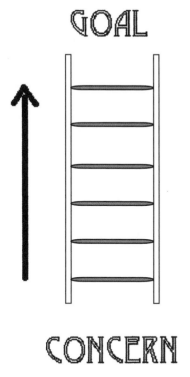

Figure 11.3   SMC goal ladder

do this. It allows expected levels of outcome to be set as a means of later evaluating the degree of achievement. Setting formal treatment goals can be especially helpful for clients with a large number of concerns who need help specifically to prioritize their goals. Conversely, clients with few concerns might need help to find additional goals for which to strive.

Component 4: Constructing Goal Ladders

It can be useful for clients to divide their long-range goals into subgoals. In fact, extensive evidence now indicates that helping people to formulate *implementation intentions* (decisions and mental imagery regarding just when, where, and how to perform the various actions that move them toward their goals) greatly enhances the likelihood of their completing their goal pursuits (Chasteen, Park, & Schwarz, 2001; Gollwitzer, 1999; Gollwitzer & Brandstätter, 1997; Oettingen, Pak, & Schnetter, 2001; Taylor & Pham, 1998–1999; Willutzki & Koban, Chapter 17, this volume). In SMC, this is done for the major long-range goals judged appropriate and realistic and not to conflict significantly with other such goals. For this exercise, *goal ladders* are used (see Figure 11.3), which consist of a hierarchical series of steps required to reach the final goal. The client completes each successive subgoal before the next one is added to the ladder.

Clinical Example

Examples of two clients' goal ladders are shown in Figures 11.4 and 11.5. They show how during weekly counseling sessions these clients were helped to formulate and work toward

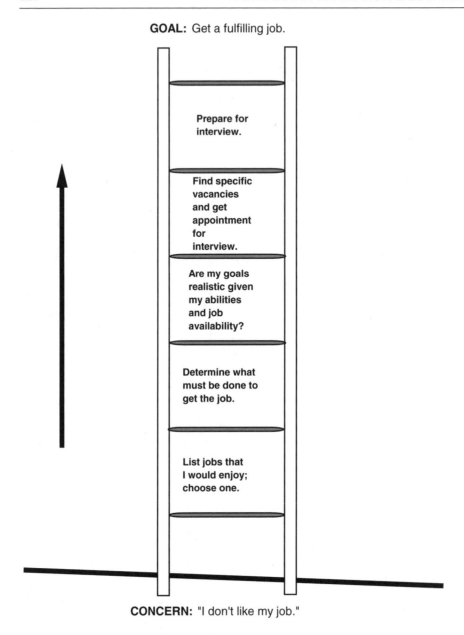

GOAL: Get a fulfilling job.

Prepare for interview.

Find specific vacancies and get appointment for interview.

Are my goals realistic given my abilities and job availability?

Determine what must be done to get the job.

List jobs that I would enjoy; choose one.

CONCERN: "I don't like my job."

Figure 11.4   SMC completed goal ladder, Example One

successive subgoals until the final goal had been achieved. Setting subgoals can also be helpful when a longed-for goal is presently out of reach. For example, someone might want to be a homeowner, although buying a house is currently financially impossible. In such a case, it might be best to postpone the ultimate goal, substituting a lesser one such as saving a specific amount of money. After the new goal is reached, the person would then have the option either of saving additional money to apply toward the first house payment or spend the money for something else.

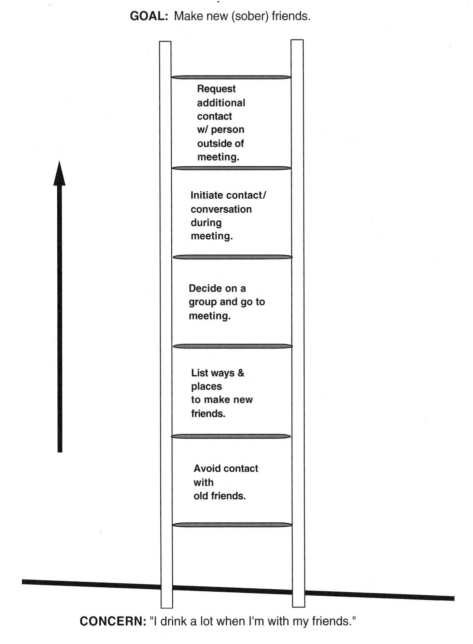

GOAL: Make new (sober) friends.

Request additional contact w/ person outside of meeting.

Initiate contact/ conversation during meeting.

Decide on a group and go to meeting.

List ways & places to make new friends.

Avoid contact with old friends.

CONCERN: "I drink a lot when I'm with my friends."

Figure 11.5 SMC completed goal ladder, Example Two

Component 5: Setting Between-Session Goals

Throughout SMC, the counselor and client together formulate activities related to goal attainments for the client to undertake between counseling sessions. There are two kinds of activities in which counselors encourage clients to become involved. The first consists of activities that are gratifying in their own right and are sources of immediate pleasure (see Component 9 below). The second type is aimed at reaching subgoals underlying the achievement of long-range goals. Between counseling sessions, the client is instructed to work on successive subgoals (e.g., from the goal ladders) that will lead to ultimate goal attainments. It is important that both kinds of goals be made concrete. As much as possible, clients should formulate them imagistically—that is, by actively imagining the process—as a way of forming connections to implicit motives (Schultheiss, in press; Willutzki & Koban, Chapter 17, this volume). This will help the client to work toward goal achievements and make it easier for goal attainments to be evaluated. During each successive session, the list of goals set at the previous session is discussed, and progress (or lack of it) evaluated.

Subsequent Counseling Components

Use of the preliminary and goal-setting counseling components will reveal several kinds of goals to be targeted during the subsequent counseling sessions. These include (a) goals that were judged to be appropriate and realistic, but for which the client needs more effective achievement strategies; (b) goals judged inappropriate or unrealistic or in significant conflict with other goals, and from which the client would be better to disengage; (c) goals that the client either over- or undervalued; and (d) goals toward which the client's level of invested energy needs to be redirected. The counselor uses the components described in this section to help clients to make these kinds of changes in their goals. The choice of which components to use with each client depends largely on that client's motivational structure and the specific goals that the client needs help to achieve. Hence, these components allow greater latitude than do the preliminary and goal-setting components.

Component 6: Improving the Ability to Reach Goals

Clients often need to enhance their ability to reach their goals. Even when goals seem appropriate and realistic, clients might lack the skills needed to reach these goals. For instance, clients with high scores on the MSQ Spectator Role index (see Cox & Klinger, Chapter 8, this volume) might need to develop assertion skills. Those who struggle with interpersonal concerns might need help with social skills. Other clients might need to acquire educational and vocational skills. Anxious clients or those otherwise under stress might need help with stress management. The counselor either helps clients acquire the needed skills or refers the person to a specialist for help.

Clinical Example

One client wanted to "become a good father," a goal whose achievement needed to be operationalized. He was helped to define specific, concrete behaviors (e.g., "get dressed and go to a nice restaurant with my wife and daughter") that to him would indicate that he was being a good father. The same client wanted to "buy a house," but to him this goal seemed financially out of reach. Accordingly, after exploring with him different neighborhoods and types of houses in which he might live, the client's counselor helped him to devise a plan to save enough money for a down payment on a house.

Component 7: Resolving Conflicts Among Goals

Whether or not clients should be helped to resolve particular goal conflicts will depend on how debilitating the conflicts are judged to be and how likely they are to be resolvable. Resolving a conflict usually involves finding another way to reach one or the other, or both, of the goals involved in the conflict.

Clinical Examples

One client's completed Goal Matrix indicated that the goal to perform well in his present job strongly interfered with the goal to complete his training at a technical school. Because the client devoted considerable energy to his full-time job as a mechanic, he could enroll only as a part-time student at the technical school, had very little time for study, and in some cases had received low marks. Having explored with his counselor other strategies for reaching his goals, the client eventually decided to take a half-time job, which would permit him to devote more time to his studies and successfully finish his degree in a timely fashion.

Another male client, recently separated from his wife, persisted in seeing women who were married or otherwise involved in committed relationships, despite the fact that he reported feeling guilty about doing so. Consequently, the counselor and client explored more appropriate ways for him to satisfy his need for a relationship with a female, such as meeting eligible women through the organization *Parents Without Partners* or social events at his church. They also specified the steps the client needed to take to realize his goal.

Component 8: Disengagement from Inappropriate Goals

Sometimes it is in clients' best interest to give up certain goals to which they have been committed. There are at least three kinds of situations where disengagement is called for: (a) when conflicts among goals cannot be resolved; (b) when goals are unachievable; and (c) when clients overvalue goals that are unlikely to bring them much satisfaction. Disengagement may also be appropriate when clients' expected Sorrow (MSQ Step 7) from failing to reach a goal considerably exceeds the expected Joy (MSQ Step 5) from succeeding.

It is not easy for clients to become disengaged from goals to which they have been committed. Rationally, they might agree that giving up a goal is the best thing for them to do. Emotionally, however, giving up the goal is quite another matter. To give up a goal means that a person will lose something that he or she values, regardless of how much sense it makes to do so in the long run. Losses are fraught with negative emotional consequences, such as anger, aggression, and depression (see Klinger, 1975). When a person starts to move away from a to-be-avoided goal, the attractiveness of the goal becomes magnified, and an approach-avoidance cycle ensues (Dollard & Miller, 1950). The SMC counselor helps the client endure and work through the pain and frustration accompanying goal relinquishment. The counselor also helps the client to find healthy sources of emotional satisfaction to take the place of the loss.

Clinical Example

One client recently divorced from his wife was still very emotionally attached to her. Despite the fact that there was no chance for the couple to be reconciled (the wife, in fact, was to be remarried and move away), the client was preoccupied with the idea of reuniting with his former wife. Requiring considerable emotional support, this client was strongly encouraged to put his past behind him and to find new pleasures to replace his loss.

Component 9: Identifying New Incentives

Many clients for whom SMC is appropriate, including those with affective and substance-use disorders, have a paucity of incentives to enjoy. Moreover, a common pattern among alcohol abusers is to strive for goals that they feel they *should* achieve, rather than for ones that they really *want* (cf. Marlatt & Gordon, 1985). Such *ought*-driven pursuits are fraught with anxiety (e.g., Higgins et al., 1994) and provide little expectation of pleasure. When alcohol abusers are trying to reduce their drinking, it is important for them to find healthy sources of immediate gratification to replace the alcohol. This entails replacing largely ought-driven goals, insofar as practicable, with goals likely to provide intrinsic pleasure.

There are several ways in which SMC counselors can help. They might start by asking clients about pleasant activities enjoyed in the past and those they imagine would be enjoyable, even though they have not tried them. Counselors might also try to identify the category of activities that clients like and find other activities in that category. Finally, counselors might use the *Pleasant Events Schedule* (MacPhillamy & Lewinsohn, 1982; see also Correia, Chapter 3, this volume) to help clients to find new pleasant activities to try.

Clinical Examples

When one client gave up drinking alcohol, he decided that he wanted to savor new, interesting, nonalcoholic beverages. Each week he would go to a speciality food store and choose either a new gourmet coffee to sample or buy an exotic fruit such as a mango or papaya from which to make a nonalcoholic drink. Another client who was an avid reader decided to volunteer to work at his local library. He enjoyed both his work and being able to help other people. At the same time, he became less preoccupied with drinking.

On the MSQ, another client wrote that he wanted to "get a dog." However, he was not strongly committed to this goal, seeming to underestimate the positive emotional impact that obtaining a dog would have on his life. Discussion revealed that dogs had always been a source of pleasure for this client and that it had been painful for him to part with his family's dogs after his recent divorce. Nevertheless, the client was at first unable to see how having a dog would help to fill the emptiness in his life. After further discussions during subsequent counseling sessions, the client eventually did decide to get a dog, and doing so had the anticipated positive effect on his life.

Component 10: Shifting from an Aversive to an Appetitive Lifestyle

It is psychologically more satisfying for people to have positive goals that they are striving to achieve than negative ones that they are trying to avoid or escape from (e.g., Elliot &

Sheldon, 1997; Roberson, 1990; Roberson & Sluss, Chapter 14, this volume). In fact, when people's negative motivation is high and their positive motivation is low, they are more likely to attempt to cope by drinking alcohol (Klinger, 1977). Therefore, SMC counselors try to help clients to shift from aversive to appetitive lifestyles, particularly when clients have high scores on the MSQ Aversive Motivation index (see Cox & Klinger, Chapter 8, this volume).

In some cases, clients need to reframe aversive goals as appetitive ones. To help them do so, SMC counselors might use cognitive-restructuring techniques to focus on positive aspects of goals, while downplaying the negative aspects. In other cases, the best strategy might be to help clients to reduce the number of negative goals they have. Sometimes people trouble themselves needlessly as a result of their faulty beliefs about how things *should* be (Ellis & Dryden, 1999; Ellis et al., 1988). SMC counselors might help clients to overcome such tendencies by exploring the possibility that the negative goals are an unnecessary source of discomfort that might be commanding too much attention.

Clinical Examples

Examples of how negative goals could be reconceptualized as positive ones are as follows: A goal of *Getting rid of my weight problem* might become *Accomplish an attractive, healthy body through good nutrition and exercise. Avoid making a fool of myself around other people* could be reformulated as *Learn to enjoy having other people appreciate me for the person I really am. Escape from my present boring job situation* could be recast as *Accomplish finding a job where I really enjoy going to work.*

Component 11: Re-Examine Sources of Self-Esteem

People with alcohol problems often hold high standards for themselves, and are unduly harsh on themselves when they are unable to achieve their high standards (Cox, 1983, 1987; Cox et al., 2001; Klinger, 1977). Problem drinkers also often pursue goals because they feel that they *ought* to do so, not because the goals are inherently satisfying. Thus, SMC counselors try to help clients to find new ways to feel good about themselves, to become less self-condemning, and to develop the capacity for self-forgiveness for goals they have not yet reached.

Clinical Example

One client accorded great importance to "keep on striving to be even better." He pursued this goal relentlessly and in doing so neglected other incentives that he might have pursued and enjoyed, thereby placing himself in a perilous *all-or-none* situation. Discussion revealed that the client's constant striving for self-improvement apparently arose from his relationship with his grandfather. The grandfather had always worked hard to *make something out of himself*, had become a *self-made man*, and successfully instilled his own values in his grandson. Wanting to live up to his image of his grandfather, the client felt compelled always to better himself. Accordingly, the client's counselor helped him not to equate his self-esteem with these kinds of accomplishments and to find new sources of self-satisfaction.

Maintenance Contacts

Initial experiences with SMC suggest that some—perhaps many—clients will need periodic maintenance contacts with their SMC counselors to prevent back-sliding. This is especially likely to be true for clients with substance-use disorders or limited mental capacities and for those who will return to resource-poor or stressful environments. The present state of knowledge is insufficient to permit specific guidelines regarding the frequency, number, or timeframe of maintenance contacts, but abrupt termination is inconsistent with maintenance of gains for at least a range of clients.

EXPERIENCES USING SMC

In addition to the use of SMC in individual sessions with substance-abusing clients, it has been used in various other formats and with people suffering from disorders other than substance abuse. Schroer, Fuhrmann, and de Jong-Meyer (Chapter 12, this volume), for instance, modified SMC for use in group sessions. The main goals of their sessions are to help clients (a) to activate their concerns and assess their motivational structure, and (b) to organize their goals into a hierarchy and then set main goals and subgoals to work on. The group technique has been used with clients with alcohol- and other substance-abuse disorders, affective disorders, personality disorders, and psychosis. Schroer et al.'s clinical experiences and research findings show the procedure to be therapeutically beneficial. De Jong-Meyer (Chapter 13, this volume) developed a self-help version of SMC, which she uses in conjunction with other self-help techniques aimed at personal-goal attainments. These strategies help individuals to set appropriate goal levels, plan concrete action steps, and implement habit-breaking strategies for approaching the chosen goals. Cox and colleagues (2003; see also Miranti & Heinemann, Chapter 15, this volume) evaluated the use of SMC in individual counseling sessions with patients who had suffered traumatic brain injuries—a population for whom motivational enhancement techniques are especially appropriate. Unlike patients in the control group, those receiving SMC showed significant improvements in motivational structure and significant reductions in negative affect and the use of substances of abuse. The use of SMC helped counselors to identify patients' needs, understand their motivational strengths and weaknesses, and plan their individualized treatments.

In addition to its clinical applications, SMC is also appropriate for use in work settings, where it leads to better management and increased employee job satisfaction and work performance (Roberson & Sluss, Chapter 14, this volume). Still others have proposed additional SMC applications, such as with offenders, to assess and change their motivation to offend (McMurran, Chapter 16, this volume), and in conjunction with other treatment strategies such as behavioral-economic approaches (Correia, Chapter 3, this volume), the Motivational Drinker's Check-Up (Emmen et al., Chapter 20, this volume), and Motivational Interviewing (Miller & Rollnick, 1991, p. 188; Resnicow et al., Chapter 24, this volume).

Finally, although clinical experiences with the newer PCI are more limited than those with the MSQ, clinicians' comments about their experiences have been positive. Samantha Wordsworth, Community Drug and Alcohol Nurse, North East Wales National Health

Service, described her experience using the PCI with a substance abuser as follows:

> Fiona and I worked together to fill in her PCI. The PCI was very user-friendly for both
> of us. In fact, there were some immediate benefits while filling it out. Doing the exercise
> highlighted the issues over which Fiona has no real influence or control. It also showed that
> some of the things that Fiona has been concerned about changing would not actually benefit
> her if they were to change. Fiona started to say, "Well, if that's the way it is, why am I so
> worried?" Reviewing life areas like *Relatives* and *Sexual Matters* allowed her to ventilate
> some of her frustrations, using humor rather than anger as she ordinarily would do. To sum
> up my impressions of the PCI: It is easy to use. It prompts discussion. I like it.

Geraint Jones, Clinical Manager of Hafan Wen Detoxification and Rehabilitation Centre, Wrexham, Wales, UK, had this to say:

The advantages of using the PCI as I see them are that it:

- allows better communication between different agencies involved in the treatment of a particular client;
- provides appropriate, alternative options for clients who present themselves for treatment time and time again;
- allows the possibility of developing a universal care plan and contract that would follow clients right through their contact with the different services involved in their care;
- provides a platform for people from different agencies to share knowledge and expertise;
- promotes the use of a recognized research-based tool that encourages universality in one aspect of our work.

REFERENCES

Chasteen, A.L., Park, D.C., & Schwarz, N. (2001). Implementation intentions and facilitation of prospective memory. *Psychological Science, 12*, 457–461.

Cox, W.M. (Ed.) (1983). *Identifying and measuring alcoholic personality characteristics.* San Francisco: Jossey-Bass.

Cox, W.M. (1987). Personality theory and research. In H.T. Blane & K.E. Leonard (Eds.), *Psychological theories of drinking and alcoholism* (pp. 55–89). New York: Guilford.

Cox, W.M., Heinemann, A.W., Miranti, S.V., Schmidt, M., Klinger, E., & Blount, J.P. (2003). Outcomes of Systematic Motivational Counseling for substance use following traumatic brain injury. *Journal of Addictive Diseases, 22*, 93–110.

Cox, W.M., & Klinger, E. (1988). A motivational model of alcohol use. *Journal of Abnormal Psychology, 97*, 168–180.

Cox, W.M., & Klinger, E. (1990). Incentive motivation, affective change, and alcohol use: A model. In W.M. Cox (Ed.), *Why people drink: Parameters of alcohol as a reinforcer* (pp. 291–314). New York: Gardner Press.

Cox, W.M., Yeates, G.N., Gilligan, P.A.T., & Hosier, S.G. (2001). Individual differences. In N. Heather, T.J., Peters, & T.R. Stockwell, (Eds.), *International Handbook of alcohol dependence and problems* (pp. 357–374). New York: John Wiley & Sons.

DiClemente, C.C., & Prochaska, J.O. (1998). Toward a comprehensive, transtheoretical model of change: Stages of change and addictive behaviors. In W.R. Miller & N. Heather (Eds.), *Treating addictive behaviors* (2nd edn.; pp. 3–24). New York: Plenum.

Dimeff, L.A., & Marlatt, G.A. (1998). Preventing relapse and maintaining change in addictive behaviors. *Clinical Psychology: Science and Practice, 5*, 513–525.

Dobson K.S. (2001). *Handbook of cognitive-behavioral therapies.* New York and London: Guilford.

Dollard, J., & Miller, N.E. (1950). *Personality and psychotherapy: An analysis in terms of learning, thinking, and culture.* New York: McGraw-Hill.

Donovan, D.M., & Chaney, E.F. (1985). Alcoholic relapse prevention and intervention: Models and methods (pp. 351–416). In G.A. Marlatt & J.R. Gordon (Eds.), *Relapse prevention: Maintenance strategies in the treatment of addictive behaviors*. New York: Guilford.

Elliot, A.J., & Sheldon, K.M. (1997). Avoidance achievement motivation: A personal goals analysis. *Journal of Personality and Social Psychology, 73*, 171–185.

Ellis, A., & Dryden, W. (1999). *The practice of REBT*. London: Free Association Press.

Ellis, A., McInerney, J.F., DiGiuseppe, R., & Yeager, R.J. (1988). *Rational-Emotive Therapy with alcoholics and substance abusers*. New York: Pergamon Press.

Emmons, R.A., & King, L.A. (1988). Conflict among personal strivings: Immediate and long-term implications for psychological and physical well-being. *Journal of Personality and Social Psychology, 54*, 1040–1048.

Gollwitzer, P.M. (1999). Implementation intentions: Strong effects of simple plans. *American Psychologist, 54*, 493–503.

Gollwitzer, P.M., & Brandstätter, V. (1997). Implementation intentions and effective goal pursuit. *Journal of Personality and Social Psychology, 73*, 186–199.

Higgins, E., Roney, C., Crowe, E., & Hymes, C. (1994). Ideal versus ought predilections for approach and avoidance: Distinct self-regulatory systems. *Journal of Personality and Social Psychology, 66*, 276–286.

Hunt, W., Barnett., L., & Branch, L. (1971). Relapse rates in addiction programs. *Journal of Clinical Psychology, 27*, 455–456.

Janis, I.L., & Mann, L. (1977). *Decision making*. New York: Free Press.

Kiresuk, T.J., Smith, A., & Cardillo, J.E. (1994). *Goal attainment scaling*. Hillsdale, NJ: Erlbaum.

Klinger, E. (1975). Consequences of commitment to and disengagement from incentives. *Psychological Review, 82*, 1–25.

Klinger, E. (1977). *Meaning and void: Inner experience and the incentives in people's lives.* Minneapolis: University of Minnesota Press.

Klinger, E., Cox, W.M., & Blount, J.P. (in press). Motivational Structure Questionnaire (MSQ) and Personal Concerns Inventory (PCI). In J.P. Allen & M. Columbus (Eds.), *Assessing alcohol problems: A guide for clinicians and researchers* (2nd edn.). Washington, DC: US Department of Health and Human Services.

Kuhl, J. (1994). A theory of action and state orientations. In J. Kuhl & J. Beckmann (Eds.), *Volition and personality: Action versus state orientation* (pp. 9–46). Seattle: Hogrefe & Huber.

Locke, E.A., & Latham, G.P. (1990). *A theory of goal setting and task performance*. Englewood Cliffs, NJ: Prentice-Hall.

MacPhillamy, D.J., & Lewinsohn, P.M. (1982). The pleasant events schedule: Studies on reliability, validity, and scale intercorrelation. *Journal of Consulting and Clinical Psychology, 50*, 363–380.

Maier, G.W., & Brunstein, J.C. (1999). *Action versus state orientation and disengagement from unrealistic goals*. Paper presented at the annual meeting of the American Psychological Assocation, Boston.

Marlatt, G.A. (1985). Cognitive factors in the relapse process. In G.A. Marlatt & J.R. Gordon (Eds.), *Relapse prevention: Maintenance strategies in the treatment of addictive behaviors* (pp. 128–200). New York: Guilford.

Marlatt, G.A., & Gordon, J.R. (Eds.) (1985). *Relapse prevention: Maintenance strategies in the treatment of addictive behaviors*. New York: Guilford.

Miller, W.R., & Rollnick, S. (1991). *Motivational interviewing: Preparing people to change addictive behavior*. New York: Guilford.

Miller, W.R., & Rollnick, S. (2002). *Motivational interviewing: Preparing people to change addictive behavior* (2nd edn.). New York: Guilford.

Oettingen, G., Pak, H., & Schnetter, K. (2001). Self-regulation of goal setting: Turning free fantasies about the future into binding goals. *Journal of Personality and Social Psychology, 80*, 736–753.

Prochaska, J.O., Johnson, S., & Lee, P. (1998). The transtheoretical model of behavior change. In S.A. Shumaker, E.B. Schron, J.K. Ockene, & W.L. McBee (Eds.), *The handbook of health behavior change* (2nd edn.; pp. 59–84). Berlin: Springer.

Riley, D.M., Sobell, L.C., Leo, G.I., Sobell, M.B., & Klajner, F. (1987). Behavioral treatment of alcohol problems: A review and a comparison of behavioral and nonbehavioral studies. In W.M. Cox (Ed.), *Treatment and prevention of alcohol problems: A resource manual* (pp. 73–115). Orlando, FL: Academic Press.

Roberson, L. (1990). Prediction of job satisfaction from characteristics of personal work goals. *Journal of Organizational Behavior, 11*, 29–41.

Schultheiss, O.C. (in press). An information processing account of implicit motive arousal. In M.L. Maehr & P. Pintrich (Eds.), *Advances in motivation and achievement. Vol. 12: Methodology in motivation research.* Greenwich, CT: JAI Press.

Scott, M. (1999). The problem-solving pilgrim. In J. Lees (Ed.), *Clinical counseling in context: An introduction* (pp. 64–79). London: Routledge.

Taylor, S.E., & Pham, L.B. (1998–1999). The effect of mental simulation on goal-directed performance. *Imagination, Cognition, and Personality, 18*, 253–268.

Whitworth, A.B., Fischer, F., Lesch, O.M., Nimmerrichter, A., Oberbauer, H., Platz, T., Potgieter, A., Walter, H., & Fleischhacker, W.W. (1996). Comparison of acamprosate and placebo in long-term treatment of alcohol dependence. *Lancet, 347* (9013), 1438–1442.

Systematic Motivational Counseling in Groups: Clarifying Motivational Structure during Psychotherapy

Bernhard M. Schroer
Psychotherapeutische Praxis, Münster, Germany
Arno Fuhrmann
Alexianer-Krankenhaus GmbH, Münster, Germany
and
Renate de Jong-Meyer
Westfälische Wilhelms-Universität of Münster, Germany

Synopsis.—The development and effectiveness of a brief intervention is described that adapts and extends techniques of *Motivational Structure Analysis* and *Systematic Motivational Counseling* to the special demands of a group setting. The development of *Systematic Motivational Counseling in Groups (SMC-G)* was stimulated by the necessity to enrich the phase of *Qualified Detoxification* in German alcoholism treatment by an intervention aimed at improving motivation for abstinence and for participating in further treatments. The group procedure was devised as an adjunct to individual sessions, and was later extended for use in different inpatient and outpatient clinics and psychotherapy practices. A manual provides detailed instructions on how to help clients clarify and approach their goals within four to five group sessions. Specifically, the following description includes the strategies for: (1) activating clients' current concerns using a combination of relaxation and guided imagery instructions; (2) assessing current concerns, and translating them into goal statements; (3) anticipating and rating various goal aspects; (4) selecting main goals; (5) drawing conclusions regarding motivational structure in a therapist-guided feedback process focusing on structural and content issues of the goals, taking into account previous goal attainment attempts and self-regulatory characteristics of individual clients; and (6) constructing goal hierarchies and defining concrete subgoals. Some strategies are illustrated by transcripts of therapeutic interactions to give a more lively impression of the procedure, namely, how diagnostic information might lead to options of change within the context of a self-management approach. As a result of this SMC-G procedure, personal goals might become treatment goals for subsequent individual sessions, where therapists can profit from the assessment

Handbook of Motivational Counseling. Edited by W. Miles Cox and Eric Klinger.
© 2004 John Wiley & Sons, Ltd.

of motivational dimensions for longitudinal evaluations. Other goals might be supported by self-help approaches. Data from a longitudinal treatment outcome study show that SMC-G is comparable in effectiveness to the established social skill training approach, and has the advantage of being less time-consuming.

Epidemiological research confirms a high prevalence of problematic alcohol drinking behavior throughout Europe with Germany in fourth place (10.8 litres) behind Portugal (11.3), Luxembourg (11.2), and France (10.9), while the UK only showed up in 19th place (7.7). Though German consumption declined slightly during recent years (Demmel, 2000), public health authorities, following criteria introduced by the ICD-10, assume that 1.6 million men and women suffer from alcohol addiction. Another 2.7 million people are estimated to abuse alcohol per day, and 4.9 million more consume 30–40 grams (men) or 20 grams (women) of pure alcohol, thus running the risk of developing an abuse or addiction disorder later in life. The projected costs of more than 20 billion euros per year are enormous for society in general and for the health insurance system in particular, because it pays the heavy burden of 7 billion euros for treatment of alcohol-related diseases.

Although treatment of addictions is considered to be fairly differentiated in Germany, relatively few clients make full use of these options. The standard treatment for alcohol addiction in Germany consists of a short detoxification treatment followed by an extended inpatient psychotherapeutic treatment that averages 13 weeks. Only 10 to 20% of clients proceed to psychotherapy after detoxification. The many reasons for this range from shortcomings of the standard detoxification intervention to clients' fear of losing their jobs by investing time in a prolonged therapy.

The epidemiological data, together with the current economic pressure to reduce treatment time and to give priority to outpatient rather than inpatient treatment, have stimulated interest in brief interventions (Aalto, Pekuri, & Seppä, 2001; Babor & Higgins-Biddle, 2000; Bien, Miller, & Tonigan, 1993; Drummond, 1997; Fleming & Graham, 2001; Moyer et al., 2002; Prochaska & DiClemente, 1986; Zweben & Fleming, 1999). This trend has increased even more since international studies (US and EU) show no clear evidence for differences in effectiveness between brief interventions and standard treatments (e.g., Project MATCH, 1997, 1998). Contrasting with this, in a meta-analysis of 44 German and Anglo-American studies, Süss (1995) found the success rate for the standard German treatment to be 14% higher than the average of the remaining European countries.

Heightened German interest within the last decade in brief interventions has resulted in *qualified detoxification programs*. These programs have been tested in many psychiatric treatment centers. Their common objective is to facilitate the clients' readiness to confront their addiction and to support their commitment to treatment. Such programs aim at two main groups: clients who are ambivalent with regard to changing their alcohol consumption and clients who disapprove of extended treatment. Both groups are prone to relapse shortly after detoxification, require multiple attempts at treatment, and ultimately face an increasing risk of severe bodily harm.

Nearly all brief interventions established throughout recent years focus directly on the problematic or addictive drinking pattern (Heather, 1995). In contrast, Cox, Klinger, and Blount (1999) take an indirect route by promoting clients' nonalcohol-related goals (see Cox & Klinger, Chapters 8 and 11, this volume). In the course of an alcohol-addiction disorder clients usually show a decreasing number of goals other than goals centering around procurement and consumption of alcohol. The corresponding state of mind is characterized by state-orientation (lack of initiative and planning) and cognitions typical of a depression

(Kuhl & Helle, 1986). Goals tend to be unrealistic and thus pave the way for frustration, which ultimately increases motivation to drink again. Over time the person experiences a decreasing rate of reinforcement from goal-directed action and an increasing rate of chemically induced reinforcement independent of goal attainment. Cox and Klinger (1988) have integrated this core dynamics into a motivational model of alcohol use, which in connection with Klinger's theory of current concerns (Klinger, 1975, 1977, 1996) serves as the theoretical background behind the SMC approach. Other theoretical approaches are related to or build upon Klinger's theory of motivation (e.g., Kaschel & Kuhl, Chapter 6, this volume; Kuhl, 2000).

SMC IN GROUPS

What are the advantages of applying SMC strategies in a group setting? For many clinicians, particularly in inpatient setting, time and personnel constraints demand a motivational intervention, capable of reaching a group of patients within a brief treatment. This must not, however, lead to a disadvantage. On the contrary, the particular social situation of a group of individuals, who sometimes even identify with each other in seeking to clarify their motivational structure, might even improve therapeutic effects. Another specific advantage is seen in conducting a procedure that is both a diagnostic tool *and* a therapeutic intervention.

This chapter describes how the diagnostic information derived from the analysis of motivational structure (see Cox & Klinger, Chapter 8, this volume) can be communicated to clients in a group setting, and how it translates into therapeutic interventions guided by a self-management heuristic (Kanfer, Reinecker, & Schmelzer, 1996). The chapter first provides the reader with detailed instructions for using these techniques in groups of clients, with special emphasis on deviations from the original SMC technique (see Cox & Klinger, Chapter 11, this volume), and on recommendations for clinical management of difficult situations in this context. Second, the chapter summarizes the findings of a controlled treatment study, where Systematic Motivational Counseling in Groups (SMC-G) was compared to a social skill training (Schroer, 2001).

Session One: Activating Clients' Current Concerns

In the initial group session clients are introduced to the procedure, its general purpose, and possible personal benefits from taking part. Another important function of this session is to evoke emotional responses by activating clients' current concerns. To think about one's current life situation and one's goals is a very personal matter. For clients, unfortunately, it often is a painful act. Thus the therapist has to be aware of a variety of defensive strategies and ambivalencies provoked by the procedure. The more the client knows in advance about the aim and the method of the first meeting, the better. This means that each participating client should be given specific information either verbally or in written form. All explanations and instructions given during the session should stress that it is the client's choice to disclose personal information during the later stages. Direct or indirect pressure to participate should be carefully avoided, because pressure might strengthen reactance to the procedure. Another problem with clients suffering from an alcohol addiction is their tendency to respond in a socially desirable way that might put restrictions on the diagnostic inferences to be drawn from answers under pressure. A subject, for example, might choose to omit important concerns, or might try to maintain an image of being highly committed, while at the same time is feeling low commitment because of strong ambivalence. To reduce the activation of such response tendencies we strictly guaranteed to clients that no therapist would read their working sheets unless they gave their permission.

Specifically, our instructions start as follows:

> I would like to invite you today, tomorrow, and on the next day to think about your current concerns. What are current concerns? The answer is quite simple. Everything that is important to you, things you think about, things that matter to you, things that are close to your heart.
>
> I will join you on this journey, but you don't need to tell me anything about your concerns unless you want to. Do it for yourself. Perhaps you will realize that this is an opportunity: to have the time to write down all the concerns that you are aware of and to have enough time to look at these concerns in various ways.

Creating Conditions for Motivational Disclosure

After a short introduction, the therapist continues with a relaxation exercise using guided imagery. This relaxation serves two functions: first, it signals the actual start of the procedure and ends the verbal explanations (which otherwise tend to take too much time); second, a relaxation employing guided imagery will probably improve the individual's sensitivity for his concerns. Klinger (1971, 1990) theoretically sees a close connection between imagination and current concerns, and empirical research showed clear evidence for this claim (Klinger, Barta, & Maxeiner, 1981). Current concerns significantly influence the stream of thoughts, i.e., in daydreaming. Relaxation facilitates such a respondent, undirected mode of thinking. We have used a sensory relaxation script that calls for a variety of highly specific images in multiple sensory modalities (vision, touch, weight, temperature, etc.). After having the subject imagine *something in the distance* as a symbolic representation of a goal state, the script leads to the subject's current situation in different life areas. It refers to the past, the present, and the future in a nonfocused general manner. The following part of the instruction illustrates this particular important phase of the procedure:

> I would now like to invite you to take part in a short guided relaxation. It can be very helpful to take some time for relaxation before one starts with another task, because it redirects your thoughts away from the things you had in mind when you came here and makes it easier to think of something else ... // ... (Sensory relaxation)[*] ... // ... Whatever it is that you see or perceive in the distance, are you now able to say goodbye to it? Confidently allow yourself to pull away from it whenever you are ready to do so. // Is it now possible for you to turn your attention to the things that you are concerned with at the moment in your everyday life, such as your concerns at home or about your work? // Can you now allow these things to come into your view by way of your inner eyes? // Whatever concern occurs to you first ... Think about positive things ... and also about negative, painful, or frustrating experiences and situations in this area of your life. // Perhaps you are thinking about the last two weeks, or about the more distant past. Maybe you will think of the future and how things might be then. // Is there something about the situation that you perhaps would like to change, or would you like for everything to stay the way it is? // Is there something that you would like to keep the way it is because

---

[*] This script can be ordered from Bernhard M. Schroer.

it pleases you, or is it because for the time being you simply cannot think of an alternative? [*Note. It is important to mention the possibility of keeping things the way they are!*]

The procedure we describe here focuses mainly on the client's present situation and develops discrepancies with former times or desired states in the future. Alternative interventions to activate motives and personal projects are conceivable, e.g., focusing attention directly into the future by having clients imagine their personal situation ten years later.

Collecting Conscious Representations of Current Concerns

After the relaxation participants are asked about their experiences and whether they were successful in imagining the things they were instructed to think about. It often happens that at least one client talks about the circumstances that brought him into treatment or the way he wants his future to be. Clients then receive the working sheets and are instructed (closely adhering here to the wording used for the original MSQ [Motivational Structure Questionnaire]) to write down whatever current concerns come to their mind.

> Please write down whatever it is that came to your mind or that you happen to think about now. We simply want you to list briefly the things that affect your life, that are important to you. This could be both the things that you consider to be problems and the ones that bring you joy and happiness. It is not necessary to list important things from the past that no longer concern you.
>
> Take your time. This is not a test and therefore it doesn't matter how fast you are or how much you write down. A few words should be enough to sketch your concern. For every new concern that you think of use a new space on the answer-sheet. Try to make each description a complete thought. If you need more sheets just let me know.

Our clinical experience with the concern-generation phase indicated that clients do not need many clear and specific instructions here. Only a limited set of initial instructions is recommended to have the clients stop talking and start writing. To assure standardization, one can, for example, use transparencies to show the definition of a current concern, and give a few examples. Further verbal instructions might interfere with clients' efforts to recall their personal concerns. The typical situation is that most clients seem to understand intuitively and start writing down their list of current concerns immediately, whereas others understand, but listen to the therapist as long as he goes on with his instructions. Still other clients need these instructions, because they have difficulties relating the abstract concept of current concerns to their own lives. In this case it is often helpful to ask the group if someone would be willing to give a personal example of a written concern. Usually this frees the reluctant client to start writing and has the positive side effect of supporting group cohesiveness. There are clients, however, who are uncomfortable with writing down very personal thoughts in the group. The tendency to avoid the task can also take the form of a statement of mistrust as to what might happen with the data, or lead to a frequently expressed belief that the client knows enough about his personal goals and therefore does not need to write them down. A good way to deal with such statements is to express an understanding of how the client feels and to accept his point of view.

> I see your point. You are not sure whether participating in all this will help you or bring you new insights, because you already know very well what your plans are. It might well be that you are right and that you do not need this. Of course, I cannot be sure about this.

It's up to you to decide. Maybe you will learn nothing from this. Maybe there is something you can learn from or gain new insights or develop new perspectives about. I suggest you take your time deciding and if at any point during the procedure you decide to stop—that will be all right.

Our experience has shown that some clients write down goals, describing changes they intend to make, whereas others simply describe situations as they experience them. Nevertheless, we do not want the verbal instructions to overemphasize the goal perspective, because this could filter out important concerns, especially goals that clients are undecided or unclear about wishing to pursue. For this reason, we use examples of current concerns that do not name goals but imply the possibility of different goals (e.g. *Andrea: She makes me so angry!*).

After 60 minutes have passed, we usually end the first group session and advise clients to complete their list of concerns after a short break later the same day.

Session 2: Now and Then

The second session should be run after only a short time interval (e.g., the next day). It starts with asking clients whether or not they have completed their list of concerns, and how many concerns they have written down. This is advisable, because some clients might produce a very long list of concerns, in which case they must be carefully instructed to work at their own pace but to accept that the timing of the upcoming sequence of questions will not allow them to answer each question for all of their concerns. They are advised in advance to complete their ratings after the group session has ended.

Rating 1: Satisfaction with Present Situation

Clients are instructed to rate each of their concerns regarding current satisfaction, and in doing this to think of all positive aspects as well as all negative aspects of the present situation.

The question and answer format (a bipolar scale ranging from -10 to $+10$) focuses clients' attention on a balanced perception of the present situation, thus promoting an integrative decisional process for either changing or maintaining the present situation. Put another way, having clients think of both advantages and disadvantages of a particular situation, before asking them what, if anything, they actually want to change, evokes dissonances by indirectly pointing to advantages of a situation one wants to change and disadvantages of a situation one would like to maintain. The resulting response is intended to be more representative of the person's needs and strivings. In addition, the rating serves as an anchor for the subject, against which changes toward or away from the intended goal can be evaluated at a later time (see the *Goal Ladder* procedure by Cox & Klinger, Chapter 11, this volume).

From Current Concerns to Goals

The therapist asks everyone in the group to think about each concern carefully, and to try to determine which goal they would see for the concern. Clients are then instructed to phrase a

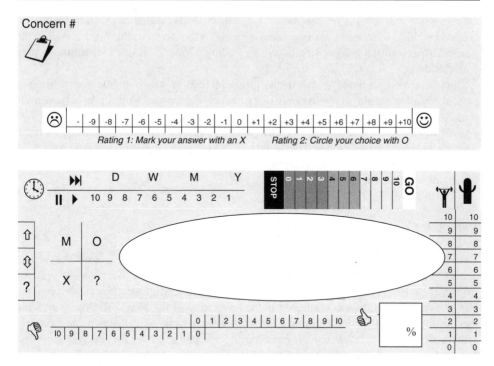

Figure 12.1 The two sides of the working sheet used with the SMC-G. The top part of the figure shows one of four fields on the front side of the working sheet, where clients sketch their concern and indicate their satisfaction with the present situation (ratings 1 and 2). The lower part of the figure displays one of four corresponding fields on the backside of the working sheet. Clients write down their goals in the white ellipse and give their ratings 3 through 12 in the surrounding subfields

goal for every concern by completing a sentence starting with *I will . . .* or *I want to. . . .* These goal sentences are to be written adjacent to the corresponding concerns.

This very central step of the procedure seldom creates problems. The therapist guiding clients through this step is advised to use examples of *translations* of concerns into goals. Both approach and avoidance goals should be used as examples. By asking clients for their examples, the therapist should also discuss that two people can come to very different solutions (goals) since they perceive the same current concern differently, and that neither goal is the one and only correct one.

Rating 2: Satisfaction with Permanence of the Present Situation

This rating requires the client to toy with the idea of how one would feel if the present situation would never change. The original MSQ contains a rating of expected *sorrow*, if the goal could not be reached. As the *sorrow* rating showed a very high correlation with *commitment*, which is theoretically plausible but represents redundant information in the clinical context, this *satisfaction with permanence* rating was devised. It is useful to sensitize the client to positive aspects of the present situation, because those aspects often create a latent conflict with goal states representing a change. Such conflict can well be the reason for not reaching a desired goal because approaching the goal would mean reducing the positive aspects of the present situation (e.g., finding a job may result in less time to play with the kids).

Questions recommended to ask in the group include to which degree a nonchanging present situation would worry the client or to which degree this would take a burden off him. At a later stage, it might become important to consider the ratings on *satisfaction with present situation* and *Commitment* together with the *satisfaction with permanence* rating. Sometimes, inconsistent ratings have to be pointed out (e.g., high commitment to change but little or no effect of a nonchanging situation on satisfaction) or have to become the subject of later therapeutic interventions.

Rating 3: Control over the Situation

By asking *Goal attainment depends on what or whom?* this rating aims at clients' beliefs about the factors influencing goal attainments. The subject then has four response options: (a) me, (b) others, (c) accident or fate, and (d) cannot say. Multiple choices are possible. Part of this information was contained in the *role* rating of the MSQ. The six-point scale used in the original format combined two important psychological dimensions, namely self-involvement (e.g., *I am actively involved . . .*) and preparedness for action (e.g., *. . . and know what to do*). We decided to separate these dimensions. In the SMC-G, *Preparedness for action* is presented later as rating 12, whereas self-involvement was broadened to this *Control of the situation* rating by including not only the self as an acting and controlling agent but also other people and circumstances. For diagnostic purposes it is important to compare the frequencies of goals whose attainment is perceived to be under the exclusive control of the client with those where goal attainment depends on the joint influence of the client and others. Some clients have interactional goals (e.g., *Develop a better understanding of my partner*) and yet see themselves as the only responsible agent, thereby neglecting influences of the partner. Those clients have to be guided to a more realistic estimate of joint responsibilities in social interactions.

Ratings 4 and 5: Joy and Unhappiness upon Goal Attainment

These ratings correspond to those in the MSQ. The scale was changed, though, from 0 to 10, and the two dimensions/ratings were presented together instead of one after the other. Asking for joy without letting clients know that an unhappiness rating will follow might skew judgments. For instance, the client could give a rating of joy adjusted for the degree of unhappiness expected despite having reached the goal. Through introducing the two dimensions together, clients are induced to evaluate each dimension independently. This step again engages the client to anticipate emotional consequences of goal attainment and to build a commitment that integrates both positive and negative expectations. Diagnostically, it is of particular interest whether the client actually expects negative feelings in conjunction with goal attainment. The higher the degree of perceived disadvantage of goal attainment, the more difficult is goal enactment and the less likely goal attainment.

Session 3: Self-Regulatory Aspects and the Decision to Act

Rating 6: Initiative versus Inhibition of Impulses

Rating 6 supplements the choice of action words to describe the intended goal approach (see Cox & Klinger, Chapter 8, this volume). This and the following two ratings were newly constructed with the aim of stimulating clients' reflection about self-regulatory functions necessary for successful goal enactment. In rating 6, clients estimate to what extent goal attainment requires a *Go Response* requiring initiative and own action (e.g., visit the doctor, start a fitness plan) or a *Stop Response requiring* inhibiting one's impulses (e.g., not to argue with the partner, maintain a dietary plan). A bipolar scale from 1 to 10 is used with *STOP* and *GO* as anchor descriptions. While choosing action words permits assessing the relative dominance of appetitive, avoidant, maintenance, or clarification goals, this rating makes more explicit which self-regulatory strategy the client actually considers for a particular goal. The same goal (e.g., *I want to shape up my physical fitness*) can be enacted focusing either on an initiative (*use the bicycle to go to work, book a course at the gym*) or on impulse control (*do not use the elevator, refrain from eating potato chips*) or a combination of both. It is not trivial for the purpose of clinical intervention whether the instrumental subgoals the client tends to form require initiative or the inhibition of impulses.

Rating 7: Difficulty of Enactment

This rating asks for an appraisal of the anticipated risk of becoming distracted from the goal or losing sight of the goal pursuit. Again, a scale running from 0 to 10 is used. The rationale for introducing this dimension is to cognitively prepare the client for difficulties that might arise along the way to goal attainment. From a diagnostic perspective it becomes important at a later point of the intervention to examine the relationship between the anticipated difficulty, the client's *Commitment*, and the *expected success* ratings (here introduced as ratings 9 and 10). When, for example, a client frequently rates the degree of enactment difficulties as high and at the same time rates his success expectancies as moderate or low, commitment might be reduced and this client should be helped to examine this resignative pattern and to change it.

Rating 8: Readiness for Action

The rating consists of choosing from among three mutually exclusive categories describing absence of any action plan (*I have no idea*), indecision (*I have not yet decided*), and a clear idea as to what action to take or which opportunity lends itself to action (*I know clearly what I will do next*). With this rating, information is collected on the client's preparedness for action and/or his knowledge of action opportunities.

Goal descriptions and goal representations may activate action schemata in specific situations to increase their probability of realization. Vague descriptions of a desired goal state can lead to unintended neglect of the goal or to overseeing opportunities to take action toward the goal. In such a situation it helps to think of intermediate goal states, i.e., to operationalize the goal for the short term (*What is it that you can do today or tomorrow to get a little closer to your goal?*).

Rating 9: Probability of Success

With this step (which corresponds to step 8 of the MSQ) clients estimate the likelihood of goal attainment given all the circumstances and aspects of which they are aware (*How do you judge your chances all in all to reach your goal?*). This dimension is a good *entry point* for therapists' comments on clients' motivational structure. The therapist can, for example, point to low probability in combination with high commitment or simply ask the client to talk about things and circumstances that would heighten or lower the perceived probability of success.

Rating 10: Commitment

As this rating is central to the whole procedure because it has the function of a summarizing parameter, it was put close to the end of the sequence of ratings. Doing so enables the client to consider various aspects (as represented by the ratings above) influencing his commitment. By the same token, a particular degree of commitment can represent quite different internal states, from a desperate insistence on an almost impossible goal (e.g., *I want to save my marriage!*) to a strongly felt obligation not to betray others (e.g., *I want to stop drinking!*). From a therapeutic perspective, discussing the degree of a client's commitment should encompass the possibility of lowering commitment and reducing effort down to a point where one would only *wait and see*. It also can be very helpful to consider disengagement from some goals, at least for a limited time, to clarify and if necessary revise one's inner attitude toward the goal. This is an option that clients sometimes do not see.

Rating 11: Urgency

This rating (on an 11-point scale from 0 = *not urgent at all* to 10 = *very urgent*) asks clients to consider how much time is left to start action or to strengthen current efforts in order to reach the goal. This step involves an implicit request to devise a time order of activities and to set priorities within the total list of one's goals—not an easy task for many clients. A typical pattern of responding shows high average values for urgency and only little variance, which either demonstrates the client's inability to differentiate the goal's importance or is an indirect sign of a weak representation of the concrete action steps necessary to approach that goal. A second typical pattern of responding is to underestimate urgency of action. This may work short term as a cognitive relief strategy but could also indicate a dysfunctional long-term strategy of postponing the critical moment of taking initiative. In discussing these aspects with the client, one has to be aware of possible interactions with the perceived preparedness for action. Indicating a low urgency of action toward a goal has different implications according to whether the client has no idea what to do next or states a clear understanding of necessary next steps.

Rating 12: Goal Distance

Clients are required here to give the number of days, weeks, months, or years they think will go by before they will have reached their goal. Whether the client differentiates between short-term, mid-term, and long-term goals is a diagnostically relevant issue here. A client who puts everything in the near term might experience maladaptive pressure and difficulty in setting priorities for action, whereas someone who sees goal attainment in the distant future might feel little incentive to work on that goal now. The therapist should generally be aware of unrealistic planning when evaluating this dimension. For the purpose of discussing ratings with the clients, it can be useful to relate this rating to the perceived *difficulty of enactment*. It is not unusual for clients to expect moderate to high difficulties during goal pursuit, but at the same time to expect reaching the goal within the next four weeks. In some cases this may work, in other cases it may be implausible and unrealistic and should therefore be made salient to the client to prevent frustration.

Selection of Focus Goals and Introduction of Goal Matrix

At the end of the third group session, clients are instructed to go carefully through their list of goals and select up to five focus goals, which they plan to pursue in the near future. This is to focus clients' attention and motivational resources onto a subset of action opportunities and thereby to enhance the probability of goal-directed action. They are also instructed to reproduce their original worksheet ratings of every goal on a special summary sheet (*goal matrix*), thus collecting all dimensional ratings on one sheet of paper. The therapist emphasizes the possibility *on second thought* of changing one's original ratings. Whether the client changes the ratings or not, one can expect him or her to check the original ratings at least partially upon completing the matrix of goal characteristics. Clients usually react favorably to this opportunity, but differ, of course, in the extent to which they make use of it. The therapist sends an important message here, namely, whatever you thought of your goals in the first place, you might have changed your thinking about them by now. It is again the general attitude of allowing individuality, giving high responsibility to clients, evoking the clients' choice for change rather than imposing choices and strategies, which makes that kind of instruction recommendable.

Sessions 4 and 5: Discussing Structural Aspects of Clients' Motivation in the Group

Whereas the first three sessions consisted of standardized self-rating modules and usually led to little interaction among group members, the following sessions are based on individual materials and experiences with working on them. These session are often characterized by a high degree of group interaction. The fourth and an optional fifth session are designed to analyze individual goal matrices and in doing so to extend each client's knowledge of his motivational structure.

In earlier stages of SMC-G development the fourth session was used to comment on different aspects of goals. Discussion of individual data was included in an unsystematic way and mainly for illustration purposes. Individual feedback and guidance was not done in the group setting but in subsequent individual sessions. It seemed like a disadvantage of the SMC that it took a lot of computing and expert knowledge to come up with something meaningful for the client. It took us quite a while to realize that by confining analysis and feedback to an individual session where the therapist had to do the homework, we had ignored a very important guideline of effective psychotherapy, namely, not to do the client's work!

Instead of drawing conclusions from the data and feeding them back to the client in the most adequate manner, we now have the clients do the analyses and draw conclusions not only from their own data but regarding the other participants of the group, too. We do this, first of all, by concentrating the feedback on structural aspects and by not discussing the actual content of the goal, unless a client starts to disclose contents. To proceed this way reduces reactance tendencies and helps to create an agreeable atmosphere of mutual interest and respect. The matrices of goals and their associated dimensional ratings, which clients had transfered from the working sheets, are used as the base material for the session(s). The therapist and the group members jointly analyze the motivational structure matrix of one client, who volunteers to have his or her matrix presented to the others. (The therapist should prepare the session by clarifying who will his or her give his consent for this!). Drawing on an individual goal matrix, clients exchange their thoughts and conclusions regarding structural goal characteristics.

The therapist complements this with his or her own insights, and questions clients' opinions using principles of cognitive therapy and the six principles of Motivational Interviewing (Miller & Rollnick, 1991; see also Resnicow et al., Chapter 24, this volume). Miller and Rollnick maintain clients' need for *feedback* about their current status and understanding of personal *responsibility* for change. The therapist, in his or her view, should give clear *advice* and present a *menu* of alternative strategies (e.g., different perspectives on a goal). *Empathy* of the therapist is an empirically well-established common element of effective interventions and an important determinant of patient motivation and change. Group therapists should seek to reinforce clients' *self-efficacy*, their belief in their competencies to change problem behaviors, and reach specific goals. These six principles are assumed to work not only for clients suffering from addictions but also for most other psychological disorders.

Excerpts from transcripts of actual group interactions of clients are used here to illustrate the procedure, for which no steps can be given. The structural group feedback approach allows for a wide range of therapeutically meaningful inferences. In the following dialog, T refers to the therapist, and A, B, C, and M are clients.

T: Last time I asked you to look at your goals and ratings. Now is the time to share your thoughts and receive feedback from others. Of course everyone is free to do so and no one should feel an obligation to disclose his personal affairs. Who wants to begin?

A: When I look at my goal matrix (Figure 12.2) I really feel pressure. It seems so much that I want to do within the next weeks. Tried to postpone some things already though it still seems a load . . .

B: Well I see what your problem is. You have 19 goals and want to pursue 11 goals at the same time. But what I find especially noteworthy is that you do not seem to know which steps to take next with four of the goals.

C: I looked at the line "commitment" first, since that is what I asked myself yesterday. Do I really want to make an effort to reach my goals? It looks as if you are highly committed to start doing something?

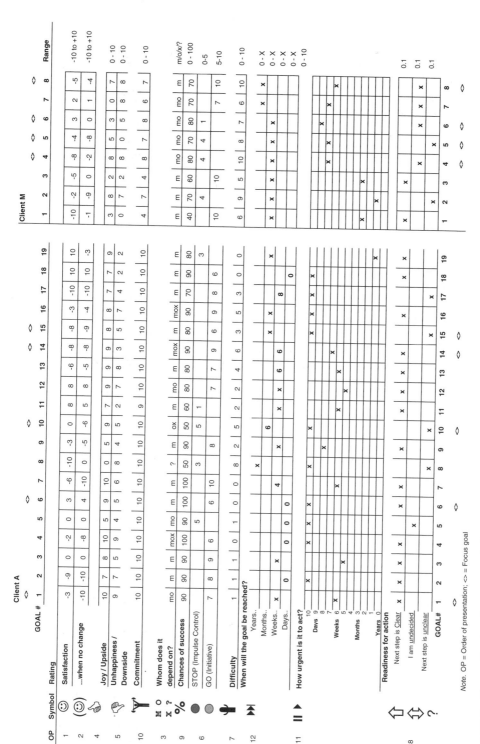

Figure 12.2 The motivational structure of clients A and M

A: Hm. . . . I have to think abou this. I mean I feel like I really should go on with that goal 15 (looks at his working sheet) but then again something holds me back . . .

T: You mean there are advantages and disadvantages to pursuing the goal?

A: Yes. I believe every time I think about the goal I think about the positive aspects of reaching the goal, whereas when it comes to action I realize how uncomfortable it would be to work for that goal.

B: Could it be that your marking "don't know what to do" actually means I don't know how to get myself started?

A: I think you're right. I seem to need some extra thrust here to overcome my doubts.

T: And you feel highly committed to make that decision for action? Do I interpret this correctly?

A: Oh yes! I do want to make a decision here. Otherwise I am afraid everything would remain the same.

For the client and the therapist it is often surprising to realize how expressive the mere numbers are. Most often client and therapist recognize very quickly the particular part of the motivational structure that is problematic in itself or points to a currently problematic aspect of the client's life. The therapist's role in this process is crucial and involves multiple tasks, e.g., to maintain an atmosphere of mutual respect, to assist in developing discrepancies that clients begin to see, to amplify or deamplify critical aspects, to re-evaluate client's comments, and to be a balanced leader of the discussion. To repeat: the process so far does not openly refer to the actual content of someone's problem. In some cases this enables the therapist to *understand* the dynamics of a client's problem without knowing the problem itself. This particular aspect of the feedback process helps to promote trust in the therapist, especially for inexperienced or suspicious clients.

M: I find it noticeable that you (A) have very many goals in comparison to me (shows his matrix containing 8 goals). I think I would feel a lot of pressure if I had that many goals. On the other hand, maybe there are advantages in having a lot of goals. Maybe your goals are more concrete than mine and relate to each other.

A: I really have a lot of goals. Sometimes I feel like I cannot see the forest for the trees. But then I begin to see a little more clearly. As a matter of fact many goals have a connection with each other.

C: You have many short-term goals, which I think is good, because you can start to do something. But don't you think it would relieve the strain on you a little bit if you could reconsider the timely manners. I mean, I would ask myself what really is the most important step to start with or how many things can I do at once without feeling so uneasy again that . . .

A: . . . I feel I have an excuse for drinking! . . . But how can I differentiate between my goals and determine what to do next?

T: A difficult question indeed. . . . Well, when you have had times of failure and misfortune, it is advisable not to begin with the most difficult goals, those that have a low probability of success, because you perceive that you have little influence on goal attainment. Your goal 10, which you have selected as a focus goal, seems to fulfill this criterion. To have rewarding experiences more quickly you should instead concentrate on goals with medium difficulty, relatively high probability of success, and a high degree of individual control. This is the case with your goal 17, which seems to be rather important too.

A: Good idea. . . . Besides, when I look at the numbers now, it seems a bit odd that with the majority of my goals I estimate the difficulties for action so low and that I would be committed to the highest degree with every single goal.

T: We often think that we should feel highly committed to every goal we follow. Though sometimes this is wishful thinking: you think you are committed, but actually you are not. It can happen easily with goals you feel ambivalent about, because of their downsides or indirect negative consequences. In many cases it makes sense to concentrate on less ambivalent goals first, and to use the energy set free by goal attainment for the more difficult goals. (*Turns to M.*) You had just mentioned an aspect of your goal matrix. OK if we turn to you now?

M: I want. . . . Well—looking at A's matrix, it struck me that I myself have almost no short-term goals. I only have "big hammers" that take months and years. Besides this I discovered three goals (*points to his goals 2, 6, and 8*) where I feel somewhat wavering, like going back and forth. With goals 6 and 8 I even see more disadvantages than advantages upon reaching the goal. Though these two goals belong to my set of focus goals. I am a strange person—don't you think so!?

A: With three of your five main goals (*focus goals*) you see a dependency on others, which means you cannot reach that goal exclusively by your own efforts. Do I understand this correctly?

M: (*stunned*) Yes. . . . Amazing that you could see this among all those numbers!

A: I would not feel good if my important goals were codetermined by others.

M: Well, that seems to be one of my biggest problems. Throughout recent years my satisfaction was directly related to the mood of my close relationships, first my mother, then my girlfriend . . . but I think this takes us too far now . . .

T: Now—this is very impressive, how both of you made a connection here and that you (*to M*) take care of yourself and draw a line here, because it becomes too personal for you . . .

Due to space limitations we have to conclude here. It is left to the reader's fantasy to imagine how this process might unfold.

Whenever we continued the group into a fifth session, typical relevant issues were (a) the individual criteria for selecting the focus goals, (b) types of goals (approach, avoidance, maintenance, clarification), and (c) individual experiences with goal-setting and goal attainment.

A therapist should also bear in mind that many clients show deficits in social competence (e.g., difficulty in saying no, perceiving and expressing own emotions and wishes, expressing a critical opinion). If such difficulties in social interactions become apparent for a group member, the recommended course is to follow general principles of social skills training.

As a means of summarizing the discussion of structural motivational aspects, we recommended introducing criteria for a well-formed goal (see Willutzki & Koban, Chapter 17, this volume). Furthermore, it can be important to focus clients' attention on goal interdependencies or possible conflicts among their goals (Emmons & King, 1988; see Michalak, Heidenreich, & Hoyer, Chapter 5, this volume) and to assist the client in resolving such conflicts.

To promote clients' chances for taking action, a final intervention consists in operationalizing goal states and in constructing a step-by-step action plan. First, we introduce clients to the important difference between final goal state and subgoals instrumental to reaching that desired state. Second, we ask the clients to define particular qualitative subgoals (e.g., a description of the situation that would leave the client satisfied to 10%, 20%, etc., to 100%) as a means of generating more realistic mid-term goals. Finally, we require clients to think in a more concrete way about *What can you do today and tomorrow to come closer to your desired goal?*

At this point, in the context of a prolonged psychotherapy, it usually makes sense to continue the process outside the group in a standard one-to-one setting. Therapist and client could perhaps evaluate the content of particular important goals in light of the overall structural pattern and the learning history of the person (past sufficient and insufficient attempts at goal attainment, self-regulatory competence). As a result of this critical reflection, a decision can be made regarding which personal goals lend themselves to being therapeutic goals.

The following empirical section describes results of a treatment study with alcohol addicts that confirms the efficacy of the procedure.

EFFECTIVENESS OF THE SMC-G IN ALCOHOL WITHDRAWAL TREATMENT

Schroer (2001) evaluated the effectiveness of SMC-G in a study with 146 inpatients diagnosed with alcohol addiction (International Classification of Diseases, ICD-10; Dilling, Mombour, & Schmidt, 1991), which were treated in a qualified detoxification program. The study design consisted of three groups of treatments. The first group of clients (A) received SMC-G alone, the second group (B) received standard social skills training, and the third group (C) was treated with both treatments, thus representing a more expensive combination therapy. Data assessment included the Volitional Components Inventory (VCI; Kuhl & Fuhrmann, 1998), a measure of self-regulatory competencies, and nine specific sociodemographic criteria that have been shown to be related to good prognosis (Küfner & Feuerlein, 1989): residence in a town with less than 100 000 inhabitants, owner of a house or a flat, living together with a partner, no loss of employment because of alcohol abuse, no inpatient rehabilitation in former times, no suicidal attempt, only one employment during the last two years, not homeless or living in a residential home for alcoholics.

Main criteria for treatment outcome at a three-month follow-up were (1) consumption of alcohol, (2) quality of life, and (3) treatment activity. The three treatments led to significant and clinically important improvements in the above criteria, with no differences among them regarding the outcome criteria. That is, the more cost-intensive combination treatment did not show an advantage beyond SMC-G alone, and SMC-G alone proved to be as effective as the social skills training, which has been shown to be one of the most effective treatment options (Miller & Wilbourne, 2002).

In addition to this main effect for treatment, there was a main effect of groups classified according to their prognosis. Clients with a good prognosis index profited more from all three treatments than clients with an unfavorable prognosis index. Related to SMC-G variables, clients with a good prognosis tended to form more short-term goals that specified concrete actions in specific situations, whereas clients with an unfavorable prognosis revealed a pattern of motivational structure that, on the one hand, was characterized by an ambitious positive goal binding with high commitment, high anticipated joy, and no ambivalence, and, on the other, a goal attainment that was perceived to be less under their own control.

As the prognosis score also was moderately related to the VCI (Fuhrmann & Kuhl, 1998), measuring the level of self-regulatory functions, one interpretation of the motivational structure pattern of clients with an unfavorable prognosis might be that they are prone to introject goals of their social environment, which are less in accordance with their self, and therefore are not supported by intrinsic motivational energy (see Kaschel & Kuhl, Chapter 6, this volume, and Kuhl, 2000, giving more background for this interpretation). Alternatively or in addition, self-regulatory competencies involved in planning, initiating, or maintaining goal-related action might have suffered in clients who have no employment, no partner, or have previously received an inpatient treatment.

CONCLUSIONS

Conclusions are based, first, on the development of the SMC-G procedure and the clinical experience with more than 400 clients over the last six years, and second, on the results of the treatment outcome study in alcohol addicts as well as on further data relating motivational structure dimensions and prognosis status to self-regulatory competencies of alcohol addicts.

In accordance with the distinction by Cox and Klinger (1990) between the diagnosis of motivational structure via the idiographic and the nomothetic dimensions of the MSQ, and the subsequent use of these informations to guide motivational counseling and interventions via the SMC, the following conclusions deal separately with diagnostic and therapeutic issues. The focus is on communalities and differences or extensions of the group adaptation relative to the original procedures.

Communalities regarding the assessment of motivational structure dimensions include the rationale given to the clients, and the use of 8 out of 12 dimensions of the MSQ in a similar way. More generally, all the features of the original motivational diagnoses were adapted that were helpful in individual applications, to enable clients to look at their concerns and goals from different, yet transparent, perspectives.

Differences include changes in wording and sequence of ratings and some additional rating dimensions (e.g., satisfaction with current situation, satisfaction when situation does not change, perceived control over situation, difficulty of enactment, and the preparedness for action). They were introduced gradually with growing experiences to adjust the procedure to the special situation of a group setting. Changes were made, in particular, to augment the therapeutic function of the diagnostic part of the procedure by making incentives for change more salient as well as realistic versus irrational expectations of clients, and by strengthening the commitment for reaching the personal goals.

Already the diagnostic procedure of the motivational structure has a therapeutic function in a way that strengthens the commitment for reaching the personal goals. Realistic and irrational expectations of the patient can become obvious.

The most important extension of the MSQ is the introduction, which uses relaxation and imagination techniques. It was developed to set the stage for an extended course of guided imagery, represented by the steps of the MSQ-G.

There are less communalities regarding the translation of diagnostic information into therapist feedback and subsequent interventions. Obviously, this step requires highly individual feedback and tailoring of interventions to the personal goal contents and to the context of the individual client. It is felt, though, that the SMC-G interventions in the third to fifth session succeeded not only to guide clients in their individual conclusions but to use the group format to the advantage of this process. Two essential differences are the self-selection of focus goals and the interactive feedback in the group. The latter concentrates on the structural aspects of individual motivation.

The following characteristics are regarded as extensions of the original procedure. The group application has advantages in relation to the individual setting. Especially after the third session, one could observe an interactive process in which observations and feedback of all group members led to strong expressions of intended therapeutic changes. It seemed that being together as a group minimized reactance and resistance to change, and helped to raise the energy for self-regulatory efforts.

Clinical experience with the SMC-G in the form presented here extends to inpatient and outpatient settings, and to clients with different diagnoses (other addictive disorders, affective disorders, personality disorders, and psychosis). They strongly support the use of this brief intervention at least as a helpful adjunct to individual treatment in a broad range of mental problems and disorders. The results of the controlled treatment study (Schroer, 2001) proved the effectiveness of SMC-G in a large sample of alcohol addicts who received this diagnostic and therapeutic intervention after their detoxification. The study shows that the effectiveness of SMC-G is comparable with an established but more time-consuming social skills training program. We found a relationship between level of severity of the addiction, self-control efficiency, and therapy success. Clients with favorable prognostic characteristics profit more from SMC-G than clients with a poor prognosis. The prognosis score we used showed a clear relationship with efficiency of self-regulation. The more efficient the self-regulation, the better the prognosis, which is theoretically plausible. Knowledge of interdependencies among sociodemographic characteristics, self-regulation, and motivational structure could be more effectively used in a withdrawal treatment, apart from already existing approaches. For treatment purposes, reference to dysfunctional self-regulatory styles (Fuhrmann & Kuhl, 1998) can also imply that therapists and advisers consider the decreased ability of these clients to pursue actions and goals compatible with their needs (see Baumann, Chapter 10, this volume; Ryan, Koestner, & Deci, 1991).

A goal of further basic as well as applied research should be to consider self-regulatory functions in addition to the motivational structure to optimize therapy planning.

REFERENCES

Aalto, M., Pekuri, P., & Seppä, K. (2001). Primary health care nurses' and physicians' attitudes, knowledge and beliefs regarding brief interventions for heavy drinkers. *Addiction, 96,* 305–311.

Babor, T.F., & Higgins-Biddle, J.C. (2000). Alcohol screening and brief intervention: Dissemination strategies for medical practice and public health. *Addiction, 95,* 677–686.

Barry, M.M., & Zissi, A. (1997). Quality of life as an outcome measure in evaluating mental health services. A review of the empirical evidence. *Social Psychiatry Epidemiology, 32,* 38–47.

Bien, T.H., Miller, W.R., & Tonigan, J.S. (1993). Brief interventions for alcohol problems: A review. *Addiction, 88,* 315–335.

Cox, W.M., & Klinger, E. (1988). A motivational model of alcohol use. *Journal of Abnormal Psychology, 97,* 168–180.

Cox, W.M., & Klinger, E. (1990). Incentive Motivation, affective change, and alcohol use: A model. In W.M. Cox (Ed.), *Why people drink: Parameters of alcohol as a reinforcer.* New York: Gardner Press.

Cox, W.M., Klinger, E., & Blount, J.P. (1999). *Systematic motivational counseling: A treatment manual.* Unpublished manuscript. University of Wales, Bangor, UK.

Demmel, R. (2000). Epidemiologie. In T. Poehlke, I. Flenker, A. Follmann, F. Rist, & G. Kremer (Eds.), *Orientierung am Weiterbildungs-Curriculum der Bundesärztekammer: Suchtmedizinische Versorgung* (pp. 15–20). Berlin, Heidelberg, and New York: Springer.

Dilling, H., Mombour, W., & Schmidt, M.H. (1991). *Internationale Klassifikation psychischer Störungen.* Bern, Göttingen, and Toronto: Huber.

Drummond, D.C. (1997). Alcohol interventions: Do the best things come in small packages? *Addiction, 92,* 1699–1704.

Emmons, R.A., & King, L.A. (1988). Conflict among personal strivings: Immediate and long-term implications for psychological and physical well-being. *Journal of Personality, 59,* 453–472.

Fleming, M.F., & Graham, A.W. (2001). Screening and brief interventions for alcohol use disorders in managed care settings. *Recent developments in alcoholism: An official publication of the American Medical Society on Alcoholism, the Research Society on Alcoholism, and the National Council on Alcoholism, 15,* 393–416.

Fuhrmann, A., & Kuhl, J. (1998). Decomposing self-regulation and self-control: The Volitional Components Inventory. In H. Heckhausen & C. Dweck (Eds.), *Lifespan perspectives on motivation and control.* Hillsdale, NJ: Erlbaum.

Heather, N. (1995). Brief Intervention Strategies. In R.K. Hester & W.R. Miller (Eds.), *Handbook of alcoholism treatment approaches* (pp. 105–122). Boston, London, Toronto, Sydney, Tokyo, and Singapore: Allyn & Bacon.

Kanfer, F.H., Reinecker, H., & Schmelzer, D. (1996). *Selbstmanagement-Therapie.* Berlin: Springer.

Klinger, E. (1971). *Structure and functions of fantasy.* New York: John Wiley & Sons.

Klinger, E. (1975). Consequences of commitment to and disengagement from incentives. *Psychological Review, 82,* 1–25.

Klinger, E. (1977). Meaning and void: Inner experience and incentives in people's lives. Minneapolis: University of Minnesota Press.

Klinger, E. (1990). *Daydreaming.* Los Angeles: Tarcher.

Klinger, E. (1996). Emotional influences on cognitive processing, with implications for theories of both. In P.M. Gollwitzer & J.A. Bargh (Eds.), *The psychology of action* (pp. 168–189). New York and London: Guilford.

Klinger, E., Barta, S.G., & Maxeiner, M.E. (1981). Current concerns: Assessing therapeutically relevant motivation. In P.C. Kendall & S.D. Hollon (Eds.), *Assessment strategies for cognitive-behavioural interventions.* New York: Academic Press.

Küfner, H., & Feuerlein, W. (1989). *Patient variables as prognostic factors. In-patient treatment for alcoholism—A multi-centre evaluation study.* Berlin: Springer.

Kuhl, J. (2000). The volitional basis of personality systems interaction theory: Applications in learning and treatment contexts. *International Journal of Educational Research, 33,* 665–703.

Kuhl, J., & Helle, P. (1986). Motivational and volitional determinants of depression: The degenerated-intention hypothesis. *Journal of Abnormal Psychology, 95,* 247–251.

Miller, W.R., & Rollnick, S. (1991). *Motivational interviewing: Preparing people to change addictive behaviour.* New York: Guilford.

Miller, W.R., & Wilbourne, P.L. (2002). Mesa Grande: A methodological analysis of clinical trials of treatments for alcohol use disorders. *Addiction, 97,* 265–277.

Moyer, A., Finney, J.W., Swearingen, C.E., & Vergun, P. (2002). Brief interventions for alcohol problems: A meta-analytic review of controlled investigations in treatment-seeking and non-treatment-seeking populations. *Addiction, 97,* 279–292.

Prochaska, J.O., & DiClemente, C.C. (1986). Toward a comprehensive model of change. In W.R. Miller & N. Heather (Eds.), *Treating addictive behaviors: Processes of change.* New York: Plenum.

Project MATCH Research Group (1997). Matching alcoholism treatments to client heterogeneity: Project MATCH posttreatment during outcomes. *Journal of Studies on Alcohol, 58,* 7–29.

Project MATCH Research Group (1998). Matching alcoholism treatments to client heterogeneity: Project MATCH three-year drinking outcomes. *Alcoholism: Clinical and Experimental Research, 22,* 1300–1311.

Ryan, R.M., Koestner, R., & Deci, E.L. (1991). Ego-involved persistance: When free choice behavior is not intrinsically motivated. *Motivation and Emotion, 15*, 185–205.

Schroer, B.M. (2001). Zielaktivierung und Zielklärung: Evaluation einer gruppentherapeutischen Kurzintervention in der Entzugsbehandlung alkoholabhängiger Merschen. (*Goal activation and goal clarification: Evaluation of a group-therapeutic brief intervention in abstinence treatment of alcohol dependent individuals.*) Unpublished doctoral: Münster.

Süss, H.M. (1995). Zur Wirksamkeit der Therapie bei Alkoholabhängigen: Ergebnisse einer Meta-Analyse. (Effectiveness of therapy with the alcohol-dependent: Results of a meta-analysis.) *Psychologische Rundschau, 46*, 248–256.

Zweben, A. & Fleming, M.F. (1999). Brief interventions for alcohol and drug problems. In J.A. Tucker, D.M. Donovan, & G.A. Marlatt (Eds.), *Changing addictive behavior. Bridging clinical and public health strategies* (pp. 251–282). New York: Guilford Press.

CHAPTER 13

Systematic Motivational Analysis as Part of a Self-Help Technique Aimed at Personal Goal Attainment

Renate de Jong-Meyer

Westfälische Wilhelms-University of Münster, Germany

Synopsis.—Clinical and basic research findings on motivational and volitional competencies stimulated the development of a self-help manual aimed at personal goal attainment. Evidence for the general effectiveness of bibliographic materials encouraged its development. The choice of components for the bibliotherapy was based on research pointing to the importance of specific mind sets or abilities between activating concerns and approaching concern-related goals. Rationale, empirical evidence, and examples for the components are presented. They are systematic motivational analysis, contemplating a preselected goal, planning necessary actions, and initiating and evaluating these actions. Three evaluation studies showed that nonclinical participants followed the instructions and for the most part liked working with the materials, which they rated as demanding but helpful. Motivational Structure Analysis, contemplating a preselected goal, and planning concrete action steps were rated favorably by the majority of participants. It was concluded that feedback in a minimal contact format would improve the choice of favorable goal levels, help in implementing habit-breaking strategies, and facilitate tailoring later parts of the self-regulatory efforts to individual goals.

INTRODUCTION AND BACKGROUND

It might not be all good news for psychotherapists and related professionals, but efforts are increasing to enable people with emotional and behavioral problems to become their own therapist, with perhaps a little professional help. Self-help books have been on bestseller lists for a long time, and nobody knows how many people have managed to solve their problems by reading Carnegie's *How to stop worrying and start living* (1984) or the hundreds of similar popular books. From a professional point of view, one can easily disregard this kind of competition by referring to lack of empirical evidence. The next sections, however, review attempts to establish the effectiveness of theory-based self-help manuals using the standards of treatment effectiveness research.

Handbook of Motivational Counseling. Edited by W. Miles Cox and Eric Klinger.

Most effectiveness studies have been conducted using a minimal contact format, in which bibliotherapy is self-paced but therapists monitor and encourage progress. Whereas earlier reviews (e.g., Glasgow & Rosen, 1978) described the effectiveness for such self-help approaches as highly variable, more recent evaluations (e.g., Gould & Clum, 1993; Marss, 1995; Scogin et al., 1996) are more optimistic, and the interest in this potentially cost-effective way of improving the physical or emotional states of clients is growing (see, e.g., Santrock, Minnett, & Campbell, 1994; Zweben & Fleming, 1999).

SELF-HELP TECHNIQUES FOR VARIOUS CLINICAL DISORDERS

Anxiety problems are among those most amenable to self-help strategies (Ghosh, Marks, & Carr, 1988; Gould & Clum, 1993; Sorby, Reavly, & Huber, 1991). Marks (1993) even concluded that manual-assisted rather than therapist-assisted confrontation with anxiety-provoking situations is the most important factor in long-term success of anxiety treatments, as long as a therapist had introduced and guided the manual-assisted treatment approach. Lidren et al. (1994), for example, compared two treatments that were both based on Clum's *Coping with panic* (1990) and found the self-help format as beneficial as the group therapy format and both significantly better than the waiting list control. Self-help books such as *Your perfect right* (Alberti & Emmons, 1970) or *I can if i want to* (Lazarus & Fay, 1975) have been used successfully with clients with social phobias. Marks (1997) demonstrated the general viability of the self-help approach even for obsessive-compulsive disorders.

A meta-analysis of six studies of bibliotherapy for *depression* (Cuijpers, 1997) led to the conclusion that bibliotherapy was as effective as individual or group therapy and produced a large effect when compared to waiting list control groups (mean effect size of .82). Clients in these studies were typically self-referred and suffered from mild-to-moderate depression. Smith et al. (1997) showed the stability of treatment gains over time in a three-year follow-up of the Jamison and Scogin (1995) study. Results were promising across a range of age groups, from adolescence (Ackerson et al., 1998) to old age. Scogin, Jamison, and Gochneaur (1989), for example, compared two different bibliotherapy groups (*Feeling good*, Burns, 1980, and *Control your depression*, Lewinsohn et al., 1986) with a delayed treatment control group in clients over 60 years old suffering from mild-to-moderate depression. Both materials led to greater reductions in depression than the control condition, and the improvements were maintained over a two-year period (Scogin, Jamison, & Davis, 1990).

According to Marss (1995), *impulse control problems*— e.g., *problem drinking, alcohol dependence, smoking*, in which an ability to delay gratification is an implicit prerequisite of success—are not among the problems where bibliotherapy has excelled in the past. On the other hand, alcohol consumption has been shown to reliably decrease in groups of self-referred participants with harmful drinking patterns when they work with the manual *How to control your drinking* (e.g., Miller & Muñoz, 1982; Miller, Gribskov, & Mortell, 1981), and effects were as lasting as those of therapist-administered behavioral self-control training in a 24-month follow-up (Miller & Baca, 1983). Heather, Kissoon-Singh, and Fenton (1990) demonstrated that working with the booklet *So you want to cut down on your drinking?: A self-help guide to sensible drinking* led to a 35% reduction in alcohol consumption among hazardous drinkers as compared to 10% in a non-intervention control group at six-months follow-up. Zweben and Fleming (1999) further summarized positive results for brief interventions, including bibliotherapy.

Others have presented evidence for a range of positive results, including reduced symptoms in people with eating disorders (e.g., Wilfley & Cohen, 1997), improved health status of medically ill persons (e.g., Hodges, Craven, & Littlefield, 1995, for lung transplant patients), increased levels of physical activity (e.g., Marcus et al., 1998), quality-of-life improvements (Grant et al., 1995), and reduced self-harming behavior of people diagnosed with personality disorder (Evans et al., 1999).

Self-help materials for clients with specific disorders or problems were mostly derived from therapist-guided treatment manuals, which in turn were based on social learning theory and cognitive-behavioral models. With growing evidence of their beneficial effects, a *stepped care approach* is currently recommended for numerous disorders with supervised or guided self-help interventions as the first option in routine treatment, followed in cases of unresponsiveness by more intense or more sophisticated treatments.

Self-Help Techniques Focusing on Self-Regulation and Problem-Solving

Whereas the majority of texts included in the reviews cited above are targeted at changing specific symptoms or illness syndromes, some self-help materials aim to teach clients more general ways of dealing with problems or better ways to approach personal goals. Such materials were published as long ago as the early 1970s (e.g., Mahoney & Thoresen, 1974; Watson & Tharp, 1972). They share many features derived from a self-management (Goldstein & Kanfer, 1979) or self-efficacy heuristic (Bandura, 1977). The promotion of motivational processes is central to these heuristics. The texts implement enhancement of motivation by, for example, stressing clients own decisions and choices, recommending small steps, breaking down general goals into more specific subgoals, and promoting self-reinforcement. They usually lead readers through the following steps: (a) specifying a behavior requiring change; (b) setting goals and developing a self-change contract; (c) self-monitoring the frequency of occurrence of the target behavior; and (d) rearranging relevant antecedents and consequences in an operant framework (Glasgow & Rosen, 1978, p. 15).

Promotion of Self-Regulation and Problem-Solving by Modifying Specific Motivational Processes

There has been much basic and applied research on motivational processes since the publication of the problem-solving and self-management concepts and their translation into self-help manuals. Theoretical refinements of the processes that occur between a person's realization of a problem, concern about resolving it, and attaining the aimed-for goal have been published by different groups (e.g., Carver & Scheier, 1996; Emmons & Kaiser, 1996; Heckhausen, Gollwitzer, & Weinert, 1987; Kuhl & Goschke, 1994).

One particular refinement was the distinction between motivational and volitional processes (Heckhausen, Gollwitzer, & Weinert, 1987; Kuhl & Goschke, 1994). Heckhausen, Gollwitzer, and Weinert proposed four self-regulatory phases between intending and ending goal-related actions: contemplating and deciding about action alternatives, planning,

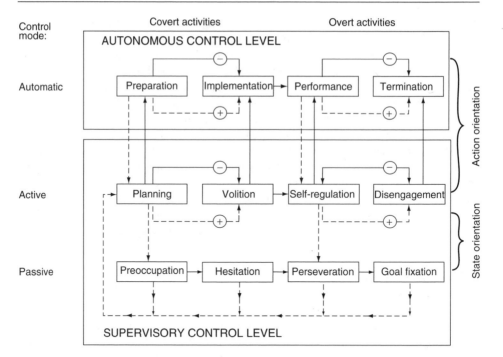

Figure 13.1   Outline of the process of action control in terms of planning (preparation), volition (implementation), self-regulation (maintenance), and disengagement (termination). (From J. Kuhl & J. Beckmann (Eds.) (1994). *Volition and personality: Action versus state orientation* (p. 109). Seattle: Hogrefe. Reproduced by permission of Hogrefe-Verlag GmbH & Co. KG, Göttingen.)

implementing actions, and evaluating them. Motivational processes—predicted by expectancy × value concepts—regulate behavior during contemplating/deciding and during post-action evaluation. The planning and the action phase, on the other hand, require "volition" or extra effort, particularly when obstacles have to be overcome. Gollwitzer (1991) expanded this distinction by defining favorable mental states to perform the phase-specific tasks (see below). Figure 13.1 shows Kuhl and Goschke's (1994) slightly different distinction between motivational and volitional processes.

Simplifying for the present purpose, motivational processes are represented by the automatic control mode. This mode is characteristic of goal approaches resembling the flow experience as described by Csikszentmihalyi (1975), in which preparation, implementation, performance, and termination are triggered by the situational demands, and are supported by intrinsic motivation. It is the active control mode where volitional competencies come into play, because strategies are required to overcome obstacles in all phases toward goal attainment. If a person engages in planning when immediate implementation is blocked, then deliberately initiates action if an opportunity occurs (volition), and then adapts the activities to situational demands (self-regulation), he or she is assumed to possess the volitional competencies to approach goals against obstacles or—equally important—to disengage from goals that have proven to be unrealistic or unattainable. Kuhl (see Kuhl & Beckmann, 1994, for an overview) coined the term *action orientation* to describe this mode of regulation. The passive control mode in Figure 13.1 depicts the processes when volitional competencies are low, *state orientation* prevails, and goal attainment will be unlikely. Such a person is preoccupied with contemplating alternatives, hesitates to initiate action, lacks flexibility in dealing with changing situational demands, and remains mentally fixated on the goal instead of disengaging when it is appropriate to do so. Action and state orientation are considered to be both traits (i.e., relatively enduring) and states (i.e., varying with external or internal eliciting stimuli). The latter makes them amenable to change. A series of experiments in nonclinical populations (Goschke & Kuhl, 2003) identified specific conditions required for changes from unfavorable to favorable prerequisites of volitional competencies.

The self-regulation model of Carver and Scheier (1998) specifies feedback loops in goal hierarchies, the role of affect in self-regulation, and how expectancies (confidence versus doubt) influence whether a person enhances efforts to attain a goal or disengages from it. From a different perspective but with similar aims, Emmons and colleagues (e.g., Emmons & Kaiser, 1996) have studied processes through which goal attainment is facilitated. The older problem-solving manuals (e.g., *Self-control: Power to the person*, Mahoney & Thoreson, 1974) contain principles that resemble those derived from these recent empirical and experimental studies, but without reference to a basic research context which, in fact, for the most part was not yet available.

In developing bibliotherapeutic materials aimed at personal goal attainment, we tried to transform the above-mentioned concepts and findings of motivational/volitional psychology into steps by which individuals can be supported to pursue their goals even in the face of obstacles. As a useful foundation for that purpose, the phase heuristic of Heckhausen, Gollwitzer, and Weinert (1987) was adopted.

COMPONENTS OF THE SELF-HELP MANUAL AIMED AT PERSONAL GOAL ATTAINMENT

In the following sections, a task profile is presented for the self-regulation phases (contemplation, planning, action, and post-actional evaluation), followed by the rationale and empirical evidence for the materials chosen, and a description of the procedure.

Contemplation

Task Profile

According to theoretical analyses and empirical findings (Gollwitzer, 1991), the activation/reactivation of personal goals is supported by the following mind set:

- Broad attentional scope
- Unselective and nonevaluative information processing regarding the consequences of different choices
- Elaborate reflection on alternatives in a defined decision space.

The advantages of the contemplation mind set for subsequent self-regulatory efforts lie in the inhibition of premature action and the opportunity to develop goals, which are compatible with the person's actual or aspired self. Coherence between day-to-day concerns and the desired self are assumed to activate emotional and motivational resources (e.g., Deci & Ryan, 1991; Emmons & Kaiser, 1996; Sheldon & Kasser, 1995), and to counteract alienation, i.e., the unreflected acceptance of other people's goals as one's own (see Kuhl & Beckmann, 1994). A possible disadvantage lies in not ending the contemplation mind set with a decision or action. This disadvantage is central to the constructs of hesitation and prospective state orientation (see Kuhl & Goschke, 1994), and must be addressed if self-regulatory competencies are deficient at this transition between contemplation and planning.

Rationale for Self-Help Steps Related to Motivational Analysis

The *Motivational Structure Questionnaire* (MSQ; Cox & Klinger, Chapter 8, this volume; Klinger, Cox, & Blount, in press) was translated into German and modified slightly to account for cultural differences (e.g., the life areas and examples of concerns in them), but Steps 1 through 12 closely follow the original MSQ. The German adaptation of the MSQ is called *Fragebogen für Lebensziele und Anliegen* (FLA) [Questionnaire of Life Goals and Concerns]. The MSQ fits the task profile of the first part of the contemplation phase in a number of ways. By giving participants the opportunity to think about personal concerns and goals in all important life areas, the questionnaire supports a broad and open mind set. Elaboration of contemplation is promoted by having participants think about the expected affective consequences and the other aspects introduced by Steps 1 through 12. Neither quick evaluation nor decision is forced, but respondents are guided to reflect on the different dimensions, compare their motivational structure across life areas, and look for functional and less functional characteristics of their goal-strivings.

Rationale for the Self-Helf Step "Questions and Suggestions"

The challenge of the bibliotherapeutic approach is to replace therapist feedback and guidance in reflecting on MSQ results (provided by subsequent Systematic Motivational Counseling) by instructing participants to analyze the results, and to draw conclusions themselves. To this end, a module *Questions and Suggestions* was developed. After participants have written down their concerns, have rephrased them in an intention format, and have rated their role in pursuing the concern (Steps 1 through 3 of the MSQ), three worksheets are introduced. On the first one, participants are asked to count their concerns and goals, reflect on this number, and look at the distribution across life areas. In the second one, they are asked to consider the approach/avoidance dimension, that is, count and reflect on the number of goals for which they used particular verb classes. Questions and suggestions of the third worksheet are related to the active versus passive role ratings in the different life areas. The second set of three *Questions and Suggestions* worksheets is introduced after all MSQ ratings have been completed. For each goal, where the expected joy upon attainment was smaller than the expected sorrow upon nonattainment, participants are asked to reflect in writing on how much it represents their own intention or is influenced by the intentions of others, what they would lose giving up that goal, and what modifications of the goal might increase the joy upon attainment or reduce the disappointment upon not reaching it. In the next worksheet dealing with ambivalent goals, participants are asked to extract the goals for which they rated both expected joy and expected unhappiness upon goal attainment high. The suggestions lead participants to focus on the emotional consequences by writing down the advantages of attaining/not attaining these goals, and by stating the expected positive and negative feelings in specific and concrete sentences. In the final worksheet, participants are led to extract subtypes of goals with high or low success expectancies after engaging actively or remaining passive. They are, for example, asked to reflect on the reasons which prevented the approach of these types of goals in the past, on prerequisites in themselves or the environment which might improve chances, or on possible substitute goals which could be achieved easier and improve chances of reaching the original goals.

Rationale for Self-Help Steps Related to Deciding about Alternative Actions

To prevent reflecting too long on concerns and goals and delaying decisions regarding goals to be pursued, two further components were included at the transition between the contemplation and the planning sections. First, participants were guided to choose a goal which, based on their previous analyses, would seem worthwhile to pursue (which becomes the "preselected" goal). Second, an elaborate decision process was introduced regarding the question, *Do I really want to pursue this preselected goal or not?*

Gollwitzer (1991) induced the mind set *contemplation* by having participants write down positive and negative consequences of yes–no decisions of this type. Information processing in nonclinical participants in subsequent tasks was improved. They showed a broader attention span, better memory for peripheral details, more thought production about incentives and expectations, and a more balanced and realistic estimate of advantages/disadvantages and of chances of success, all compared to an induction aimed at a planning mind set (see below). We adapted the worksheets that Gollwitzer (1991) used in these experiments.

Both immediate and delayed and positive and negative consequences of the decision alternatives *Yes, I will pursue . . .* versus *No, I will not pursue my preselected goal* are assessed. Participants are instructed to think separately on short-term and long-term consequences, and to see the positive consequences of engaging in goal pursuit independently from the negative consequences of leaving things as they are, that is, not to just reverse their phrasing. The concreteness of the four types of expected consequences is modeled in examples. After having written down all expected consequences of their decision alternative, respondents are asked to rate the importance of each consequence. Then, they are encouraged to decide. In case of *Yes*, they enter the planning phase, in case of *No*, an alternative goal might become the subject of deciding.

Planning

Task Profile

A different cognitive set is necessary once a goal has been chosen. Planning promotes the initiation of actions by allowing the person to anticipate concrete steps and action opportunities. Concreteness of goal-related actions predicts actual goal attainment (e.g., Emmons & Kaiser, 1996; Locke et al., 1981). According to Gollwitzer (1996), the planning task will be facilitated by a mind set with the following characteristics:

- Preferential processing of information regarding the when, where, and how of intended actions
- Focusing on incentive and expectancy related information that is biased in favor of goal approach
- Inhibition of distracting information.

Rationale of Self-Help Steps related to planning

It has been shown that nonclinical participants can be induced with a planning mind set through written exercises that focus on the when, where, and how of an intention (Gollwitzer, 1991). This mind set had positive effects on subsequent tasks. It led to a narrower and less flexible attentional focus, with less memory for peripheral details and better memory for concrete circumstances related to implementation of action. More thoughts about the when, where, and how of acting were produced, and participants were optimistic about their chances of succeeding, all in comparison to respondents who had received the contemplation induction.

We adapted the materials used in Gollwitzer's experiments for the self-help manual. They guide participants into defining the concrete circumstances of the first five steps toward their goal, and model the process through an example that meets concreteness criteria. First, participants have to write down the steps (or subgoals) they have to take to approach their goal. For each step they are asked to name the when, where, and what of the goal-related activity as specifically as possible.

Because visualizing supports the initiation of goal-related actions (e.g., Taylor & Pham, 1996), an *imaginary exercise* is included after the planning worksheet. Participants are encouraged to imagine as many details of the planned situation as possible. Examples of different sensory qualities (sight, sound, smell, tactile sensations) are given, and it is stressed that feelings and changes in feelings are an essential part of this exercise (e.g., to evoke the feeling of anxiety if the step concerns an unpleasant conversation, and one feels afraid saying a certain sentence, and also to imagine the changes in physical and emotional sensations after having successfully said the sentence). Participants are advised to prepare the imagination by choosing a comfortable place, reading the planned steps and the instructions again, closing their eyes, and focusing on the imaginary exercise for one to five minutes.

Action and Post-Actional Evaluation

Theory and empirical evidence hold that the initiation of the goal-related action will be primed once the situation defined via the planning procedure occurs. Therefore, promoting self-regulation in the action and post-actional evaluation phases means dealing with goal approaches against obstacles and failure experiences.

Task Profile of the Action Phase

Initiating and continuing actions in the face of obstacles depends on the volitional competencies as differentiated by Kuhl and coworkers (e.g., Kuhl & Fuhrmann, 1998). Shielding against external or internal distractions from initiating and pursuing goal-related actions may require:

- filtering attention
- strengthening emotional and motivational resources
- enhancing effort
- flexibility in changing goal-related actions according to situational demands.

Rationale for Self-Help Steps in the Action Phase

Hesitation is the central construct in prospective state orientation. Empirical findings (e.g., Dibbelt & Kuhl, 1994; Hautzinger, 1994; de Jong-Meyer et al., 1999; Kammer, 1994) demonstrate that prospective state orientation is related to depression.

The bibliotherapy text introduces participants to this problem and delineates steps to overcome hesitation about starting planned actions. Comments and examples are given for different strategies (e.g., increasing trust in the correctness of one's decision; keeping in mind the positive consequences; selectively shifting attention to aspects of situations that support the intention; withstanding interferences from actions of other people; starting actions independently of current mood; changing situations in ways that support the intended action).

External and internal threats to goal pursuance are then explained. Types of external threats included *There was not enough time. The occasion demanded an action that wasn't connected to the goal. Other persons behaved obstructively because they pursued their own conflicting intentions. Other persons criticized or called the goal into question.* Strategies to deal with these threats are described. In the case of criticism participants were advised, for example, to not reject the criticism immediately, but to examine if there is some point in the criticism that might be worthwhile taking into account for future actions. Rules of functional communication are given for responding to criticism, for explaining the importance of one's action, and for working toward a compromise. Strategies for overcoming types of internal threats (e.g., *Difficulties in maintaining concentration and effort; Decreasing attractiveness of the goal*) are described next.

Task Profile of Functional Post-Actional Evaluation

Theoretical analyses and empirical results of Beckmann (1994) suggest the following sequence of a functional evaluation process:

- Stating the result in concrete terms
- Analyzing one's contribution (strengths and weaknesses) in the specific situation
- Defining the next step in terms of when, where, and how to act next. On, defining an alternative goal if disengagement from the previous one is necessary
- Engaging in a different activity to avoid oscillating between the first and second steps of this sequence.

Rationale for Self-Help Steps in the Post-Actional Evaluation Phase

The above-mentioned sequence of steps was chosen to prevent self-oriented evaluation of failure experiences and to promote a task-oriented functional way of dealing with unsuccessful action attempts. Empirical evidence particularly supports the importance of defining a next step or a substitute action if failure has occurred (Brunstein et al., 1995). Oscillation between focusing on what went wrong and self-oriented thinking about it is avoided or shortened by focusing on concrete future steps. Empirical evidence related to the negative consequences of disengagement failure dates back to early experimental work on uncompleted intentions and their intrusive potential (Zeigarnik, 1927), which was reconfirmed by Klinger (1987), Kuhl and Helle (1986), Kazén-Saad and Kuhl (1989), and McIntosh (1996).

This section of the bibliotherapy text starts with describing how to deal with a failure outcome in a functional way. The reasons for each step of the above-mentioned task profile are explained, and then instructions are given. For the first step—*state the result in concrete terms*—it was stressed that the statement should be specifically related to the previous intention and the situation that had just occurred, and that participants should take time to write it down as soon after the situation as possible. Instructions for the second step—*analyzing one's contribution to the result*—introduced the distinction between task-related and self-related failure attribution, and advised confining evaluation of the task. Instructions for the third step included an explanation as to when it is appropriate to define the next step in the goal approach, and to when it might be necessary to disengage from the current goal. Finally, a change of activity was recommended to end evaluation at this point.

Compilation of the Self-Help Manual

The different components of the bibliotherapy were arranged under two main headings. The first was *Analysis of Concerns and Goals*, and consisted of the adaptation of the MSQ/FLA and the *Questions and Suggestions*. The second part was termed *Toward Goal Attainment* (TGA), and consisted of the materials for preselecting a goal, contemplation whether to approach it or not, and modules for planning as well as action and post-actional evaluation. Within each module, there were psychoeducational texts, instructions, examples for recommended steps, and separate booklets with worksheets related to these steps.

EMPIRICAL RESEARCH

Three studies have evaluated the self-help manual and its components, and have addressed the following questions related to motivational-structure variables: (1) How do participants in the bibliotherapy respond to the nomothetic part of the motivational structure analysis, the MSQ/FLA dimensions, and what are the relationships between these dimensions? (2) What relationships exist between MSQ/FLA dimensions and variables that are related to the theoretical background of the additional self-help components (e.g., *action orientation*)? (3) What can be learned from participants' feedback after they have worked with the materials?

Motivational Structure Dimensions

Descriptive data on MSQ/FLA dimensions in nonclinical participants who share an interest in improving their personal goal attainments can help to establish comparison standards when extending the approach to clinical groups. Robustness of descriptive characteristics in different nonclinical samples would lend support to this aim. Correlations between MSQ/FLA dimensions and results of factor analysis contribute to methodological knowledge regarding the internal validity of this part of the materials, and to practical questions, e.g., whether all dimensions are needed or a more parsimonious assessment would be justified.

Ratings on FLA dimensions were available for two samples (Study I, Bruns, 1997; Study II, unpublished data) with a high educational level (Study I: 41 students in a Catholic college, age range between 19 and 42, 26 women, 15 men; Study II: 39 participants, 82.1% students or people with qualification for university admission, age range between 23 and 44, 25 women, 14 men). Both samples were introduced to the bibliotherapeutic materials (Study I: FLA plus *Questions and Suggestions*; Study II: all materials, including the TGA components) in an introductory session. The general usefulness of learning about personal concerns and goals was stressed. Examples were given for FLA Steps 1 and 2, and the main worksheets were introduced. The subsequent dimensions were not commented on to avoid promoting any answering sets. Participants were not requested to reveal their personal goals and concerns but only to number them and rate them on the different dimensions.

Table 13.1 shows the means and standard deviations for dimensions with acceptable scale and distribution criteria.

Descriptive characteristics between the two samples did not differ from each other, with two exceptions. Respondents in Study I named more goals/concerns ($t = 2.53$, $p = .014$), and were more often uncertain about the time perspective for reaching their goals ($t = 3.01$, $p = .004$). All respondents showed a relatively broad area of goals/concerns (over 30 on average). They saw themselves in an active role for around 75% of these. Commitment was rated in the medium range (above 3 on a scale from 1 to 5). The expected joy on average was higher than the expected unhappiness upon goal attainment. This was also reflected in the ambivalence index, showing that more than 70% of the goals were unambivalent in the sense of expected joy exceeding expected unhappiness. Disappointment upon not attaining the goals (sorrow) was rated in the medium range. For approximately 70% of the goals, the expected disappointment upon not reaching them exceeded the expected joy upon reaching them (Sorrow Greater Than Joy index). The mean probability of attaining the goals if actively pursuing them (over 60%) was considerably higher than the probability of reaching them just by waiting (around 15%). For more than 50% of the goals the beginning of action was considered to lie within weeks, but actual goal attainment was expected for less than 20% of the goals within weeks. The respondents did not specify the beginning of action for nearly one-third of the goals, and the time perspective for reaching them for about half of the goals (approximately 60% in Study I and 40% in Study II).

Correlations between the FLA indices are shown in Table 13.2 for both samples combined, after separate analyses showed comparable relationships.

Two dimensions (*Number of Goals* and *Chances if no Action*) showed independence from all the others. For the other, dimensions, interrelationships supported the internal

Table 13.1 Means (M) and standard deviations (SD) of the 14 FLA indices in Study I
($N = 34$) and Study II ($N = 39$)

	Study I		Study II	
	M	SD	M	SD
1. Number of Goals	40.8	15.41	31.4	16.14
2. Active Role	73.4	18.37	77.4	18.85
3. Commitment	3.4	.46	3.2	.67
4. Joy	3.6	.43	3.7	.48
5. Unhappiness	1.5	.36	1.6	.59
6. Sorrow	3.4	.51	3.3	.47
7. Chances of Success	62.1	12.42	67.2	10.83
8. Chances if no Action	16.0	11.22	15.5	8.52
9. Begin Uncertain	27.3	23.14	29.0	24.09
10. Begin Within Weeks	57.1	23.69	53.5	26.17
11. Attainment Time Uncertain	60.5	24.70	41.7	28.01
12. Attainment Within Weeks	14.4	18.06	19.1	18.98
13. Sorrow Greater Than Joy index	70.0	15.52	16.7	16.61
14. Ambivalence	26.6	15.95	30.0	19.53

Note:

Number of Goals	= Number of goals named by respondents
Active Role	= Proportion of goals for which respondents assumed an active role
Commitment	= Mean commitment to goals (on a 1–5 scale)
Joy	= Mean expected joy upon goal attainment (on a 1–5 scale)
Unhappiness	= Mean expected unhappiness upon goal attainment (on a 1–5 scale)
Sorrow	= Mean expected sorrow if goals are not attained (on a 1–5 scale)
Chances of Success	= Mean expected chance of success
Chances if no Action	= Mean expected chance of success if no action is taken
Begin Uncertain	= Proportion of goals for which no action date is given
Begin Within Weeks	= Proportion of goals with action dates being less than four weeks
Time of Goal Attainment Uncertain	= Proportion of goals for which no attainment date was given
Time of Goal Attainment Within Weeks	= Proportion of goals with less than four weeks until attainment
Sorrow Greater Than Joy index	= Proportion of goals for which expected sorrow upon attainment exceeds expected joy upon nonattainment
Ambivalence Index	= Proportion of goals for which expected joy and expected unhappiness upon goal attainment are not more than one point apart

validity of the constructs. Correlations were not as high, though, as rendering the dimensions redundant (with the exception of $-.75$ between *Proportion of Goals With no Action Date* and *Proportion With an Action Date Within Weeks*). Factor analysis was done to facilitate interpretation of the correlational pattern. Loadings on the six-factor solution (six factors had eigenvalues > 1, scree plots also led to the acceptance of this solution) are presented in Table 13.3 together with the percentages of explained variances.

A total variance of 76.8% was explained by this solution. Factors were named as follows: Factor I: *Goals With Joy and Success Expectation*; Factor II: *Anticipating and Being Committed to Goal-Related Actions Within Weeks*; Factor III: *Non-Appetitive Goals (Shoulds)*; Factor IV: *Uncertainty About Time Perspective of Goal Attainment in a Diversified Goal Space (Dissipation)*; Factor V: *Active Role*; Factor VI: *Chances of Goal Attainment if no Action*. These results speak in favor of the level of complexity chosen for the MSQ/FLA procedure.

Table 13.2 Intercorrelations[a] between MSQ/FLA dimensions (Study I and Study II samples combined, $N = 73$)

	1	2	3	4	5	6	7	8	9	10	11	12	13	14
1. Number of Goals	—													
2. Active Role	.02	—												
3. Commitment	.11	-.05	—											
4. Joy	.02	-.03	.34**	—										
5. Unhappiness	.06	-.16	-.25*	-.33**	—									
6. Sorrow	-.05	-.03	.49**	.54**	-.11	—								
7. Chances of Success	-.09	.27*	.08	.35**	-.26*	.26*	—							
8. Chances if no Action	.05	-.10	.04	.02	.20	-.05	.21	—						
9. Start Uncertain	-.11	-.16	-.36**	-.05	.51**	-.06	-.19	.01	—					
10. Start Within Weeks	.12	.35**	.44**	.05	-.38**	.14	.11	.00	-.75**	—				
11. Attainment Time Uncertain	.14	-.06	.16	.03	.11	.24*	-.09	-.04	.30*	-.10	—			
12. Attainment Within Weeks	.03	.34**	.02	.03	-.21	-.05	.18	.03	-.23*	.30**	-.53**	—		
13. Appetitive Index	.10	.14	-.28*	.07	.03	-.57**	-.06	.10	.15	-.08	.01	.06	—	
14. Ambivalence	.01	-.09	-.38**	-.55**	.69**	-.42**	-.34**	.18	.31**	-.21	-.03	.02	.05	—

[a] Bravais–Pearson product-moment correlation coefficient.
* Correlation is significant with $p = .05$ (two-tailed).
** Correlation is significant with $p = .01$ (two-tailed).

Table 13.3 Factor loadings and percentages of explained variances of the MSQ/FLA
dimensions

	Factor					
	I	II	III	IV	V	VI
4. Joy	.83					
5. Unhappiness	.65	−.42				
7. Chances of Success	.53				.46	
14. Ambivalence	−.85					
3. Commitment		.56	.43			
9. Start Uncertain		−.83				
10. Start Within Weeks		.85				
6. Sorrow	.43		.78			
13. Appetitive Index			−.89			
1. Number of Goals		.42		.46		
11. Attainment Time Uncertain				.88		
12. Attainment Within Weeks				−.60	.41	
2. Active Role					.92	
8. Chances if no Action						.89
Explained variance (total)	24.6%	15.7%	10.6%	9.3%	9.0%	7.6%

Note: Loadings > .40 are reported.

Relationships Between Motivational Structure Dimensions and Other Variables

There are, as yet, no empirical findings on the relationships between dimensions of motivational structure and self-regulatory (volitional) competencies subsumed under the construct of action orientation. Theoretically and clinically it would be of interest to know how motivational dimensions (e.g., expected joy upon goal attainment) are related to the competencies of people to reach their goals against obstacles, represented by high scores on the Action Control Scale (ACS-90; Kuhl, 1994).

According to Bruns (1997), correlational patterns of Study I participants between MSQ/FLA dimensions and *Prospective Action Control* (HOP) as well as *Failure-Related Action Control* (HOM) were similar, with slightly higher correlations regarding the prospective (planning-oriented) dimension. Significant relationships (Kendall's Tau-b) were found for *Commitment* (with HOP: .28; $p < .05$), *Joy* (with HOP: .22; $p < .05$), *Chances of Success* (with HOP: .32; $p < .01$; with HOM: .36; $p < .01$), and *Chances if no Action* (with HOP: .35; $p < .01$; with HOM: .31, $p < .01$).

Negative affectivity as reflected by depressiveness scores on the Beck Depression Inventory (BDI Beck; et al., 1961) can be assumed to interfere with a favorable pattern of motivational variables. *Unhappiness* and *Chances of Success* were correlated significantly ($r = .27$ and $r = −.22$, respectively, both $p < .05$) but moderately with the BDI in sample I ($N = 34$). No other correlations reached significance in this student sample scoring primarily in the nondepressed range on the BDI (M: 8.3; SD: 6.6; range: 0–28).

The ratings on how near respondents had actually come toward attaining their goals (10-point scale, 1 = goal is far away, 10 = goal is reached) while being guided through the

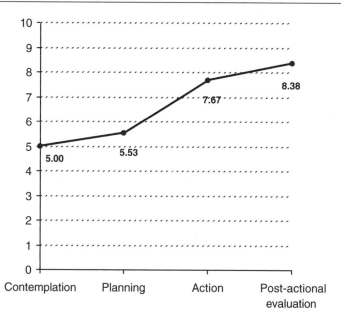

Figure 13.2 Ratings of sample II participants ($n = 27$) on *Nearness to Goal* on a scale from 1 (goal is far away) to 10 (goal attained) after having completed different phases of "TGA" materials

self-regulatory phases were the central outcome measures for the TGA materials. Figure 13.2 shows the longitudinal course of these ratings for Study II participants.

MSQ/FLA dimensions were correlated with the final rating after having completed work with all components of the materials. Relationships for most dimensions did not reach significance (mainly because of outliers). As an exception to this, *Commitment* was significantly related to actual approaching the goal ($r = .39$, $p = .03$), and there was also a nearly significant negative relationship for the *Ambivalence Index* ($r = -.35$, $p = .051$).

Feasibility and Subjective Usefulness of the Materials

An *Evaluative Interview* was developed in Study I: 22 questions/ratings covered strategic (e.g., time, understanding of instructions, use of worksheets) and content aspects (e.g., ratings regarding helpfulness, difficulty or clarity of materials; questions related to experienced changes). The one-hour interview took place three to seven weeks after the FLA plus *Questions and Suggestions* had been given. As the answers of this student sample supported the general feasibility of the approach, another study was conducted to extend the evaluation to a more representative, primarily nonstudent, sample, and to the materials of the TGA part.

For Study III (Grothenrath & Schneider, 1996), 41 participants (32 females, 9 males; age range between 20 and 53) were recruited in consultation centers for occupational orientation. Their education level was intermediate and lower than that of Study I participants; the majority were employed. The *Evaluative Interview* covered the same aspects as in Study I,

Table 13.4 Percentages of respondents rating an evaluative dimension with "agree completely" or "agree predominantly"

	Study I (%)	Study III (%)	Study II (%)
General feasibility	88.6	74.1	88.9
Clarity	—	77.8	92.6
Adequateness of size/comprehensiveness	—	29.6	55.6
Effort	—	96.0	81.5
Effort rated as positive	—	25.0	57.1
General liking	—	60.0	84.6
General helpfulness	—	61.9	84.6

Note: Dashes indicate that in this study no ratings were assessed for these items.

but used more ratings and fewer open questions. Also, it included ratings for the TGA materials and on nearness to goal approach. This format had also been used in Study II.

Evaluative ratings and comments are available for 35 participants of Study I, 27 participants of Study II, and 27 participants of Study III. Drop-out percentages (respondents not showing up for the evaluative interview) were 10, 21, and 34%, respectively. The feedback of participants was primarily used to improve wording and layout of the materials. Here, only feasibility issues are addressed.

General Evaluative Dimensions Across all Parts of the Materials

The majority of respondents liked working with the materials and rated them favorably regarding feasibility, clarity, and helpfulness (see Table 13.4). There was strong agreement that the texts and worksheets demanded effort. In Study II, the majority rated in terms of less materials and less effort would be more adequate. Ratings of Study III participants were split on the adequacy of size, comprehensiveness, and positive valence of the required effort.

Evaluation of Different Parts

More variable ratings resulted when participants were asked about the different parts of the materials and about steps within these parts (see Figure 13.3 as an example, showing the frequencies of Study I respondents, who rated specific steps of the MSQ/FLA and the *Questions and Suggestions* part as particularly helpful or difficult).

Asked about the reasons for rated helpfulness of these parts, the most frequent answers were: *Goals/concerns became clearer; the procedure was concrete; motivation was improved; clustering of goals became apparent; the work helped me to become conscious about life perspective; the suggestions helped me focus on my own role.* Reasons for rated difficulty were, e.g., *too many goals/concerns; too many dimensions to rate; loss of overview; the phrasing of goals was a challenge; questions and suggestions were too repetitive; the materials did not apply to own long-term goals.*

Regarding the TGA materials, ratings and comments of the majority of Study II and III participants stressed the clarity of the decision and the planning module. The most frequent reasons for rated helpfulness were *materials forced an intensive working-through of own*

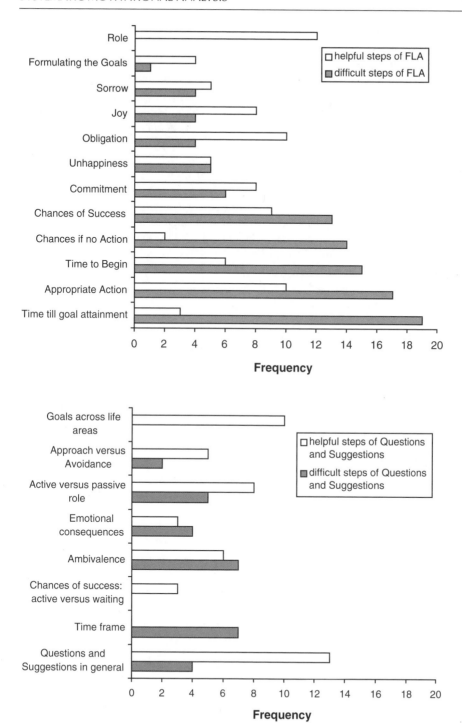

Figure 13.3 Number of respondents rating different MSQ/FLA dimensions and Questions and Suggestions as helpful and/or difficult

expectations with the preselected goal; looking at adverse consequences was enlightening; having to write down things in a concrete way; degree of structure in the examples and worksheets; planning in small steps and with a short time perspective; commitment grew. The comments of participants who rated the decision and planning modules as difficult focused on the point that such an elaborate look at consequences and such a small-step planning approach might be helpful for big, complex goals/concerns but that the *procedures were too detailed, and the steps too redundant for their particular goals.* The materials for the action and post-actional evaluation phase received approval from fewer participants than the preceding parts. Fewer than half rated them as particularly helpful. Positive feedback included: *gave new ideas; being more aware of the goal approach and where I stand; being more prepared for difficulties, seeing disengagement as an alternative, becoming more aware of my strengths.* Reasons for rated difficulty had, in common, that the recommended strategies could not be applied to the individual goal approach. For other participants, whose goal approach went smoothly, and who did not need to overcome difficulties, these materials were rated as unhelpful because of being unnecessary. In addition, there were participants who experienced failures and expressed their lack of motivation to continue with the materials of this phase.

DISCUSSION

Systematic motivational analysis was chosen as the first component of a self-help manual aimed at personal goal attainment. Data from our pilot studies with nonclinical participants lend support to the nomothetic dimensions, which require participants to elaborate on different aspects of their concerns and goals. First, the descriptive characteristics of most dimensions were comparable in the two student samples which allowed for this analysis. Second, the dimensions correlated moderately with each other but not high enough to render them redundant, which also was reflected in the six-factor solution of the factor analysis. A diversified assessment of the aspects seems justified in bibliotherapy, which fits well with the task profile of the contemplation phase, asking for an open mind set and for elaborate reflecting of a broad range of concern and goal-related aspects.

The theoretical considerations which led to the construction of the different dimensions of motivational structure (Cox & Klinger, Chapter 8, this volume) were supported by the relationships between dimensions. It was of interest to note, though, that some dimensions did *not* load on a common factor in our nonclinical samples. For instance, the anticipated negative affect upon goal attainment failure (sorrow) loaded on a different factor than anticipated positive and negative emotions upon reaching a goal. Also, the time perspective for starting actions was independent of the time perspective for actual goal attainments. These findings perhaps reflect characteristics of ambitious (disappointment upon goal attainment failure exceeding anticipated joy upon reaching goals) young people with a less limited temporal goal space (high percentages of goals with extended time frames). Further basic research is needed to address this issue in more heterogeneous samples, including clinical groups.

Being committed to a goal and having positive success expectations were the dimensions related to action orientation, where higher scores reflect more volitional competencies. Being committed also was the only MSQ/FLA dimension that correlated significantly with actual goal approach for participants working with the self-help materials. Clinically and theoretically, it seems important to study the prerequisites of commitment in experimental designs (e.g., Is an expected goal approach within weeks a prerequisite for commitment, or vice versa?). In addition, results of factor analysis suggested that the motivational–volitional distinction might also apply to the MSQ dimensions, with commitment presumably tapping more a volitional than a motivational dimension.

Based on theoretical concepts and empirical findings reviewed in the introduction, the motivational structure analysis was complemented by interventions promoting subsequent phases toward goal approach, that is, preselecting *one* particular concern/goal, contemplating its expected consequences, planning actions, initiating and pursuing actions even in the face of obstacles, and concluding self-regulatory effort with functional post-actional evaluations. It is premature—after only three evaluative studies with nonclinical participants—to address rigorous questions about the effectiveness of the self-help manual. This still has to be established in controlled studies using different comparison groups (e.g., with varying degree of therapist support, or contrasting bibliotherapy with training or treatment interventions). There are, nevertheless, several questions that the evaluation studies already undertaken do address.

First, is it possible to translate theoretically delineated self-regulatory steps into a self-help manual that can be followed by participants without further guidance? The answer is a tentative *yes*. Instructions about the sequence and timing of working on the materials were generally followed both by students and a limited number of less-well-educated individuals, although some initial omissions occurred. Participants found the procedures required effort but were helpful.

Second, did some aspects of the materials seem more helpful than others? The self-help components rated most helpful were the motivational structure analysis via MSQ/FLA, and the TGA components related to contemplating advantages and disadvantages of preselected goals and the stepwise planning. Within the MSQ/FLA materials, the most helpful steps included looking with a broad perspective on the whole scope of life areas, reflecting one's own role, and rephrasing concerns into a goal format. In general, aspects related to strategies of problem approach (e.g., taking time, being concrete, following a highly detailed and structured procedure, being guided by examples and worksheets, writing down the results of reflections, decisions, and experiences) received more positive feedback than learning about content issues (e.g., being instructed to consider goals with no action necessity, estimating timeframes of goal attainment, separating different kinds of emotional consequences, or learning about strategies to overcome obstacles). Difficulties occurred if the chosen goals were either too easy or too difficult. Participants with concrete goals of known short-time perspective tended to rate the materials as too complicated or redundant. Other participants with more abstract, more complicated goals expressed difficulties in adapting the materials to their own needs. Results of the *Evaluative Interview* thus suggest that the materials are best suited for goals of an intermediate level of complexity and difficulty, and that even nonclinical participants need some professional support early on for selecting and structuring goals that fit such an intermediate level. A minimal contact format with some therapist guidance would probably help in two other types of reported difficulties. Support and exercises might, first, improve adherence to steps that involve breaking habits, e.g., interrupting daily activities to prepare or evaluate goal-related actions by focused thinking and writing. Second, guidance in applying the recommended strategies to overcome difficulties or to cope with failures at the individual goals might help participants to continue working with the materials.

As having goals and striving for them is strongly related to well-being (e.g., Martin & Tesser, 1996) the range of nonclinical and clinical groups that might profit from this self-help approach is considered large. Likely nonclinical candidates are, for example, people in transition phases of their lives (e.g., before entering a career path, during unemployment, after divorce, at the beginning of retirement). In the clinical range, clients with emotional and behavioral problems and/or physical symptoms might profit from this approach even without formal treatment, as was shown for different kinds of bibliotherapies in the introductory section. The feedback of our nonclinical subjects suggests, however, a minimal contact format, in which working with the materials is self-paced but therapists monitor, guide, and encourage progress rather than a totally self-administered format in clinical settings. The module-like structure of the materials also allows them to be used as adjuncts in a broad range of treatments. Motivational structure analysis via the MSQ/FLA, the contemplating on decision alternatives, and the planning module could, for example, be given as homework assignments, as could the action and post-actional evaluation parts, after they are tailored to the goal of the individual client. To summarize, we feel optimistic that the self-help manual is a useful tool to promote goal clarification and goal approaches.

REFERENCES

Ackerson, J., Scogin, F., McKendree-Smith, N., & Lyman, R.D. (1998). Cognitive bibliotherapy for mild and moderate adolescent depressive symptomatology. *Journal of Consulting and Clinical Psychology, 66* (4), 685–690.

Alberti, R.E., & Emmons, M.L. (1970). *Your perfect right: A guide to assertive behaviour.* San Louis Obispo, CA: Impact.

Bandura, A. (1977). Self-efficacy: Toward a unifying theory of behavioral change. *Psychological Review, 84,* 191–215.

Beck, A.T., Ward, C.H., Mendelson, M., Mock, J., & Erbaugh, H. (1961). An inventory for measuring depression. *Archives of General Psychiatry, 4,* 561–571.

Beckmann, J. (1994). Ruminative thought and the deactivation of an intention. *Motivation and Emotion, 18* (4), 317–334.

Bruns, T. (1997). *Der Fragebogen zu Lebenszielen und Anliegen. Eine Pilotuntersuchung.* Unpublished diploma thesis. University of Münster, Münster, Germany.

Brunstein, J.C., Lautenschlager, U., Nawrot, B., Pöhlmann, K., & Schultheiß, O. (1995). Persönliche Anliegen, soziale Motive und emotionales Wohlbefinden. *Zeitschrift für Differentielle und Diagnostische Psychologie, 16* (1), 1–10.

Burns, D. (1980). *Feeling good.* New York: Guilford.

Carnegie, D. (1984). *How to stop worrying and start living.* Pocket Books.

Carver, C.S., & Scheier, M.F. (1996). Self-regulation and its failures. *Psychological Inquiry, 7* (1), 32–40.

Carver, C.S., & Scheier, M.F. (1998). *On the self-regulation of behavior.* New York: Cambridge University Press.

Clum, G.A. (1990). *Coping with panic.* Pacific Grove, CA: Brooks-Cole.

Csikszentmihalyi, M. (1975). *Beyond boredom and anxiety.* San Francisco: Jossey-Bass.

Cuijpers, P. (1997). Bibliotherapy in unipolar depression: A meta-analysis. *Journal of Behaviour Therapy and Experimental Psychiatry, 2* (2), 139–147.

Deci, E.L., & Ryan, R.M. (1991). A motivational approach to the self: Integration in personality. In R. Dienstbier (Ed.), *Nebraska Symposium on Motivation, 38,* 237–288. Lincoln: University of Nebraska Press.

Dibbelt, S., & Kuhl, J. (1994). Volitional processes in decision making: Personality and situational determinants. In J. Kuhl & J. Beckmann (Eds.), *Volition and personality* (pp. 177–194). Seattle: Hogrefe.

Emmons, R.A., & Kaiser, H.A. (1996). Goal orientation and emotional well-being: Linking goals and affect through the self. In L.L. Martin & A. Tesser (Eds.), *Striving and feeling: Interactions among goals, affect, and self-regulation* (pp. 79–98). Mahwah, NJ: Erlbaum.

Evans, K., Tyrer, P., Catalan, J., Schmidt, U., Davidson, K., Dent, J., Tata, P., Thornton, S., Barber, J., & Thompson, S. (1999). Manual-assisted cognitive-behaviour therapy (MACT): A randomized controlled trial of a brief intervention with bibliotherapy in the treatment of recurrent deliberate self-harm. *Psychological Medicine, 29* (1), 19–25.

Ghosh, A., Marks, I.M., & Carr, A. (1988). Therapist contact and outcome of self-exposure treatment for phobias. *British Journal of Psychiatry, 152,* 234–238.

Glasgow, R.E., & Rosen, G.M. (1978). Behavioral bibliotherapy: A review of self-help behavior therapy manuals. *Psychological Bulletin, 85* (1), 1–23.

Goldstein, A.P., & Kanfer, F.H. (Eds.) (1979). *Maximizing treatment gains: Transfer enhancement in psychotherapy.* New York: Academic Press.

Gollwitzer, P.M. (1991). *Abwägen und Planen: Bewußtseinslagen in verschiedenen Handlungsphasen.* Göttingen, Germany: Hogrefe.

Gollwitzer, P.M. (1996). Das Rubikonmodell der Handlungsphasen. In J. Kuhl & H. Heckhausen (Eds.), *Enzyklopädie der Psychologie (Themenbereich C, Serie IV, Bd. 4: Motivation, Volition und Handlung)* (pp. 531–582). Göttingen, Germany: Hogrefe.

Goschke, T., & Kuhl, J. (2003). *Retrieval of intentions and wishes from memory: Cognitive and motivational determinants of accessibility.* Manuscript submitted for publication.

Gould, R.A., & Clum, G.A. (1993). A meta-analysis of self-help treatment approaches. *Clinical Psychology Review, 13* (2), 169–186.

Grant, G.M., Salcedo, V., Hynan, L.S., Frisch, M.B., & Puster, K. (1995). Effectiveness of quality of life therapy for depression. *Psychological Reports, 76,* 1203–1208.

Grothenrath, A., & Schneider, A. (1996). *Entwicklung und empirische Überprüfung eines Leitfadens zur Auseinandersetzung mit Lebenszielen und Anliegen.* Unpublished diploma thesis. Westfälische Wilhelms-Universität Münster, Münster, Germany.

Hautzinger, M. (1994). Action control in the context of psychopathological disorders. In J. Kuhl & J. Beckmann (Eds.), *Volition and personality* (pp. 209–215). Seattle: Hogrefe.

Heather, N., Kissoon-Singh, J., & Fenton, G.W. (1990). Assisted natural recovery from alcohol problems: Effects of self-help manual with and without supplementary telephone contact. *British Journal of Addictions, 85,* 1177–1185.

Heckhausen, H., Gollwitzer, P.M., & Weinert, F.E. (1987). *Jenseits des Rubikon: Der Wille in den Humanwissenschaften.* Berlin: Springer.

Hodges, B., Craven, J., & Littlefield, C. (1995). Bibliotherapy for psychological distress in lung transplant patients and their families. *Psychosomatics, 36* (4), 360–368.

Jamison, C., & Scogin, F. (1995). The outcome of cognitive bibliotherapy with depressed adults. *Journal of Consulting and Clinical Psychology, 63* (4), 644–650.

de Jong-Meyer, R., Schmitz, S., Ehlker, M., Greis, S., Hinsken, U., Sonnen, B., & Dickhöver, N. (1999). Handlungsorientierte Interaktionsbeiträge in verschiedenen Therapien: Prozesssteuerung und Erfolgsrelevanz. *Zeitschrift für Klinische Psychologie, Psychiatrie und Psychotherapie, 47* (2), 172–190.

Kammer, D. (1994). On depression and state orientation: A few empirical and theoretical remarks. In J. Kuhl & J. Beckmann (Eds.), *Volition and personality* (pp. 351–362). Seattle: Hogrefe.

Kanfer, F.H., Reinecker, H., & Schmelzer, D. (1996). *Selbstmanagement-Therapie* (2nd rev. edn.). Berlin: Springer.

Kazén-Saad, M., & Kuhl, J. (1989). Motivationale und volitionale Aspekte der Depression: Die Rolle der Lageorientierung. In R. Straub, G. Hole, & M. Hautzinger (Eds.), *Denken, Fühlen, Wollen und Handeln bei depressiven Menschen* (pp. 30–57). Bern, Switzerland: Lang.

Klinger, E. (1987). Current concerns and disengagement from incentives. In F. Halisch & J. Kuhl (eds.), *Motivation, intention and volition* (pp. 337–347). Berlin: Springer.

Klinger, E., Cox, W.M., & Blount, J.P. (in press). Motivational Structure Questionnaire (MSQ) and Personal Concerns Inventory (PCI). In J.P. Allen & M. Columbus (Eds.), *Assessing alcohol problems: A guide for clinicians and researchers* (2nd edn.). Washington, DC: US Department of Health and Human Services.

Kuhl, J. (1994). Action versus state orientation: Psychometric properties of the Action Control Scale (ASC-90). In J. Kuhl & J. Beckmann (Eds.), *Volition and personality: Action versus state orientation* (pp. 47–59). Göttingen, Germany: Hogrefe.

Kuhl, J., & Beckmann, J. (1994). *Volition and personality: Action versus state orientation*. Göttingen, Germany: Hogrefe.

Kuhl, J., & Fuhrmann, A. (1998). Decomposing self-regulation and self-control: The Volitional Components Inventory. In J. Heckhausen & C. Dweck (Eds.), *Lifespan perspectives on motivation and control*. Hillsdale, NJ: Erlbaum.

Kuhl, J., & Goschke, T. (1994). State orientation and the activation and retrieval of intensions from memory. In J. Kuhl & J. Beckmann (Eds.), *Volition and personality: Action versus state orientation* (pp. 127–154). Göttingen, Germany: Hogrefe.

Kuhl, J., & Helle, P. (1986). Motivational and volitional determinants of depression: The degenerated-intention hypothesis. *Journal of Abnormal Psychology, 95* (3), 247–251.

Lazarus, A., & Fay, A. (1975). *I can if I want to*. New York: Morrow.

Lewinsohn, P., Muñoz, R., Youngren, M.A., & Zeiss, A. (1986). *Control your depression*. Englewood Cliffs, NJ: Prentice-Hall.

Lidren, D.M., Watkins, P.L., Gould, R.A., Clum, G.A., Asterino, M., & Tulloch, H.L. (1994). A comparison of bibliotherapy and group therapy in the treatment of panic disorder. *Journal of Consulting and Clinical Psychology, 62* (4), 865–869.

Locke, E.A., Shaw, K.N., Saari, L.M., & Latham, G.P. (1981). Goal setting and task performance. *Psychological Bulletin, 90*, 125–152.

Mahoney, M.J., & Thoresen, C.E. (1974). *Self-control: Power to the person*. Monterey, CA: Brooks-Cole.

Marcus, B.H., Owen, N., Forsyth, L.H., Cavill, N.A., & Fridinger, F. (1998). Physical activity interventions using mass media, print media, and information technology. *American Journal of Preventive Medicine, 15* (4), 362–378.

Marks, I. (1993). *Ängste. Verstehen und bewältigen*. Berlin: Springer

Marks, I. (1997). Behaviour therapy for obsessive-compulsive disorder: A decade of progress. *Canadian Journal of Psychiatry, 42* (10), 1021–1027.

Marss, R.W. (1995). A meta-analysis of bibliotherapy studies. *American Journal of Community Psychology, 23* (6), 843–870.

Martin, L.L., & Tesser, A. (Eds.) (1996). *Striving and feeling—interactions among goals, affect, and self-regulation*. Mahwah, NJ: Erlbaum.

McIntosh, W.D. (1996). When does goal nonattainment lead to negative emotional reactions, and when doesn't it?: The role of linking and rumination. In L.L. Martin & A. Tesser (Eds.), *Striving and feeling—interactions among goals, affect, and self-regulation* (pp. 53–77). Mahwah, NJ: Erlbaum.

Miller, W.R., & Baca, L.M. (1983). Two-year follow-up of bibliotherapy and therapist-directed controlled drinking training for problem drinkers. *Behavior Therapy, 14* (3), 441–448.

Miller, W.R., Gribskov, C., & Mortell, R. (1981). The effectiveness of a self-control manual for problem drinkers with and without therapist contact. *International Journal of the Addictions, 16*, 829–839.

Miller, W.R., & Muñoz, R.F. (1982). *How to control your drinking: A practical guide to responsible drinking* (rev. edn.). Albuquerque, NM: University of New Mexico Press.

Santrock, J.W., Minnett, A.M., & Campbell, B.D. (1994). *The authoritative guide to self-help books*. New York: Guilford.

Scogin, F., Floyd, M., Jamison, C., Ackerson, J., Landreville, P., & Bissonnette, L. (1996). Negative outcomes: What is the evidence on self-administered treatments? *Journal of Consulting and Clinical Psychology, 64* (5), 1086–1089.

Scogin, F., Jamison, C., & Davis, N. (1990). Two-year follow-up of bibliotherapy for depression in older adults. *Journal of Consulting and Clinical Psychology, 58*, 665–667.

Scogin, F., Jamison, C., & Gochneaur, K. (1989). Comparative efficacy of cognitive and behavioral bibliotherapy for mildly and moderately depressed older adults. *Journal of Consulting and Clinical Psychology, 57* (3), 403–407.

Sheldon, K.M., & Kasser, T. (1995). Coherence and congruence: Two aspects of personality integration. *Journal of Personality and Social Psychology, 68*, 531–543.

Smith, N.M., Floyd, M.R., Scogin, F., & Jamison, C.S. (1997). Three-year follow-up of bibliotherapy for depression. *Journal of Consulting and Clinical Psychology, 65* (2), 324–327.

Sorby, N.D.G., Reavly, W., & Huber, J.W. (1991). Self-help programme for anxiety in general practice: Controlled trial of an anxiety management booklet. *British Journal of General Practice, 41*, 417–420.

Taylor, S.E., & Pham, L.B. (1996). Mental stimulation, motivation, and action. In P.M. Gollwitzer & J.A. Bargh (Eds.), *The psychology of action: Linking cognition and motivation to behaviour* (pp. 219–235). New York: Guilford.

Watson, D.L., & Tharp, R.G. (1972). *Self-directed behavior: Self-modification for personal adjustment*. Monterey, CA: Brooks-Cole.

Wilfley, D.E., & Cohen, L.R. (1997). Psychological treatment of bulimia nervosa and binge eating disorder. *Psychopharmacology Bulletin, 33* (3), 437–454.

Zeigarnik, B. (1927). Über das Behalten von erledigten und unerledigten Handlungen. *Psychologische Forschung, 9*, 1–85.

Zweben, A., & Fleming, M.F. (1999). Brief interventions for alcohol and drug problems. In J.A. Tucker, D.M. Donovan, & G.A. Marlatt (Eds.), *Changing addictive behavior. Bridging clinical and public health strategies* (pp. 251–282). New York: Guilford.

CHAPTER 14

Systematic Motivational Counseling at Work: Improving Employee Performance, Satisfaction, and Socialization

Loriann Roberson*

and

David M. Sluss

Arizona State University, Tempe, USA

Synopsis.—Although originally developed for use in clinical settings, Systematic Motivational Counseling (SMC) is also appropriate and valuable for use in work settings. Research in organizational behavior has consistently shown that aspects of goal systems are important for critical job outcomes, such as productivity, job satisfaction, organizational commitment, and job retention. Managers are frequently advised to use goal-setting for their employees as a part of good management practice. Indeed, major performance management techniques such as Management by Objectives are built on the notion of setting and monitoring task performance goals. SMC provides a more comprehensive approach for managing employee work goals. Past research on SMC in clinical settings has shown it can result in desired behavioral change, and in increases in life satisfaction, positive affect, and well-being (Cox et al., in press). In this chapter, we discuss how SMC can have a similar positive impact in work settings, leading to better management, and increased employee job satisfaction and work performance.

In this chapter we first review the theory and research in Organizational Behavior that focus on goals and the characteristics of goals that influence important outcomes. These characteristics are assessed in the Motivational Structure Questionnaire (MSQ). We then discuss how managers can use both the MSQ and SMC for performance management, with particular focus on new employees during the socialization period—the period of adjustment to a new job and organization, which is critical for both organizations and individuals (Harris & DeSimone, 1994). Turnover rates tend to be high during this time, and inadequate socialization is often cited as a major reason why new employees leave their jobs (Hom & Griffeth, 1995). New employees experience difficulties in learning new job tasks, adjusting to organizational climate and culture, and balancing work and nonwork roles. Our analysis

---

* Please address all correspondence to Loriann Roberson.

Handbook of Motivational Counseling. Edited by W. Miles Cox and Eric Klinger.
© 2004 John Wiley & Sons, Ltd.

of goals and socialization suggests how SMC can be used by managers to help employees during this difficult transition.

RESEARCH ON GOALS IN ORGANIZATIONAL BEHAVIOR: MOTIVATION AND PERFORMANCE

Goal-Setting Theory

Most research and theory regarding goals in Organizational Behavior is concentrated on explaining work motivation and task performance. Within this area, goal-setting theory (Locke & Latham, 1990) has been the dominant framework guiding research. This theory, which grew out of experimental research where goals were assigned to subjects, argues that goals are the central determinant of action, controlling effort, persistence, and direction of action (Locke & Latham, 1990). Numerous studies have provided support for the basic principles of goal-setting theory (Ambrose & Kulik, 1999; Latham & Locke, 1991). (1) Specific difficult goals lead to higher performance than do specific easy goals, vague goals, or no goals. For example, a goal to "walk for 30 minutes during my lunch break every day" will be more effective in increasing exercise than a goal to "be more active". (2) Goal-setting is more effective in increasing performance when feedback showing progress is provided. So monitoring and checking off the days when one completes the lunch-time walk should also increase the amount of exercise completed.

The positive relationship between assigned goals and performance assumes that the individual is committed to attaining the goal (Locke & Latham, 1990). Thus, in order to influence performance, the assigned goal must become a personal goal of the individual. Research has also focused on identifying factors that increase commitment to assigned goals. Most propose an expectancy theory framework for predicting commitment (Klein et al., 1999). The value or attractiveness and the expectancy of goal attainment are viewed as the most direct determinants of commitment. Evidence suggests that several management techniques, especially participation in goal-setting and financial incentives, can increase commitment to goals (Kanfer, 1990). In addition, self-efficacy is also associated with goal commitment (Wofford, Goodwin, & Premack, 1992). This evidence supports the theory that those who feel confident that they can reach the goal are more likely to be committed to attaining it.

Goal conflict has been identified and studied as another characteristic of goals that can influence commitment and performance (Locke & Latham, 1990). For example, Locke et al. (1994) found that the conflict between faculty members' teaching and research goals was negatively related to performance, although this effect was not mediated by goal commitment. In addition, research suggests that task complexity can moderate the relationship between difficult goals and performance (Wood, Mento, & Locke, 1987), such that, on complex tasks, the relationship between goal difficulty and performance is reduced. Dividing a complex task into subtasks and setting goals for each subtask has been proposed as a more effective strategy than setting a goal for the entire task (Cropanzano, James, & Citera, 1993).

In sum, research on goal-setting has typically focused on single, externally set goals and their influence on primarily one outcome—performance. Although a limited number of goal characteristics have been studied in relation to goal commitment and performance, the findings provide clear guidance to managers in setting performance goals for their subordinates—goals should be specific, challenging, and not conflicting. In order to increase commitment, the perceived value and probability of goal attainment should be high. Feedback on goal progress must be provided, and if the task is complex, subgoals should be set.

Goal Orientation

A second theoretical perspective for examining the effects of goals on motivation and task performance is provided by work on goal orientation (Dweck, 1986; Nicholls, 1984). In this theory and research, the focus is on the content or framing of the individual's personal achievement goal and the impact of this framing on behavior. Dweck (1986) and Dweck and Leggett (1988) proposed two broad classes of goals that individuals can pursue in an achievement setting: learning or performance. With a learning-goal orientation, the individual's goals are to develop and increase task competence. With a performance-goal orientation, the individual's goals are to demonstrate or prove competence by seeking a positive evaluation and avoiding a negative evaluation of one's abilities. Brett and Vandewalle (1999) demonstrated this impact of goal orientation on the content of personal goals in a study of MBA students taking a training program on presentation skills. Individual students with a learning-goal orientation set skill improvement goals for the course (e.g., develop my presentation skills; refine my presentation skills). Students with a performance-goal orientation set comparison goals (e.g., do better than others in the class; not look incompetent).

Goal orientation influences the content of the achievement goal and how people interpret and respond to the achievement setting, influencing cognition, behavior, and affect. Individuals with a learning-goal orientation tend to view competence as malleable, as something that can increase through effort (Dweck, 1986). The expenditure of effort, therefore, is viewed and experienced as positive, as it is seen as a way of meeting one's goal to increase competence. In contrast, people with a performance-goal orientation view competence as static, a fixed and stable attribute of people. Effort is not seen as developing proficiency. Rather, high effort is believed necessary only for those with low competence, along with the belief that highly competent people don't need to expend effort in order to succeed. Therefore, the expenditure of effort is viewed and experienced as negative, as it is interpreted as a sign of low proficiency and lack of goal attainment.

In addition, goal orientation influences preferences for and interpretations of feedback. Individuals with a learning-goal orientation prefer feedback that provides information on task strategies and how to improve (Butler, 1993). Negative feedback is viewed as useful information for meeting the goal of developing one's competence. Individuals with a performance-goal orientation prefer feedback that provides information on relative standing, rather than task information. Negative feedback is not viewed as useful information, but as a sign of low competence. Under a performance-goal orientation, the frequency of seeking feedback is related to performance level, with those doing well engaging in more feedback seeking than those doing poorly (Butler, 1993). Vandewalle and Cummings (1997) also reported a relationship between goal orientation and frequency of feedback seeking. Individuals with a learning-goal orientation sought feedback from superiors and peers more frequently than those with a performance-goal orientation.

Much research on goal orientation has focused on how it influences responses to task difficulty, a situation that results in negative feedback to the individual. With a learning-goal orientation, responses to task difficulty are described as "adaptive" (Dweck, 1986; Vandewalle, 1999). Individuals persist at the task, often escalate their effort, engage in problem-solving self-talk with high task focus, and report positive affect, enjoying the challenge. This response pattern is predictable as effort and negative feedback are viewed as instrumental to the individual's overarching goal of improving competence. With a performance-goal orientation, responses to task difficulty are "maladaptive." Individuals withdraw from the task, decreasing their effort. They engage in negative ability attributions and lose task focus, reporting negative affect and decreased task interest. This pattern is also predictable as effort and negative feedback are viewed as signs that the goal of demonstrating competence is not being met. Therefore, in order to avoid negative judgments of one's ability, withdrawal is necessary.

Thus, the framing of the achievement goal can have profound effects on feelings, motivation, and performance, especially when task difficulty is encountered. It is particularly in these circumstances that goal orientation has a differential relationship to performance. On complex and difficult tasks, a learning-goal orientation is associated with higher performance than a performance-goal orientation (Steele-Johnson et al., 2000). However, with less difficult or demanding tasks, a performance-goal orientation is associated with higher performance than a learning-goal orientation (Steele-Johnson et al., 2000).

Research has also examined the causes of goal orientation. Goal orientation is believed to have both trait and state components. Many researchers conceptualize and measure goal orientation as a dispositional trait (e.g., Button, Mathieu, & Zajac, 1996). However, research has also demonstrated that goal orientation can be induced by situational cues. For example, competition, punishment of mistakes, and evaluative, relative appraisal systems have been found to induce a performance-goal orientation (Ames & Archer, 1988; Nicholls, 1984; Vandewalle, 1999). Cooperation, the encouragement of experimentation, and developmental appraisals can result in a learning-goal orientation. Butler (1987) found that the type of feedback provided could influence goal orientation. Both simple praise (e.g., very good) and grades on performance shifted individuals toward a performance-goal orientation, whereas individualized comments on performance encouraged a learning-goal orientation. Explicit goal assignments have also been used to induce goal orientations. For example, Roberson and Alsua (2002) told participants that the purpose of engaging in a managerial problem-solving task was either to demonstrate and prove their competence as managers (performance-goal orientation), or to develop and improve their competence (learning-goal orientation). Such goal assignments have also been effective in eliciting the intended goal orientations.

This research, then, highlights the importance of one aspect of personal achievement goals—the content or framing. This one characteristic has been shown to be important for a wide range of self-regulation activities and outcomes. Although individuals may differ in their tendencies to approach achievement tasks with either a learning- or performance-goal orientation, goal orientation can also be influenced through setting goals, the use of feedback and appraisal strategies, and other techniques. Although this research has yet to have a major impact on management practice, recent prescriptions for the *learning organization* (McGill & Slocum, 1995; Senge, 1990) are consistent with its findings. Characteristics of a learning organization include a culture that promotes the pursuit of continuous improvement and learning from mistakes. These characteristics are believed to result in higher organizational performance.

Theories of Intrinsic Motivation

A third and related theoretical perspective on motivation and performance with implications for personal goals concerns intrinsic motivation. These theories argue that there are two classes of motivated behavior: intrinsic and extrinsic, which differ in terms of the individual's reasons or goals for performing the behavior. Intrinsically motivated behavior is performed for its own sake, for the satisfaction inherent in the activity itself. Extrinsically motivated behavior is performed as a means to an end, to accomplish some other external goal such as rewards or the avoidance of punishment (Vallerand, 1997). These two forms of motivation differ not only in the personal goal of the individual in performing the act, but also in the experience of goal pursuit. With intrinsic motivation, individuals experience pleasure and positive emotion. They are focused on the task and experience little pressure to perform. With extrinsic motivation, individuals experience negative emotion, less task focus, and feel pressured and tense. Research has found that intrinsically motivated individuals are more likely than extrinsically motivated people to persist at the task. In work situations, intrinsic motivation is associated with higher job satisfaction and less propensity to quit (Vallerand, 1997).

Much research on intrinsic and extrinsic motivation has focused on the relationship between the two, finding that the two forms are not additive. Rather, evidence suggests that adding extrinsic motivation can undermine intrinsic motivation (Kanfer, 1990). Many of the techniques for adding extrinsic motivation are commonly advocated management tools such as deadlines, rewards, competition, and surveillance. Research suggests that these situational variables will decrease intrinsic motivation to the extent that they decrease feelings of competence and lead to the individual's feeling controlled (Kanfer, 1990; Vallerand, 1997). Conversely, situational interventions or variables that enhance feelings of mastery and autonomy will increase intrinsic motivation. The provision of choice (for example, choice of tasks, or choice of timing of tasks) and positive feedback on task performance have been effective in this regard (Jussim et al., 1992). Again, this research suggests the importance of the content of the individual's personal goal for performing an activity and the influence of management strategies in helping to shape goal content. Similar to the recommendations stemming from goal orientation research, the intrinsic motivation literature suggests that, ideally, employees should be performing job tasks to increase their feelings of competence, to learn, and to enjoy the task. Thus, managers should gain goal commitment by stressing these outcomes, not through the use of rewards or threats.

RESEARCH ON GOALS IN ORGANIZATIONAL BEHAVIOR: WORK ATTITUDES

Although most research and theory in organizational behavior regarding personal goals has focused on their influence on behavior and performance, some work has emphasized the importance of goals for work attitudes. Job satisfaction has been the most heavily investigated work attitude (Brief, 1998). One prominent definition of job satisfaction, that of Locke (1976), argued that job satisfaction is "a pleasurable or positive emotional state resulting from the attainment of values." There are two aspects of this definition that suggest the importance of personal goals: the definition of job satisfaction as an emotional state, and the role of value attainment in determining job satisfaction.

Job Satisfaction as an Emotional State

Locke (1976) defines job satisfaction as an emotional state. As noted by Brief and Weiss (2000), job satisfaction is not typically measured as affect or emotion. But, theoretically, construing satisfaction as an emotion suggests the relevance of those theories that conceptualize emotions as arising from goal attainment and goal-striving. Several theoretical perspectives have proposed that emotion and affect arise from degree of goal attainment (Bandura, 1991; Klinger, 1975; Tomkins, 1979), the rate of progress toward goal attainment (Carver & Scheier, 1990), or anticipated goal attainment (Bandura, 1989). Theories of life satisfaction have also proposed that goal commitment is related to satisfaction and well-being. Happiness is dependent on being involved in meaningful activities (Diener, 1984).

Higgins (1987) suggested that not only the extent of goal attainment but also the content of the goal determined emotion. His theory of self-discrepancy proposes that goals can be categorized into self- or other-generated, and ideal or ought goals. Different emotions are generated by different kinds of goal discrepancies. For example, discrepancies from one's ideal own goals generate frustration-related emotions, whereas discrepancies from ideal other goals generate dejection-related emotions.

Other theorists have proposed that the valence of the goal (approach or avoidance) can influence emotion, with approach goals generating more positive emotion than avoidance goals (Klinger, 1977). In addition, perceptions of goal conflict, when the pursuit of one goal detracts from the pursuit of another, have been proposed and studied as a precursor to negative emotion (Austin & Vancouver, 1996; Emmons, 1986).

Thus, considering job satisfaction as an emotion suggests several relevant characteristics of personal goals. Goal attainment, framing as positive or negative, and conflict are important determinants of emotions, and may also determine satisfaction with one's job.

Value Attainment as a Determinant of Satisfaction

The second aspect of Locke's definition of satisfaction that suggests the relevance of personal goals is his statement that satisfaction results from the degree to which values are attained, and his definition of a value as that which one acts to gain or keep (Locke, 1976). This definition suggests that the individual's own personal values are what influence satisfaction; that personal goals are the important determinant. The idea that attainment of personal goals is the key to satisfaction has also been voiced by others (Katzell, 1964; Meyer & Allen, 1997). However, most research has not examined personal goals of workers as an influence on job satisfaction. Instead, research on the relationship of job satisfaction to value attainment has been guided by general taxonomies of needs or values, and measured the degree to which these have been attained (Brief, 1998). Research on conflict has not assessed conflict among actual goals, but rather perceptions of role conflict- and work–family conflict-related constructs. Both of these forms of conflict are consistently negatively related to job satisfaction, and positively related to turnover. Work–family conflict is also positively related to a variety of mental health symptoms (Frone, 2000).

An exception to this trend was provided by Roberson (1990) who measured personal work goals of employees and predicted job satisfaction from characteristics of those goals. Consistent with theoretical predictions, expectancies of goal attainment, valence (positive or negative), and goal commitment were related to satisfaction. In addition, Maier and Brunstein (2001) also measured the personal goals of new employees and found that the interaction of goal commitment and goal attainability predicted changes in satisfaction during the first months of employment. Satisfaction increased for those committed to their goals who perceived that attainment was possible, but declined if individuals perceived that their important goals would not be met.

RESEARCH ON GOALS IN ORGANIZATIONAL BEHAVIOR: GROUPS/TEAMS

As much work in organizations is now conducted in teams, research has also examined how the individual's personal goals influence team-level outcomes. Zander (1980) suggested that four types of goals can be relevant in a team situation: (1) each member's goal for the group; (2) each member's goal for him or herself (3) the group's goal for each member; and (4) the group's goal for itself. The fourth type of goal, the group's goal for itself, has been shown to affect performance. Just as for individual goals, the specificity and difficulty of the group's performance goal is related to group performance (O'Leary-Kelly, Martocchio, & Frink, 1994).

However, the role that individual-level (type 2) goals play in team performance appears to depend on the nature of the group task. Mitchell and Silver (1990) argued that the degree of interdependence (the extent to which members must work together) influences the relationship between individual goals and performance. They found that given interdependence, the use of individual performance goals reduced team performance. Crown and Rosse (1995) suggested that task summativity (the extent to which group performance is the sum of individual performance) is an additional important factor. When the task is summative, a group member's focus on maximizing his or her individual output can enhance team performance. Crown and Rosse (1995) found that this was not true when the task is nonsummative. Under these conditions, personal goals to maximize individual performance (egocentric goals) were less effective than personal goals to maximize individual contributions to the group (groupcentric goals). Thus, care must be given to framing personal goals in a team setting. If group performance is more than the sum of individual performance, a group member's focus on his or her own performance can be detrimental.

Other studies have examined the congruence of individual team members' goals. When individuals perceive that the personal goals of other team members are similar to their own, they are more likely to believe that the team will facilitate attainment of their own valued outcomes. Kristoff-Brown and Stevens (2001) found that congruence of individual members' goals was related to satisfaction with the team and interpersonal contributions to the team. Peer goal congruence is also related to job satisfaction and organizational commitment (Reichers, 1986; Vancouver & Schmitt, 1991).

Summary of Research on Goals in Organizational Behavior

In summary, this brief review indicates a number of characteristics of individuals' personal work goals that influence performance and job satisfaction. Goal content has been studied in goal orientation and intrinsic motivation research, suggesting that achievement goals result in better outcomes when framed as learning goals and as intrinsically motivating, being performed for learning and enjoyment. Framing goals in positive terms is also better for satisfaction than framing them in negative terms. In addition, goal content that is congruent with others (supervisor and team) will enhance work attitudes and interpersonal contributions to the job and team. Independent of goal content, the variables of goal commitment, expectancy of attainment, specificity, availability of feedback, and goal conflict also influence performance and satisfaction. Thus, motivational assessment and counseling should focus on these characteristics of employee goals.

SYSTEMATIC MOTIVATIONAL COUNSELING AT WORK

Systematic Motivational Counseling (SMC) would focus on the aspects of goals reviewed above in diagnosing and addressing problems of motivation, performance, and satisfaction at work. A focus on goals to improve performance and work attitudes is not new in management science. Goal-setting techniques such as Management by Objectives (MBO) are widely used at managerial levels for performance management and appraisal (Bernardin & Russell, 1998). MBO systems start at the top management level with the statement of organizational objectives, and these goals are handed down to lower levels. At each consecutive level, managers take the upper level objective, and from it derive objectives for their own jobs that will contribute to the higher level goal. To be most effective, it is recommended that these objectives be stated in quantifiable terms, with specific timeframes and deadlines attached (Quinn et al., 1996). Once objectives have been agreed on, there is periodic review and comparison of actual performance against the objectives. Research has shown that MBO can result in improved productivity (Bernardin & Russell, 1998).

Goal-setting is also a major feature or activity of most career counseling and management approaches (Greenhaus, 1987). After exploring options and engaging in self-awareness activities, individuals set career goals and plans for accomplishing them. Progress toward goals is monitored, and feedback from both work and nonwork sources used to revise goals and plans. The career management process is cyclical and ongoing; managers aid employees by giving help in setting goals and in providing feedback.

SMC differs from these traditional approaches in several ways. First is in its emphasis on a broader variety of work-related goals. MBO focuses only on job tasks and those objectives derived from corporate goals. In practice, the requirement for quantifiable objectives also tends to limit goals to those that can be objectively measured. This can result in the neglect of other important aspects of performance that are less quantifiable (Gomez-Mejia, Balkin, & Cardy, 2001). In contrast, career management programs focus on broader, long-term career goals that may have little to do with the current work situation. SMC is not limited by either of these constraints. It focuses on a wide variety of employee concerns within the current work situation, and can include both task and nontask, long- and short-term goals.

A second distinguishing feature of SMC is its emphasis not only on specificity and feedback, goal characteristics prominent in MBO and career management, but other important goal cognitions discussed above such as framing, expectancies, and conflict. As our review has shown, these characteristics are important for work outcomes; they are also assessed in this comprehensive technique.

Table 14.1 Categories of personal work goals

Categories, in decreasing order of frequency of mention (left column first)	
Personal performance	Self-image
Professional development	Client relationships
Pay/benefits	Positive/negative feedback
Working conditions and resources	Organizational performance
Career advancement	Work schedule
Managerial relationships	Coworker effectiveness
Job task type	Autonomy/independence
Coworker relationships	Work group morale

Note: Table adapted from "Identifying valued work outcomes through a content analysis of personal goals" by Roberson, L., Houston, J.M., & Diddams, M., in *Journal of Vocational Behavior*, **35**, 30–45. (Copyright ©1989, Elsevier Science (USA), reproduced with permission from the publisher.)

DOING SMC AT WORK

SMC begins by having the employee list major work-related goals. The Work Concerns Inventory (WCI; Roberson, 1989), based on the MSQ (Cox & Klinger, Chapter 8, this volume; Klinger, Cox, & Blount, in press), provides one method for assessing goals. This instrument uses a free response format, with two prompts to structure and guide the individual's goal elicitation. First, the instrument contains a list of content areas about which individuals may have goals. Roberson, Houston, and Diddams (1989) conducted a content analysis of personal work goals generated by 175 employees on the WCI. Table 14.1 shows the most frequently mentioned goal content categories. These content areas can be used to aid people's memories in thinking about their current goals. Second, as with the MSQ, individuals are asked to write goals using a list of action verbs. Both positive verbs (e.g., get, keep, do) and negative verbs (e.g., avoid, prevent, escape) are included so that individuals can accurately state their intentions. The WCI allowed listing many (50–60) goals but, for practical use, 10–20 items would be most useful. Once goals are listed, as with the MSQ, individuals use scales for rating goal characteristics.

The other important goal characteristics and cognitions discussed in this chapter can be assessed via examination of goal content, along with discussion for clarification. For example, intrinsic motivation and goal orientation would be reflected by positively stated task goals for learning and development, with high expectancies of success and high value. Conversely, negatively or positively framed goals about evaluation concerns or comparisons with coworkers would reflect extrinsic and performance-goal orientations. Alternatively, a user might wish to add scales to the existing MSQ scales to assess variables of special interest. For example, goal orientation could be measured by asking respondents to rate each goal on a scale from 1 (I am pursuing this goal to develop and improve my skills) to 10 (I am pursuing this goal to demonstrate my competence). In this way, the MSQ can be easily adapted to a variety of research objectives and applications.

Other maladaptive patterns to look for include general low expectancies of success, lack of specificity in framing and timeframes, low value of goals, and conflict among goals. Managers would seek to alter these patterns through discussion. For example, they can help employees see more and different outcomes of goal attainment, and link specific work goals to broader organizational and individual goals, enhancing the value of goal attainment.

They can also discuss and talk about specific strategies for goal attainment and offer help or resources, increasing expectancies of success. Because research has shown that goal orientation can be manipulated by goal assignment, managers can ask employees to adopt learning goals for task achievement instead of, or in addition to, performance goals. This would also increase intrinsic motivation. Additionally, they can help employees to adopt groupcentric rather than egocentric goals where appropriate.

This type of discussion is valuable as part of ongoing performance management and might be used as part of a yearly appraisal discussion for development and coaching purposes. In addition, we believe that a time when SMC would be most profitably used is during work transitions, and especially for new employees during the socialization period.

NEW-EMPLOYEE SOCIALIZATION AND GOAL SYSTEMS

The new-employee socialization process involves a transition in which individuals move from one role identity (organizational outsider) to another (organizational insider) (Ashforth, 2001). During this transition, newcomers have a high probability of experiencing a motivational crisis or "identity deficit" (Baumeister, Shapiro, & Tice, 1985). Baumeister, Shapiro, and Tice (1985) suggest that individuals in transition experience an inadequate definition of self because their previous role, which provided a sense of identity, is now deficient and the new role is still ambiguous and uncertain. As a result, individuals experiencing identity deficits "lack a basis for making consistent choices and decisions" (Baumeister, Shapiro, & Tice, 1985, p. 408). This uncertainty leads to difficulty in accepting and setting goals, which makes adjustment to the new work environment more problematic. At the same time, newcomers desire certainty and try to make sense out of what they are experiencing (Louis, 1980; Weick, 1995). In an effort to move from uncertainty to certainty, newcomers move through three distinct stages when transitioning from outsider to insider (Feldman, 1976). The stages are described as anticipatory socialization ("getting in"), accommodation ("breaking in"), and role management ("settling in") (Wanous, 1992). Through all these stages, newcomers have goals of adjusting within the organization while still maintaining some coherent sense of self (Baumeister, Shapiro, & Tice, 1985). This means that a wide array of goals exists during the socialization process all the way from "learn to use the new software application" and "prepare for management position in finance department" to "make time to go hiking on weekends." However, lack of experience and knowledge in the new work role hinder optimal goal-setting and self-regulatory activity. As a result, the newcomer-socialization process is a fruitful area in which to focus on assessing and shaping goal systems and appropriate goal characteristics through the MSQ and SMC.

Socialization simultaneously occurs in two directions—organizations act to socialize newcomers (through socialization tactics) and newcomers act to socialize themselves (through proactive socialization). Given the importance of goal systems during a time of transition (Baumeister, Shapiro, & Tice, 1985), the following sections analyze both organizational and proactive socialization tactics in terms of their impact on newcomer goal systems. Previous sections mentioned the importance of several goal system characteristics for performance and satisfaction: goal content, lack of conflict, goal commitment, attainability, specificity, and feedback. Evidence suggests that newcomers who receive (through organizational tactics) or obtain (through proactive tactics) these goal characteristics through the socialization process tend to experience increased job satisfaction and performance.

Institutionalized Socialization

Van Maanen and Schein (1979) posited that organizations use a mixture of six main tactics or processes when helping newcomers to adjust to their new jobs. Jones (1986) simplified the six tactics to fit parsimoniously onto a continuum between institutionalized and individualized socialization processes. Institutionalized tactics include organizational processes in which newcomers are collectively indoctrinated in a formal, sequential, and fixed way. Military basic training and medical and other professional schools epitomize the use of institutionalized socialization tactics. On the other hand, individualized tactics are organizational processes in which newcomers are individually and informally indoctrinated in a "hit and miss" or random pattern. For example, smaller entrepreneurial organizations tend not to pay explicit attention to socializing their employees, instead immersing newcomers in their position and expecting work from day one. As a result, newcomers receive help and orientation in informal, individualized, disjointed, randomized, and varied ways.

Overall, institutionalized tactics give newcomers a structured experience in which to make sense of their new role (Jones, 1986). First, institutionalized tactics provide solutions for resolving seemingly conflicting assigned goals. For example, a telemarketing center may assign goals concerning both the quality and quantity of completed sales calls. Collective and formal tactics allow the organization to explain how both are relatively weighted. If such explanation is absent, newcomers may be left to their own to "divine" which of the two goals are of priority and in what situations.

Second, formal training and indoctrination (collective, formal, sequential, and fixed tactics) increase newcomer job proficiency. This increases perceived goal attainability.

Third, institutionalized tactics focus on job-related goals and issues (Saks & Ashforth, 1997). Formal training and indoctrination provide rationale for why assigned goals are important for both the individual and the organization (Klein & Weaver, 2000). As a result, goal commitment should increase (Latham, Erez, & Locke, 1988).

Fourth, sequential and fixed socialization tactics provide newcomers with specificity regarding their job-related goals. Sequential and fixed tactics translate into repeatable and reliable patterns wherein newcomers are given specific information regarding their job expectations, organizational goals, and other related data (Wanous, 1992).

Finally, institutionalized tactics provide feedback through both formal orientation training and sequential tactics in which progression to the next step necessitates performance feedback. As mentioned earlier, performance feedback will increase the probability of goal achievement and is needed for goals to affect performance. Consistent with this analysis, research has found the use of institutionalized socialization processes to be related to job satisfaction, job performance, organizational commitment, and organizational identification (Saks & Ashforth, 1997).

Individualized Socialization

In contrast to institutionalized tactics, individualized tactics provide less structure to personal work goals. Instead, individualized and informal tactics allow individuals to take more control over the goal-setting process. As a result, newcomers will tend to set goals more aligned with personal desires and values than with organizational initiatives. Additionally, the newcomer will tend to set goals depending upon personal disposition, according to a learning orientation or performance orientation. These goals are likely to be intrinsically motivating, which will then increase goal commitment and satisfaction. In support of this notion, Orpen (1995) found individualized tactics to be positively related to long-term career satisfaction.

On the other hand, random and variable individualized tactics challenge the newcomer's ability to maintain goal specificity. Additionally, these tactics may decrease expectancies of success. The lack of pattern or sequence for events during the socialization process (i.e., training, skill development, performance evaluations, etc.) may not provide sufficient information or skills needed for the newcomers to understand or obtain goals.

The socialization process is a learning process. As such, newcomers will not learn as effectively when new information is not presented in a coherent and logical manner. For example, two new doctoral students may have an overall goal to learn data analysis procedures. One doctoral student is instructed to follow a sequenced and fixed process (i.e., a statistics course during the first semester, a simple project during the second semester, a more difficult project during the summer, followed by another statistical course, etc.) that results in a series of specific goals increasing in difficulty. The second doctoral student, on the other hand, follows a random and variable learning process (i.e., involvement in a complicated data analysis project during the first several months, an adviser-prompted statistical short course due to errors in the data analyses, followed by a second project using different statistical analyses). Both socialization tactics generally support an overall goal of learning data analysis procedures. However, the second student will have initial difficulty formulating specific task goals (due to lack of familiarity with analysis), and will likely experience low expectancies of success.

Additionally, random tactics deprive newcomers of rationales to resolve goal conflicts. For example, a newcomer who receives conflicting goals from two different managers will have difficulty resolving the conflict without an overarching organizational policy or strategy regarding task priorities. This is unlikely to be provided when information is random and variable.

Variable individualized tactics may also decrease goal commitment. Variable tactics imply that there is no definite time schedule for socialization events. The variability of timing would prolong the sense of surprise during the socialization period (Louis, 1980), increasing levels of uncertainty. For example, a new sales representative may not commit to attaining sales goals in a timely fashion if the scheduling of performance evaluations (in which the newcomer would receive a bonus or merit increase) is nebulous.

Finally, disjunctive tactics (being socialized by individuals outside the newcomer's functional area) may cause newcomers to receive inaccurate feedback due to the informal mentor's lack of knowledge, or no feedback at all due to the informal mentor's lack of personal investment in the newcomer's adjustment. Disjunctive tactics may also be more likely to result in goal conflict as mentors from different functional areas have different goal priorities.

In summary, institutionalized tactics impose and structure newcomer goals in ways that can enhance performance. Individualized tactics provide less structure but allow newcomers more freedom in setting and structuring personally relevant work and career goals. Although this freedom can enhance satisfaction, it also adds uncertainty and puts a greater burden on newcomers at a time when stress and uncertainty are already high. Thus, SMC may be most useful when organizations use individualized tactics. However, because institutionalized tactics tend to focus on assigned task goals, SMC can be used to give more attention to personal nontask work goals.

Proactive Socialization

Recently, socialization researchers have begun to look at how individuals attempt to manage their own socialization and adjustment to work (Saks & Ashforth, 1997), finding that newcomers employ proactive behaviors in their own efforts to adjust to the new roles and work environment. Evidence suggests that as the organization is less involved in the newcomer's socialization (i.e., using individualized socialization tactics), newcomers will increase proactive socialization behaviors in an effort to reduce uncertainty and increase goal achievement. In essence, where one is absent, the other may substitute and produce similar results.

Proactive socialization traditionally has concerned itself with how newcomers acquire information needed to adjust to the job and work environment (Bauer, Morrison, & Callister, 1998). Generally speaking, research has found information acquisition to be positively related to task mastery, social integration, role clarity, and job satisfaction, and negatively related to intentions to leave (Morrison, 1993).

Ashford and Black (1996) expanded the definition of proactive socialization to include (in addition to information acquisition) feedback seeking, relationship building, positive framing, and job-change negotiating. Positive framing imposes cognitive restructuring of a potentially difficult or negative event. For example, a medical resident may not particularly enjoy a 36-hour "in-house" call (wherein the resident has to be in the hospital and working continuously for 36 hours). However, the resident may cognitively reframe the situation as a great learning experience wherein one can have uninterrupted study time (free from family or friends) or a great learning experience wherein the resident can handle a wide variety of cases and get a true feeling for the hospital inner workings. The result of positive framing is a change of a negatively valued goal into a positively valued one. Job-change negotiating is attempting to change the job (tasks, role expectations, etc.) to better align with personal needs and values.

Ashford and Black (1996) found that proactive tactics were positively related to job satisfaction and job performance. Individuals engaged in proactive socialization tactics are engaging in goal-striving behavior. Newcomers are able to reduce uncertainty and increase feelings of control through actively participating in their own work adjustment (Ashford & Black, 1996). Specifically, both information acquisition and feedback seeking increase the amount of relevant goal feedback (Renn & Fedor, 2001). Relationship building increases the number of knowledgeable people in the newcomer's social network. The increase in network resources will tend to raise the probability that the newcomer will attain the goal. Positive framing will assist the newcomer in gaining a positive perspective of assigned goals, thus increasing goal commitment and job satisfaction. Additionally, positive framing may help newcomers to resolve goal conflict through cognitively framing the paradoxical goals as both desirable and attainable, even though this is an illusion. Job-change negotiating will tend to increase the intrinsic motivation component of the goal, and increased intrinsic motivation leads to increased goal commitment (Deci & Ryan, 1980; Latham, Erez, & Locke, 1988). will seek to resolve goal conflict. It seems that newcomers, depending upon personality differences, may choose either job-change negotiating or positive framing as their tactic of choice when resolving goal conflict.

On the other hand, proactive tactics should be analyzed with caution. Proactive tactics will tend to focus upon personally relevant instead of assigned organizational goals. Thus, proactive tactics may still not lead to increased job performance and organizational commitment if personal goals are incongruent with organizational goals. Moreover, proactive tactics are sometimes used as a form of impression management (Morrison & Bies, 1991). This may be indicative of a performance-goal orientation, which may result in decreased performance and satisfaction. During socialization—a time when tasks are perceived as difficult and complex—a learning-goal orientation may be more functional.

In summary, proactive socialization tactics are used by newcomers to regulate goal-striving. SMC can aid newcomers in this activity, helping to balance both personal goals and performance-critical assigned goals.

USING SMC DURING SOCIALIZATION

The MSQ and SMC can be used to elicit newcomers' personal work-related concerns and their perceptions of job-task goals. Managers can introduce assigned task goals, creating linkages between assigned and personal concerns. To increase perceived probability of goal attainment, managers should discuss strategies for goal attainment and sources of help such as coworkers. Because proactive socialization tactics are positively related to satisfaction and task mastery, managers should create a culture where asking questions, obtaining feedback, building relationships, and negotiating job changes are valued. However, managers must balance the need for strict adherence to assigned goals with flexibility to include personal work and career aspirations.

CONCLUSION

As noted by Cropanzano, James, and Citera (1993), good leaders are those who influence the personal goals of their employees. As discussed in this chapter, the MSQ and SMC provide valid and established methods for accomplishing this outcome. Use of these techniques moves beyond the simple tenets of goal-setting, which focus on influencing productivity, to using the wealth of knowledge of how goals affect behavior and affective experience to accomplish not only performance improvements, but improvements in job satisfaction and in the socialization experience. Both the MSQ and the SMC are valuable management tools.

REFERENCES

Ambrose, M.L., & Kulik, C.T. (1999). Old friends, new faces: Motivation research in the 1990s. *Journal of Management, 25*, 231–292.
Ames, C., & Archer, J. (1988). Achievement goals in the classroom: Student's learning strategies and motivational processes. *Journal of Educational Psychology, 80*, 260–267.
Ashford, S.J., & Black, J.S. (1996). Proactivity during organizational entry: The role of desire of control. *Journal of Applied Psychology, 81*, 199–214.
Ashforth, B.E. (2001). *Role transitions in organizational life*. Hillsdale, NJ: Erlbaum.
Austin, J.T., & Vancouver, J.B. (1996). Goal constructs in psychology: Structure, process, and content. *Psychological Bulletin, 120*, 338–375.

Bandura, A. (1989). Self-regulation of motivation and action through internal standards and goal systems. In L.A. Pervin (Ed.), *Goal concepts in personality and social psychology* (pp. 19–85). Hillsdale, NJ: Erlbaum.

Bandura, A. (1991). Social cognitive theory of self-regulation. *Organizational Behavior and Human Decision Processes, 50*, 248–287.

Bauer, T.N., Morrison, E.W., & Callister, R.R. (1998). Organizational Socialization: A review and directions for future research. *Research in Personnel and Human Resources Management, 16*, 149–214.

Baumeister, R.F., Shapiro, J.P., & Tice, D.M. (1985). Two kinds of identity crisis. *Journal of Personality, 53*, 407–424.

Bernardin, H.J., & Russell, J.E.A. (1998). *Human resource management: An experiential approach* (2nd edn.). Boston: Irwin McGraw-Hill.

Brief, A.P. (1998). *Attitudes in and around organizations*. Thousand Oaks, CA: Sage.

Brief, A.P., & Weiss, H.M. (2002). Organizational behavior: Affect in the workplace. *Annual Review of Psychology, 33*, 279–307.

Brett, J.F., & Vandewalle, D. (1999). Goal orientation and goal content as predictors of performance in a training program. *Journal of Applied Psychology, 84*, 863–873.

Butler, R. (1987). Task-involving and ego-involving properties of evaluation. Effects of different feedback conditions on motivational perceptions, interest, and performance. *Journal of Educational Psychology, 79*, 474–482.

Butler, R. (1993). Effects of task- and ego-achievement goals on information-seeking during task engagement. *Journal of Personality and Social Psychology, 65*, 18–31.

Button, S.B., Mathieu, J.E., & Zajac, D.M. (1996). Goal orientation in organizational research: A conceptual and empirical foundation. *Organizational Behavior and Human Decision Processes, 67*, 26–48.

Carver, C.S., & Scheier, M.F. (1990). Origins and functions of positive and negative affect: A control process view. *Psychological Review, 97*, 19–35.

Cox, W.M., Heinemann, A.W., Miranti, S.V., Schmidt, M., Klinger, E., & Blount, J. (in press). Outcomes of systematic motivational counseling for substance use following traumatic brain injury. *Journal of Addictive Diseases*.

Cropanzano, R., James, K., & Citera, M. (1993). A goal hierarchy model of personality, motivation, and leadership. *Research in Organizational Behavior, 15*, 267–322.

Crown, D.F., & Rosse, J.G. (1995). Yours, mine, and ours: Facilitating group productivity through the integration of individual and group goals. *Organizational Behavior and Human Decision Processes, 64*, 138–150.

Deci, E.L., & Ryan, R.M. (1980). The empirical exploration of intrinsic motivational processes. *Advances in Experimental Social Psychology, 13*, 39–80.

Diener, E. (1984). Subjective well-being. *Psychological Bulletin, 95*, 542–575.

Dweck, C.I. (1986). Motivational processes affecting learning. *American Psychologist, 41*, 1040–1048.

Dweck, C.I., & Leggett, E.L. (1988). A social-cognitive approach to motivation and personality. *Psychological Review, 95*, 256–273.

Emmons, R.A. (1986). Personal strivings: An approach to personality and subjective well-being. *Journal of Personality and Social Psychology, 51*, 1058–1068.

Feldman, D.C. (1976). A contingency theory of socialization. *Administrative Science Quarterly, 21*, 433–452.

Frone, M.R. (2000). Work–family conflict and employee psychiatric disorders: The national comorbidity survey. *Journal of Applied Psychology, 85*, 888–896.

Gomez-Mejia, L.R., Balkin, D.B., & Cardy, R.L. (2001). *Managing human resources* (3rd edn.). Upper Saddle River, NJ: Prentice-Hall.

Greenhaus, J.H. (1987). *Career management*. Hinsdale, IL: The Dryden Press.

Harris, D.M., & DeSimone, R.L. (1994). *Human resource development*. Fort Worth, TX: The Dryden Press.

Higgins, E.T. (1987). Self-discrepancy: A theory relating self and affect. *Psychological Review, 94*, 319–340.

Hom, P.W., & Griffeth, R.W. (1995). *Employee turnover.* Cincinnati, OH: South-Western College Publishing.

Jones, G. (1986). Socialization tactics, self-efficacy, and newcomers' adjustments to organizations. *Academy of Management Journal, 29*, 262–279.

Jussim, L., Soffin, S., Brown, R., Ley, J., & Kohlhepp, K. (1992). Understanding reactions to feedback by integrating ideas from symbolic interactionism and cognitive evaluation theory. *Journal of Personality and Social Psychology, 62*, 402–421.

Kanfer, R. (1990). Motivation theory and industrial/organizational psychology. In M.D. Dunnette & L.M. Hough (Eds.), *Handbook of industrial and organizational psychology* (Vol. 1; pp. 75–170). Palo Alto, CA: Consulting Psychologists Press.

Katzell, R.A. (1964). Personal values, job satisfaction, and job behavior. In H. Borow (Ed.), *Man in a world at work* (pp. 341–361). Boston: Houghton Mifflin.

Klein, H.J., & Weaver, N.A. (2000). The effectiveness of an organizational-level orientation training program in the socialization of new hires. *Personnel Psychology, 53*, 47–66.

Klein, H.J., Wesson, M.J., Hollenbeck, J.R., & Alge, B.J. (1999). Goal commitment and the goal setting process: Conceptual clarification and empirical synthesis. *Journal of Applied Psychology, 84*, 885–896.

Klinger, E. (1975). Consequences of commitment to and disengagement from incentives. *Psychological Review, 82*, 1–25.

Klinger, E. (1977). *Meaning and void: Inner experience and the incentives in people's lives.* Minneapolis: University of Minnesota Press.

Klinger, E., Cox, W.M., & Blount, J.P. (in press). Motivational Structure Questionnaire (MSQ) and Personal Concerns Inventory (PCI). In J.P. Allen & M. Columbus (Eds.), *Assessing alcohol problems: A guide for clinicians and researchers* (2nd edn.). Washington, DC: US Department of Health and Human Services.

Kristoff-Brown, A.L., & Stevens, C.K. (2001). Goal congruence in project teams: Does the fit between members' personal mastery and performance goals matter? *Journal of Applied Psychology, 86*, 1083–1095.

Latham, G.P., Erez, M., & Locke, E.A. (1998). Resolving scientific disputes by the joint design of crucial experiments by the antagonists: Application to the Erez–Latham dispute regarding participation in goal setting. *Journal of Applied Psychology, 73*, 753–772.

Latham, G.P., & Locke, E.A. (1991). Self-regulation through goal setting. *Organizational Behavior and Human Decision Processes, 50*, 212–247.

Locke, E.A. (1976). The nature and causes of job satisfaction. In M.D. Dunnette (Ed.), *Handbook of industrial-organizational psychology* (1st edn.; pp. 1297–1349). Chicago: Rand-McNally.

Locke, E.A., & Latham, G.P. (1990). *A theory of goal setting and task performance.* Englewood Cliffs, NJ: Prentice-Hall.

Locke, E.A., Smith, K.G., Erez, M., Chah, D., & Schaffer, A. (1994). The effects of intra-individual goal conflict on performance. *Journal of Management, 20*, 67–91.

Louis, M.R. (1980). Surprise and sense-making: What newcomers experience in entering unfamiliar organizational settings. *Administrative Science Quarterly, 25*, 226–251.

Maier, G.W., & Brunstein, J.C. (2001). The role of personal work goals in newcomers' job satisfaction and organizational commitment: A longitudinal analysis. *Journal of Applied Psychology, 86*, 1034–1042.

McGill, M.E., & Slocum, J.W. (1995). Executive development in learning organizations. *American Journal of Management Development, 1*, 23–30.

Meyer, J.P., & Allen, N.J. (1997). *Commitment in the workplace: Theory, research, and application.* Thousand Oaks, CA: Sage.

Mitchell, T.R., & Silver, W.S. (1990). Individual and group goals when workers are interdependent: Effects on task strategies and performance. *Journal of Applied Psychology, 75*, 185–193.

Morrison, E.W. (1993). A longitudinal study of newcomer information seeking: Exploring types, modes, sources, and outcomes. *Academy of Management Journal, 36*, 557–589.

Morrison, E.W., & Bies, R.J. (1991). Impression Management in the feedback seeking process: A literature review and research agenda. *Academy of Management Review, 16*, 522–541.

Nicholls, J.G. (1984). Achievement motivation: Conceptions of ability, subjective experience, task choice, and performance. *Psychological Review, 91,* 328–346.

O'Leary-Kelly, A.M., Martocchio, J.J., & Frink, D.D. (1994). A review of the influence of group goals on group performances. *Academy of Management Journal, 37,* 1285–1301.

Orpen, C. (1995). The effect of socialization tactics on career success and satisfaction: A longitudinal study. *Psychological Studies, 40,* 93–96.

Quinn, R.E., Faerman, S.R., Thompson, M.P., & McGrath, M.R. (1996). *Becoming a master manager: A competency framework* (2nd edn.). New York: John Wiley & Sons.

Reichers, A.E. (1986). Conflict and organizational commitments. *Journal of Applied Psychology, 71,* 508–514.

Renn, R.W., & Fedor, D.B. (2001). Development and field test of a feedback seeking, self-efficacy, and goal setting model of work performance. *Journal of Management, 27,* 563–583.

Roberson, L. (1989). Assessing personal work goals in the organizational setting. Development and evaluation of the Work Concerns Inventory. *Organizational Behavior and Human Decision Process, 44,* 345–367.

Roberson, L. (1990). Prediction of job satisfaction from characteristics of personal work goals. *Journal of Organizational Behavior, 11,* 29–41.

Roberson, L., & Alsua, C.J. (2002). Moderating effects of goal orientation on the negative consequences of gender-based preferential selection. *Organizational Behavior and Human Decision Processes, 87,* 103–135.

Roberson, L., Houston, J.M., & Diddams, M. (1989). Identifying valued work outcomes through a content analysis of personal goals. *Journal of Vocational Behavior, 35,* 30–45.

Saks, A.M., & Ashforth, B.E. (1997). Organizational socialization: Making sense of the past and present as a prologue for the future. *Journal of Vocational Behavior, 51,* 234–279.

Senge, P. (1990). *The fifth discipline: The art and practice of the learning organization.* New York: Doubleday.

Steele-Johnson, D., Beauregard, R.S., Hoover, P.B., & Schmidt, A.M. (2000). Goal orientation and task demand effects on motivation, affect, and performance. *Journal of Applied Psychology, 85,* 724–738.

Tomkins, S.S. (1979). Script theory: Differential magnification of affects. In H.E. Howe & M.M. Page (Eds.), *Nebraska Symposium on Motivation* (pp. 201–236). Lincoln, NB: University of Nebraska Press.

Vallerand, R.J. (1997). Toward a hierarchical model of intrinsic and extrinsic motivation. *Advances in Experimental Social Psychology, 29,* 271–360.

Vancouver, J.B., & Schmitt, N.W. (1991). An exploratory examination of person–organization fit: Organizational goal congruence. *Personnel Psychology, 44,* 333–352.

Vandewalle, D. (August, 1999). *Goal orientation comes of age for adults: A literature review.* Paper presented at the annual meeting of the Academy of Management, Chicago.

Vandewalle, D., & Cummings, L.L. (1997). A test of the influence of goal orientation on the feedback-seeking process. *Journal of Applied Psychology, 82,* 390–400.

Van Maanen, J., & Schein, E.H. (1979). Toward a theory of organizational socialization. In B.M. Staw (Ed.), *Research in organizational behavior* (Vol. 1; pp. 209–264). Greenwich, CT: JAI Press.

Wanous, J.P. (1992). *Organizational entry: Recruitment, selection, orientation, and socialization of newcomers* (2nd edn.; pp. 187–235). Reading, MA: Addison-Wesley.

Weick, K.E. (1995). *Sensemaking in organizations.* Thousand Oaks, CA: Sage.

Wofford, J.C., Goodwin, V.L., & Premack, S. (1992). Meta-analysis of the antecedents of personal goal level and of the antecedents and consequences of goal commitment. *Journal of Management, 18,* 595–615.

Wood, R.E., Mento, A.J., & Locke, E.A. (1987). Task complexity as a moderator of goal effects: A meta-analysis. *Journal of Applied Psychology, 72,* 416–425.

Zander, A. (1980). The origins and consequences of group goals. In L. Festinger (Ed.), *Retrospectives on social psychology* (pp. 205–235). New York: Oxford University Press.

CHAPTER 15

Systematic Motivational Counseling in Rehabilitation Settings

S. Vincent Miranti
Schwab Rehabilitation Hospital, Chicago, USA

and

Allen W. Heinemann
Rehabilitation Institute of Chicago, USA

Synopsis.—This chapter describes applications of Systematic Motivational Counseling (SMC; see also Chapters 11–14 and 16, this volume) in rehabilitation settings. Although motivation is an important variable in rehabilitation, few studies have investigated its application to populations with physical disabilities. Motivation can be an asset or barrier in rehabilitation and subsequent community integration. Participants in rehabilitation programs often struggle with ways of finding emotional satisfaction in the face of new physical or cognitive limitations. These struggles can be exacerbated for patients with neurological conditions, such as brain injury, with which motivational deficits can be reactive, neurologically based, or both. SMC techniques are useful in helping rehabilitation participants to identify new sources of satisfaction and clarify goals of therapy. Moreover, the rate of substance abuse is high among certain subgroups of rehabilitation participants; their substance abuse must be addressed to assure success in physical rehabilitation. SMC may be integrated into physical rehabilitation efforts as a means of helping clients to achieve rehabilitation goals as well as develop alternative sources of satisfaction. Brain injury rehabilitation issues are emphasized here due to the richness of the examples and the complexity of the condition.

INTRODUCTION

Bombardier (2000) characterized motivational interviewing as a "Brief Intervention" for problem drinking and reported the adaptation of this intervention to inpatient rehabilitation settings. He cited preliminary results of data obtained from 9 of 12 patients with traumatic brain injury (TBI). Other studies (Stephens, Roffman, & Curtin, 2000) demonstrate the effectiveness of motivational interventions with other drugs such as marijuana. This chapter expands the application of SMC from substance use treatment to various rehabilitation populations. To focus our efforts, this chapter primarily emphasizes use of systematic

Handbook of Motivational Counseling. Edited by W. Miles Cox and Eric Klinger.

motivational counseling with individuals who have sustained brain injury. We begin the chapter by describing the context within which rehabilitation interventions are provided, particularly rehabilitation psychology.

REHABILITATION STRUCTURE

Rehabilitation psychology is a health care specialty focusing on the treatment and care of individuals with disabling conditions (Frank & Elliott, 2000). It was one of the first applied clinical specialties of professional psychology and is undergoing a rapid evolution. Psychologists employed in rehabilitation settings work collaboratively with professionals from multiple disciplines including physiatry, rehabilitation nursing, psychiatry, other medical specialties, physical therapy, occupational therapy, patient advocacy, recreational therapy, art therapy, spiritual counselors, addiction experts, vocational therapists, social workers, case managers, financial experts, and community integration professionals. Rehabilitation psychologists use a wide variety of skills ranging from clinical and counseling interventions, family consultations, group therapies, behavioral technologies, and neuropsychological assessments. These services are provided in a wide variety of settings other than mental health settings.

Medicare's new prospective payment system for inpatient medical rehabilitation introduced new incentives to control costs and may result in reduced services from rehabilitation psychologists. Hagglund, Kewman, and Ashkanazi (2000) describe the Prospective Payment System which limits payment to a lump sum for each admission. The burden for controlling health care costs is left to each facility, thereby having potential impacts on the quality and quantity of services provided to patients. While the system is designed for Medicare-insured patients, Medicare provides coverage for 70% of admissions to rehabilitation hospitals and units; other payers are expected to emulate Medicare's payment system. These changes will impact indirectly individuals in acute care hospitals; skilled nursing facility care; home health care; hospice; and outpatient physical, occupational, and speech therapy programs. With the decreasing lengths of stay over the last decade (now, in our experience, down to as little as three weeks after a moderate to severe brain injury), "success depends on facilitating the development of and participation in integrated health delivery systems" that are "cost-efficient" and "high quality" (pp. 612–613). Rehabilitation psychologists, in particular, with their integrative, multidisciplinary, and "whole person" approaches can play a key role in this evolution.

With sudden-onset neurological disabilities such as TBI, spinal cord injury, and stroke, individuals enter rehabilitation after medical stabilization in an acute hospital setting. They may be referred to an acute inpatient rehabilitation setting if they are able to benefit from three or more hours of therapy daily. They may be referred to a subacute program if unable to endure therapy. Other kinds of nursing homes and extended care facilities provide care for individuals with fewer medical needs. Individuals capable of returning home may receive home health services or outpatient services depending upon their rehabilitation goals and resources. For individuals with a terminal diagnosis, hospice may be the best rehabilitation program. Regardless of the setting, family education is essential. These disabilities typically result in chronic limitations in multiple life functions.

Individuals with chronic disabling conditions may be admitted for an acute hospitalization after an episodic flare-up or exacerbation, development of medical complications such as decubitis ulcers (bed sores), or a slow deterioration in functional status that decreases their abilities to live in their current environment. A number of health and behavioral conditions impact chronic disability and quality of life, including obesity, smoking, high blood pressure, pain, gastrointestinal problems, and Type A coronary behavior. Lifestyle changes can ameliorate and perhaps even reduce the handicapping effects of many conditions. Blanchard (1994) showed that multicomponent psychological interventions using cognitive and behavioral strategies can be effective in health care settings.

Glueckauf (2000) identified several key principles that guide rehabilitation service planning, including; (1) the client remains the center of the process; (2) individual, behavioral and social factors interact to determine outcomes; (3) effective care is research based; and (4) cultural diversity demands a sensitive and informed approach to the problems and challenges presented. Blanchard (2000) also recommends a "stepped care approach relying initially on mass communication and education but backed up by physician advice (and specific treatment)...at the individual level, and finally by intensive, group (and) behavioral interventions" (p. 704). We recommend that rehabilitation systems maintain an "open door" policy that allows individuals to re-enter the system throughout their lives. Cost savings and humanitarian issues are paramount in providing treatment on an as-needed basis. People who incur traumatic brain injury are particularly likely to need and benefit from such an open door policy.

BRAIN INJURY

Each year an estimated 1.5 million people experience TBI; approximately 80 000 individuals experience continuing, significant disability; and there are currently 5.3 million Americans living with a brain-injury-related disability (M.W. Schmidt, pers. com., 2002) Alcohol and other drug (AOD) abuse is a major risk factor for acquired brain injury. Although alcohol is the primary drug associated with acquired brain injury, the use of other drugs, such as benzodiazepines, marijuana, opiates, barbiturates, and amphetamine, has also been linked with acquired brain injury (Boyle, Vella, & Maloney, 1991; Kreutzer et al., 1991). Alcohol use is implicated in 48% of all fatal motor vehicle crashes and upward to 72% of all brain injuries (Kreutzer et al., 1990, 1991; Sparadeo, Strauss, & Barth, 1990). Moreover, alcohol abusers are more likely to be involved in repeat motor vehicle crashes (McLellan et al., 1993) and other traumatic, injury-producing events such as falls.

The connection between AOD abuse and the occurrence of TBI is well established. Corrigan, Rust, and Lamb-Hart (1995b) noted that approximately two-thirds of patients admitted to brain injury rehabilitation programs have a history of AOD abuse that can be described as abusive. Among a sample of people interviewed one year after discharge from inpatient rehabilitation for brain injury, at least one-half reported resumption of alcohol use (Schmidt & Garvin, 1994). Kreutzer and colleagues (1996) reported that alcohol use patterns often return to pre-injury levels by two years after injury.

A history of AOD abuse has been associated with deterioration of functioning after brain injury (Dunlop et al., 1991). This finding may be explained by a number of factors. For example, intoxication may interact with the neurological consequences of brain injury to exacerbate the cognitive and motor impairments (Kreutzer et al., 1991). People with a history of AOD abuse, especially chronic abuse, may have fewer financial, social, and medical resources to facilitate continued recovery. In addition, the use of substances following acquired brain injury is potentially dangerous when combined with prescription medications and may increase the likelihood of seizures (Murray, 1987). Resumption of substance use following brain injury is associated with continued significant cognitive deficits (Parsons, 1987). Other negative sequelae of substance use after brain injury include increased balance problems, depression, and increased suicide risk (as cited by Langley & Kiley, 1992).

Interestingly, some symptoms and behaviors are shared by people who have brain injury and people whose primary disability is substance abuse. These symptoms include short-term memory loss, slowed thinking, diminished judgment, and poor attention. Impulsivity, emotional dysregulation, depression, fatigue, decreased tolerance for frustration, personality changes, and sleep problems may also be present. Last, difficulty with balance and coordination may be seen. Substance-abuse counselors often may help clients manage these limitations without problem and view this as another way of individualizing treatment for the greatest success.

Several cognitive and behavioral problems are unique to brain injury. These problems include word-finding difficulties, trouble tracking conversations, especially group conversations, difficulty initiating meaningful activity, sequencing difficulties, limited insight, and difficulty generalizing from one situation to another. People with brain injury may also have a number of motor problems, from poor balance to hemiplegia to gait problems. Some people with brain injury have tremendous difficulty with abstract thinking and have a concrete understanding of metaphors. These cognitive and motor problems, particularly decreased initiation, difficulty generalizing, and decreased insight, may prevent a person with brain injury from meaningful or successful participation in existing, nonadapted substance abuse programs (Corrigan, Lamb-Hart, & Rust, 1995a).

Prigatano (1992) observed that "injury to the brain obviously changes the biological state of the organism and can, consequently, produce temporary and permanent changes in emotional and motivational responses" (p. 360). He classifies 25 affective disturbances that might impair motivation after brain injury as active or passive. "Active" disturbances include: irritability, agitation, anger, paranoia, manic-like states, over-reactivity to noise or stress, unexpected acts of violence, anxiety, emotional lability, and inappropriate social responses. Passive disturbances include: depression, fatigue, lack of initiation or desire, lack of goals, sluggishness, loss of interest in the environment, lack of spontaneity, and child-like behavior. To illustrate the frequency of these problems, he cites research documenting: (1) prevalence of irritability ranging from 39 to 71%; (2) frequency of head injury history in populations being treated for episodic and violent behavior, including 35% with uncontrollable rage and recurrent physical attacks and 61% of cases referred for marital violence; (3) estimated prevalence of emotional lability at 63%; (4) 63% incidence of clinical depression; and (5) estimates of "aspontaneity ranging up to 100%." All of these disturbances impair individuals' abilities to function; derive satisfaction in daily life; set, prioritize, and achieve goals; and survive changing environments or complex interpersonal interactions. As an example, he points out that both dyscontrol, depression, and amotivational problems are all major factors in impairing independence and return to work. These problems impair patient participation and ability to benefit from rehabilitation services.

Prigatano (1992) illustrates the difficulty of identifying behavioral or reactionary components as well as the neurological and neurochemical substrates involved in these motivational disturbances. He points out that individuals' emotional responses may be in reaction to lost coping or cognitive skills, organic, or an interaction of these factors. Patients may grieve the loss of prior accomplishments, status, and lifestyle. He notes, "When patients are unable to cope with environmental demands that they previously could have handled with ease . . . they have a difficult time thinking through a solution . . . and may become overwhelmed emotionally" (p. 367). In evaluating the various contributions of organicity and environmental or reactive responses, he points out that given the "static nature" of TBI deficits, persistent problems probably reflect neuropathological deficits, and worsening problems probably "reflect a complicated interaction between neuropathologically mediated affective disturbances and the patients' reactions to environmental factors" (p. 366). Again, he states that "angry TBI patients are unable to sustain employment," TBI patients with aspontaneity "do not look for jobs or are unwilling to actively engage in rehabilitation," and "TBI patients with impaired self- or social awareness recognize neither the need for rehabilitation nor their social impact on others" (p. 366).

Six years after Prigatano's review article, Al-Adawi, Powell, and Greenwood (1998) discussed the impact of motivational deficits on specialized rehabilitation training and on poor psychosocial outcomes. Based on multiple empirical studies, they suggest that damage to the frontal lobes, various dopaminergic pathways, and prefrontal lesions may all contribute to dysfunctional motivation. They point out that deficits can be exhibited both as failure to respond appropriately to incentives or excessive passivity with low levels of participation in therapy. They developed the Card-Arranging Reward Responsivity Objective Test (CARROT) and the Percent Participation Index (PPI). These are relatively simple measures, with the CARROT measuring response speed and psychomotor speed in rewarded and nonrewarded conditions and the PPI estimating the actual percentage of time in which therapists judged patient participation to be above a minimal necessary level. In a study with 54 patients diagnosed with TBI or nonfocal vascular injury and assessed on multiple measures, they found poor motivation associated with impaired reward responsivity and frontal lobe deficits. Low PPI scores were associated both with poor motivation and impairments in frontal lobe tasks such as the Wisconsin Card Sort Test and the Oral Word Test. A factor they called Initiation-Motivation accounted for 63% of the variance in PPI. They conclude, "the assessment techniques developed here for assessing clinical motivation (PPI) and reward responsivity (the CARROT) have both individually shown psychometric properties that suggest that they have promise as tools for use in future motivational research with clinical and nonclinical populations" (p. 121).

The major goal in rehabilitation is improvement in impairment, activity level, and community participation. While reliable measurement is necessary to demonstrate improvement, the priority is different. It is incumbent upon rehabilitation professionals to demonstrate effective therapy techniques and strategies.

McGlynn (1990) reviewed several studies with brain-injured populations to illustrate that behavioral interventions are effective. She cited studies demonstrating reduced aggressiveness, improved cognitive performances (including memory), reduced inappropriate and impulsive behaviors, anger and frustration management, awareness of deficits, and self-instructional training for attention. Specifically with motivational deficits, she cited data demonstrating that participation and benefit from participation could be increased, including not just brain-injured or stroke patients but also demented patients. Typically these studies were with individual patients and use strategies that included emphasis on consequences of the behavior, shaping, fading, behavioral rehearsal, practice, and "time out." While some of the cited studies were reported in terms of self-monitoring and self-reinforcement, a few emphasized a more "metacognitive" approach to rehabilitation. Ylvisaker and Szekeres (1989) recommended "training in goal setting, self-monitoring and self-evaluation" in a "self-discovery" approach emphasizing "natural consequences . . . in a relevant context" for "*mildly impaired adults with high premorbid levels of functioning*" (p. 428) (emphasis added). Especially with regard to incentive motivation, rewards, goal-setting, self-monitoring, self-evaluation, and self-reinforcement, these studies highlight the import of motivational interventions and strategies with neurologically impaired populations.

In a federally funded demonstration project, the authors of this chapter demonstrated at least a limited effectiveness of SMC with a brain-injured population (Cox et al., in press). Participants receiving SMC were compared with a group receiving usual care and were evaluated on a number of cognitive and personality measures, including the Motivational Structure Questionnaire (MSQ; see Chapters 8–10, this volume). Assessments were scheduled prior to intervention, immediately after intervention, and at a follow-up 6 to 18 months after the intervention. Significant effects were demonstrated on the MSQ including a reduction in the number of concerns and a change from passive to active means of addressing concerns. In addition, self-report of drug/alcohol use declined immediately after intervention but the effect dissipated at follow-up. While the quasi-experimental nature of the design limits generalizability of results, the results are encouraging. The limited number of sessions (12) in the treatment protocol prevented us from estimating the number of sessions that would be needed for optimal improvement (consistent with McGlynn, 1990).

ROLE OF MOTIVATIONAL INTERVENTIONS DURING REHABILITATION

Motivational interventions initially were applied among people seeking to change maladaptive behavior patterns, such as problematic alcohol use. Such interventions are client-centered counseling techniques for eliciting behavior change by helping clients to find emotional satisfaction in a positive manner. Motivational interventions arise from a philosophical stance that holds that the motivation to change is elicited from the client, and not imposed from without (Miller & Rollnick, 1995). SMC specifically targets clients' motivation for recovery (Cox & Klinger, 1988). SMC helps to identify and mobilize clients' intrinsic values and goals to stimulate behavior change. Motivational interventions seek to shift the satisfaction the person expects to find by using alcohol to nonchemical sources by increasing the probability of entering, continuing, and complying with an active change strategy (Miller, 1985).

Although initially designed to facilitate recovery from alcohol abuse, SMC can be adapted for use with people recovering from new-onset disability in physical rehabilitation. Instead of targeting substance use as the behavior to change, motivational interventions can facilitate engagement in physical rehabilitation itself. Diminished motivation for, and participation in, physical rehabilitation are common reactions to sudden disabling conditions. Frequently people feel as if "my life is over" or "I will never get any better." Such beliefs are major barriers to successful rehabilitation. Often, the person who feels "life is over" sees no point in "doing rehab." This unwillingness to participate in treatment, or the change process itself, is similar to the lack of motivation that accounts for treatment failures among substance abusers. Adaptations to SMC can be used to help clients to shift the balance between "staying the same" or adapting to changes in physical or cognitive functioning.

The philosophy of motivational counseling (i.e., motivation for change must come from within the client) is shared by physical rehabilitation. Both fields view individuals' experiences, personality characteristics, and sociocultural factors as influencing present circumstances. For example, one person may have social support for change, another may not. Another person may feel comfortable trusting authority; another may resist directives from anyone other than family. The decision to engage in the often challenging process of making positive adaptations to disability can be influenced by positive and negative affective incentives in other life areas. Such affects can influence the beliefs and thoughts about the expected outcome of rehabilitation. For example, if someone believes that a romantic partner may leave if he "becomes a disabled person," he may resist therapy to avoid "becoming disabled" but instead try to "still be me."

Participation in physical rehabilitation occurs when the factors that contribute to the decision to participate outweigh the factors that contribute to the decision not to participate. Physical rehabilitation often is a challenging process. To persist in their efforts, people need to learn about the expected benefits and positive outcomes of participating in rehabilitation. They often need help to identify "why" they want to recover. Adaptations to SMC can be useful in this process. Systematic motivational approaches can help people to identify incentives, understand their thoughts, beliefs, and perceptions about their condition, delineate expected benefits, and identify goals for their recovery. By keeping this adapted motivational model of change in mind, the counselor can shape questions and focus interventions to help patients to formulate goals for recovery.

A critical modification of standard rehabilitation practice that must be implemented for motivational counseling is to address the attitudes of therapists and other rehabilitation staff. Instead of evaluating, judging, diagnosing, and then prescribing, the staff must adopt an attitude of understanding, caring, and believing that the patient, rather than the staff, may best be able to identify goals. Despite our best intentions to have physical rehabilitation be a "client-centered" endeavor, many in the rehabilitation field tend to believe they know what is best for a patient.

Basic motivational principles can be applied equally well to counseling in the physical rehabilitation setting. One of the first principles involves empathy, or a way to see the world through the patient's eyes. When patients feel understood, they are better able to share their feelings and experiences. Another basic principle in motivational counseling is to avoid arguing. "Persuasion is gentle, subtle, always with the assumption that change is up to the client (Miller et al., 1992, p. 7). Self-efficacy should be supported. One way to help bolster patients' belief that they are capable of change is to inquire about other healthy changes or successful coping episodes and highlight the skills the person has demonstrated. Last, motivational counselors develop discrepancies. "Motivation for change occurs when people perceive a discrepancy between where they are and where they want to be" (Miller et al., 1992, p. 9). When rehabilitation patients realize that their current coping efforts are not helping them to achieve therapy goals, they may become more determined to make important life changes and follow recommended modifications to achieve independent functioning.

As with any therapeutic endeavor, the counselor who intends to use a variant of SMC in the physical rehabilitation setting spends some time initially getting to know the patient and establishing a rapport and a therapeutic bond. The counselor also sets the stage for the application of motivational counseling. Because SMC requires the use of the MSQ to begin treatment, the adaptations presented here do not meet the criteria of "Systematic Motivational Counseling." However, an adaptation to the MSQ can be used to set goals, identify patients' role in goal-strivings, and determine commitment to particular goals. It is also helpful to assess whether clients anticipate joy, unhappiness, or sorrow if they are or are not successful in reaching their goals. It is also important to evaluate whether expectations of success are realistic. This task is especially relevant in work with people with new brain injury or spinal cord injury. Often, a person's physical condition may preclude goals such as walking or returning to work. In circumstances such as these, the construction of goal ladders with short-term and intermediate goals can be helpful in maintaining motivation to engage in rehabilitation.

GROUP INTERVENTIONS

Group psychotherapy is more effective than placebos, no treatment, some "nonspecific treatments," and some well-known psychological interventions (Bednar & Kaul, 1994). Indeed, in a meta-analysis of individual vs. group psychotherapy effectiveness, McRoberts, Burlingame, and Hoag (1998) argue that the individual and group formats are equally effective although a lack of current research limited their conclusions in terms of curative processes, populations and settings of interest, and targets of behavioral change. For greater elaboration the reader is also referred to reviews by Orlinsky and Howard (1986) and Sternbarger and Budman (1996), as well as multiple others cited in Bednar and Kaul (1994).

Two recent studies are relevant to the use of group therapies in rehabilitation with neurocognitively impaired patients (Miranti, Hantsch, & Pick, 2002; Miranti et al., 2002). Both studies used retrospectively collected data for quality improvement and billing purposes. The primary measures were the change in functional status as measured by the Functional Independence Measure (FIM) instrument and the number of group or psychological interventions conducted during inpatient rehabilitation. The FIM measures motor and cognitive function with a rating scale that ranges from dependent to independent task performance (see the review by Heinemann, 2000). We reported a positive and significant correlation between the number of group sessions and FIM gains for participants on the brain injury unit ($r = .35$, $p < .001$, $n = 275$) but only a similar trend for participants on the stroke unit ($r = .09$ and $p < .10$). Participants on the stroke unit may have had less access to the groups, which had originally been designed for the brain injury population and were located on a different floor of the hospital. On both the TBI and the stroke units, the correlations between FIM gains and the total number of psychology sessions were significant ($r = .33$, $p < 001$, $n = 239$ and $r = .22$, $p < .001$, $n = 403$, respectively).

Quasi-experimental strategies (Campbell & Stanley, 1968) were used to examine the effects of cognitive interventions, specifically a reality orientation group for low-level patients and a cognitive stimulation group for patients demonstrating specific deficits but consistent orientation. Patients admitted in 2000 and 2001 to the brain injury and stroke units at Schwab Rehabilitation Hospital, an inner-city rehabilitation facility, were randomly selected. Retrieved were data from the quality improvement and billing data sets, including specific group therapies (reality orientation, cognitive stimulation, stroke, brain injury, and pain management) attended separately, combined total for all psychology sessions conducted, age, length of stay, and FIM scores (admission, discharge, and change). Of the 143 randomly selected cases, subjects were categorized into three groups based on the number of group sessions they attended. Group 1 cases did not attend any reality orientation or cognitive stimulation groups; Group 2 cases attended one to five sessions total of either or both groups; Group 3 cases attended six or more sessions. The number of reality orientation and cognitive stimulation group sessions attended ranged from none to 13. The hypothesis that greater FIM change would be associated with more group attendance was supported in a one-way analysis of variance. Results of an analysis of covariance demonstrated significant group effects ($p = .04$, with no interactions) while holding constant the year of treatment, length of stay, pain management session, total of all psychology sessions, and total attendance in all adjustment or cognitive groups. While the authors were unable to test hypotheses about mechanisms of change, the results suggest that multiple factors were responsible, including motivation, group cohesion, acceptance and belonging, respect, goal-setting, decision-making, and learning. The groups emphasized neurocognitive change, an area of group intervention apparently absent from the literature.

These studies are included here for several reasons. First, there is the pressing need for more cost-effective and efficient treatment methods, whereas there are few studies examining appropriate outcome and process variables (McRoberts et al., 1998). Second, the TBI literature emphasizes potentials and humanistic concerns (cf., Pepping, 1998). Third, these studies demonstrate change on a measurement tool that is ecologically valid and not primarily focused on traditional mental health variables. Fourth, data include both adjustment (a more traditional psychological variable) and cognition (an area still in need of experimental validation with this population). But—perhaps most importantly, in discussions with these researchers—motivation to attend and participate are assumed to impact the patient's ability to learn and benefit from the relatively expensive rehabilitation experience.

MILIEU INTERVENTIONS

Staff at the Rusk Institute of Rehabilitation Medicine (see Ben-Yishay et al., 1980; Rattok et al., 1992) have developed a rehabilitation model that integrates rehabilitation therapies with psychological interventions in a "milieu" setting for persons with TBI. Rattok and associates demonstrated the effectiveness of "multimodal" interventions on cognitive variables, functional outcomes in daily life, and inter- and intrapersonal variables. They make a cogent argument for treatment of the whole person using a balanced approach. The impact of motivational interventions was not assessed.

Although perhaps not the original intent, Dunn's (2000) review illustrates that rehabilitation activities across settings can be viewed as a "milieu." She states,

> (B)ehavior is seen through a rehabilitative lens . . . (F)actors are evaluated on the basis of their potential to promote the assessment, amelioration and treatment of chronic . . . disorders. Whether disabilities are acquired, induced by trauma, or developmental in origin, some of the same personal and situational factors . . . come into play. (With) the bulk of research (and intervention) . . . directed toward reducing societal (and personal) barriers preventing people from achieving life goals, often creating an amalgam of knowledge from psychology, medicine, physical therapy and education, in the process. (Dunn, 2000, p. 566).

Clearly, the disciplines within rehabilitation and the practices within each discipline are not independent. Gait and balance activities in physical therapy should have reciprocal effects on occupational therapy activities involving the upper extremities and ability to transfer safely to a bed, chair, or toilet. Language therapies should have reciprocal effects with cognitive and self-instructional training, including mood or affect, in psychology. Medications might facilitate some functions through specific mechanisms such as reduction of spasticity or infectious or metabolic dysfunctions, or they might inhibit others including attention, balance, and strength, all of which would impact rehabilitation outcome. Nursing care, hygiene, adequate rest, recreation, and diet might impact any intervention across all disciplines. Family, friends, and other support from the involvement and cooperation of the community have been repeatedly shown to impact rehabilitation outcome (see Chwalisz & Vaux, 2000). Finally, although many recent studies emphasize social psychological models, it is possible to approach these interventions with models that include neurorehabilitation, neuropsychology, and motivation principles. The roles of rehabilitation psychologists are diverse.

SMC AND REHABILITATION INTERACTION

The accreditation standards for rehabilitation promulgated by the Rehabilitation Accreditation Commission (CARF, 2002) and the Joint Commission for the Accreditation of Healthcare Organizations (JCAHO, 2002) are quite congruent with the multicomponent counseling that comprises SMC (Cox & Klinger, 1988). The person served is central to program planning and implementation. The consumer begins the process with an expression of needs and statement of goals. Therapists work with consumers to develop goals into hierarchical steps with realistic timeframes. Therapists may restructure goals to point out and resolve goal conflicts and define priorities that are achievable in the available time. They place emphasis on individual responsibility and decision-making, and promote lifestyle changes in order to maintain community involvement. When necessary, consumers are encouraged to assume a more active role in their care, decisions, and ultimately their lives. Environmental and personal barriers (e.g., inaccessible communities, social acceptance, depression, fear, and anxiety) are countered. Consistent with the rehabilitation standards, psychologists using SMC can emphasize emotional satisfaction and positive goals to minimize negative goals and sources of frustration. Issues of identity, self-confidence, and self-esteem are involved. However, from a therapist and therapy efficacy perspective, four of the most gratifying similarities are the provision of respectful, empathic, supportive, and nonjudgmental conditions in treatment. There is a "good fit" between SMC and rehabilitation.

Other adaptations are necessary for individuals incurring brain injury. One of the most helpful modifications of technique and practice is to assume an active, involved stance. Psychological work may involve greater and more frequent between-session efforts to cue homework and follow-through. For example, during the research demonstration of SMC, we found that we needed to make telephone calls to patients between sessions and remind them of homework expectations. During sessions, it was helpful to cue them when to take notes. Occasionally, we allowed clients to make an audiotape for later review. A multidisciplinary approach is also needed. With the client's consent, one should make contact with rehabilitation providers, therapists, or physicians. One should consult with clinicians to tailor sessions to the client's learning style. For example, a neuropsychologist suggested that one patient could remember better by pairing new information with old information whereas another patient benefited more from having new information written down. For best results, it is important to individualize each program as necessary.

Some general pointers for working with people with cognitive limitations include:

- working at the clients' pace
- checking frequently for understanding
- decreasing the number of topics included in a session
- increasing the number of sessions provided
- breaking goals into smaller objectives
- keeping instructions brief and clear
- reducing the tempo in sessions
- giving clients extra time or individual attention
- simplifying language and avoiding metaphors or analogies
- repeating information using short, simple phrases
- encouraging note-taking or providing printed notes
- anticipating a higher frequency of off-topic remarks
- redirecting clients when they go off topic, talk excessively, or behave inappropriately
- requesting feedback frequently—asking questions that verify understanding
- gently correcting or restating misunderstood points, and
- summarizing ideas and points throughout the session.

Clients with brain injury need to know that the provider is sensitive to their cognitive difficulties and is willing to tailor the process. Providers should ask directly, "What would help?"

With these provisos in mind, let us turn to the application of SMC among people with brain injury. The next section reviews specific issues.

SMC FOR PEOPLE WITH BRAIN INJURY

In view of the extensive introduction to SMC in previous chapters of this volume (especially Chapter 11), this section provides only a brief summary and focuses instead on adapting SMC in the rehabilitation setting. Miranti, Cox, Klinger, and colleagues adapted this technique for use with people with brain injury as part of a federally funded demonstration project coordinated by Heinemann and colleagues (1995). They found that SMC techniques could be used successfully with people with brain injury by focusing jointly on individuals' motivation for recovery from brain injury and substance abuse.

SMC operationalizes Cox and Klinger's (1988; Chapter 7, this volume) motivational model of substance use. The following definitions of basic motivational principles (see also Klinger & Cox, Chapter 1, this volume) will facilitate understanding of this model. First, *affect* is the experiential or psychological component of an emotional response. Motivational theorists think of affect as being either positive or negative. Positive affect means pleasurable engagement with the environment whereas negative affect is unpleasurable. *Affective change* is a change in affect from its present state, and most people are motivated to change negative affect to positive affect. Substances often are used to achieve affective change. An *incentive* is any object or event that a person expects will bring about an affective change. Incentives can be positive (things the person wants to obtain) or negative (things the person wishes to avoid). Every goal is an incentive, but not every incentive is a goal. For example, a woman with brain injury might expect that having a million dollars would increase her positive affect, but will not be committed to having a million dollars because that may be unachievable. A *current concern* is a person's motivational state between the time a decision is made to pursue an incentive and the time the goal is reached or relinquished. During this time, people appear vigilant to cues that have an impact on obtaining their goals. Many current concerns may be operative at the same time.

For people with brain injury, self-concept is often a primary concern. Frequently, patients focus on differences between the "old (pre-injury) self" and the "new self" (i.e., handicapped, impaired, broken, incomplete, or "less than human"). Concerns focus on reclaiming or resurrecting the old self, creating a new but acceptable self, or finding ways to cope with the injured self. A goal of therapy linked to this concern may include seeing one's self as a "whole" even if "imperfect" person. Concrete reminders that prior life experiences offer possibilities for future coping are often helpful.

This motivational model illuminates the principles by which substances or other nonchemical events can be incentives. For people with brain injury, they are often motivated to pursue nonchemical incentives such as clarifying self-concept, for example, to improve positive mood or avoid negative affect. The relative balance between chemical and nonchemical incentives is a critical determinant of the motivation to use alcohol. SMC operates on the idea that it is possible to empower people to increase their nonchemical sources of emotional satisfaction that are incompatible with substance use, thereby shifting the balance in favor of decisions not to use. For example, a person with brain injury may want to improve cognitive skills so that he or she can feel more like the "old self." Learning that substance use can decrease cognitive functioning and limit neurological recovery may be a sufficient incentive to avoid chemical use.

GETTING STARTED

The therapist who intends to use SMC will spend some time initially becoming acquainted with the client, establishing rapport, and beginning to establish a therapeutic bond. For clients with brain injuries, this process may be slower than with persons without cognitive impairments. The therapist also introduces SMC by explaining its rationale and eliciting the client's reactions to determine if he or she wants to proceed. Assuming that there is a desire to go forward, the therapist then begins to understand the client's motivations for substance use and how this relates to other life areas. Some areas to be explored include the circumstances surrounding the beginning of counseling, the person's history of substance use, the client's view of the problem, and his or her goals for counseling.

SMC is initiated by assessing people's motivational patterns through the use of the MSQ (Cox & Klinger, Chapter 8, this volume; Klinger, Cox, & Blount, in press). Beyond that, the SMC technique is an individualized one that does not use a session-by-session agenda that is identical for all clients. Although certain components are used with all clients, others may or may not be used with specific clients, depending on their motivational characteristics.

Preliminary counseling components include reviewing the individual's MSQ to review goals and analyzing the interrelationships among goals. Goal-setting is the next component, and treatment goals are established. Goal ladders, with short-term, session-to-session subgoals designed to achieve major long-term goals, are constructed. Subsequent sessions focus on improving the client's ability to meet goals and resolving the conflicts among goals. There is also a focus on empowering clients to disengage from inappropriate goals and identifying new incentives.

In SMC, the therapist works with the client to achieve positive goals rather than to avoid negative goals, as an appetitive lifestyle is psychologically more satisfying (see Klinger & Cox, Chapter 1, this volume). For some clients, this may be accomplished by cognitive reframing to help them focus on positive aspects of their goals. In other cases, more success might be gained by helping clients reduce the number of negative concerns in their lives. Associated with this is an effort to help people re-examine their sources of self-esteem. Low self-esteem is a pervasive problem for people with substance abuse as well as people with brain injury. Some people tend to hold high standards for themselves and are unduly harsh on themselves when they are unable to achieve high standards (Klinger, 1997). This may be especially true for people with brain injury who cling to the image of themselves before the injury, and who, because of neurocognitive and motor impairments, are no longer able to perform activities that they once did with ease. Dissatisfaction with current achievements because they are not commensurate with previous achievements is often seen among people with brain injury who continue to abuse substances and presents a major barrier to adjustment. Thus, counselors try to help clients to find new ways of affirming themselves, to become less self-condemning, and to develop self-forgiveness for goals they have not attained.

Field evaluation of this model with people with brain injury (Cox et al., in press) showed that approximately 20% of people became abstinent and 41% maintained abstinence during treatment. Participants showed significantly fewer concerns and greater movement toward an appetitive lifestyle than did a no-treatment control group. Early sessions relied heavily on reviewing the MSQ, discussing the profile, and setting treatment goals. The most frequently used counseling components were re-examining sources of self-esteem and constructing goal ladders. It was particularly difficult to encourage disengagement from goals related to "complete recovery," but this was often accomplished by shifting the focus of sessions to the "here and now" in asking participants to identify and build on current successes.

PRIMARY ADAPTATIONS OF SMC TO THE REHABILITATION SETTING

Two primary categories of adaptations of SMC were implemented. The first category involved the role and activity of the therapists in SMC implementation. The second category involved adaptations to address cognitive changes. We discuss each category and provide examples for illustration.

In general, the emphasis of SMC is on the preliminary or core counseling components. However, with the brain injury participants that we served, we found that we needed to emphasize the "Subsequent Counseling Components," including (1) improving the ability to meet goals, (2) identifying new incentives, (3) shifting from an aversive to appetitive lifestyle, and (4) re-examining sources of self-esteem. For example, we found it helpful to help people focus on their refusal to "give up on the old self" and instead focus on current sources of esteem.

We found it useful to provide an empathic, respectful, nonjudgmental, and positive therapeutic relationship. People with brain injury frequently experience rehabilitation as devaluing—most of their therapies focus on remediating deficits. In addition, people with brain injury feel socially isolated from their peer groups. One participant compared his experience of brain injury to being "stuck on an island by myself while everyone else is floating away on the river." In addition to the cognitive adaptations made, we found it useful to emphasize the need to find positive satisfaction in life and to adopt a constructive, involved lifestyle rather than a passive, avoidant style.

The clinicians implementing SMC focused on producing change that was not necessarily centered on substance use. Motivation for recovery from brain injury was an equally important target. Motivation to change is enhanced by addressing the person's expectations of emotional change, satisfaction, goal attainment, and probability of success and failure. We were able, in turn, to influence the decision of whether or not to use substances. We learned that it was equally valuable to target the motivation to recover from brain injury, that is, the decision of whether or not to improve, as a means of reducing substance use. For many people with brain injury, a sense of hopelessness and powerlessness pervades these decisions. In these cases, it was important that the therapist facilitate a success experience that could compete with the previous satisfaction derived from using substances. For example, the therapist might facilitate the person's effective problem-solving in other areas to encourage feelings of empowerment that might carry over into motivation to change substance use. Thus, the person who feels powerless to effect any change may be supported in obtaining reliable transportation to and from sessions as a means to increase concrete success and feelings of efficacy, with the expectation that this feeling may improve other efforts for change. Last, given their cognitive difficulties, people with brain injuries have trouble generalizing information learned in counseling to their everyday lives. It is vital that rehabilitation providers and family members actively reinforce and support clients to follow through on new routines and behaviors.

SUMMARY AND FUTURE DIRECTIONS

In this chapter, we identified ways that SMC can be integrated into rehabilitation practice. The complexity of rehabilitation services was illustrated by describing issues involving settings, populations, disciplines, financing, social and developmental or life span issues. We focused on individuals with brain injury to demonstrate the multi- and interdisciplinary concerns in a diverse population, and the multifocal concerns and multiple levels at which issues can be addressed. We advocate an integrated approach that emphasizes a problem-solving focus. We emphasized assisting patients to take active roles in their lives, to regain or maintain independence, and to pursue satisfactions including health and well-being. We emphasized that, no matter what the suspected problem or how severe the behavior, motivation and personal choice are central mechanisms in behavior change. We described how SMC can be adapted to address life adjustment issues using group interventions and milieu programs. We view therapists in general, and psychologists in particular, as change agents. We point out the correspondence of SMC with the standards set forth by the major accreditation organizations in rehabilitation. It should be clear that motivational principles can help therapists ally themselves with clients and promote favorable life changes. Nobody, neither patient nor therapist, has to be powerless in the face of adversities or challenges posed by a disability.

REFERENCES

Al-Adawi, S., Powell, J., & Greenwood, R. (1998). Motivational deficits after brain injury: A neuropsychological approach using new assessment techniques. *Neuropsychology, 12* (1), 115–124.

Bednar, R., & Kaul, T. (1994). Experiential group research: Can the canon fire? In A.E. Bergen & S.L. Garfield (Eds.), *Handbook of psychotherapy and behavior change* (pp. 631–663). New York: John Wiley & Sons.

Ben-Yishay, Y., Lakin, P., Ross, B., Rattok, J., Cohen, J., & Diller, L. (1980). Developing a core "curriculum" for group exercises designated for head trauma patients who are undergoing rehabilitation. In Y. Ben-Yishay (Ed.), *Working approaches to remediation of cognitive deficits in brain damaged persons* (Rehabilitation Monograph, 61; pp. 175–235). New York: New York University Medical Center.

Blanchard, E.B. (1994). Behavioral medicine and health psychology. In A.E. Bergen & S.L. Garfield (Eds.), *Handbook of psychotherapy and behavior change* (pp. 701–733), New York: John Wiley & Sons.

Bombardier, C.H. (2000). Alcohol and traumatic disability. In R.G. Frank & T.R. Elliott (Eds.), *Handbook of rehabilitation psychology* (pp. 399–416). Washington, DC: American Psychological Association.

Boyle, M.J., Vella, L., & Maloney, E. (1991). Role of drugs and alcohol in patients with head injury. *Journal of the Royal Society of Medicine, 84*, 608–610.

Campbell, D.T., & Stanley, J.C. (1968). *Experimental and quasi-experimental designs for research.* Chicago, IL: Rand McNally.

CARF . . . The Rehabilitation Accreditation Commission (2002). CARF standards manual: Medical rehabilitation (July 2002–June 2003). Tucson, AZ: CARF.

Chwalisz, K., & Vaux, A. (2000). Social support and adjustment to disability. In R.G. Frank & T.R. Elliott (Eds.), *Handbook of rehabilitation psychology* (pp. 537–552). Washington, DC: American Psychological Association.

Corrigan, J.D., Lamb-Hart, G.L., & Rust, E. (1995a). A programme of intervention for substance abuse following traumatic brain injury. *Brain Injury, 9*, 221–236.

Corrigan, J.D., Rust, E., & Lamb-Hart, G.L. (1995b). The nature and extent of substance abuse problems in persons with traumatic brain injury. *Journal of Head Trauma Rehabilitation, 10*, 29–46.

Cox W.M., Heinemann, A.W., Miranti, S.V., Schmidt, M., Klinger, E., & Blount, J. (in press). Outcomes of systematic motivational counseling for substance use following traumatic brain injury. *Journal of Addictive Diseases.*

Cox, W.M., & Klinger, E. (1988). A motivational model of alcohol use. *Journal of Abnormal Psychology, 97* (2), 168–180.

Dunlop, T.W., Udvahelyi, G.B., Stedem, A.F., & O'Connor, J.M. (1991). Comparison of patients with and without emotional/behavioral deterioration during the first year after traumatic brain injury. *Journal of Neuropsychiatry, 3*, 150–156.

Dunn, D.S. (2000). Social psychological issues in disability. In R.G. Frank & T.R. Elliott (Eds.), *Handbook of rehabilitation psychology* (pp. 565–584). Washington, DC: American Psychological Association.

Frank, R.G., & Elliott, T.R. (2000). Rehabilitation psychology: Hope for a psychology of chronic conditions. In R.G. Frank & T.R. Elliott (Eds.), *Handbook of rehabilitation psychology* (pp. 3–9). Washington, DC: American Psychological Association.

Gauggel, S., Wietasch, A., Bayer, C., & Rolko, C. (2000). The impact of positive and negative feedback on reaction time in brain-damaged patients. *Neuropsychology, 14* (1), 125–133.

Glueckauf, R.L. (2000). Doctoral education in rehabilitation and health care psychology: Principles and strategies for unifying subspecialty training. In R.G. Frank & T.R. Elliott (Eds.), *Handbook of rehabilitation psychology* (pp. 615–628). Washington, DC: American Psychological Association.

Haglund, K.J., Kewman, D.G., & Ashkanazi, G.S. (2000). Medicare and prospective payment systems. In R.G. Frank & T.R. Elliott (Eds.), *Handbook of rehabilitation psychology* (pp. 603–612). Washington, DC: American Psychological Association.

Heinemann, A.W. (2000). Functional status and quality-of-life measures. In R.G. Frank & T.R. Elliott (Eds.), *Handbook of rehabilitation psychology* (pp. 261–286). Washington, DC: American Psychological Association.

Heinemann, A.W., Cox, M., Schmidt, M., Langley, M., & Miranti, V. (1995). *Final report: Substance abuse as a barrier to employment for persons with traumatic brain injury.* Demonstration project funded by the National Institute on Disability and Rehabilitation Research.

JCAHO (2002). *Hospital accreditation standards: Accreditation policies standards intent statements.* Oakbrook Terrace, IL: Joint Commission on Accreditation of Healthcare Organizations.

Klinger, E. (1997). *Meaning and void: Inner experience and the incentives in people's lives.* Minneapolis: University of Minnesota Press.

Klinger, E., Cox, W.M., & Blount, J.P. (in press). Motivational Structure Questionnaire (MSQ) and Personal Concerns Inventory (PCI). In J.P. Allen & M. Columbus (Eds.), *Assessing alcohol problems: A guide for clinicians and researchers* (2nd edn.). Washington, DC: US Department of Health and Human Services.

Kreutzer, J.S., Doherty, K.R., Harris, J.A., & Zasler, N.D. (1990). Alcohol use among persons with traumatic brain injury. *Journal of Head Trauma Rehabilitation, 5,* 9–20.

Kreutzer, J.S., Wehman, P., Harris, J., Burns, C., & Young, H. (1991). Substance abuse and crime patterns among persons with traumatic brain injury referred for supported employment. *Brain Injury, 5,* 177–187.

Kreutzer, J.S., Witol, A.D., Sander, A.M., Cifu, D., Marwitz, J.H., & Demonic, R. (1996). A prospective, longitudinal, multicenter analysis of alcohol patterns among persons with traumatic brain injury. *Journal of Head Trauma Rehabilitation, 11* (5), 58–69.

Langley, M.J., & Kiley, D. (1992). Prevention of substance abuse in persons with neurological disabilities. *Neurorehabilitation, 2,* 56–64.

McGlynn, S. (1990). Behavioral approaches to neuropsychological rehabilitation. *Psychological Bulletin, 108* (3), 420–441.

McLellan, B.A., Vingilis, E., Larkin, E., Stoduto, G., Filgate, M., & Sharkey, P.W. (1993). Psychosocial characteristics and follow-up of drinking and non-drinking drivers in motor vehicle crashes. *Journal of Trauma, 35,* 245–250.

McRoberts, C., Burlingame, G.M., & Hoag, M.J. (1998). Comparative efficacy of individual and group psychotherapy: A meta-analytic perspective. *Group Dynamics: Theory, Research and Practice, 2* (2), 101–117.

Miller, W.R. (1985). Motivation for treatment: A review with special emphasis on alcoholism. *Psychological Bulletin, 98,* 84–107.

Miller, W.R., & Rollnick, S. (1995). *Motivational interviewing.* New York: Guilford.

Miller, W.R., Zweben, A., DiClemente, C.C., & Rychtarik, R.G. (1992). *Motivational enhancement therapy manual: A clinical research guide for therapists treating individuals with alcohol abuse and dependence.* Rockville, MD: National Institute on Alcohol Abuse and Alcoholism.

Miranti, S.V., Hantsch, P., Liljedahl, E., McMorrow, M., & Gertz, B. (2002). *Reality orientation and cognitive stimulation group psychotherapy in acute rehabilitation.* Poster presented at the 2002 Annual American Psychological Association Convention, August 24.

Miranti, S.V., Hantsch, P., & Pick, S. (2002). *Psychology service and group psychotherapy impact: Correlations with rehabilitation outcome.* Poster presented at the 2002 Annual American Psychological Association Convention, August 24.

Murray, P.K. (1987). Clinical pharmacology in rehabilitation. In B. Caplan (Ed.), *Rehabilitation psychology desk reference* (pp. 501–525). Rockville, MD: Aspen.

Orlinsky, D., & Howard, K. (1986). Process and outcome in psychotherapy. In S.L. Garfield & A.E. Bergen (Eds.), *Handbook of psychotherapy and behavior change* (3rd edn.; pp. 311–381). New York: John Wiley & Sons.

Parsons, O.A. (1987). Intellectual impairment in alcoholics: Persistent issues. *Acta Medica Scandinavica, 717,* 33–46.

Pepping, M. (1998). The value of group psychotherapy after brain injury: A clinical perspective. *Brain Injury, 2* (1n).

Prigatano, George P. (1992). Personality disturbances associated with traumatic brain injury. *Journal of Consulting and Clinical Psychology, 60* (3), 360–368.

Rattok, J., Ross, B., Ben-Yishay, Y., Ezrachi, O., Silver, S., Lakin, P., Vakil, E., Piasetsky, E., Zide, E., & Diller, L. (1992). Outcome of different treatment mixes in a multidimensional neuropsychological rehabilitation program. *Neuropsychology, 6* (4), 395–415.

Schmidt, M.F., & Garvin, L.J. (1994). *Substance abuse patterns one year after inpatient rehabilitation.* Poster presented at the National Head Injury Eleventh Annual Meeting, Chicago, Illinois.

Sparadeo, F.R., Strauss, D., & Barth, J.T. (1990). The incidence, impact and treatment of substance abuse in head trauma rehabilitation. *Journal of Head Trauma Rehabilitation, 5*, 1–8.

Stephens, R.S., Roffman, R.A., & Curtin, L. (2000). Comparison of extended vs. brief treatments for marijuana use. *Journal of Consulting and Clinical Psychology, 68* (5), 898–908.

Sternbarger, B., & Budman, S. (1996). Group psychotherapy and managed behavioral health care: Current trends and future challenges. *International Journal of Group Psychotherapy, 46*, 297–309.

Ylvisaker, M., & Szekeres, S. (1989). Metacognitive and executive impairments in head-injured children and adults. *Topics in Language Disorders, 9*, 34–49.

CHAPTER 16

Assessing and Changing Motivation to Offend

Mary McMurran

University of Wales, Cardiff, UK

Synopsis.—Working with offenders to reduce their offending behavior is an enterprise of some social significance and cost to the public. Ensuring that the offender is motivated to change is crucial for effective therapy. Assessing offenders' motivation to change is important in making decisions about incarceration, treatment, and release, yet there are currently no psychometrically developed assessments specifically for motivation to change offending. Treatments for offending can be effective, and motivating offenders to engage is important, yet there are currently no treatments specifically designed to address offenders' motivation to change. The development of assessment and treatment should be based on a theoretical model of motivation to change offending, but integrated theoretical models are a rarity. This chapter reviews the literature on offending in relation to the motivational model of Cox and Klinger (1988, 1990, and Chapter 7, this volume), concluding that there is sufficient supportive evidence to develop similar motivational models in relation to offending. Following from this, a case is made for the psychometric development of an assessment instrument based upon the Motivational Structure Questionnaire (MSQ; Cox & Klinger, Chapter 8, this volume; Klinger & Cox, Chapter 9, this volume; Klinger, Cox, & Blount, in press). Finally, the principles of Systematic Motivational Counseling (SMC; Cox & Klinger, Chapter 11, this volume; Cox, Klinger, & Blount, 1999) appear to fit well with what works with offenders, and a case is made for developing this approach for offenders.

INTRODUCTION

Working with offenders to reduce their offending behavior is an enterprise of some social significance, and prison, probation, and mental health services world-wide devote considerable resources to offender treatments. Treatments for offending can be effective (Lösel, 2001; McGuire, 2001), and encouraging offenders to enter into treatment, engage in the process, and complete programs are all central to the success of this enterprise. Indeed, preventing dropout from treatment programs is of great importance, because in some cases those who drop out are more likely to recidivate than are those who have not been treated at all (Cullen, 1994; Hanson & Bussière, 1998).

Willingness to enter into treatment, engagement in the process, and completion of programs are taken to indicate an offender's motivation to change, although these more accurately describe motivation to engage in treatment or therapy. Where crime is concerned,

---

Handbook of Motivational Counseling. Edited by W. Miles Cox and Eric Klinger.

estimates of offenders' motivation to change are really predictions of whether offenders will recidivate or not. Motivation for therapy can be indicative of motivation to change, but offenders are rational beings and some will choose to participate in treatment programs because it puts them in good light with those responsible for making decisions about their freedom rather than from any genuine intention to change.

Interventions aimed at reducing offending depend for their effectiveness upon offenders at least being motivated to engage in therapy and, ideally, upon their being motivated to change. In some cases, only offenders deemed motivated to change are selected for treatment programs, whereas, in other cases, motivation is seen more as a treatment need, with programs containing components that are specifically designed to enhance motivation to change. Specifying motivation to change as a selection criterion for treatment programs makes it important to use valid and reliable assessments of motivation (McMurran, 2002). Identifying motivation to change (or lack of it) as a target for treatment makes it important to understand the nature of the offender's motivation in order that effective treatments can be designed. In the UK, this latter point assumes additional (though ethically dubious) significance in light of recent legislative developments regarding the detention of dangerous offenders for treatment regardless of their motivation to change or engage in therapy (Department of Health/Home Office, 2000), a situation that already pertains in some states of the USA (La Fond, 2001).

Whether selection criterion or treatment target, an offender's motivation to change should be thoroughly assessed and understood. Despite this, there are currently no theory-driven and psychometrically developed assessments of offenders' motivation to change and no comprehensive methods of intervention. This has recently been stated explicitly by Tierney and McCabe (2002) in relation to sex offenders, but is true of all types of offenders. In this chapter, the aim is to determine whether there is sufficient evidence in the offending literature to suggest that the motivational model of Cox and Klinger (1988, 1990, and Chapter 7, this volume) might justifiably be applied to offending. If there is, then this might support the adaptation of the assessment protocol and the motivational treatment that are derived from Cox and Klinger's model. The end product of this chapter will be to suggest a research direction, recommending further development and empirical testing of a motivational model of offending, the psychometric development of an assessment methodology, and the development and evaluation of a motivational intervention for offenders.

A MOTIVATIONAL MODEL OF OFFENDING

The motivational model of Cox and Klinger (1988, 1990, and Chapter 7, this volume) is a comprehensive model of alcohol use based on incentive motivation and decision-making. Despite the focus upon drinking, the underlying principles of this model should be able to describe any behavior. Indeed, the notion that substance-use behaviors and nonsubstance-use behaviors may be described using the same principles is well accepted (Brown, 1997; Davies, 1997; Orford, 2001).

Cox and Klinger's model, in brief, holds that:

(1) the person has a learning history that is based upon constitutional, sociocultural, and experiential factors;
(2) this learning history is summarized in a person's incentive motivations, beliefs, and expected effects of the behavior; and

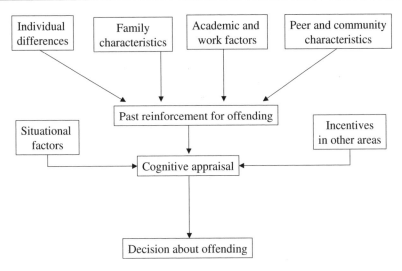

Figure 16.1   A motivational model of offending (based on Cox & Klinger, 1988)

(3) in the present, situational factors, cognitions, and the availability of alternative sources of reward combine to predict the likelihood of the behavior.

An adaptation of this model for offending is outlined diagrammatically in Figure 16.1, and some of the existing knowledge about offenders will be examined here for goodness of fit.

Studies of the development of offending behavior and offender characteristics have provided a considerable body of knowledge about risk factors for offending. These lie in a number of different domains, including physical, psychological, familial, and social. An illustrative summary of risk factors for violent offending, taken from reviews and meta-analyses (Hawkins, et al., 1998; Lipsey & Derzon, 1998; Lösel, 2002), is presented in Table 16.1.

Although useful in accurately targeting those factors related to crime in prevention and treatment efforts, this list of risk factors does not, as it stands, tell us much about the specifics of the development of criminal behavior for any one individual. We need to look to the interplay of these risk factors to understand any one individual's motivations for offending, by integrating these risk factors into developmental models that assume feedback loops (Lösel, 2002; McMurran, 1996; Tolan & Gorman-Smith, 1998). Some of the factors listed in Table 16.1 will be described with regard to how they link together, as shown diagrammatically in Figure 16.1. There is no intention to be exhaustive in the coverage of the factors listed, nor is there any intention to suggest one definitive offending pathway. Significantly different types of offending (e.g., acquisitive, violent, sexual) and different types of people (e.g., males versus females) will doubtless follow different pathways. The intention is, rather, to give a flavor of how such factors may link together in principle, thus describing a motivational pathway.

Individual Differences

Studies of the development of antisocial behavior implicate biologically based individual attributes, such as brain functioning (Hare, 1998), psychophysiological functioning

Table 16.1 Summary of risk factors for violence (from Hawkins et al., 1998; Lipsey & Derzon, 1998; Lösel, 2002)

Individual risk factors	*Physical* Male Prenatal trauma Pregnancy complications Low resting heart rate Deficits in prefrontal functioning High testosterone levels *Psychological* Low IQ Hyperactivity, impulsivity, attention deficit Internalizing disorders Aggressiveness Early violence and delinquency Antisocial behaviors Substance use Antisocial attitudes and beliefs Biases in social information processing Skills deficits
Family risk factors	Parental criminality Child maltreatment Poor family management Parent–child interaction Family bonding Family and marital conflict Parental attitudes favorable to violence Stressful family events Residential mobility Early separation from parents
School risk factors	Academic failure Low bonding to school Truancy and school dropout Changing schools High-school delinquency rate Aspirations to lower-status jobs
Peer risk factors	Delinquent siblings Delinquent peers Gang membership
Community risk factors	Poverty Disorganization Low neighborhood attachment Availability of drugs Presence of adults involved in crime Exposure to violence Exposure to racial prejudice

(Raine, 1997), neurochemical functioning (Berman, Tracy, & Coccaro, 1997), and personality traits (Widiger, 1998). Biologically based risk factors operate by determining what individuals find reinforcing, how they respond to reward and punishment, what they experience emotionally, and how easy or difficult it is for them to regulate their behavior.

Family Characteristics

The development of antisocial behavior is, however, mediated or moderated by the social environment, where reciprocal relationships pertain. The child's temperament, responsiveness, and abilities influence how carers respond to him or her, and those responses in turn shape the child's view of the world. Laboratory studies, for example, have shown that hyperactive and inattentive children are stressful for parents to deal with, and these lapse into family management practices that are predictive of later delinquency, namely ignoring good behavior and punishing bad behavior (Pelham & Lang, 1993). The mismanaged child will be less likely to acquire the self-control skills that underpin prosocial behaviors, and in the absence of prosocial means of acquiring rewards, antisocial means prevail. This is especially true for those whose parents and siblings are antisocial.

Academic and Work Factors

Children's learning experiences are reflected in their later functioning, such as intellectual capacity (Farrington, 2000) and social information-processing skills (Keltikangas-Järvinen & Pakaslahti, 1999). Low intelligence, particularly low verbal intelligence, and poor social problem-solving skills are associated with aggressive and antisocial behavior. Persistent antisocial behavior increases the likelihood of school failure, association with delinquent peers, and the eventual acquisition of a criminal record. Inadequate behavioral self-control, low intelligence, and poor social problem-solving all militate against good school performance, and poor school performance has been shown to be an important variable in the development of delinquency and the continuity of criminality into adulthood (Le Blanc, 1994). School performance is further influenced by social factors, such as the way classes are taught and managed, and the parents' attitudes about education and schooling. Depending upon the child's level of success and integration, and the value placed upon school work, schooling will be a more or less pleasant experience, with consequent effects on attendance and achievement. The effects of erratic school attendance and poor academic achievement take their effect in predicting later-life criminality because these early risk factors are unlikely to lead to successful job finding and satisfactory work-related behaviors. Although unemployment is not a direct cause of offending, unemployed offenders are more likely to reoffend (May, 1999).

Peer and Community Characteristics

Over time, opportunities to engage in the noncriminal world diminish. With a criminal record and lack of work experience, employment becomes difficult to find, and without an income, housing may be poor and insecure (Webster et al., 2001). Offenders may gravitate toward peers and social venues where they meet with similar others, thus increasing the likelihood of further antisocial behavior, particularly where there are few alternative survival strategies. Unemployment, poor and insecure housing, and involvement in crime all conspire to make intimate relationships hard to sustain. A lifestyle of crime develops from which it is difficult to escape (Walters, 1998).

Table 16.2   Reinforcements for offending

Type of reinforcement	Positive	Negative
Affective	Positive affect from offending, e.g., pleasure, excitement	Reduction of an aversive affective states, e.g., boredom, deprivation
Material	Acquisition of goods, e.g., through theft, robbery	Prevent loss of possessions, e.g., aggression as a defense
Social	Enhancement of status and reputation	Prevent isolation, e.g., by belonging to a group

Past Reinforcement for Offending

Antisocial behaviors can include a variety of offenses, in the broad categories of violent, sexual, or acquisitive. Offending of all types can bring rewards affectively, materially, and socially, both positively (by enabling offenders to acquire something that they want) and negatively (by enabling them to avoid something that they do not want) (see examples in Table 16.2). Offending may fundamentally be intrinsically rewarding, but the reward value develops over time, based upon past experience of gains from offending along with failure to gain from alternative, nonoffending behaviors. Thus offending acquires the status of an *incentive*, which Cox, Klinger, and Blount (1999) define as "any object or event that a person expects will bring about an affective change" (p. 5).

Cognitive Appraisal

A person's learning history is the lens through which he or she views the current situation. Cognitive representations of past experience are represented as attributions, expectancies, attitudes, and beliefs. The undercontrolled and aggressive child typically experiences the world as a hostile place, being unpopular with prosocial peers and frequently chastized by authority figures, and, under these conditions, becomes more likely to attribute hostile intentions to others' behavior (Lochman & Dodge, 1994). Hostile attributional biases are associated with aggressive conduct disorder, reactive aggression, and violent crimes (Dodge et al., 1990).

Outcome expectancies are cognitive representations of the "if–then" relationship between behavior and specific outcomes. These have been studied thoroughly in the alcohol field (e.g., Goldman, Del Boca, & Darkes, 1999; Jones, Chapter 19, this volume), but rarely in studies of criminal behavior. Positive outcome expectancies for crime are postulated to maintain criminal behavior, and a study by Walters (2000) revealed complex relationships among positive expectancies, negative consequences, and fear. McMurran and Bellfield (1993) studied sex-related alcohol expectancies in rapists, finding that those who had offended while intoxicated were most likely to believe that in future they might do something sexually risky after drinking. The concern was that this belief would become a self-fulfilling prophecy, and it was recommended that such expectancies should be addressed in interventions.

As a criminal lifestyle develops, it is bolstered by a criminal identity and antisocial attitudes and beliefs. Walters (1995a, 1995b, 1996), for example, has identified thinking styles associated with criminality, such as entitlement, cognitive indolence, and rationalization. Through the lens of hostile attributions, positive outcome expectancies for crime, and antisocial thinking styles, the likelihood of a decision to commit crime is increased.

Situational Factors

The importance of situational factors in relapse to offending has been widely recognized (Laws, 1989). A high-risk situation for a rapist might be seeing a woman walking into a park alone, and that for a child molester might be babysitting a youngster for a neighbor. Many experts believe that high-risk situations are engineered by the offender, who makes "seemingly unimportant decisions" (which used to be known as "apparently irrelevant decisions") that are actually covert plans to relapse (Pither, 1990). The rapist, for instance, may decide to take a shortcut through a park because it is a quicker route home, and the child molester may befriend a single parent who would be likely to need a babysitter.

Incentives in Other Areas

Brown (1997), in his investigation of crime as a behavioral addiction, describes the development of a "motivational monopoly," where activities—including criminal behaviors—that lead to enhanced mood and emotional states become the sole source of reward for the individual. The behavior to which a person is addicted is likely to be highly rewarding for the individual in terms of managing moods and emotions (i.e., "hedonic tone") and also highly reliable in producing rewards. Addictive behaviors occur at the expense of behaviors aimed at achieving rewards from other sources, which eventually disappear from the person's repertoire. Typically, the addictive behavior brings instant reward, and rewards that require long-term planning and behavioral self-control are those that disappear. The addictive behavior acquires high subjective value in relation to the available alternatives, and "addictive decision-making" ensures the choice of the addictive behavior over the alternatives. Whether or not a person can become addicted to certain types of crime is debatable, but the development of motivational monopolies does seem credible.

Decision-Making

In a cost–benefit analysis of the decision to offend or not, the potential benefits of offending would be weighed against the likelihood of being punished and how "punishing" the punishment is likely to be. With regard to offending, the perceived benefits are, as illustrated in Table 16.2, affective, material, and social. These short-term gains from offending, compared to the longer-term costs of offending, often carry greater weight in many offenders' decision-making processes. The potential negative costs are criminal justice sanctions, from fines, through community rehabilitation orders, to imprisonment. Linked with these are potential affective costs, such as guilt and shame, material costs, such as loss of housing and loss of employment, and social costs, such as breakdown of relationships and loss of access to children.

The chances of being caught and processed through the criminal justice system are often slim. In the UK, at least, with the exception of homicide, it is not certain that the police will be informed about an offense, and, even when they are informed, there will not always be enough evidence to warrant bringing the case to court. Where an offense is processed by the criminal justice system and the defendant is found guilty, the penalty is often intended to be harsh, but the harshness is assumed by people with different incentive values than the offender. For some offenders, there is little to lose by having a criminal record or spending time in prison in that incentives in other areas are few and prison can be a place of more regular care and attention than the outside world. Prison can serve to diminish those other incentives that do exist in the outside world, for instance, stable housing, relationships, and job prospects, thus making imprisonment less and less of a relative hardship.

A MOTIVATIONAL MODEL

The factors contributing to offending fit a motivational model, as outlined in Figure 16.1. That is, individual attributes, family characteristics, academic and work factors, and peer and community characteristics all interact to shape the individual's learning history. Current triggers to offending are viewed through the lens of past experience and, in light of other available incentives, lead to a decision-making process that may or may not lead to offending. However, these factors require further integration to advance our understanding of offending, a task that has been undertaken for sexual offending by Ward and colleagues.

Ward and Hudson (1998) and Ward and Siegert (2002) have begun to investigate sexual offending pathways in greater detail, identifying the processes that lead from the development of individual vulnerabilities to offending, through offense triggers, to the occurrence of an offense. Their approach integrates existing theories, knitting together their best parts, to construct a new framework. In Ward's approach, attempts are made to link together those distal and proximal factors implicated in offending, creating what might be termed a developmental motivational map.

Ward and Hudson (1998) suggested nine phases leading to a sexual offense:

1. A life event, such as an argument, a hassle, or a memory, automatically activates knowledge structures related to the individual's needs and goals.
2. A desire for the deviant activity is triggered, accompanied by memories, fantasies, and rehearsal of deviant acts.
3. The individual decides what to do, in light of his or her affective state (e.g., craving for excitement, difficulty handling negative feelings, or fear of the consequences), and an approach goal (i.e., offend) or an avoidance goal (i.e., not offend) is set.
4. A strategy is selected from four possible offense pathways:
   (a) *approach-automatic*, which is impulsive offending as a result of overlearned behavioral scripts;
   (b) *approach-explicit*, which is a planned strategy for attaining an illegal goal;
   (c) *avoidant-passive*, which is a decision not to offend that fails because of deficits in those skills required to control emotion and regulate behavior; and
   (d) *avoidance-active*, which is a decision not to offend that fails because of the use of inappropriate control strategies, such as using alcohol and drugs.

5. A high-risk situation is encountered, either deliberately or mistakenly, and the risk of offending is increased in different ways depending on the offense pathway:
   (a) succumbing to immediate gratification (approach-automatic);
   (b) deliberate choice (approach-explicit);
   (c) the triggering of automatic behavioral sequences (avoidant-passive); or
   (d) failure of self-control along with feelings of inadequacy (avoidance-active).
6. In the high-risk situation, approach goals are pursued and avoidance goals become approach goals. This latter situation resembles the "abstinence violation effect" (Marlatt, 1985), where attempts to control behavior are abandoned.
7. The offender commits the offense.
8. The offense is evaluated, with different types of offender perhaps feeling differently about their actions. Approach offenders may feel positive affect, whereas avoidant offenders may feel guilt and shame.
9. These evaluations shape attitudes about future offending. Those with approach goals will have their offending reinforced; those with avoidance goals may reassert their intention to avoid, or they may give up attempts to control their behavior.

Ward and Siegert (2002) describe different pathways to child sexual abuse, depending upon the dominant causal mechanism (intimacy deficits, deviant sexual scripts, emotional dysregulation, or antisocial cognitions). Polaschek et al. (2001) have applied a similar model specifically to rape, with interactions between the offender's goals and strategies and the victim's responses explaining various "typologies" of rape, such as those motivated by anger, sadism, power, and immediate gratification. These models proposed by Ward and colleagues show several decisional routes from trigger to offense, and such detailed accounts could be used to describe other types of offense.

The evidence presented so far supports the notion that the motivational model of Cox and Klinger (1988, 1990, and Chapter 7, this volume) fits offending behavior. There is work to be done on augmenting this model—a task that has been begun by Ward and colleagues. From this position, what suggestions might be made with regard to assessment of offenders' motivation to change?

ASSESSING OFFENDERS' MOTIVATION TO CHANGE

In many cases, offenders' motivation to change is gauged simply by their expression of an intention to change and their willingness to participate in therapeutic programs. Such transparent assessments are not to be disregarded, but they are rather superficial measures. An expression of an intention to change and engage in an intervention is prudent for the offender whose incarceration or liberation may depend upon how he or she responds. Although it may be important to establish the genuineness of an offender's commitment to change, an arguably more productive pursuit is to capitalize on this early expression of willingness to change by examining the structure of the offender's motivation in a person-centered style, thus nourishing whatever level of motivation to change is present and whatever its origins—external or internal.

Conversely, the offender may actually be motivated to change but not motivated to participate in therapy. This may be because the therapy does not appeal, for example, because of the risk of being publicly identified as a sex offender through joining a recognized treatment group. Alternatively, the offender may wish to change but feel hopeless about the prospect, perhaps because of having tried and failed in the past. It is, therefore, important to understand the nature of an offender's motivation. Where the goal is to enhance motivation to change in treatment, efficacy is likely to be highest where the factors influencing motivation are fully understood and treatments are designed accordingly. Thus, it is important to understand the structure of an offender's motivation to change.

To date, the assessment of motivation to change offending has been largely clinical, rather than actuarial, in terms of knowing the right questions to ask, comparing the offender's behavior with his or her assertions, and making a judgment on the basis of the responses given (e.g., Jones, 2002). There are few psychometrically developed measures of motivation to change offending (Tierney & McCabe, 2002). When measures of motivation to change are used, these are based largely upon Prochaska and DiClemente's (1986) model of stages of change in psychotherapy. In this model, change is described as a process in which people move through the following stages: (1) *precontemplation*, which is failure to recognize a problem or lack of recognition of the need for change; (2) *contemplation*, which is recognition of a problem and the need for change, along with ambivalence about taking action to effect change; (3) *action*, which is taking steps to change; and (4) *maintenance*, which is when change is well established. Sutton (2001) noted that the stages-of-change model derives largely from research on smoking, and may not be generalizable even to alcohol and drug-taking, to which it is widely applied. One must, therefore, question the applicability of the stages-of-change model to offending. Very little research on the stages-of-change model as applied to offending has been conducted.

The University of Rhode Island Change Assessment (URICA), also known as the Stages of Change Questionnaire (McConnaughy, Prochaska, & Velicer, 1983; McConnaughy et al., 1989), has been used in assessment of offenders. This questionnaire is useful in that it refers to "my problem," and can therefore be applied to offending, unlike other questionnaires that refer to specific problem behaviors. Some work has been done to investigate the URICA's reliability and validity with offenders. McMurran et al. (1998) reported mean scores, test–retest reliability, and validation information for offender patients legally detained under the UK mental health legislation as suffering from "psychopathic disorder." Hemphill and Howell (2000) administered the URICA to adolescent offenders, finding evidence for its validity in the correlation of constituent scales (precontemplation, contemplation, action, and maintenance) with other relevant questionnaires. They did, however, find that a three-factor solution rather than a four-factor solution was a better fit to the data from this adolescent sample, these three factors being fear of relapse, action, and wanting to change. This difference could mean that offenders are different from nonoffenders. Overall, further psychometric development of the URICA with offenders is needed.

One alternative method to using the URICA is to ask raters to make judgments about the offender's stage of change for various behaviors (Wong & Gordon, 2000). This has the advantage of relying less on the offender's self-report, but may suffer validity problems for reasons related to inferring others' motivational states. Clearly, the repertoire of measures for assessing offenders' motivation to change could usefully be developed.

The Motivational Structure Questionnaire (MSQ; Klinger, Cox, & Blount, in press) is one comprehensive motivational assessment that could be adapted to address motivation to change offending. The MSQ invites people to list their current concerns in a number of major life areas, and then describe what their goals are regarding each concern. In this way, the relative strengths of a person's positive motivation (i.e., achievement oriented) and negative motivation (i.e., avoidance oriented) can be identified. The relevance of positively and negatively motivated goals has been described by Ward and Hudson (1998), who asserted that acquisitional goals require attention to information indicating success, and avoidance goals require attention to information signaling failure. An acquisitional goal that would reduce the likelihood of offending might be finding and sustaining employment. The offender can measure success in terms of completing application forms, being interviewed, being offered jobs, attending work on time, and so on. By contrast, an avoidance goal—to desist from offending—requires attention to risk situations, for instance, what thoughts, feelings, and behaviors were noticed on occasions when a lone child was present, when an insult or injustice was perceived, or when an unattended purse was observed. When it comes to behavior change, success is more likely when the focus is on the positive.

The MSQ further asks respondents to indicate how active they are in striving to meet their goals, along with their commitment, emotional involvement, self-efficacy, and amount of time before achieving goals. Finally, respondents are asked about the impact of the problem behavior, which is alcohol use in the case of the original MSQ, on the achievement of goals. Clearly, motivation to desist from offending is influenced not only by the rewards gained by offending (see Table 16.2), but the availability of reinforcement from alternative sources. Alternative reinforcement is not always readily available. For example, there are few affordable ways to recreate the emotional high of "joyriding" and few high-salaried career opportunities to replace acquisitive offending. Alternatives may not be as reinforcing as the criminal behavior. For example, consensual sex may not be as reinforcing as rape for the sexual deviant, and negotiation not as reinforcing as violence for the violent offender. Thus, ambivalence to change may be high and commitment low. There are no easy answers to these issues, but understanding the offender's motivational profile is crucial for effective motivational enhancement.

At a commonsense level, it is plain that the MSQ could be translated to address offending, and psychometrically developed in terms of establishing its reliability and validity. The MSQ could be revised to address offending generally or to address specific types of offense. Ward and Siegert (2002) suggest that specificity is important when studying offense pathways, and researchers should be precise about the offense and the offender. Their reasoning rightly relates to theory, and is supported by the psychometric failure to develop a tool to measure motivation to change "offending" generally (McMurran et al., 1998). "Offending" is a class of many and varied behaviors that need to be studied separately. Further support for different pathways comes from Loeber (1988, 1990), who identified distinct typologies of aggressive-versatile criminality, nonaggressive criminality, and substance misuse, as illustrated in Table 16.3.

Table 16.3 Developmental pathways (after Loeber, 1990)

Early childhood →	Late childhood/ → early adolescence	Adolescence →	Adulthood
Aggressive-versatile			
Difficult temperament/ → hyperactivity	Conduct problems → with aggression	Problem behaviors →	Aggression and property offenses
Nonaggressive	Conduct problems →	Problem behaviors →	Property offenses
Substance misuse			Substance misuse

INTERVENTIONS TO ADDRESS OFFENDERS' MOTIVATION TO CHANGE

Offender treatment programs generally require attention to be paid to motivational issues in the early stages of intervention, yet there are few, if any, theoretically driven, structured treatments aimed at motivation alone. Clearly, this is a risky gap, given the concerns commonly expressed about offenders' motivation to change.

The motivational model and the assessment of motivational structure described above led to the development of Systematic Motivational Counseling (SMC; Cox & Klinger, Chapter 11, this volume; Cox, Klinger, & Blount, 1999), which focuses on clients' "current concerns" (Cox & Klinger, 1988; Klinger, Barta, & Maxeiner, 1981). A "current concern" is defined as "the state of an organism between the time that it becomes committed to pursuing a particular goal and the time that it either consummates that goal or abandons its pursuit and disengages from the goal" (Klinger, Barta, & Maxeiner, 1981, p. 162). The basic components of SMC are to review these current concerns with the client, interpret the client's motivational profile, set treatment goals, and work toward achieving these goals.

The general approach of SMC is nonconfrontational and collaborative, rather than confrontational and prescriptive—an approach that is consistent with what seems to work best with offenders (Kear-Colwell & Pollock, 1997). SMC also pays attention to the reasons for engaging in the behavior under scrutiny, on the assumption that the behavior is guided by normal contingencies rather than some inherent abnormality. Serious offending is often attributed to an inherent quality of "evil," or construed as inhuman behavior committed by a "monster" or "beast." Taking the perspective of offending as a rational act, albeit a socially unacceptable one, not only helps the offender maintain self-esteem, but also suggests that there are rational ways of changing offending behavior, both of which are essential for effective therapy.

Many of the techniques of SMC have been used to good effect with offenders, although evaluative research is scant at present. Motivational interviewing (Miller & Rollnick, 1991, 2002) has been effective with offenders in tackling denial in a rapist, preventing a sex offender from dropping out of treatment, and encouraging offenders with alcohol problems to consider changing (Mann, Ginsberg, & Weekes, 2002). Decision matrices (Janis & Mann, 1977) have proved effective in reducing anger and aggression in young offenders (McDougall & Boddis, 1991) and have been rated as useful in alcohol treatment by offenders in a secure forensic psychiatric hospital (McMurran & Thomas, 1991).

SMC components—such as setting goals, breaking down large goals into achievable steps, and encouraging offenders to work on goals between sessions—all work to good effect with offenders. For example, social problem-solving skills training that required personality-disordered offenders to identify problems, set goals, devise action plans, and implement them led to significant improvements on a self-report measure of social problem-solving abilities (McMurran et al., 2001).

In terms of treatment, motivational pathways elucidate what is appropriate for different offenders. Ward and Hudson (1998) suggested that offenders with approach-automatic pathways require increased awareness of the contingencies controlling their behavior, self-monitoring skills, and cognitive restructuring. Those with approach-explicit pathways require schema-focused therapy and reconditioning. Those with avoidant-passive pathways need coping-skills training and efficacy enhancement. Finally, those with avoidance-active pathways need training in appropriate coping skills, to replace those that are counter-productive.

In summary, the evidence suggests that SMC could provide a theory-driven, assessment-based, systematic direction in which to move forward interventions aimed at motivating offenders to change.

CONCLUSIONS

The purpose of this chapter was to examine Cox and Klinger's (1988, 1990, and Chapter 7, this volume) motivational model for goodness of fit to offending. If the evidence suggested a reasonable fit, a further aim was to suggest a research direction to develop and test the model. First, we saw that Cox and Klinger's motivational model resonates with the offense pathways described by Ward and colleagues for sexual offending, and similar pathway descriptions could be developed for other types of offense. All pathways, including those of Ward, require empirical examination and consequent refinement. Second, in practical terms, we saw the necessity and urgency to develop psychometrically robust instruments to assess offenders' motivation to change. Many important decisions about an offender's destiny—incarceration or hospitalization, treatment or punishment, release or continued detention—are often made on a very flimsy understanding of an offender's motivational structure. Adaptation of the MSQ specifically for offenders is one viable option for resolving this problem. Finally, interventions aimed at motivating offenders to change are, at best, embryonic compared to interventions targeting specific offenses or offense-related behaviors. This fundamental issue needs systematic attention to improve treatment outcomes, and the adaptation of SMC specifically for offenders would be a fruitful endeavor.

ACKNOWLEDGMENT

The grant support of the National Program for Forensic Mental Health Research and Development is gratefully acknowledged.

REFERENCES

Berman, M.E., Tracy, J.I., & Coccaro, E.F. (1997). The serotonin hypothesis of aggression revisited. *Clinical Psychology Review, 17*, 651–665.

Brown, I. (1997). A theoretical model of the behavioural addictions—applied to offending. In J.E. Hodge, M. McMurran, & C.R. Hollin (Eds.), *Addicted to crime?* (pp. 13–65). Chichester, UK: John Wiley & Sons.

Cox, W.M., & Klinger, E. (1988). A motivational model of alcohol use. *Journal of Abnormal Psychology, 97*, 168–180.

Cox, W.M., & Klinger, E. (1990). Incentive motivation, affective change, and alcohol use: A model. In W.M. Cox (Ed.), *Why people drink: Parameters of alcohol as a reinforcer* (pp. 291–314). New York: Amereon Press.

Cox, W.M., Klinger, E., & Blount, J.P. (1999). *Systematic motivational counselling: Treatment manual.* Unpublished manuscript. University of Wales, Bangor, UK.

Cullen, E. (1994). Grendon: The therapeutic prison that works. *Therapeutic Communities, 15*, 301–311.

Davies, J.B. (1997). *The myth of addiction* (2nd edn.). Amsterdam: Harwood.

Department of Health/Home Office (2000). *Reforming the Mental Health Act: Part II: High risk patients*, Cm. 5016-II. Norwich, UK: The Stationery Office.

Dodge, K.A., Price, J.M., Bachorowski, J., & Newman, J.P. (1990). Hostile attributional biases in severely aggressive adolescents. *Journal of Abnormal Psychology, 99*, 385–392.

Farrington, D.P. (2000). Psychosocial predictors of adult antisocial personality and adult convictions. *Behavioral Sciences and the Law, 18*, 605–622.

Goldman, M.S., Del Boca, F.K., & Darkes, J. (1999). Alcohol expectancy theory: The application of cognitive neuroscience. In K.E. Leonard & H.T. Blane (Eds.), *Psychological theories of drinking and alcoholism* (2nd edn.; pp. 203–246). New York: Guilford.

Hanson, R.K., & Bussière, M.T. (1998). Predicting relapse: A meta-analysis of sexual offender recidivism studies. *Journal of Consulting and Clinical Psychology, 66*, 348–362.

Hare, R.D. (1998). Psychopathy, affect and behavior. In D.J. Cooke, A.E. Forth, & R.D. Hare (Eds.), *Psychopathy: Theory, research and implications for society* (pp. 105–137). Dordrecht, The Netherlands: Kluwer Academic.

Hawkins, J.D., Herrenkohl, T., Farrington, D.P., Brewer, D., Catalano, R.F., & Harachi, T. (1998). A review of predictors of youth violence. In R. Loeber & D.P. Farrington (Eds.), *Serious and violent juvenile offenders* (pp. 106–146). Thousand Oaks, CA: Sage.

Hemphill, J.F., & Howell, A.J. (2000). Adolescent offenders and stages of change. *Psychological Assessment, 12*, 371–381.

Janis, I.L., & Mann, L. (1977). *Decision making.* New York: Free Press.

Jones, L. (2002). An individual case formulation approach to the assessment of motivation. In M. McMurran (Ed.), *Motivating offenders to change: A guide to enhancing engagement in therapy* (pp. 31–154). Chichester, UK: John Wiley & Sons.

Kear-Colwell, J., & Pollock, P. (1997). Motivation and confrontation: Which approach to the child sex offender? *Criminal Justice and Behavior, 24*, 20–33.

Keltikangas-Järvinen, L., & Pakaslahti, L. (1999). Development of social problem solving strategies and changes in aggressive behavior: A 7-year follow-up from childhood to late adolescence. *Aggressive Behavior, 25*, 269–279.

Klinger, E., Barta, S.G., & Maxeiner, M.E. (1981). Current concerns: Assessing therapeutically relevant motivation. In P.C. Kendall & S.D. Hollon (Eds.), *Assessment strategies for cognitive-behavioral interventions* (pp. 161–196). New York: Academic Press.

Klinger, E., Cox, W.M., & Blount, J.P. (in press). Motivational Structure Questionnaire (MSQ) and Personal Concerns Inventory (PCI). In J.P. Allen & M. Columbus (Eds.), *Assessing alcohol problems: A guide for clinicians and researchers* (2nd edn.). Washington, DC: US Department of Health and Human Services.

La Fond, J.Q. (2001). Clinical, legal, and ethical issues for mental health professionals in implementing a sexual predator law in the Unites States. In D.P. Farrington, C.R. Hollin, & M. McMurran (Eds.), *Sex and violence: The psychology of crimes and risk assessment* (pp. 105–122). London: Harwood Academic.

Laws, D.R. (1989). *Relapse prevention with sex offenders.* New York: Guilford.

Le Blanc, M. (1994). Family, school, delinquency, and criminality: The predictive power of an elaborated social control theory for males. *Criminal Behaviour and Mental Health, 4*, 101–117.

Lipsey, M.W., & Derzon, J.H. (1998). Predictors of violent or serious delinquency in adolescence and early adulthood. In R. Loeber & D.P. Farrington (Eds.), *Serious and violent juvenile offenders* (pp. 86–105). Thousand Oaks, CA: Sage.

Lochman, J.E., & Dodge, K.A. (1994). Social-cognitive processes of severely violent, moderately aggressive and non-aggressive boys. *Journal of Consulting and Clinical Psychology, 62*, 366–374.

Loeber, R. (1988). Natural histories of conduct problems, delinquency, and associated substance use. In B.B. Lahey & A.E. Kazdin (Eds.), *Advances in clinical child psychology* (Vol. 11; pp. 73–124). New York: Plenum.

Loeber, R. (1990). Development and risk factors of juvenile antisocial behavior and delinquency. *Clinical Psychology Review, 10*, 1–41.

Lösel, F. (2001). Evaluating the effectiveness of correctional programs: Bridging the gap between research and practice. In G.A. Bernfeld, D.P. Farrington, & A.W. Leschied (Eds.), *Offender Rehabilitation in practice: Implementing and evaluating effective programs* (pp. 67–92). Chichester, UK: John Wiley & Sons.

Lösel, F. (2002). Risk/need assessment and prevention of antisocial development in young people: Basic issues from a perspective of cautionary optimism. In R.R. Corrado, R. Roesch, S.D. Hart, & J.K. Gierowski (Eds.), *Multi-problem violent youth* (pp. 35–57). Amsterdam: IOS Press.

Mann, R.E., Ginsberg, J.I.D., & Weekes, J.R. (2002). Motivational interviewing with offenders. In M. McMurran (Ed.), *Motivating offenders to change: A guide to enhancing engagement in therapy* (pp. 87–102). Chichester, UK: John Wiley & Sons.

Marlatt, G.A. (1985). Relapse prevention: Theoretical rationale and overview of the model. In G.A. Marlatt & J.R. Gordon (Eds.), *Relapse prevention: Maintenance strategies in the treatment of addictive behaviors* (p. 370). New York: Guilford.

May, C. (1999). *Explaining reconviction following a community sentence: The role of social factors.* Research Study, No. 192. London: Home Office.

McConnaughy, E.A., DiClemente, C.C., Prochaska, J.O., & Velicer, W.F. (1989). Stages of change in psychotherapy: A follow-up report. *Psychotherapy, 26*, 494–503.

McConnaughy, E.A., Prochaska, J.O., & Velicer, W.F. (1983). Stages of change in psychotherapy: Measurement and sample profiles. *Psychotherapy: Theory, Research and Practice, 20*, 368–375.

McDougall, C., & Boddis, S. (1991). Discrimination between anger and aggression: Implications for treatment. In M. McMurran & C. McDougall (Eds.), *Proceedings of the First DCLP Annual Conference*, Vol. II: Issues in Criminological and Legal Psychology, No. 17. Leicester: The British Psychological Society, pp. 101–106.

McGuire, J. (2001). What works in correctional intervention? Evidence and practical implications. In G.A. Bernfeld, D.P. Farrington, & A.W. Leschied (Eds.), *Offender rehabilitation in practice: Implementing and evaluating effective programs* (pp. 25–43). Chichester, UK: John Wiley & Sons.

McMurran, M. (1996). Substance use and delinquency. In C.R. Hollin & K. Howells (Eds), *Clinical approaches to working with young offenders* (pp. 210–235). Chichester, UK: John Wiley & Sons.

McMurran, M. (Ed.) (2002). *Motivating offenders to change: A guide to enhancing engagement in therapy.* Chichester, UK: John Wiley & Sons.

McMurran, M., & Bellfield, H. (1993). Sex-related alcohol expectancies in rapists. *Criminal Behaviour and Mental Health, 3*, 76–84.

McMurran, M., Fyffe, S., McCarthy, L., Duggan, C., & Latham, A. (2001). "Stop & Think!"—Social problem-solving with personality disordered offenders. *Criminal Behaviour and Mental Health, 11*, 273–285.

McMurran, M., & Thomas, G. (1991). An intervention for alcohol-related offending. *Senior Nurse, 11*, 33–36.

McMurran, M., Tyler, P., Hogue, T., Cooper, K., Dunseath, W., & McDaid, D. (1998). Measuring motivation to change in offenders. *Psychology, Crime, and Law, 4*, 43–50.

Miller, W.R., & Rollnick, S. (1991). *Motivational interviewing: Preparing people to change addictive behavior.* New York: Guilford.

Miller, W.R., & Rollnick, S. (2002). *Motivational interviewing: Preparing people for change* (2nd edn.). New York: Guilford.

Orford, J. (2001). *Excessive appetites: A psychological view of addictions* (2nd edn.). Chichester, UK: John Wiley & Sons.

Pelham, W.E., & Lang, A.R. (1993). Parental alcohol consumption and deviant child behavior: Laboratory studies of reciprocal effects. *Clinical Psychology Review, 13*, 763–784.

Pithers, W.D. (1990). Relapse prevention with sexual aggressors: A method for maintaining therapeutic change and enhancing external supervision. In W.L. Marshall, D.R. Laws, & H.E. Barbaree (Eds.), *The handbook of sexual assault: Issues, theories, and treatment of the offender* (pp. 363–385). New York: Plenum.

Polaschek, D., Ward, T., Hudson, S.M., & Siegert, R.J. (2001). Developing a descriptive model of the offence chains of New Zealand rapists: Taxonomic implications. In D.P. Farrington, C.R. Hollin & M. McMurran (Eds.), *Sex and violence: The psychology of crime and risk assessment* (pp. 153–174). London: Routledge.

Prochaska, J.O., & DiClemente, C.C. (1986). Toward a comprehensive model of change. In W.R. Miller & N. Heather (Eds.), *Treating addictive behaviors: Processes of change* (pp. 3–27). New York: Plenum.

Raine, A. (1997). Antisocial behavior and psychophysiology: A biosocial perspective and a prefrontal dysfunction hypothesis. In D.M. Stoff, J. Brieling, & J.D. Maser (Eds.), *Handbook of antisocial behavior* (pp. 289–304). New York: John Wiley & Sons.

Sutton, S. (2001). Back to the drawing board? A review of applications of the transtheoretical model to substance use. *Addiction, 96*, 175–186.

Tierney, D.W., & McCabe, M.P. (2002). Motivation for behavior change among sex offenders: A review of the literature. *Clinical Psychology Review, 22*, 113–129.

Tolan, P.H., & Gorman-Smith, D. (1998). Development of serious and violent offending careers. In R. Loeber & D.P. Farrington (Eds.), *Serious and violent juvenile offenders* (pp. 68–85). Thousand Oaks, CA: Sage.

Walters, G.D. (1995a). The psychological inventory of criminal thinking styles: Part I. Reliability and preliminary validity. *Criminal Justice and Behavior, 22*, 307–325.

Walters, G.D. (1995b). The psychological inventory of criminal thinking styles: Part II. Identifying simulated response sets. *Criminal Justice and Behavior, 22*, 437–445.

Walters, G.D. (1996). The psychological inventory of criminal thinking styles: Part III. Predictive validity. *International Journal of Offender Therapy and Comparative Criminology, 40*, 105–112.

Walters, G.D. (1998). *Changing lives of crime and drugs: Intervening with substance-abusing offenders.* Chichester, UK: John Wiley & Sons.

Walters, G.D. (2000). Outcome expectancies for crime: Their relationship to fear and the negative consequences of criminal involvement. *Legal and Criminological Psychology, 5*, 261–272.

Ward, T., & Hudson, S.M. (1998). A model of the relapse process in sexual offenders. *Journal of Interpersonal Violence, 13*, 700–725.

Ward, T., & Siegert, R.J. (2002). Toward a comprehensive theory of child sexual abuse: A theory knitting perspective. *Psychology, Crime and Law 8*, 319–351.

Webster, R., Hedderman, C., Turnbull, P.J., & May, T. (2001). *Building bridges to employment for prisoners.* Home Office Research Study, No. 226. London: Home Office.

Widiger, T.A. (1998). Psychopathy and normal personality. In D.J. Cooke, A.E. Forth, & R.D. Hare (Eds.), *Psychopathy: Theory, research and implications for society* (pp. 47–68). Dordrecht, The Netherlands: Kluwer Academic.

Wong, S., & Gordon, A. (2000). *Violence risk scale.* Unpublished manuscript. Regional Psychiatric Center, PO Box 9243, Saskatoon, Saskatchewan, Canada S7K 3X5.

PART IV

Other Motivational Approaches to Changing Behavior

Enhancing Motivation for Psychotherapy: The Elaboration of Positive Perspectives (EPOS) to Develop Clients' Goal Structure

Ulrike Willutzki
and
Christoph Koban
Ruhr-University of Bochum, Germany

Synopsis.—At the beginning of psychotherapy patients are demoralized. Their experience is dominated by negative affect and they have difficulties describing goals other than a reduction of symptoms. In addition, goal conflicts may further hamper their motivation for treatment. Patients thus have difficulty in envisioning a positive future beyond the mere alleviation of problems and how the strain of psychotherapy might be worth while. To enhance patients' motivation, the intervention EPOS (Elaboration of POSitive perspectives) was developed to (re)connect patients to personally relevant goals as a context for psychotherapy. Its theoretical basis is action psychology and resource-oriented perspectives. Action psychology reconstrues human behavior as goal-driven and particularly points to the impact of self-related goals on regulating action. Resource-oriented perspectives stress the importance of positive perspectives in psychotherapy and the relevance of the person's competencies and achievements. The intervention consists of an imagery phase in which positive perspectives beyond the current problems are activated, and an analysis phase in which personally relevant goals are concretized and related to the psychotherapy. Preliminary research points to its usefulness and indicates which process aspects are relevant for success. A case example shows how the intervention can be integrated into therapy. The limits as well as the potential of the intervention for psychotherapy and training in psychotherapy are delineated.

Handbook of Motivational Counseling. Edited by W. Miles Cox and Eric Klinger.
© 2004 John Wiley & Sons, Ltd.

INTRODUCTION

At the beginning of psychotherapy clients are regularly demoralized and helpless; they don't have much hope that their life will develop in a positive direction (Frank & Frank, 1991; Wampold, 2001). This state goes hand in hand with a negative mood, low self-esteem and often much tension/apprehension. The client's focus rests on his or her current problems and thus is rather oriented toward the past (Kanfer, Reinecker, & Schmelzer, 1996).

In this situation clients have the impression that there is no positive future for them and that they will never be able to pursue or even attain personal projects and goals (Little, 1983; Little & Chambers, Chapter 4, this volume). If they have a concept of the future, this often seems depressingly far away, particularly as intermediate goals and steps are not salient or even present for them. Moreover, goal conflicts destabilize the clients and prevent their developing a structure for their life.

At the same time psychotherapists look for a useful orientation during the therapeutic process: The focus should be on what a person wants to strive for (Emmons & Kaiser, 1996), on concrete goals and personal projects (Little & Chambers, Chapter 4, this volume), and on things that can make the client's life better—which at the same time leads to an understanding of why it is worth taking on the strains of psychotherapy. The intervention described in this chapter was developed to support the Elaboration of POSitive perspectives (EPOS) in psychotherapy; its purpose is to help clients and psychotherapists to develop a goal perspective for their collaborative work (see also Willutzki & Koban, 1996).

The next sections first provide a short overview of the theoretical background, followed by a more detailed description of the intervention (including a case example) and some empirical results and ideas for training psychotherapists.

CONCEPTUAL AND EMPIRICAL BACKGROUND

The theoretical background for the EPOS comes mainly from two traditions: The action-oriented perspective reconstrues the relevance of goals in the context of action-regulation theories; the resource-oriented perspective substantiates the positive evaluative focus in the intervention.

Action Regulation

From an action-oriented perspective, any behavior can be construed as goal oriented; thereby it points generally to the values and future perspectives of the person. Which goals are relevant in motivating the person must be determined for the individual client. In psychotherapy the elaboration of motivational aspects is also relevant for the question of whether the therapeutic approach matches the particular goals and whether the client is open to the intervention (see Orlinsky, Rønnestad, & Willutzki, in press). Clients at the beginning of therapy often have unclear or only implicit goal perspectives. Moreover, more or less conscious goal conflicts may prevail (Michalak, Heidenreich, & Hoyer, 2001; Michalak, Heidenreich, & Hoyer, Chapter 5, this volume). The orientation problems that arise from these constellations may lead to rumination, worry, and high distress. The person's actions are rather push-motivated; that is, avoidance goals dominate (Kanfer, Reinecker, &

Schmelzer, 1996; Pöhlmann, 1999). The less clients know and experience about how the hardships of psychotherapy may actually make their lives better, the less they will engage in the process. A strong pull motivation, future-oriented ideas/concepts about perspectives and personal projects, thus facilitates the therapeutic change process.

Self-relevant goals to which the person is explicitly connected make it easier for the client to plan further action, pursue long-term goals, and shield them from competing intentions (Heckhausen & Gollwitzer, 1987; Pöhlmann, 1999; Willutzki, 2000). These approach goals should be differentiated and made explicit so that they may become salient orientation points for the client and the therapeutic process. Moreover, Franken (1994) regards goal-setting skills as metastrategies that are a basic competency for managing the person's motivation.

Thus it becomes the therapists' task, together with their clients, to activate positive goal concepts and support the person in developing appropriate goals for him- or herself and for the therapy. The motivational process relies not only on rational information processing, but also on imaginative and emotional processing (Epstein, 1990; Franken, 1994). In such images, all senses are to be addressed, particularly visual, auditory, and olfactory "images." Utopian ideas that are developed in this context point to the person's wishes. From them, concrete goals that are personally important and thereby relevant for action regulation can be deduced (Klinger, 1987). Some support for these contentions was found by James, Thorin, and Williams (1993), who showed that setting concrete goals within cognitive-behavioral treatment for chronic headache pain enhanced treatment efficacy.

In summary, a focus on positive affects, positive goals, and positive perspectives is expected to be supportive and helpful for functional action-regulation processes; ideally they initiate a positive upward spiral of positive beliefs, affects, and behaviors (Gilham & Seligman, 1999). An orientation toward the person's resources plays a major role in this context.

Resource Orientation

What does resource orientation in psychotherapy mean? In general, such an approach begins with the person's current intrapersonal, interpersonal, and external possibilities (Willutzki, 2000). In the context of goal elaboration, this presupposes that the person has abilities to develop positive perspectives that are just to be activated in therapy with support from the therapist. At the same time the therapist assumes that the future-oriented ideas are likely to be valuable for the therapeutic change process; they are not suspected to be pathological. In the course of goal specification, the therapist focuses on positive self-aspects, abilities and skills, positive aspects in social relationships, as well as the client's positive anticipations. Moreover, therapist and client continuously work out what the person has already achieved and how this was done. On the one hand, such an activation and clarification of resources may suggest how to use the resources for the ongoing change process. On the other hand, the orientation toward positive abilities and skills that the person has developed should help to counter the client's negative basic attitude and mood (Grawe, 1998; MacLeod & Moore, 2000).

From this theoretical background the following features of the EPOS emerge:

• Regarding the action-regulation process, one of the targets of the intervention is the production of personal wishes and goals.

- The development of positive affects and concrete behavioral steps is supported by a vivid imagery.
- Positive emotions are used as vehicles for identifying the particular positive aspects of the person's goals.
- The intervention is resource-orientated and also focuses on goals the person likes to maintain or on goals already reached (maintenance goals).

ELABORATION OF POSITIVE PERSPECTIVES AND GOALS WITH THE EPOS

The starting point for creating the EPOS-manual (Willutzki & Koban, 1996) was Schmelzer's (1983; see also Kanfer, Reinecker, & Schmelzer, 1996) *goal-value-clarification* method. This was supplemented by concepts from solution-focused therapy (Berg & Miller, 1992; de Shazer, 1988) and also integrated concepts for the analysis of the generated goals. Since 1994 the EPOS has been used regularly at the Center for Psychotherapy at the Ruhr-University of Bochum, a large outclient unit with a clinical psychology training course.

The Structure of the Exercise

In general the EPOS takes two to three hours of therapy. The intervention has three parts (Figure 17.1): First, the client is stimulated to develop positive, even unrealistic, future images; second, the client and therapist separately prepare for the analysis on the basis of audiotape or video recordings of the therapy session; third, the imagery is analyzed collaboratively by both client and therapist. The EPOS results in the explication of the

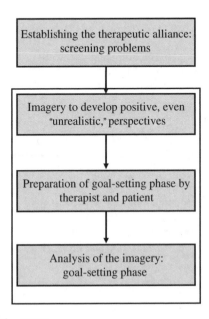

Figure 17.1 Structure of the EPOS

person's goal structure, including a specification of the steps already achieved and the choice of relevant goals for the collaborative therapeutic work.

Preconditions for the EPOS

The EPOS is primarily suited for adult clients. It is particularly indicated if (a) clients suffer from a loss of goal perspectives (e.g., connected with questions about the meaning of life during early adulthood), (b) the current problems seem to be very complex, (c) goal conflicts are apparent, or (d) the client is so demoralized that it is very difficult for her or him to imagine a life without problems. Moreover, the EPOS can generally be used to give the therapist an impression of the client's goal perspectives and improve coordination and cooperation in psychotherapy. Ideally the developed goals can be used as a central thread for the whole therapy.

The EPOS appears unnecessary if the client already expresses well-elaborated goals; but even in these cases, after some progress in therapy, this intervention can develop new goal perspectives and support structural changes to maintain improvements.

The intervention is contraindicated if clients suffer from a severe depressive mood. In such cases the gap between current state and future perspectives may widen further during the intervention and may thus intensify the client's hopelessness (Salovey & Birnbaum, 1989).

Before starting the EPOS the therapist should make sure that the client is at least marginally willing to think about possible goal perspectives. Such willingness is not static; the therapist can support the client's acceptance by explaining the exercise beforehand. The client should have had enough time to describe her or his problems and difficulties; the therapeutic alliance should not be under particular strain.

The therapist's attitude plays a major role in the success of the exercise. In addition to a general therapeutic attitude—respectful, interested, open, supportive, and empathic—the therapist should be comfortable with the therapeutic emphasis on positive contents and goals.

The Imagery

The most important goal of the imagery phase is to enable clients to develop positive life perspectives while turning their attention away from their actual problems and state of demoralization. The connections between the client's actual state and the new life perspectives developed during the imagery are clarified afterwards during the goal-setting phase.

The client's images may be totally unrealistic or far beyond her or his actual life situation. For example, during the imagery the client may talk about being on a tropical island, meeting people quite unlikely ever to be met again, or doing things she or he usually would not do.

The person should be in a holistic information-processing mode (Fiedler, 1988; Kelly, 1955; Kuhl, 1983, 2001) to make it easier for her or him to develop new solutions and ideas concerning the current problems. Characteristics of this state of mind are positive affects, free-floating associations, few explanations, a low level of self-evaluation, and a creative point of view.

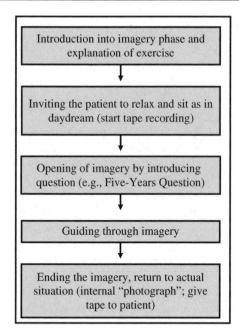

Figure 17.2   Structure of the imagery

As shown in Figure 17.2, the imagery component consists of different parts. During the introductory phase, the therapist explains how the intervention works and why it is used at this point in the therapy:

> So far we have talked about topics and problems that put you under pressure. Today and in the next one to two sessions I would like to use an exercise that should help us to find out which ideas, goals, and wishes you have for your life in the future. I would like to know more about how you see your future life and how the therapy can help you to reach these goals. In this session we start with an imagery exercise to develop a picture of what your future could look like ideally. We will not think about possible ways of realizing these ideas and goals today; this is going to be the topic of the next session.

After the introduction the therapist asks the client to sit down and relax, for example, as in a daydream, to help the client to concentrate on her or his images. The imagery phase should be audiotaped (on 100 minute cassettes) for the client and videotaped for the therapist.

Guiding the Client through the Imagery

There are several ways to begin with the creation and investigation of a person's goal perspectives. For example, the person can be asked to imagine her or his ideal life three, five, ten, or more years later, living on a tropical island, or having only one year left to live. In choosing a starting point for the client, the therapist decides whether the imagery should be linked thematically to the client's problems or have no connection with the client's current situation. The major objective of the imagery is to help the client to vividly experience positive thoughts, emotions, and situations.[*] A relatively neutral start for the imagery is the Five-Years Question: "Imagine that I meet you in 5 years [or 3 or 15] from today and up to then everything has turned out well in your life. You have reached certain personal goals that were important for you, and many other things went just the way you wanted. Where am I meeting you, what are you doing (in 5 years), and how do you feel?" (Further information about beginning with imagery can be found in, e.g., Kanfer, Reinecker, & Schmelzer, 1996 [pp. 430ff], or de Shazer, 1988.)

If the client has difficulties putting her or his current problems aside, the therapist can ask the client to relax and take as much time as necessary to get into the situation. In some cases it can make sense to use the *backpack metaphor*: the therapist asks the client to go on a trip into the mountains and to carry all his or her major problems in a backpack. During the mountain trip the client leaves the problems along the path one by one. The aim of this exercise is to leave all problems behind without denying or reducing them and to make it easier for the client to think about positive topics (see Kanfer, Reinecker, & Schmelzer, 1996).

Usually the imagery takes 30 to 40 minutes. There should be enough time for a possible extension so that the imagery can be adjusted to the needs of the client. The therapist should support the client, following the guidelines in imaginative therapy (Leuner, 1981):

- Probably the most important rule for the therapist is to consistently use the present tense/indicative form and not the subjunctive. Instead of saying "and you would sit in a coffee shop and have breakfast," the therapist says "and you are sitting in a coffee shop and having breakfast right now. How do you feel?" Whereas the present tense makes it easier for the client to develop lively images that activate cognitive-emotional schemata, the subjunctive establishes distance between the content and the current situation and thus hinders the activation of personally relevant topics.
- The therapist uses open questions that stimulate the client's creativity rather than implying particular topics or contents. Possible questions could be: "Where are you right now?", "What does it look like and how are you feeling?", and "What are you doing?"
- The therapist adjusts his or her contributions to the client's pace. Quite likely—but not always—this will mean that the therapist's pace is slower than in normal interactions.
- The therapist tries to ask concrete questions that address all of the client's sense modalities: "What does it look like? How does it smell? How does it taste?"
- Positive feelings play a major role during the imagery; therefore, the therapist tries to focus on them: "And how do you feel in this situation? You are feeling . . . ?" The therapist also gives the client enough time to experience and enjoy these feelings.
- In general the therapist pays attention to the words and metaphors the client uses and picks up on them; he or she avoids adding own personal contents and images. The therapist asks no questions while the client is talking nor comments on the importance of the client's images. The therapist can often support the flow of images by reflecting the client's feelings, thoughts, and actions.
- The therapist supports a holistic-associative and nonanalytical information-processing mode. That means that he or she does not use questions that impose explanations (e.g., "Why" questions). If the client starts to explain the imagined situation, the therapist gently

---

[*] Again, we want to stress that an explicit connection between the person's current problems and the imagery will be established later.

focuses again on the situation and what is going on there. Reasons and causal relationships will be looked at later, either directly after the imagery or during the goal-setting phase.

To get an idea of how the client imagines different areas of life (e.g., when asking the Five-Years Question), it can make sense to accompany some clients in imagery through one whole day. For others, it is more important to stay in just one particular situation and to describe this in depth. Therapists consider the client's current self-relatedness (see Orlinsky, Rønnestad, & Willutzki, in press) and his or her actual mood in choosing their interventions.

The imagery is slowly brought to an end, and the client is carefully helped to return to the actual situation. It can be helpful to guide the client briefly through the different situations developed in the imagery. The therapist may also ask the client to take an internal "photograph" of the most important moment and perhaps find a title for it.

After the imagery the client has the opportunity to evaluate the exercise briefly. Usually clients start talking about the major contents of the imagery. The therapist should not spend too much time discussing these topics directly as a more in-depth analysis of the content will follow in the next session. After finishing with the imagery the therapist pays particular attention to the mood of the client. For some clients the focus on future perspectives widens the subjective gap between the imagined and the current situation; this discrepancy may induce negative feelings and a depressive mood. In this case the therapist points out that this is a normal reaction and makes it clear that the development of future perspectives is important for therapy in helping to find concrete ways to realize them. To help the client to improve his or her mood, the therapist tries to activate examples in which the client has already attained some part of what he or she wants. The therapist may then point out that the development of future perspectives itself is a step in the right direction. Visions of the future are helpful in solving current problems and provide a clearer description of personal goals.

Possible Difficulties during the Imagery

Sometimes it is difficult to activate deep, vivid imagery. Still, in our experience therapists are more likely to help clients by introducing and accompanying the exercise. Certainly one must consider the state of the client at the beginning of the exercise. Demoralized clients who have focused on their current problems for years may seem uninvolved in the imagery; yet even such little steps—little from an outside perspective—can become more important later than the therapist first supposes. Moreover, it is almost impossible to anticipate whether a client is easily involved in or has problems with the exercise. Clients who seem a bit shallow and unimaginative during prior conversation often develop lively and elaborated ideas about their future during the imagery.

Therefore, it seems relevant to focus on the therapist's behavior and the possibilities of supporting the client:

• A good introduction of the exercise is important for the success of the imagery. The client must understand the rationale for the exercise and gain information about ensuing therapeutic steps. The therapist patiently tries to solve difficulties and uncertainties before starting the imagery.

- The therapist is careful not to use directive and extensive expressions as these might hinder the client's imagery. The client is made aware that there are no right or wrong images and that the aim of the exercise is just to develop positive, future-directed, and personally relevant images.
- The therapist is careful to develop a good working alliance. Before engaging in such an imaginative "adventure," the client has to trust the therapist, believe in the therapist's competence, and feel comfortable and understood while talking about personal problems.
- Some clients have habits that generally interfere with exercises and problem-solving. They may tend to intellectualize, have a strong rationalistic orientation, or do both. For them an initial success may be to enter into a positive holistic information-processing mode for short periods of time. Persistent as well as personal and concrete support by the therapist is particularly relevant here.

Preparation for the Goal-Setting Phase

At the end of the imagery session the client receives an audiotape of the exercise and the therapist asks the client to listen to it for the next session. The suggestions for listening to the tape should not be too concrete: "While listening to the tape, just think about: What might be important for you? Which of the things you said have an impact on you?" Moreover, the client is informed that a concrete analysis of the content will take place during the next session.

Between the sessions the therapist listens to the tape in order to prepare for the following session and makes notes about the relevant aspects of the imagery that can later be used to supplement the client's ideas. At the same time the therapist thinks about what meaning these aspects may have for the client, where he or she has questions, and which aspects to talk about in the next session. These preparations help to orient the therapist in the therapeutic process; they do not represent strict guidelines for the topic of the following session.

Goal-Setting Phase

The aim of the goal-setting phase is to elaborate and analyze, together with the client, concrete goals and the connections among these goals, on the basis of the future perspectives developed during the imagery (see Table 17.1). Ideally this phase results in an explicit goal structure, characterized by personal relevance, from which to draw first connections to the

Table 17.1   Aims of the goal-setting phase

The goal-setting phase should lead to:

- Explication of goals that were implicit before
- Working out the connection between goals and actual situation
- Working out the personal relevance and self-reference of explicated goals
- Differentiation between values, goals, and utopias (see Kanfer, Reinecker, & Schmelzer, 1996)
- Evaluation of goals and utopias
- Clarifying functional relations between different goals
- Agreement on the goals that are relevant for the work in psychotherapy

---

client's current state. Furthermore, client and therapist work on differentiating between goals relevant for psychotherapy on the one hand, and, on the other, further life goals for which the client strives without therapeutic support. In the following we first generally characterize the goal-setting phase and then describe its stages more concretely.

Because clients often generate many ideas during the imagery, it sometimes becomes difficult to select those aspects that are relevant for the therapeutic work. In this context it makes sense to differentiate between values, goals, and utopias (Kanfer, Reinecker, & Schmelzer, 1996). Values are regarded as personal preferences without particular need for action ("It would be quite nice to have more fun, weigh less, . . . "). Concrete actions can sometimes be derived from these personal values; more often clients are not willing to put much effort into reaching these wishes. Goals are simple to more complex anticipations of certain final future states implying—in contrast to values—greater personal meaning and more personal commitment. It is particularly this personal relevance and the commitment component that can make goals relevant for action. Utopias are defined as ideas or wishes likely not to be fulfilled, considering the outer circumstances and individual competencies of the person. Utopias can nevertheless be used to derive concrete goals by focusing the client's attention on certain emotional and behavioral aspects. For example, the therapist may ask: "What would you like about being the boss of a big company?" The client may answer: "I would like telling people what to do and I would enjoy deciding myself what is going to happen. I would take care that everybody is treated fairly and nobody suffers in my company." In this regard, the client could pursue a goal to have an "independent job" and to "create a friendly atmosphere" in the client's current life situation, even without having a leading position in her or his job.

At the end of the goal-setting phase, client and therapist will have developed a number of well-defined goals (Walter & Peller, 1992, 2000). Such goals are characterized by the following criteria:

- Well-defined goals are characterized by positive formulations, by the presence of some-thing rather than its absence. If the client says "I do not want to be lonely anymore," the therapist can contribute to a positive formulation by asking, "How would you like to be *instead*?"
- Well-defined goals are personally relevant; that is, the clients are convinced that their lives would be better and their personality changed in a positive way when the goals are reached.
- Goals should be characterized by process or action orientation. This means that the therapist asks, "How will you do that?" instead of "What will you do?"
- Goals should be formulated in specific and preferably in behavioral and concrete terms: "What do the particular steps look like?"
- Well-defined goals focus on the here and now instead of the final state to be achieved much later. This means that they deal with the beginning of new patterns: "What would be the first little sign that you are on the way to reach the goal?"
- Well-defined goals are within the client's control. Instead of "I don't want to have problems with alcohol any longer" the client commits him- or herself to "I want to learn to manage critical situations without drinking alcohol."
- Finally, the client should be aware that it is not always easy to reach goals and that much effort and commitment is needed.

The following paragraphs describe the steps in the goal-setting phase more concretely.

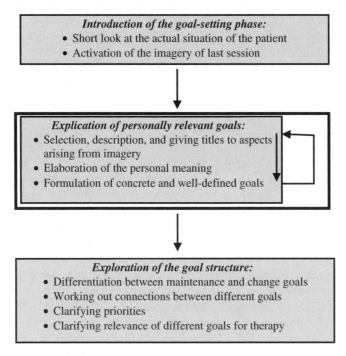

Figure 17.3   Structure of the goal-setting phase

Introducing the Goal-Setting Phase

At the beginning of the first session in which the imagery is analyzed, the client is asked how he or she feels at the moment and what happened after the imagery exercise. From this the therapist may gain a first impression about the meaning of the imagery for the client. The therapist takes care not to postpone an evaluation of the imagery or let it be overshadowed by current and/or dramatic problems in the client's life. If necessary, client and therapist may relatively quickly decide to divide the session into two sections: the first part for the discussion of current, pressing problems and the second part for analyzing the imagery. The analysis begins by briefly activating the content of the imagery (e.g., by describing aspects of the particular images). This is especially important if the clients neglected to prepare themselves by listening to the imagery recording.

Making Personally Important Goals Explicit

The centerpiece of the analysis is to clarify in a number of recursive steps the personal meaning—the affective relevance—of the material produced in the imagery. The topics that emerge as relevant are written down (e.g., on index cards) as preliminary results of the analysis. As a first step, the therapist and the client may try to collect potential topics for further elaboration or may deepen one topic before turning to the next. Here they draw on the aspects named by the client and additional themes regarded as relevant by the therapist. The further steps (elaborating personal meanings as well as concretizing goals and giving them working titles) are described in the following sections.

First the client (or the therapist) selects and briefly describes an aspect arising from the imagery that is important for him or her. Then he or she tries to find a provisional title for this aspect. By elaborating the personal meaning of this aspect, particular details can be linked to his or her superordinate goals. For example, if the client saw him- or herself as weighing much less in the future, the therapist may ask the client what it means for him or her to weigh less, what is important about it, and what that would change in his or her life. The answers may reveal that losing weight is important either because he or she would feel much healthier or because he or she believes that others would then be more accepting. In particular, relatively abstract themes such as health and appreciation can be superordinate goals that he or she pursues in varying situations. Exploring the personal meaning of particular aspects of the imagery should lead to more information about what goals drive his or her behavior and what goal relevance specific situations have for him or her (see also the concept of plan analysis: Caspar, 1995). By abstracting from the concrete contents, and by elaborating their personal meaning, it becomes possible to extract the aspects of the imagery that are goal relevant; the more abstract formulations in turn allow one to look for new or other operationalizations of the personally relevant dimensions. For example: Which other, probably more easily attainable or less problematic, behaviors or intermediate steps are suited to reach the personally relevant goal? Moreover, abstracting from concrete details of the imagery facilitates differentiating between goals and utopias. If the client described a day without professional or private obligations during the imagery, it may be particularly relevant for him or her to be able to freely schedule his or her time. This superordinate goal may lead to therapy goals, such as arranging to have time without a fixed schedule.

The following questions can be helpful to elaborate the personal meaning of certain ideas:

- "What is important for you here?"
- "What does it mean for you when you do this?"
- "Why is it important for you?"
- "How do you realize that it is important for you?"

When clients recognize and experience the personal meaning of particular aspects, they often show some emotional involvement, a certain contemplation, or may even have experiences of sudden insight.

The goals explicated in this part of the intervention will quite likely simultaneously lie on different levels of abstraction. On the one hand, there may be more general goals such as being appreciated by others, and on the other hand there may be more concrete goals such as making more new suggestions at work. During the elaboration of personal meaning the therapist takes care to stay on a level that is emotionally relevant for the person. Sometimes a high level of abstraction (e.g., "I want to be independent") is experienced as trivial and irrelevant by the client; it may be more important for him or her to identify a particular life area in which he or she wants to be more independent (Caspar, 1995).

Once the relevant aspects of the imagery have been explicated, they are formulated as concrete goals. The therapist helps the client to construe the goals according to the criteria for well-formulated goals (see above). It is useful at this point to write the concrete goals on index cards; thereby it becomes possible to show the client all his or her goals simultaneously.

The different steps in this phase—selecting a particular topic arising from the imagery, elaborating personal meanings, concretizing goals, and giving them working titles—are repeated iteratively. The therapist may introduce aspects that seemed important while preparing for the analysis. Some aspects may be clarified easily, whereas others may require more investigation. The criterion for a sufficient elaboration is, on the one hand, that the goal has great importance for the client and, on the other, that the therapist understands the goal's personal meaning for the client. At this point it is unnecessary to decide whether the goal is relevant for the therapeutic work; this will be clarified during later discussion of the client's priorities.

Often many different topics emerge from the imagery that may all seem to point to important goals; and sometimes the wealth of ideas seems almost overwhelming. Particularly in such instances it is the therapist's job to enable the client to select some aspects, for example, by differentiating explicitly between values and goals and exploring their importance. The aim of the intervention is not to collect all possible goals, but to elaborate the currently relevant ones. As goal development and orientation are generally regarded as dynamic processes (Walter & Peller, 2000), the imagery is also meant to help the client to develop general abilities to elaborate personally relevant goals and to strive for them.

Exploring the Goal Structure

In this phase of the evaluation, the qualities of the explicated goals and their relations are further analyzed; moreover, priorities for the ensuing work are clarified.

Initially therapist and client explore whether the goals that have been formulated are maintenance or change goals. Particularly from a resource perspective, maintenance goals are of great interest. The person has worked on and created an aspect of his or her life in a way that is satisfying and makes him or her content (e.g., a positive partnership, getting appreciation from others, a high qualification). By analyzing such aspects clients can come to recognize that they are able to achieve something—even when their situation is generally difficult. When the therapist points out that maintaining such life aspects can itself be a goal, this further stresses their positive qualities and the client's active contribution to them. Moreover, maintenance goals can become a topic for therapeutic work (e.g., maintaining health through sports).

The relationships between different goals are established by directly asking the client about the connections—positive correlations or negative relations—between goals. Implicative relations and temporal dependencies can be visualized by sorting the index cards accordingly. Sometimes contradictory goals activate tendencies in clients to justify themselves; in order to soften this it may be useful to name these as different self-aspects ("Some part of you would like to get more appreciation from your colleagues; another part opts for independence."). This helps to differentiate between contexts in which one or the other of the two contradictory aspects may be more relevant or when the two themes are in conflict. Priorities concerning different goals can be clarified by questions such as "What is most important for you at the moment?"; "What should change straightaway in your life?"; and "Are you working on this on your own or should it be a topic in our work?" These questions offer starting points for the therapeutic collaboration, and common decisions about what comes first or later become possible. The therapist clarifies that a delay of certain goals is preliminary and that goal priorities can be changed during the therapy.

The elaboration of the goal structure ends by reaching an agreement about the goals that are relevant for therapy. Which projects are to be pursued in therapy? Where should the work start? Now therapist and client focus on the one project that will play an immediate role in therapy. This decision can be visualized by putting the particular goal card on the table during the next therapy sessions. It implies at the same time that the goals developed during the intervention are integrated into the therapy process and other therapy steps and strategies are used to pursue them. Directly after selecting a particular goal for therapy, it makes sense to ask the following questions: "What would be the first steps to strive for this goal?"; "How do you recognize that you are on the way to reach this goal?"; and "On a scale from 1 to 10 (10 = you reached the goal, 1 = start of the therapy), at what point are you at the moment?" as well as "How much time are you allowing yourself to reach this goal?" In the following section we provide a case example of how the intervention can be used to explicate goals and use them in therapy.

THE DEVELOPMENT OF POSITIVE GOALS DURING THE THERAPEUTIC PROCESS: AN EXAMPLE

The client, Mr. L. (a 31-year-old photographer working at a photo laboratory), began individual psychotherapy because he suffered from panic disorder with agoraphobia according to DSM-IV criteria (American Psychiatric Association, 1994). The therapy process was first structured according to current cognitive-behavioral concepts for the treatment of panic disorder (Barlow et al., 1989; Margraf & Schneider, 1989). After 14 sessions, the panic attacks had disappeared and the client's agoraphobic avoidance behavior was markedly reduced. Mr. L. still felt uneasy about his situation because he did not know what to do with his life; moreover, he often felt a nagging uncertainty about whether he did the right things. He reported that he constantly ruminated about the way he was living and that he often compared himself unfavorably to others, which in turn put him under pressure and stress. The high level of pressure sometimes even led to the impression that new panic attacks could arise directly.

On the one hand, the lack of goal perspectives was a direct indication for the EPOS; on the other hand, a potential reduction of the stress level might have a prophylactic effect on the panic disorder.

The EPOS was started in session 15. During the imagery (Five-Years Question) Mr. L. developed several very positive scenes:

• He saw himself in the evening sitting with his girlfriend and talking about what they experienced during the day. In this situation he imagined how they would make plans for their futures and make small talk.
• He was going on a photo trip to Scotland.
• He saw himself as the owner of a photo laboratory. He enjoyed his work, had good relationships with his clients, and was creative during photo productions.
• He went to a pool and swam relaxed from one end to the other.
• In yet another scene he imagined himself being at an administrative office and acting self-confident.

In the week following the imagery, Mr. L. listened to the tape several times. In the following session he reported that some of the images were rather surprising for him (e.g., swimming, traveling, ...) and that they carried a great number of new and helpful perspectives. Figure 17.4 gives a brief overview of the personally relevant goals elaborated

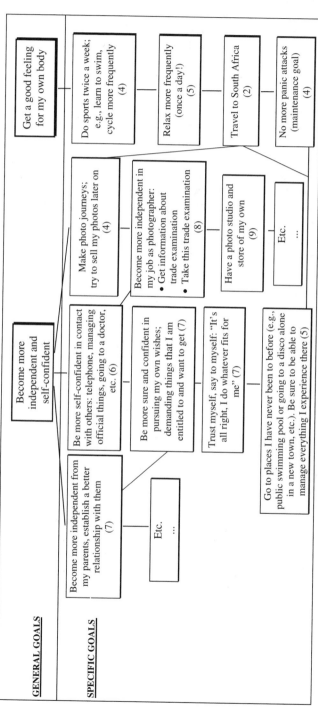

GENERAL GOALS

SPECIFIC GOALS

Become more
independent and
self-confident

Become more independent from
my parents, establish a better
relationship with them
(7)

Etc.
…

Be more self-confident in contact
with others: telephone, managing
official things, going to a doctor,
etc. (6)

Be more sure and confident in
pursuing my own wishes;
demanding things that I am
entitled to and want to get (7)

Trust myself, say to myself: "It's
all right, I do whatever fits for
me" (7)

Go to places I have never been to before (e.g.,
public swimming pool or going to a disco alone
in a new town, etc.). Be sure to be able to
manage everything I experience there (5)

Make photo journeys;
try to sell my photos later on
(4)

Become more independent in
my job as photographer:
• Get information about
  trade examination
• Take this trade examination
  (8)

Have a photo studio and
store of my own
(9)

Etc.
…

Get a good feeling
for my own body

Do sports twice a week;
e.g., learn to swim,
cycle more frequently
(4)

Relax more frequently
(once a day!)
(5)

Travel to South Africa
(2)

No more panic attacks
(maintenance goal)
(4)

Figure 17.4 Example of the goal structure of Mr. L., which was established through the EPOS (excerpt). Every goal was fixed on an index card and these cards were used later in therapy. Numbers represent the difficulty of the particular goal (1 = easy; 10 = very difficult). The lines represent implications between different goals, which were seen by the client: "If I reach A, I am going ahead with B too."

with Mr. L., the relations between these goals, and which explicit goals he initially decided to pursue.

It deeply impressed the client to realize that he had already reached some of his personally relevant goals. On the basis of this hopeful stance he started to work on several "projects" simultaneously in therapy. During every session the index cards were put on the table, sometimes with additional cards that Mr. L. had developed between sessions.

On the basis of the elaborated goal structure, the client decided to work first on the project of "feeling certain and self-confident while in contact with others." Different exercises and role plays were developed that enabled him to feel more self-confident when calling and talking with unknown people. This first project was important because his second project was "becoming more independent professionally." At the same time he started to learn to swim and regularly went to the pool, sometimes alone and sometimes with his girlfriend. A few weeks later he told his parents that he no longer wanted to see them so often (daily); this was the first step toward establishing a relation with them based more on partnership, which gave him more self-confidence in the long term.

Mr. L. was well motivated during the following therapy sessions. During the last session, which took place after a trip to Scotland, Mr. L. already had an appointment for an admissions examination for a trade school. He finished therapy after 31 sessions and was very satisfied with the outcome. After working on the panic disorder, he found his goals well clarified and had found good ways to reach them with the support of the therapist. The differentiated view of positive perspectives played a major role for him and his therapeutic progress. He planned to pursue the remaining projects on his own.

SOME EMPIRICAL IMPRESSIONS OF THE GOAL ELABORATION PROCESS

To evaluate the intervention, six therapists at the Center for Psychotherapy at the Ruhr-University of Bochum were trained in the EPOS manual (Willutzki & Koban, 1996). They used the EPOS intervention during the first four sessions in a total of 17 different therapies in an outpatient unit. This group was compared to a group of 17 other out-clients undergoing a cognitive-behavioral treatment during the same period of time (working with another seven therapists). All 13 therapists taking part in this study were trained in cognitive-behavioral treatment. Most clients suffered from anxiety disorders according to DSM-IV (American Psychiatric Association, 1994). The aim of the study was to investigate whether the EPOS counteracts demoralization and thus supports remoralization and whether it has effects on a person's self-esteem.

The average time for the imagery intervention was 30.5 minutes (SD = 9.0, ranging from 19 to 46 minutes). Compared to the control group, the clients in the EPOS group showed a trend toward stronger reduction in demoralization and greater improvement in self-esteem (Koban & Jancyk, 1995), particularly when they achieved a holistic information-processing mode during the imagery.

Further process analysis of the therapy sessions of the EPOS group pointed to positive effects for the therapy process (Behr & Lüthke-Steinhorst, 1998). The analysis showed that the clients' self-relatedness (Kolden, 1991; Orlinsky, Rønnestad, & Willutzki, in press), as a central link between therapeutic interventions and changes on the clients' side, was improved significantly in the EPOS group.

Moreover, the greater the use of specific interventions to concretize—identify and elaborate—personally relevant goals, the more the clients became self-related to such goals ($r = .87$; $p < .01$). The quality of the therapeutic alliance also correlated highly with the clients' self-relatedness ($r = .75$; $p < .01$). While the number of goals developed did not seem to have an effect on the perceived usefulness of the EPOS, stringency and depth of the goal elaboration seemed to be more relevant. The less client and therapist talked about negative topics during the session, the better the clients evaluated the session ($r = -.56$) and the more goal relevant realizations took place ($r = -.62$). Also, in retrospect the whole goal elaboration process was judged as more helpful by the therapists when the focus of the EPOS was more positive. These results give preliminary support to the contention that clients can profit from the EPOS not only in the short term but also in the intermediate term.

When evaluating these empirical results, it has to be kept in mind that the sample is much too small to allow general statements. The ecological validity of the study is further hampered by the fact that, because of the research constraints allowing only regular implementation of the EPOS in the first phase of therapy, the need for the EPOS was not always indicated. This may have resulted in smaller effects for clients not needing goal elaboration (Willutzki, 2000).

The study, nevertheless, shows that a careful identification and in-depth analysis of personally relevant goals can have positive effects both on clients' remoralization and self-esteem and the therapy process. A positive evaluative focus and a good therapeutic alliance represent intermediate steps on the way to therapeutic success. Therapists should monitor these aspects continually to secure a favorable therapeutic outcome. Preconditions for using the EPOS intervention are a clear indication and good timing.

FINAL REMARKS

As an example of difficulties that may arise when using the EPOS, we describe reactions of a colleague when he learned about our concepts in a workshop. In the beginning he pointed out that the intervention carries the risk that therapists impose goals on their clients that are not the clients' own. Further on during the workshop, this colleague voiced concerns that client goals may emerge that cannot be supported by the therapist for ethical reasons. Both of these problems are inherent in any goal-clarification process. On the one hand, discussions about therapeutic goals are always a co-constructive process between client and therapist during which they clearly influence each other. Both the solely process-directive—and not content-directive—approach of the EPOS and its focus on the personal meaning of goals are supposed to give clients room to develop perspectives that are relevant for them. On the other hand, the possibility that clients have goals that therapists do not share cannot be ruled out with any method. The advantage of our approach is that the goals are visualized, which facilitates an open discussion. In some cases higher-order goals that therapists can share may provide new ways to cooperate; but there may be cases—though rarely, in our experience—in which clients and therapists disagree on goals in principle and cooperation is impossible. From our perspective, even in such cases open discussion of the disagreement is preferable to implicit disputes or attempts to manipulate clients.

Besides the EPOS there are a number of other therapeutic approaches that are directed to the clarification of motives and goals. We see the advantage of both our concept and that of goal-value clarification (Schmelzer, 1983, 1986) in the pronounced orientation toward positive goals and resources of the client. In a similiar vein, positive states and positive perspectives on one's life have increasingly been stressed by the so-called positive psychology movement (Seligman & Csikszentmihalyi, 2000; Snyder & Lopez, 2002). We are, however, well aware of the fact that there is no one method that can always solve clients' motivational problems.

The approach we described for the development of positive perspectives has also been useful in psychotherapy training courses; it is possible to teach the basic structure of the intervention in a workshop in 12 to 18 hours. In this context psychotherapists have profited most from an action-oriented approach where the goal perspectives of the workshop participants were explored through the EPOS. Beyond improving their therapeutic competence, the therapists can benefit personally from such an experience-oriented approach. On the basis of research on the professional development of psychotherapists, Skovholt and Rønnestad (1992) stress that the development of long-term goals—professional as well as personal—has a positive effect on the career and professional satisfaction of psychotherapists. When therapists get to know the EPOS they also become more sensitive to the goal and striving aspect of other human behaviors (e.g., emotions, habits, assessments, standards, etc.; Kanfer, Reinecker, & Schmelzer, 1996). Instead of going through all the steps delineated in the EPOS, goal aspects can be highlighted in many ways and single elements of the intervention—such as the imagery or the explication of personal meaning—can be used throughout therapy (Schmelzer, personal communication) in order to use the motivational power of positive goals.

REFERENCES

American Psychiatric Association (1994). *Diagnostic and statistical manual for mental disorders* (4th edn.). Washington, DC: American Psychiatric Press.

Barlow, D.H., Craske, M.G., Cerny, J.A., & Klosko, J.S. (1989). Behavioral treatment of panic disorder. *Behaviour Therapy, 20,* 261–282.

Behr, B., & Lüthke-Steinhorst, E. (1998). *Die Elaboration wohlformulierter Ziele in der Psychotherapie. Zur Rolle allgemeiner und spezifischer Interventionen [Elaboration of well-formulated goals in psychotherapy. The role of general and specific interventions].* Unpublished thesis. Faculty of Psychology, Ruhr-University of Bochum, Germany.

Berg, I.K., & Miller, S.D. (1992). *Working with problem drinkers.* New York: W.W. Norton.

Caspar, F. (1995). *Plan analysis. Toward optimizing psychotherapy.* Seattle: Hogrefe.

De Shazer, S. (1988). *Clues. Investigating solutions in brief therapy.* New York: W.W. Norton.

Emmons, R.A., & Kaiser, H.A. (1996). Goal orientation and emotional well-being: Linking goals and affect through the self. In L.L. Martin & A. Tesser (Eds.), *Striving and feeling: Interactions among goals, affects and self-regulation* (pp. 79–98). Hillsdale, NJ: Erlbaum.

Epstein, S. (1990). Cognitive-experiential self-theory. In L.A. Pervin (Ed.), *Handbook of personality: Theory and research* (pp. 165–192). New York: Guilford.

Fiedler, K. (1988). Emotional mood, cognitive style, and behaviour regulation. In K. Fiedler & J.P. Forgas (Eds.), *Affect, cognition and social behaviour* (pp. 100–119). Toronto: Hogrefe.

Frank, J.D., & Frank, J.B. (1991). *Persuasion and healing.* Baltimore: Johns Hopkins University Press.

Franken, R.E. (1994). *Human motivation.* Belmont: Wadsworth.

Gilham, J.E., & Seligman, M.E.P. (1999). Footsteps on the road to a positive psychology. *Behaviour Research and Therapy, 37,* 163–173.

Grawe, K. (1998). *Psychologische Therapie [Psychological therapy].* Göttingen: Hogrefe.

Heckhausen, H., & Gollwitzer, P.M. (1987). Thought contents and cognitive functioning in motivational versus volitional states of mind. *Motivation and Emotion, 11*, 101–120.

James, L.D., Thorin, B.E., & Williams, D.A. (1993). Goal specification in cognitive-behavioral therapy for chronic headache pain. *Behavior Therapy, 24*, 305–320.

Kanfer, F.H., Reinecker, H., & Schmelzer, D. (1996). *Selbstmanagement-Therapie [Self-management-therapy]* (2nd edn.). New York: Springer.

Kelly, G.A. (1955). *The psychology of personal constructs.* New York: W.W. Norton.

Klinger, E. (1987). Current concerns and disengagement from incentives. In F. Halisch & J. Kuhl (Eds.), *Motivation, intention and volition* (pp. 337–347). New York: Springer.

Koban, C., & Jancyk, L. (1995). *Zur Relevanz der Zielklärung für die Handlungssteuerung von Klienten [The relevance of clarifying goals for action regulation of clients]*. Unpublished thesis. Faculty of Psychology, Ruhr-University of Bochum, Germany.

Kolden, G.G. (1991). The generic model of psychotherapy: An empirical investigation of patterns of process and outcome relationships. *Psychotherapy Research, 1*, 62–73.

Kuhl, J. (1983). Emotion, Kognition und Motivation. II. Die funktionale Bedeutung der Emotionen für das problemlösende Denken und für das konkrete Handeln [Emotion, cognition and motivation. II. The functional meaning of emotions for problem-solving thinking and for concrete action]. *Sprache und Kognition, 4*, 228–253.

Kuhl, J. (2001). *Motivation und Persönlichkeit [Motivation and Personality]*. Göttingen: Hogrefe.

Leuner, H. (1981). *Katathymes Bilderleben [Guided affective imagery]*. Stuttgart: Thieme.

Little, B.R. (1983). Personal projects: A rationale and methods for investigation. *Environment and Behavior, 15*, 273–309.

MacLeod, A.K., & Moore, R. (2000). Positive thinking revisited: Positive cognitions, well-being and mental health. *Clinical Psychology and Psychotherapy, 7*, 1–10.

Margraf, J., & Schneider, S. (1989). *Panik: Angstanfälle und ihre Behandlung [Panic: Anxiety attacks and their treatment]*. New York: Springer.

Michalak, J., Heidenreich, T., & Hoyer, J. (2001). Konflikte zwischen Patientenzielen—Konzepte, Ergebnisse und Konsequenzen für die Therapie [Conflicting goals of patients—Concepts, findings, and consequences for therapy practice]. *Verhaltenstherapie und psychosoziale Praxis, 34*, 273–280.

Orlinsky, D.E., Rønnestad, M.H., & Willutzki, U. (in press). Fifty years of psychotherapy process-outcomes research: Continuity and change. To appear in M.J. Lambert (Ed.), *Handbook of psychotherapy and behavior change* (5th edn.). New York: John Wiley & Sons.

Pöhlmann, K. (1999). *Die Entwicklung von Zielsystemen und ihre Veränderung durch Intervention: Persönliche Ziele von seelisch Gesunden und PsychotherapieklientInnen [Development of goal-systems and their change by intervention: Personal goals of mentally healthy people and psychotherapy clients]*. Unpublished manuscript. Philosophical Faculty, Friedrich-Alexander-University Erlangen/Nürnberg, Germany.

Salovey, P., & Birnbaum, D. (1989). Influence of mood on health-relevant cognitions. *Journal of Personality and Social Psychology, 57*, 539–551.

Schmelzer, D. (1983). Problem- und zielorientierte Therapie. Ansätze zur Klärung der Ziele und Werte des Klienten [Problem- and goal-orientated therapy. Approaches to clarify goals and values of the client]. *Verhaltensmodifikation, 4*, 130–156.

Schmelzer, D. (1986). Problem- und zielorientierte Verhaltenstherapie, Teil II. Das OPTIMIZE-Prozessmodell als Orientierungsrahmen für die Praxis [Problem- and goal-orientated therapy II. The OPTIMIZE-process-model as a framework for practice]. *Verhaltensmodifikation, 6*, 101–151.

Seligman, M., & Csikszentmihalyi, M. (2000). Positive psychology: An introduction. *American Psychologist, 55*, 5–14.

Skovholt, T.M., & Rønnestad, H.M. (1992). *The evolving professional self.* Chichester: Plenum.

Snyder, C.R., & Lopez, S.J. (Eds.) (2002). *The handbook of positive psychology.* Oxford: Oxford University Press.

Walter, J.F., & Peller, J.E. (1992). *Becoming solution-focused in brief therapy.* New York: Brunner/Mazel.

Walter, J.F., & Peller, J.E. (2000). *Recreating brief therapy. Preferences and possibilities.* New York: W.W. Norton.

Wampold, B.E. (2001). *The great psychotherapy debate: Models, methods, and findings.* Mahwah, NJ: Erlbaum.

Willutzki, U. (2000). *Positive Perspektiven in der Psychotherapie [Positive perspectives in psychotherapy].* Unpublished manuscript. Ruhr-University of Bochum, Faculty for Psychology.

Willutzki, U., & Koban, C. (1996). *Manual zur Elaboration wohlgestalteter Ziele in der Therapie (EPOS). [Manual for elaboration of well-defined goals in psychotherapy (EPOS)].* Research Bulletin. Faculty of Psychology, Ruhr-University of Bochum, Germany.

CHAPTER 18

Viktor E. Frankl's Existential Analysis and Logotherapy

Manfred Hillmann

Meppen, Germany

Synopsis.—Logotherapy is a school of psychotherapy that was founded by the Vienna neurologist and psychiatrist Viktor E. Frankl (1905–1997). To complement the dimensions of *soma* and *psyche*, Frankl introduced the spiritual dimension for healing purposes. The starting point of logotherapy is an outline of an anthropology, a reflection on the human image and the world view. It is within the spiritual dimension that the human capacity for self-distancing and self-transcendence occur. The *will to meaning* is a basic striving of the human being, which leads to inner fulfilment. Indeed this is such a strong human incentive that it helps one to cope with even the worst conditions. If the *will to meaning* becomes distorted or hindered, existential frustration or even noogenic-neuroses can ensue. Meaning can be realized in different ways, namely through realizing creative values, experiential values, and attitudinal values, this latter in the face of unalterable suffering. Even in human suffering fulfilment can ultimately be found. Humans need to recognize their potential freedom to act upon their lives and the responsibility to engage meaningfully with life. Finally, from the anthropological concept methods are developed, e.g., paradoxical intention, dereflection, attitudinal adjustment, and sensitization training for meaning.

INTRODUCTION

Logotherapy is a school of psychotherapy that was founded by the Vienna neurologist and psychiatrist Viktor E. Frankl (1905–1997) (Frankl, 1997). (The term "existential analysis" is often used coterminously with logotherapy.) The prefix "logo" derives from the Greek *logos* and has the sense of "meaning" or "spirit" (in Greek, *nous*, in German, *das Geistige*). Logotherapy, then, is a "meaning-centered psychotherapy," including and drawing on the capacities of the human spiritual dimension for psychotherapeutic purposes.

As a student, Frankl had already studied Sigmund Freud's psychoanalysis, and later became a member of the circle of Alfred Adler, the founder of "individual psychology." Frankl paid tribute to their fundamental achievements, but pointed out that their theories addressed only some aspects of the human person, not the human person in its totality, which would include the spiritual dimension—the *essential* human dimension. In practice

Handbook of Motivational Counseling. Edited by W. Miles Cox and Eric Klinger.

this can lead to an inadequate treatment of the patient, who is seen within a reductionist view, reduced to psychodynamics and biological forces. In approaching the whole person by also considering the spiritual dimension, Frankl intends the rehumanization of the medical field and of psychotherapy. Within the spiritual dimension phenomena occur that are important for healing. The patient has to be assisted in the perception of personal freedom as opposed to leaning toward fate and determinism, thus making him or her aware of his or her responsibility for the shaping of a personal life story, and of life as such. The questions of meaning and values come to the fore within this dimension.

In Frankl's approach one senses a convincing genuineness. What Frankl teaches is what he also experienced in his personal life. In his youth he had to grapple with the question of meaning and had to wrestle with the prevalent nihilistic philosophy of that time. Later, because he was a Jew, he was deported, together with his family, into Nazi concentration camps. But precisely this experience was the occasion for verifying a paraphrase of a saying of Nietzsche, in which Frankl saw his logotherapy epitomized, namely, "He who has a *why* to live for can bear with almost any *how*." Human beings need aims, meaningful aims, for living and surviving, for remaining psychologically stable and physically strong.

Interestingly, logotherapy became well known abroad, first of all in the United States, to which Frankl made 92 trips, whereas in Europe it has become well known only since the 1980s. A decisive contribution toward this has been the work of Frankl's pre-eminent pupil, Dr. Elisabeth Lukas (Lukas, 1981, 1985, 1994), who founded the *South German Institute of Logotherapy* in Fürstenfeldbruck, near Munich. She has published more than 30 books on logotherapy, and has trained several hundred logotherapists.

Presumably, Frankl's existential analysis and logotherapy will be absorbed to the full only now after his death, and this will give even further stimulation to psychotherapy.

EXISTENTIAL ANALYSIS AND LOGOTHERAPY

> *Every psychotherapy rests on its anthropological foundation—on its answer as to what human nature essentially is. This answer will point to what can be expected, assumed, and demanded of a human being in particular circumstances.*
>
> (Polak, 1980, pp. 46–48)

Physicians, psychologists, psychotherapists, social workers, educators, and nurses all understand, act, and work against the background of their personal perceptions of their image of the human, and their world view. It is all the more important, therefore, that all this be consciously reflected upon.

Frankl's approach is structured into two areas: existential analyst and logotherapist. Generally, only the term *logotherapy* is in use, in this way leaving the term *existential analysis* to be implicitly understood. Existential analysis deals with the anthropological philosophical foundation on which basis logotherapy, as "applied anthropology" (Böschemeyer, 1997, p. 10), is developed and put into psychotherapeutic practice.

Frankl's approach, both as existential analyst and logotherapist, "portrays a psychotherapy focused 'on the spirit (nous)'" (Frankl, 1996, p. 172).

Existential analysis incorporates human existence into psychotherapy. It investigates how far the human being, as such, is able to perceive and act freely, and in what way it is responsible for shaping itself and involving itself in life. Existential analysis analyzes the human being in terms of its possibility for realizing a spiritual existence. It is an analysis directed to the spiritual dimension, and "challenges existence to a sense of the always possible" (Frankl, 1996, p. 172).

Logotherapy then sets out from the spirit. "Logotherapy not only assumes the spiritual, the objective world of meaning and values, but it also brings them into play, establishes them in the psychiatric process" (Frankl, 1996, p. 172). Logotherapy helps patients to become more sensitive to meaning and values and encourages their spiritual capacities to respond to them.

THE SPIRITUAL DIMENSION

> *Today, man knows only too well that he has drives, what we have to show him is rather the opposite, namely, that he also has a spirit—a spirit, freedom, and responsibility.*
> (Frankl, 1992, p. 126)

This is the primary theme of the logotherapeutic approach. Whereas the human being is passive as regards the physical and psychical dimension (inherited body, conditioned behavior patterns), through the spiritual dimension one can rise above the physical and the psychical, at least on occasion. Thus it is that one can actively intervene and is open to change and formation. To illustrate this point, Frankl gives us a graphic example:

> Naturally, an airplane does not cease to be an airplane if it moves only on the ground. It can, and indeed must over and over again move on the ground, but that it really is an airplane only becomes evident when it lifts off into the sky. And, analogically, the human is only then acting as a human being when he goes beyond the level of psychophysical facticity, and is able to take a stand towards himself. It is precisely this ability that we call existence, and to exist means to have already achieved such a going beyond oneself.
> (Frankl, 1998, p. 73)

Logotherapy indicates to the patient that he has yet undiscovered abilities, which he can utilize for his own healing and personal growth. Frankl's example above makes clear that it is not a question of leaving the physical and psychical dimension behind, but that one should, again and again, transcend them in order to gain another perspective from which to deal differently with oneself. In this respect, Frankl himself called logotherapy a "height-psychology" (Frankl, 1998, p. 86). The spiritual dimension is a higher dimension than the others. But just as the child awakes into the consciousness of his own *ego*, the mature human being must become awake to the consciousness of his spiritual dimension. In this recognition, he will also grasp that he thereby has the innate capacity to discern, decide, and act.

What, more precisely, is the spiritual dimension? It is the locus, within the human being, where he is a person in the deepest sense. It is where the conscience is, the deepest intuitive faculty, the center of action, the unity from where human experience and action flow. The conscience, which is the center of the human person, is the meaning-organ of the person. Here, also, ethical sensitivity is located, and the apprehension of values. Within the spiritual dimension all those human phenomena, which are not found in the animal world, come to the fore. The phenomenon of intelligence is, therefore, not identical with the spiritual ability. Two spiritual phenomena are especially important in logotherapy, and Viktor Frankl referred to them again and again: the capacity for self-distancing, and that of self-transcendence. Figure 18.1 illustrates these two phenomena which are so central to logotherapy.

The illustration clarifies the special status of the spiritual dimension over the psychophysical dimension. The ability for self-distancing allows the person to take a stand toward a

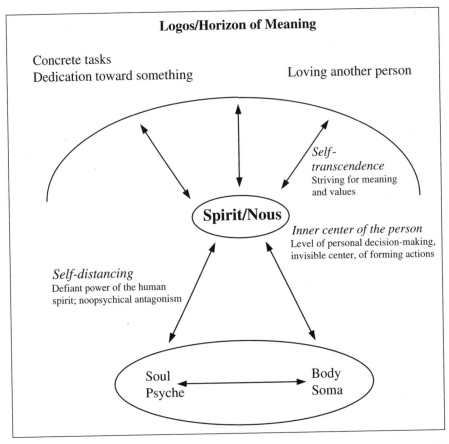

Logos/Horizon of Meaning

Concrete tasks
Dedication toward something   Loving another person

Self-
transcendence
Striving for meaning
and values

Spirit/Nous

Inner center of the person
Level of personal decision-making,
invisible center, of forming actions

Self-distancing
Defiant power of the human
spirit; noopsychical antagonism

Soul   Body
Psyche   Soma

Figure 18.1   The view of the human in logotherapy: Nous–Psyche–Soma (Spirit–Soul–Body)

situation or toward himself. Frankl describes this as follows:

> By virtue of this capacity man is capable of detaching himself not only from a situation but
> also from himself. He is capable of choosing his attitude towards himself. By so doing he
> really takes a stand towards his own somatic and psychic conditions and determinants. This
> is, understandably, a crucial issue for psychotherapy and psychiatry, education and religion.
> For, seen in this light, a person is free to shape his own character, and man is responsible
> for what he may make of himself. What matters is not the features of our character, or the
> drives and instincts per se, but rather the stand we take towards them. And the capacity to
> take such a stand is what makes us human beings. (Frankl, 1988, p. 17)

Only through the spiritual phenomenon for self-distancing does it become possible to
constructively tackle anxieties, compulsions, traumatic experiences, and strokes of fate. In
this practice of self-distancing, we have the act of freedom which cannot be found within
the animal world.

Another spiritual ability, which Frankl holds to be an essential trait of our human existence, is self-transcendence. This capacity puts the human being in a position to reach
beyond himself, toward the world and the logos. He can relate to values and spiritual ideals,
can relate lovingly to other human beings, and precisely by this means realizes his own

humanness. On this point a further quotation by Viktor Frankl:

> By self-transcendence I understand the fundamental anthropological fact that being human
> is to always reach out beyond self, towards something which is not just once more itself—
> towards something or towards someone: towards a meaning, which may be fulfilled by a
> human being, or towards a fellow human being who may have been encountered out there.
> Only to the extent to which a human being transcends itself in such a way as this does it
> actualize itself, in serving a cause or in loving another person! (Frankl, 1982, p. 160)

In the achievement of self-transcendence the human being encounters himself in the fullness
of his human capacity, and avoids all neurotic self-centeredness.

THE WILL TO MEANING

There are a variety of motivational forces in human beings, like the *will to lust* (Freud) or
the *will to power* (Adler). "But there is something with still deeper roots in man, what I call
the 'will to meaning'; this is man's endeavour towards achieving the best possible sense to
his existence" (Frankl, 1998, p. 116).

The will to meaning is the authentic motive force of human living, and is innate in
humans. If the patient becomes aware of it he is willing "to give himself to important tasks
with dedication and the readiness for sacrifice that may be necessary—in the service of
those he loves, in doing what is dear to his heart, and in being busy with what is his own
area of interest" (Lukas, 1998b, p. 276).

Meaning orientation is a massive healing power, which penetrates all levels of the human
being. Frankl writes:

> There is nothing in this world, be it ever so enabling, that can so help someone to overcome
> inner problems and outer difficulties, as the knowledge of one's specific task. This is the
> knowledge of a very concrete meaning, not of the whole of one's life but of the here and
> now, in the very situation in which one finds oneself. (Frankl & Kreuzer, 1994, p. 26)

The example of the iron filings used by Frankl is relevant here: these filings are lying on
a slab, just lying there unsorted. Then someone holds a magnet under the slab and the iron
filings all face the same direction (Frankl & Kreuzer, 1994). So it is with our psychic and
bodily powers, if they are drawn by meaning.

One has to discover the innate will to meaning lying within, and then focus upon it.
Suffering people are often especially fine-tuned for this task, because, once thrown off the
track, they are in search of discovering a new meaning and togetherness to latch on to.

Here one might well recall the case of Christy Brown (*My left foot,* an autobiography
especially worth reading from the logotherapeutic standpoint), who suffered from cerebral
palsy. He writes: "I wanted something to live for, and there was nothing. I wanted my life
to have a purpose, a value" (Brown, 1998, p. 101). Indeed, he found this in writing, and to
achieve this he had his left foot, the only member over which he had some control.

The painter Vincent van Gogh, who failed in many of his life-tasks, was also an inde-
fatigable searcher after meaning: "I am good for something then, I have some justification
for my existence!" he wrote. Time and again he posed himself the question: "Could I be of
some use for something, what purpose might I possibly serve?" (Nemeczek, 2001, p. 11).
This is the crucial logotherapeutic question, which was eventually answered by van Gogh
through and in his paintings.

In logotherapy the question about meaning always remains concrete. It arises from the uniqueness of the patient, within his or her unique life-situation (Frankl, 1982). From this question meaning can be deciphered, that is to say, the concrete life-task and the particular human relationships implied.

THE FRUSTRATED WILL TO MEANING

> *What man himself is really about, at least in original intention, is the fulfilment of meaning and the realisation of values. This is, in a word, his existential fulfilment. According to our opinion the existential has to do, not only with human life but, with the meaning that this life has. The opposite of existential fulfilment then would be existential emptiness, or, as logotherapy says, an "existential vacuum".*
>
> (Frankl, 1996, p. 24)

If the will to meaning is really the authentic purpose in life, that which brings fulfillment, then it will not be inconsequential if the will to meaning is frustrated. This will be the case if a personal meaningful task is not found, and meaningful human relationships are not established. An *existential frustration* will result if an "object of meaning adequate to the situation" (Lukas, 1997, p. 59) is not found and the person begins to suffer under this lack of meaning-orientation. In itself, that is not yet of a pathological nature, but it is quite a common phenomenon with which human beings are confronted. As a normal reaction, a person is stimulated to overcome the inner emptiness by a search for new possibilities of meaning. The logotherapist's task is to assist in the search for meaning, so that blockages can be broken through, and new meaningful perspectives can be opened up (Riedel, Deckart, & Noyon, 2002).

But the feeling of meaninglessness within the existential frustration can turn into an inner void. Life movements become paralyzed because the noodynamics, that is, the healthy, stimulating tension between the status quo and a meaning yet to be fulfilled, has collapsed and with that the motivational structure (Riedel, Deckart, & Noyon, 2002). The living bond between person and logos, horizon of meaning and values, has been broken. The human being no longer lives in a self-transcending way, but focuses back on himself. The object of attention now is the feeling of inner void and emptiness, by which he is plagued, and that drives him into an ever deeper feeling of discontent. This leads, further, to a general deterioration of emotions, and of the functioning of the nervous system, which will tend toward depressive conditions (Riedel, Deckart, & Noyon, 2002). Here, then, we have arrived at the point that crosses over into *noogenic neurosis*, which is defined as an existential frustration that has become pathological.

The existential frustration is not always manifest, but can hide behind manifold masks of negative ways of living. Something must fill the vacuum—this is intuitively felt by everyone. But not everyone realizes that the vacuum actually wants to be filled with meaning in order to be authentically satisfied. Instead, the feeling of inadequacy is anesthetized by a senseless work mania, by a general attitude of obsession—be it for drinking, hedonism, gambling, or simply gossip. But this is a futile effort to fill such an existential vacuum.

NOOGENIC NEUROSIS

The roots of neurosis may not be in the psyche only, but can originate beyond that, namely, in the spiritual dimension. Frankl defines noogenic neurosis as follows: "In cases where a noetic problem, a moral conflict, or an existential crisis is etiologically the basis of the neurosis, we speak of noogenic neurosis" (Frankl, 1998, p. 147).

These make up about 20% of all neuroses. Noogenic neurosis is an existential frustration that has become pathological. Existential frustration is not pathological as such, but it can take on a form that defines it as pathological. The precise reason why an existential frustration becomes pathological is when it is united with a somatic affectivity or weakness. It is this combination that defines noogenic neurosis. The psychosomatic involvement loses its importance when the conflict within the spiritual dimension finds a solution. Therapeutically, therefore, the problem must be solved on the level of the spiritual dimension and not only on the psychophysical level. A depression, for example, can have a biological cause—this is endogenous depression—in which case logotherapy cannot be the first therapeutic choice. But if depression is based on an unresolved problem within the spiritual level—reactive depression—then the therapeutic intervention must be a logotherapeutic one. This does not, however, exclude the support of adequate and simultaneous medication.

Existential frustration is a state of dissatisfaction, a spiritual state of emergency, which calls for rescue measures. But the psychophysical aspect hampers the forces that usually correct and overcome such an existential frustration. The person is now trapped in a kind of vicious circle and succumbs to neurotic attitudes, leading to either passivity and boredom, or to a meaningless overactivity.

Elisabeth Lukas writes:

> A noetic crisis can lead to psychic illness, as when a person misunderstands the signals from his deepest conviction; when he only finds wrong answers for the most important existential

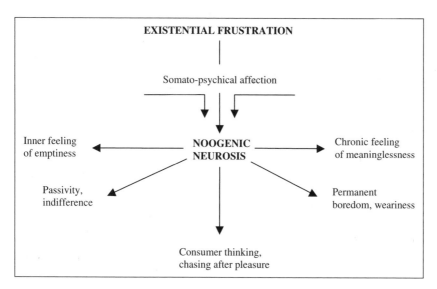

Figure 18.2 Existential frustration. (From Lukas, E. (1998a). *Lehrbuch der Logotherapie*, p. 163. Reproduced by permission of Profil Verlag, München-Wien.)

questions or no answers at all; when he cannot sense the "what for" of being in the world; when he cannot connect meaning with his existence and becomes depressed with feelings that it does not matter whether or not he is here at all. (Lukas, 1998a, p. 162)

The unsuccessful search for meaning, one's task in life not found, frustrated or inadequately lived relationships, a conflict of values, or the disorientation and complicated nature of a living situation are the bases on which noogenic neurosis can develop.

For example, the reason why a patient has neurotic stomach problems and insomnia could be a dilemma of values, a problem of conscience—that is to say, it could be a spiritual problem. The patient wants to leave his job because he feels he is no longer able to cope with its demands. At the same time, his hands are tied because he has to support a family. He is able to see the need to stay in the job for obvious financial reasons, yet he is unable to discern a real meaning that would convince him. He simply puts up with the situation. But, because he cannot solve it spiritually, he builds up inner tensions which, in turn, are the cause of his dysfunctional stomach and his insomnia.

The logotherapeutic task is, now, to make conscious the conflict of values, and also the various meaningful reasons for or against a change of working place. This enables the patient to discover, on the one hand, new, and more, reasons to consider, and, on the other hand, to weigh these up. Let's say this leads to the decision to stay in the particular job, but now with a different perspective, enabling him to be more at peace, and more in harmony. This, eventually, leads to a disappearance of the stomach problems and to better sleep. The change of attitude takes place within the process of widening the patient's perspective on a meaningful involvement in life. He might, indeed, have discovered that leaving his job would even increase his problems. But, on the basis of this insight, he has suddenly accepted the necessity for improving his work situation, by creatively looking at things that can be changed within his job, instead of running away from it.

Noogenic neuroses arise when the spiritual attempt to come to terms with the world has come to a halt, and when someone begins to suffer from inner emptiness, and meaninglessness in his life. Dealing spiritually with life should already be practiced early on in life, which is why logotherapy has a preventive task.

THREE PATHWAYS TO MEANING

The realization of meaning through values in everyday life can be categorized into the following three pathways to meaning, namely: creative values, experiential values, and attitudinal values.

The realization and experience of meaning through creative values plays a prominent role in Western culture. It is an active involvement in, and shaping of, life. Working in a job, building a house, shaping a garden, writing a book, painting or composing, all these are creative values in which a person's part is an active role.

But meaningful living does not depend only on creative values. The receptive apprehension of reality, through which a person is impressed, is equally important. "They are realized by taking in the world, for example through an appreciation of, and devotion to, beauty in nature and art. The wealth of meaning they can give to humans must not be underestimated" (Frankl, 1982, p. 60). Frankl writes:

> There is a third category of realising values and meaning in life: attitudinal values. They are, at one and the same time, a provocation and a challenge.

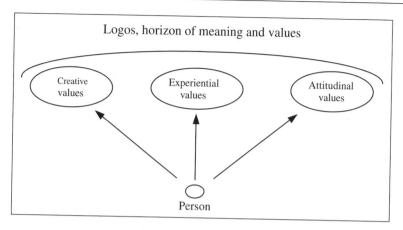

Figure 18.3   Three pathways to meaning

> We must never forget that we may also find meaning in life even when confronted with a hopeless situation, when facing a fate that cannot be changed. For, what matters then, bears witness to the uniquely human potential at its best, which is to transform a personal tragedy into a triumph, to turn one's predicament into a human achievement. When we are no longer able to change a situation—just think of an incurable disease such as inoperable cancer—we are challenged to change ourselves. (Frankl, 1985, p. 135)

Here Frankl's uncompromising attitude toward the meaningfulness of life finds expression. The human being must not throw in the towel too soon, but is challenged to squeeze meaning even out of unavoidable suffering, by taking a stance toward it.

The three pathways to meaning should be made conscious as soon as possible in life, and our everyday lives should be lived under the umbrella of these categories. A missed bus, for example, represents a situation in which a person can work on his inner attitude, by not getting stressed, but by accepting the situation as it is. Personal stability is made manifest by flexible adjustment to all three categories of values.

The theme of the three pathways to meaning is often mentioned in logotherapy, because it plays a fundamental role in everyday human living, all the more so in crisis situations. The aim is to broaden the patient's outlook about the meaningfulness of life, and to change his personal attitude toward life, in that life is accepted as a personal challenge, and a possibility for realizing meaning to the last.

THE SUFFERING PERSON

When Viktor Frankl talks about meaning in suffering his words are validated by his own experience as he himself had to suffer through four concentration camps, during three years. In his book, *Man's search for meaning*, he writes:

> What was really needed was a fundamental change in our attitude toward life. We had to learn ourselves and, furthermore, we had to teach the despairing men, that it *did not really matter what we expected from life, but rather what life expected from us.*
>
> (Frankl, 1985, p. 98)

This is a complete existential changeover, a change of paradigm. The human being is not the ultimate center of everything, but is related to something outside, which demands a response. Human freedom, thinking, and action are informed by the texture of life. Life

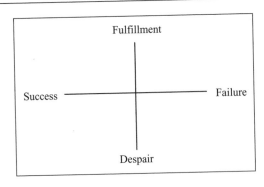

Figure 18.4 Reticle

presents itself as a task. Human freedom, then, is to realize the possibility of accepting suffering as a task that has, somehow, to be coped with.

Logotherapy's assignment is to assist and encourage people in the process of changing their perspectives and basic habits. "Where no more action is possible to shape fate, there, it is necessary to face up to fate with the right attitude" (Frankl, 1998, p. 131). In this context human experience comes to our aid: "Suffering makes human beings perceptive and the world transparent" (Frankl, 1998, p. 136). The one confronted with suffering often becomes very sensitive toward value possibilities, and reality becomes transparent, insofar as he can better distinguish between what is essential and what is not.

To be able to see meaning in suffering, the patient must undergo a change of paradigm. Those whose main aim is to strive for success will fail, when confronted with the demands of suffering. It has to be grasped that "human existence at its deepest, and in the end, is passive, that the essence of the human being is to be a suffering one: *homo patiens*" (Frankl, 1998, p. 137).

The suffering person can become aware of a dimension perpendicular to the dimension of the *homo faber*, that is to say, the vertical dimension, with its poles of despair and fulfillment. And now a new perspective, often unsuspected, comes into view, allowing one to undergo the vision of meaning, that of the *homo sapiens*. From this a new strength and a new vitality can flow.

Attitudinal values—which arise in the face of inalterable suffering—when compared with creative and experiential values, make the greatest demands on human beings. This is why they rank highest.

I have often observed this process of change in a medical rehabilitation clinic, where, for example, parents are confronted with a daughter's or a son's irreversible brain damage. In the first phase, parents are full of hope that their child will become reasonably normal again, even if this runs against medical assessment. Only after a considerable time, and after an inner struggle and process of adjustment, will a change of attitude take place. The unavoidable is gradually accepted, and meaning is no longer looked for in the fruitless hope of medical healing, but in good care, together with personal love and affection toward their child. This is a gain for both—for the parents, who are now open to the most suitable encounter with their beloved child, and for the child, who, despite the heavy cognitive restrictions, can profit from the caring and more peaceful atmosphere around it.

The acceptance of suffering and the change of paradigm to the realization that suffering constitutes a personal task is not so much the result of logical reasoning, but rather of a personal insight into the deepest existential levels of life. The mediation of this insight is possible most of all through personal witness, such as Frankl's own experience in the concentration camps. But role models and witnesses to the meaning of suffering are found everywhere in ordinary life. Humans should encourage each other by showing each other how to live a meaningful life, despite its tragedies.

METHODS OF LOGOTHERAPY

Viktor Frankl frequently stressed the uniqueness of every human being. He was always skeptical when, in psychotherapy, methods and techniques were overemphasized. There is a great danger that the human being may be pressed into a system, and a system does not do justice to the uniqueness of the individual.

In the logotherapeutic approach anthropology is of primary importance, and, from that point of view, logotherapy has a strong philosophical basis. Experience has shown "that simply confronting the patient with his (Frankl's) concept of the human has a healing effect" (Lukas, 1998b, p. 275). This is communicated in interpersonal dialog and encounter. This anthropology, then, is the texture from which methods can be shaped, often easily, for practical application. Logotherapy is very open to methods and techniques developed outside logotherapy, if only they fit with some basic logotherapeutic tenets. Indeed, Frankl understood his own contribution, not as a replacement but as a supplement to other forms of psychotherapy. Many current methods achieve a new lease of life in reconnecting with Frankl's anthropological views, in that they are linked into a wider context.

In the following we describe four established, specific, logotherapeutic methods and strategies (according to E. Lukas), namely, paradoxical intention, dereflexion, attitudinal adjustment, and meaning sensitization training.

Paradoxical Intention

Paradoxical intention finds its application most of all in dealing with anxiety disorders (Ascher & Schotte, 1999), phobias, panic disorders, compulsory disorders, insomnia (Ascher, 1980; Ladouceur & Gros-Louis, 1986), and social phobias. Paradoxical intention is an exceptional and successful psychotherapeutic technique. It aims to put a stop to a neurotic vicious circle of symptoms.

Let us take a patient suffering from extreme insomnia. The experience of not being able to fall asleep awakens an anticipatory anxiety and at the same time induces an increased effort to force oneself to sleep. But even more insomnia results from this.

In paradoxical intention the neurotic vicious circle is broken by expressing a wish for exactly what one fears. Here the ability for self-distancing is mobilized in a humorous way. Gordon W. Allport once said: "The neurotic who learns to laugh at himself may be on the way to self-management, perhaps to a cure" (Frankl, 1998, p. 164). Paradoxical intention validates this statement. Elisabeth Lukas's description is as follows:

> Paradoxical intention is more than the treatment of symptoms. With the aid of humor, the patient elevates himself beyond the self. He no longer submits the self to his psycho-physical impulses, he rather experiences the self as strong, he evidences courage, seizes "the bull by the horns", and faces anxiety-filled situations intentionally and deliberately. All this

introduces an inner growth that would never be attainable through mere rational fighting against anxieties. He alters his general attitude toward life and regains basic confidence. This cultivates the best protection against any neurotic upset wherever its roots may be located. (Lukas, 2000, p. 105)

Applied to the example mentioned above, the patient with insomnia is instructed that instead of struggling for sleep he is to wish deliberately not to go to sleep, at least not at the moment, and if possible not at all. After all, before developing insomnia he slept too much anyway, so now it is only right that he lie awake all night, at least this night. His tired eyes the next morning could possibly be kept open with match-sticks or some cellophane tape. The moment the patient really wishes this, the fear of not falling asleep will vanish, because the fear of not falling asleep cannot coexist with the actual wish not to go to sleep. The fact that the patient then miserably fails in this project by immediately falling asleep can be laughed at the next day.

This method will need to be explained and demonstrated by examples, only once to some patients. For others, one will need to develop an understanding and appreciation. In the end, the patient must understand that, as the acting person, he or she can deal with the neurotic contents of the psyche in a humorous, playful, and subtle way. I remember a patient whose hands kept trembling when she had to read a text in the church. I explained the mechanics of paradoxical intention to her, but she judged it to be rather implausible. She wanted to get rid of the trembling, not intensify it! However, two months later she reported that her hands were no longer trembling when reading in the church. One day, when her hands were again trembling, she tried what I had explained to her, and to her utter surprise the trembling stopped. She then understood that sometimes the psyche has to be dealt with in unusual ways.

Dereflection

Whereas in paradoxical intention it is the human capacity for self-distancing that is mobilized, in the case of dereflection it is self-transcendence. Dereflection finds its application in therapeutic work with every form of hyper-reflection, that is, neurotic self-obsession— for example, with sexual disorders, insomnia, somatoform disorders, and a variety of other problems. Hyper-reflection cuts off the connection with the logos, with values and meaning, with what transcends, and thus it throws the human being back onto itself. This can lead to considerable difficulties and disturbances.

Whoever is too concerned about falling asleep, interferes with the normal process of falling asleep. Whoever anxiously looks out for the recurrence of a disruption of the heart rhythm will actually produce the disruption. It is the same with many other symptoms, such as headaches, trembling, or noises in the ear. One's own behavior or what one says can also be hyper-reflected. All this leads to a blockage of the natural course of life. The therapeutic aim is to detach the attention from the symptom and from concern with the self. What we are here dealing with is actually not a distraction technique but a reorientation toward the logos:

To ignore something—in order to achieve the required dereflection—is only possible by by-passing this something through directing oneself towards something other. This is where logotherapy goes over into existential analysis, whose essential aim is, more or less, that the human being is geared to and turned towards the concrete meaning of his personal existence. This meaning itself has, at times, to be clarified by analysis. (Frankl, 1998, p. 179)

It is about bringing the patient back into contact with meaningful tasks and with human relationships.

> The human being does not exist to observe and reflect on himself before a mirror. Rather is he there to offer and sacrifice himself, to dedicate himself consciously and with devotion.
> (Frankl, 1998, p. 81)

Within the therapeutic process it can be a challenging task to detach the patient from these symptoms of self-concern to which he clings. It often needs creativity and perseverance to find something that is more attractive than hyper-reflection. But sometimes, also, it is very easy, as in the following example to which Viktor Frankl refers:

> Ladies and gentlemen, you all surely remember the film *Moulin Rouge*, and perhaps also, the gripping scene where Toulouse Lautrec has decided to take his own life? We already hear the gas flowing and hissing, then his eye falls on the easel and on a painting resting there in which he notices a mistake. He gathers himself together, hobbles over, picks up a paintbrush and puts things right. Then he turns off the gas. What do I want to say with this story? That he was able to overcome his depression, which sparked off the impulse to suicide, only because of, and thanks to, his *being fully devoted to a task*.
> (Frankl & Kreuzer, 1994, p. 73)

In working with people suffering from tinnitus it has become obvious that dereflection is at the center of the healing process. Naturally a person with loud noises in the ear is inclined to focus on the noises. Only a strong meaningful goal, something regarded as more important than the noise, can distract him from the fixation on the troublesome noises. Paradoxical intention and attitudinal adjustment are also part of the therapeutic procedure.

Meaningful personal goals and relationships allow people to grow beyond their problems and suffering. The psychiatrist Ernst Kretschmer describes it as follows:

> One should give to one's life a strong positive current, with goals suited to one's personality. Neurotic complexes best proliferate in standing water, a strong, fresh current sweeps them away. (Frankl, 1982, p. 199)

Attitudinal Adjustment

Having focused on the spiritual qualities of self-distancing through paradoxical intention, and on self-transcendence through dereflection, now we move toward self-formation and inner growth through attitudinal adjustment (Lukas, 1998a).

Whether a person copes and comes to grips with a difficult life-situation, or suffers and breaks down under its burden, will largely depend on his or her personal attitude toward it. Attitudinal adjustment, therefore, is of invaluable importance in counseling and therapy. Attitudinal adjustment touches on the core of the person, deep into mentality and disposition, the point from where basic attitudes influence the person as a whole.

> Attitudinal adjustment is principally aimed at modifying pathogenic attitudes, and this is especially necessary if the problems that give rise to these attitudes cannot themselves be changed. As a result, the attitudinal adjustment then comes to have all the more importance the more the limits for modifying such reality are restricted.
> (Riedel, Deckart, & Noyon, 2002)

A shift of view, in logotherapeutic terms a "Copernican revolution," has to take place: "It is life itself that asks the questions, not man. His task is to answer life's questions, to respond, to take responsibility in the face of life" (Frankl, 1998, p. 141).

What has to be worked out and achieved is a "stronger, improved, ethically more valuable, more hope-filled . . . attitude" (Lukas, 1998a, p. 115). This can entail, for example, physical appearance, disadvantageous living conditions, acceptance of chronic illness, of pain, tinnitus, neurodermatitis, etc., even mental illness. It may concern interhuman relationships or work conditions.

Elisabeth Lukas points out that attitudinal adjustment is not only important and necessary in the face of negative fate, but also in the face of positive fate. Toward favorable circumstances one should behave responsibly. A wealthy person can do a lot of good for others. Good health provides energy to do meaningful tasks. Intelligence can be used to solve difficult problems. Power, also, can be used for the realization of meaningful goals.

A human being's personal attitude decides whether outer fate also becomes inner fate, whether one gains inner freedom in the face of outer circumstances. In this context another reference to the autobiography of Christy Brown, who suffered from cerebral palsy, seems relevant: "Now I can speak quite well if only I take my time about it and do not get flustered when I cannot get out a word clearly. Basically, the whole cause of my speech difficulty lies in my own attitude to it. Once I have conquered that queer hot feeling of panic, almost of shame, that brings the blood in a warm swift rush to my cheeks whenever anyone strange tries to converse with me, I will have destroyed the root-cause of my trouble" (Brown, 1998, p. 163).

Sensitization Training for Meaning

Elisabeth Lukas has developed a sensitization training for meaning (Lukas, 1998a), with a five-stage set of questions, which helps the patient to find out the most meaningful action within a particular unresolved, problematic situation. The questions are:

1. What is my problem?
2. What "scope for free action" do I have?
3. What choices do I have?
4. Which choice is the most meaningful?
5. This one choice I want to realize!

One can take a sheet of paper and divide it into two halves. The left half stands for the scope of fate, for what is given and unchangeable, at least for the moment. Let us assume that the given problem is a new working colleague who destroys the harmony between the other colleagues. We now attend to the right half of the page, which represents the scope for free action, which is there despite the given problem.

In the third step possible choices and actions are to be noted. Here, unrestricted and unlimited fantasy should prevail. Everything thinkable, even if it looks impossible, is to be listed under the scope for free action. For example, it is thinkable that the new colleague could be ignored by the group, or be reported to the personnel manager. But it is also thinkable that someone suitable might talk to the colleague, or that the group be supportive of each other in order to calm personal anger, and so deal with the situation in an open manner.

Then in the fourth step the most meaningful option is to be chosen. Reporting the colleague to the personnel manager might not be a meaningful step because it may only add to the tension. But encouraging each other and dealing openly with the situation in hand could be the most meaningful action in this case. Such will demand courage from all involved, and readiness to sustain the continuing conflict; but it can mostly be assumed that such problems do not necessarily snowball.

In the fifth and last step the resolution must be put into action. Here, again, the group members can support one another. This may, in the end, lead to the result that misunderstandings and disagreements are cleared up within a few weeks, and that the new colleague learns to integrate himself into the group more harmoniously.

This set of questions leads to more sensitive awareness and clarity within a problem situation. The scope for free action is made clear to the patient, and he is encouraged toward a creative dealing with the problem at hand. Thus, the danger of getting stuck within the confining scope of fate is prevented.

CONCLUDING REMARKS

By developing logotherapy and existential analysis Viktor Frankl has made an outstanding contribution to humankind. His approach has won worldwide acknowledgment and inspires not only the fields of medicine, psychology, and psychotherapy but also the fields of pedagogy, teaching, sociology, business, and many others.

The human being, in his orientation toward a trans-subjective meaning, a meaningful task to dedicate himself to, and meaningful relationships to engage in, is the center of logotherapeutic attention. Meaning as a motive helps one to survive even the worst conditions in life, which was also Frankl's very own experience.

But the question of meaning can only be answered within the spiritual dimension. Therefore, it is the primary task of logotherapeutic intervention to make this specific human dimension conscious, which will then enable the patients to see themselves in the light of their abilities and possibilities. The image one has of oneself is essential for one's ability to cope with life. Therefore, it is logotherapy's assignment to help the patient to correct distorted self-images and to understand reality from within an adequate concept of life. In practice, simply the presentation of the anthropological concepts, as worked out in logotherapy, has healing effects on the patient (Lukas, 1998b).

Frankl convincingly highlighted the potential freedom to grow, which a person has, in the face of and despite a burdensome and crisis-laden life. He encourages the responsibility of this person to engage meaningfully in life. He saw the essential movements of human life to lie in the realization of spiritual abilities for self-distancing and self-transcendence. These movements correspond to human nature; they psychically stabilize and physically vitalize the human person.

Frankl's major contribution is the renewed focus on the anthropological foundations of psychotherapeutic practice. In the rectification of the human image and world view, the logotherapist establishes a basic attitude that is the foundation for any practical realization. Although in logotherapy a number of techniques and methods have been developed, the stress remains on the development of a deepened existential understanding with which the logotherapist encounters the patient. "Fundamentally, the strength of logotherapy consists in excellent guidelines for the art of improvization, rather than in a polished and extensive repertoire of methods. This allows the therapist to match his therapy to the unique characteristics of each patient in his particular life- crisis-situation" (Lukas, 1998a, p. 85).

Frankl's logotherapy aspires to a holistic view of the human being. Therefore, the perspective must always be bigger than an exclusively natural scientific approach, which may run the danger of overemphasizing the biochemical or psychodynamic make-up of the human being. Frankl's focus is on the human person, who is always more than symptoms and psychology. One has to perceive human beings in all their dimensions—physical, psychological, and spiritual. Logotherapy's healing approach is to help the patient to become aware of this last dimension, to feel at home there, to trust in it and to make use of the spiritual resources for healing that are to be found there.

REFERENCES

Ascher, L.M. (1980). Paradoxical intention. An experimental investigation. In A. Goldstein & E.B. Foa (Eds.), *Handbook of behavioral interventions* (pp. 266–321). New York: John Wiley & Sons.

Ascher, L.M., & Schotte, D.E. (1999). Paradoxical intention amd recursive anxiety. *Journal of Behavior Therapy and Experimental Psychiatry, 30*, 71–79.

Böschemeyer, U. (1997). Über Gründe zum Leben [About reasons for living]. *Zeitschrift des Hamburger Instituts für Existenzanalyse und Logotherapie, 2*, 3–13.

Brown, C. (1998). *My left foot.* London: Vintage/Random House.

Frankl, V.E. (1982). *Ärztliche Seelsorge [Medical spiritual counseling].* Wien: Deuticke.

Frankl, V.E. (1985). *Man's search for meaning.* New York: Washington Square Press.

Frankl, V.E. (1986). *The doctor and the soul: from psychotherapy to logotherapy.* New York: Vintage Books.

Frankl, V.E. (1988). *The will to meaning: Foundations and applications of Logotherapy.* New York: Meridian Printing.

Frankl, V.E. (1992). *Psychotherapie für den Alltag [Psychotherapy for everyday life].* Freiburg i.Br.: Herder Verlag.

Frankl, V.E. (1996). *Der leidende Mensch: Anthropologische Grundlagen der Psychotherapie [The suffering human: Anthropological foundations of psychotherapy].* Bern: Verlag Hans Huber.

Frankl, V.E. (1997). *Recollections—an autobiography.* New York: Plenum.

Frankl, V.E. (1998). Grundriß der Existenzanalyse und Logotherapie [Outline of existential analysis and logotherapy]. In *Logotherapie und Existenzanalyse: Texte aus sechs Jahrzehnten [Logotherapy and existential analysis]* (pp. 57–184). Weinheim: Psychologie Verlags Union.

Frankl, V.E., & Kreuzer, F. (1994). *Im Anfang war der Sinn [In the beginning was meaning].* München: Piper.

Ladouceur, R., & Gros-Louis, Y. (1986). Paradoxical intervention vs. stimulus control in the treatment of severe insomnia. *Journal of Behavior Therapy and Experimental Psychiatry, 17* (4), 267–269.

Lukas, E. (1981). A validation of logotherapy. *The International Forum for Logotherapy, 4* (2), Fall/Winter, 116–125.

Lukas, E. (1985). The meaning of logotherapy for clinical psychology. *The International Forum for Logotherapy, 8* (1), Spring/Summer, 7–10.

Lukas, E. (1994). Zur Validierung der Logotherapie [Toward the validation of logotherapy]. In V. Frankl, *Der Wille zum Sinn: Ausgewählte Vorträge zur Logotherapie [The will to meaning: Selected lectures on Logotherapy]* (pp. 283–316). München: Piper.

Lukas, E. (1997). *Urvertrauen gewinnen [Gaining basic trust].* Freiburg i.Br.: Herder Verlag.

Lukas, E. (1998a). *Lehrbuch der Logotherapie [Textbook of logotherapy].* München: Profil Verlag.

Lukas, E. (1998b). Logotherapie—Viktor E. Frankl 1905–1997 [Logotherapy—Viktor E. Frankl 1905–1997]. *Wiener Klinische Wochenschrift—The Middle European Journal of Medicine, 110* (8), 275–278.

Lukas, E. (2000). *Logotherapy textbook.* Toronto: Liberty Press.

Nemeczek, A. (2001). *Van Gogh: Das Drama von Arles [Van Gogh: The drama at Arles].* München: Prestel Verlag.

Polak, P. (1980). The Anthropological Foundations of Logotherapy. *The International Forum for Logotherapy, 3*, Spring, 46–48.

Riedel, C., Deckart, R., & Noyon, A. (2002). *Existenzanalyse und Logotherapie: Ein Handbuch für Studium und Praxis [Existential analysis and logotherapy: A handbook for study and practice].* Darmstadt: Primus Verlag.

CHAPTER 19

Changing Alcohol Expectancies: Techniques for Altering Motivations for Drinking

Barry T. Jones
University of Glasgow, UK

Synopsis.—The expected reinforcing properties of alcohol consumption outcomes are thought to impact on current and future consumption. Called "expectancies" and stored in memory reflecting past direct and indirect consumption experiences, positive expectancies are thought to represent a significant part of the motivation to drink, and negative expectancies are thought to represent a significant part of the motivation to restrain. This formulation has led to the speculation that procedures that might reduce the number or intensity of positive expectancies held might cause a commensurate reduction in consumption and, more recently, to speculation that increasing the number or intensity of negative expectancies might also bring this about. This chapter provides a background on what is known about positive and negative expectancies dealing first with "implicit" expectancies before moving on to "explicit" expectancies. A basic process designed to *reduce* the number or intensity of positive expectancies held, experiential expectancy challenge, is described and the studies that have evaluated its effectiveness are reviewed. Most of this work has been carried out with heavy drinking students (principally in the USA). A basic process designed to *increase* the number and intensity of negative expectancies held by individuals in treatment is also described. This process has the touch and feel of a motivational interview and is described in detail. Both the reduction in positive expectancies and the increase in negative expectancies has been shown to have limited success in addressing excessive consumption. It remains to be seen whether the procedures currently used with heavy drinking students can be usefully extended to individuals in treatment and whether the quite different procedures used with those in treatment can be useful in the student context.

MEMORY, ON GOING BEYOND THE INFORMATION GIVEN

Memory affords individuals the opportunity to "go beyond the information given" (given by the perceptual moment, Bruner, Goodnow, & Austin, 1956). It is a process that provides them with the capability of responding appropriately to current and future events on the basis of past experiences. These experiences might have impinged on consciousness as they

Handbook of Motivational Counseling. Edited by W. Miles Cox and Eric Klinger.
© 2004 John Wiley & Sons, Ltd.

unfolded and sometimes they might not have. Memories from the experiences might have been laid down consciously and with effort, but sometimes they might have been laid down without the individual's being aware of it occurring. When the memories are brought into play, it might be through a conscious decision to do so, and sometimes it might not. Finally, in going beyond the information given, the memories' actions and effects might impinge on current consciousness, but sometimes they might not. Whatever the circumstance, it provides new experiences and the wheel of memory continues to turn. Going beyond the information given by the perceptual moment might benefit, for example, processes such as catching a ball, contacting emergency services, switching on an electric light in a room, looking in an appropriate direction when crossing the street, and understanding spoken and written sentences. But going beyond the information given does not *always* deliver benefit; for example, an American visitor to the United Kingdom might be able to catch a ball appropriately but also might incorrectly dial 911 in an emergency (it should be 999), switch up to turn on the room lights (it should be down), and look left when leaving the sidewalk (it should normally be right when leaving the pavement). It appears that decisions about whether to consume an alcoholic drink might be another set of processes in which going beyond the information given (through the application of "memory") does not always deliver benefit. It has been part of the core business of psychology to explore and understand conscious and unconscious memory and its explicit and implicit role in the process of going beyond the information given. Such knowledge about memory has been used by scientists to help to explain the variability found in the quantity of alcohol that individuals consume—variability in consumption both *between* different individuals and variability *within* an individual, from one day to another. The purpose of this chapter is to describe some of this work. The bottom line is to identify psychological structures (memory structures) that might be the target of intervention. The chapter begins with some typical drinking decision scenarios.

TYPICAL DRINKING SCENARIOS

Consider decisions to "have a drink"—decisions of the sort that might be made by any alcohol user or abuser, or an alcohol-dependent person. First, consider some circumstances that might relate to those who *use* alcohol (loosely categorized as individuals who have few if any problems as a result of the alcohol they drink). Such a decision "to have a drink" might be planned: knowing that there is going to be a hard day at the office and things will finish late, it might be planned to go to a bar for a drink with coworkers after work. Or it might be unplanned: walking along the street after a job interview recalling the events of the day and seeing across the street an illuminated logo of a well-known beer hanging over the entrance of a bar, the decision might be made to cross the street and go in for a drink. Second, consider some other circumstances but this time involving individuals who consume alcohol at levels of *abuse* or *dependency* (loosely categorized as levels and frequencies of consumption that regularly bring significant problems). The decision "to have a drink" might also be planned: sitting on jury service all day, during which time there is no access to alcohol, a juror might have planned to bring in a small bottle so that a drink might be consumed surreptitiously in the court house or immediately on leaving it. It might also be unplanned: feeling somewhat troubled or depressed while alone at a movie and seeing an advertisement showing an ice bucket being filled with crushed ice, the decision might be made to leave the theater to find a bar for a drink. These sketches illustrate two quite different types of explanation provided by scientists of the possible roles of memory in alcohol consumption variability, which have generated two quite different research areas—one on *alcohol cue–reactivity* and the other on *alcohol outcome expectancies*. Two aspects of alcohol cue–reactivity will be described as an introduction to alcohol expectancies.

Drinking Decisions as Automated Processes

Alcohol cue–reactivity has traditionally been studied within a conditioned learning framework. Within this framework, scientists describe how objects that were once alcohol neutral may, after repeatedly being paired with alcohol consumption, begin to elicit similar responses that had previously only surrounded consumption initiation or consumption itself (Heather & Greeley, 1990). Responses such as changes in salivary flow (Rubonis et al., 1994), skin conductance (Stormark et al., 1993), reaction time (Sayette et al., 1994), craving and urges (Bradizza et al., 1999), and intention and desire to drink (Schulze & Jones, 1999, 2000) have been used to measure how neutral objects can acquire an alcohol-related status through experience with alcohol consumption. Two examples of objects with this change of status might be the illuminated beer logo (hanging above the entrance to the bar in the sketch described earlier) and the ice bucket filled with crushed ice (the advertisement), both cueing "alcohol" responses such as salivary flow or other responses that might give rise to thoughts about alcohol when such thoughts might not have otherwise occurred. These thoughts might, in turn, increase the likelihood of subsequent consumption should they occur. Alcohol cue-exposure treatment has been designed to reduce this likelihood by changing the conditioned link between the cue and the response by exposing the alcohol cue to the client in the absence of subsequent consumption opportunities. Not only does this procedure promote habituation and extinction (weakening the link), it also provides an opportunity to practice other coping and control skills that might be formally taught as part of combined treatment programs (e.g., Monti et al., 2001; Rohsenow et al., 2001). Although the evidence on the effectiveness of cue-exposure treatment *per se* as a means of helping to reduce consumption is equivocal, its effectiveness when combined with another program appears to be much better.

To a large extent, the conditioning model used to explain alcohol cue reactivity has been superseded by a more contemporary model. Within this model, it is proposed that memory holds associations between internal representations of *behaviors* (such as drinking alcohol) and internal representations of behavioral *outcomes* (such as feeling relaxed) and that the strength of any particular association is a function of the number of times the two have occurred together in an individual's past (Stacy, 1997; Stacy, Leigh, & Weingardt, 1994). It is postulated that the internal representations are held in memory as nodes in an interconnecting network. When such a node is activated through use (i.e., input from the sensory or cognitive systems), it spreads activity outwards through the network. Although the ubiquitous inverse-square law for propagating effects severely limits the spread, repeated activation of a particular pathway is thought to increases the ease with which activity is propagated along it. In this way, two nodes repeatedly being activated at the same time will become increasingly connected, to the extent that if only one is activated, the other will be also. For example, when activated alone through thinking about the need to relax after a hard day at the office, the node for "relaxation" would spread its activation through the network. The activation would spread preferentially to those nodes connected by paths streamlined through previous experience. This might be to the node for "drinking alcohol" in individuals with a history of relaxing by drinking alcohol but to different nodes in individuals without this history (such as nodes representing eating or reading a novel). Once an activity such as drinking alcohol has (unconsciously) popped into the drinker's mind through the process of spreading activation, it is more likely to be incorporated into the (consciously generated) plans for the evening such as described in one of the sketches above. In the movie theater sketch, nodes representing a troubled or depressed state (a state perhaps partially generated through being alone at the theater) might be activated and then preferentially spread activation to nodes representing the behavior for "alcohol consumption" in individuals who had often obtained relief from negative feelings by consuming alcohol. Indeed, activation of these nodes might be augmented by additional activation preferentially spreading from nodes responsive to the sight of the ice bucket and the sound of the crushed ice. This simple example illustrates how complex the dynamics of the process can be. The similarity between the alcohol cue–reactivity framework described earlier and the associative memory framework described above is clear. Each represents experience captured in memory either as S–R/S–S links, or as more complex associations. Each recognizes the importance of its respective memory structure built up through experience in explaining current and future consumption. Although both represent explanations of how an individual might go beyond the information given by the perceptual moment, the more contemporary associative framework is becoming increasingly used within the cue–reactivity domain (Glautier & Spencer, 1999; Jones & Schulze, 2000; Schulze & Jones, 2000).

A feature both of the alcohol cue–reactivity framework and the associative memory framework is that the *generation* and *triggering* of the links or the associations do not normally impact on consciousness. There is fairly good evidence that the triggering process does not reach consciousness in individuals at the abusive/dependent pole of alcohol consumption, as shown, for example, by studies using the alcohol–Stroop paradigm (e.g., Cox et al., 2002). Individuals at the pole of social use have also shown automated processing such as this in studies using the Stroop paradigm (Bauer & Cox, 1998) and a flicker paradigm for inducing change blindness (Jones et al., 2002, 2003). Change blindness describes the surprisingly long time it takes to detect any change in a visual scene. Such change-detection latency can be measured using a flicker paradigm in which two versions of a visual scene (the original and a changed one) are shown in an alternating series of half-second presentations until the change is detected. The number of "flicks" required to detect the change is the measure of change blindness, which is shorter in heavy than in light social drinkers when the change is made to an alcohol-related object. The relationship between change-detection latency and alcohol consumption is comparable to the relationship between interference on the alcohol–Stroop task and consumption. Although the processes underpinning change detection in the flicker paradigm and the interference effect in the alcohol–Stroop paradigm might not reach consciousness, they give rise to responses, feelings, and thoughts related to alcohol that become conscious and are capable of influencing current and future cognitions and planned behavior. In general, alcohol cue–reactivity research has been directed toward cognitions and behaviors at the abusive/dependent pole of the drinking continuum, but associative memory research toward the use/misuse pole. Although treatment is unlikely to directly *modify* the links or associations, it can raise awareness of their existence, how they operate, what effects they might create, and how these effects might be countered (e.g., Rohsenow et al., 2001).

Drinking Decisions as Nonautomated Processes

The intelligent layperson might not be inclined to call the links and associations central to these two memory frameworks *expectancies*, even though they are instrumental in going beyond the information given by the perceptual moment. The lack of such an inclination might be driven by the fact that the activities underpinning this process do not themselves reach consciousness, even though the end product might. Whether or not these activities underpin a construct that can be usefully called an expectancy construct is probably unimportant. What is important is that the term has usually been used for an expectancy construct that has quite different properties. In evaluating whether or not expectancy constructs help to explain drinking variability and whether or not they might be a focus of intervention for excessive drinking, the dual use of the term *expectancy* is a likely source of confusion. This point leads us to a consideration of the second expectancy construct that assists in going beyond the information given, which was introduced at the start of this chapter and with which the remainder of this chapter is concerned. It appears that this expectancy construct might be an easier target for interventions designed to change alcohol consumption than the expectancy construct represented by links or associations described earlier.

If expectancies represented by S–R/S–S links or associations are thought of as unconsciously held, then the following type of expectancies might be thought of as consciously held. These expectancies, alcohol consumption outcome expectancies, are conceived of as a different type of memory structure from the associations described earlier. Although they are also formed through direct and indirect experience, they are best characterized as *if–then* rules rather than S–R/S–S links or associations. For example, in the case of the individual knowing that he or she will have a hard day at the office, past experiences with alcohol and the information acquired about alcohol might well have been recorded as memory structures containing information such as "if I go for a drink *then* I will meet friends," or "*if* I go for a drink *then* I will feel happy," or "*if* I go for a drink *then* I will feel relaxed," or "if I go for a drink *then* I will have dating opportunities." These are positive expectancies, which, it has been claimed, broadly represent the motivation to *drink*. On the other hand, the motivation to *restrain* (from drinking) is thought to be broadly represented by negative expectancies. For example, "*if* I go for a drink *then* I will spend all my money," or "*if* I go for a drink *then* I will end up being sick," or "*if* I go for a drink *then* I will have a bad hangover," or "*if* I go for a drink *then* I will get argumentative." Any drinking decision should, therefore, emerge from the balance between the motivation to drink and the motivation to restrain (Jones & McMahon, 1998).

EXPECTANCIES AND EXPECTANCY QUESTIONNAIRES

The interest in understanding alcohol consumption motivations through the use of *if–then* rules has led scientists to develop catalogs of the different expectancies about alcohol that might be held by people in general. In other words, a full and comprehensive catalog of expectancies might be derived from a large and representative sample of what a particular society expects to happen when alcohol is consumed. A comprehensive (if not exhaustive) catalog of expectancies could be identified from such a collective exercise and the catalog could then be subjected to a series of statistical procedures designed to condense and categorize the expectancy items. Such compacted catalogs have been called expectancy questionnaires. Expectancy questionnaires generated in this way are then given to other individuals who are invited to endorse those items that they expect would happen to them should they "have a drink." Expectancy researchers have posited that the number of items so endorsed by an individual should predict that person's level of consumption. Expectancy questionnaires were developed in this manner for *positive* expectancies (e.g., Brown, Christiansen, & Goldman, 1987; Brown et al., 1980), for *negative* expectancies (e.g., Jones & McMahon, 1994a), and for both *positive* and *negative* expectancies (e.g., Fromme, Stroot, & Kaplan, 1993; Young & Knight, 1989). These questionnaires typically comprise between 50 and 100 items of the *if–then* type. Different patterns of results have been obtained for positive and negative expectancies. The results with positive expectancies will be considered first.

Positive Alcohol Consumption Outcome Expectancies

Research over 20 years has demonstrated that the more positive expectancies that individuals endorse on positive expectancy questionnaires (or the positive subscale of composite positive/negative questionnaires), the more they drink (see Goldman, Del Boca, & Darkes, 1999, and Jones, Corbin, & Fromme, 2001, for reviews). These results have suggested the possibility that positive expectancies might be a target for intervention: reducing positive expectancies should reduce consumption. Whether or not the expectancies held are valid is unimportant—if they are believed, they can have an impact on behavior. Indeed, the fact that they might be subjectively "true" but objectively "untrue" has led to the development of a procedure in which alcohol expectancies are *challenged, and which could potentially be used as a therapeutic intervention.* The procedure, known as the Expectancy Challenge (Darkes & Goldman, 1993), was designed to provide individuals with opportunities to learn that some of the positive expectations they hold about alcohol consumption might be wrong. If alcohol is indeed consumed because it is believed that its consumption will deliver certain positive outcomes, and if, through their experience with the challenge, drinkers can be "persuaded" that the assumption is incorrect, then the procedure might have an impact on their consumption. The simplest sort of expectancy challenge has provided *information only.* For example, Gustafson (1986) provided university students with information about alcohol that was designed to contradict many of their expectancies about it. Unfortunately, this procedure did not produce a reduction in the expectancies challenged, nor a reduction in consumption. Therefore *experiential* challenges were subsequently developed.

To some extent, the migration from informational to experiential challenges reflects a change in therapy during the 1980s from confrontational to nonconfrontational approaches, as typified by motivational counseling, motivational interviewing, and motivational enhancement therapy. In a typical experiential challenge, participants are randomly assigned to receive either a drink containing alcohol or a placebo (e.g., Darkes & Goldman, 1993). After consuming their drink in a social setting providing the opportunity for interaction, participants were asked to judge who, among the other participants, had consumed alcohol and who had not. The task proved more difficult than expected. Participants who thought they had drunk alcohol (but had been given a placebo) showed similar behavioral changes to those who correctly thought they had drunk alcohol, and this collective observation provided experiences from which it was predicted that expectancies would change. Although Darkes and Goldman did indeed report that a reduction in the positive alcohol expectancies occurred following this procedure and that there was also a reduction in subsequent consumption, Jones, Corbin, and Fromme (2001), in their review of expectancy challenges, concluded that the design of the expectancy challenge experiment did not allow the conclusion to be made that the reduction in expectancies *caused* the reduction in consumption. In other words, although the expectancy challenge might lead to reduced consumption, the reduction was not necessarily mediated by a reduction in positive expectancies. Developing and evaluating expectancy challenges are still new and there have been few replications of Darkes and Goldman's finding (Darkes & Goldman, 1998; Dunn, Lau, & Cruz, 2000; Wiers & Kummeling, 2001) and as many failures to replicate (Corbin, McNair, & Carter, 2001; Jones, Silvia, & Richman, 1995; Maddock et al., 1999). Wiers (2002), however, noted that the failures to replicate Darkes and Goldman's finding used single rather than multiple-challenge sessions (as in the original experiment), and this change in methodology could account for the discrepant results.

It is clear that more experimentation is needed to identify the precise conditions under which positive expectancies might be reduced by challenging them. Experimental designs need to be developed that would allow causal links between changed expectancies and subsequent changes in consumption to be identified. Extending expectancy challenge procedures to applied situations would also be fruitful. For example, expectancy challenges could be used in counseling contexts to more formally enhance clients' perception of the contrast between what they expect and what actually occurs.

Negative Alcohol Consumption Outcome Expectancies

There has been considerable focus on challenging positive expectancies in efforts to modify consumption, but much less focus on the role of negative expectancies. This difference is surprising because there have been strong suggestions, apart from the expectancy research, that negative expectancies are closely tied to drinking restraints. Although not usually called *negative expectancies*, the anticipated negative consequences of excessive drinking have been identified as a major influence on abusive and dependent drinkers' decisions to change (Amodeo & Kurtz, 1990; Ludwig, 1985; Tuchfeld, 1981; Tucker & Sobell, 1992). Eastman and Norris (1982) demonstrated how important perceptions about negative consequences of drinking could be when they found that among clients in treatment who expected positive consequences from drinking, 75% subsequently relapsed, but among those who expected negative consequences fewer than 10% relapsed. Encouraged by these results and similar ones reported by Adams and McNeil (1991), Jones and McMahon initiated formal studies of negative alcohol expectancies, particularly among drinkers in treatment.

From responses of clients in treatment and those of light, moderate, and heavy drinkers not in treatment, Jones and McMahon compiled a catalog of negative expectancies that drinkers in general hold. The instrument that resulted is the Negative Alcohol Expectancies Questionnaire (NAEQ; Jones & McMahon, 1994a; see Appendix). The items on the NAEQ are grouped into three temporal contexts: expectancies about what will happen when the drinking is consuming; those about what will happen the next day; and those about what will happen if the drinker continues to drink at the current level. With the NAEQ, Jones and McMahon have shown that drinkers who hold more negative expectancies at the time of treatment have higher rates of abstinence after discharge than those who hold fewer negative expectancies (Jones & McMahon, 1994a, 1994b, 1996a). Jones and McMahon (1996b) showed that clients whose negative expectancies increase during treatment (even though the treatment did not specifically target negative expectancies) had better drinking outcomes than those whose negative expectancies did not change. Just as efforts had been made to *reduce* positive expectancies through expectancy challenges (described above), Jones and McMahon argued that comparable procedures could be used to *increase* negative expectancies. Accordingly, they designed such an intervention.

Jones and McMahon (1998) used a racing car analogy to show how targeting abusive or dependent drinkers' negative expectancies can be more effective than targeting their positive expectancies. The driver of a racing car who is approaching a tight bend at high speed could reduce the car's speed in order to negotiate the bend safely either by lifting off the gas pedal or applying the brake. In their analogy, speed represents the effects of alcohol consumption, lifting off the gas pedal represents reducing positive expectancies, and applying the brake represents increasing negative expectancies. Although lifting off the gas pedal could allow moderate turns to be negotiated, braking would also be required for a larger speed reduction needed for more substantial turns. In the same way, the prior research (e.g., Eastman & Norris, 1982) suggests that increasing negative consequences of drinking is a more critical determinant of drinkers' ability to reduce their consumption than is decreasing their positive expectancies. Adopting the general strategy used in motivational interviewing (Miller & Rollnick, 2002; see also Resnicow et al., Chapter 24, this volume), Jones and McMahon used the NAEQ to identify those negative consequences of consumption that clients *expected* and those that they thought were only *possible*. The motivational interview was designed to confirm the former kind of expectancy and change the status of the latter. Results showed that, relative to individuals who showed no increase, individuals in treatment whose negative expectancies rose from admission to discharge had better outcomes both in terms of rates of abstinence and typical amounts consumed (Jones & McMahon, 1998, 2001).

A Brief Intervention Using Negative Expectancies

Using a computerized version of the NAEQ, Jones and McMahon (2001) tested a brief intervention specifically focusing on negative expectancies. The brief intervention was given prior to clients' beginning a conventional week-long outpatient treatment for alcohol problems at a local hospital. Unlike the brief intervention, the hospital program was itself not specifically designed to alter negative expectancies.

Clients were tested individually with the computer-administered NAEQ. The items appeared one at a time with clients having the opportunity to respond to each item by clicking a mouse. Earlier studies had shown that completion rates of this phase of the intervention were erratic if clients were left to their own resources. Therefore, a therapist was present but did not necessarily see the client's responses. The therapist demonstrated how to use the mouse and offered encouragement from time to time. Under these conditions, completion rates became nearly perfect. Items were presented to the client in the order shown in the Appendix. A stem (context) for each item first appeared alone at the top of the screen for three seconds (e.g., "if I went for a drink *now*"), after which the item itself appeared beneath the stem in a larger font (e.g., "I would become argumentative"). Both the context and the expectancy item remained on the screen until the client responded from among the five choices: "highly likely," "likely," "possible," "unlikely," and "highly unlikely." Respondents could change their response to the current item should they wish to do so before clicking "next" to continue, after which the response could not be changed. The slowest clients took less than ten minutes to complete this first phase.

Once the last item had been answered, the items were scored and ranked by the computer program. Ten items were then randomly selected from those that the client had indicated were "highly likely" or "likely" to occur. Clients always endorsed more than ten items in this manner. An additional ten items were automatically selected from those identified as "possible." Clients almost always endorsed more than ten items in this manner, but on rare occasions when they did not, the program chose additional items that had been endorsed as "unlikely" to make a full set of ten items. The computerized scoring, rankings, and selections took only a few seconds. This meant that the second phase of the intervention could take place almost immediately after the assessment had been completed.

The second phase comprised structured feedback based on the 20 items selected from the client's NAEQ. Following the selection process, the computer program generated an order of feedback for the 20 items, so that "highly likely" or "likely" items were more densely represented in the earlier part of the feedback session than the later part. This arrangement was designed to improve the client's engagement with the feedback. The 20 items of the feedback phase were presented one at a time as follows. A single item was presented at the top of the screen along with its temporal context and the client's response. For example, appearing at the top of the screen might be "You believe that if you were to go for a drink now, it's highly likely you'd become argumentative." This statement would remain at the top of the screen until the therapist (more critically involved in the feedback than in the assessment phase) clicked the mouse to display under the item in a larger font the question, "What makes you believe this?" When the therapist judged that the client's responses to this question had run their course, the therapist displayed a second question beneath the first one, "Does this happen when you are not drinking?" Finally, once the client's responses to this question had run their course, the question "Do you think this is becoming more or less of a problem?" appeared. The next item in the feedback session was presented when the therapist thought it appropriate to move on from the current item.

As the density of feedback items changed from those believed by the client to be "highly likely" or "likely" to those believed to be "possible," a discrepancy developed between what the client appeared to believe on the basis of the NAEQ and what emerged from the discussion, as commonly observed in motivational interviewing. It is through this discrepancy that the negative expectancies seemed to be "experientially" challenged and modified. Experience had shown that there was little benefit from including feedback about those consequences that had been identified as "unlikely" or "highly unlikely" to occur. These items prompted little, if any, discussion and did not lead to the same discrepancy as the other items. The feedback phase typically lasted 30 minutes.

Jones and McMahon (2001) administered the brief intervention to 60 clients and compared them with 40 clients comprising a control group. Group assignments occurred randomly and therapists delivering the five-day program for alcohol problems following the brief intervention were blind to clients' group assignment. A greater increase in negative expectancies from admission to discharge occurred in the brief intervention group than in the control group. A survival analysis with day of first drink as the dependent variable showed that the experimental group survived significantly longer than the control group. At 90 days follow-up, 38% of the experimental group had not drunk, whereas only 9% of the control group had not. It appears likely, therefore, that the brief intervention motivationally primed clients to take better advantage of the treatment program.

In summary, Jones and McMahon built on evidence from outside mainstream expectancy research, which suggests that anticipated negative consequences are more important in decisions to reduce excessive drinking than are positive expectancies. They showed that when negative expectancies are measured during treatment with the NAEQ, clients whose negative expectancies increase most remain drink-free for longer periods. They also showed that negative expectancies can be manipulated (through a brief intervention given prior to treatment), and that this manipulation can affect post-treatment outcomes.

Negative Expectancies in Other Kinds of Drinkers

Studies with nonproblem drinkers have been less persuasive about the role of negative expectancies in explaining alcohol consumption. Nonproblem drinkers appear to hold few negative expectancies, and these expectancies show little relationship to actual consumption (e.g., Brown et al., 1980). However, one difficulty is that most of the studies have been with young college students with limited experience with consumption, and have not yet had the opportunity to experience many negative consequences of drinking. As experience with consumption increases, the likelihood of negative outcomes should increase, as should negative expectancies about drinking. Consequently, one should expect a positive relationship between consumption and negative expectancies to develop. Accordingly, McMahon, Jones, and O'Donnell (1994) found that adult, heavy, social drinkers held greater negative expectancies than moderate drinkers. They suggested that negative expectancies reach a threshold (of number or intensity) before they impact on decisions about drinking and actual behavior, either to reduce consumption or to seek help.

CONCLUSIONS

This chapter suggests that negative expectancy is the construct on which motivational interviewing has been focused. A difference between motivational interviewing and Jones and McMahon's approach is that the latter assesses negative expectancies with items shown to be closely associated with post-intervention reductions in consumption. Motivational interviewing, by contrast, is more open-ended and subjective. Using the more formal approach might allow the effectiveness of motivational interviewing to be more fully evaluated—not only in terms of drinking *outcomes* but also in terms of the *processes* that mediate the change. In addition, the principles that underpin motivational interviewing in combination with Jones and McMahon's procedure could be a practical alternative to the experiential expectancy challenge currently in use. However expectancies are challenged, there remains the possibility that effective interventions for abusive or dependent drinkers might not be effective for less severe kinds of excessive drinking.

APPENDIX

NEGATIVE ALCOHOL EXPECTANCY QUESTIONNAIRE

Barry T. Jones and John McMahon

Please read these instructions carefully.

Below is a list of things that you might or might not expect to happen to you during or after drinking. Please will you indicate the likelihood of each of these things happening to you if you were to go for a drink NOW.

Do this by circling the appropriate number on the 1-2-3-4-5 scale. Please be sure to answer every question.

		Highly likely	Likely	Possible	Unlikely	Highly unlikely
If I went for a drink now...						
1	I would become argumentative	1	2	3	4	5
2	I would become aggressive	1	2	3	4	5
3	I would become violent	1	2	3	4	5
4	I would become anxious	1	2	3	4	5
5	I would have an accident	1	2	3	4	5
6	I would become depressed	1	2	3	4	5
7	I would get drunk	1	2	3	4	5
8	I would get in a fight	1	2	3	4	5
9	I would have memory lapses	1	2	3	4	5
10	I would lie about how much I had to drink	1	2	3	4	5
11	I would end up in jail	1	2	3	4	5
12	I would argue with my spouse	1	2	3	4	5
13	I would have difficulty sleeping	1	2	3	4	5
14	I would wet the bed	1	2	3	4	5
15	I would become boastful	1	2	3	4	5
16	I would borrow money	1	2	3	4	5
17	I would consider taking other drugs	1	2	3	4	5
18	I would take other drugs	1	2	3	4	5
19	I would lose my driving licence	1	2	3	4	5
20	I would drink more than the others in my company	1	2	3	4	5
21	I would have difficulty in stopping drinking	1	2	3	4	5
If I went for a drink now, then tomorrow...						
22	I would miss work	1	2	3	4	5
23	I would have "the shakes"	1	2	3	4	5
24	I would have "the sweats"	1	2	3	4	5
25	I would have a hangover	1	2	3	4	5
26	I would feel depressed	1	2	3	4	5
27	I would have low self-esteem	1	2	3	4	5

Appendix (*continued*)

		Highly likely	Likely	Possible	Unlikely	Highly unlikely
28	I would crave a drink	1	2	3	4	5
29	I would have difficulty sleeping	1	2	3	4	5
30	I would feel generally ill	1	2	3	4	5
31	I would feel frightened	1	2	3	4	5
32	I would feel guilty	1	2	3	4	5
33	I would feel remorseful	1	2	3	4	5
34	I would feel anxious	1	2	3	4	5
35	I would be shy of meeting people	1	2	3	4	5
36	I would feel restless	1	2	3	4	5
37	I would be sick	1	2	3	4	5
38	I would be unable to eat	1	2	3	4	5
39	I would go on a binge	1	2	3	4	5

If I continued to drink at my present level, then ...

		Highly likely	Likely	Possible	Unlikely	Highly unlikely
40	I would lose my wife/husband	1	2	3	4	5
41	I would lose my house	1	2	3	4	5
42	I would lose my job	1	2	3	4	5
43	I would have the DTs	1	2	3	4	5
44	I would have convulsions	1	2	3	4	5
45	I would lose my friends	1	2	3	4	5
46	I would get into debt	1	2	3	4	5
47	I would end up in hospital	1	2	3	4	5
48	I would end up sleeping rough	1	2	3	4	5
49	I would consider suicide	1	2	3	4	5
50	I would attempt suicide	1	2	3	4	5
51	I would feel frightened	1	2	3	4	5
52	I would feel depressed	1	2	3	4	5
53	I would feel self-loathing	1	2	3	4	5
54	I would feel self-pity	1	2	3	4	5
55	I would lose all respect for myself	1	2	3	4	5
56	I would end up in jail	1	2	3	4	5
57	I would damage my liver	1	2	3	4	5
58	I would feel I was going mad	1	2	3	4	5
59	I would choke on my own vomit	1	2	3	4	5
60	I would die	1	2	3	4	5

REFERENCES

Adams, S.L., & McNeil, D.W. (1991). Negative alcohol expectancies reconsidered. *Psychology of Addictive Behaviors, 5*, 9–14.

Amodeo, M., & Kurtz, N. (1990). Cognitive processes and abstinence in a treated alcoholic population. *The International Journal of Addictions, 25*, 983–1009.

Bauer, D., & Cox, W.M. (1998). Alcohol-related words are distracting to both alcohol abusers and non-abusers in the Stroop colour-naming task. *Addiction, 93*, 1539–1542.

Bradizza, C.M., Gulliver, S.B., Stasiewicz, P.R., Torrisi, R., Rohsenow, D.J., & Monti, P.M. (1999). Alcohol cue reactivity and private self-consciousness among male alcoholics. *Addictive Behaviors, 24*, 543–549.

Brown, S.A., Christiansen, B.A., & Goldman, M.S. (1987). The Alcohol Expectancy Questionnaire: An instrument for the assessment of adolescent and adult alcohol expectancies. *Journal of Studies on Alcohol, 48*, 483–491.

Brown, S.A., Goldman, M.S., Inn, A., & Anderson, L.R. (1980). Expectations of reinforcement from alcohol: Their domain and relation to drinking patterns. *Journal of Consulting and Clinical Psychology, 48*, 419–426.

Bruner, J.S., Goodnow, J., & Austin, G. (1956). *A study of thinking.* New York: John Wiley & Sons.

Corbin, W.R., McNair, L.D., & Carter, J.A. (2001). Evaluation of a treatment-appropriate cognitive intervention for challenging alcohol outcome expectancies. *Addictive Behaviors, 26*, 475–488.

Cox, W.M., Hogan, L.M., Kristian, M.R., & Race, J.H. (2002). Alcohol attentional bias as a predictor of alcohol abusers' treatment outcome. *Drug and Alcohol Dependence, 68*, 237–243.

Darkes, J., & Goldman, M.S. (1993). Expectancy challenge and drinking reduction: Experimental evidence for a mediational process. *Journal of Consulting and Clinical Psychology, 61*, 344–353.

Darkes, J., & Goldman, M.S. (1998). Expectancy challenge and drinking reduction: Process and structure in the alcohol expectancy network. *Experimental and Clinical Psychopharmacology, 6*, 64–76.

Dunn, M.E., Lau, H.C., & Cruz, I.Y. (2000). Changes in activation of alcohol expectancies in memory in relation to changes in alcohol use after participation in an expectancy challenge program. *Experimental and Clinical Psychopharmacology, 8*, 566–575.

Eastman, C., & Norris, H. (1982). Alcohol dependence, relapse and self-identity. *Journal of Studies on Alcohol, 43*, 1214–1231.

Fromme, K., Stroot, E., & Kaplan, D. (1993). Comprehensive effects of alcohol: Development and psychometric assessment of a new expectancy questionnaire. *Psychological Assessment, 5*, 19–26.

Glautier, S., & Spencer, K. (1999). Activation of alcohol-related associative networks by recent alcohol consumption and alcohol-related cues. *Addiction, 94*, 1033–1041.

Goldman, M.S., Del Boca, F., & Darkes, J. (1999). Alcohol expectancy theory. In K.E. Leonard & H.T. Blane (Eds.), *Psychological theories of drinking and alcoholism* (2nd edn.; pp. 203–246). New York: Guilford.

Gustafson, R. (1986). Can straight-forward information change alcohol related expectancies? *Perceptual and Motor Skills, 63*, 937–938. See page 378.

Heather, N., & Greeley, J. (1990). Cue exposure in the treatment of drug dependence: The potential of a new method for preventing relapse. *Drug and Alcohol Review, 9*, 155–158.

Jones, B.C., Jones, B.T., Blundell, L., & Bruce, G. (2002). Social users of alcohol and cannabis who detect substance-related changes in a change blindness paradigm report higher levels of use than those detecting substance-neutral changes. *Psychopharmacology, 165*, 93–96.

Jones, B.T., Corbin, W.R., & Fromme, K. (2001). A review of expectancy theory and alcohol consumption. *Addiction, 96*, 57–72.

Jones, B.T., Jones, B.C., Smith, H., & Copely, N. (2003). A flicker paradigm for inducing change blindness reveals alcohol and cannabis information processing biases in social users. *Addiction, 98*. 235–244.

Jones, B.T., & McMahon, J. (1994a). Negative alcohol expectancy predicts post-treatment abstinence survivorship: The whether, when and why of relapse to a first drink. *Addiction, 89*, 1653–1665.

Jones, B.T., & McMahon, J. (1994b). Negative and positive alcohol expectancies as predictors of abstinence after discharge from a residential treatment program: A one-month and three-month follow-up study in men. *Journal of Studies on Alcohol, 55*, 543–548.

Jones, B.T., & McMahon, J. (1996a). A comparison of positive and negative alcohol expectancy and value and their multiplicative composite as predictors of post-treatment abstinence survivorship. *Addiction, 91*, 89–99.

Jones, B.T., & McMahon, J. (1996b). Changes in alcohol expectancies during treatment relate to subsequent abstinence survivorship. *British Journal of Clinical Psychology, 35*, 221–234.

Jones, B.T., & McMahon, J. (1998). Alcohol motivations as outcome expectancies. In W.R. Miller & N. Heather (Eds.), *Treating addictive behaviors* (2nd edn.; pp. 75–91). New York: Plenum.

Jones, B.T., & McMahon, J. (2001). *Motivational priming of alcohol problems treatment improves outcome*. Paper presented at the British Psychological Society Centenary Conference, Glasgow, UK.

Jones, B.T., & Schulze, D. (2000). Alcohol-related words of positive effect are more accessible in social drinkers' memory than are other words when sip-primed by alcohol. *Addiction Research, 8*, 221–232.

Jones, L.M., Silvia, L.Y., & Richman, C.L. (1995). Increased awareness and self-challenge of alcohol expectancies. *Substance Abuse, 16*, 77–85.

Ludwig, A.M. (1985). Cognitive processes associated with "spontaneous" recovery from alcohol. *Journal of Studies on Alcohol, 46*, 53–58.

Maddock, J.E., Wood, M.D., Davidoff, S.M., Colby, S.M., & Monti, P.M. (1999). *Alcohol expectancy challenge and alcohol use: Examination of a controlled trial*. Paper presented at the Annual Scientific Meeting of the Research Society on Alcoholism, Santa Barbara, CA.

McMahon, J., Jones, B.T., & O'Donnell, P. (1994). Comparing positive and negative alcohol expectancies in male and female social drinkers. *Addiction Research, 1*, 349–365.

Miller, W.R., & Rollnick, S. (2002). *Motivational interviewing: Preparing people to change addictive behavior* (2nd edn.). New York: Guilford.

Monti, P.M., Rohsenow, D.J., Swift, R.M., Gulliver, S.B., Colby, S.M., Mueller, T.I., Brown, R.A., Gordon, A., Abrams, D.B., Niaura, R.S., & Asher, M.K. (2001). Naltrexone and cue exposure with coping and communication skills training for alcoholics: Treatment process and 1-year outcomes. *Alcoholism: Clinical and Experimental Research, 25*, 1634–1647.

Rohsenow, D.J., Monti, P.M., Rubonis, A.V., Gulliver, S.B, Colby, S.M., Binkoff, J.A., & Abrams, D.B. (2001). Cue exposure with coping skills training and communication skills training for alcohol dependence: 6- and 12-month outcomes. *Addiction, 96*, 1161–1174.

Rubonis, A.V., Colby, S.M., Monti, P.M., Rohsenow, D.J., Gulliver, S.B., & Sirota, A.D. (1994). Alcohol cue reactivity and mood induction in male and female alcoholics. *Journal of Studies on Alcohol, 55*, 487–494.

Sayette, M.A., Monti, P.M., Rohsenow, D.J., Gulliver, S.B., Colby, S.M., Sirota, A.D., Niaura, R., & Abrams, D.B. (1994). Effects of cue exposure on reaction time in male alcoholics. *Journal of Studies on Alcohol, 55*, 629–633.

Schulze, D., & Jones, B.T. (1999). The effects of alcohol cues and an alcohol priming dose on a multi-factorial measure of subjective cue reactivity in social drinkers. *Psychopharmacology, 145*, 452–454.

Schulze, D., & Jones, B.T. (2000). Desire for alcohol and outcome expectancies as measures of alcohol cue–reactivity in social drinkers. *Addiction, 95*, 1015–1020.

Stacy, A.W. (1997). Memory activation and expectancy as prospective predictors of alcohol and marijuana use. *Journal of Abnormal Psychology, 106*, 61–73.

Stacy, A.W., Leigh, B.C., & Weingardt, K.R. (1994). Memory accessibility and association of alcohol use and its positive outcomes. *Experimental and Clinical Pharmacology, 2*, 269–282.

Stormark, K.M., Laberg, J.C., Bjerland, T., & Hugdahl, K. (1993). Habituation of electrodermal reactivity to visual alcohol stimuli in alcoholics. *Addictive Behaviors, 18*, 437–443.

Tuchfeld, B.S. (1981). Spontaneous remission in alcoholics: Empirical observations and theoretical implications. *Journal of Studies on Alcohol, 42*, 626–641.

Tucker, J.A., & Sobell, L.C. (1992). Influences on help-seeking for drinking problems and on natural recovery without treatment. *The Behavior Therapist* (January), 12–14.

Wiers, R.W. (2002). Half full or half empty, what are we drinking? Some comments on the discussion of the causal role of alcohol expectancies as a mechanism of change. *Addiction, 97*, 599– 600.

Wiers, R.W., & Kummeling, R.H.C. (2001). An experimental test of an expectancy challenge in heaving drinking male and female university students. *Alcoholism: Clinical and Experimental Research, 25* (Suppl. 5), 39A.

Young, R.McD., & Knight, R.G. (1989). The Drinking Expectancy Questionnaire: A revised measure of alcohol beliefs. *Journal of Psychopathology and Behavioural Assessment, 11*, 99–112.

CHAPTER 20

The Motivational Drinker's Check-Up: A Brief Intervention for Early-Stage Problem Drinkers

Maria J. Emmen
Gerard M. Schippers
Amsterdam Institute for Addiction Research, The Netherlands
and
Gijs Bleijenberg
Hub Wollersheim
University Medical Center, Nijmegen, The Netherlands

Synopsis.—Brief interventions can reduce alcohol consumption and problems for early-stage problem drinkers. Brief motivational interventions are a subcategory of brief alcohol interventions, which aim mainly to increase the awareness of alcohol problems and enhance the motivation to change. The Motivational Drinker's Check-Up is an example of a brief motivational intervention, which consists of an assessment session followed by a feedback session. The assessment tests are selected to detect early manifestations of alcohol-related impairment. Shortly after the assessment, the drinker returns for the second session, which consists of personalized feedback of the assessment results. The preferred style for the feedback session is motivational interviewing, a directive, client-centered style which elicits behavior change by helping the client to explore and resolve ambivalence, and applies stage-specific strategies according to the stages of change model. This chapter presents the Dutch Motivational Drinker's Check-Up (DVA), an adaptation of Miller's original Drinker's Check-Up (DCU), which is shorter, more compact, and follows a manual. The components of the DVA are described and illustrated by a case example. The chapter also presents evidence for the effectiveness of the Motivational Drinker's Check-Up and discusses implementation issues. It is concluded that the Motivational Drinker's Check-Up is a feasible and effective early intervention for problem drinkers that can be applied in a variety of health-care facilities.

INTRODUCTION

Across a diversity of cultural settings, clinical research teams have demonstrated that relatively brief interventions can have significant beneficial effects in reducing alcohol

Handbook of Motivational Counseling. Edited by W. Miles Cox and Eric Klinger.
© 2004 John Wiley & Sons, Ltd.

consumption and problems. They involve less time than the usual intensive treatment and can be delivered by professionals other than specialists in substance abuse. Brief interventions can be used both to impact drinking behavior directly and facilitate referral to more intensive treatments. Most brief interventions aim for moderate or harm-free drinking rather than total abstinence. Target groups for brief intervention are hazardous drinkers who drink in excess of guidelines for safe drinking, problem drinkers with low or moderate dependence, and high-dependence problem drinkers who are not reached by conventional treatment services. From the literature, Moyer et al. (2002) and Miller and Wilbourne (2002) concluded that brief interventions for alcohol problems are significantly more effective than no treatment, and are often as effective as more extensive treatments. According to Heather (1995), brief interventions are not a type of treatment, but a category of interventions that are restricted to one to four or more sessions of assessment, advice, and optional counseling with educational components, often supported by self-help manuals or other forms of bibliotherapy. Interventions of more than one session include a follow-up, which is aimed at repeating the advice given during the feedback session and monitoring the progress that was made subsequently. One-session interventions are referred to as minimal interventions. The advice may be based on feedback on an individual's risk status, and may include setting a goal for moderate drinking or to accept referral for additional help. Most brief interventions emphasize the personal responsibilities of drinkers, aim at enhancing their self-efficacy, and stress the importance of the counselor's empathy (see Miller, 1995). A subcategory of brief interventions, called brief motivational interventions, aim mainly to increase the awareness of alcohol problems and enhance the motivation to change. An example is the Motivational Drinker's Check-Up, originated by Miller and colleagues as the DCU (Miller & Sovereign, 1989; Miller, Sovereign, & Krege, 1988). This chapter describes this intervention and discusses its effectiveness. It presents a manual-guided version developed in the Netherlands: the Dutch Motivational Drinker's Check-Up (DVA; Schippers, Brokken, & Otten, 1994a).

BRIEF MOTIVATIONAL INTERVENTIONS FOR PEOPLE WITH ALCOHOL PROBLEMS

Miller and Rollnick (2002) suggested that the primary impact of brief interventions is on motivation for change and that once such motivation has been impacted, individuals may proceed to change their behavior with minimal assistance. The often observed evidence in favor of brief treatment over no treatment suggests that brief interventions instigate natural change processes that otherwise would not occur or would be delayed in onset. Miller and Rollnick further suggested that brief interventions contain the critical conditions needed to instigate change in a substantial proportion of the cases seen. The emphasis on the motivational character of brief interventions fits into the transtheoretical perspective proposed by Prochaska and DiClemente (1986; Prochaska, DiClemente, & Norcross, 1992). They described the process of changing addictive behaviors as moving from early stages of change (precontemplation and contemplation), through the determination and action stages, where the actual behavior change takes place, and finally into the maintenance stage, or possibly relapse. According to the stage model, there are active agents in interventions for addictive behaviors: motivational enhancement, self-control empowerment, and relapse prevention. Motivational interventions focus mainly on the first element: enhancing the motivation to change. Because not all people need active assistance in self-controlled behavior change and the prevention of relapse, motivational enhancement will itself, for some people, function as an effective intervention. Brief motivational interventions can be carried out in different communication styles. Confrontational and directive styles have been used, as described in Walters' (2000) review. Miller and Rollnick (2002), however, recommend a motivational style called motivational interviewing (see Resnicow et al., Chapter 24, this volume). Motivational interviewing is a client-centered counseling style for eliciting behavior change by helping clients to explore and resolve ambivalence. The style is distinguished from other approaches by being empathic, nonconfrontational, and applying stage-specific strategies. It appraises motivation not as a stable, trait-like characteristic of a client but as the result of an interaction between the drinker and those around him or her. This means that there are things a therapist can do to increase motivation for change. Miller and Rollnick (2002) described four broad clinical principles underlying motivational interviewing: expressing empathy, developing discrepancy, rolling with resistance, and supporting self-efficacy.

The Drinker's Check-Up

Miller's Drinker's Check-Up (DCU; Miller & Sovereign, 1989; Miller, Sovereign, & Krege, 1988) was derived from a health promotion model for early identification of emerging alcohol-related problems. It consists of two hours of assessment that yields several dozen objective indicators of alcohol-related problems, followed by a one-hour feedback session. Miller and coworkers presented the DCU as a check-up for drinkers who wanted to find out whether their drinking was causing them any harm. The DCU was free of charge and not part of any treatment program. It was intended for drinkers in general rather than alcoholics and did not result in labeling or diagnosis. The check-up provides clear, objective, personal feedback with which the drinker may do as he or she pleases.

For the assessment part of the DCU, specific tests were selected for their ability to detect some of the earlier manifestations of alcohol-related impairment. The assessment consisted of:

1. The Brief Drinker's Profile (Miller & Marlatt, 1987)—a structural clinical interview to assess drinking patterns, drinking-related life problems and family history, symptoms of pathological drinking, and levels of alcohol dependence.
2. The Alcohol Use Inventory (Horn, Wanberg, & Foster, 1987)—a self-report inventory that helps to identify distinct patterns of behavior, attitudes, and symptoms associated with the use and abuse of alcohol.
3. Collateral interviews to confirm clients' self-reports (Miller, Crawford, & Taylor, 1979).
4. A serum-chemistry battery of tests that detect alcohol's impact on bodily systems.
5. A battery of eight neuropsychological tests sensitive to alcohol's chronic effects on the brain (Miller & Saucedo, 1983).

The content of the assessment package is not fixed, however. Other valid measures of alcohol use and its consequences can be included. The instruments are administered in a straightforward, objective, and friendly manner, carefully following the instructions in the test manuals. No interpretation of results is given at the time of the assessment.

Following the assessment, all tests are scored; the serum sample is assayed; and a summary evaluation is prepared. The drinker's scores on all dimensions are displayed within normative ranges to inform the drinker about his or her position relative to the general population, or to a population of alcohol-impaired individuals.

Within a week of the assessment, the drinker returns for a personalized feedback session. A personal profile of the results measured during the assessment is presented orally, and the client is given a written explanation of the results to take home. A personalized blood alcohol concentration table (Matthews & Miller, 1979) is also provided. The information is presented as objective data, but the focus is on the client's own concerns and reactions rather than the counselor's interpretations. At the conclusion of the feedback, the drinker's overall reactions to the information are determined.

The content of the last part of the DCU's feedback session depends on where the client is in the process of change. Precontemplating clients are not yet considering the possibility of change. They need the information and feedback to raise awareness of the problem and the importance of change. Drinkers enter the contemplation stage when they become aware that there is a problem. This stage is characterized by ambivalence: the contemplator both considers change and rejects it. Often people in this stage are responsive to the DCU. For such clients, personal feedback from the check-up should be emphasized, but also information and advice should be offered about the possibilities and desirability of behavior change with or without help. If the client is in the action or determination stage, he or she is considered to be motivated to change and will take action or return to contemplation. The counselor's task with clients in this stage is to help them find a change strategy that is acceptable, appropriate, and effective. Information and advice about the possibility and desirability of professional help are given.

Applications of the DCU

According to its developers, the DCU can be applied in a variety of settings and for several different purposes. Firstly, it can be used as part of routine health-screening procedures in hospitals and medical practices. Secondly, the DCU provides a comprehensive range of information appropriate for use in matching patients with optimal treatment approaches and is also applicable as an assessment procedure for clients, such as drunk driving offenders, who are mandated to receive treatment. Further, the DCU can be advertized to the general public as a method for discovering whether or not one's drinking is having detrimental effects. Finally, the DCU provides a wealth of individual patient data that can be useful in outcome assessments.

The DCU formed an important element in Motivational Enhancement Therapy (MET; Miller et al., 1992), one of the three treatment modalities evaluated in Project MATCH (Project MATCH Research Group, 1997a). The four-session intervention did not guide clients through recovery, but employed motivational strategies to mobilize their own change resources. The first session of MET was organized as the DCU feedback session, presenting clients with selected data collected in the Project MATCH research assessment battery. MET is more extensive than the DCU, with three more counseling sessions, and with a significant other usually being involved. MET used a manual for all sessions, and included a Personal Feedback Report, a written statement with feedback data.

Marlatt and colleagues (Blume & Marlatt, Chapter 21, this volume; Dimeff et al., 1999) have recently developed BASICS, a motivational module for problem-drinking college students. This is an individualized, manual-guided assessment and feedback intervention delivered in two 50-minute sessions, with referral to substance abuse treatment for those requiring services beyond the two sessions. Several studies have demonstrated the effectiveness and efficacy of BASICS with high-risk college students (Baer et al., 2001; Dimeff et al., 1999; Marlatt et al., 1998; Murphy et al., 2001).

THE DUTCH MOTIVATIONAL DRINKER'S CHECK-UP

Modeled after the DCU, the Dutch Motivational Drinker's Check-Up (DVA: Doorlichting, Voorlichting Alcoholgebruik) was developed by Schippers, Brokken, and Otten in 1994. The DVA differs from the DCU in that the DVA is shorter, more compact, and fully manual-guided. The manual is detailed, and includes three DVA instructional videotapes. The first tape gives instruction on motivational interviewing; the second gives an overview of the DVA; and the third gives instruction on the DVA feedback procedure. No blood tests are included, as in the original DCU, because psychologists in the Netherlands are not allowed to interpret medical tests. The neurological tests are more selective and finer-tuned than in the original DCU. Feedback is given in the form of bar graphs, comparing the subtest results with each other. Data for the feedback are presented in a Personal Feedback Report. After the DVA face-to-face contacts, the counselor sends a personal letter to the client, summarizing the results, including the data that had been fed back to the client, the conclusions drawn, and the advice given.

Protocol of the DVA

The different elements of the DVA are illustrated here with a case example. For each element, short descriptions of the *assessment phase* and *feedback phase* are presented consecutively.

Case Study: Peter

Peter is a 50-year-old man. The internist advised him to reduce his alcohol consumption after a consultation for pain in his upper abdomen. He had never sought help for alcohol problems before and was in the early contemplation stage. Because on the hospital ward a counselor was available who could deliver the intervention, the internist recommended that Peter participate.

The counselor began with a short introduction:

> I would like to follow a procedure to look at the role that alcohol plays in your life. We will meet two times. The first time we will discuss your drinking behavior. There are some questionnaires for you to complete, and I would also like to test your skill at certain tasks. During our second appointment, we will discuss the results of the earlier meeting, and you will receive a written report of the results. It is up to you to decide what, if anything, you want to do with the feedback that you are given. Is the procedure clear to you? Do you have any questions? Do you want to take part?

Demographic Information (Interview)

The procedure starts with the counselor's recording a few of the person's demographic characteristics, such as gender, age, education, weight, and names of medications taken.

Alcohol Use (Interview)

Assessment. Alcohol use is assessed by several questions concerning the person's current and past drinking behavior. The timeline follow-back (TLFB) technique (Sobell & Sobell, 1992) is used to assess quantity, frequency, and location of drinking. Detailed information is first collected about drinking during the prior week. A typical drinking week is also analyzed to establish a representative quantity and frequency of alcohol use. Further questions are asked about highest alcohol consumption ever, periods of excessive drinking in the past, and contacts with treatment services.

Feedback. The counselor discusses with the client the number of standard drinks per week that the person consumes and his or her estimated blood–alcohol levels (BALs). A table is used to illustrate the meaning of BALs. If the client does not experience the effects that normally occur at particular BALs, the phenomenon of tolerance to alcohol can be discussed.

C: You remember that during the assessment part of the DVA we went through a typical week of drinking for you. After the assessment, I added up how much you usually drink in a week. It came out to about 50 standard drinks a week. One "drink" is a standard size glass of beer or wine, or about a 33 milliliter serving of spirits. What do you think about that?

P: It seems like a lot. I never really added it up before, but I don't think of myself as a heavy drinker.

C: You are surprised.

P: Yes, I didn't think it would be that much.

C: We also estimated your blood–alcohol levels based on your drinking patterns. The estimate is that you reach .25 g/ml. In the table you can see that at this level people usually feel that they are intoxicated.

P: But I don't ever feel that drunk. How is that possible?

C: It's common for heavy drinkers not to feel their alcohol like other people do. This is called tolerance. You can have a fairly high blood–alcohol level, enough to affect your driving and even to do damage to your internal organs, without feeling intoxicated.

Now let's look at the blood–alcohol level you reach when you drink the heaviest. Your level gets as high as .30 g/ml.

Family History (Interview)

Assessment. To get an impression of whether the person has a family history of alcohol problems, he or she is asked to describe the father's, mother's, and partner's drinking, by placing each of them into a drinking category. By sorting cards, the client assigns each person to one of the following categories: abstainer, light drinker, moderate drinker, heavy drinker, problem drinker, or alcoholic. To assess genetic risk factors, the client is also asked about alcohol problems in other biological relatives.

Feedback. When none of the family members is described as having had alcohol problems, it can be explained that it is unlikely that the drinking problem is genetically determined.

This usually means that heavy drinking patterns did not occur early in life but were acquired later. When there is evidence for alcohol problems in the family, the implications that this might have for the person's own drinking in the future are discussed.

C: You told me your father had some drinking problems.
P: Yes, he was a real alcoholic, which was terrible for my mom. After he lost his job, he would spend long hours in the pub every day. And sometimes I am afraid I will become like him.
C: How does your drinking seem like your father's?
P: Lately, there have been some times when I was late getting to work, because I was drinking too much the night before. And sometimes I can't concentrate on my work very well.

Drinking Styles in the Social Environment (Interview)

Assessment. The drinker categories are used in two other ways. First, a drinking style is assigned to the person. Second, the categories are used to determine the client's perception of the drinking style that important other people assign to him. Making use of the same Q-sort, clients also choose a drinker category for themselves, and are asked which category the partner, a best friend, and most people who know them would choose.

Feedback. Clients' own perception of their drinking is compared with the imagined perceptions of other people. If there is a discrepancy between the two sets of perceptions, clients might be concealing their drinking from other people, and the meaning of hiding one's drinking can be discussed.

C: You think that your best friend would describe you as drinking less than you actually do.
P: Yes, that's right. I would call myself a heavy drinker, but I think my best friend would say that I am a moderate drinker.
C: So your best friend doesn't know how much you drink?
P: No, he knows I like to drink beer, but most of the time he is not there when I am drinking.

Structured Diagnostic Interview for Alcohol Dependence (DSM-IV)

Assessment. With this semistructured diagnostic interview, the diagnosis of alcohol abuse and alcohol dependence according to the DSM-IV criteria (American Psychiatric Association, 1994) can be established. Alcohol abuse is described as a destructive pattern of alcohol use, leading to significant social, occupational, or medical impairment. Important criteria for the diagnosis of alcohol dependence are: alcohol tolerance (the need for increased amounts of alcohol to achieve intoxication or diminished effects with continued use of the same amount of alcohol), alcohol withdrawal symptoms (such as sweating, rapid pulse, increased hand tremor, and insomnia), and loss of control over or preoccupation with drinking.

Feedback. Feedback about having or not having a diagnosis of alcohol abuse or dependence can easily be experienced as a demotivating form of labeling. In some cases, however, it can have a motivating effect. In cases where the client is seriously wondering whether or not he or she is an alcoholic or in cases where such a diagnosis has been made, an open discussion with concrete answers given nonjudgmentally can be reassuring.

Alcohol-Related Problems and Consequences (Q-Sort)

Assessment. Information is gathered about current life problems by having the client sort 18 cards depicting a variety of these problems. The clients select those cards with life problems that pertain to them, and rank these cards in terms of their importance. The influence of alcohol use on the selected and ranked life problems is identified. For each alcohol-related life problem, the client is asked if drinking alcohol preceded or followed the life problem, or both.

Feedback. In the feedback session, current life problems and their possible relationship to drinking alcohol are discussed. For each of the problems, whether alcohol-related or not, the client is asked about any prior sources of help, professional or otherwise. The counselor then assesses whether the help was adequate. For unresolved mental health problems in particular, clients are advised to visit a professional counselor.

C: You mentioned different problems that are occurring in your life. The problem that concerns you most is your physical health, especially the problems with your stomach.
P: Yes, I'm really worried about my stomach. Sometimes the pain is unbearable.
C: You also told me a week ago that the stomach problems are related to your drinking. Can you tell me more about it?
P: Sometimes when my stomach is hurting so badly, I take a drink to relieve the pain.
C: Does it give you relief?
P: Yes, at first, but after a while the pain comes back even worse than before.
C: So the drink can relieve the pain in the short term, but in the long term it makes the problem worse?
P: Yes, I'm afraid that's right.
C: What conclusion would you draw from this?
P: Drinking seems to be bad for my stomach.

Neuropsychological Tests

Assessment. Feedback of impairment in neuropsychological functioning that is possibly or probably related to excessive alcohol use can provide a potent motivational boost, because such information is new to the person and not available from his or her ordinary daily experiences. In the DCU, Miller, Sovereign, and Krege (1988) used the Wechsler Adult Intelligence Scale (WAIS; Wechsler, 1955) and subtests of the Halstad–Reitan (Reitan, 1986) to assess neuropsychological functioning. The selection of these tests was based on a review of the literature on neuropsychological impairment and brain damage in alcohol-dependent patients as assessed by different psychological tests (Miller & Saucedo, 1983).

Miller and Saucedo sought to find combinations of tests of neuropsychological functioning that would reflect excessive alcohol use. They wanted to compile a test battery comprising pairs of subtests, one of which was alcohol-sensitive and the other alcohol-insensitive. Alcohol-sensitive subtests were defined as those on which people with alcohol dependence score lower than comparable nonalcohol-dependent people. Alcohol-insensitive subtests were those unaffected by alcohol use.

For the DVA, an updated selection of such tests was made using data from Dutch patients. Existing test results were reviewed from a total of 359 patients with a primary diagnosis of alcohol dependence. The information included demographic characteristics, drinking history, and scores from a variety of tests for which normative scores on nonalcoholic populations were also available. The tests included the WAIS (Dutch version), Trail Making Test (subtest of the Halstad–Reitan; Dutch version), and the Stroop Color-Word Test (which tests concentration and attention; Dutch version). Three pairs of subtests were identified as appropriate for use in the DVA (Schippers, Brokken, & Otten, 1994a), because alcoholics perform differently on these subtests from nonalcoholics, i.e., on one subtest from each set alcoholics matched for age and gender perform the same as nonalcoholic normative samples, whereas on the other subtest alcoholics perform markedly lower than normative groups. The groups of subtests administered to the clients were the Similarities (alcohol-insensitive) and Digit Symbol (alcohol-sensitive) portions of the WAIS; Part A (alcohol-insensitive) and Part B (alcohol-sensitive) of the Trail Making Test; and the color-congruent (alcohol-insensitive) and color-incongruent (alcohol-sensitive) cards from the Stroop Color-Word Test. Scores on these subtests range from 0 to 10, corresponding to the 0 to 100 percentiles.

Feedback. The client is told that his or her drinking could influence the scores on the tests administered. Damaging effects of alcohol may be seen in the person's cognitive abilities, and can be measured by psychological tests. Clients are shown bar graphs representing their scores on the alcohol-insensitive and alcohol-sensitive tests. It is explained that the scores are presented in relationship to scores of people of the same age and gender from the general population, and that a score of "5" means average performance. A low score on any one of the tests does not necessarily give cause for concern, because there can be many reasons for a particular individual's low score. However, if there is a clear pattern of low scores (i.e., most or all of the alcohol-sensitive scores are lower than the non-sensitive ones), it is emphasized that the low scores probably result from the person's drinking. On the other hand, in cases where there is no evidence for alcohol-related impairment, the client is reassured accordingly. In any case, the counselor emphasizes that the tests are not a full neuropsychological assessment. Further, the counselor explains that impairment, when found, might very well be reversible. If the client were to quit drinking, for example, the neuropsychological functioning would likely improve. However, the longer and the greater the quantity of drinking has been, the greater the chance of cognitive impairment, and the slower the improvement will be.

C: Here you can see that your scores on the alcohol-sensitive tests are lower than on the alcohol-insensitive tests. That could mean that alcohol has affected your brain and especially your mental ability and concentration.

P: You mean that drinking alcohol has already destroyed some part of my brain?

C: Well, it seems that there is some impairment, indeed. We cannot say for sure from these few tests that it was caused by alcohol, but the possibility cannot be ruled out either.

Knowledge about Alcohol (Questionnaire)

Assessment. A knowledge-about-alcohol test is administered that was developed in the Netherlands (Kayser, 1990). The 17-item true–false questionnaire measures clients' knowledge about alcohol and its effects. Examples of items are: *Alcohol increases the body's temperature. Drinking coffee decreases the effects of alcohol on the body. Regularly drinking alcohol causes brain damage.* Clients choose from three answers: "true," "false," or "don't know." The questionnaire ends with an open-ended question about the legal blood–alcohol level for driving.

Feedback. The client is informed about the number of correct answers. Items that were answered incorrectly are discussed, and the correct answers explained. The client is then given a take-away information booklet with all the questions, correct answers, and an explanation for each of them. Although no normative scores are available for this test, experience shows that most clients know the correct answer to 12 or more of the items.

Drinking and Craving Situations (Questionnaire)

Assessment. Clients are administered the Dutch Drinking Habit Scale (SVD: Schaal Voor Drinkgewoonten). Walburg and Van Emst (1985) modeled this test after the Inventory of Drinking Situations (IDS; Annis, Graham, & Davis, 1987). For six kinds of situations, clients rate on a five-point Likert scale how much craving they experience and how often they drink while experiencing unpleasant emotions, while feeling embarrassed, while experiencing unpleasant physical sensations, in high-risk and nonhigh-risk drinking situations, and during social interactions.

Feedback. The counselor first discusses the situations in which the client does and does not usually drink, and then characterizes the situations in which the client often drinks.

C: I would like to give you some feedback on your drinking habits. You don't drink in all situations. In some situations, such as being in a pub, with friends, or at parties, you usually drink, but when you feel guilty, depressed, or alone you almost never drink. Correct?

P: Yes.

C: When you are with friends you often drink, but is that always the case?

P: Most of the time it is, but not always. One of my friends has a liver disease. When I am with him, I don't drink. I know he likes alcohol very much, but is not allowed to drink anymore, and I don't want him to see me drinking.

C: Can you give examples of other situations in which you are with friends and you don't drink?

P: Yes, when I have a football game the next day. I know that I play really awful if I drank the day before.

C: So you can also have a good time with friends without drinking alcohol?

Further the counselor compares the client's degree of craving in the different situations with the frequency of drinking in them. Habitual drinking without craving or craving without drinking can be pointed out.

C: In situations where people can feel embarrassed about something, you seem to crave a drink, but you don't actually drink.

P: Yes, that's true. For example, when I feel guilty about not being nice to my wife. I really want a drink, but I know if I drink I will feel even more guilty. I would do better to do something nice for my wife.

C: So when you crave a drink, you can resist it.

Finally, the counselor asks the client how he or she would interpret the results.

C: We discussed situations in which you usually drink and those in which you don't drink. You often drink during holidays or when you are in a pub or with friends. You also told me that being with friends does not always mean drinking alcohol. Although your craving is high in situations where you feel embarrassed about something, you don't drink in these situations. What does this information mean to you?

P: Maybe I don't need alcohol as much as I thought. I can resist the urge to drink when I feel embarrassed. I also enjoy spending time with friends without drinking.

Self-Evaluation Questionnaire

Assessment. The Self-Evaluation Questionnaire is a Dutch modification of Appel and Miller's (1984) Self-Evaluation of Drinking Questionnaire. Clients complete the self-evaluation by answering 14 questions on a five-point scale about perceived consequences of drinking on different life areas. Each consequence is illustrated with a short text elaborating the topic.

Feedback. Clients' answers on the Self-Evaluation Questionnaire are represented in a decisional balance sheet. Systematically evaluating the positive and negative effects of alcohol on all life areas can help the client to clarify the relative effects of drinking in the different areas.

C: Your answers about perceived consequences of drinking are shown in this balance sheet. This side of the sheet represents the benefits of drinking, and that side the disadvantages. Here you can see that alcohol seems to benefit your mood and social life. On the other side, you can see that alcohol has negative consequences for your physical health and mental functioning.

P: Yes, that's the problem. I am used to drinking with my wife and friends and to have a good time, but I know that drinking is not good for my body.

C: For you, drinking means having a good time, but you are also concerned about your health.

The last question on the Self-Evaluation Questionnaire concerns the client's motivation to reduce the drinking. The person's answer to this question is used to discuss the pros and cons of reducing or stopping. If clients are not interested in cutting down, they are asked about their reluctance. If they do want to cut down, they are asked the reasons for wanting to.

C: On the question about the importance of reducing your drinking, you answered that it is very important for you to cut down. Can you say more about this?

P: I think that I have to change my drinking, especially for my health. I know that drinking alcohol is bad for my stomach. The doctor said so. Besides, I know now that drinking might have already destroyed some of my brain cells. I don't like that at all!

C: To take care of your stomach and brain, you would like to reduce your drinking. Are there other reasons for reducing it?

P: Yes, I am also afraid of becoming like my father who was a real alcoholic.

Conclusions, Information about Options for Support, and Advice

After discussing the assessment results, the last part of the feedback session is devoted to conclusions, giving information about support, and advice. Strict rules for this part of the intervention are not followed, because the content will depend on the information from the assessment and the client's reactions to it. Nevertheless, it is important to follow the order conclusions, information on options for support, and advice. The counselor gives no information and advice before the client has drawn conclusions from the results of the DVA. Advice to change is not provided until information about options for support is given, if this is necessary. In this way, the client is maximally motivated to self-interpret the results presented, to consider the desirability of change, and to present self-committing statements for future change.

Conclusions

Generally, a good way to prompt clients to draw their conclusions from the results is to ask their overall reactions to the whole procedure.

C: We've covered a lot of ground. I wonder what you think about all these results?

At this point, the counselor asks the clients what the results mean to them, if it changed their way of thinking about drinking, if they think change is important, if they would like to change something, and if so, what, and over what period of time. If clients are resistant to change or still wonder if change is necessary, their doubts will be reflected back to them. To draw a conclusion from the results does not necessarily mean making a decision to change. The counselor summarizes clients' conclusions to confirm that they were understood.

Information about Options for Support

Whether or not information about options for support is provided depends on what clients need and want. Accordingly, the counselor should be familiar with all available and appropriate professional and nonprofessional treatment resources and self-help programs. The counselor should describe the available options in a way that is understandable to clients. The counselor needs to be able to evaluate whether clients' unwillingness to accept help is due to their lack of knowledge about treatment possibilities, practical barriers like cost or transportation issues, or simply resistance to accept help. Furthermore, the counselor should be prepared to answer questions about controlled drinking.

P: Maybe drinking is not so good for my health. I am damaging my stomach and brain and I want to stop that.

C: What would you like to do to stop damaging your stomach and brain?

P: I don't know. I would like to cut down my drinking, but I am afraid I cannot do that by myself. Do you know how I could do that?

C: I can tell you about different kinds of help, but I cannot decide what you need. You have to decide that for yourself. May I give you some information about different kinds of help?

Advice

If the client is unable to draw a conclusion from the DVA results or is still precontemplating changing his or her drinking, the counselor does not give advice about change. Rather, the client is encouraged to take the time to consider the DVA results and later to draw a conclusion from them. However, often clients want advice about the need to change their drinking and how they can accomplish it. Counselors offer the best advice they can, based on the information from the DVA. They can advise about drinking limits, changing drinking with or without treatment, and about the kinds of treatment. Of course, the advice should be consistent with the client's needs, preference, treatment experiences, and readiness to accept help. If a client is ready to change his or her drinking, commitment to a plan for change is elicited.

P: You told me about different kinds of help. I am certain that I don't want to go to a clinic for alcoholics because my problem isn't that big. But I really don't know what kind of help will be best for me. What would you advise?

C: It is difficult to say what approach is best for you. But we can talk about the options that appeal to you, and I will try to help you to find the approach that is right for you.

Closing the Session and Follow-Up Letter

At the end of the feedback session, the counselor summarizes the most important findings on assessment results, the client's conclusions about the need for and willingness to change, and change options. The client is given the opportunity to correct the counselor's conclusions. The counselor indicates that the client will receive a personal letter with the summary and offers the client the Personal Feedback Report with the assessment results. The counselor closes the feedback session by wishing the client success in reaching the goals selected.

As soon as possible after the last contact, the counselor sends the personal letter to the client. Points discussed in the letter include the risks and problems that the assessment revealed and the client's own reaction to the feedback, including self-motivational statements that the client may have made. Additional points to cover include the person's need for and willingness to change and accept professional or nonprofessional help, and concrete decisions that were reached about when the change would be made.

Example

In your typical drinking week that we discussed, you drank 50 beers. You usually drink when you are in the pub with your friends or at parties. You experience problems with your health and mental functioning. You have stomach pain and problems concentrating on your work. Both of these problems are related to your alcohol use. Alcohol can relieve the stomach pain for a short time, but the long-term effects of the drinking are to make the pain worse. You also think that your alcohol use affects your ability to concentrate, which is also shown in the results of the neuropsychological tests that you took. You are afraid that you are becoming more and more like your father who had severe alcohol problems and lost his job as a result of them. The pain in your stomach, problems with concentrating, and your fear that you are getting the same alcohol problems as your father are all reasons for you to reduce your drinking. You don't think you can reduce your drinking by yourself, and you prefer some kind of help. We discussed different treatment possibilities. Because you mostly drink when you are with your friends and at parties, it is important for you to learn to say "no" in these situations when someone offers you a drink of alcohol. As we decided, it would be good for you to take a course to learn assertiveness skills.

Administering the DVA

The DVA can be given at the request of a referring professional. In such cases, the referring person is usually informed of the results of the DVA. The information could be limited to the fact that the client was seen on the two occasions. Usually, however, it is desirable also to give information about the conclusions that were drawn. This information could be given verbally, or by sending the referring person a copy of the letter sent to the client. Users of the DVA have had good experiences with referrals from a department of internal medicine at a general hospital, where the physicians regularly refer clients with probable alcohol problems. In this case, the written DVA conclusions are sent to the patient and the medical specialist, and are added to the patient's medical record.

EFFECTIVENESS OF THE MOTIVATIONAL DRINKER'S CHECK-UP

Empirical Evidence for the Effectiveness of the DCU

Miller, Sovereign, and Krege (1988) first evaluated the DCU in a study of 42 problem drinkers recruited through media advertizements. These problem drinkers were randomized to receive an immediate or delayed DCU. In the immediate DCU group, both alcohol consumption and peak intoxication were significantly reduced from baseline at both the six-week and 18-month follow-ups. While the delayed group waited to receive the DCU, they showed no change in their drinking. After receiving it, they too showed a significant reduction in alcohol consumption and peak levels of intoxication. Family members and other collateral informants verified the self-reported changes in both groups. Across both groups, 14% had sought help for their alcohol problems within six weeks after feedback, and 33% had done so within 18 months of having the DCU.

Miller, Benefield, and Tonigan (1993) replicated the findings of the first study. They assigned 42 problem drinkers randomly to three groups: immediate DCU with directive confrontational counseling; immediate DCU with client-centered counseling; or delayed DCU. Participants receiving the immediate DCU demonstrated significantly less weekly alcohol consumption, lower peak blood–alcohol levels, and fewer drinking days relative to the delayed DCU group at a six-week and 12-month follow-up. Analysis of therapist style indicated that the directive confrontational counseling style evoked significantly more client resistance behavior like arguing, ignoring, and interrupting which in turn predicted poorer drinking outcomes.

Two other studies were conducted in treatment settings. Patients being admitted to a residential substance-abuse program were randomly assigned to receive or not receive a DCU prior to treatment (Brown & Miller, 1993). Therapists in the residential program who were unaware of patients' group assignment perceived patients who had received the DCU to be more motivated and involved during treatment than the patients who had not received it. Moreover, the patients who had received the DCU showed significantly lower alcohol consumption than the other patients three months after discharge.

Bien, Miller, and Boroughs (1993), using the same design with severely alcohol-impaired outpatients in a Veteran Affairs Medical Center, reported similar findings. A three-month follow-up analysis using a composite drinking measure (total consumption, peak blood–alcohol level, and days abstinent) for the prior 30 days showed significantly lower values for the DCU than the control group.

Miller et al. (1992) developed MET, with the DCU as an integral part, for Project MATCH, a multi-site clinical trial designed to test a series of *a priori* hypotheses on how patient–treatment interactions relate to outcome (Project MATCH Research Group, 1997a). Clients were recruited from outpatient settings or from aftercare settings and randomized to MET, Cognitive-Behavioral Therapy (CBT), or Twelve-Step Facilitation (TSF). All clients achieved significant improvements in drinking outcomes (percent days abstinent and drinks per drinking day) during a one-year post-treatment period, but there was little difference in outcomes across the types of treatment. Four sessions of MET produced similar drinking outcomes to 12 sessions of each of the other treatments. For outpatients, these results were sustained over a three-year follow-up period (Project MATCH Research Group, 1998). Probably in accordance with the accepting nature of MET, clients receiving it who were high in anger had better drinking outcomes at both one-year and three-year follow-ups than those receiving either of the other two treatments (Project MATCH Research Group, 1997b, 1998).

Empirical Evidence for the Effectiveness of the DVA

The DVA has been evaluated in several different settings. First, in an outpatient alcohol and drug treatment center, 35 patients given the standard intake procedure were compared with 20 patients given the DVA at intake. At six-months follow-up, significantly more of the DVA patients accepted and received alcohol treatment, although there was no difference between the two groups in the amount of drinking (Schippers, Brokken, & Verweij, 1994b).

The same design was used on a psychiatric ward of a general hospital. Twenty patients with primary or secondary diagnosis of alcohol abuse or dependence who received the DVA were compared with 12 patients with the same diagnosis who received care as usual. Patients receiving the DVA accepted and received alcohol treatment more often than those not receiving it. Again, there was no difference between the two groups in the amount that they drank (Schippers, Brokken, & Verweij, 1994b).

IMPLEMENTING THE MOTIVATIONAL DRINKER'S CHECK-UP

Over the years we have learned that implementing the Motivational Drinker's Check-Up in general and specialized health care is not an easy task. One of the obstacles is to convey the potential value of the procedure to health-care professionals. One reason for the difficulty is that the procedure does not readily fit into the familiar categories of either a complete diagnostic instrument or a complete treatment technique. Further, questions arise about whether the Motivational Drinker's Check-Up should be used within general health care or specialized addiction treatment. Another obstacle is that applying the Motivational Drinker's Check-Up requires special skills for which special training is needed. Although the procedure could be appropriate to use as opportunistic intervention in general health-care settings, most health-care providers lack the necessary counseling skills to use it properly. Professional supervision is necessary for the nonmoralizing attitude that must be assumed. In addiction treatment centers, the providers of care usually do have the counseling skills needed, and it is sometimes difficult to convince them that the intervention is intense enough for their clientele.

In the Netherlands, the Motivational Drinker's Check-Up has also been more readily accepted in other than health-care settings; for example, in *Employee Assistance Programs*. Because the DVA is both a structured and a brief intervention, it is appropriate for use in the workplace to identify problem drinkers and motivate them to start a change process. In companies, the focus with persons with alcohol problems has been primarily on referral rather than on intervention. The possibility to deal on-site with some employees has advantages. It is easier to motivate employees to participate in the DVA than to refer them for a full treatment. In employee assistance programs, collaboration between the medical officer (who administers the DVA) and an off-site counselor (who delivers the treatment) works quite well.

THE MOTIVATIONAL DRINKER'S CHECK-UP AND SYSTEMATIC MOTIVATIONAL COUNSELING

How is the Motivational Drinker's Check-Up related to Systematic Motivational Counseling (SMC; Cox & Klinger, Chapter 11, this volume; Cox, Klinger, & Blount, 1991, 1999; Cox et al., 2003)? When used with alcohol abusers, the first session of SMC resembles the Motivational Drinker's Check-Up. In this session, both techniques attempt to establish why drinking alcohol has a high incentive value for the drinker. Going beyond the Motivational Drinker's Check-Up, however, the SMC assesses which nonchemical incentives in people's lives might motivate them to bring about affective changes by drinking alcohol. The SMC is a more extensive procedure for assessing and modifying the drinker's motivational structure than the Motivational Drinker's Check-Up. The SMC is broader in scope and based upon an explicit theoretical model (Cox & Klinger, 1988, 1990, and Chapter 7, this volume).

In a sense, the SMC begins where the Motivational Drinker's Check-Up ends. SMC offers a technique to enhance motivation to change among people who have already decided they wanted to change their drinking. It does so by framing the drinking behavior within the person's broader motivational structure. In contrast, the Motivational Drinker's Check-Up is a pragmatic technique for use during early phases of problem identification, more in the context of opportunistic interventions.

In treatment settings, the Motivational Drinker's Check-Up could also be used after SMC. That is, if a client undergoing SMC discovered that drinking alcohol played an important role in the larger network of his or her goals and motivations, that role could be explored further with the problem-focused Motivational Drinker's Check-Up.

CONCLUSIONS

The Motivational Drinker's Check-Up is a structured brief intervention based on constructive-confrontational feedback of personalized information about drinking and drinking-related problems using motivational interviewing. Evidence suggests that it is a feasible and effective early intervention for problem drinkers. Although the number of studies evaluating it is still small, the available results support the effectiveness of the Motivational Drinker's Check Up. Although progress of the Motivational Drinker's Check-Up has been slow, the procedure has found its way into a growing number of health-care facilities, where it is seen as an important addition to existing ways of addressing alcohol problems in society. When pleas for reform of the existing system for treating alcohol problems are voiced loudly (e.g., Humphreys & Tucker, 2002; Marlatt & Witkiewitz, 2002), ready-made, harm-reduction modules like the Motivational Drinker's Check-Up are highly welcomed.

REFERENCES

American Psychiatric Association (1994). *Diagnostic and statistical manual of mental disorders* (4th edn.). Washington, DC: Author.

Annis, H.M., Graham, J.M., & Davis, C.S. (1987). *Inventory of Drinking Situations (IDS): User's guide.* Toronto: Addiction Research Foundation.

Appel, G.P., & Miller, W.R. (1984). *Self-evaluation of drinking.* Internal report. University of New Mexico, Albuquerque.

Baer, J.S., Kivlahan, D.R., Blume, A.W., McKnight, P., & Marlatt, G.A. (2001). Brief intervention for heavy-drinking college students: 4-year follow-up and natural history. *American Journal of Public Health, 91*, 1310–1316.

Bien, T.H., Miller, W.R., & Boroughs, J.M. (1993). Motivational interviewing with alcohol outpatients. *Behavioural and Cognitive Psychotherapy, 21*, 347–356.

Brown, J.M., & Miller, W.R. (1993). Impact of motivational interviewing on participation and outcome in residential alcoholism treatment. *Psychology of Addictive Behaviors, 7*, 211–218.

Cox, W.M., Heinemann, A.W., Miranti, S.V., Schmidt, M., Klinger, E., & Blount, J.P. (2003). Outcomes of Systematic Motivational Counseling for substance use following traumatic brain injury. *Journal of Addictive Diseases, 22*, 93–110.

Cox, W.M., & Klinger, E. (1988). A motivational model of alcohol use. *Journal of Abnormal Psychology, 97* (2), 168–180.

Cox, W.M., & Klinger, E. (1990). Incentive motivation, affective change, and alcohol use: A model. In W.M. Cox (Ed.), *Why people drink: Parameters of alcohol as a reinforcer* (pp. 291–314). New York: Amereon Press.

Cox, W.M., Klinger, E., & Blount, J.P. (1991). Alcohol use and goal hierarchies: Systematic motivational counseling for alcoholics. In W.R. Miller & S. Rollnick (Eds.), *Motivational interviewing: Preparing people to change addictive behavior* (pp. 260–271). New York: Guilford.

Cox, W.M., Klinger, E., & Blount, J.P. (1999). *Systematic motivational counseling: A treatment manual.* Unpublished manuscript. University of Wales, Bangor, UK.

Dimeff, L.A., Bear, J.S., Kivlahan, D.R., & Marlatt, G.A. (1999). *Brief alcohol screening and intervention for college students (BASICS): A harm reduction approach.* New York: Guilford.

Heather, N. (1995). Brief intervention strategies. In R.K. Hester & W.R. Miller (Eds.), *Handbook of alcoholism treatment approaches: Effective alternatives* (2nd edn.; pp. 105–122). Needham Heights, MA: Allyn & Bacon.

Horn, J.L., Wanberg, K.W., & Foster, F.M. (1987). *The alcohol use inventory.* Minneapolis, MN: National Computer Systems.

Humphreys, K., & Tucker, J.A. (2002). Toward more responsive and effective intervention systems for alcohol-related problems. *Addiction, 97,* 126–132.

Kayser, R.E. (1990). *Rijden onder invloed. Evaluatie van een lesprogramma voor rijscholen [Drunken driving. Evaluation of an education program for driving schools].* Nijmegen, The Netherlands: Katholieke Universiteit.

Marlatt, G.A., Baer, J.S., Kivlahan, D.R., Dimeff, L.A., Larimer, M.E., Quigley, L.A., et al. (1998). Screening and brief intervention for high-risk college student drinkers: Results from a 2-year follow-up assessment. *Journal of Consulting and Clinical Psychology, 66,* 604–615.

Marlatt, G.A., & Witkiewitz, K. (2002). Harm reduction approaches to alcohol use: Health promotion, prevention, and treatment. *Addictive Behaviors, 27,* 876–886.

Matthews, D.B., & Miller, W.R. (1979). Estimating blood alcohol concentration: Two computer programs and their applications in therapy and research. *Addictive Behaviors, 4,* 55–60.

Miller, W.R. (1995). Increasing motivation for change. In R.K. Hester & W.R. Miller (Eds.), *Handbook of alcoholism treatment approaches: Effective alternatives* (2nd edn.; pp. 89–104). Needham Heights, MA: Allyn & Bacon.

Miller, W.R., Benefield, R.G., & Tonigan, J.S. (1993). Enhancing motivation for change in problem drinking: A controlled comparison of two therapist styles. *Journal of Consulting and Clinical Psychology, 61,* 455–461.

Miller, W.R., Crawford, V.L., & Taylor, C.A. (1979). Significant others as corroborative sources for problem drinkers. *Addictive Behaviors, 4,* 67–70.

Miller, W.R., & Marlatt, G.A. (1987). *Comprehensive Drinker Profile Manual Supplement.* Odessa, FL: Psychological Assessment Resources.

Miller, W.R., & Rollnick, S. (2002). *Motivational interviewing: Preparing people for change* (2nd edn.). New York: Guilford.

Miller, W.R., & Saucedo, C.F. (1983). Assessment of neuropsychological impairment and brain damage in problem drinkers. In C.J. Golden, J.A. Moses, Jr., J.A. Coffman, W.R. Miller, & F.D. Strider (Eds.), *Clinical neuropsychology: Interface with neurological and psychiatric disorders* (pp. 141–195). New York: Grune & Stratton.

Miller, W.R., & Sovereign, R.G. (1989). The Check-Up: A model for early intervention in addictive behaviors. In T. Løberg, W.R. Miller, P.E. Nathan, & G.A. Marlatt (Eds.), *Addictive behaviors: Prevention and early intervention* (pp. 219–231). Amsterdam: Swets & Zeitlinger.

Miller, W.R., Sovereign, R.G., & Krege, B. (1988). Motivational interviewing with problem drinkers: II. The Drinker's Check-Up as a preventive intervention. *Behavioural Psychotherapy, 16,* 251–268.

Miller, W.R., & Wilbourne, P.L. (2002). Mesa Grande: A methodological analysis of clinical trials of treatments for alcohol use disorders. *Addiction, 97,* 265–277.

Miller, W.R., Zweben, A., DiClemente, C.C., & Rychtarik, R. (1992). *Motivational enhancement therapy manual: A clinical research guide for therapists treating individuals with alcohol abuse and dependence.* Project MATCH Monograph Series, Vol. 2. Rockville, MD: National Institute on Alcohol Abuse and Alcoholism.

Moyer, A., Finney, J.W., Swearingen, C.E., & Vergun, P. (2002). Brief interventions for alcohol problems: A meta-analytic review of controlled investigations in treatment-seeking and non-treatment-seeking populations. *Addiction, 97,* 279–292.

Murphy, J.G., Duchnick, J.J., Vuchinich, R.E., Davison, J.W., Karg, R.S., Olson, A.M., et al. (2001). Relative efficacy of a brief motivational intervention for college student drinkers. *Psychology of Addictive Behaviors, 15,* 373–379.

Prochaska, J.O., & DiClemente, C.C. (1986). Toward a comprehensive model of change. In W.R. Miller & N. Heather (Eds.), *Treating addictive behaviors: Processes of change* (pp. 3–27). New York: Plenum.

Prochaska, J.O., DiClemente, C.C., & Norcross, J.C. (1992). In search of how people change: Applications to addictive behaviors. *American Psychologist, 47*, 1102–1114.

Project MATCH Research Group (1997a). Matching alcoholism treatments to client heterogeneity: Project MATCH posttreatment drinking outcomes. *Journal of Studies on Alcohol, 58*, 7–29.

Project MATCH Research Group (1997b). Project MATCH secondary a priori hypotheses. *Addiction, 92*, 1671–1698.

Project MATCH Research Group (1998). Matching alcoholism treatments to client heterogeneity: Project MATCH three-year drinking outcomes. *Alcoholism: Clinical and Experimental Research, 23* (60), 1300–1311.

Reitan, R.M. (1986). *Trail making test. Manual of administration and scoring.* Tucson, AZ: Reitan Neuropsychology Laboratory.

Schippers, G.M., Brokken, L.C.M.H., & Otten, J. (1994a). *Doorlichting, Voorlichting Alcoholgebruik. Handleiding [Manual, Dutch Motivational Drinker's Check-Up].* Nijmegen, The Netherlands: Bureau Beta.

Schippers, G.M., Brokken, L.C.M.H., & Verweij, J.W.M. (1994b). Doorlichting voorlichting alcoholgebruik: Een protocol voor motivatie en assessment ten behoeve van vroegtijdige interventie bij alcoholproblematiek [Evaluating a protocol for motivation and assessment of early intervention in alcohol problems]. *Tijdschrift voor Alcohol, Drugs en Andere Psychotrope Stoffen, 20*, 88–94.

Sobell, L.C., & Sobell, M.B. (1992). Timeline follow-back: A technique for assessing self-reported alcohol consumption. In R.Z. Litten & J.P. Allen (Eds.), *Measuring alcohol consumption: Psychosocial and biological methods* (pp. 14–72). Totawa, NJ: Humana Press.

Walburg, J.A., & Van Emst, A.J. (1985). *Schaal voor drinkgewoontes [Drinking habit scale].* Lisse, The Netherlands: Swets & Zeitlinger.

Walters, G.D. (2000). Behavioral self-control training for problem drinkers: A meta-analysis of randomized control studies. *Behavior Therapy, 31*, 135–149.

Wechsler, D. (1955). *Wechsler Adult Intelligence Scale Manual.* New York: Psychological Corporation.

CHAPTER 21

Motivational Enhancement as a Brief Intervention for College Student Drinkers

Arthur W. Blume
University of Texas at El Paso, USA
and
G. Alan Marlatt
University of Washington, USA

Synopsis.—Heavy drinking is common among college and university students, and often leads to a variety of risky behaviors while drinking alcohol. College students with a history of alcohol or other substance abuse in the family, antisocial behavior, impulse control problems, or who join fraternities or sororities seem to be at the greatest risk for problematic drinking behavior while in college. College students' lack of motivation to change their drinking is influenced by positive expectancies related to consuming alcohol, the perpetuation of myths that provide inaccurate information about drinking and its potential consequences, peer pressures that tend to induce overdrinking in social situations, beliefs that alcohol is a useful coping strategy for reducing academic and social stress, and underestimating personal risks related to drinking behavior. Behavioral interventions to increase college students' motivation to change abusive drinking practices have shown some success. Those interventions that seem to motivate change often challenge positive alcohol expectancies, teach resistance to peer pressure, and debunk drinking myths and misperceptions about negligible risks associated with drinking behavior. Particularly effective is the Alcohol Skills Training Program/Brief Alcohol Screening and Intervention for College Students (ASTP/BASICS) program, which educates students about binge- and heavy-drinking risks while teaching them how to cope effectively with stress and social situations without the abuse of alcohol. Key components of the ASTP/BASICS program include education about physical effects of alcohol, using social norms to enhance motivation to reduce abnormal drinking, and teaching skills to cope without overdrinking in a variety of drinking situations. Recent technological advances offer new methods for motivating college students to change their risky drinking practices. Virtual reality and Internet interventions can provide both information to college students in a nonthreatening way and opportunities to learn and practice new skills imaginally.

Heavy- and binge-drinking practices are quite common among college students. In the United States, young adults 18–24 years old, usually the age for attending college, have the highest drinking rates of all age groups (Kandel & Logan, 1984), with estimates that nearly 90% of all college students drink (Barnes, Welte, & Dintcheff, 1992; Haworth-Hoeppner et al., 1989; Meilman et al., 1990; Salz & Elandt, 1986; Wechsler & Isaac, 1992).

Handbook of Motivational Counseling. Edited by W. Miles Cox and Eric Klinger.
© 2004 John Wiley & Sons, Ltd.

Approximately 25–50% of college students binge or drink heavily (Engs & Hanson, 1985; Haworth-Hoeppner et al., 1989; Wechsler & Isaac, 1992; Wechsler et al., 1995a; Werner & Greene, 1992), although there is some debate as to what constitutes binge drinking and whether consumption rates alone are a useful way to conceptualize the problem (e.g., deJong, 2001; Wechsler & Nelson, 2001). Heavy drinking often places college students at high risk for a variety of negative drinking-related consequences, such as poor academic performance; antisocial and aggressive behavior; sexual assaults, unplanned pregnancies, and sexually transmitted diseases; traumatic injuries and death; and increased risk for alcohol dependence (Berkowitz & Perkins, 1986; Engs & Hanson, 1985; Hingson & Howland, 1993; Institute of Medicine, 1990; Larimer et al., 1999; McCormick & Ureda, 1995; Quigley & Marlatt, 1996; Rivinus & Larimer, 1993; Wechsler & Isaac, 1992; Wechsler et al., 1994; 1995b).

Problems with self-regulation have been identified as a risk factor for problem drinking among young adults (Chassin & DeLucia, 1996). Young, single male student drinkers under age 35 are often at highest risk for engaging in binge drinking (Johnston, O'Malley, & Bachman, 1996; Quigley & Marlatt, 1996). Although many young adults "mature out" of the heavy-drinking patterns typical in college as they assume greater familial and work-related responsibilities (e.g., Baer et al., 2001), a small subset of binge drinkers seem to have increasing difficulties with drinking and its negative consequences into later adulthood (e.g., Schulenberg et al., 1996a, 1996b).

Several subgroups of college students seem to be at high risk for heavy drinking and its aversive consequences. For instance, students whose family members abuse alcohol are at increased risk for risky drinking in college (Kushner & Sher, 1993), as are students who have a history of antisocial behavior (Jessor, Donovan, & Costa, 1991). One college subgroup that seems at great risk for heavy- and binge-drinking practices are members of fraternities and sororities (Larimer, 1992). In the United States, members of these organizations often identify drinking as an important part of group identity and may perceive that heavy drinking is the norm. In some cases fraternities and sororities find strong reinforcement for acquiring heavy-drinking reputations, viewing the label of being a heavy-drinking "house" as positive (Larimer et al., 1997). One study found that heavy or binge drinking in fraternities and sororities may be attributable to high rates of student–parent conflict among these groups (Turner, Larimer, & Sarason, 2000).

FACTORS THAT INFLUENCE MOTIVATION TO CHANGE ALCOHOL USE

Expectancies

Positive alcohol expectancies seem to be strongly associated with higher numbers of heavy- and binge-drinking episodes and drinking-related problems among college students (Evans & Dunn, 1995; Mooney et al., 1987). College students who engage in heavy or binge drinking often have positive expectancies related to alcohol's ability to enhance the enjoyment of social situations, such as parties and other social interactions (Carey, 1995; Fromme, Stroot, & Kaplan, 1993). With regard to motivating change, negative expectancies about drinking behavior often are not as strongly considered by students as are positive expectancies (Gerrard et al., 2000; Whaley, 1986), possibly because of less experience or concern about negative consequences. However, there is reason to believe that teaching college students about misconceptions regarding alcohol expectancies may be useful to increase their motivation to change. Controlled trials have found that expectancy challenges are associated with significant reductions in alcohol consumption (Darkes & Goldman, 1993, 1997; Jones, Silvia, & Richman, 1995). Expectancy challenges can involve different cognitive therapy strategies, such as thinking through the behavior chain to its natural consequences, data collecting to refute positive expectancies, and hypothesis testing to check out personal assumptions about the positive qualities of alcohol consumption.

Drinking Myths

Positive expectancies often are perpetuated through drinking myths concerning misinformation about the power of alcohol. Marketing strategies often target these myths in order to sell their product, making drinking glamorous. One drinking-myth theme includes stories about the powers of alcohol to improve personality or performance. An example of this type of myth is the belief by many young adults (and some older ones!) that drinking enhances sexual performance, so that more drinking would cause better sexual performance (Bills & Duncan, 1991). Of course, the reality is that alcohol in high doses tends to hinder sexual performance (Miller & Gold, 1988).

Other drinking myths concern how to avoid the negative consequences of heavy alcohol consumption. Such myths often place a person at risk because acting upon the myth provides the illusion of safety. Examples include beliefs that certain behaviors before heavy drinking, such as drinking olive oil or milk, will prevent hangovers, or that drinking coffee sobers a person (Dolan, 1975; Engs & Hanson, 1989). Belief in these myths can lead to very risky behavior, such as driving while intoxicated with the belief that coffee has taken away the impairment.

One way to motivate drinking behavior change is to challenge drinking myths (Dolan, 1975; Engs & Hanson, 1989). College students can be educated about the many drinking myths, either through challenging stories (or advertizement) about the abilities of alcohol to improve personality or performance, or by challenging the assumption that the aversive consequences of heavy drinking are avoidable through some form of superstitious behavior. Education conducted in a disarming fashion can debunk the veracity of these tales, and is an important component of enhancing college students' motivation to change their risky drinking practices.

Peer Pressures and Socially Sanctioned Drinking Behavior

College student drinking practices tend to be highly influenced by peers. For instance, students often seem to take cues about their own drinking behavior by modeling their peers (Caudill & Marlatt, 1975; Collins, Parks, & Marlatt, 1985). Furthermore, college students tend to overestimate how much their peers are drinking, thereby underestimating how much their own drinking deviates from peer norms (Baer, Stacy, & Larimer, 1991; Haines & Spear, 1996; Larimer et al., 1997; Perkins & Berkowitz, 1986; Presley, Meilman, & Lyerla, 1994). Taking such cues from others may also indicate that students lack skills for controlling their alcohol consumption, such as drink refusal and behavioral self-regulation skills (e.g., Marlatt, Baer, & Larimer, 1995).

Because college students often have misperceptions about their drinking practices in relationship to their peers, enhancing college students' motivation to reduce their drinking usually involves education about peer (or other social) norms. This may include education about drinking norms at the local university, or national college student drinking norms. For instance, in programs designed to motivate changes in college student drinking behavior, such as the Alcohol Skills Training Program (ASTP; Fromme et al., 1994), the Brief Alcohol Screening and Intervention for College Students (BASICS; Dimeff et al., 1999), or other programs that use peer norms to motivate change, these norms are presented factually and without judgment in order to disarm students' defensiveness about their drinking. These programs will be described in detail later.

"Self-Medication" for Stress

Many college students report using alcohol to relieve stress, and many heavy-drinking events occur in reaction to periods of high stress, such as examinations, homework demands, or the end of the semester. Other times drinking is related to stress in personal relationships or difficulties with parents. In fact, research indicates that anxiety about social situations is a significant predictor of heavy drinking among college students (Burke & Stephens, 1999).

To reduce the likelihood that alcohol will be used to reduce stress, the college student needs to have a larger repertoire of stress-reducing skills, such as exercise, the ability to tolerate distress, meditation, or other alternative activities that reduce stress without alcohol (Marlatt, 1985a, 1985b; Marlatt & Kristeller, 1999). Students are taught that using alcohol to cope with stress and anxiety is not particularly useful because alcohol can increase stress via aversive consequences, and heavy alcohol use increases rather than decreases anxiety over time (Allan, 1995). Alternatively, students are taught other skills to cope with stress and anxiety in a more effective manner (Rohsenow, Smith, & Johnson, 1985). Coping skills for stress and anxiety are important components of interventions such as ASTP or BASICS to motivate college students to change their drinking behavior.

Underestimation of Threat

Research has found that college students tend to underestimate personal dangers associated with drinking, and that while drinking they become even less aware of those dangers (Heck, 1997; Maiman & Becker, 1974). The lack of attentiveness to cues about potential dangers during heavy-drinking episodes is akin to "alcohol myopia." Alcohol myopia is a narrowing of perception during intoxication which interferes with accurate awareness and processing of environmental cues. The drinker becomes increasingly less able to accurately perceive and interpret complex cues in the environment as he or she becomes increasingly intoxicated (Steele & Josephs, 1990). Alcohol myopia might impair thoughtful responses to environmental cues, resulting in disinhibited (sometimes aggressive) behavior that places a person at risk for danger (e.g., Cheong & Nagoshi, 1999; George & Stoner, 2000).

Motivating college students to change their drinking behavior includes educating them about risks associated with alcohol myopia. Because alcohol myopia tends to leave people vulnerable, it is recommended that college students travel in pairs or groups to social gatherings where alcohol is served. For instance, in ASTP or BASICS programs, friends are encouraged to watch out for one another during social events, and to intervene to protect one another from potentially risky behavior, such as driving while intoxicated or engaging in drinking games. This strategy may include designating certain friends to remain sober in order to chaperone those who drink during such events.

Neurocognitive Factors

Researchers have been increasingly interested in the neurocognitive risks associated even with short-term heavy or binge drinking. Alcohol researchers once believed that neurocognitive deficits associated with drinking alcohol were found only among alcohol-dependent adults, but recent research has found neurocognitive difficulties among early to middle adolescents with a history of heavy alcohol use (Brown et al., 2000). Furthermore, chronic abuse of alcohol by adolescents has been associated with attention problems that increase over time (Tapert & Brown, 1999), and some research has identified problems with executive control functions among heavy-drinking college students, which are often associated with deficits in behavioral regulation skills, judgment, and decision-making; and impaired ability to attend to contextual cues (Blume, Marlatt, & Schmaling, 2000). Executive control dysfunction may adversely affect motivation in that a heavy drinker may not process information related to drinking behavior in an efficient manner. The key, unanswered question is the extent to which these deficits are a predisposition to or a consequence of heavy alcohol use.

MOTIVATING CHANGE AMONG COLLEGE STUDENT DRINKERS: INTERVENTIONS

Successful interventions for motivating risky drinkers to change have been evaluated and refined. Effective education programs have targeted young adults' inaccurate perceptions that their high-risk drinking patterns are the norm (e.g., Baer, Stacy, & Larimer, 1991), have provided skills training to counter peer pressures to drink (Caudill & Marlatt, 1975; Collins, Parks, & Marlatt, 1985), and challenged positive expectancies related to drinking (e.g., Carey, 1995). These programs have also taught students how to refuse drinks and how to develop safety plans (such as designating sober drivers, using peer support systems at social gatherings, and monitoring one's own behavior; e.g., Marlatt, Baer, & Larimer, 1995).

One particularly promising program is the ASTP (Fromme et al., 1994), which integrates all of these educational tools. The original ASTP program included eight weekly sessions (Kivlahan et al., 1990). A two-session version, called the BASICS program, was first used with the entering first-year class at the University of Washington in 1990. The intervention was conducted during the first year of college, and periodic feedback of drinking behavior such as consumption rates and consequences were mailed to participants. The feedback also consisted of a comparison of the student's drinking behavior with the normative drinking behavior of college students across the United States. The students were followed for four years to determine the long-term effects of the intervention. Participants who received the BASICS program had clinically and statistically greater reductions in alcohol-related problems than a matched control group at four-year follow-up (Baer et al., 2001; Marlatt et al., 1998; Roberts et al., 2000).

The BASICS program educates students about drinking myths, challenges positive drinking expectancies (beliefs about the positive effects of alcohol), provides accurate peer norms about drinking practices, and teaches about the physical effects of alcohol and how to resist peer pressure. BASIC participants monitor their alcohol consumption between the two educational sessions to increase their awareness of their own drinking habits. They are also provided with a personalized Blood–Alcohol Level chart on a laminated wallet-sized card as a personal reminder to avoid heavy drinking, and are taught how to use this and other cues to promote safe drinking. The leaders of BASICS sessions use an enjoyable audiovisual presentation to maintain participants' interest in the program (Dimeff et al., 1999). In ASTP and BASICS, leaders use motivational interviewing techniques (Miller & Rollnick, 2002; Resnicow et al., Chapter 24, this volume) for increasing motivation to reduce alcohol use.

In more recent trials to evaluate BASICS, peer leaders (either advanced graduate students or mature students in their final undergraduate year) have conducted the intervention with the other students. Peer leaders were chosen because of research suggesting that the behavior of young adults is more influenced by peers than by older adults (e.g., Caudill & Marlatt, 1975; Collins, Parks, & Marlatt, 1985). Having peer leaders is intended to provide positive modeling of safe drinking behavior, and increase the credibility of BASICS among college student peers (Miller, 1999).

THE COMPONENTS OF THE ASTP/BASICS INTERVENTION

The ASTP/BASICS program consists of educational components designed to motivate college students to change their drinking behavior. First, the physical effects of alcohol are described in detail, including information refuting myths about the effects of alcohol. Physical effects discussed can range from severe (e.g., cirrhosis of the liver) to unpleasant (e.g., weight gain) and pleasant (mild euphoria at low doses). Possible interactions of alcohol with other psychoactive substances are included in this discussion. Potentiation is explained, as are antagonistic effects, with examples of how drug and alcohol interactions can greatly exaggerate intoxication and even be lethal. Potentiation occurs when alcohol and another central nervous system depressant interact in a synergistic fashion, causing an exaggerated depressant effect, whereas antagonistic effects occur when alcohol is combined with a drug that counteracts the depressant effects of alcohol.

During the discussion about physical effects, the biphasic effects of alcohol are discussed in an effort to educate participants about the value of moderate consumption. A principal message of ASTP/BASICS is that alcohol can have stimulating and euphoric effects at lower doses, but that drinking to intoxication causes depressive effects and a variety of aversive consequences (the biphasic effects of alcohol). Furthermore, ASTP/BASICS emphasizes that chronic heavy drinking can cause health problems. The goal of this discussion is to motivate college students to reduce their drinking to safe levels in order to maximize the pleasurable effects of alcohol while minimizing risks of aversive consequences. The recommended target of .055 grams of alcohol per 100 milliliters of blood (the blood–alcohol level, or BAL) or below has been labeled by researchers as the point of diminishing pleasurable returns from alcohol consumption. Drinking to a BAL below this point of diminishing returns is thought to help to reduce the risks of negative health consequence drinking and of developing tolerance (Dimeff et al., 1999), although some research has found that different people may have different points of diminishing returns (e.g., Conrod et al., 1997). The ASTP/BASICS program also introduces to college students alcohol myopia and its relationship to risky behavior. College students are encouraged to use the .055 BAL target to avoid alcohol myopia.

Tolerance for the effects of alcohol is discussed in an effort to encourage moderate drinking. The myth that tolerance can be helpful by allowing a person to drink more while experiencing less physical effects is disputed by evidence that tolerance can diminish the body's ability to detect the intoxicating effects of alcohol. In addition, tolerance increases the amount of alcohol needed to feel pleasurable effects, which would cost college student drinkers more money.

ASTP/BASICS also include strategies for challenging inaccurate expectancies about the effects of alcohol. An aim of the educational component of the program is to encourage discussions about common misconceptions about the chemical effects of alcohol. In connection with this discussion, the placebo effects of alcohol are described through Marlatt, Demming, and Reid's (1973) classic study in which they found that drinkers' beliefs about the effects of alcohol more strongly influenced their behavior while drinking than did the pharmacological effects of alcohol. Participants who believed they were drinking alcohol, but who were not, acted more intoxicated than people who were drinking but believed they were not.

Another tool to enhance motivation to change is simply to encourage self-monitoring of alcohol use. Self-monitoring has been found to be an effective method for reducing risky drinking among college students (Cronin, 1996; Garvin, Alcorn, & Faulkner, 1990). In ASTP/BASICS, a session is devoted to teaching students how to self-monitor, and they are asked to monitor their drinking between sessions, and bring the results to the next session. Often people are not aware of how much they drink, but self-monitoring allows students to reflect on how much they are actually drinking. Other types of monitoring are also encouraged, such as one's mood while drinking, or peers' behavior while drinking heavily as compared to drinking moderately.

Participants are taught how to record their drinking on diary cards. In addition, personalized BAL charts can be provided as laminated wallet-sized cards in order to remind participants to drink moderately. Participants can also use the cards to plan safe drinking events by calculating how many drinks they should limit themselves to in order to maximize pleasurable effects while minimizing risks. Participants use the BAL wallet card and other cues to remind themselves to track their drinking, thereby enhancing their motivation through self-awareness (Dimeff et al., 1999).

Social norms are used in conjunction with the self-monitoring data. The self-monitoring results are discussed in relationship to college student drinking norms, encouraging participants to compare their behavior to that of other students. Students' discovery that they drink more than their peers can motivate them to reduce the amount they drink. However, for some students, a heavy-drinking reputation may be seen as a badge of honor (Larimer et al., 1997), so the use of peer norms to enhance motivation should be used with caution.

Finally, ASTP/BASICS allows participants to learn new skills for reducing risky drinking, and opportunities to rehearse newly learned skills. ASTP/BASICS manuals use vignettes to illustrate how people can successfully use such coping skills as drink refusal and self-assertion. As the ASTP/BASICS participants practice the material and develop their competence using the new skills, their motivation to maintain changes in risky drinking practices seems to be enhanced.

OTHER WAYS TO MOTIVATE CHANGE

Other interventions to motivate college students to change risky drinking behavior have been developed using computer technology. For example, an interactive program called "Alcohol 101" (The Century Council and the University of Illinois, 1997) uses many of the components found in ASTP/BASICS. The user learns about the effects of alcohol, and is allowed to experience consequences of choices about drinking made during a virtual party. Another creative intervention involves the use of web-base technology to motivate change. Recent evidence suggests that Internet-based assessments are effective in motivating college students to reduce their risky drinking behavior (Miller, 1999).

One currently popular strategy is to curb alcohol consumption through university community policies about drinking. The most extreme example is that of "dry" campuses that have a policy of "zero tolerance" for alcohol consumption. Recent evidence suggests that nondrinking campuses have fewer binge-drinking episodes than drinking ones, but it is unclear whether university policies contributed to the changes in drinking (Wechsler et al., 2001). Others have suggested that policies would be more effective if they encouraged safe drinking practices rather than banning drinking altogether, arguing that zero-tolerance policies have not succeeded in the past (e.g., Lewis, 2001). The focus would be on preventing aversive consequences of drinking behavior rather than eliminating the drinking itself. Such a policy might be more effective, inasmuch as it is unclear whether prohibition of alcohol on college campuses actually reduces students' drinking, or simply encourages them to drink off campus. Furthermore, there is no evidence that prohibiting drinking changes students' attitudes about drinking and their motivation to change.

MOTIVATING COLLEGE STUDENTS TO DRINK SAFELY: FUTURE DIRECTIONS

One promising new direction is to use interventions before students enter college in order to prevent problem drinking, or to provide for interventions prior to important events frequently associated with heavy-drinking celebrations and parties, such as the final examination week, or a student's 21st birthday. In the United States, the legal drinking age is 21 years of age, and a student's 21st birthday is a time of heavy drinking, often encouraged by bars and taverns that offer free alcoholic drinks as birthday gifts.

Some students choose to drink regardless of their campus's policy about drinking. Because prohibitions against drinking might not be effective, it seems prudent to continue to develop interventions that reduce the risks associated with students' drinking. Further development of harm-reduction strategies that guide students through successive approximations toward a goal of moderation or abstinence (e.g., Marlatt, 1998) would be a fruitful direction for enhancing students' motivation. Also the use of new technology, such as interactive Internet sites, is another promising direction. More could be done with virtual reality and web-based technologies, both of which afford ease of access and a sense of anonymity. These new technologies allow drinkers the opportunity to rehearse new skills, and to be exposed to risky situations and potential aversive consequences imaginally (via virtual reality technology). New technology could afford college students the chance to experience virtual parties where they could practice refusing drinks and avoiding dangerous consequences and be reinforced for doing so. Finally, using individual and community interventions conjunctively to motivate healthy drinking behavior would seem beneficial. The community reinforcement model might be helpful in this regard (e.g., Miller, Meyers, & Hiller-Sturmhofel, 1999; Wong, Jones, & Stitzer, Chapter 22, this volume). College students' motivation for change would likely be enhanced if environmental controls and individual interventions were aimed toward a common goal. Such a program would require integrated campus–community efforts in which university officials, student representatives, community tavern owners, therapists, and local citizens worked together to develop consistent drinking policies with well-specified contingent rewards and punishments attached to them. A clear and consistent message concerning norms and expectations about university student drinking behavior would be conveyed by involving the entire community. An integrated approach using combinations of empirically supported strategies would appear to hold the greatest promise for promoting safe drinking among college students.

REFERENCES

Allan, C.A. (1995). Alcohol problems and anxiety disorders—a critical review. *Alcohol and Alcoholism, 30*, 145–151.

Baer, J.S., Kivlahan, D.R., Blume, A.W., McKnight, P., & Marlatt, G.A. (2001). Brief intervention for heavy drinking college students: Four-year follow-up and natural history. *American Journal of Public Health, 91*, 1310–1316.

Baer, J.S., Stacy, A., & Larimer, M. (1991). Biases in the perception of drinking norms among college students. *Journal of Studies on Alcohol, 52*, 580–586.

Barnes, G.M., Welte, J.W., & Dintcheff, B. (1992). Alcohol misuse among college students and other young adults: Findings from a general population study in New York State. *International Journal of the Addictions, 27*, 917–934.

Berkowitz, A.D., & Perkins, H.W. (1986). Problem drinking among college students: A review of recent research. *Journal of American College Health, 35*, 1–28.

Bills, S.A., & Duncan, D.F. (1991). Drugs and sex: A survey of college students' beliefs. *Perceptual and Motor Skills, 72*, 1293–1294.

Blume, A.W., Marlatt, G.A., & Schmaling, K.B. (2000). Executive cognitive function and heavy drinking behavior among college students. *Psychology of Addictive Behaviors, 14*, 299–302.

Brown, S.A., Tapert, S.F., Granholm, E., & Delis, D.C. (2000). Neurocognitive functioning of adolescents: Effects of protracted alcohol use. *Alcoholism: Clinical and Experimental Research, 24*, 164–171.

Burke, R.S., & Stephens, R.S. (1999). Social anxiety and drinking in college students: A social cognitive theory analysis. *Clinical Psychology Review, 19*, 513–530.

Carey, K.B. (1995). Alcohol-related expectancies predict quantity and frequency of heavy drinking among college students. *Psychology of Addictive Behaviors, 9*, 236–241.

Caudill, B.D., & Marlatt, G.A. (1975). Modeling influences in social drinking: An experimental analogue. *Journal of Consulting and Clinical Psychology, 43*, 405–415.

Chassin, L., & DeLucia, C. (1996). Drinking during adolescence. *Alcohol Health and Research World, 20*, 175–180.

Cheong, J., & Nagoshi, C.T. (1999). Effects of sensation seeking, instruction set, and alcohol/placebo administration on aggressive behavior. *Alcohol, 17*, 81–86.

Collins, R.L., Parks, G.A., & Marlatt, G.A. (1985). Social determinants of alcohol consumption: The effects of social interaction and model status on the self-administration of alcohol. *Journal of Consulting and Clinical Psychology, 53*, 189–200.

Conrod, P.J., Peterson, J.B., Pihl, R.O., & Mankowski, S. (1997). Biphasic effects of alcohol on heart rate are influenced by alcoholic family history and rate of alcohol ingestion. *Alcohol: Clinical and Experimental Research, 21*, 140–149.

Cronin, C. (1996). Harm reduction for alcohol-use-related problems among college students. *Substance Use and Misuse, 31*, 2029–2037.

Darkes, J., & Goldman, M.S. (1993). Expectancy challenge and drinking reduction: Experimental evidence for a mediational process. *Journal of Consulting and Clinical Psychology, 61*, 344–353.

Darkes, J., & Goldman, M.S. (1997). Expectancy challenge and drinking reduction: Process and structure in the alcohol expectancy network. *Experimental and Clinical Psychopharmacology, 6*, 64–76.

deJong, W. (2001). Finding common ground for effective campus-based prevention. *Psychology of Addictive Behaviors, 15*, 292–296.

Dimeff, L.A., Baer, J.S., Kivlahan, D.R., & Marlatt, G.A. (1999). *Brief alcohol screening and intervention for college students.* New York: Guilford.

Dolan, J.S. (1975). Drinking myths: A guided tour through folklore, fantasy, humbug, and hogwash. *Journal of Drug Education, 5*, 45–49.

Engs, R.C., & Hanson, D.J. (1985). The drinking patterns and problems of college students. *Journal of Alcohol and Drug Education, 31*, 65–82.

Engs, R.C., & Hanson, D.J. (1989). The alcohol knowledge and drinking myths of a national sample of university students. *Journal of College Student Development, 30*, 180–182.

Evans, D.M., & Dunn, N.J. (1995). Alcohol expectancies, coping responses and self-efficacy judgments: A replication of Copper et al.'s study in a college sample. *Journal of Studies on Alcohol, 56*, 186–193.

Fromme, K., Marlatt, G.A., Baer, J.S., & Kivlahan, D.R. (1994). The alcohol skills training program: A group intervention for young adult drinkers. *Journal of Substance Abuse Treatment, 11*, 143–154.

Fromme, K., Stroot, E.A., & Kaplan, D. (1993). Comprehensive effects of alcohol: Development and psychometric assessment of a new expectancy questionnaire. *Psychological Assessment, 5*, 19–26.

Garvin, R.B., Alcorn, J.D., & Faulkner, K.K. (1990). Behavioral strategies for alcohol abuse prevention with high-risk college males. *Journal of Alcohol and Drug Education, 36*, 23–34.

George, W.H., & Stoner, S.A. (2000). Understanding acute alcohol effects on sexual behavior. *Annual Review of Sex Research, 11*, 92–124.

Gerrard, M., Gibbons, F.X., Reis-Bergen, M., & Russell, D.W. (2000). Self-esteem, self-serving cognitions, and health risk behavior. *Journal of Personality, 68*, 1177–1201.

Haines, M., & Spear, S.F. (1996). Changing the perception of norm: A strategy to decrease binge drinking among college students. *Journal of American College Health, 45*, 134–140.

Haworth-Hoeppner, S., Globetti, G., Stem, J., & Morasco, F. (1989). The quantity and frequency of drinking among undergraduates at a southern university. *International Journal of Addictions, 24*, 829–857.

Heck, M.J. (1997). *Risk perception and alcohol consumption in college students.* Unpublished dissertation, Virginia Commonwealth University.

Hingson, R., & Howland, J. (1993). Alcohol and non-traffic unintended injuries. *Addiction, 88*, 877–883.

Institute of Medicine (1990). *Broadening the base of treatment for alcohol problems.* Washington, DC: National Academy Press.

Jessor, R., Donovan, J.E., & Costa, F.M. (1991). *Beyond adolescence: Problem behavior and young adult development.* New York: Cambridge University Press.

Johnston, L.D., O'Malley, P.M., & Bachman, J.G. (1996). *National survey results on drug use from monitoring the future study, 1975–1994. Volume II: College students and young adults.* Washington, DC: US Government Printing Office.

Jones, L.M., Silvia, L.Y., & Richman, C.L. (1995). Increased awareness and self-challenge of alcohol expectancies. *Substance Abuse, 16*, 77–85.

Kandel, D.B., & Logan, J.A. (1984). Patterns of drug use from adolescence to young adulthood: I. Periods of risk for initiation, continued use, and discontinuation. *American Journal of Public Health, 74*, 660–666.

Kivlahan, D.R., Marlatt, G.A., Fromme, K., Coppel, D.B., & Williams, E. (1990). Secondary prevention with college drinkers: Evaluation of an alcohol skills training program. *Journal of Consulting and Clinical Psychology, 58*, 805–810.

Kushner, M.G., & Sher, K.J. (1993). Comorbidity of alcohol and anxiety disorders among college students: Effects of gender and family history of alcoholism. *Addictive Behaviors, 18*, 543–552.

Larimer, M.E. (1992). *Alcohol abuse and the Greek system: An exploration of fraternity and sorority drinking*. Unpublished doctoral dissertation, University of Washington, Seattle.

Larimer, M.E., Irvine, D.L., Kilmer, J.R., & Marlatt, G.A. (1997). College drinking and the Greek system: Examining the role of perceived norms for high risk behavior. *Journal of College Student Development, 38*, 587–598.

Larimer, M.E., Lydum, A.R., Anderson, B.K., & Turner, A.P. (1999). Male and female recipients of unwanted sexual contact in a college student sample: Prevalence rates, alcohol use, and depression symptoms. *Sex Roles, 40*, 295–308.

Lewis, D.C. (2001). Urging college alcohol and drug policies that target adverse behavior, not use. *Journal of American College Health, 50*, 39–41.

Maiman, L.A., & Becker, M.H. (1974). The health belief model: Origins and correlates in psychological theory. *Health Education Monographs, 2*, 336–353.

Marlatt, G.A. (1985a). Lifestyle modification. In G.A. Marlatt & J.R. Gordon (Eds.), *Relapse prevention: Maintenance strategies in the treatment of addictive behaviors* (pp. 280–348). New York: Guilford.

Marlatt, G.A. (1985b). Relapse prevention: Theoretical rationale and overview of the model. In G.A. Marlatt & J.R. Gordon (Eds.), *Relapse prevention: Maintenance strategies in the treatment of addictive behaviors* (pp. 3–70). New York: Guilford.

Marlatt, G.A. (1998). Basic principles and strategies of harm reduction. In G.A. Marlatt (Ed.), *Harm reduction: Pragmatic strategies for managing high-risk behaviors*. New York: Guilford.

Marlatt, G.A., Baer, J.S., Kivlahan, D.R., Dimeff, L.A., Larimer, M.E., Quigley, L.A., Somers, J.M., & Williams, E. (1998). Screening and brief intervention for high-risk college student drinkers: Results from a two-year follow-up assessment. *Journal of Consulting and Clinical Psychology, 66*, 604–615.

Marlatt, G.A., Baer, J.S., & Larimer, M.E. (1995). Preventing alcohol abuse in college students: A harm reduction approach. In J. Howard & R. Zucker (Eds.), *Preventing alcohol abuse among adolescents: Pre-intervention and intervention research*. (pp. 147–172). Mahwah, NJ: Lawrence Erlbaum Associates.

Marlatt, G.A., Demming, B., & Reid, J.B. (1973). Loss of control drinking in alcoholics: An experimental analogue. *Journal of Abnormal Psychology, 81*, 233–241.

Marlatt, G.A., & Kristeller, J. (1999). Mindfulness and meditation. In W.R. Miller (Ed.), *Integrating spirituality into treatment*. Washington, DC: American Psychological Association.

McCormick, L.K., & Ureda, J. (1995). Who's driving? College students' choices of transportation home after drinking. *Journal of Primary Prevention, 16*, 103–115.

Meilman, P.W., Stone, J.E., Gaylor, M.S., & Turco, J.H. (1990). Alcohol consumption by college undergraduates: Current use and 10-year trends. *Journal of Studies on Alcohol, 51*, 389–395.

Miller, E.T. (1999). *Preventing alcohol abuse and alcohol-related negative consequences among freshmen college students: Using emerging computer technology to deliver and evaluate the effectiveness of brief intervention efforts*. Unpublished doctoral dissertation. University of Washington, Seattle.

Miller, N.S., & Gold, M.S. (1988). The human sexual response and alcohol and drugs. *Journal of Substance Abuse Treatment, 5*, 171–177.

Miller, W.R., Meyers, R.J., & Hiller-Sturmhofel, S. (1999). The community-reinforcement model. *Alcohol and Research World, 23*, 116–121.

Miller, W.R., & Rollnick, S. (2002). *Motivational interviewing: Preparing people for change* (2nd edn.). New York: Guilford.

Mooney, D.K., Fromme, K., Kivlahan, D.R., & Marlatt, G.A. (1987). Correlates of alcohol consumption: Sex, age, and expectancies relate differentially to quantity and frequency. *Addictive Behaviors, 12*, 235–240.

Perkins, H.W., & Berkowitz, A.D. (1986). Perceiving the community norms of alcohol use among students: Some research implications for campus alcohol education programs. *The International Journal of the Addictions, 21*, 961–976.

Presley, C.A., Meilman, P.W., & Lyerl. (1995). Development of the core alcohol and drug survey: Initial findings and future directions. *Journal of American College Health, 42*, 248–255.

Quigley, L.A., & Marlatt, G.A. (1996). Drinking among young adults: Prevalence, patterns, and consequences. *Alcohol Health and Research World, 20*, 185–191.

Rivinus, T.M., & Larimer, M.E. (1993). Violence, alcohol, other drugs, and the college student. *Journal of College Student Psychotherapy, 8*, 71–119.

Roberts, L.J., Neal, D.J., Kivlahan, D.R., Baer, J.S., & Marlatt, G.A. (2000). Individual drinking changes following a brief intervention among college students: Clinical significance in an indicated preventive context. *Journal of Consulting and Clinical Psychology, 68*, 500–505.

Rohsenow, D.J., Smith, R.E., & Johnson, S. (1985). Stress management as a prevention program for heavy social drinkers: Cognitions, affect, drinking, and individual differences. *Addictive Behaviors, 10*, 45–54.

Salz, R.F., & Elandt, D. (1986). College student drinking studies 1976–1985. *Contemporary Drug Problems, 13*, 117–159.

Schulenberg, J., O'Malley, P.M., Bachman, J.G., Wadsworth, K.N., & Johnston, L.D. (1996a). Getting drunk and growing up: Trajectories of frequent binge drinking during the transition to young adulthood. *Journal of Studies on Alcohol, 57*, 289–304.

Schulenberg, J., Wadsworth, K.N., O'Malley, P.M., Bachman, J.G., & Johnston, L.D. (1996b). Adolescent risk factors for binge drinking during the transition to young adulthood: Variable- and pattern-centered approaches to change. *Developmental Psychology, 32*, 659–674.

Steele, C.M., & Josephs, R.A. (1990). Alcohol myopia: Its prized and dangerous effects. *American Psychologist, 45*, 921–933.

Tapert, S.F., & Brown, S.A. (1999). Neuropsychological correlates of adolescent substance abuse: Four-year outcomes. *Journal of the International Neuropsychological Society, 5*, 481–493.

The Century Council and the University of Illinois (1997). *Alcohol 101: CD ROM*. Urbana-Champagne, IL: Authors.

Turner, A.P., Larimer, M.E., & Sarason, I.G. (2000). Family risk factors for alcohol-related consequences and poor adjustment in fraternity and sorority members: Exploring the role of the parent–child conflict. *Journal of Studies on Alcohol, 61*, 818–826.

Wechsler, H., Davenport, A., Dowdall, G., Moeykens, B., & Castillo, S. (1994). Health and behavioral consequences of binge drinking in college. *Journal of the American Medical Association, 272*, 1672–1677.

Wechsler, H., Dowdall, G.W., Davenport, A., & Castillo, S. (1995a). Correlates of college student binge drinking. *American Journal of Public Health, 85*, 921–926.

Wechsler, H., Dowdall, G.W., Davenport, A., & Rimm, E.B. (1995b). A gender-specific measure of binge drinking among college students. *American Journal of Public Health, 85*, 982–985.

Wechsler, H., & Isaac, N. (1992). "Binge" drinkers at Massachusetts Colleges. *Journal of the American Medical Association, 267*, 292–293.

Wechsler, H., Lee, J.E., Gledhill-Hoyt, J., & Nelson, T.F. (2001). Alcohol use and problems at colleges banning alcohol: Results of a national survey. *Journal of Studies on Alcohol, 62*, 133–141.

Wechsler, H., & Nelson, T.F. (2001). Binge drinking and the American college student: What's five drinks? *Psychology of Addictive Behaviors, 15*, 287–291.

Werner, M.J., & Greene, J.W. (1992). Problem drinking among college freshmen. *Journal of Adolescent Help, 13*, 487–492.

Whaley, A.L. (1986). Cognitive processes in adolescent drug use: The role of positivity bias and implications for prevention policy. *International Journal of the Addictions, 21*, 393–398.

CHAPTER 22

Community Reinforcement Approach and Contingency Management Interventions for Substance Abuse

Conrad J. Wong
Hendrée E. Jones
and
Maxine L. Stitzer
Johns Hopkins University, Baltimore, USA

Synopsis.—Contingency management interventions have been demonstrated to be effective in treating substance-use disorders in various populations, including primary cocaine-dependent and methadone-maintenance patients. Operant principles of reinforcement are at the heart of contingency management interventions. Two of the most effective contingency management interventions for the treatment of substance-abuse disorders have been abstinence reinforcement procedures and the Community Reinforcement Approach (CRA). The primary objective of both treatments is to modify drug-using behavior by increasing the density of alternative reinforcers that are incompatible with the drug-using lifestyle. The primary premise of both treatments is that if sufficient numbers of alternative reinforcers can be made available, they might effectively compete with the pharmacological reinforcing effects of drugs and nondrug reinforcers that are associated with the drug-using lifestyle. The CRA achieves this goal by increasing the number of alternative reinforcers in the drug abusers' natural environment or community. In contrast, abstinence reinforcement procedures utilize tangible or more contrived reinforcers to reinforce drug abstinence more directly. The purpose of this chapter is to highlight the CRA and abstinence reinforcement procedures. Their conceptual background and rationale are described and seminal studies to support the effectiveness of these interventions are reviewed. The chapter also discusses how to implement these treatments using effective reinforcement contingencies to reward therapeutically desired behaviors, especially drug abstinence.

The purpose of this chapter is to highlight new therapeutic interventions for substance abuse based on operant principles of reinforcement. In particular, the chapter focuses on the Community Reinforcement Approach (CRA) and abstinence reinforcement procedures. Their conceptual background and rationale are described, and seminal studies to support the

Handbook of Motivational Counseling. Edited by W. Miles Cox and Eric Klinger.
© 2004 John Wiley & Sons, Ltd.

effectiveness of these interventions are reviewed. The chapter also discusses how to implement these treatments using effective reinforcement contingencies to reward therapeutically desired behaviors, especially drug abstinence.

CONCEPTUAL FRAMEWORK

Contingency management interventions, including abstinence reinforcement procedures and the CRA, are based on extensive basic and applied research. The theoretical foundation of contingency management interventions for drug abuse was derived from fundamental principles of operant conditioning (see Glasner, Chapter 2, this volume) and behavioral pharmacology. The primary tenets of operant conditioning are that behaviors are learned and reinforced by interactions with environmental contingencies. Furthermore, behavior is orderly, controlled by its consequences, and is amenable to change by altering its consequences. The fundamental operant principles of reinforcement exert a powerful modulating influence on behavior. Consequences that increase the likelihood of behavior occurring under similar circumstances in the future are considered reinforcing; those that decrease the likelihood of behavior occurring are considered punishing.

Reinforcement has been demonstrated to shape a wide range of behaviors in a diverse range of organisms, including humans. Moreover, a wide variety of events and consequences function as reinforcers, including water, food, electrical brain stimulation, heat, and the opportunity to engage in other behaviors (Kish, 1966; Sidman et al., 1955; Skinner, 1938; Weiss & Laties, 1960;). The fundamental principle of reinforcement is the heart of contingency management interventions designed to elicit and maintain therapeutically desired behaviors.

Building on operant conditioning, the field of behavioral pharmacology emerged and demonstrated that drug use is also a learned behavior that is maintained through the reinforcing effects of the pharmacological actions of drugs in combination with other reinforcement associated with drug use (e.g., social reinforcement; Higgins & Katz, 1998). Behavioral pharmacology studies with animals and humans have demonstrated that drugs of abuse function as reinforcers similar to primary reinforcers, such as food, water, and sex (Griffiths, Bigelow, & Henningfield, 1980; Higgins, 1997). Moreover, studies have shown that drug taking is amenable to change in the same way that other behaviors are altered when alternative reinforcers are available in the organism's environment (Carroll & Bickel, 1998).

Within this conceptual framework, contingency management interventions for treating drug abuse were developed based upon observations that drugs function as reinforcers and that drug-taking behavior is amenable to change. Based upon those observations, an overarching goal of contingency management interventions is to systematically weaken the influence of reinforcement derived from drug use and the related lifestyle and to increase the frequency and magnitude of reinforcement derived from healthier alternative activities, especially those that are incompatible with drug use.

APPLICATION TO SUBSTANCE-ABUSE TREATMENT

Two of the most effective contingency management interventions for the treatment of substance-abuse disorders have been abstinence reinforcement procedures and the CRA.

The primary objective of both treatments is to modify drug-using behavior by increasing the density of alternative reinforcers that are incompatible with the drug-using lifestyle. The primary premise of both treatments is that if sufficient numbers of alternative reinforcers can be made available, they might effectively compete with the pharmacological reinforcing effects of drugs and nondrug reinforcers that are associated with the drug-using lifestyle.

Abstinence reinforcement procedures have been studied for almost three decades and have been shown to be effective in promoting abstinence from a wide range of drugs and in diverse patient populations (Higgins & Silverman, 1999; Robles, Silverman, & Stitzer, 1999). Under abstinent reinforcement procedures, patients are offered some attractive options, including tangible goods and services, immediately contingent on demonstrating objective evidence of drug abstinence (i.e., drug-negative urine samples). Contingencies that offer immediate and tangible benefits for behavior change have been demonstrated to be effective in increasing the frequency of therapeutically desired behaviors in drug abusers, in particular drug abstinence.

The CRA was originally developed as a treatment for chronic alcohol abusers (Hunt & Azrin, 1973); later adapted to treat cocaine-dependent patients (Higgins et al., 1994); and more recently used with opiate-dependent patients (Abbott et al., 1998). The CRA is a comprehensive behavioral treatment that is designed to systematically facilitate changes in the patient's daily environment that will reduce drug abuse and promote a healthier lifestyle. In implementing the CRA, systematic efforts are made to increase the frequency and amount of reinforcement the drug-abuse patient derives from his vocation, family relations, and social and recreational activities, so that such reinforcers might compete successfully with the allure of the pharmacological and social reinforcement obtained through drug use.

Although both the CRA and abstinence reinforcement procedures were derived from principles of operant conditioning (see Glasner, Chapter 2, this volume) and behavioral pharmacology, the treatments differ in several important ways. One important difference is the derivation of the alternative reinforcers used to reinforce drug abstinence in the drug abuser. Specifically, the CRA attempts to increase the density of alternative reinforcers in the drug abuser's natural environment or community, including reinforcement from social interactions or recreational activities. In contrast, abstinence reinforcement procedures tend to use predetermined tangible reinforcers, including monetary vouchers that can be exchanged for goods and services.

Second, the CRA is delivered in individual or group sessions by therapists or counselors trained in behavior therapy. A CRA therapist attempts to arrange positive consequences for drug abstinence in the patient's community by encouraging patients to come in contact with community reinforcers for alternative behaviors that are incompatible with the drug-using lifestyle. Therapists might also recruit the help of a patient's significant others to reinforce the patient's abstinence and compliance with treatment regimens. The CRA therapy is a proactive and labor-intensive treatment that often requires the therapist to actively engage the patient in alternative reinforcing activities, sometimes accompanying them during the activity. This procedure promotes sampling of novel and potentially reinforcing events by the drug-abuse patient. One limitation of the CRA is that primary reinforcement contingencies for abstinence are ultimately controlled by agents in the community, and are not under the direct control of the therapist. Specifically, the CRA therapists primarily manipulate antecedents of patients' behaviors and not necessarily consequences of them.

In contrast with abstinence reinforcement procedures, reinforcers are applied as a direct consequence of drug abstinence, can be offered by a variety of different intervening agents (treatment provider, employer, probation officer), and require relatively little training to administer. All aspects of the reinforcement contingency, including procedures for verification of the target behavior (e.g., monitoring of drug abstinence) and procedures for delivery of consequences (e.g., monetary vouchers), are clearly stated to the patient at the beginning of treatment. In contrast to the CRA therapist, the agent providing abstinence reinforcement has greater direct control of the primary reinforcement contingencies.

As mentioned earlier, the CRA therapy and abstinence reinforcement procedures have both been demonstrated to be effective contingency management interventions for the treatment of substance abuse when used alone and in combination with each other. The remainder of this chapter focuses on how each of these treatments can effectively modify drug-taking behavior when used independently or in combination with each other.

ABSTINENCE REINFORCEMENT INTERVENTIONS

Over 30 years of human laboratory and applied research have shown abstinence reinforcement procedures to be effective in modifying drug-taking behavior (see reviews by Higgins & Silverman, 1999; Petry, 2000; Robles, Silverman, & Stitzer, 1999; Stitzer & Higgins, 1995). The primary goal of abstinent reinforcement procedures is to identify tangible and effective reinforcers that can be delivered to the drug-abuse patient contingent upon objective measures of drug abstinence (e.g., observed urinalysis testing).

Tangible reinforcers that have been demonstrated to be effective in promoting drug abstinence include money, vouchers exchangeable for goods and services, retail items, and small prizes (Higgins & Silverman, 1999; Petry, 2000). The use of treatment privileges or services such as methadone take-home doses, flexible dosing schedules, and changes in methadone dose have also been demonstrated to be effective in promoting abstinence from cocaine and opiates in methadone-maintenance patients (Robles, Silverman, & Stitzer, 1999).

The Voucher Procedure

One of the most effective abstinence reinforcement procedures first developed to treat cocaine addiction is the voucher procedure (Higgins et al., 1993a, 1994, 2000). Under the voucher procedure, patients earn vouchers that are exchangeable for goods and services contingent on documented drug abstinence (i.e., negative urine samples). Other studies have demonstrated the voucher procedure to be effective in treating other drugs of abuse, including opiates and marijuana (Budney et al., 2000; Sigmon et al., 2000; Silverman et al., 1996).

Under the voucher procedure, drug-abuse patients provide urine samples under staff observation three times per week and earn monetary vouchers exchangeable for goods and services when they provide drug-free urine samples. Vouchers rather than money are used to reduce the chance that patients will use earnings to purchase drugs. There are two important features of the voucher intervention that promote sustained drug abstinence. First, drug-abuse patients earn vouchers under a schedule of escalating reinforcement for sustained abstinence. Under this type of schedule, the monetary value of the voucher starts low and then increases at a fixed amount for every consecutive drug-free urine sample provided. Because each consecutive drug-free urine sample is worth more than the last one, this feature of the schedule emphasizes the importance of sustained abstinence. Second, there is a penalty for using drugs. If a patient provides a drug-positive urine sample or fails to provide a mandatory urine sample, the patient forgoes the opportunity to earn a voucher and the monetary value of the next voucher is reset to the initial low value. This feature of the voucher procedure provides patients with the motivation to sustain abstinence and avoid relapsing to drug use.

The voucher procedure was first developed as part of a multicomponent behavioral treatment for primary cocaine-dependent outpatients (Higgins et al., 1991, 1993a, 1994). In a randomized-controlled trial (Higgins et al., 1994), the voucher procedure improved treatment outcomes in cocaine-dependent outpatients when added to an intensive behavioral treatment based on the CRA. In that study, patients received intensive CRA counseling either with or without the voucher intervention (Higgins et al., 1994). Urinalysis monitoring was conducted three times per week for 12 weeks and then twice weekly during weeks 13–24 of the 24-week intervention. The voucher intervention was in effect during weeks 1–12; during weeks 13–24 patients received a $1 Vermont state lottery ticket for every cocaine-free urine sample. The voucher intervention significantly improved treatment retention and cocaine abstinence. Seventy-five percent of patients who received the voucher intervention completed 24 weeks of abstinence compared to 40% in the group that did not receive vouchers. Furthermore, rates for continuous cocaine abstinence were almost doubled in patients who received vouchers compared to those who did not (11.7 ± 2.0 weeks vs. 6.0 ± 1.5 weeks).

Other studies have evaluated the voucher intervention in injection drug users receiving methadone treatment for their heroin addiction, but who persisted in their use of cocaine (Silverman et al., 1996, 1998). In those studies, the initial value of the voucher started at $2.50 and increased by $1.50 for every consecutive cocaine-free urine sample provided thereafter. In addition, patients earned bonus vouchers worth $10 for every three consecutive cocaine-free urine samples. The voucher procedure was in effect for 12 weeks when patients could earn approximately $1000 in vouchers. In one controlled trial, patients who continued to use cocaine during methadone treatment were randomly assigned to a group that received vouchers contingent on cocaine abstinence or to a group that received vouchers independent of their urinalysis results (noncontingent vouchers; Silverman et al., 1996). Patients assigned to the contingent voucher group were exposed to the voucher procedure described above. Patients in the contingent voucher group achieved significantly longer periods of cocaine abstinence compared to patients in the noncontingent voucher group (5 weeks vs. 1 week). Studies have also demonstrated the voucher intervention to be effective in promoting abstinence from heroin in methadone patients who persist in using heroin during methadone treatment (Robles et al., 2002; Silverman et al., 1998).

Although the voucher intervention is effective in promoting abstinence in chronic drug abusers, not all patients respond equally well. In the controlled trials conducted by Silverman et al. (1996, 1998), approximately half of the patients receiving the voucher intervention achieved long periods of sustained drug abstinence, whereas the other half failed to achieve any significant periods of abstinence.

One possible explanation for treatment failures was that the value or magnitude of the vouchers was not sufficient to compete with drug use. Two studies have evaluated whether increasing the magnitude of voucher reinforcement could promote abstinence in patients who failed to achieve significant periods of abstinence when exposed to the standard voucher intervention (Dallery et al., 2001; Silverman et al., 1999). In one study, methadone patients who failed to initiate abstinence after receiving the standard 12-week voucher intervention were exposed in counterbalanced order to three nine-week voucher conditions that varied in magnitude of voucher reinforcement (Silverman et al., 1999). Each patient was exposed to a zero-, low-, and high-magnitude condition in which it was possible to earn $0, $382, or $3380 in vouchers for providing cocaine-free urine samples. When participants were exposed to a condition in which they could earn $3400 in vouchers for providing cocaine-free urine samples during a nine-week intervention, about half (10 of 22 patients, 45%) of the patients achieved four or more weeks of sustained cocaine abstinence. In contrast, only one patient (1 of 22 patients, 5%) achieved more than two weeks of sustained abstinence when exposed to a condition in which it was possible to earn $382 in vouchers over nine weeks for providing cocaine-free urine samples, and no patients achieved more than two weeks of abstinence in the condition in which vouchers had no monetary value. These data provided the support that treatment outcomes could be improved in treatment-resistant patients by simply increasing the magnitude of voucher reinforcement.

The voucher intervention has also been demonstrated to sustain long-term abstinence when the intervention is extended for significant periods of time. For example, Silverman and colleagues (2000) evaluated a one-year voucher program as a potential maintenance intervention. Seventy-eight patients were randomly assigned to a Usual Care Control condition or to one of two abstinence reinforcement groups. All three groups received standard methadone-maintenance treatment throughout the year-long study, which included daily methadone, weekly counseling, and observed urine sample collection on Monday, Wednesday, and Friday of each week. Patients in the Usual Care Control group received no other services. Patients in one of the abstinence reinforcement groups could earn a take-home methadone dose every day they provided a urine sample that was negative for opiates and cocaine (Take-Home Only group). Take-home methadone doses have been shown in previous studies to function as reinforcers in many methadone patients (e.g., Stitzer, Iguchi, & Felch, 1992). The other abstinence reinforcement group could earn take-home methadone doses under the same contingencies, but could also earn vouchers for providing cocaine-free urine samples (Take-Home plus Voucher group). Over the entire year, patients in the Take-Home plus Vouchers group could earn up to $5800 in vouchers for providing cocaine-free urine samples. Cocaine use by patients in the Usual Care Control group persisted throughout the year-long study; while cocaine abstinence increased in the Take-Home Only group, particularly during the first nine months of the study. Cocaine abstinence was greatest in the Take-Home plus Voucher group; about 60% of their urine samples were negative for cocaine, compared with 40% in the Take-Home Only and 15% in the control group. Moreover, a greater percentage of patients in the Take-Home plus Voucher group were completely cocaine abstinent at the end of the year-long intervention period.

EFFECTIVE IMPLEMENTATION OF THE VOUCHER INTERVENTION

Controlled studies with varying drug-abuse populations have shown the voucher procedure to be an effective intervention for substance abuse. This section describes key features of the voucher procedure that have probably contributed to its success.

Describing the Voucher Procedure to Patients

The voucher intervention is indeed an unconventional drug-abuse intervention with which clients are unlikely to be familiar. As a result, it is essential to provide a clear explanation of the abstinence reinforcement contingency and what is expected of the patients in order to earn a voucher. This explanation should include a description of the target drug that will be monitored, frequency of urinalysis testing, escalating voucher schedule for sustained abstinence, the temporary reset of the voucher value to the initial low value following a drug-positive urine sample, and the process of how and when to redeem vouchers for goods and services in the community. Providing actual exposure to an initial voucher and voucher exchange may be useful in introducing the intervention to the patient. After describing the voucher procedure, administration of a short true/false quiz reviewing the fundamental elements of the voucher procedure is useful in assessing whether the patient fully understands the contingency or requirement necessary to earn vouchers during the treatment period.

Reinforcement Schedule

Two of the defining characteristics of the voucher procedure have been the escalating pay schedule for sustained drug abstinence and the reset contingency in the event of drug use once abstinence has been initiated. Under the escalating pay schedule, the value of the voucher begins at a relatively low value, around $1.50–$2.50, and then increases at a constant amount of $1.25 for every subsequent drug-free urine sample. As a result, a drug-abuse patient who has initiated and maintained abstinence for a significant period of time will be earning relatively high-value vouchers for each subsequent drug-free urine sample provided. The escalating voucher schedule provides motivation for the drug-abuse patient to first initiate and then maintain abstinence, especially as the value of the voucher increases over longer and longer periods of drug abstinence.

The second important characteristic of the voucher intervention is the practice of resetting the value of the voucher to the initial low amount for a drug-positive urine sample or failure to provide a sample on a mandatory urine sample day. Once a reset in voucher value has been implemented, the value of the voucher escalates again after a patient begins to provide consecutive drug-free urine samples. After nine days of consecutive drug-free urine samples, the value of the next voucher for a drug-free urine sample is returned to the value of the voucher before the patient provided the last drug-positive urine sample. This reset contingency represents a relatively severe penalty for drug-abuse patients who are earning vouchers for abstinence, especially for those who have achieved a substantial period of abstinence and are earning vouchers that have high monetary value. However, the escalating pay schedule for consecutive drug-free urine samples and the return of the value of a voucher prior to the reset after nine consecutive drug-free samples provides motivation for the patient to return to drug abstinence as quickly as possible. The importance of the escalating voucher pay schedule with the reset contingency has been shown in controlled research with cigarette smokers. Specifically, a reinforcement schedule with these features was more effective in promoting sustained abstinence from cigarette use than was a fixed amount pay schedule without a reset contingency (Roll, Higgins, & Badger, 1996).

Targeting Abstinence

The number of drugs that are targeted at any one time during the voucher intervention must be given careful consideration. The majority of studies demonstrating the efficacy of voucher-based contingency management procedures have targeted single drugs, including alcohol (Petry et al., 2000), marijuana (Budney et al., 2000), opiates (Silverman et al., 1996), and cocaine (Higgins et al., 1993a, 1993b, 1994, 2000; Silverman et al., 1996, 1998, 1999). In contrast, relatively few studies have investigated the use of vouchers to promote abstinence from multiple drugs among methadone patients, and these studies have reported only modest results. For example, Piotrowski et al. (1999) implemented a voucher program designed to promote abstinence from alcohol and six illicit drugs. Patients were randomly assigned to one of two treatment groups: methadone treatment alone or methadone treatment with contingency management. During the first month of the contingency management treatment, patients were contracted to abstain from illicit opioids and cocaine; during months 2–4, voucher earnings were based on abstinence from alcohol, amphetamines, barbiturates, benzodiazepines, and marijuana, as well as opioids and cocaine. Overall, participants could earn $755 during the four-month study. Methadone patients receiving the contingency management program achieved mean periods of continuous abstinence that were twice as long as those observed in the usual care methadone-maintenance control group (7.6 vs. 3.3 days for voucher vs. usual care groups, respectively, at study month 4), and produced more drug-free urine specimens (28.5% vs.16.3% drug-free samples at study month 4). However, these results are clinically modest and nearly half of the participants who were offered the voucher program failed to produce a single drug-free urine specimen. The authors suggested that the relatively low value of the initial incentive ($0.35 for the first substance-free urine specimen) and requirement of abstinence from multiple drugs may have contributed to the high number of nonresponders.

Results discussed above support the clinical recommendation that abstinence from one drug at a time should be the clinical goal. Once a period of abstinence has been achieved from the primary target drug, abstinence from other drugs can be required for the patient to earn additional vouchers. By initially targeting only one drug, patients who are using several drugs may have a greater chance of becoming abstinent and coming into contact with the reinforcement contingency for abstinence than if they were required to abstain from all drugs at once.

Frequent Urine Monitoring

Frequent and regular urine monitoring has been an important element in implementing effective voucher interventions for at least two reasons. First, urinalysis monitoring provides an objective measure of the target behavior that is being reinforced, which is drug abstinence. Without collecting observed urine samples from the drug-abuse patient, abstinence or continued drug use is difficult to assess. Secondly, a urinalysis monitoring schedule of Monday, Wednesday, and Friday provides frequent and regular assessment of drug abstinence. A frequent urinalysis schedule provides systematic and regular opportunity to reinforce the drug-abuse patient for abstaining from drugs. Finally, frequent and regular urinalysis schedule allows for the detection of drugs that are short acting, such as cocaine.

Community drug-abuse clinics may be deterred from collecting and testing urine samples for drugs due to the belief that sophisticated laboratory equipment and trained technicians are required. This is no longer the case with the availability of hand-held urine tests that allow for simple accurate urinalysis testing with minimal training and space requirements.

Providing Feedback

Feedback and social reinforcement have typically been incorporated and may be an important element of an effective voucher intervention. Feedback regarding the results of the urine sample can be provided in a preprinted or written form that simply states whether the urine sample was positive or negative for the target drug. In addition, positive social reinforcement from clinic staff should also be provided whenever the drug-abuse patient provides a drug-free urine sample and receives a voucher. For example, when a clinic staff member gives a voucher and urine result indicating abstinence, the staff should show a positive attitude when telling patients what a great job they are doing in achieving their abstinence. Furthermore, the staff should point out how much the patients are earning in vouchers and exactly how much in voucher earnings they have accumulated. In contrast, social reinforcement should be withheld when patients provide drug-positive urine samples. By using differential reinforcement, patients learn that drug abstinence is associated with only positive and desirable consequences, including the monetary vouchers and social praise. Additional research is needed to determine the influence of feedback and social reinforcement on treatment outcomes.

Minimizing Delay in Voucher Exchange

Minimizing the delay between the time a patient places a request for vouchers to be redeemed and the time the patient actually receives the requested item is an important feature of an effective voucher intervention. In general, a request to redeem or exchange a voucher for a retail item or service should be made as promptly as possible. One way of improving immediacy is to have available gift certificates from local vendors at the clinic for patients to redeem their vouchers. When a specific retail item is requested, the patient should be informed that the item will be available within 48 hours from the time the request was submitted, if not sooner. Minimizing the amount of time that patients are able to receive their reward for drug abstinence should help to maintain the reinforcing value of the voucher.

Frequent and Regular Voucher Spending

Patients should be encouraged to redeem their vouchers as they are earning them. Frequent use of vouchers permits patients to come in contact with the positive consequences of drug abstinence achieved during treatment. With frequent and regular contact with the vouchers, the drug-abuse patient will learn that the positive consequences associated with vouchers are a direct result of drug abstinence and that a drug-using lifestyle is incompatible with the opportunity to earn incentives for abstinence.

Voucher Redemption

In general, patients should be allowed to redeem their vouchers for goods and services in the local community that they find desirable, with the exception of tobacco or alcohol. Some items that are typically requested when redeeming vouchers include movie passes, gift certificates to restaurants, clothes and shoes for the patients or their children, course tuition, rent payments, and utility payments.

Often the process of redeeming vouchers for retail items and services in the community can be labor intensive for clinic staff, especially if several patients are receiving vouchers contingent on drug abstinence and are initiating and maintaining abstinence. Maintaining a regular supply of gift certificates from various local merchants with monetary value at the clinic is an efficient means of exchanging vouchers for items desired by the patient. By having gift certificates readily available at the clinic, patients are able to redeem voucher earnings immediately, which may be an important attribute that contributes to the effectiveness of the intervention.

Abstinence Reinforcement Summary

We have briefly discussed key features of the voucher procedure that have recently become the centerpiece of abstinence reinforcement interventions for drug abusers. Key features contributing to its success have been described, including the voucher pay schedule, frequent urinalysis testing, and prompt exchange of vouchers for goods or services, to name a few. We now turn to another effective contingency management intervention that is also based on operant principles of reinforcement, the CRA. In the following sections, a brief review of clinical trials providing the empirical support for the effectiveness of the treatment and a description of the treatment and implementation considerations are provided.

THE CRA

The CRA is a multicomponent behavioral treatment that was originally developed for the treatment of severe alcoholics (Hunt & Azrin, 1973). The CRA was designed to systematically facilitate changes in the client's daily environment in order to reduce substance abuse and promote a healthier lifestyle. There have been several recent reviews of the empirical support for the CRA therapy in treating various kinds of substance-abuse disorders, including primary cocaine-dependent and opiate-dependent outpatients (Higgins & Abbott, 2001; Higgins, Sigmon, & Budney, in press; Smith, Meyers, & Miller, 2001).

The first matched control trial was conducted with alcohol abusers receiving inpatient treatment. In that study, the CRA therapy was compared to standard hospital care that was based on the 12-step program of Alcoholics Anonymous (AA; Hunt & Azrin, 1973). The goal of the CRA therapy was to systematically weaken the influence of reinforcement derived from alcohol use and the alcohol-using lifestyle, and to increase the frequency of reinforcement derived from healthier alternative activities, especially those that were incompatible with alcohol use. During treatment patients received counseling in improving the quality and frequency of participating in social and recreational activities. Patients who were unemployed received vocational counseling and assistance in seeking employment. Patients also received relapse prevention training, being taught how to handle situations that had previously resulted in drinking in a different way.

At the six-month follow-up, patients assigned to the CRA therapy reported drinking on 14% of the follow-up days, compared to 79% for patients who had received standard treatment. Furthermore, compared to patients in the standard treatment group, the CRA patients had lower rates of unemployment days (5% vs. 62%), and were hospitalized for fewer days (2% vs. 27%).

In the second controlled study, the CRA also included monitoring patients taking disulfiram (Antabuse) and reinforcing them for doing so, a "buddy" system for social support, and group rather than individual counseling (Azrin, 1976). Compared to a standard treatment group that only received advice to take disulfiram, the CRA group again showed significantly better outcomes with reduced time spent drinking, less time institutionalized, and increased rates of employment. Subsequent controlled trials with outpatient alcohol abusers have provided further support for the efficacy of the CRA with monitored disulfiram therapy incorporated (Azrin et al., 1982). Other studies have evaluated the various components of the CRA, including couples counseling, an alcohol-free recreational and social club, and a job club intervention to assist individuals in obtaining satisfying employment (Azrin, Flores, & Kaplan, 1975; Azrin, Naster, & Jones, 1973; Mallams et al., 1982).

Finally, Smith, Meyers, and Delaney (1998) conducted a controlled trial with homeless alcohol-dependent participants. Participants were randomly assigned to either a CRA group or a group that received 12-step AA counseling with employment counseling. Participants in the CRA group had significantly better outcomes on various drinking measures. However, there was no difference between the two groups at the 12-month follow-up on other outcome measures, including disulfiram compliance, rates of employment, or homelessness.

Abbott and coworkers (1998) conducted a controlled trial with methadone-maintained patients who were randomly assigned to one of three treatment groups: standard counseling, the CRA, or the CRA with relapse prevention. A greater percentage of patients assigned to the CRA groups than to the standard counseling group achieved three weeks of continuous opiate abstinence (89% vs. 78%). Furthermore, the CRA groups showed greater improvements on outcome measures on problems associated with drug use compared to the standard counseling group.

IMPLEMENTING THE CRA

The controlled trials reviewed provide empirical support for the CRA, a multicomponent behavior therapy, as an effective treatment for alcohol, cocaine, and opiate dependence. The following section describes the primary components of the CRA that contribute to its success. Individuals who are interested in a comprehensive and detailed description and methods for implementation are referred to published treatment manuals for that purpose (Budney & Higgins, 1998; Meyers & Smith, 1995).

The CRA can be implemented in either individual or group counseling sessions. Both types of sessions focus on four general issues. The first step is to instruct patients in how to recognize the antecedents and consequences of their drug use. This process is known as functional analysis of behavior, which in this case is drug use by the patient. During this process, therapists and patients learn about the conditions under which drug use occurs most frequently by the patient. For example, in performing a functional analysis of a patient's cocaine use, the therapist and patient might identify other drug users who frequently use cocaine with the patient in some common setting (e.g., restroom in a local tavern). The therapist would help the patient in making the connection between his or her involvement with the drug-using individuals in this situation and the actual drug use.

Based upon information from the functional analysis, patients are then counseled to restructure their daily activities to minimize contact with known antecedents of their use, find healthy alternatives to drug use, and make explicit the negative consequences of their drug use. For example, there might be explicit goals of avoiding individuals or places associated with the patient's drug use. The therapist and client together monitor the goals in the treatment plan during each therapy session by simply graphing changes in the targeted behaviors.

Unemployed patients are offered participation in a job club intervention, which is an effective method for assisting chronically unemployed individuals to obtain employment (Azrin & Besalel, 1980). During the job club intervention, the CRA therapist assists the unemployed patient in identifying jobs that are of interest to patients and match their vocational abilities. The CRA therapist can also assist the patient to develop a resume, find potential job opportunities in the classified ads, send resumes to potential employers, and practice interviewing techniques with the patient. The CRA therapist might also make a referral to a professional vocational or employment counselor who is trained in assessing vocational skill, aptitude, and interests and make recommendations for suitable employment. Some patients may express interest in pursuing educational goals or new vocational interests. For example, many patients begin treatment without a high-school diploma and wish to earn a general education degree (GED). A therapist might help the patient to identify GED programs in the local community, and, once enrolled, monitor the patient's progress in the program. Through monitoring, the therapist can assist the patient in problem-solving difficulties that might arise and impede progress.

In an attempt to develop a nondrug-using lifestyle, patients are counseled to develop new recreational activities or to become reinvolved in those pursued prior to the drug use. Therapists and patients work together to identify potentially reinforcing activities by having the patient complete a leisure interest inventory (Rosenthal & Rosenthal, 1985). Using such a list helps to prompt ideas about activities that the patient enjoyed in the past and is willing to engage in again. Furthermore, patients are encouraged to sample new recreational activities even if they are unsure whether or not they would like them. Therapists might accompany patients, individually or in groups, in new recreational activities, helping them to develop their interests. When counseling patients on engaging in recreational activities, the CRA therapist and the patient might agree upon a goal of participating in at least one new novel recreational activity a week. Once the patient has identified a recreational activity of interest, the CRA therapist and patient should agree on a level of participation in that recreational activity on a regular basis. For example, patients may find attending a gym to exercise as an activity of interest. As a result, the CRA therapist might suggest that the patient attend the gym on some regular and frequent schedule (e.g., three times per week). Once a goal has been set, the CRA therapist and patient should monitor the patient's level of participation in recreational activities to ensure compliance.

To assist the patient to develop a new social network of nondrug-using individuals, patients are counseled to increase spending time with nondrug-using people and discontinuing interactions with drug abusers. Attending AA or Narcotics Anonymous meetings is an excellent way for patients to begin establishing relationships with nondrug-using individuals. Religious and community organizations are also excellent resources to establish social networks of nondrug-using individuals. Finally, family members who are nondrug users can play an important role in the initiation and maintenance of drug abstinence.

Patients and their nondrug-using significant other might together participate in reciprocal relationship counseling. This is a validated intervention for helping couples to negotiate positive changes in their relationship (Azrin et al., 1973). The intervention is designed to teach couples positive communication skills and how to negotiate reciprocal contracts for desired changes in each other's behavior.

Finally, alcohol-dependent and polysubstance-abusing patients might be offered disulfiram, and newly abstinent opiate-dependent patients might be offered Naltrexone. These medications are effective in promoting abstinence from alcohol (disulfiram), cocaine (disulfiram), and opiates (Naltrexone), and have become an integral part of the CRA (Azrin et al., 1982; Carroll et al., 1998; Higgins et al., 1993b; Preston et al., 1999). To ensure medication compliance, clinic staff is encouraged to dispense the medication when patients report to the clinic for urinalysis testing. On other days, a significant other, family member, or friend should monitor medication compliance. The therapist should explain to the monitor the importance of observing the patient taking the medication and encouraging reporting of noncompliance.

THE CRA COMBINED WITH VOUCHER REINFORCEMENT

Controlled trials have recently been conducted to evaluate the CRA combined with the voucher procedure with primary cocaine-dependent outpatients (Higgins et al., 1991, 1993a, 2000) and opiate-dependent outpatients participating in a detoxification protocol (Bickel et al., 1997). By combining both interventions, the drug-abuse disorder can be treated using two complementary approaches with common roots in operant conditioning. When the CRA and vouchers are used together during the initial phase of treatment, the abstinent reinforcement procedure can assist in initiating abstinence while the CRA therapist simultaneously helps patients to restructure their lives so that natural sources of reinforcement can be identified to sustain drug abstinence.

Two controlled trials have compared the CRA plus vouchers to standard outpatient drug-abuse counseling based upon the disease model (Higgins et al., 1991, 1993a). Both studies demonstrated that the CRA plus vouchers was superior to standard treatment in retaining patients in treatment and promoting sustained abstinence. For example, in the randomized-controlled study, a greater percentage of patients assigned to the CRA plus vouchers group completed the 24 weeks of treatment than patients assigned to standard drug-abuse counseling (56% vs. 11%). Moreover, 42% of patients in the behavioral treatment achieved eight and 15 weeks of continuous cocaine abstinence compared to only 5% of patients in the standard counseling group.

Bickel and coworkers (1997) evaluated the CRA plus vouchers with opiate-dependent patients participating in a buprenorphine detoxification protocol. Buprenorphine is a partial mu agonist/antagonist that has been demonstrated to be an effective medication in treating heroin addiction (Bickel & Amass, 1995). Patients were randomly assigned to the CRA plus vouchers or standard detoxification treatment. In the CRA plus vouchers condition, patients received vouchers both for opioid-free urine samples and for participating in specified CRA activities. In the standard detoxification treatment, patients received individual case management counseling. Patients assigned to the CRA plus vouchers group were more likely to complete the 24-week detoxification treatment (53% vs. 20%) and achieve at least eight weeks of continuous abstinence from opioids (47% vs. 15%). The results of this study provide support for the CRA plus vouchers in improving outcomes from participating in opiate detoxification.

ISSUES IN IMPLEMENTING THE CRA PLUS VOUCHERS METHOD

The combination of the CRA plus vouchers reinforcement has been shown to be an effective drug-abuse treatment, in particular for cocaine and opiate dependence. This section discusses conceptual and practical issues that arise when combining the CRA therapy with abstinence reinforcement procedures.

There is reason to think that the CRA and abstinence reinforcement procedures can have complementary benefits. For example, one advantage of vouchers is that they can improve and promote treatment attendance. The CRA therapists can take advantage of early treatment compliance by ensuring that the CRA therapy is being implemented fully from the outset of treatment. A second benefit when abstinence reinforcement procedures are integrated into the patient's treatment is that money earned by abstinent patients can be used to support other aspects of the treatment plan. For example, if the CRA therapist is encouraging the patient to engage in a new healthy recreational activity that may be initially cost prohibitive, voucher earnings for abstinence can be used to offset these costs. Similarly, vouchers could be spent on recreational activities that involve the patient's drug-free family members to increase contact with drug-free social networks.

Vouchers can also be used to improve patients' motivation for treatment. For example, if a patient does not actively participate in treatment, the CRA therapist should review with the patient the opportunity to earn a substantial amount of money in vouchers that could be redeemed or many desirable goods and services. The CRA therapist can also ensure that patients are utilizing vouchers that have been earned for abstinence, especially when patients are having difficulty in making recent progress in treatment. Reviewing the benefits of the vouchers with the patient can often motivate patients to become actively involved in their treatment.

SUMMARY AND CONCLUSIONS

The scientific literature has accumulated impressive empirical support for the effectiveness of contingency management interventions in the treatment of substance-abuse disorders. Principles of operant conditioning (see Glasner, Chapter 2, this volume) are the heart of contingency management interventions. Abstinence reinforcement procedures, wherein vouchers are delivered contingent on drug abstinence, have proven efficacious in increasing treatment retention and initiating and sustaining abstinence. Researchers are increasingly accepting these methods, although there remain barriers to their implementation in community treatment programs. The CRA also has good theoretical underpinnings, but with less empirical support than the voucher procedure, especially with drug abusers. Further research is needed to compare the CRA with other psychosocial treatments for drug abusers. In addition, incremental efficacy of voucher reinforcement and the CRA treatment also needs to be tested. A recent controlled trial has just been completed in which patients were randomly assigned to receive either the CRA plus abstinence contingent vouchers or abstinence contingent vouchers alone. The results from that study, which have yet to be published (Heil et al., 2002), will be important for understanding the incremental efficacy of vouchers and the CRA as well as the utility of vouchers when delivered alone. Both the CRA procedure and the voucher system have clear standard operating methods that can be applied in community settings with appropriate training and supervision of staff. However, because one barrier to their use is that both treatments may appear more costly and labor intensive than usual care procedures, cost–benefit studies are needed. Such studies would provide useful information to treatment providers, funding agencies, and policy-makers. If the cost–benefit ratio of these efficacious therapies were positive, this would support more widespread dissemination and implementation in community treatment programs.

Overall, the CRA and abstinence reinforcement procedures have shown impressive results in treatment outcomes for drug abuse. This demonstrates that drug-taking behavior can be usefully conceptualized within an operant conditioning framework and that drug-taking behavior is amenable to change through interventions grounded in the principles of learning and behavior change.

ACKNOWLEDGMENT

Preparation of this chapter was supported by research grants from the National Institutes of Health: R01DA12564, R0IDA13107, R0IAA12154.

REFERENCES

Abbott, P.J., Weller, S.B., Delaney, J.D., & Moore, B.A. (1998). Community Reinforcement Approach in the treatment of opiate addicts. *American Journal of Drug and Alcohol Abuse, 24*, 17–30.

Azrin, N.H. (1976). Improvements in the community reinforcement approach to alcoholism. *Behaviour Research and Therapy, 14*, 339–348.

Azrin, N.H., & Besalel, V.A. (1980). *Job club counselor's manual.* Baltimore: University Park Press.

Azrin, N.H., Flores, T., & Kaplan, S.J. (1975). Job-finding club: A group-assisted program for obtaining employment. *Behavior Research and Therapy, 13*, 17–27.

Azrin, N.H., Naster, B.J., & Jones, R. (1973). Reciprocity counseling: A rapid learning-based procedure for marital counseling. *Behavior Research and Therapy, 11*, 365–382.

Azrin, N.H., Sisson, R.W., Meyers, R.J., & Godley, M. (1982). Alcoholism treatment by disulfiram and community reinforcement therapy. *Journal of Behavior Therapy and Experimental Psychiatry, 13*, 105–112.

Bickel, W.K., & Amass, L. (1995). Buprenorphine treatment of opioid dependence: A review. *Experimental and Clinical Psychopharmacology, 3*, 477–489.

Bickel, W.K., Amass, L., Higgins, S.T., Badger, G.J., & Esch, R.A. (1997). Effects of adding behavioral treatment to opioid detoxification with buprenorphine. *Journal of Consulting and Clinical Psychology, 65*, 803–810.

Budney, A.J., & Higgins, S.T. (1998). *A community reinforcement plus vouchers approach: Treatment cocaine addiction.* National Institute on Drug Abuse. NIH Pub. No. 98-4309. Washington, DC: US Government Printing Office.

Budney, A.J., Higgins, S.T., Radonovich, K.J., & Novy, P.L. (2000). Adding vouchers-based incentives to coping-skills and motivational enhancement improves outcomes during treatment for marijuana dependence. *Journal of Consulting and Clinical Psychology, 68*, 1051–1061.

Carroll, M.E., & Bickel, W.K. (1998). Behavioral–environmental determinants of the reinforcing functions of cocaine. In S.T. Higgins & J.L. Katz (Eds.), *Cocaine abuse: Behavior, pharmacology, and clinical applications.* San Diego: Academic Press.

Carroll, K.M., Nich, C., Ball, S.A., McCance, E., & Rounsaville, B.J. (1998). Treatment of cocaine and alcohol dependence with psychotherapy and disulfiram. *Addiction, 93*, 713–727.

Dallery, J., Silverman, K., Chutuape, M.A., Bigelow, G.E., & Stitzer, M.L. (2001). Voucher-based reinforcement of opiate plus cocaine abstinence in treatment-resistant methadone patients: Effects of reinforcer magnitude. *Experimental and Clinical Psychopharmacology, 9*, 317–325.

Griffiths, R.R., Bigelow, G.E., & Henningfield, J.E. (1980). Similarities in animal and human drug-taking behavior. In N.D. Mellow (Ed.), *Advances in substance abuse* (pp. 1–90). Greenwich, CT: JAI Press.

Heil, S.H., Higgins, S.T., Wong, C.J., Sigmon, S.C., Donham, R., Anthony, S., Dantona, R., & Badger, G.J. (2002). Further observations on the role of CRA in the CRA plus vouchers treatment for cocaine dependence. *Drug and Alcohol Dependence, 66*, 285.

Higgins, S.T. (1997). The influence of alternative reinforcers on cocaine use and abuse: A brief review. *Pharmacology, Biochemistry, and Behavior, 57*, 419–427.

Higgins, S.T., & Abbott, P. (2001). Community reinforcement approach and treatment of cocaine and opioid dependence. In R.J. Meyers & W.R. Miller (Eds.), *A community reinforcement approach to addiction treatment* (pp. 123–146). Cambridge, UK: Cambridge University Press.

Higgins, S.T., Budney, A.J., Bickel, W.K., Hughes, J.R., & Foerg, F. (1993a). Disulfiram therapy in patients abusing cocaine and alcohol. *American Journal of Psychiatry, 150*, 675–676.

Higgins, S.T., Budney, A.J., Bickel, W.K., Hughes, J.R., Foerg, F., & Badger, G. (1993b). Achieving cocaine abstinence with a behavioral approach. *American Journal of Psychiatry, 150*, 763–769.

Higgins, S.T., Budney, A.J., Bickel, W.K., Foerg, F.E., Donham, R., & Badger, G.J. (1994). Incentives improve treatment retention and cocaine abstinence in ambulatory cocaine-dependent patients. *Archives of General Psychiatry, 51*, 568–576.

Higgins, S.T., Delaney, D.D., Budney, A.J., Bickel, W.K., Hughes, J.R., Foerg, F., & Fenwick, J.W. (1991). A behavioral approach to achieving initial cocaine abstinence. *The American Journal of Psychiatry, 148*, 1218–1224.

Higgins, S.T., & Katz, J.L. (1998). *Cocaine abuse: Behavior, pharmacology, and clinical applications.* San Diego, CA: Academic Press.

Higgins, S.T., Sigmon, S.C., & Budney, A.J. (in press). Psychosocial treatment of cocaine dependence: The community reinforcement plus vouchers approach. In S.G. Hofmann & M.C. Tompson (Eds.), *Handbook of psychosocial treatments for severe mental disorders.* New York: Guilford.

Higgins, S.T., & Silverman, K. (1999). *Motivating behavior change among illicit-drug abusers: Research on contingency-management interventions.* Washington, DC: American Psychological Association.

Higgins, S.T., Wong, C.J., Badger, G.J., Ogden, D.E., & Dantona, R.L. (2000). Contingent reinforcement increases cocaine abstinence during outpatient treatment and one year of follow-up. *Journal of Consulting and Clinical Psychology, 68* (1), 64–72.

Hunt, G.M., & Azrin, N.H. (1973). A community reinforcement approach to alcoholism. *Behavior Research and Therapy, 11*, 91–104.

Kish, G.B. (1966). Studies of sensory reinforcement. In W.K. Honig (Ed.), *Operant behavior: Areas of research and application* (pp. 109–159). New York: Appleton-Century-Crofts.

Mallams, J.J., Godley, M.D., Hall, G.M., & Meyers, R.J. (1982). A social-systems approach to resocializing alcoholics in the community. *Journal of Studies on Alcohol, 43*, 1115–1123.

Meyers, R.J., & Smith, J.E. (1995). *Clinical guide to alcohol treatment: The community reinforcement approach*. New York: Guilford.

Petry, N.M. (2000). A comprehensive guide to the application of contingency management procedures in clinical settings. *Drug and Alcohol Dependence, 58*, 9–25.

Petry, N.M., Martin, B., Cooney, J.L., & Kranzler, H.R. (2000). Give them prizes, and they will come: Contingency management for treatment of alcohol dependence. *Journal of Consulting and Clinical Psychology, 68*, 250–257.

Piotrowski, N.A., Tusel, D.J., Sess, K.L., Reilly, P.M., Banys, P., Meek, P., & Hall, S.M. (1999). Contingency contracting with monetary reinforcers for abstinence from multiple drugs in a methadone program. *Experimental and Clinical Psychopharmacology, 7*, 399–411.

Preston, K.L., Silverman, K., Umbricht, A., DeJesus, A., Montoya, I.D., & Schuster, C.R. (1999). Improvement in naltrexone treatment compliance with contingency management. *Drug and Alcohol Dependence, 54*, 127–135.

Robles, E., Silverman, K., & Stitzer, M.L. (1999). Contingent management therapies. In E.C. Strain & M.L. Stitzer (Eds.), *Methadone treatment for opioid dependence*. Baltimore, MD: The Johns Hopkins University Press.

Robles, E., Stitzer, J.L., Strain, E.C., Bigelow, G.E., & Silverman, K. (2002). Voucher-based reinforcement of opiate abstinence during methadone detoxification. *Drug and Alcohol Dependence, 65*, 179–189.

Rosenthal, T.L., & Rosenthal, R.H. (1985). Clinical stress management. In D. Barlow (Ed.), *Clinical handbook of psychological disorders* (pp. 145–205). New York: Guilford.

Sidman, M., Brady, J.V., Bore, J.J., Conrad, D.G., & Schulman, A. (1955). Reward schedules and behavior maintained by intracranial self-stimulation. *Science, 122*, 830–831.

Sigmon, S.C., Steingard, S., Badger, G.J., Anthony, S.L., & Higgins, S.T. (2000). Contingent reinforcement of marijuana abstinence among individuals with serious mental illness: A feasibility study. *Experimental and Clinical Psychopharmacology, 8*, 508–517.

Silverman, K., Chutuape, M.A., Bigelow, G.E., & Stitzer, M.L. (1999). Voucher-based reinforcement of cocaine abstinence in treatment-resistant methadone patients: Effects of reinforcement magnitude. *Psychopharmacology, 146*, 128–138.

Silverman, K., Higgins, S.T., Brooner, R.K., Montoya, I.D., Cone, E.J., Schuster, C.R., & Preston, K.L. (1996). Sustained cocaine abstinence in methadone maintenance patients through voucher-based reinforcement therapy. *Archives of General Psychiatry, 53*, 409–415.

Silverman, K., Robles, E., Bigelow, G.E., & Stitzer, M.L. (2000). Long-term exposure to abstinence reinforcement in methadone patients. In L.S. Harris (Ed.), *Problems of drug dependence, 1999* (p. 144). NIDA Research Monograph 180. Washington, DC: US Government Printing Office.

Silverman, K., Wong, C.J., Umbricht-Schneiter, A., Montoya, I.D., Schuster, C.R., & Preston, K.L. (1998). Broad beneficial effects of reinforcement for cocaine abstinence in methadone patients. *Journal of Consulting and Clinical Psychology, 66*, 811–824.

Skinner, B.F. (1938). *The behavior of organisms: An experimental analysis*. Englewood Cliffs, NJ: Prentice-Hall.

Smith, J.E., Meyers, R.J., & Delaney, H.D. (1998). The community reinforcement approach with homeless alcohol-dependent individuals. *Journal of Consulting and Clinical Psychology, 66*, 541–548.

Smith, J.E., Meyers, R.J., & Miller, W.R. (2001). The community reinforcement approach to the treatment of substance use disorders. *The American Journal on Addictions, 10*, 51–59.

Stitzer, M.L., & Higgins, S.T. (1995). Behavioral treatment of drug and alcohol abuse. In F.E. Bloom & D.J. Kupfer (Eds.), *Psychopharmacology: The fourth generation of progress. 1807–1819*. New York: Raven Press.

Stitzer, M.L., Iguchi, M.Y., & Felch, L. (1992). Contingent take-home: Effects on drug use of methadone maintenance patients. *Journal of Consulting and Clinical Psychology, 60*, 927–934.

Weiss, B., & Laties, V.G. (1960). Magnitude of reinforcement as a variable in a thermoregulatory behavior. *Journal of Comparative Physiological Psychology, 53*, 603–308.

CHAPTER 23

Goal-Setting as a Motivational Technique for Neurorehabilitation

Siegfried Gauggel

and

Martina Hoop

University of Technology, Chemnitz, Germany

Synopsis.—This chapter emphasizes the importance of goals and goal-setting in rehabilitation, especially in the rehabilitation of patients with brain injuries. After the main theoretical components of an empirical basis for goal-setting theory (Locke & Latham, 1990) and guidelines for goal-setting, the chapter discusses how this approach can be applied in the assessment and treatment of brain-damaged patients. Several studies are discussed in which goal-setting techniques (i.e., the assignment of specific, difficult goals instead of unspecific, easy ones) have been used to improve the performance of patients with brain injuries. The findings indicate that the assignment of specific, difficult goals leads to significantly better performance than easy, unspecific goals. The chapter also discusses the application of Goal-Attainment Scaling (GAS), a procedure for measuring individualized needs and outcomes in rehabilitation programs. GAS has a broad clinical impetus and can be used both as a measurement tool and a therapeutic technique to improve individuals' awareness of their performance in relation to an established standard or goal level. In addition, patients with brain injuries, who are often characterized by limited goal-setting skills, may learn to adapt their performance in order to meet varying standards. Finally, the chapter describes possible future developments of the goal-setting approach in neuropsychology and neurorehabilitation.

INTRODUCTION

As discussed in other chapters in this volume, it is evident that goals play a fundamental role in human behavior. Everyone knows that one has to set goals in order to accomplish anything in life. Goals serve as significant regulators of human actions because they act as a standard against which perceptions and anticipations can be compared. The goal construct, therefore, is a central component of many psychological theories (e.g., control theory, social-cognitive-learning theory, goal-setting theory) and helps to explain why people (their ability and knowledge aside) differ in their choice (direction), persistence, and intensity of behavior (see Austin & Vancouver, 1996, for a review).

Handbook of Motivational Counseling. Edited by W. Miles Cox and Eric Klinger.
© 2004 John Wiley & Sons, Ltd.

The goal construct is also an important component of motivational counseling. Clarifying clients' personal standards (i.e., goals) and identifying discrepancies between their current behavior and personal goals provides the basis for motivational counseling and behavior change. In the motivational counseling process, the counselor and client should work out clear, realistic goals regarding behavior changes and develop strategies to reach these goals.

Locke and Latham's (1990, 2002) goal-setting theory describes mechanisms and variables which are important for the goal-setting process that affects performance. Goal-setting theory was developed in the context of industrial and organizational psychology but can also be applied to a wide range of fields concerned with changes in human performance or behavior in general. Thus, goal-setting theory usefully complements motivational counseling by explaining why goal-setting is important in motivational counseling and stating the rules that have to be considered to make goal-setting effective.

GOAL-SETTING THEORY

In the three decades since the publication of Locke's (1968) seminal article in which he proposed a model of motivation based on conscious goals and intentions, a vast amount of research has been conducted in industrial, organizational, and laboratory settings to empirically test the effects of goal-setting and related variables on task performance (Locke & Latham, 2002). Goal-setting theory states that specific, difficult goals, if they are accepted, lead to better performance than generalized and unspecific goals (such as "do your best"), easy goals, or no goals (Locke & Latham, 1990). This increase in performance from setting specific, difficult goals is called the *goal-setting effect*, whereas the procedure of setting these difficult specific goals is called the *goal-setting technique*. Figure 23.1 depicts the

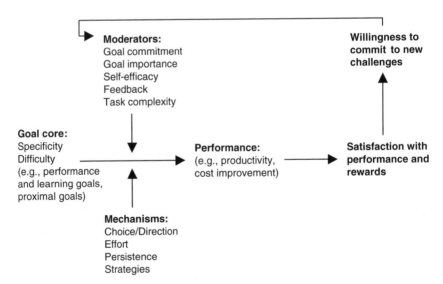

Figure 23.1 Depiction of important components of Locke and Latham's goal-setting theory. (From Locke, E.A., & Latham, G.P. (2002). Building a practically useful theory of goal-setting and task motivation: A 35-year odyssey. *American Psychologist, 57*, 714. Copyright ©2002 by the American Psychological Association. Reprinted with permission of the authors.)

major constructs of goal-setting theory and the components of the associated motivational processes (Locke & Latham, 1990).

Locke and Latham's goal-setting theory asserts that goals are immediate regulators or causes of behavior (e.g., task or work performance). This is contrary to motive or need theories in which basic needs or motives have only regulatory functions. Although needs and motives are important to fully understand human action, they are several steps away from action itself. This is the reason why Locke (1968) formulated goal-setting theory, which starts with situationally specific, conscious, motivational factors closest to action: goals and intentions. The theory then worked backward to determine what caused goals to be formed and what made them effective (Locke & Latham, 1990, 2002).

Since 1968, goal-setting research has repeatedly replicated the positive influence of goal difficulty (and goal specificity) on performance. The relationship between goal difficulty and performance is linear, i.e., the higher the goal difficulty, the higher the level of performance. Nearly 400 studies involving 40 000 participants have replicated this finding (see Locke et al., 1981; Mento, Steel, & Karren, 1987, for reviews or meta-analyses). Furthermore, these findings have shown the effect to have external validity across a wide variety of tasks (e.g., reaction-time tasks, word-naming), and across laboratory and field settings, short and long time spans, easy and difficult performance criteria, quantitative and qualitative measures, and individual and group situations (Locke & Latham, 1990).

Mechanisms of Goal-Setting

The performance benefit from difficult goals appears to stem from the influence that such goals have on directing attention, effort, and persistence in individual performance (Locke & Latham, 1990). These mechanisms correspond to the three common attributes of motivated action: direction (choice of behavior), intensity, and duration (persistence of behavior). Individuals learn at an early age that they perform better on a task if they focus their attention on the task, exert effort at it, and persist over time. In addition to these three direct mechanisms, goals can affect performance indirectly by motivating the individual to develop task-specific strategies or plans.

Moderating Factors

Goal-setting research has shown that the goal-setting effect is moderated by several factors, with feedback and commitment as the most important. Further moderators include ability and task complexity.

Goal commitment is one of the most important moderating factors; challenging goals can lead to high performance only if the individual is committed to them. Erez and Zidon's (1984) experiment nicely illustrates the influence of goal commitment on performance: if commitment declined in response to increasing goal difficulty, performance also declined. Many factors (e.g., peer group influences, incentives, and rewards) influence and determine goal commitment (Locke, Latham, & Erez, 1988). Most of these influences can be explained within the framework of expectancy theory. However, it has also been shown that perceived authority is a very powerful determinant of goal commitment; goals assigned by authority figures typically affect individuals' personal goals.

It is surprising that participation in goal-setting does not lead to greater goal commitment or productivity than having the authority figure simply assign the goal (Latham & Lee, 1986; Tubbs, 1986). However, there are exceptions to these findings, with research having shown that the kind of instructions used in goal-setting studies played an important role. The assignment of goals is as effective as participative goal-setting, provided the goals are accompanied by a reasonable explanation and the experimenter is supportive.

Besides commitment, *feedback* is another important moderating factor in the goal-setting process (Neubert, 1998). Feedback can inform individuals about the accuracy and progress of their performance. In addition, feedback can motivate them by affecting their perceptions of competence and accomplishment. However, feedback in the form of praise by itself is not sufficient to improve performance. Although positive findings have frequently been reported for the effects of feedback (e.g., Ammons, 1956; Annett, 1969; Kopelman, 1982), they probably stem from the deliberate or inadvertent confounding of feedback with goal-setting or other factors (e.g., information regarding better task strategies; recognition or other rewards). Moreover, in a meta-analysis, Kluger and DeNisi (1996) showed that feedback can also have detrimental effects; the influence of feedback is primarily determined by the participants' cognitive appraisal of the feedback (Kluger & DeNisi, 1996). On the other hand, research has also shown that goal-setting in the absence of feedback is ineffective (Erez, 1977; Locke et al., 1981). Both goals and feedback are needed to affect performance. Whereas goals direct and energize action, feedback allows the tracking of progress in relation to the goal.

Ability is a third moderating factor, which generally limits the individual's capacity to respond to a challenge. Performance cannot increase after the limit of ability has been reached. This has been found in many goal-setting studies. Goal-setting research has also provided some evidence that goal-setting has stronger effects among high-ability than among low-ability individuals, and that ability has stronger effects among individuals with high goals than among those with low goals (Locke, 1965, 1982). One reason for the latter finding could be that when goals are set low and people are committed to them, output is limited to a level below what is possible.

Finally, *task complexity* seems also to have a moderating influence on goal-setting. In a meta-analysis, Wood, Mento, and Locke (1987) investigated the moderating effects of task complexity. To do this, task complexity was defined in terms of three dimensions: component complexity (number of elements in the task), coordinative complexity (the number and nature of the relationship between the elements), and dynamic complexity (number and types of elements and the relationships between them over time) (Wood, 1986). They generally found that goal-setting effects were strongest for easy tasks (e.g., reaction time, brainstorming; $d = .76$), and weakest for more complex tasks (e.g., business-game simulations, scientific and engineering work; $d = .42$). It seems that on simple tasks, the effort induced by the goal leads relatively directly to task performance. On more complex tasks, however, effort does not necessarily pay off so directly. One must decide where and how to allocate effort. Moreover, one has to use strategies to be efficient and successful. Thus, in more complex tasks, the plans, tactics, and strategies used by the individual play a more important role in task performance than they do in simpler tasks, where the number of different strategies is more limited and the strategies are generally known to all performers.

Expectancy and Self-Efficacy

Expectancy and perceived self-efficacy are further mediators of the performance process. Partly on the basis of beliefs about personal efficacy, people choose what challenges to undertake, how much effort to expend at the endeavor, and how long to persevere in the face of difficulties. That is, high expectancy and self-efficacy lead to high levels of goal commitment and also to high goal levels (Locke et al., 1984). Expectancy and self-efficacy influence the individual's response to feedback concerning progress in relation to goals and may even affect the efficiency of task strategies (Wood & Bandura, 1989).

Rewards

Internal and external rewards provide the individual with what he or she wants or considers appropriate or beneficial. Once high performance has been demonstrated, rewards can become important as inducements to continue. Internal, self-administered rewards that can occur following high performance include a sense of achievement based on attaining a certain level of excellence, pride in accomplishment, and feelings of success and efficacy. The experience of success will depend on reaching one's goal or "level of aspiration" (Lewin, 1936, 1938) or making progress toward the goal.

Guidelines for Effective Goal-Setting

More than 35 years of goal-setting research have shown the strength and limitations of the goal-setting technique (Locke & Latham, 2002). To make goal-setting effective, several aspects have to be considered. Essential guidelines for the application of goal-setting that Locke (1996) formulated are depicted in Table 23.1.

Table 23.1   Guidelines for successful goal-setting (adapted from Locke, 1996)

1. The more difficult the goal, the greater the achievement.
2. The more specific or explicit the goal, the more precisely performance is regulated.
3. Goals that are both specific and difficult lead to highest performance.
4. Commitment to goals is most critical when goals are specific and difficult.
5. High commitment to a goal is achieved when:
   (a) the individual is convinced that the goal is important
   (b) the individual is convinced that the goal is attainable.
6. In addition to having a direct influence on performance, self-efficacy influences:
   (a) the difficulty level of the goal chosen or accepted
   (b) commitment to goals
   (c) the response to negative feedback or failure
   (d) the choice of task strategies.
7. Goal setting is most effective when there is feedback showing progress in relation to the goal.
8. Goals affect performance by affecting the direction of action, the degree of effort exerted, and the persistence of action over time.

Problems with Goal-Setting Theory

Despite the large number of convincing studies supporting the goal-setting approach, there are several problems with goal-setting theory. First, the *quality of goals* has been neglected. Both quantity and quality are important components of performance in many jobs or daily life situations. Although both aspects are important, there has been little research on the quality of goal performance. Although quality is subordinate to quantity in many situations (e.g., work performance), quantity is not the sole dimension of performance.

Second, goal-setting theory does not consider *goal conflicts*, although they obviously occur in many daily life situations and may have dysfunctional effects on performance (Michalak, Heidenreich, & Hoyer, Chapter 5, this volume). Multiple goals might arise from multiple role sets, supervisors, or multiple system requirements.

Third, the influence of goal difficulty and specificity has been investigated mainly as it affects intensity of behavior. To our knowledge, there are only a few studies that have considered the direction (choice) and persistence of behavior. No study has investigated direction, intensity, and persistence simultaneously.

Fourth, the nature of criteria used in goal-setting research is limited. In order to meet the specificity requirement of goal-setting, performance measures generally take the form of countable criteria. Experimental tasks (e.g., solving anagrams or sorting cards into piles) yield concrete scores, such as "number of cards sorted" or "number of errors made." However, real life criteria are less clear and sometimes very subjective.

Finally, although numerous studies have found that goal-setting leads to performance improvement, there are only a few studies that have tried to explain how goal-setting works by analyzing the dynamics responsible for goal-setting effects, e.g., the process by which task–goal attributes affect performance (e.g., Schmidt, Kleinbeck, & Brockmann, 1984). It seems likely that there are boundaries beyond which goal-setting will not have an effect. For instance, Huber (1985) argued that, for complex or heuristic tasks, goals may be dysfunctional because they may serve to misdirect an individual's attention. In addition, goals may be dysfunctional if an individual is already stressed or under pressure or when the assignment of a specific, difficult goal creates excessive pressure and degrades performance.

APPLICATION OF GOAL-SETTING IN NEUROREHABILITATION

The principles of goal-setting can, of course, be applied in different settings and are not limited to the industrial and organizational domain. Locke (1991) wrote at length about the application of goal-setting to sports. In addition, Locke and Latham (1990) discussed how goal-setting can be applied to education, psychotherapy, and personal health management (see also Strecher et al., 1995). In psychotherapy, goal-setting and the attainment of chosen goals is at the core of training in self-management and self-regulation. For example, Kanfer's self-management therapy teaches clients to assess problems, to set specific, difficult goals in relation to those problems, to monitor ways in which the environment facilitates or hinders goal attainment, and to identify and administer reinforcers for working toward goal attainment, and punishers for failing to do so (Kanfer & Gaelick-Buys, 2002; Schefft et al., 1997).

However, psychotherapy is not the only fruitful area for the application of goal-setting principles. In rehabilitation settings also, the selection of appropriate treatment goals is

Table 23.2 Importance of goals and goal-setting in rehabilitation

Goals appear useful for:
(1) monitoring progress in a time-limited era of care
(2) structuring team conferences
(3) planning and making decisions about ongoing rehabilitation
(4) insuring concise, relevant communication
(5) guiding the delivery of social reinforcement
(6) evaluating programs
(7) encouraging patients to develop more accurate self-awareness
(8) redeveloping patients' capacity for goal-setting

a very important element and provides a means of concentrating on desired and achievable outcomes and measuring progress toward those outcomes (Prigatano et al., 1997; Rockwood, 1994). Schut and Stam (1994) listed several arguments supporting the use of goal-setting in rehabilitation, especially in rehabilitation teamwork:

1. Goals are essential in rehabilitation because all the involved professionals, patients, and relatives should work together to achieve common rehabilitation goals.
2. Goal-setting improves communication between all participants (e.g., patient, therapists, significant others) in the rehabilitation process because all of them know what they are aiming for.
3. Goal-setting provides a platform for interdisciplinary teamwork, because all team members are involved in problem analysis and decision-taking, including allocation of actions or tasks to the team members and drawing up a time schedule and an evaluation.
4. Goals influence the choice (direction), intensity, and persistence of behavior. Therefore, goal-setting has a motivational aspect for both patients and team members.
5. The evaluation of attained goals can be used to measure rehabilitation outcome and to document treatment progress.

Table 23.2 provides a more detailed list of useful functions of goal-setting in rehabilitation (Malec, 1999).

To summarize, goal-setting can structure rehabilitation in a specific way if the goals are relevant, attainable, allow planning, and state what should be accomplished. Moreover, if goals are positively defined, are put in behavioral terms, are measurable, and can easily be understood by all the team members, they offer a powerful framework for rehabilitation (Schut & Stam, 1994). For example, in a prospective study of chronic musculoskeletal pain patients, Tan et al. (1997) showed that the goal "return-to-work" was the single best predictor of outcome. They concluded that the assessment of an individual's motivation as defined by goal-setting might be a key factor in predicting a favorable outcome.

The next section briefly reviews findings of a series of empirical studies in which goal-setting was used to influence performance of patients with brain injuries. Thereafter, Goal-Attainment Scaling (GAS) is introduced as another application of goal-setting.

Goal-Setting with Brain-Injured Patients

A large number of studies in industrial and organizational psychology have shown that goal difficulty has an influence on performance. Specific, difficult goals lead to better

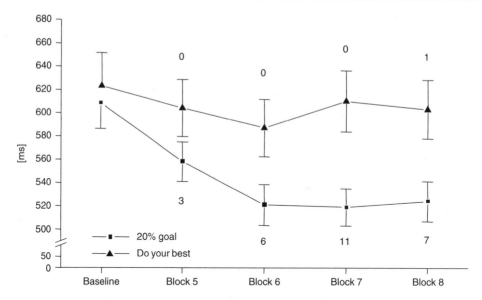

Figure 23.2 Mean reaction times (ms) during baseline performance on four blocks after goal-setting, shown separately for brain-damaged patients with a high, specific goal and those with a "do-your-best" goal. Vertical lines depict standard deviations of the means. Integers at the top or bottom of vertical lines indicate the number of patients who showed a 20% improvement (i.e., decrease in RT) from baseline. (From Gauggel, S., Leinberger, R., & Richardt, M. (2001). Goal-setting and reaction time performance in brain-damaged patients. *Journal of Clinical and Experimental Neuropsychology*, **23**, 357. Copyright ©2001 by Swets & Zeitlinger. Adapted with permission of the authors.)

performance than easy, unspecific goals. In a series of studies, Gauggel and colleagues have shown that this relationship can also be applied to patients with brain injuries. In the first of these studies, Gauggel, Leinberger, and Richardt (2001) used the goal-setting technique to examine the way in which 62 patients with closed-head injuries (CHI) or cerebral-vascular accidents (CVA) and 47 orthopedic control patients altered their performance on a four-choice reaction-time (RT) task. Both patient groups were randomly assigned to one of two conditions: one that set a specific, hard goal and one that set a "do-your-best" goal. Patients given a specific, difficult goal responded significantly faster on the task than patients given a "do-your-best" goal (see Figure 23.2). No clinical or neuropsychological variables (e.g., attention, memory) had a moderating influence on the goal-setting effect.

The findings of this study were replicated in a second experiment in which an arithmetic task was used instead of the reaction-time task (Gauggel & Billino, 2002). Again, patients with a specific, difficult goal outperformed patients with a "do-your-best" goal in the number of calculations performed. There was again no moderating influence on the goal-setting effect of clinical or neuropsychological variables (e.g., time since onset of illness, memory function, executive function). These results indicate that even brain-damaged patients with cognitive and executive dysfunctions are able to efficiently self-regulate their behavior after the assignment of a difficult, specific goal in a simple laboratory task.

The results of the studies just described were expanded by a third study. Gauggel and Fischer (2001) used the Purdue Pegboard Test, a simple fine-motor test, as the task to be performed by patients with brain injuries. Participants assigned a specific, difficult goal again performed better than those assigned a "do-your-best" goal. But, most interestingly, the attained improvement in performance did not disappear in this group after ten minutes of rest. Unlike the first two studies, there were slight moderating influences of mood, self-efficacy, and memory on goal-setting performance.

In the last study, the effect of goal origin (i.e., self-set vs. assigned) was assessed in a simple arithmetic task (Gauggel, Hoop, & Werner, 2002). Patients were randomly assigned to one of three conditions: (1) one that set a specific, difficult goal, (2) one that set a "do-your-best" goal, and (3) one in which patients stated their own goal. The results indicate that assigned, difficult goals lead to better performance than assigned easy goals or self-set goals. The reason that participants with self-set goals did not perform better is that they chose only moderately difficult goals, and their actual performance approximated the goal that they had set, except for one patient with an extremely high goal. These findings indicate that although brain-damaged patients are responsive to goals that they set for themselves, letting patients self-set their performance goals does not always lead to maximal performance.

To summarize, almost all of the findings from goal-setting studies with brain-damaged patients are consistent with those from the industrial and organizational domain. Difficult, specific goals lead to better performance than easy goals. Furthermore, although the goals were assigned, commitment to them seemed high and stable. As a further finding, cognitive impairments and major clinical variables (e.g., time since onset, current mood) had only a small moderating influence, or none at all, on the goal-setting effect, suggesting that a wide variety of people respond to goal-setting. This result is not surprising, because previous studies had shown that even retarded individuals respond to goal-setting (see Copeland & Hughes, 2002, for a review). In conclusion, goal-setting theory delivers an empirically grounded model of motivation with a specific emphasis on goals. The findings of four studies showed that the goal-setting approach can successfully be applied to patients with brain injuries.

Although the first studies indicated positive effects of goal-setting, one must exercise caution in applying goal-setting techniques in neurorehabilitation. There are situations in which goal-setting does not enhance performance. The effects of goal-setting and the goal difficulty-performance relationship are not so strong when (1) tasks that are complex for an individual are set as goals, (2) the individual is unable to perform behaviors related to the goals, and (3) the individual is not committed to the goals.

Clearly, further studies are needed, both to establish a sounder empirical basis and to investigate the influence of specific task characteristics. So far, only simple laboratory tasks (e.g., reaction-time tasks, arithmetic calculation) have been used. The question arises as to how patients with brain injuries would respond when more realistic life tasks (e.g., managing finances, practicing physical therapy exercises) are targeted.

GAS

GAS is another application of goal-setting with a broad clinical impetus. Kiresuk and Sherman (1968) introduced GAS as a methodology for program evaluation in mental health services that allows progress toward individualized goals to be measured.

The method has been used subsequently to evaluate outcomes in diverse settings (e.g., social work, psychiatric hospitals, nursing homes, rehabilitation centers) and programs

Table 23.3 Examples of GAS in neurorehabilitation. For three problem areas (food preparation, mood, and decision-making), five possible goal levels and time for goal attainment are formulated. Expected level of outcome is set to 0

Level of attainment	Goal 1 Food preparation	Goal 2 Mood	Goal 3 Decision-making
Much greater than expected +2	Can accomplish food preparation at home without any help or supervision	Scores 6 or less on the Beck Depression Scale	Makes concrete plans and can carry them out without help
Somewhat more than expected +1	Can prepare basic meals without supervision	Scores 7–9 on the Beck Depression Scale	Makes concrete plans and has begun to carry them out with therapist's help
Expected level of outcome 0	Can prepare frozen or canned food without supervision	Scores 10–14 on the Beck Depression Scale	Can make concrete plans and can consider pros and cons
Somewhat less than expected −1	Can prepare a sandwich without supervision	Scores 15–19 on the Beck Depression Scale	Makes global plans, but cannot consider pros and cons
Much less than expected −2	Able to drink without supervision	Scores 20 or more on the Beck Depression Scale	Can consider certain alternatives but cannot make decisions
Designated completion/time for goal attainment	4 weeks	2 months	2 months

(e.g., substance-abuse treatment, family therapy). Kiresuk, Smith, and Cardillo (1994) provided an extensive review of GAS, its conceptual background, measurement techniques, and examples of its application. Malec (1999) reviewed the use of GAS in neurorehabilitation and described its application in a brain-injury outpatient program.

Kiresuk and Sherman (1968) were confronted with the problem of how to evaluate a public service quantitatively in terms of the unique goals it set for its clients. They devised a method of evaluation in which a set of five-point scales of possible goals or outcomes for each client had to be created. These goal attainment scales were then used to evaluate the client's performance at the end of the treatment program or during another specified time period. Table 23.3 gives an example of such a five-point scaling of goals in neurorehabilitation and describes the behaviors and levels of attainment for three problem areas.

In general, the development and scaling of goals can be realized in a few steps, which involve (1) identifying and selecting treatment goals, (2) selecting an indicator for each goal, (3) weighting goals, (4) designating a follow-up time period, (5) specifying the expected level of outcome for each treatment goal, (6) specifying the "somewhat more than" and "somewhat less than" expected levels of outcome for the goal, and (7) assessing the GAS level on admission and at follow-up (Malec, 1999; Ottenbacher & Cusick, 1990; Smith, 1994).

In the first step of GAS, only those problems, symptoms, or issues are considered that the treatment is expected to change. Several specific top priority goals must be formulated that become the main focus of the intervention. Cardillo (1994), for example, selected on average of three specific goals that were scaled for possible outcomes and then evaluated at pre- and post-treatment. For brain-damaged patients, selecting and specifying goals is not easy, because these patients often have difficulties generating goals or specifying them in a concrete and realistic way. Therefore, it is not uncommon in neurorehabilitation for goals to be assigned to, rather than formulated with, the patient. In a second step, therapists identify what behaviors, events, or other criteria will indicate improvement, or lack of it, in each of the areas selected. For this step, it is important to determine a verifying source that can be expressed concretely in behavioral terms (e.g., performance measure, behavioral rating). In addition, this step also includes determining the methodology that will be used to collect the desired information. For example, if remembering appointments has been identified as a problem area, then the number of remembered appointments per week might be selected as one measurable indicator of improvement.

The third step in the GAS process is to apply weights to the goals that have been negotiated with or assigned to the patient. Weights define the hierarchy of goals by indicating the importance of each goal to the overall treatment plan. If there is no hierarchy of goals, all goals would be given a weight of "1." In fact, weighting goals is not a necessary step in GAS, as the lack of consensus about the weighting indicates. Kiresuk and Sherman (1968), for example, were not clear about whether or not goal weights should sum to one. Because of the lack of agreement about how goals should be prioritized or weighted, some authors argue against the use of weights in rehabilitation settings (Grenville & Lyne, 1995). Malec (1999) noted that weights have typically not been used in studies of GAS in rehabilitation settings.

The fourth step is to define the time period after which the GAS will be performed a second time. The period often coincides with the projected length of stay in the treatment program or the time required for successful treatment.

The specification of the expected level of outcome for each treatment goal is the fifth step in GAS. This step is an important one and relies heavily on the therapist's clinical experience and his or her realistic appraisal of the client's competencies. As Ottenbacher and Cusick (1990) noted, the specification of the expected level of outcome is a weakness of GAS, because it is assumed that the therapist will be able to reliably predict treatment outcomes. The "expected level of outcome" is a level of goal achievement that is realistic in the sense that the client should be able to achieve this outcome in the specified time period with a reasonable, but not exceptional, degree of effort (Malec, 1999). Typically, a value of "0" is assigned to the "expected level of outcome." In the sixth step, "greater than expected" and "less than expected" levels of outcome for each goal are specified. These levels are "somewhat more than expected" $(+1)$, "much more than expected" $(+2)$, "somewhat less than expected" (-1), and "much less than expected" (-2) (which is defined as the client's current level). Thus, these additional levels allow the most favorable outcome and the least favorable outcome to be defined. A disadvantage of this procedure is that it leaves no room for regression. The worst outcome is that the client remains at the "-2" level on the final evaluation. In this system, it is not possible to document a decline in performance or level of functioning. Generally, by determining outcome levels, care must be taken not to have goals that are either too easily accomplished or too difficult. Realistic expectations for outcomes should be used to accurately evaluate the program.

The final step of GAS is to assess the GAS level at follow-up. To increase the reliability of the assessment, it is recommended that a therapist who is not involved in the treatment program and who is unaware of the actual treatment goals should do this step. However, it is often difficult to realize such a blind evaluation in clinical settings.

After all of these steps have been completed and the follow-up levels of performance have been evaluated, computation of a goal-attainment score or scores (depending on the number of selected goals) is possible. The computed GAS scores (i.e., the client's outcome levels) are transformed into standard scores with a mean of 50 and a standard deviation of 10. These T-scores provide a value for each client's improvement or lack of it and can be used to see how attained level of performance on one goal compares with the person's attainment on some other goal or with attained goals of other patients.

The formula used to compute the goal-attainment score for a selected goal at follow-up is:

$$T = 50 + \frac{10 \sum w_i x_i}{(1 - r) \sum w_i^2 + r \left(\sum w_i \right)^2}$$

where x_i is the outcome score of the ith scale at follow-up; w_i is the numerical weight assigned to the ith scale; and r is the weighted average intercorrelation of the scale scores. The r-value in the formula reflects the estimated average intercorrelation between the outcome scores. Kiresuk and Sherman (1968) argued that an r-value of .30 could be safely assumed and used as a constant in the formula. Cardillo and Smith (1994) pointed out that *if* $r = .30$ and the scales are not differentially weighted (i.e., each scale receives equal weight, so that w_i is set to 1), then the formula for the GAS T-score can be simplified to:

$$T = 50 + C \left(\sum x_i \right)$$

where C is a constant that depends only on the number of scales at follow-up. The value of C for one scale is 10.0, with $r = .30$. For two scales, the C value is 6.2; for three scales it is 4.56; for four scales it is 3.63; and for five scales it is 3.01 (see Cardillo & Smith, 1994, for a detailed discussion of psychometric issues and derivation of the different formulas). Note that the formula produces T-scores when each scaled score is on the -2 to $+2$ scale.

Illustration of GAS

This section illustrates the application of GAS with a typical patient found in a neurological rehabilitation center. Mr. L. was a 67-year-old male admitted to the center 18 days after a right-hemisphere stroke. The stroke caused a hemiplegia on his left-hand side and a visual neglect (visual inattention to the left side, including unawareness of the impairment).

Step One of GAS was to define the treatment goals. After a comprehensive neurological and neuropsychological assessment, the rehabilitation team selected three treatment goals: (1) *ambulation:* to be able to walk for short distances with the use of an appropriate assisting device; (2) *awareness:* to improve Mr. L.'s awareness of his visual inattention; and (3) *visual attention:* to improve his visual attention of his left side. The three goals (ambulation, awareness, visual attention) reflected the primary focus of the treatment program that was planned for Mr. L.

Step Two was the selection of an indicator for each goal. The indicator for ambulation was in terms of the number of meters walked with the device for assistance (e.g., a walker).

The indicator for awareness was the staff's rating of the patient's degree of awareness, as shown on a standard five-point Likert-type scale. The indicator for visual attention was the number of targets detected on the left side during a computerized visual scanning task.

Step Three, "goal weights," was optional, but if completed, resulted in weights being given to each of the three goal areas described above, according to how problematic (or important) it was for the patient to execute the goal-related tasks (e.g., ranging from "1" for a minor problem to "5" for a very severe problem).

For Step Four, a follow-up period was selected. The average length of stay of stroke patients in the rehabilitation center is four to five weeks. A follow-up period of five weeks was, therefore, selected as reasonable for Mr. L.

In Steps Five and Six the expected levels of outcome were specified for each treatment goal together with the "somewhat more than" or "somewhat less than" expected levels of outcome. Because Mr. L. had been fully independent prior to the stroke, this was his first stroke, and he showed substantial improvement during the first 18 days—walking a distance of 120 meters with the use of a walker was selected as the expected goal outcome for ambulation. The goal was set lower for Mr. L. than for other patients with such a movement disorder because of his visual inattention. "Somewhat less than expected" was defined as being able to walk only half the distance of the expected outcome (i.e., 60 meters), without resting, but using a walker. The "much less than expected" outcome was defined as being unable to walk even 60 meters without resting. On the other hand, the "somewhat more than expected" outcome was that Mr. L. would walk a distance of about 200 meters. The "much more than expected" level of outcome was that he would be able to walk for short distances (5–10 meters) without using any device for assistance.

For the second and third goal, awareness and visual inattention, the staff took into consideration the fact that treatment of visual inattention and the patient's unawareness of the deficit is not easy and can be attained only after a long period of time. Therefore, it was expected that Mr. L. would show a slight improvement in awareness (a rating of "3" on the standardized measure) and a 20–30% improvement on his detection rate on the scanning task. To complete our example, a "somewhat better than expected" outcome might have been a rating of "4" on the awareness questionnaire and a 50% improvement in the detection rate. A "much better than expected" outcome might have been a rating of "5" (full awareness in almost all situations) and a 70% or higher improvement in detection rate. The rehabilitation team believed that attaining a 70% higher detection rate and full awareness of the problem was unlikely, but possible. A "somewhat less than expected" outcome might have been a rating of "2" on the awareness questionnaire and a 10% improvement in detection rate. A "much less than expected" outcome might have been an awareness rating of "1" (the patient's being unaware of his impairment in almost all situations) and no improvement in the detection rate.

After setting the expected levels of outcome, the treatment program was started, and outcome was measured after five weeks, i.e., at the end of the program. By convention, the goal-attainment level on admission and discharge was indicated by different symbols. If the attained outcome was between two goal levels, it would have been scored midway between the two levels, with the score thus reflecting the average of the two levels. In this way, a discharge earlier than expected (e.g., after four weeks instead of the planned five weeks) could be considered and documented with a symbol between two goal levels.

Provided that the correlation between the three scale scores was .30 (Kiresuk & Sherman, 1968, regarded this as a reasonable correlation between scale scores in mental health settings) and the scales are not differentially weighted, the patient's GAS score was calculated according to the formula:

$$\text{Goal-attainment score} = 50 + C\left(\sum x_i\right)$$

where C is a constant that depends only on the number of scales at follow-up (in our example, the value of C for three scales is 4.56, with $r = .30$).[1] If all goals were achieved to the extent expected, then all the x values would be zero and the GAS score would be 50 $(50 + (4.56 \times 0))$. Scores above 50 would indicate a better outcome than expected; scores below 50 indicate a worse-than-expected outcome.

Limitations of GAS

In neurorehabilitation and probably also in other clinical domains, GAS can be used not only to identify needed outcomes and progress toward them during treatment, but also as a means of managing patients' specific problems. For example, GAS can be used to facilitate patients' problem-solving efforts and increase their motivation to improve. In addition, GAS can be used to systematically encourage more accurate self-awareness and to retrain patients' goal-setting abilities (Malec, 1999; Malec, Smigielski, & DePompolo, 1991).

However, there are several limitations of GAS (see Cytrynbaum et al., 1979, for a review). First, individualized measures are not without problems. GAS, for example, is not free of arbitrariness, so that different therapists or therapeutic teams might differ in the goals that they formulate. The process of goal selection, scaling the levels of attainment, and assigning relative importance (weights) to each scale are difficult and highly subjective tasks. Second, using GAS and developing an inventory of goals is more time-consuming and takes greater effort than using standardized assessment instruments. Third, GAS may give a false sense of measurement precision due to the quantitative nature of the behavioral anchors. Finally, the reliability and validity of GAS depends on the objectivity with which the behavioral anchors or verifying sources for the outcome levels are selected or described.

Despite these limitations, GAS seems to be a fruitful additional approach to the measurement of outcome in neurorehabilitation. However, GAS is not offered as a solution to all evaluation needs. Due to its limitations, it should be used to augment standardized measures of classification and outcome (e.g., measures of level of functioning, symptom rating scales, neuropsychological tests). Given the heterogeneity of patients treated in most rehabilitation centers, GAS can help to focus the evaluation process on only those characteristics, behaviors, or symptoms that treatment, or any other intervention, is intended to change or alleviate. Moreover, GAS (and related goal-setting techniques as described in previous sections of this chapter) can be used as a promising intervention

---

[1] See Cardillo and Smith (1994) for details about the derivation of the formula for calculation of the GAS *T*-score and for simplifications of the GAS *T*-score formula. In addition, Cardillo and Smith calculated values of C for different goal scale numbers.

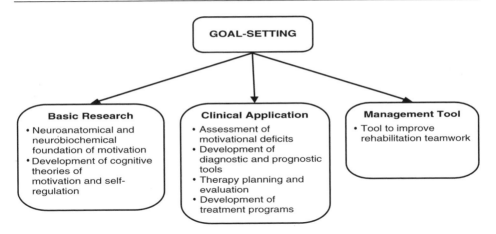

Figure 23.3 Possible applications of and research on goal-setting concepts and goal-setting techniques in neuropsychology and neurorehabilitation

technique. Therapeutic potentialities of GAS are encouraging and worthy of further research.

FUTURE PERSPECTIVES

It is expected that future research on the goal construct and goal-setting theory will open the door to several interesting avenues in neuropsychology and neurorehabilitation. As Figure 23.3 suggests, goal-setting techniques could be used to (1) investigate the neuroanatomical and neurobiochemical foundations of motivation and self-regulation, and (2) better understand the functional architecture of cognitive motivational processes. In the clinical domain, for example, findings from basic research could be used to (1) develop new diagnostic tools for outcome assessment, (2) improve rehabilitation teamwork (i.e., increase staff and patient agreement and cooperation), and (3) help to stimulate the development of new treatment techniques (see, e.g., Levine et al., 2000).

An important issue is the cognitive dysfunction of brain-damaged patients. Brain-injured individuals typically have poor organizational skills, and are often not goal-directed. Some patients have severe impairments in self-regulation and motivation. It would be interesting for future research to investigate how these patients perform when confronted with goal conflicts and when goal-setting techniques are used as intervention techniques. Are these patients' difficulties more related to goal development, to comparing and choosing between several alternative and attractive goals, or to initiating activities to reach desired goals? Descriptive and experimental studies could help to broaden our understanding of these issues. Descriptive studies could inform clinicians about the prevalence of motivational impairments (e.g., apathy) and their comorbidity with other problems in various cerebral disorders. Correlational and experimental studies would be useful for identifying how motivational deficits can predict treatment outcome and affect clinical prognosis. These paths will likely lead to a broader understanding of the concept of motivation, its neurological basis, and its implications for assessment and treatment.

REFERENCES

Ammons, R.B. (1956). Effects of knowledge of performance: A survey and tentative theoretical formulation. *Journal of General Psychology, 54*, 279–299.

Annett, J. (1969). *Feedback and human behavior.* Baltimore: Penguin.

Austin, J.T., & Vancouver, J.B. (1996). Goal constructs in psychology: Structure, process, and content. *Psychological Bulletin, 120*, 338–375.

Cardillo, J.E. (1994). Goal setting, follow-up, and goal monitoring. In T.J. Kiresuk, A. Smith, & J.E. Cardillo (Eds.), *Goal attainment scaling* (pp. 39–104). Hillsdale, NJ: Erlbaum.

Cardillo, J.E., & Smith, A. (1994). Psychometric issues. In T.J. Kiresuk, A. Smith, & J.E. Cardillo (Eds.), *Goal attainment scaling* (pp. 173–212). Hillsdale, NJ: Erlbaum.

Copeland, S.R., & Hughes, C. (2002). Effects of goal setting on task performance of persons with mental retardation. *Education and Training in Mental Retardation and Developmental Disabilities, 37* (1), 40–54.

Cytrynbaum, S., Ginath, Y., Birdwell, J., & Brandt, L. (1979). Goal attainment scaling. A critical review. *Evaluation Quarterly, 3*, 5–40.

Erez, M. (1977). Feedback: A necessary condition for the goal setting–performance relationship. *Journal of Applied Psychology, 62*, 624–627.

Erez, M., & Zidon, I. (1984). Effect of goal acceptance on the relationship of goal difficulty to performance. *Journal of Applied Psychology, 69*, 69–78.

Gauggel, S., & Billino, J. (2002). The effects of goal setting on the arithmetic performance of brain-damaged patients. *Archives of Clinical Neuropsychology, 17* (3), 283–294.

Gauggel, S., & Fischer, S. (2001). The effect of goal setting on motor performance and motor learning in brain-damaged patients. *Neuropsychological Rehabilitation, 11*, 33–44.

Gauggel, S., Hoop, M., & Werner, K. (2002). Assigned vs. self-set goals and their impact on the performance of brain-damaged patients. *Journal of Clinical and Experimental Neuropsychology, 24*, 1070–1080.

Gauggel, S., Leinberger, R., & Richardt, M. (2001). Goal setting and reaction time performance in brain-damaged patients. *Journal of Clinical and Experimental Neuropsychology, 23* (3), 351–361.

Grenville, J., & Lyne, P. (1995). Patient-centred evaluation and rehabilitative care. *Journal of Advanced Nursing, 22*, 965–972.

Huber, V.L. (1985). Effects of task difficulty, goal setting, and strategy on performance of a heuristic task. *Journal of Applied Psychology, 70*, 492–504.

Kanfer, F.H., & Gaelick-Buys, L. (2002). Self-management methods. In F.H. Kanfer & A.P. Goldstein (Eds.), *Helping people change: A textbook of methods* (4th edn.; pp. 305–360). New York: Pergamon Press.

Kiresuk, T.J., & Sherman, R.E. (1968). Goal attainment scaling: A general method for evaluating comprehensive mental health programs. *Community Mental Health Journal, 4*, 443–453.

Kiresuk, T.J., Smith, A., & Cardillo, J.E. (1994). *Goal attainment scaling.* Hillsdale, NJ: Erlbaum.

Kluger, A.N., & DeNisi, A. (1996). The effects of feedback interventions on performance: A historical review, a meta-analysis, and a preliminary feedback intervention theory. *Psychological Bulletin, 119*, 254–284.

Kopelman, R.E. (1982). Improving productivity through objective feedback: A review of the evidence. *National Productivity Review, 2*, 43–55.

Latham, G.P., & Lee, T.W. (1986). Goal setting. In E.A. Locke (Ed.), *Generalizing from laboratory to field settings* (pp. 101–118). Lexington, MA: Lexington Books.

Levine, B., Robertson, I.H., Clare, L., Carter, G., Hong, J., Wilson, B.A., Duncan, J., & Stuss, D.T. (2000). Rehabilitation of executive functioning: An experimental-clinical validation of goal management training. *Journal of the International Neuropsychological Society, 6*, 299–312.

Lewin, K. (1936). Psychology of success and failure. *Occupations, 13*, 926–930.

Lewin, K. (1938). The conceptual representation and the measurement of psychological forces. Durham, NC: Duke University.

Locke, E.A. (1965). Interaction of ability and motivation in performance. *Perceptual and Motor Skills, 21*, 719–725.

Locke, E.A. (1968). Toward a theory of task motivation and incentives. *Organizational Behavior and Human Performance, 3*, 157–159.

Locke, E.A. (1982). Relation of goal level to performance with a short work period and multiple goal levels. *Journal of Applied Psychology, 67*, 512–514.

Locke, E.A. (1991). Problems with goal setting research in sports—and their solution. *Journal of Sports and Exercise Psychology, 13*, 311–316.

Locke, E.A. (1996). Motivation through conscious goal setting. *Applied and Preventive Psychology, 5*, 117–124.

Locke, E.A., Frederick, E., Lee, C., & Bobko, P. (1984). Effect of self-efficacy, goals, and task strategies on task performance. *Journal of Applied Psychology, 69*, 241–251.

Locke, E.A., & Latham, G.P. (1990). *A theory of goal setting and task performance.* Englewood Cliffs, NJ: Prentice-Hall.

Locke, E.A., & Latham, G.P. (2002). Building a practically useful theory of goal setting and task motivation: A 35-year odyssey. *American Psychologist, 57*, 705–717.

Locke, E.A., Latham, G.P., & Erez, M. (1988). The determinants of goal commitment. *Academy of Management Review, 13*, 23–39.

Locke, E.A., Shaw, K.N., Saari, L.M., & Latham, G.P. (1981). Goal setting and task performance: 1969–1980. *Psychological Bulletin, 90*, 125–152.

Malec, J.F. (1999). Goal Attainment Scaling in rehabilitation. *Neuropsychological Rehabilitation, 9*, 253–275.

Malec, J.F., Smigielski, J.S., & DePompolo, R.W. (1991). Goal attainment scaling and outcome measurement in postacute brain injury rehabilitation. *Archives of Physical Medicine and Rehabilitation, 72*, 138–143.

Mento, A.J., Steel, R.P., & Karren, R.J. (1987). A meta-analytic study of the effects of goal setting on task performance: 1966–1984. *Organizational Behavior and Human Decision Processes, 39*, 52–83.

Neubert, M.J. (1998). The value of feedback and goal setting over goal setting alone and potential moderators of this effect: A meta-analysis. *Human Performance, 11* (4), 321–335.

Ottenbacher, K.J., & Cusick, A. (1990). Goal attainment scaling as a method of clinical service evaluation. *American Journal of Occupational Therapy, 44*, 519–525.

Prigatano, G.P., Wong, J.L., Williams, C., & Plenge, K.L. (1997). Prescribed versus actual length of stay and inpatient neurorehabilitation outcome for brain dysfunctional patients. *Archives of Physical Medicine and Rehabilitation, 78*, 621–629.

Rockwood, K. (1994). Setting goals in geriatric rehabilitation and measuring their attainment. *Reviews in Clinical Gerontology, 4*, 141–149.

Schefft, B.K., Malec, J.F., Lehr, B.K., & Kanfer, F.H. (1997). The role of self-regulation therapy with the brain-injured patient. In M.E. Maruish & J.A. Moses (Eds.), *Clinical neuropsychology.* Mahwah, NJ: Erlbaum.

Schmidt, K.-H., Kleinbeck, U., & Brockmann, W. (1984). Motivational control of motor performance by goal setting in a dual-task situation. *Psychological Research, 46*, 129–141.

Schut, H.A., & Stam, H.J. (1994). Goals in rehabilitation teamwork. *Disability and Rehabilitation, 16*, 223–226.

Smith, A. (1994). Introduction and overview. In T.J. Kiresuk, A. Smith, & J.E. Cardillo (Eds.), *Goal attainment scaling* (pp. 1–14). Hillsdale, NJ: Erlbaum.

Strecher, V.J., Seijts, G.H., Kok, G.J., Latham, G.P., Glasgow, R., DeVellis, B., Meertens, R.M., & Bulger, D.W. (1995). Goal setting as a strategy for health behavior change. *Health Education Quarterly, 22*, 190–200.

Tan, V., Cheatle, M.D., Mackin, S., Moberg, P.J., & Esterhai, J.L. Jr. (1997). Goal setting as a predictor of return to work in a population of chronic musculoskeletal pain patients. *International Journal of Neuroscience, 92*, 161–170.

Tubbs, M.E. (1986). Goal-setting: A meta-analytic examination of the empirical evidence. *Journal of Applied Psychology, 71*, 474–483.

Wood, R.E. (1986). Task complexity: Definition of the construct. *Organizational Behavior and Human Decision Processes, 37*, 60–82.

Wood, R.E., & Bandura, A. (1989). Impact of conceptions of ability on self-regulatory mechanisms and complex decision making. *Journal of Personality and Social Psychology, 56*, 407–415.

Wood, R.E., Mento, A.J., & Locke, E.A. (1987). Task complexity as a moderator of goal effects: A meta-analysis. *Journal of Applied Psychology, 72*, 416–425.

CHAPTER 24

Motivational Interviewing in Health Promotion and Behavioral Medicine

Ken Resnicow
University of Michigan, Ann Arbor, USA
Monica L. Baskin
Simone S. Rahotep
Santhi Periasamy
Emory University, Atlanta, USA
and
Stephen Rollnick
University of Wales, Cardiff, UK

Synopsis.—Motivational interviewing (MI), a counseling technique initially used to treat addictions, has increasingly been applied in public health (PH), medical, and health promotion settings. This chapter provides an overview of MI, and its philosophic orientation and essential strategies, with an emphasis on its application to health promotion and chronic disease prevention. MI has been defined as an interpersonal orientation: an egalitarian, empathetic, "way of being" that manifests through specific techniques and strategies, e.g., reflective listening, agenda setting, and eliciting change talk. An essential element of MI is assisting individuals to work through their ambivalence about behavior change and having clients explore how their current health behavior affects their ability to achieve their life goals or live out their core values. We compare MI to Systematic Motivational Counseling (SMC) and other models of behavior change, such as the Transtheoretical Model, and discuss the nuances that distinguish its use for modifying nonaddictive behaviors and how its application in medical and PH settings differs from traditional psychotherapy and addiction counseling. These include differences in the nature of the behaviors themselves as well as constraints on providing MI counseling in these settings, such as limited client contact time and practitioner training. We review major outcome studies where MI has been used to modify chronic disease behaviors and then conclude with future research directions.

INTRODUCTION

Motivational interviewing (MI), originally described by Miller (1983) and more fully discussed in a seminal text by Miller and Rollnick (1991), has been used extensively in

Handbook of Motivational Counseling. Edited by W. Miles Cox and Eric Klinger.
© 2004 John Wiley & Sons, Ltd.

the addiction field (Heather et al., 1996; Kadden, 1996; Miller, 1983; Rollnick et al., 1992). There has been considerable recent interest from public health (PH) and medical researchers and practitioners in adapting MI to address various health-related behaviors, such as smoking, diet, physical activity, cancer screening, sexual behavior, and medical adherence (Berg-Smith et al., 1999; Colby et al., 1998; DiIorio et al., 2003; Dunn, Deroo, & Rivara, 2001; Emmons & Rollnick, 2001; Ershoff et al., 1999; Miller, 1996; Resnicow et al., 2001, 2002a; Smith et al., 1997; Stott, Rollnick, & Pill, 1995; Velasquez et al., 2000).

This chapter provides an overview of MI and its philosophic orientation and essential strategies, with an emphasis on its application to health promotion and chronic disease prevention. We compare MI to Systematic Motivational Counseling (SMC) and other models of behavior change, and discuss the nuances that distinguish its use when modifying nonaddictive behaviors.

MI OVERVIEW

MI is neither a discrete nor an entirely new intervention paradigm but an amalgam of principles and techniques drawn from extant models of psychotherapy and behavior change. MI can be thought of as an interpersonal orientation: an egalitarian, empathetic "way of being" that manifests itself through specific techniques and strategies—e.g., reflective listening, agenda setting. One of the goals of MI is assisting individuals to work through their ambivalence about behavior change. It appears to be particularly effective for individuals who are initially less ready to change (Butler et al., 1999; Heather et al., 1996; Miller & Rollnick, 1991; Resnicow et al., 2001; Rollnick & Miller, 1995).

The Spirit and Process of MI

The tone of MI is nonjudgmental, empathetic, and encouraging. Counselors establish a nonconfrontational and supportive climate where clients feel comfortable expressing both the positive and negative aspects of their current behavior. Unlike some psychotherapeutic models that rely heavily on therapist insight or traditional patient education that focuses on providing information, in MI, the client is expected to do much of the psychological work. There is generally no direct attempt to dismantle denial, to confront irrational or maladaptive beliefs, to convince or persuade. Instead, the goal is to help clients to think about and verbally express their own reasons for and against change, how their current health behavior may conflict with their health goals, and how their current behavior or health status affects their ability to achieve their life goals or live out their core values. A goal of MI is to encourage clients to make fully informed and deeply contemplated life choices, even if the decision is not to change. To achieve these ends, MI counselors rely heavily on reflective listening and positive affirmations. The assumption is that behavior change is affected more by motivation than information.

Employing a neutral yet inquisitive tone, the MI counselor addresses discrepancies in clients' knowledge, beliefs, or behaviors without instilling defensiveness or attempting to refute their position. For example, when the counselor is concerned about the feasibility of a client's plans for change, such concerns are gently raised in a neutral, nonjudgmental manner with comments such as "I am wondering how well your plan to delay quitting smoking fits into your overall goals and family situation." The goal is to help clients to acknowledge and process the limitations of their plans or inconsistencies between their beliefs and practices.

THE CORE TECHNIQUES OF MI

Whereas the essence of MI lies in its spirit, there are specific techniques and strategies that, when used effectively, help to ensure that such a spirit is evoked. Core MI techniques include the use of reflective listening, allowing the client to interpret information, agenda setting, rolling with resistance, building discrepancy, and eliciting self-motivational statements or "change talk."

Reflective Listening

Reflective listening can be conceptualized as a form of hypothesis testing. The hypothesis in generic terms, is "If I heard you correctly, this is what I think you are saying." Reflections, particularly by counselors who are new to the technique, often begin with the stem "It sounds like . . ." More skilled counselors often phrase their reflections as more direct statements, "You are having trouble with . . ," leaving off the assumed "It sounds like." The goals of reflecting include demonstrating that the counselor has heard and is trying to understand the client, affirming client thoughts and feelings, and helping the client to continue the process of self-discovery. One of the most important elements of mastering MI is suppressing the instinct to respond with questions or advice rather than reflections. Questions can be biased by what the counselor may be interested in hearing about rather than what the client wants or needs to explore. Reflecting helps ensure that the direction of the encounter remains client-driven.

Reflections involve several levels of complexity or depth (Carkhuff, 1993). The simplest level tests whether the counselor understood the content of the client's statement, i.e., what was said. Deeper levels of reflection attempt to reveal and explore the meaning or feeling behind what was said, i.e., "What you meant by" or "What you are feeling." Examples of each are shown in Table 24.1. Effective deeper-level reflections can be thought of as the next sentence or next paragraph in the story, i.e., "where the client is going with it." Deeper-level reflecting entails a degree of insight beyond the ability to paraphrase. A high level of reflective listening involves selectively reinforcing positive change talk that may be embedded in a litany of barriers for why the client cannot change his or her behavior. Similarly, skilled MI counselors selectively reflect statements that build efficacy by focusing on prior successful efforts or reframing past unsuccessful attempts as practice rather than failure. These are examples of how MI is more directive than traditional client-centered counseling.

Allowing the Client to Interpret Information

In the patient–education paradigm, the health practitioner often provides information about the risks of continuing a behavior or the benefits of change with the intent of persuasion.

Table 24.1 Levels of reflection

Client statement	"I want to quit smoking because I don't want another heart attack; I want to see my kids grow up."
Content reflection	"You see a connection between your smoking and the possibility of having another heart attack."
Feeling reflection	"You are scared that you might have another heart attack."
Meaning reflection	"Your children are important to you and you want to be there for them."

Statements may include "This is very important for your health because . . .," "This behavior poses great risk," or "It is essential that you change because . . ." Implicit in such statements is a directional interpretation of the information. In contrast, in MI, information is presented in a neutral manner, and the client is asked to interpret what it means for him or her. For example, rather than saying "It is important for you to quit smoking because it places you at great risk of having another heart attack," in MI, the counselor might say, "You may have heard that smoking can increase a person's chances of having another heart attack, and I have seen this happen to several of my patients. But what is important to me is how you think about this, and what you think the risks are for you." MI practitioners avoid persuasion with "predigested" health messages, and instead allow clients to process information and find their own personal relevance.

Rolling with Resistance

Confronting clients often makes them defensive and leads to poor therapeutic outcomes (Miller, 1983). MI counselors, therefore, avoid argumentation; they "roll with resistance" rather than contest it. As Rollnick, Mason, and Butler (1999) noted, the MI encounter resembles a dance more than a wrestling match, *Judo rather than boxing.* For example, if a client questions the association between his or her diet and disease risk, rather than stating facts to counter that belief, the counselor may simply reflect the doubt to the client or provide opportunities for the client to express any doubts he or she may have. In cases where the client's resistance is intractable, the counselor may use a therapeutic paradox or "negative reverse" by stating that "it appears that you see no benefit in changing your diet," or, in the case of smoking, "Cigarettes really work for you and you see little reason to give them up." This risky strategy is designed to "unstick" the entrenched client by short-circuiting the "yes–but" cycle. It is important to use a nonsarcastic, neutral tone.

Agenda Setting and Asking Permission

To ensure that clients are active and willing participants in the process, they are asked to help set the agenda for the encounter. This may include deciding what behavior(s) to talk about and what goals they have for the session (or the intervention in general). If there are multiple behaviors to focus on, such as for a cardiac rehabilitation patient, the agenda setting may prioritize the behaviors to work on, and their order. Permission is sought at key transitional points to ensure that the client is continually engaged. For example, the counselor may ask permission to provide information, to list possible solutions, or to discuss the client's next step.

Self-Motivational Statements: Eliciting Change Talk

A core principle of MI is that individuals are more likely to accept and act upon that which they voice (Bem, 1972). The more a person argues for a position, the greater his or her commitment often becomes. Therefore, considerable effort is made to allow clients to express their own reasons and plans for change (or lack thereof). This is referred to as eliciting self-motivational statements or change talk.

A technique to elicit change talk was developed by Rollnick, Mason, and Butler (Butler et al., 1999; Rollnick, Butler, & Stott, 1997; Rollnick, Mason, & Butler, 1999). The technique begins with two questions: (1) "On a scale from 0 to 10 (with 10 the highest), how motivated/interested are you in . . . (modifying target behavior)?" and (2) "On a scale from 0 to 10 (with 10 the highest), assuming you wanted to change, how confident are you that you could . . . ?" The two questions tap readiness and efficacy for change, respectively (Rollnick, Butler, & Stott, 1997; Rollnick et al., 1992). The first question could also ask about the importance of change rather than interest. Using the client's numeric response, the counselor asks two questions: (1) "Why did you not choose a lower number, like a 1 or 2 (which elicits positive self-motivating statements)?" and (2) "Why did you not choose a higher number (which elicits barriers or cons)?" If barriers are presented, the counselor prompts the client to suggest solutions. To elicit solutions the counselor may further ask, "What would it take to get you to a 9 or a 10?" When the client responds with a 0 or 10, the respective "lower" or "higher" probes are usually omitted.

Another method for evoking change talk is to help clients to develop a discrepancy between their current behavior and their behavioral goals. For example, for clients who have expressed interest in changing a particular behavior, but have not been willing or able to accomplish their goal, the counselor may "softly confront" this discrepancy. This is accomplished with a low-key, inquisitive tone, rather than by expressing disappointment or imparting guilt.

A related strategy is to help clients to establish discrepancy between their current behavior and their personal core values or life goals. A values card sort (Miller & C'deBaca, 1994) has been developed to facilitate the exploration of a client's core values and the relationship of those values to the behavior being discussed. In the original method, clients sorted a list of about 70 values in terms of personal importance and selected the three to five that were most important to them. The counselor next asked whether clients saw any connection between the health behavior and their ability to achieve these goals or realize these values. Alternatively, the counselor may ask how changing the health behavior would be related to these goals or values. A variation on the values sort involves a modified and shorter set of values or attributes such as that shown in Table 24.2 (Resnicow et al., 2002b). The list of values and attributes can be tailored to the particular client population or the health behavior being addressed. For example, the list for adolescents may include values such as "being popular" or "mature," whereas for an elderly population the list may include values related to independent living, youth, or vitality. Alternatively, some practitioners obtain goals and values from clients using open-ended questions rather than a list.

Table 24.2   List of values, attributes, and goals

Good parent	Respected at home	Respected at work
Good spouse/partner	Good Christian (or Jew, Muslim, etc.)	Athletic
Good community member	Successful	Not hypocritical
Strong	Attractive	Energetic
On top of things	Disciplined	Considerate
Competent	Responsible	Youthful
Spiritual	In control	

COMPARISON WITH OTHER MODELS

SMC

What are the similarities and differences between SMC, as applied in the treatment of problem alcohol and drug use, and MI, as applied in health promotion and behavioral medicine settings?

In a broad sense, both MI and SMC consider individual motivation as a driving force in behavior change. Yet they conceptualize the construct of motivation somewhat differently. These differences are driven, at least in part, by the nature of the problem behaviors they address. SMC, for example, views problem alcohol use as serving a major function in the individual's life, a major source of enjoyment and coping, and a vehicle for retreat or release (Cox, 1987, 1998; Cox & Klinger, 1988 and Chapter 7, this volume Cox et al., 2000;). SMC treatment is predicated on the assumption that individuals drink alcohol because of inadequate emotional satisfaction. SMC assumes that a number of contributing factors influence an individual's motivation to drink. Among these are sociocultural and environmental factors, situational factors, past experiences, and incentives. The influence of these factors in the decision to drink varies by individual and context; however, a change in value of any one factor can impact the individual's expectations of positive and negative consequences of drinking. SMC treatment, therefore, logically emphasizes cognitive and lifestyle restructuring to increase satisfaction from nonchemical sources that are incompatible with drinking, and encourages the patient to delineate, pursue, and achieve goals that provide positive reinforcement and decrease the need for and positive expectations from drinking (Cox, 1987, 1998; Cox & Klinger, 1988 and Chapter 11, this volume; Cox, Klinger, & Blount, 1999; Cox et al., 2000). A fundamental assumption is that problem alcohol use pervades many aspects of the client's functioning and that, therefore, treatment must be equally comprehensive.

In contrast, some of the behaviors addressed through MI in health promotion and behavioral medicine settings do not, at least at first blush, convey the same degree of global, often cataclysmic, psychological, social, and family implications as can problem substance use. For example, the social and psychological implications of low levels of fruit and vegetable intake or physical activity are generally not as profound, and interventions often focus more on health consequences as opposed to family, social, and vocational implications. Nonetheless, there are situations where finding alternative sources of satisfaction and joy to replace a health compromising behavior may be equally applicable to chronic disease behaviors. For example, losing weight or practicing safer sex may convey some of the same types of salient life consequences and adjustment challenges as does reducing problem alcohol use. Clients may need to identify new behaviors that provide pleasure, relaxation, entertainment, or affect management to replace the functions served by their health compromising behavior.

There are few, if any, inherent contradictions between MI and SMC. In fact, Cox and Klinger suggest that MI might be a useful component of SMC, particularly as a means for eliciting motivation from ambivalent clients. Similarly, Miller and Rollnick (1991, p. 188) note that:

> W. Miles Cox, Eric Klinger, and Joseph Blount make the important point that drug use is only one behavior within the larger network of a client's life goals and motivations. Their "systematic motivational counseling" approach seeks to clarify how the problem behavior (in this case, drinking) fits into the client's bigger motivational picture. Where does drinking fit in[to] the person's overall goal hierarchy? How does it serve to detract from other goals? The structured goal attainment counseling procedures ... nicely complement our more problem-focused discussions of motivational interviewing.

Although MI certainly entails more than resolving ambivalence, SMC is a more structured and comprehensive approach for addressing the cognitive and behavioral components of behavior change that come into play after ambivalence has been resolved. SMC treatment is comprised of two main components: assessment of the individual's current motivational structure and restructuring motivational structure to exclude alcohol. The first component involves identifying the goals and incentives that help to maintain the problem behavior, whereas the second component involves a multistep process for changing the goals and incentives that support drinking alcohol. Thus, SMC provides a more structured framework for addressing not only "why" a client might want to change but delineates "how" the individual goes about this change, whereas MI is somewhat more focused on the former.

To the extent that the Motivational Structure Questionnaire (MSQ) is an essential element of SMC, it can be viewed as a distinguishing factor between MI and SMC (Stuchlíková, Klinger, & Man, 1998). The MSQ is a systematic and comprehensive tool used to identify not only motivational issues related to the target behavior, but goals, aspirations, and sources of motivation across all areas of the client's life. In part due to the generally briefer nature of MI interventions in public health/behavioral medicine settings compared to SMC, such comprehensive assessment is not feasible. Nonetheless, there are some elements of the MSQ that many MI practitioners routinely could incorporate into their practice. For example, during Steps 1 and 2 of the MSQ, clients are asked to list major concerns and goals across major life domains and the action to be taken to resolve each of them. Then, in Step 12, clients are asked to indicate how drinking alcohol or using other drugs impacts the goals and action steps described in Steps 1 and 2, ranging from prevent, impair, improve, or assure. This process is similar to the values clarification strategy described earlier, whereby clients first delineate three or four important values, traits, and goals and then explore how their current health-related behavior or changing the behavior may impact these major values or goals. Therefore, common to both SMC and MI is an emphasis on clients' articulating how giving up their current health compromising behavior may impact their ability to achieve their broader life goals and core values.

Another similarity between SMC and MI can be seen in Steps 4 and 8 of the MSQ, where clients are asked to rate their level of commitment to achieving their goals and their expected chances of success. In MI many practitioners use two questions, scaled from 0 to 10, as starting points to gauge clients' perceived importance of and confidence in changing their health behavior. Although the scope of this "readiness" assessment in SMC is considerably more comprehensive, as it includes goals beyond the health behavior of focus, both treatment approaches appreciate the importance of understanding a client's interest in achieving change, and their expectations regarding their ability to do so.

Similarly, in Steps 5–7 on the MSQ, clients are asked to rate the positive and negative implications of achieving or not achieving the goals and actions delineated in Steps 1 and 2. This task is similar to the pros and cons exercise used by some MI counselors, whereby clients delineate the reasons for and against changing and continuing their current behavior. Again, in SMC this task is more global in nature, extending beyond the target health behavior. Yet both models emphasize the need for understanding the client's subjective reality, including "fears of success," or the elements of the risky behavior the client will miss and what elements of new behaviors, even if largely positive, the person may fear.

There are situations in behavioral medicine and health promotion settings where MI clinicians may have the opportunity for extended treatment, and where the health behavior in questions might have the type of life-altering implications that alcohol and other drug abuse often does. The potential role that the MSQ and SMC might play in such circumstances merits examination. Key questions would include: (1) for which problems and types of clients would the MSQ and SMC be appropriate?; (2) which steps of the MSQ would be most useful?; and (3) how could MI practitioners best learn and incorporate the techniques and treatment philosophy of SMC?

Other Theoretical Models

Conceptually, MI is deeply rooted in Carl Rogers's client-centered approach to psychotherapy. Rogers challenged the ethics and effectiveness of advice giving and the view that the client should be a passive recipient of the counselor's insight and wisdom (Corey, 1991; Rogers, 1986, 1987). He developed a nondirective counseling, in which the counselor communicates unconditional positive regard for the client and expresses understanding and empathy, often through reflective listening. The counselor makes considerable effort to understand the client's subjective reality. Robert Carkhuff described many of the person-centered techniques which are often utilized in MI (Carkhuff, 1993; Carkhuff & Berenson, 1969; Carkhuff et al., 1979).

In many ways, MI is consistent with the philosophy and style of nondirective counseling, in that both postulate that change is ultimately up to the client. However, MI can be more directive and goal-oriented than client-centered therapy. For example, when MI is used in health promotion and PH, there is often implicit or explicit expectations that clients should modify their behavior in a specific direction—e.g., stop smoking, increase fruit and vegetable intake, etc. In contrast, in nondirective psychotherapy, emphasis is often placed on helping clients to accept themselves as they are. In MI the counselor is equally nonjudgmental, but the therapeutic contract may specify that one course of action will result in more positive health outcomes than another.

Nevertheless, the MI counselor assumes that some individuals are not ready to change. In such cases, the clients may simply be allowed to express disinterest or ambivalence about change, with the discrepant feelings perhaps emphasized, and the door left open for future intervention.

MI and the transtheoretical model (TTM) are similar in that they both emphasize the need to match an intervention to the client's readiness for change (DiClemente et al., 1991; Prochaska et al., 1992). There are differences, however, between the two. TTM interventions often must "lock" a person into a particular stage, which, together with their pros and cons, determines what messages they receive. For example, a person in precontemplation may receive health-related information intended to shift decisional balance, whereas an individual in the action phase might receive concrete behavioral information (Campbell et al., 1999; King et al., 1998; Marcus & Simkin, 1994; Velicer et al., 1999; Zimmerman, Olsen, & Bosworth, 2000). In MI, on the other hand, stage of change is more fluid. Within a single intervention session a person's stage may fluctuate in either direction.

A related key distinction between MI and the TTM is that MI is delivered person-to-person, whereas most TTM interventions are delivered through audiovisual modalities with no direct interpersonal contact. The interpersonal element of MI allows for a more fluid conceptualization stage. In this sense, MI could perhaps be considered a "real time" application of stage-based counseling. Finally, whereas many TTM messages are intended to persuade individuals to change, MI discourages such direct appeals. Rather, the goal is to help clients to write their own "advertisement for change."

With regard to behavior therapy, when ambivalence has been resolved and the client is ready to change, strategies such as self-monitoring, goal-setting, shaping, and reinforcement can be incorporated in an MI-consistent manner, and presented as possible options rather than prescriptions.

CONCEPTUAL AND PRAGMATIC ISSUES

MI for Addictive Behaviors vs. Nonaddictive Behaviors

The increased use of MI for nonaddictive behaviors raises important questions about its delivery and effectiveness in this context. As noted above, an essential element of MI is clients working through their ambivalence about change. The nature and degree of ambivalence (which in the extreme can manifest itself as denial) and reasons for change may differ for addictive and nonaddictive behaviors. Changing nonaddictive behaviors, such as fruit and vegetable intake or physical activity, may not entail the same degree of resistance or convey the depth of psychological and interpersonal meaning as does changing problem alcohol or heroin use. One implication is that less time (though not necessarily less skill) might be needed to resolve ambivalence about changing nonaddictive behaviors. Changing such behaviors may involve the use of more behavioral than cognitive strategies. Resnicow et al. (2001) used MI to modify fruit and vegetable intake in a sample of healthy adults. Unlike excessive drinkers or drug users who might not have decided that they want to change, in this study the participants initially expressed strong interest in wanting to eat more fruit and vegetables (mean rating of 7.0 on a 1-to-10 scale). In addition, the major perceived barriers to change were more pragmatic (e.g., unavailability of foods or insufficient time to prepare them) than psychological.

Another difference between the two kinds of behaviors is that changing an addictive behavior, such as cigarette use, typically involves a clearly articulated goal of cessation and a "quit day." The target goals and plans for reaching them are generally less clearly defined in the case of changing nonaddictive behaviors. Similarly, the concepts of abstinence and relapse may be less tangible for changing many of these behaviors.

The process of changing many chronic disease behaviors generally involves modifying rather than eliminating the behavior; reshaping rather than abstaining. Additionally, MI interventions for chronic disease behaviors such as diet, physical activity, or medication adherence may be incorporated within multiple risk factors programs. Particularly for secondary prevention, the changes need to be long-term, if not for a lifetime. Thus, ambivalence may center around the long-term burden of change. MI in such cases may focus on helping people to come to grips with the chronic nature of their condition and identifying ways to reduce what might be perceived as an overwhelming burden. However, similar to addictive behaviors, reducing or eliminating a favorite food or reducing preferred sedentary behaviors can be perceived as a major sacrifice, with reactions similar to withdrawal. Thus, a key goal for an MI counselor might be to help an individual to reframe the change in positive terms, e.g., what is gained vs. what is lost.

MI in Medical and PH

There are important considerations related to feasibility and efficacy when using MI in medical and PH settings that are different from treating addictions. These include time, mode of delivery, and whether the counseling is practitioner vs. or client initiated.

Proactive vs. Reactive Counseling

Addicted people typically refer themselves for help or are referred by someone else. In medical and PH settings, however, clients typically have sought care for a specific medical condition, and the practitioner may proactively raise issues such as smoking, diet, or exercise. In these circumstances, where clients may not have initiated the discussion, clients may be less interested or willing to address these behaviors. On the other hand, some patients may schedule a periodic check-up with their physician, with the explicit expectation that their health behaviors will be addressed. Whether practitioner-initiated interventions function differently from those that are client initiated merits examination.

Time Limitations

Perhaps the greatest challenge in using MI in medical and PH settings is the limitations on time. Whereas traditional MI for addiction counseling or psychotherapy may involve multiple extended sessions, in medical and PH settings patients are typically seen for ten to 15 minutes (Emmons & Rollnick, 2001; Goldstein et al., 1998). In fact, medical practitioners may have only a single contact in which to address a patient's health behavior (Emmons & Rollnick, 2001; Goldstein et al., 1998). Even when care is ongoing, it can be difficult to be reimbursed for behavioral counseling, which may discourage use of MI in these settings. For these reasons, in many of the health promotion and medical settings where MI is being applied, the quantity and quality of counseling may be quite different than in other contexts. From a research perspective, failure to differentiate traditional MI from other permutations could result in Type III error, i.e., erroneously concluding that MI does not work when in fact it was not delivered with adequate dose or fidelity (Basch et al., 1985).

Given the diversity of clinical applications and variability in the time available for counseling across health care settings, it may be useful to differentiate between MI as a form of therapy and adaptations of MI more suited to health care settings and briefer intervention. Rollnick et al. (2002) have delineated a continuum model that presents three levels of intervention: (1) brief advice; (2) behavior change counseling; and (3) MI. These differ not only by the skills involved but by the context and purpose of the consultation. *Brief advice* can be used in a wide range of circumstances with a large number of patients, and by professionals with limited skills and training. *Behavior change counseling* is more advanced and involves moderate use of MI techniques, such as open-ended questions and reflective listening, to ensure that patients direct the discussion and make informed decisions about change. *MI* is more specialized, involving sophisticated reflective listening and counseling skills to help clients to resolve ambivalence and explore behavior change and its relation to their personal values. MI is presumed to be better suited for more intractable problems and/or clients. Research is clearly needed to elucidate which level of intervention is most appropriate for different clinical situations and professional disciplines. Similarly, it will be important to determine the active ingredients of MI and its permutations and the optimal dose of intervention needed for effective behavior change.

Mode of Delivery

The method of delivering MI may differ in medical and PH settings, where it is often part of a multicomponent intervention (Glasgow et al., 2000; Resnicow et al., 2000, 2001, 2002b). MI is often delivered via telephone (Berg-Smith et al., 1999; Ludman et al., 1999; Resnicow et al., 2001, 2002b; Sims et al., 1998; Taplin et al., 2000; Woollard et al., 1995), in which case counselors and clients operate with limited nonverbal cues, compromising depth of rapport and treatment effectiveness (Soet & Basch, 1997). The efficacy and cost benefit of telephone vs. in-person intervention merits further study.

MI as used in health promotion and behavioral medicine is different from other settings in that the intervention often relies on structured protocols or prepared scripts (DiIorio et al., 2003; Resnicow et al., 1997, 2000, 2001, 2002b). The use of scripts has methodological and clinical advantages. They can help to ensure standardization across practitioners and thereby maximize internal and external validity. Among clinicians with limited counseling backgrounds, scripts can be a useful tool for integrating MI into their repertoire. They also allow for criterion-based assessment of intervention fidelity. The use of such tools, however, comes at some expense. Scripted interventions can result in less free-flowing and less client-centered counseling. Practitioners may become overly concerned with following the script at the expense of spontaneity. Similarly, reflective listening may be truncated due to concerns about covering the full script. Clients may perceive such interventions as less empathetic and client-centered. In addition, the use of scripts may serve to mask skills deficits among counselors or provide them with a false sense of preparedness to deal with problems or issues that are beyond those outlined in the protocol.

Professional Development and Training Issues

In the addiction field, MI has typically been delivered by individuals with training in counseling or psychology. Training such professionals to use MI often represents only a moderate reorientation of their skills. Although in medical and PH settings, psychologists and social workers (Ludman et al., 1999; Resnicow et al., 2002b; Smith et al., 1997; Velasquez et al., 2000) have been used to deliver MI interventions, other professions such as nurses (Doherty et al., 2000; Velasquez et al., 2000; Woollard et al., 1995), physicians (Doherty et al., 2000; Rollnick, Butler, & Stott, 1997), dietitians (Berg-Smith et al., 1999; Mhurchu, Margetts, & Speller, 1998; Resnicow et al., 2000, 2001), or health educators (Harland et al., 1999) are commonly used to deliver interventions. Although physicians, nurses, and dietitians have traditionally been trained to provide expert advice about the benefits of health behavior change (Goldstein et al., 1998), such providers often rely heavily on instructional methods and sharing of information (Glanz, 1979; Rollnick, 1996).

Practitioners not fully trained in MI may be able to learn its basic techniques, but without extensive training they might be unable to achieve the whole that is greater than the sum of its parts. In terms of Rollnick et al.'s three levels described above, many practitioners may be able to effectively deliver behavior change counseling or brief advice, though not full-fledged MI. Technical skills are necessary but insufficient to achieve the spirit of MI. Such professionals may be able to acquire some basic MI skills within a few hours or days of training, such as asking open-ended questions and basic reflective listening. However, mastering deeper levels of reflection, dealing with resistant clients, and being able to apply MI across a range of health behaviors often requires a degree of training, practice, and supervision that is not practical in most health care settings (Velasquez et al., 2000).

REVIEW OF OUTCOME STUDIES

The efficacy of MI in the treatment of substance use and other problem behaviors has been examined in numerous prior studies (Anonymous, 1997; Burke, Arkowitz, & Dunn, in press; Heather et al., 1996; Miller & Rollnick, 1991; Noonan & Moyers, 1997). In addition, there is emerging evidence that MI may be effective in modifying chronic disease behaviors, as discussed below.

Diet and Physical Activity

There have been five controlled outcome studies and one nonexperimental study in which MI was used to modify diet and physical activity behaviors. These studies include four secondary prevention trials (Berg-Smith et al., 1999; Mhurchu, Margetts, & Speller, 1998; Smith et al., 1997; Woollard et al., 1995) and two primary prevention trials (Harland et al., 1999; Resnicow et al., 2000, 2001).

The first secondary prevention study was conducted by Smith et al. (1997). In this pilot study, 22 overweight women (41% African American) with Non-Insulin Dependent Diabetes Mellitus were randomized to receive either a 16-week behavioral weight control group intervention or the same intervention with the addition of three individual MI sessions, delivered by experienced psychologists. One MI session was delivered before the group treatment began and two were delivered at mid-treatment. The MI included individualized feedback on glycemic control to help to develop discrepancy between current status and desired goals. At the four-month post-test, the 16 women who received the MI showed significantly better glycemic control, they better monitored their blood glucose, and they had attended more sessions than those in the comparison group.

Mhurchu, Margetts, and Speller (1998) randomly assigned 121 patients with hyperlipidemia, usually secondary to coronary heart disease, to receive either three MI sessions or a standard dietary intervention, both delivered by a dietitian. At three-month follow-up, both groups showed a significant improvement in dietary habits and body mass/index. However, there were no significant differences between groups for any of the main outcomes. Analysis of tape-recorded counseling sessions indicated greater use of MI techniques such as reflective listening in the experimental condition, whereas more advice giving occurred in the standard intervention. As the authors suggested, the efficacy of MI may have been compromised because 80% of the sample was already making some dietary changes at baseline (i.e., they were in an advanced stage of change) and thus may have been better matched to a behavioral intervention.

Woollard and colleagues (1995) randomly assigned 166 hypertensive patients in general medical practices to receive either high-intensity MI, consisting of six 45-minute sessions every fourth week, or low-intensity MI, comprising a single face-to-face session plus five brief telephone contacts, or a control group. The MI interventions were delivered by nurse counselors. Both MI groups also received their usual General Practitioner (GP) care and an educational manual. At the 18-week follow-up, there were no significant differences between the two MI groups. However, the high-intensity MI group had significantly reduced their weight and blood pressure relative to controls, whereas the low-intensity MI group significantly decreased their alcohol and salt intake relative to controls. Physical activity and smoking were not significantly altered in any of the groups.

In the Dietary Intervention Study in Children, children initially eight to ten years of age with elevated LDL cholesterol received three years of dietary intervention (Berg-Smith et al., 1999). As the cohort moved into adolescence, the investigators elected to add an MI-based intervention to "renew" adherence to the prescribed diet among the original intervention group. (There was no control group for this phase.) The counselors were primarily masters-level health educators and dietitians who received 18 hours of training. There was one in-person session, and one follow-up session, either in person or by telephone. Data from the first 127 youths to complete the two-session protocol indicated that the proportion of calories from fat and dietary cholesterol was significantly reduced at three-month follow-up, and overall adherence scores improved.

With regard to primary prevention, Harland recruited 523 adult patients from a general medical practice (Harland et al., 1999). Participants were sedentary but otherwise healthy. The study had four intervention groups. Two groups received a single 40-minute MI session and two received six 40-minute MI sessions delivered over 12 weeks. Approximately half of the participants in the MI groups also received vouchers for free aerobics classes. There was also a control group that received neither MI nor vouchers. At the 12-week follow-up, self-reported physical activity improved in the four aggregate intervention groups relative to the controls (38% improved vs. 16%), but there were no significant differences between the "high" and "low" MI groups. At one-year follow-up, there were no significant differences in physical activity between the intervention groups, either combined or separately, and to the control group. A limitation of this study is that the median number of MI sessions attended by those in the "high" groups was only three of a possible six sessions.

Resnicow and colleagues (2001) conducted the Eat-for-Life (EFL) trial, a multicomponent intervention designed to increase fruit and vegetable consumption among African American adults, recruited through churches. Fourteen churches were randomly assigned to one of three treatment conditions: (1) comparison; (2) culturally tailored self-help (SH) intervention with one telephone cue; and (3) SH intervention, with one cue call, and three MI counseling calls. The cue calls were intended to increase the use of the SH intervention materials, and were not structured as MI contacts.

The MI counselors, who were either registered dietitians or dietetic interns, had three two-hour training sessions and received ongoing supervision. Self-reported fruit and vegetable intake at one-year follow-up was significantly greater in the MI group than the comparison and SH groups.

Smoking Cessation

Several studies have used MI for smoking cessation, primarily in clinical settings (Butler et al., 1999; Colby et al., 1998; Ershoff et al., 1999; Glasgow et al., 2000; Lando et al., 2001; Rollnick, Butler, & Stott, 1997; Rollnick, Heather, & Bell, 1992; Schubiner, Herrold, & Hurt, 1998; Velasquez et al., 2000).

Glasgow and co-workers (2000) compared a brief MI with advice to quit among 1154 women attending planned parenthood clinics. Clinic staff delivered the MI intervention (in-person and telephone follow-up), discussed a motivational video, and developed personalized strategies with the patients based on their readiness to quit. The MI group had significantly higher seven-day abstinence rates at six weeks (10.2% vs. 6.9%), but not at six-month post-treatment. At both six weeks and six months, continuing smokers in the MI group showed a greater reduction in the number of cigarettes smoked than those in the comparison group. The study is limited by the relatively brief counselor training in MI, lack of information about counselor competence, and the low rate of completing the telephone follow-up calls (43%).

Two other studies evaluated the effectiveness of MI in prenatal clinic settings (Ershoff et al., 1999; Valanis et al., 2001). The first study (Ershoff et al., 1999) did not find a treatment effect for MI on smoking cessation. However, Valanis et al. (2001) found significant intervention reductions on self-reported quit rates both during pregnancy (29% vs. 39%) and six to 12 months after delivery (15% vs. 18%). One reason for these mixed results is that pregnant smokers may be more highly motivated to quit than other smokers.

In another study (Butler et al., 1999; Rollnick, Butler, & Stott, 1997), 536 smokers from Gp practices were randomly assigned to receive either one session of MI or brief advice to quit smoking from their GP. At the six-months follow-up, significantly more participants in the MI group than in the brief advice group reported having quit in the past 24 hours (8% vs. 3%, respectively). The two groups did not differ in self-reported 30-day abstinence. There was also a significant positive result for MI vs. brief advice for the percentage making a quit attempt (18.8% vs. 11.4%, respectively). The differences between the MI and the brief advice group were generally larger for participants in the pre-contemplation stage as opposed to later stages of change. Because practitioners were trained in both interventions, contamination between groups may have compromised the effects of MI.

MI has also been used with adolescent smokers (Colby et al., 1998; Lawendowski, 1998; Schubiner, Herrold, & Hurt, 1998). Colby et al. (1998) compared MI with brief advice in 40 adolescent smokers, recruited in a single hospital, who were seeking care for conditions generally unrelated to smoking. Participants in the MI group viewed four videotaped vignettes aimed to stimulate discussion. At follow-up, 20% reported seven-day abstinence in the MI group compared to 10% in the brief advice group. In the MI group, 72% made a quit attempt compared to 60% in the advice group. Due, in part, to the small sample size, however, these differences were not statistically significant.

Medical Adherence

Kemp and colleagues tested the use of MI to promote medication adherence among people with psychosis (Hayward et al., 1995; Kemp et al., 1996, 1998). In one study, psychiatric patients were randomly assigned to receive either MI-based compliance therapy or supportive counseling (Kemp et al., 1996). Each group received four to six sessions of counseling by a research psychiatrist or clinical psychologist trained in MI techniques. Participants receiving MI showed significantly greater improvements in attitudes to drug treatment, greater insight into their illness, and more compliance with their treatment than participants in the supportive counseling group at six-month follow-up. In a subsequent study, participants who received four to six sessions of MI-based compliance therapy delivered by a trained therapist had significantly greater insight, more positive attitudes toward treatment, and greater observer-rated compliance than participants receiving nonspecific counseling. These changes persisted over the 18-month follow-up period (Kemp et al., 1998).

HIV Risk Behaviors

Carey and coworkers (1997) randomly assigned 102 women considered at risk for HIV infection to an MI-based treatment or waiting list control group. The MI group met in groups of eight to 13 participants for four 90-minute sessions. Intervention participants had significant increases in HIV knowledge and risk awareness, intentions to adopt safer sexual practices, and engaged in fewer acts of unprotected intercourse relative to controls.

Carey and colleagues (2000) replicated their first study using a second sample of 102 low-income women. Participants in the MI group had increased knowledge and better intentions to reduce their risky behaviors.

Belcher et al. (1998) used MI as the basis for a single two-hour session to promote HIV risk reduction practices among low-income urban women. They found that the participants' knowledge and self-efficacy did not improve compared to a control group who received a two-hour session on AIDS education. However, participants in the intervention did report significantly higher rates of condom use at follow-up.

SUMMARY OF OUTCOME STUDIES

These studies indicate that MI can be incorporated into a wide range of health-promotion and disease-prevention interventions, and it appears to have potential application across diverse professionals and health care settings. The outcomes of these initial published interventions, though promising, have nonetheless been mixed. Negative findings in some studies could be attributable to methodological limitations, such as inadequate length of follow-up or low rates of treatment completion (Glasgow et al., 2000). A larger problem that may have impacted study outcomes is intervention fidelity, which has generally not been adequately assessed or controlled for statistically. Negative or weak results in some studies may have been the result of poor intervention delivery as opposed to ineffective intervention per se. Few studies provided evidence of counselor competence or fidelity to MI. Conversely, in positive studies, internal validity is threatened by the fact that the MI interventions were often additive to other interventions. Client contact was often not comparable across conditions, as the comparison groups did not receive any "sham" or alternative counseling.

CONCLUSION

Ultimately, the essential question may not be whether MI works in medical and PH settings, but how well, in what populations, at what dose, and at what cost? Which professions are best able to deliver MI with sufficient fidelity, and how much training is needed to raise competence to adequate levels? How will different health care delivery systems (e.g., public vs. private hospitals; HMOs vs. preferred provider plans) be willing and able to incorporate MI into clinical practice? How will practitioners be reimbursed for training and delivery of MI? These are only a few of the questions that will need to be addressed.

An important question that should be explored is the extent to which the effects of an "MI" intervention can be attributed to aspects that are unique to this approach as opposed to more generic elements of counseling, such as attention effects and empathy. Determining the internal validity of MI interventions can be achieved by comparing MI head-to-head with other counseling methods, while holding dose and delivery modality constant. Additionally, by coding MI encounters according to the degree of fidelity to the spirit and techniques of MI, with such systems as the Motivational Interviewing Skill Code (Miller & Mount, 2001), dose–response analyses can be performed. It can be hypothesized that individuals who receive counseling that was of higher fidelity should have better outcomes than those who received less skilled MI counseling. Studies that measure dose and fidelity of MI interventions will help to illuminate the essential elements and optimal dose to achieve lasting behavior change.

ACKNOWLEDGMENTS

Preparation of this manuscript was supported in part by US National Cancer Institute Grant CA-69668 and US National Heart, Lung, Blood Institute grants HL-64959 and HL-62659 to the first author. Correspondences concerning this article should be addressed to Ken Resnicow, School of Public Health University of Michigan, 1420 Washington Heights, Ann Arbor, MI 48109, USA (e-mail: Kresnic@sph.emory.edu).

The authors would like to thank Jacki Hecht, Colleen DiIorio, Johanna E. Soet, Belinda Borrelli, and Denise Ernst for their contribution to previous manuscripts which have greatly informed this chapter.

REFERENCES

Anonymous (1997). Matching Alcoholism Treatments to Client Heterogeneity: Project MATCH posttreatment drinking outcomes. *Journal of Studies on Alcohol, 58* (1), 7–29.

Basch, C.E., Sliepcevich, E.M., Gold, R.S., Duncan, D., & Kolbe, L. (1985). Avoiding type III errors in health education program evaluations: A case study. *Health Education Quarterly, 12,* 315–331.

Belcher, L., Kalichman, S., Topping, M., Smith, S., Emshoff, J., Norris, F., & Nurss, J. (1998). A randomized trial of a brief HIV risk reduction counseling intervention for women. *Journal of Consulting and Clinical Psychology, 66,* 856–861.

Bem, D. (1972). Self-perception theory. In L. Berkowitz (Ed.), *Advances in experimental social psychology* (Vol. 6; pp. 1–62). New York: Academic Press.

Berg-Smith, S., Stevens, V., Brown, K., Van Horn, L., Gernhofer, N,, Peters, E., Greenberg, R., Snetselaar, L., Ahrens, L., & Smith, K. (1999). A brief motivational intervention to improve dietary adherence in adolescents. *Health Education Research, 14* (3), 399–410.

Burke, B., Arkowitz, H., & Dunn, C. (in press). The efficacy of motivational interviewing and its adaptations: What we know so far. In W. Miller & S. Rollnick (Eds.), *Motivational interviewing.* New York: Guilford.

Butler, C., Rollnick, S., Cohen, D., Bachman, M., Russell, I., & Stott, N. (1999). Motivational consulting versus brief advice for smokers in general practice: A randomized trial. *British Journal of General Practice, 49,* 611–616.

Campbell, M.K., Demark-Wahnefried, W., Symons, M., Kalsbeek, W.D., Dodds, J., Cowan, A., Jackson, B., Motsinger, B., Hoben, K., Lashley, J., Demissie, S., & McClelland, J.W. (1999). Fruit and vegetable consumption and prevention of cancer: The Black Churches United for Better Health project. *American Journal of Public Health, 89* (9), 1390–1396.

Carey, M.P., Braaten, L.S., Maisto, S.A., Gleason, J.R., Forsyth, A.D., Durant, L.E., & Jaworski, B.C. (2000). Using information, motivational enhancement, and skills training to reduce the risk of HIV infection for low-income urban women: A second randomized clinical trial. *Health Psychology, 19* (1), 3–11.

Carey, M.P., Maisto, S.A., Kalichman, S.C., Forsyth, A.D., Wright, E.M., & Johnson, B.T. (1997). Enhancing motivation to reduce the risk of HIV infection for economically disadvantaged urban women. *Journal of Consulting and Clinical Psychology, 65* (4), 531–541.

Carkhuff, R. (1993). *The art of helping* (7th edn.). Amherst, MA: Human Resource Development Press.

Carkhuff, R.R., & Berenson, B.G. (1969). The nature, structure, and function of counselor commitment to client. *Journal of Rehabilitation, 35* (5), 13–14.

Carkhuff, R.R., Wa, A., Cannon, J., Pierce, R., & Zigon, F. (1979). *The skills of helping: An introduction to counseling skills* (p. 261). Amherst, MA: Human Resource Development Press.

Colby, S.M., Monti, P.M., Barnett, N.P., Rohsenow, D.J., Weissman, K., Spirito, A., Woolard, R.H., & Lewander, W.J. (1998). Brief motivational interviewing in a hospital setting for adolescent smoking: A preliminary study. *Journal of Consulting and Clinical Psychology, 66* (3), 574–578.

Corey, G. (1991). *Theory and practice of counseling and psychotherapy* (4th edn.). Pacific Grove, CA: Brooks/Cole.

Cox, W.M. (1987). *Treatment and prevention of alcohol problems: A resource manual.* San Diego, CA: Academic Press.

Cox, W.M. (1998). Motivational variables for addiction research. *Addiction Research, 6* (4), 289–293.

Cox, W.M., Blount, J.P., Bair, J., & Hosier, S.G. (2000). Motivational predictors of readiness to change chronic substance abuse. *Addiction Research, 8* (2), 121–128.

Cox, W.M., & Klinger, E. (1988). A motivational model of alcohol use. *Journal of Abnormal Psychology, 97* (2), 168–180.

Cox, W.M., Klinger, E., & Blount, J.P. (1999). *Systematic motivational counseling: A treatment manual.* Unpublished manuscript. University of Wales, Bangor.

DiClemente, C.C., Prochaska, J.O., Fairhurst, S.K., Velicer, W.F., Velasquez, M.M., & Rossi, J.S. (1991). The process of smoking cessation: An analysis of precontemplation, contemplation, and preparation stages of change. *Journal of Consulting and Clinical Psychology, 59* (2), 295–304.

DiIorio, C., Resnicow, K., McDonnell, M., Soet, J., McCarty, F. & Yeager, K. (2003). Using motivational interviewing to promote adherence to antiretroviral medications: A pilot study. *Journal of the Association of Nurses in AIDS care, 14* (2), 52–62.

Doherty, Y., Hall, D., James, P., Roberts, S., & Simpson, J. (2000). Change counselling in diabetes: The development of a training programme for the diabetes team. *Patient Education and Counseling, 40,* 263–278.

Dunn, C., Deroo, L., & Rivara, F. (2001). The use of brief interventions adapted from motivational interviewing across behavioral domains: A systematic review. *Addiction, 96* (12), 1725–1742.

Emmons, K., & Rollnick, S. (2001). Motivational interviewing in health care settings: Opportunities and limitations. *American Journal of Preventive Medicine, 20* (1), 68–74.

Ershoff, D.H., Quinn, V.P., Boyd, N.R., Stern, J., Gregory, M., & Wirtschafter, D. (1999). The Kaiser Permanente prenatal smoking cessation trial: When more isn't better, what is enough? *American Journal of Preventive Medicine, 17* (3), 161–168.

Glanz, K. (1979). Strategies for nutritional counseling. Dietitians' attitudes and practice. *Journal of the American Dietetic Association, 74* (4), 431–437.

Glasgow, R., Whitlock, E., Eakin, E., & Lichtstein, E. (2000). A brief smoking cessation intervention for women in low-income planned parenthood clinics. *American Journal of Public Health, 90* (5), 786–789.

Goldstein, M., DePue, J., Monroe, A., Willey Lesne, C., Rakowski, W., Prokhorov, A., Niaura, R., & Dube, C. (1998). A population-based survey of physician smoking cessation counseling practices. *Preventive Medicine, 27,* 720–729.

Harland, J., White, M., Drinkwater, C., Chinn, D., Farr, L., & Howel, D. (1999). The Newcastle exercise project: A randomised controlled trial of methods to promote physical activity in primary care. *Britain Medical Journal, 319* (7213), 828–832.

Hayward, P., Chan, N., Kemp, R., & Youle, S. (1995). Medication self-management: A preliminary report on an intervention to improve medication compliance. *Journal of Mental Health, 4* (5), 511–517.

Heather, N., Rollnick, S., Bell, A., & Richmond, R. (1996). Effects of brief counselling among male heavy drinkers identified on general hospital wards. *Drug and Alcohol Review, 15* (1), 29–38.

Kadden, R.M. (1996). Project MATCH: Treatment main effects and matching results. *Alcoholism, Clinical and Experimental Research, 20* (8 Suppl.), 196A–197A.

Kemp, R., Hayward, P., Applewhaite, G., Everitt, B., & David, A. (1996). Compliance therapy in psychotic patients: Randomized controlled trial. *British Medical Journal, 312,* 345–349.

Kemp, R., Kirov, B., Hayward, E.P., & David, A. (1998). Randomised controlled trial of compliance therapy. *British Journal of Psychiatry, 172,* 413–419.

King, A.C., Sallis, J.F., Dunn, A.L., Simons-Morton, D.G., Albright, C.A., Cohen, S., Rejeski, W.J., Marcus, B.H., & Coday, M.C. (1998). Overview of the Activity Counseling Trial (ACT) intervention for promoting physical activity in primary health care settings. Activity Counseling Trial Research Group. *Medicine and Science in Sports and Exercise, 30* (7), 1086–1096.

Lando, H.A., Valanis, B.G., Lichtenstein, E., Curry, S.J., McBride, C.M., Pirie, P.L., & Grothaus, L.C. (2001). Promoting smoking abstinence in pregnant and postpartum patients: A comparison of 2 approaches. *American Journal of Managed Care, 7* (7), 685–693.

Lawendowski, L.A. (1998). A motivational intervention for adolescent smokers. *Preventive Medicine, 27,* A39–A46.

Ludman, E., Curry, S., Meyer, D., & Taplin, S. (1999). Implementation of outreach telephone counseling to promote mammography participation. *Health Education and Behavior, 26* (5), 689–702.

Marcus, B.H., & Simkin, L.R. (1994). The transtheoretical model: Application to exercise behavior. *Medicine and Science in Sports and Exercise, 26* (11), 1400–1404.

Mhurchu, C.N., Margetts, B.M., & Speller, V. (1998). Randomized clinical trial comparing the effectiveness of two dietary interventions for patients with hyperlipidaemia. *Clinical Science, 95* (4), 479–487.

Miller, W., & C'deBaca, J. (1994). Quantum change: Toward a psychology of transformation. In T. Heatherton & J. Weinberger (Eds.), *Can personality change?* (pp. 253–280). Washington, DC: American Psychological Association.

Miller, W., & Mount, K. (2001). A small study of training in motivational interviewing: Does one workshop change clinician and client behavior? *Behavioural and Cognitive Psychotherapy, 29,* 457–471.

Miller, W., & Rollnick, S. (1991). *Motivational interviewing: Preparing people to change addictive behavior*. New York: Guilfords.

Miller, W.R. (1983). Motivational interviewing with problem drinkers. *Behavioural Psychotherapy, 11* (2), 147–172.

Miller, W.R. (1996). Motivational interviewing: Research, practice, and puzzles. *Addictive Behaviors, 21* (6), 835–842.

Noonan, W., & Moyers, T. (1997). Motivational interviewing: A review. *Journal of Substance Misuse, 2*, 8–16.

Prochaska, J.O., DiClemente, C.C., Velicer, W.F., & Rossi, J.S. (1992). Criticisms and concerns of the transtheoretical model in light of recent research. *British Journal of Addiction, 87* (6), 825–828; discussion, 833–825.

Resnicow, K., Coleman-Wallace, D., Jackson, A., DiGirolamo, A., Odom, E., Wang, T., Dudley, W., Davis, M., & Baranowski, T. (2000). Dietary change through Black Churches: Baseline results and program description of the *Eat for Life* trial. *Journal of Cancer Education, 15*, 156–163.

Resnicow, K., DiIorio, C., Soet, J., Borrelli, B., Ernst, D., & Hecht, J. (2002a). Motivational interviewing in health promotion: It sounds like something is changing. *Health Psychology, 21*, 444–451.

Resnicow, K., Jackson, A., Braithwaite, R., DiIorio, C., Blissett, D., Periasamy, S., & Rahotep, S. (2002b). Healthy body/healthy spirit: Design and evaluation of a church-based nutrition and physical activity intervention using motivational interviewing. *Health Education Research, 17* (2), 562–573.

Resnicow, K., Jackson, A., Wang, T., Dudley, W., & Baranowski, T. (2001). A motivational interviewing intervention to increase fruit and vegetable intake through Black Churches: Results of the eat for life trial. *American Journal of Public Health, 91*, 1686–1693.

Resnicow, K., Vaughan, R., Futterman, R., Weston, R., & The Harlem Health Connection Study Group (1997). A self-help smoking cessation program for inner-city African Americans: Results from the Harlem Health Connection Project. *Health Education and Behavior, 24* (2), 201–217.

Rogers, C.R. (1986). Carl Rogers on the development of the person-centered approach. *Person Centered Review, 1* (3), 257–259.

Rogers, C.R. (1987). The underlying theory: Drawn from experience with individuals and groups. Special Issue: Carl R. Rogers and the person-centered approach to peace. *Counseling and Values, 32* (1), 38–46.

Rollnick, S. (1996). Behaviour change in practice: Targeting individuals. *International Journal of Obesity and Related Metabolic, 20* (Suppl. 1), S22–S26.

Rollnick, S., Allison, J., Ballasiotes, S., Barth, T., Butler, C., Rose, G., & Rosengren, D. (2002). Variations on a theme: Motivational interviewing and its adaptations. In W. Miller & S. Rollnick (Eds.), *Motivational interviewing* (2nd edn.). New York: Guilford.

Rollnick, S., Butler, C.C., & Stott, N. (1997). Helping smokers make decisions: The enhancement of brief intervention for general medical practice. *Patient Education and Counseling, 31* (3), 191–203.

Rollnick, S., Heather, N., & Bell, A. (1992). Negotiating behaviour change in medical settings: The development of brief motivational interviewing. *Journal of Mental Health, 1* (1), 25–37.

Rollnick, S., Heather, N., Gold, R., & Hall, W. (1992). Development of a short "readiness to change" questionnaire for use in brief, opportunistic interventions among excessive drinkers. *British Journal of Addiction, 87* (5), 743–754.

Rollnick, S., Mason, P., & Butler, C. (1999). *Health behavior change: A guide for practitioners*. London: Churchill Livingstone (Harcourt Brace Inc).

Rollnick, S., & Miller, W.R. (1995). What is motivational interviewing? *Behavioural and Cognitive Psychotherapy, 23* (4), 325–334.

Schubiner, H., Herrold, A., & Hurt, R. (1998). Tobacco cessation and youth: The feasibility of brief office interventions for adolescence. *Preventive Medicine, 27*, A47–A54.

Sims, J., Smith, J., Duffy, A., & Hilton, S. (1998). Can practice nurses increase physical activity in the over 65's? Methodologic considerations form a pilot study. *British Journal of General Practice, 48*, 1249–1250.

Smith, D., Heckemeyer, C., Kratt, P., & Mason, D. (1997). Motivational interviewing to improve adherence to a behavioral weight-control program for older obese women with NIDDM. *Diabetes Care, 20* (1), 52–54.

Soet, J.E., & Basch, C.E. (1997). The telephone as a communication medium for health education. *Health Education and Behavior, 24* (6), 759–772.

Stott, N.C.H., Rollnick, S., & Pill, R.M. (1995). Innovation in clinical method: Diabetes care and negotiating skills. *Family Practice, 12* (4), 413–418.

Stuchlíková, I., Klinger, E., & Man, F. (1998). Motivational Structure Questionnaire: Comparative study of Czech and American students. *Ceskoslovenska Psychologie, 42* (3), 206–217.

Taplin, S., Barlow, W., Ludman, E., MacLehose, R., Meyer, D., Seger, D., Herta, D., Chin, R., & Curry, S. (2000). Testing reminder and motivational telephone calls to increase screening mammography: A randomized study. *Journal of the National Cancer Institute, 92* (3), 233–242.

Valanis, B., Lichtenstein, E., Mullooly, J.P., Labuhn, K., Brody, K., Severson, H.H., & Stevens, N. (2001). Maternal smoking cessation and relapse prevention during health care visits. *American Journal of Preventive Medicine, 20* (1), 1–8.

Velasquez, M., Hecht, J., Quinn, V., Emmons, K., DiClimente, C., & Dolan-Mullen, P. (2000). Application of motivational interviewing to prenatal smoking cessation: Training and implementation issues. *Tobacco Control, 9* (Suppl. III), 36–40.

Velicer, W.F., Norman, G.J., Fava, J.L., & Prochaska, J.O. (1999). Testing 40 predictions from the transtheoretical model. *Addictive Behaviors, 24* (4), 455–469.

Woollard, J., Beilin, L., Lord, T., Puddey, I., MacAdam, D., & Rouse, I. (1995). A controlled trial of nurse counselling on lifestyle change for hypertensives treated in general practice: Preliminary results. *Clinical and Experimental Pharmacology and Physiology, 22* (6–7), 466–468.

Zimmerman, G.L., Olsen, C.G., & Bosworth, M.F. (2000). A "stages of change" approach to helping patients change behavior. *American Family Physician, 61* (5), 1409–1416.

PART V

Conclusion

CHAPTER 25

Motivational Counseling: Taking Stock and Looking Ahead

W. Miles Cox
University of Wales, Bangor, UK
and
Eric Klinger
University of Minnesota, Morris, USA

Synopsis.—In recent years, the interest in motivational counseling has steadily increased. To account for people's motivated behavior or the lack of it, motivational theory has also developed, as have motivational assessments for identifying the dimensions of motivation. Grounded in motivational theory, a variety of interventions have been developed for use in both clinical and nonclinical contexts for enhancing people's motivation for healthy, desirable behaviors and reducing their motivation for unhealthy, undesirable behaviors. This chapter briefly summarizes the motivational theories and concepts, motivational assessment techniques, and motivational interventions that the earlier chapters present. The chapter then suggests how in the future the various techniques might be integrated for a more comprehensive Systematic Motivational Counseling (SMC) for use in treatment and nontreatment settings.

MOTIVATIONAL COUNSELING: TAKING STOCK AND LOOKING AHEAD

During the past decade, interest in motivational counseling has steadily increased. A search of the *PsycINFO* database using the search terms *motiv** and *counsel** revealed that the number of publications related to motivational counseling more than doubled from 1988–1990 to 2000–2002. The proportion of publications on motivational counseling to the total number indexed in *PsycINFO* doubled during the same period (see Table 25.1).

Accompanying this growth in interest has been growing sophistication in theory and application. Most people would agree that appropriate motivation is important and that lacking it is problematic. Theory is now rich enough to generate new assessment tools and theory-based interventions. The applications described in these chapters represent a formidable

Handbook of Motivational Counseling. Edited by W. Miles Cox and Eric Klinger.
© 2004 John Wiley & Sons, Ltd.

Table 25.1 Number of articles related to
motivational counseling in the *PsycINFO* database
1988–2002 and percent of these articles to total
number of entries

Years	No. of Articles	Percent of articles
1988–1900	85	.052
1991–1993	114	.063
1994–1996	153	.085
1997–1999	172	.092
2000–2002	196	.107

armamentarium of approaches, many of them with encouraging empirical validation. There is much left to do, but this is a promising start.

Consistent with a basic definition of motivation—"the internal states of the organism that lead to the instigation, persistence, energy, and direction of behavior toward a goal"— people's lives literally revolve around forming and pursuing goals. Goal pursuits constitute an organizing structure for cognition, emotion, and action. To counsel people effectively, therefore, requires understanding the principles of motivation and the processes involved in people's choices of goals and their pursuit of them.

BASIC CONCEPTS AND THEORIES

The chapters in Part I of the book lay the foundation for motivational counseling by introducing basic motivational concepts and theories of motivation. Chapter 1 details the ways in which people's behavior and experiences are organized around the pursuit and enjoyment of goals. When someone becomes committed to pursuing a goal, the person is changed motivationally. This is because commitment to a goal sets into motion an internal process—called a current concern—that causes the person to attend to, think about, and act upon stimuli related to pursing and attaining the goal. The process continues until the person either reaches the goal or gives up the pursuit. Knowing the kinds of things that people think about, talk about, pay attention to, and react to can therefore tell us a lot about their motivation. Motivational problems can result from the particular goals that a person chooses to pursue or not to pursue. For instance, some people commit themselves to socially undesirable or self-destructive goals; others are unable to find compelling goals to make their life meaningful, perhaps, as Chapter 7 discusses, turning to alcohol to try to find emotional satisfaction.

In Chapter 4, Brian Little and Neil Chambers discuss *personal projects*, a motivational construct roughly equivalent to a goal pursuit. These authors show how individuals' personal projects can be elicited and their structure assessed for the purpose of facilitating motivational counseling. Little and Chambers' central thesis is that the quality of a person's life and the course of his or her progress in therapy depend on whether or not the person has sustainable core projects to pursue.

Although people come into the world with certain hard-wired preferences, they learn which specific things to value, which goals to pursue, and how to pursue them. There is now a rich literature regarding these learning processes. Both Suzette Glasner (Chapter 2) and Christopher Correia (Chapter 3) describe principles of learning and conditioning that can help to explain why individuals are motivated to pursue particular incentives. As Glasner demonstrates, basic principles of learning identified in the laboratory have helped to elucidate why some people are strongly motivated to drink alcohol excessively or abuse other substances. Glasner shows how animal models have been useful in studying the processes involved, particularly in cases where precise control of experimental variables is not possible with humans. Correia discusses the principles of behavioral economics and shows how the variables controlling an individual's choice of one incentive over another can be identified and controlled. Two of the most important variables are the relative availability of different incentives and the constraints on access to each of them. Glasner's and Correia's chapters both demonstrate how the principles of learning and motivation can be used to help people to alter their motivation for unhealthy incentive choices over healthy ones.

People are involved at any given time with many goals, large and small. Sometimes they are compatible or even synergic, but sometimes they conflict with each other. In Chapter 5, Johannes Michalak, Thomas Heidenreich, and Jürgen Hoyer underscore the importance to counseling and psychotherapy of conflicts among individuals' goals. Goal conflicts can both precipitate psychological distress and impede clients' progress in psychotherapy. These authors propose ways to identify goal conflicts and how to use therapeutic interventions to help clients to resolve them.

There have been few new broad and yet detailed theories of personality since the mid-twentieth century, but very recent years have seen the emergence of such a theory that is much better grounded in empirical science than its predecessors. In Chapter 6, Reiner Kaschel and Julius Kuhl summarize Kuhl's comprehensive Personality Systems Interaction Theory and show how it forms a basis for motivational assessment and counseling. The theory focuses on interactions among different levels of personality, including temperament and affect, cognitive systems, needs and motives, coping styles, and self-regulatory functions. Individual differences in the nature of these interactions moderate the effectiveness of various counseling tactics and hence call for individually tailored interventions.

ASSESSING MOTIVATION

Assessing motivation is an indispensable first step in helping people to enhance their motivation for desirable goal pursuits and reduce their motivation for undesirable ones. Motivational assessments reveal both the content of clients' goals and the manner in which they strive for them, with degrees of precision that are not possible or would likely take much longer to formulate on the basis of only unstructured interactions with clients. A motivational assessment might reveal, for example, that a person is caught up in self-defeating patterns resulting from his or her misjudgments about the likelihood of attaining desired goals or the degree of fulfillment that such goals might bring. Motivational assessments can uncover such patterns and point clinicians toward ways to help clients to change their maladaptive patterns.

The Motivational Structure Questionnaire (MSQ) and the Personal Concerns Inventory (PCI), presented in Chapter 8, are two instruments that identify the content of respondents' goals and their patterns of striving for them (i.e., their motivational structure). Motivational dimensions that the MSQ and PCI measure include, among others, the value that people attribute to their goals (i.e., their anticipated positive and negative emotional reactions upon successful or unsuccessful goal attainments), their perceived control over the desired outcomes, expectancies about succeeding, the amount of time available to prepare for the pursuits, and the imminence of the goal attainments. People's patterns of responding on the MSQ or PCI yield individualized motivational profiles, pointing clinicians to areas on which to focus change.

Because the PCI is a recent derivative of the MSQ, the majority of psychometrics studies have been performed with the MSQ itself. These studies, described in Chapter 9, have been conducted with clinical and nonclinical participants in a variety of settings. The MSQ's test–retest and internal-consistency reliability have been assessed, and it has been validated with a variety of measures, including physiological, cognitive, and mental processes; behavioral patterns; work satisfaction; associated personality characteristics; and treatment outcome. The results show that the MSQ is a reliable, valid, and clinically useful motivational assessment device. In Chapter 10, Nicola Baumann presents additional evidence for the construct validity of the MSQ. The studies that Baumann reviews show how MSQ indices are related to personality (e.g., state vs. action orientation), clinical states (e.g., anxiety and depression), and motivational outcomes (e.g., difficulties with goal enactment). The results support hypotheses that MSQ indices reflecting maladaptive motivational structure predict poorer psychological functioning in a variety of other domains.

SYSTEMATIC MOTIVATIONAL COUNSELING AND ITS APPLICATIONS

Systematic Motivational Counseling (SMC) is a technique for restructuring clients' maladaptive motivational structure, in order to help them to improve their psychological functioning and achieve the goals that they want and need. The technique first utilizes the MSQ or PCI to identify clients' maladaptive motivational patterns, and then helps clients to change those patterns through individually selected counseling components. As described in Chapter 11, these components include: (1) jointly reviewing and reconsidering the client's list of goals and concerns and their ratings; (2) interpreting the motivational profile, and helping the client to identify facilitating or interfering effects of goals on one another; (3) setting treatment goals; (4) constructing goal ladders; (5) setting between-session goals; (6) acquiring the skills needed to meet goals; (7) resolving conflicts among goals; (8) disengaging from unrealistic goals and ones likely to be emotionally unsatisfying; (9) identifying new healthy incentives to enjoy; (10) shifting from negative to positive thinking; and (11) bolstering self-esteem.

The SMC technique has been used in individual counseling sessions with substance-abusing clients, as illustrated in Chapter 11, and with persons who have sustained traumatic brain injuries, as Vincent Miranti and Allen Heinemann detail in Chapter 15. People who have sustained traumatic brain injuries in particular need help to overcome motivational deficits, and they have responded well to SMC as a means of doing so. The SMC technique has also been used in various formats other than individual counseling sessions. For instance, Bernhard Schroer, Arno Fuhrmann, and Renate de Jong-Meyer describe in Chapter 12 their adaptation of SMC for use in group sessions. Their group work has assisted clients suffering from alcohol and other substance abuse, affective disorders, personality disorders, or psychosis. Additionally, Renate de Jong-Meyer discusses in Chapter 13 a self-help version of SMC that she has developed and used with nonclinical participants to help them to set appropriate goals, plan concrete steps in pursuit of them, and break maladaptive habits. Loriann Roberson and David Sluss have developed workplace applications as an additional nonclinical use of SMC procedures. Their work, presented in Chapter 14, demonstrates that the SMC approach leads to better styles of management and increased employee job satisfaction and work performance.

In an area ripe for motivational procedures in offender populations, Mary McMurran in Chapter 16 observes that there are no psychometrically sound instruments specifically for assessing offenders' motivation to change prior to engaging them in therapy. She proposes a theoretical model of offending based on the motivational model of alcohol use (see Cox & Klinger, Chapter 7) and an intervention built on this model, using an adaptation of the MSQ (see Cox & Klinger, Chapter 8; Klinger & Cox, Chapter 9) and of SMC (see Cox & Klinger, Chapter 11) for assessing and changing offenders' motivation.

OTHER MOTIVATIONAL APPROACHES FOR CHANGING BEHAVIOR

The motivational Zeitgeist has generated a variety of other goal-related approaches for helping people to improve their motivation to attain desirable goals. All of the techniques presented in Part IV are compatible with SMC, and can be used to enhance its effectiveness.

The authors of two of the chapters focus specifically on clients' motivation during psychotherapy. Ulrike Willutzki and Christoph Koban in Chapter 17 characterize clients entering therapy as having difficulty identifying meaningful goals beyond ones to alleviate their immediate suffering. Accordingly, they developed an intervention called Elaboration of Positive Perspectives to help clients to connect to personally relevant goals. It utilizes imagery techniques to help clients to adopt a positive perspective beyond their immediate problems. It provides an analysis of clients' goals to make them concrete and relevant to their psychotherapy and to prompt clients to take action to reach their goals.

Manfred Hillmann in Chapter 18 describes logotherapy, Viktor Frankl's venerable approach, which is organized around the principle that human beings' will to meaning represents a fundamental goal for which humans continually strive. To lack a sense that one's life is meaningful is to leave the individual vulnerable to distress and psychopathology. Logotherapy is designed to restore this sense of meaning, which can manifest itself in a variety of ways and can be sustained during even the most adverse of circumstances.

Motivational techniques for helping people to overcome their problematic use of alcohol make up four of the chapters in Part IV of the book. Barry Jones in Chapter 19 describes procedures for altering drinkers' expectancies about the positive and negative effects of drinking, thus helping them to reduce their consumption of alcohol. In this method, the experiential expectancy challenge is designed to reduce positive expectancies, whereas a motivational assessment and interview are used to increase negative expectancies. In Chapter 20, Maria Emmen, Gerard Schippers, Gijs Bleijenberg, and Hub Wollersheim discuss brief motivational interventions for early-stage drinking problems, with a focus on the Dutch adaptation of the Motivational Drinker's Check-Up. Using a case example for illustration, these authors show how the check-up elicits behavior change by helping clients to explore and resolve their ambivalence about reducing their drinking. Arthur Blume and Alan Marlatt in Chapter 21 present a motivational enhancement technique designed for use with heavy-drinking college students. The intervention educates students about the effects of alcohol, places their drinking in the context of social norms, and teaches them coping skills for resisting temptations and pressures in situations in which they are likely to drink excessively.

Enlisting a broader environment in treatment, Conrad Wong, Hendrée Jones, and Maxine Stitzer in Chapter 22 present two contingency-management interventions for substance abuse: abstinence-reinforcement procedures and the Community Reinforcement Approach. Both interventions aim to reduce alcohol and other drug use by increasing the density of alternative reinforcers that are incompatible with a substance-using lifestyle. The first intervention focuses on increasing alternative reinforcers in the substance abuser's natural environment; the second one directly reinforces abstinence and withholds reinforcement for nonabstinence.

Brain injury presents special motivational challenges. Siegfried Gauggel and Martina Hoop, the authors of Chapter 23, emphasize the importance of goals and goal-setting in the rehabilitation of patients with brain injuries. The research that they present identifies the characteristics of goals (e.g., specific, difficult) that optimize the performance of brain-injured patients, and they discuss Goal-Attainment Scaling as a way to measure patients' individualized needs and outcomes in rehabilitation programs.

A major, clearly motivational set of problems in health care is patients' neglect of their health and noncompliance with professional advice. Specific interventions are now available to address these problems. Ken Resnicow, Monica Baskin, Simone Rahotep, Santhi Periasamy, and Stephen Rollnick in Chapter 24 discuss the basic principles of Motivational Interviewing (MI) and its specific application in public health, medical, and health-promotion settings. They also discuss the similarities and differences between MI and other motivational techniques, viz., SMC and those derived from the Transtheoretical Model of Change. Finally, they review outcome studies in which MI has been used to modify behaviors associated with chronic diseases.

FUTURE DIRECTIONS

The innovative work of recent decades has clearly left us with a wide array of tools for improving motivational structure. Where might we go from here? Although a number of these innovations sprang from the root of current-concerns theory and the early formulations of SMC, their adaptations to group settings and special populations, as well as the development of new techniques, proceeded to some extent in isolation from one another. Other motivational methods grew largely independently of the current-concerns framework and of one another. For the most part, however, these methods complement rather than compete with one another.

Toward a More Comprehensive SMC

One obvious need is to develop a comprehensive program of interventions that would bring together the many techniques described in these pages. In an integrated form, such a program could be applied flexibly to clients and taught systematically to practitioners. There is no reason to restrict practitioners to only one (or even a fraction) of the methods available.

What would such a comprehensive approach look like? SMC already includes many features suggested by basic theory and shared by some other viewpoints. A prominent example is the central proposition of SMC—the importance of helping substance abusers shift to alternative goals (in other words, alternative reinforcers)—as suggested by work in incentive learning (Glasner, Chapter 2, this volume) and behavioral economics (Correia, Chapter 3, this volume). Another example is that SMC aims to bring clients' expectancies into better accord with presumed reality, an aim also emphasized by such expectancy approaches as are described by Jones (Chapter 19, this volume). Yet another example is the use of goal-setting in SMC, a method also used in other contexts (e.g., Gauggel & Hoop, Chapter 23; Roberson & Sluss, Chapter 14; this volume).

Nevertheless, even though SMC includes many such features, people working in allied areas have developed both perspectives and specific techniques that would enrich a broadened SMC. Thus, beginning with the components and techniques of SMC (Chapter 11, this volume, and summarized above in this chapter), one could imagine incorporating the following as they appear appropriate:

- community reinforcement and related contingency-management methods (Wong, Jones & Stitzer, Chapter 22, this volume), such as the use of vouchers, as a way to inject more potent, healthy incentives into a client's life;
- referral to professionals who may be able to assist some clients with social, financial, and educational arrangements;
- use of the Pleasant Events Schedule to help clients to locate positive incentives that they may have overlooked as enjoyable alternatives to unwanted behaviors (Correia, Chapter 3, this volume);
- formalized cost–benefit analyses as a way of persuading clients to shift to healthier goals, including goals entailing delayed gratification (Correia, Chapter 3, this volume);
- additional rating scales for goals so as to obtain more precise information about the kinds of emotional reactions they evoke (Little & Chambers, Chapter 4, this volume);
- joint cross-impact matrices that would assess the compatibility of a client's goals with the goals of the people with whom the client most interacts (Little & Chambers, Chapter 4, this volume);
- more effectively distinguishing goals that involve core projects, which are most central in an individual's life, from other goals (Little & Chambers, Chapter 4, this volume);
- Gendlin's focusing technique as a way of more precisely identifying the emotions associated with conflicting goals (Michalak, Heidenreich, & Hoyer, Chapter 5, this volume);
- systematic use of *Evolvement-Oriented Scanning* as a *Personality Systems Interaction* assessment tool to assist with clinical judgments and formulations of interventions (Kaschel & Kuhl, Chapter 6, this volume);
- group SMC as a treatment option (Schroer, Fuhrmann, & de Jong-Meyer, Chapter 12, this volume);
- systematic use of mental imagery and relaxation to identify, characterize, and explore goal pursuits (Schroer, Fuhrmann, & de Jong-Meyer, Chapter 12; Willutzki & Koban, Chapter 17; this volume);
- having clients rate their satisfaction with the permanence of the status quo as a way of sensitizing them to sources of dissatisfaction with their current situations and hence motivating change (Schroer, Fuhrmann, & de Jong-Meyer, Chapter 12, this volume);

- use of the Volitional Components Inventory to assess volitional patterns and identify dysfunctional coping skills (Schroer, Fuhrmann, & de Jong-Meyer, Chapter 12, this volume);
- the option of a self-help manual to help clients to reconsider their goals, plan actions, and initiate and evaluate these actions (de Jong-Meyer, Chapter 13, this volume);
- logotherapeutic techniques of paradoxical intention, dereflection, attitudinal adjustment, and sensitization training for meaning (Hillmann, Chapter 18, this volume);
- the *experiential challenge* technique, in which, for instance, some clients are given placebo versions of substances as a way of altering expectancies about them (Jones, Chapter 19, this volume);
- for substance-abuse cases, the Motivational Drinker's Check-Up method (Emmen, Schippers, Bleijenberg, & Wollersheim, Chapter 20, this volume) or the Brief Alcohol Screening and Intervention for College Students (BASICS; Blume & Marlatt, Chapter 21, this volume) as brief methods for focusing on impairment and risk from substance abuse, to supplement the more broadly designed SMC;
- programs for training coping skills, such as the *Alcohol Skills Training Program* (Blume & Marlatt, Chapter 21, this volume);
- more systematic goal-setting techniques (Roberson & Sluss, Chapter 14; Gauggel & Hoop, Chapter 23, this volume);
- goal-attainment scaling as a quantitative method for assessing the success of interventions (Gauggel & Hoop, Chapter 23; this volume);
- some of the techniques worked out within MI (Resnicow, Baskin, Rahotep, Periasamy, & Rollnick, Chapter 24, this volume), such as systematically inquiring into the reasons clients did not choose different ratings.

Beyond the Treatment Setting

SMC is moving beyond the clinic into other spheres of the community. Its collaborative stance toward reconfiguring lives may suit it well for work with prison populations (McMurran, Chapter 16, this volume), suggesting a dimension of SMC applicable to recalcitrant populations for whom motivational issues are at the core of their difficulties. Applying SMC to such populations will no doubt require the development of additional techniques.

In another nonclinical setting—employment situations—SMC is both being adapted to these settings and benefiting from a long history of organizational research (Roberson & Sluss, Chapter 14, this volume). Thus, enlightened managers try to fuse their organization's goals with their employees' personal goals and sources of satisfaction. The Work Concerns Inventory and variants of SMC can provide the basis for doing so for particular employees. Especially for new employees, this may become an important part of "proactive socialization."

THE CONTINUING NEED FOR EMPIRICAL VALIDATION, RE-EVALUATION, AND BASIC RESEARCH

Although the empirical evidence obtained so far on the methods described in this book is promising, it constitutes only a beginning. There is a need for far larger-scale research on process and outcome. This should investigate the incremental utility of motivational methods, both in effectiveness and in efficiency, when they serve as parts of comprehensive treatment systems.

The innovations of recent years will presumably not be the last in the field. Talented practitioners are constantly entering the professions and will make their own contributions. Techniques and, indeed, theory and metatheory need continuing development, and as they are originated they will need to be evaluated for their contribution to science and to effective treatment. As new methods arise, it will also be necessary to re-evaluate older methods for their incremental value, to determine whether they are worth keeping.

Existing evidence relates to outcomes of whole approaches to treatment. Within an integrated treatment program, however, there is also the need to perform componential analyses to determine the incremental utility of each component technique. For example, do goal ladders really add to treatment effectiveness? Do imagery techniques? How much do occasional post-termination maintenance sessions help to maintain and enhance treatment gains?

As in any treatment field, it is not enough to think in terms of the treatment process as such. The value of a method will most likely vary according to type of problem, type of client population and culture, individual personalities of clients and of practitioners, and practitioners' training. SMC and its variants have been applied with apparent success to a wide range of clients—from affluent, intact individuals to lower-socioeconomic, traumatically brain-injured people, and in at least three countries speaking at least two different languages—but for a relatively new method such as motivational counseling, there is little or no specific evidence to indicate how its effectiveness may differ according to these client and practitioner variables. This clearly needs systematic investigation.

One of the components of SMC is to help clients to gain the skills they need to attain their goals. This simple idea is a departure from most nonvocational forms of counseling and psychotherapy, and when considered carefully it is anything but simple. Inasmuch as most treatment personnel have neither the authority nor the expertise to teach skills other than inter- and intrapersonal ones, this component of SMC suggests the need for its practitioners to interface with other professionals, such as social workers and educators. For the many kinds of clients—from those in physical rehabilitation through substance abusers to offender populations—who would benefit from such services, this SMC component suggests the creation of a more comprehensive treatment model that draws on broader community resources. Such a model will require institution-building.

There is, of course, a host of basic questions that await careful research. Much more work needs to be done on distinctions among clients that affect treatment. For example, the same phenotypical problem behavior, such as substance use, may be appetitive, aimed at enhancing positive affect, or aversive, aimed at reducing or averting negative affect. How can one determine the difference, and what are the implications for treatment? Is adaptive motivational structure a unitary variable or the result of statistically related but functionally separable components? How much depression and how much withdrawal from incentives form a necessary part of disengaging from lost causes; and how much is too much or how long is too long? What specific kinds of personality $\times$ situation interactions lead to what specific kinds of psychological problems, and what do these differences require by way of different interventions? And so on. With any luck, it will be a rich future!

Author Index

Subject Index

ability 442
abstinence
  from alcohol 129, 220, 424, 428
  from cocaine 424, 425, 426
  reinforcement for 422, 423–6, 484
  violation effect 327
access to alcohol/substances 55, 56–7
achievement-goal orientation 286–7
ACS *see* Action Control Scale
action 67, 70, 328
  alternatives 207, 261
  control 85, 113
  effects of current concerns on 15–17
  evaluation 262
  goal-related 32–5, 241, 261, 266, 267
  initiation 247, 263, 277
  opportunities 200, 247, 249
  orientation *see* action orientation
  phase 262, 267, 276
  planning 247, 253, 261, 262, 277
  post-actional 266–8, 276, 277, 278
  preparedness 255
  readiness 247–8
  regulation 338–9
  steps 267, 268
  see also learning theories of addiction
Action Control Scale (ACS) 142, 202, 272
Action orientation 16, 102, 203–6, 247, 262,
  268, 276
  decision-related (AOD) 200, 205–6
  failure-related (AOF) 200, 203, 204, 206
  performance-related (AOP) 200, 206
activation 340
activation control 113
active control mode 262
adaptive motivation 193, 194
adaptive motivational patterns 220
adaptive responses to task difficulty 286
addiction 29–33, 256
  behavior 325, 465–6
  biopsychosocial models of 122, 128
  crime as 325
  decision model of 123
  "drug liking" 127

"drug wanting" 127
  incentive-sensitization theory of 127
ADHD 54
adherence 471
advice 250
affect 74–5, 101, 311, 481
  negative 100, 102, 104, 105, 106, 115, 122,
    124, 126, 129, 131–3, 145, 234, 276,
    286, 291
  positive 100, 102, 104, 105, 106, 115, 122,
    124, 126, 131–3, 145, 201, 205, 339, 340
  see also emotion
affect modulation hypothesis
  negative 201
  positive 201
affective change 122, 124, 126, 130, 133, 311
affective disorders 78, 90, 234, 256
affective disturbance 304
Affective Intensity Measure 16
aggression 107, 231, 330, 410
agoraphobia 350
alcohol
  abstinence from 129, 220, 428
  abuse 130, 218–19, 240, 254, 374
  abuse *see* alcohol abuse
  addiction 240, 241
  alternatives to 131
  anxiolytic effects of 127, 129
  appetitively-based responses 129
  aversion reaction to 127
  biochemical reactions to 124, 128, 129
  biphasic effects 414
  classically conditioned reactions to 128
  cognitive reactions to 132
  conditioned responses to 128
  consumption *see* alcohol consumption
  costs 240
  dependence *see* alcohol dependence
  detoxification 240, 254, 256
  expectancies 416, 417
  instrumental effects 131
  metabolism 127
  "myopia" 412–13, 415
  pharmacological effects of 124, 126